Computers!

Fourth Edition

Timothy N. Trainor
Diane Krasnewich

Mitchell McGRAW-HILL
New York St. Louis San Francisco Auckland Bogotá Caracas
Lisbon London Madrid Mexico Milan Montreal New Delhi Paris
San Juan Singapore Sydney Tokyo Toronto

Mitchell McGRAW-HILL
San Francisco, CA 94133

Computers! Fourth Edition

3 4 5 6 7 8 9 0 VNH VNH 9 0 9 8 7 6 5

ISBN 0-07-065248-1

Sponsoring editor: Erika Berg
Director of production: Jane Somers
Production supervisor: Leslie Austin
Project management: Greg Hubit Bookworks
Text illustration: Alexander Teshin Associates
Photo research: Monica Suder & Associates
Composition: GTS Graphics
Cover and interior design: Christy Butterfield
Printer and binder: Von Hoffmann Press, Inc.

Library of Congress Card Catalog No. 93-79185

This book is printed on acid-free paper.

When ordering this title, use ISBN 0-07-113700-9

We dedicate this book to Erika and Steve Mitchell
—Good friends on a new journey.

Brief Contents

UNIT ONE **INFORMATION TECHNOLOGY AT WORK** **2**

CHAPTER 1: END-USER COMPUTING 4
CHAPTER 2: COMPUTER INFORMATION SYSTEMS 30
CHAPTER 3: SOFTWARE CONCEPTS 60

UNIT TWO **PERSONAL PRODUCTIVITY TOOLS** **98**

CHAPTER 4: WORDPROCESSING AND DESKTOP PUBLISHING 100
CHAPTER 5: ELECTRONIC SPREADSHEETS 138
CHAPTER 6: GRAPHICS AND MULTIMEDIA 170
CHAPTER 7: FILE AND DATABASE MANAGEMENT 206

UNIT THREE **HARDWARE AND COMMUNICATIONS** **240**

CHAPTER 8: PROCESSING HARDWARE 242
CHAPTER 9: INPUT/OUTPUT HARDWARE 280
CHAPTER 10: STORAGE HARDWARE 314
CHAPTER 11: NETWORKS AND DATA COMMUNICATIONS 340

UNIT FOUR **INFORMATION SYSTEMS** **380**

CHAPTER 12: MANAGEMENT AND DECISION SUPPORT SYSTEMS 382
CHAPTER 13: SYSTEMS DESIGN AND IMPLEMENTATION 414
CHAPTER 14: SOFTWARE DEVELOPMENT 454

UNIT FIVE **TECHNOLOGICAL TRENDS** **498**

CHAPTER 15: PRIVACY, ETHICS, CRIME, AND SECURITY 500
CHAPTER 16: KEEPING UP WITH CHANGE 532

APPENDICES

A: INTRODUCTION TO MS-DOS/PC-DOS 568
B: INTRODUCTION TO MICROSOFT'S WINDOWS 596
C: INTRODUCTION TO THE APPLE MACINTOSH 628
D: PROGRAMMING PERSONAL COMPUTERS IN BASIC 650
E: BUYING A PERSONAL COMPUTER SYSTEM 696

Detailed Contents

UNIT ONE **INFORMATION TECHNOLOGY AT WORK** **2**

CHAPTER 1 END-USER COMPUTING 4

From the User's Point of View 5
Increasing Your Productivity 5
Who's Who: Blaise Pascal 9
Turning Data into Useful Information 10
In the News: Computer Literacy 12
The Impact of Information Technology 16
In the News: Fighting Fear of Change 18
Who's Who: Steve Jobs and Steve Wozniak 20
A Closer Look . . . Personal Computing 22
Chapter Facts 25
Terms to Remember 26
Mix and Match 26
Review Questions 28
Applying What You've Learned 28
Answers to Mix and Match 29

CHAPTER 2 COMPUTER INFORMATION SYSTEMS 30

From the User's Point of View 31
System Components 31
People 31
In the News: Computer Chips 32
Data 36
Procedures 39
Hardware 41
Who's Who: John Mauchly and J. Presper Eckert 42
In the News: Caring for Your Floppy Disks 44
Software 46
A Closer Look . . . Buying a Computer System 49
Chapter Facts 54
Terms to Remember 55
Mix and Match 56
Review Questions 57
Applying What You've Learned 58
Answers to Mix and Match 59

CHAPTER 3 SOFTWARE CONCEPTS 60

From the User's Point of View 61
User Interfaces 61
Evaluating Software Features 66
In the News: Operating Systems: Top 10 User Priorities 66
Systems Software 75
In the News: Desktop Operating Systems 75
In the News: The Futz Factor 77
Who's Who: William (Bill) Gates 79
Where to Find Software 83
A Closer Look . . . Comparing Popular Operating Environments 87
Chapter Facts 93
Terms to Remember 94
Mix and Match 94
Review Questions 96
Applying What You've Learned 97
Answers to Mix and Match 97

UNIT TWO PERSONAL PRODUCTIVITY TOOLS 98

CHAPTER 4 WORD PROCESSING AND DESKTOP PUBLISHING 100

From the User's Point of View 101
Word Processing 101
Who's Who: Bruce Bastian and Alan Ashton 110
Desktop Publishing 113
In the News: How to Improve Your Computer Communication 118
Automating the Office 122
In the News: 10 Ways to Make Your Office Environment-Friendly 123
A Closer Look . . . Selecting a Word Processing Package 129
Chapter Facts 133
Terms to Remember 134
Mix and Match 134
Review Questions 135
Applying What You've Learned 136
Answers to Mix and Match 137

CHAPTER 5 ELECTRONIC SPREADSHEETS 138

From the User's Point of View 139
Presenting and Processing Numbers 139
Electronic Spreadsheets: Features and Functions 142
In the News: Selecting Software 143
Who's Who: Daniel Bricklin and Robert Frankston 158
Spreadsheets as a Tool 158
A Closer Look . . . Designing a Better Worksheet 162
Chapter Facts 166
Terms to Remember 167
Mix and Match 167
Review Questions 168
Applying What You've Learned 169
Answers to Mix and Match 169

CHAPTER 6 GRAPHICS AND MULTIMEDIA 170

From the User's Point of View 171
Graphical Tools 171
Presentation Graphics 173
In the News: Trends in Computer Graphics Market 174
In the News: Presentation Rules of Thumb 177
Free-Drawing Graphics 181
Multimedia 185
Graphics and Multimedia Applications 191
Who's Who: Marshall McLuhan 193
A Closer Look . . . Presentation Software 198
Chapter Facts 202
Terms to Remember 203
Mix and Match 203
Review Questions 204
Applying What You've Learned 205
Answers to Mix and Match 205

CHAPTER 7 FILE AND DATABASE MANAGEMENT 206

From the User's Point of View 207
Data Processing 207
Who's Who: Edgar F. Codd 209
File Management 212
In the News: Characteristics of Good Information 218
Database Management 219
Applications for Data Management Software 227
A Closer Look . . . Hypermedia 233
Chapter Facts 236
Terms to Remember 237
Mix and Match 237
Review Questions 238
Applying What You've Learned 239
Answers to Mix and Match 239

UNIT THREE HARDWARE AND COMMUNICATIONS 240

CHAPTER 8 PROCESSING HARDWARE 242

From the User's Point of View 243
Processing in the Past 243
Binary Codes for Data and Instructions 247
The Central Processing Unit 250
Who's Who: William Shockley, John Bardeen, and Walter Brattain 251
In the News: Before Calling Technical Support 253
In the News: The History of Electronic Computing 256
Who's Who: Jack Kilby, Robert Noyce, Marcian Hoff, and Gilbert Hyatt 261
Hardware to Solve Different Problems 263
A Closer Look . . . The Making of a Microprocessor 271
Chapter Facts 275
Terms to Remember 276
Mix and Match 277
Review Questions 278
Applying What You've Learned 279
Answers to Mix and Match 279

CHAPTER 9 INPUT/OUTPUT HARDWARE 280

From the User's Point of View 281
Input Hardware Options 281
In the News: Ergonomics of Input 291
Output Hardware Solutions 293
In the News: Tips for Reducing Computer Vision Syndrome 293
Who's Who: Joseph Marie Jacquard 296
Peripheral Design and Safety 304
A Closer Look . . . Peripherals for Special Applications 307
Chapter Facts 309
Terms to Remember 310
Mix and Match 310
Review Questions 312
Applying What You've Learned 313
Answers to Mix and Match 313

CHAPTER 10 STORAGE HARDWARE 314

From the User's Point of View 315
Magnetic Disk Storage 315
In the News: Backup Tips 319
Optical Disk Storage 323
In the News: Optical Storage Disks 325
Magnetic Tape Storage 326
Who's Who: Herman Hollerith 328
Specialized Storage Hardware 330
Maximizing Hardware Performance 331
A Closer Look . . . Building a Personal Computer 333
Chapter Facts 336
Terms to Remember 337
Mix and Match 337
Review Questions 338
Applying What You've Learned 339
Answers to Mix and Match 339

CHAPTER 11 NETWORKS AND DATA COMMUNICATIONS 340

From the User's Point of View 341
The Need for Data Communications 341
Networks 343
In the News: Don't Be Overloaded 349
Data Communications 354
Who's Who: Augusta Ada Byron (Countess of Lovelace) 358
Network Applications 361
Who's Who: George Boole 363
In the News: The Ten Deadly Network Sins 368

A Closer Look . . . Information Utilities 371
Chapter Facts 374
Terms to Remember 375
Mix and Match 376
Review Questions 377
Applying What You've Learned 378
Answers to Mix and Match 379

UNIT FOUR INFORMATION SYSTEMS 380

CHAPTER 12 MANAGEMENT AND DECISION-SUPPORT SYSTEMS 382

From the User's Point of View 383
Management Information Systems 383
In the News: The Winds of Change 390
Decision-Support Systems 392
In the News: Expensive Executive Toys or Productivity Tools 395
Who's Who: Thomas John Watson, Sr. 396
Tools to Enhance Decision Making 398
A Closer Look . . . Developing an Expert System 407
Chapter Facts 409
Terms to Remember 410
Mix and Match 410
Review Questions 412
Applying What You've Learned 412
Answers to Mix and Match 413

CHAPTER 13 SYSTEMS DESIGN AND IMPLEMENTATION 414

From the User's Point of View 415
Handling Information Problems 415
Life-Cycle Step One: Requirements 418
In the News: How Secure Is It? 422
Life-Cycle Step Two: Alternative Evaluation 423
Who's Who: Charles Babbage 426
In the News: A Properly Planned Interview Can Be An Analyst's Best Tool 428
Life-Cycle Step Three: Design 429
Life-Cycle Step Four: Implementation 438
A Closer Look . . . Project Management Software 446
Chapter Facts 449
Terms to Remember 450
Mix and Match 450
Review Questions 452
Applying What You've Learned 453
Answers to Mix and Match 453

CHAPTER 14 SOFTWARE DEVELOPMENT 454

From the User's Point of View 455
People and Programming 455
Designing the Program 458
In the News: User-Driven Computer Training Tips 458
Who's Who: John G. Kemeny and Thomas E. Kurtz 468
Writing Program Code 469
In the News: Advantages over Traditional Methods 471
Testing and Debugging 485
Documentation and Training 486
A Closer Look . . . Programming Languages (No Matter How You Say It) 489
Chapter Facts 493
Terms to Remember 494
Mix and Match 494
Review Questions 496
Applying What You've Learned 496
Answers to Mix and Match 497

UNIT FIVE TECHNOLOGICAL TRENDS 498

CHAPTER 15 PRIVACY, ETHICS, CRIME, AND SECURITY 500

From the User's Point of View 501
Privacy 501
Ethics 504
Crime 508
In the News: Taking a Byte Out of Crime 510
Security 516
Who's Who: Seymour Papert 518
A Closer Look . . . Privacy—Is It Still Possible? 525
Chapter Facts 528
Terms to Remember 528
Mix and Match 529
Review Questions 529
Applying What You've Learned 530
Answers to Mix and Match 531

CHAPTER 16 KEEPING UP WITH CHANGE 532

From the User's Point of View 533
An Information Society 533
In the News: Rise of the Visual Communicator 541
Skills Updating 547
Career Paths 550
Who's Who: J. Georg Bednorz and Karl Müller 554
Who's Who: Alan Turing 556
A Closer Look . . . Emerging Technologies 559
Chapter Facts 563
Terms to Remember 564
Mix and Match 564
Review Questions 565
Applying What You've Learned 566
Answers to Mix and Match 567

APPENDIX A INTRODUCTION TO MS-DOS/PC-DOS 568

From the User's Point of View 569
Personal Computer Start-Up Procedures 569
DOS Commands and Utility Programs 577
System Shut-Down 591
Chapter Facts 592
Terms to Remember 593
Mix and Match 593
Review Questions 594
Applying What You've Learned 595
Answers to Mix and Match 595

APPENDIX B INTRODUCTION TO MICROSOFT WINDOWS 596

From the User's Point of View 597
Personal Computer Start-Up Procedures 597
The Program Manager 603
Common Window Features 607
The File Manager 611
System Shut-Down 622
Chapter Facts 624
Terms to Remember 625
Mix and Match 625
Review Questions 626
Applying What You've Learned 627
Answers to Mix and Match 627

APPENDIX C INTRODUCTION TO THE APPLE MACINTOSH 628

From the User's Point of View 629
Personal Computer Start-Up Procedures 629
Using a Mouse and Initializing a Diskette 632
Common Window Features 637
Applications, Documents, and Folders 640
Shutting Down the System 645
Chapter Facts 646
Terms to Remember 647
Mix and Match 647
Review Questions 648
Applying What You've Learned 648
Answers to Mix and Match 649

APPENDIX D PROGRAMMING PERSONAL COMPUTERS IN BASIC 650

From the User's Point of View 651
The Basics about BASIC 651
Performing Computations 657
Repeating Program Instructions 661
Controlling Program Loops 668
Applying What You've Learned 674
Working with Text 676
More on Loops 680
Tying It All Together 685
Chapter Facts 690
Terms to Remember 691
Mix and Match 692
Review Questions 693
Applying What You've Learned 694
Answers to Mix and Match 695

APPENDIX E BUYING A PERSONAL COMPUTER SYSTEM 696

From the User's Point of View 697
Needs Analysis 697
Hardware Requirements 703
Complete System Requirements 712
Chapter Facts 714
Review Questions 715
Applying What You've Learned 716

GLOSSARY 717

CREDITS 742

INDEX 743

Preface to the Instructor

As we prepared to write the fourth edition of *Computers!*, we were again reminded of the speed at which technological change takes place. This technological revolution has quickened the pace of life for everyone. The core knowledge demanded of the productive worker and the informed citizen has increased dramatically. Regardless of past experiences or future career choices, today's (and tomorrow's) members of society must be technologically literate, as well as computer literate.

The difficulty comes in conveying to students *why* certain knowledge is essential, *what* is important, and *how* this information can be applied. The wealth of information available can be overwhelming. *Computers!* has proved that this information is relevant and easy to understand by students young and old who have little technological experience. To these people, your students, we hope to provide an up-to-date guide to information technology.

NEW TO THIS EDITION

Connectivity and increased integration of personal computers into the workplace continue to be underlying themes in *Computers!*. We have been closely watching these and other technological trends that are changing what a computer literate person needs to know. Incorporating coverage of these trends, as well as integrating suggestions from educators who have taught from earlier editions, has resulted in some important changes to the fourth edition:

Early Presentation of Personal Computer Concepts

We know most students are eager to start the hands-on part of a computer class. Therefore, software and hardware concepts necessary for operating personal computers are discussed in the first three chapters. Terms associated with graphical user interfaces, like click and drag, have been added. As with earlier editions, the fourth edition is designed to provide educators and their students with maximum flexibility in the coverage of computer concepts. Once Unit One is completed, students will be ready to read any chapter in Unit Two (Personal Productivity Tools) or Unit Three (Hardware and Data Communications).

Splitting Peripherals into Storage and I/O Components

Several topics are reorganized in the fourth edition to better meet user expectations and to make the topics as practical as possible. In response to wider utilization of CD technology and the explosion of multimedia applications, the chapter on peripheral hardware has been split in two: Input and output equipment, such as color monitors and laser printers, are covered in Chapter 9, and Chapter 10 now focuses on magnetic and optical storage hardware. By dividing this information into two chapters, the number of new terms and concepts students cover at one time is more manageable.

Putting Historical Developments into Perspective

Expanded coverage of hardware innovations challenged us to reexamine how we introduce technological concepts. In doing so we realized that technological breakthroughs might be better understood from an applications rather than an historical point of view. As a result, people and concepts that once appeared together in the Technological Progress chapter have become special "Who's Who" features. Microsoft's founder Bill Gates, for example, is featured in Chapter 3 on Software Concepts. Herman Hollerith of punched-card fame is discussed in Chapter 10 on Storage Hardware.

Graphics Evolves into Multimedia

New user interfaces, virtual realities, applications for voice and sound, and the wider acceptance of Macintosh microcomputers and Microsoft's Windows have placed a new generation of tools into our computerized toolboxes. Along with coverage of these new tools, more emphasis is placed on the uses, limits, and operation of the technology currently available to your students. These changes are clearly evident in the reorganization of information on graphics into a new Graphics and Multimedia chapter.

New Appendix on Purchasing a Personal Computer

A new appendix that walks students through the process of purchasing a personal computer has been added by popular demand. We are often asked by our students which personal computer system we would recommend. Appendix E helps students answer this question by identifying personal applications and providing a closer look at the trade-offs and decisions people must make when buying a personal computer system.

Personal Productivity

The fourth edition is also updated with the latest innovations in personal productivity. Personal digital assistants and pen-based computers are discussed from a user's perspective in Chapter 8 on Processing Hardware. The impact of networks, personal computers, and interactive services is discussed in Chapter 11 on Networks and Data Communications. Other chapters have expanded coverage of multiprocessing computers along with fourth and fifth generation computer languages. Chapter 15 on Privacy, Ethics, Crime, and Security asks students to examine the rights of others when making decisions that concern ethical standards and privacy issues.

KEY FEATURES

Educators who have used earlier editions of *Computers!* have stated that its enduring strengths lie in its readability, comprehensive coverage, and modular design. We have tried to build on these strengths in the following ways:

Flexible Design

This textbook contains much more than just explanations of current computer concepts. You can deliver this information to your students by using different chapter combinations and a variety of teaching tools. A hands-on introduction to DOS, Windows, Macintosh System 6 or System 7, and BASIC programming are available in the appendices. A practical guide to purchasing a personal computer system is found in Appendix E. Furthermore, over three dozen tutorial lab manuals for popular application packages and user interfaces can be integrated with the concepts covered in *Computers!*.

Pedagogy

As in previous editions, *Computers!* emphasizes the integration of terms and concepts with the students' need to apply this information to their present and future work. Each chapter contains the following pedagogical features to support this goal.

- **Key Ideas**—topical outline of the chapter.
- **From the User's Point of View**—aids students' continuous search for relevance in what they are asked to learn.
- **Chapter Facts**—succinct presentation of the most important information in each chapter.
- **Terms to Remember**—listing of key words and phrases.

- **Mix and Match (new)**—asks students to match key terms to their definitions.
- **Review Questions**—objective questions about the key points in the chapter, easily answerable from the text.
- **Applying What You've Learned**—questions and projects requiring creative thought and independent research by the student.

Additional assignments, accompanying worksheets, and crossword puzzles using Terms to Remember are provided in the accompanying Student Study Guide. Together, these materials will help to motivate and reinforce student learning.

Real World Applications and Examples

The fourth edition includes many scenarios using technology in real situations. This alerts students to how all-encompassing technology really is. In addition, three features of special interest appear in each chapter:

- **"In the News"**—clips from the media that highlight topics of practical or special interest to students.
- **"Who's Who"**—a brief look at the people responsible for the technological innovations that change our lives:

Chapter 1	Pascal; Jobs and Wozniak
Chapter 2	Mauchly and Eckert
Chapter 3	Gates
Chapter 4	Bastian and Ashton
Chapter 5	Bricklin and Frankston
Chapter 6	McLuhan
Chapter 7	Codd
Chapter 8	Bardeen, Brattain, and Shockley; Hoff, Hyatt, Kilby, and Noyce
Chapter 9	Jacquard
Chapter 10	Hollerith
Chapter 11	Lovelace and Boole
Chapter 12	Watson, Sr.
Chapter 13	Babbage
Chapter 14	Kemeny and Kurtz
Chapter 15	Papert
Chapter 16	Bednorz and Muller; Turing

- **"A Closer Look"**—an in-depth and graphical investigation of a topic presented in each chapter:

Chapter 1	Personal Computing
Chapter 2	Buying a Computer System
Chapter 3	Comparing Popular Operating Environments
Chapter 4	Selecting a Word Processing Package
Chapter 5	Designing a Better Worksheet
Chapter 6	Presentation Software
Chapter 7	Hypermedia
Chapter 8	The Making of a Microprocessor

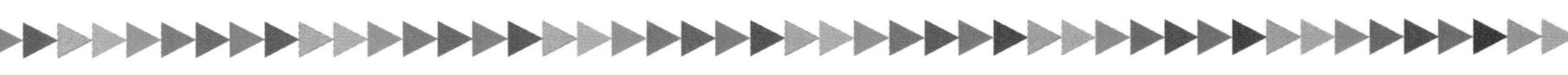

Chapter 9 Peripherals for Special Applications
Chapter 10 Building a Personal Computer
Chapter 11 Information Utilities
Chapter 12 Developing an Expert System
Chapter 13 Project Management Software
Chapter 14 Programming Languages (No Matter How You Say It)
Chapter 15 Privacy ... Is It Still Possible?
Chapter 16 Emerging Technologies

The result, *Computers!,* is a comprehensive, flexible, multimedia package designed to help you introduce computer concepts and promote computer awareness to students with various backgrounds and needs.

SUPPLEMENTARY MATERIALS

The following supplementary materials were developed to help customize *Computers!* to your unique teaching style and course objectives:

Complete Instructor's Manual

The Instructor's Manual for this edition contains detailed support material for each chapter:

- lecture outline
- transparency masters keyed to the lecture outline
- additional material for lectures not found in the text
- teaching tips
- complete answers to the Review Questions
- suggestions for related lab assignments and class projects not included in the Student Study Guide
- bibliographic list for additional research

Student Study Guide

The Student Study Guide includes space for answering in-text review questions, projects with related worksheets, crossword puzzles, and references for each chapter. Answers are not printed in the Study Guide; they can be found in the Instructor's Manual only.

Computerized and Printed Testbank

Over 2000 true/false, multiple-choice, and fill-in questions correspond to the Review Questions in the text. These are available both in printed form and on disk with the McGraw-Hill Test Generator.

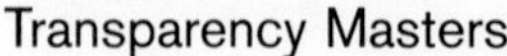

Transparency Masters

Two sets of transparency masters support the text. The first contains black and white reproductions of figures found in *Computers!*. These masters are keyed to the lecture outline in the Instructor's Manual. The second set is in full color. These color transparencies were designed to supplement figures and concepts from the text.

Broadcast Quality Videotapes

"Computers at Work," the popular documentary-style videocourse that is broadcast extensively by PBS and numerous statewide consortia, complements this new edition of *Computers!*. This video series can be supplemented by the Student Videocourse Manual, which keys reading assignments in *Computers!* to each of the following video lessons:

1. The Information Age
2. The Computer System
3. Computer Hardware
4. Computer Software
5. Business Systems Development
6. Computer Communications
7. Database Systems
8. Microcomputers
9. Computers and Society
10. Artificial Intelligence and the Future
11. Computer Crime, Viruses, and Security
12. Computer Careers

Application Software and Manuals

A variety of hands-on tutorials are available both with and without software. Applications packages covered include current versions of IBM and Macintosh operating systems; wordprocessing, spreadsheet, database, and integrated software; and commercial software and shareware. For a current list of these materials, contact your McGraw-Hill sales representative.

SPECIAL ACKNOWLEDGMENTS

It is impossible for textbook authors to produce a book alone. Many people have been involved in this project. Some deserve our special thanks for their care and help. At the top of our list is Erika Berg of Mitchell/McGraw-Hill. She has been a welcome constant in our writing lives. With her endless sense of humor and talent for compromise, she invigorated us. We wish her luck in her future plans. We will miss her.

The wonderful presentation of text is due to fine production experts, including Jennifer Gilliland and Jane Somers of Mitchell/McGraw-Hill, Greg Hubit of Bookworks, Christy Butterfield, and Monica Suder.

David R. Adams contributed material for the Macintosh tutorial in Appendix C. C. Brian Honess developed the BASIC tutorial for

Appendix D. Many of the "conventional wisdoms" presented in Appendix E can be credited to Roger Carlson, whose own wisdom was a great contribution to this manuscript. Jeff Stipes' work on spreadsheets from *Software Tools in Business* (Mitchell/McGraw-Hill, 1991) was the inspiration for Chapter 5. Nor can we forget David Kroenke's five-component model and insights about business systems, which are still solid after four editions. To each of these individuals, a very special thank you.

Finally, we would like to thank these people for their assistance with *Computers!* in both this and previous editions: Geoff Alexander, Cabrillo College; Julius Archibald, Plattsburgh State University; Gary Armstrong, Shippensburg University; Kathryn Baalman, St. Charles County Community College; Dr. Bauers, Fairmont State College; Jim Blaisdale, Humboldt State University; Don Bogema, Muskegon Community College; Jack Breglio, Rancho Santiago College; Susan Brender, Boise State University; Harry Brown, Muskegon Community College; Bruce Burns, Fish-Are-Us; Keith Carver, Sacramento City College; Lee Cornell, Mankato State University; William Cornette, Southwest Missouri State University; Steve Deam, Milwaukee Area Technical College; Kent DeYoung, Muskegon Community College; Pat Fenton, West Valley College; Marie Flatley, San Diego State University; Janet Gerth, Essex Community College; Professor Haag, University of South Florida; Terry Hamberger, York College of Pennsylvania; Rick Hamill, Beech Tree Farm; Cindy Hanchey, Oklahoma Baptist College; Frank Hannum, Eight-Bit Corner; Greg Hodge, Northwestern Michigan College; Enid Irwin, Santa Monica College; Peter Irwin, Richland College; Maribeth King, Kigore College; Linda Knight, Northern Illinois University; Linda Lantz, Community College of Aurora; Thom Luce, Ohio University; James Mathews, Siena College; Lynn McAustin, Cuesta College; Paula McClurg-Ziemelis, Muskegon Community College; Richard Otto, REO Consulting; Michael Michaelson, Palomar College; Blair Morrissey, Muskegon Community College; Patti Nunnally, John Tyler Community College; Randy Pidhayny, Silicon Graphics; Robert Pobasco, University of Idaho; Daniel Randles, General Telephone; Herb Rebhun, University of Houston - Downtown; John Salzsieder, Phillips University; Rosemary Skeele, Seton Hall University; Rod Southworth, Laramie County Community College; Jesse Sprayberry, Muskegon Area Skills Training Center; Roger Stoel, Muskegon Community College; Earl Talbert, Central Piedmont Community College; Nancy Tate, Washburn University; Antony Tiona, Broward Community College; Todd Trainor, Dow Chemical Corporation; Kenneth Walker, Weber State University; Randy Weinberg, St. Cloud State University; David Wen, Diablo Valley College; Dave Wenk, Martin-Marietta Corporation; David Whitney, San Francisco State University; Francis Whittle, Dutchess Community College; and Louis Wolff, Moorpark College.

Timothy N. Trainor
Diane Krasnewich

Muskegon, Michigan

UNIT ONE

Information Technology at Work

Throughout history people have turned to technology to help them solve problems. Chapter 1 discusses reasons for studying about computers and overviews how these problem-solving machines are used in society. It also examines the four-step cycle that computers and other tools employ when working. Additionally, the chapter explores situations where the computer cannot or should not be used.

Computers are just one component of a unified system. Besides the actual machines, a computer system also requires people, procedures, data, and programs. Chapter 2 examines how these components fit together to increase the user's productivity. The five-component model is a common thread tying together the diverse applications for computer systems presented throughout this book.

Chapter 3 overviews the common properties of application and systems software. The chapter starts off by examining common user interfaces people employ when interacting with a computer system. Sources for computer programs and the need to choose software based on the user's needs and level of understanding are discussed at length.

1

End-User Computing

- **From the User's Point of View**
- **Increasing Your Productivity**
  - **Impact on critical thinking**
  - **Promoting the competitive edge**
- **Turning Data into Useful Information**
  - **The IPOS cycle**
  - **What is a computer?**
  - **Computer software**
  - **Types of data**
- **The Impact of Information Technology**
  - **Expanding your capabilities**
  - **What computers can, cannot, and should not do**
  - **Mastering change**
- *A Closer Look . . . Personal Computing*

FROM THE USER'S POINT OF VIEW

Computers are changing the way we work, play, and live. This chapter sets the tone of the book by introducing you to the fundamental computer concepts behind the input, processing, output, and storage cycle; programmable tools; and data communications. After we explain what computers can and cannot do, you are challenged to question what they should not be asked to do.

INCREASING YOUR PRODUCTIVITY

As John Morse and Sally Anderson watched, the building began to vibrate. The shaking was slight at first, then increasing. Finally, as the building swayed its main entrance crumpled and collapsed. After a few seconds, the vibrations stopped, leaving the building only partially standing. The two observers had watched in silence from the first shocks.

"Let's see if we can pinpoint the problem," Sally said. She made a few entries on a keyboard connected to a computer. They had viewed the simulated effects of an earthquake on the attached screen. A printer also located in the small architectural office clattered for several seconds. John tore off a sheet of paper and showed it to Sally.

"I'm not sure, but I think we need to beef up the strength of that crossbeam over the entrance. Let's send these results to Juan's computer downtown to see if he agrees."

Sally was enthusiastic. "This is great," she said, as she keyed in the downtown office's number. "With hand calculations, it would have taken us days to do this analysis. By using the computer, we have our answers in a matter of minutes. Better still, we can send the information across town or around the world."

"And we have more assurance that our building will be safe," John concluded. "It's hard to remember how we did things before computers."

John stopped to think about how the computer had changed his professional life and had increased his personal productivity. Architects have known formulas to measure structural strength for over 100 years. Computers have taken professionally accepted techniques and improved them. A computer can complete computations in minutes that used to take days for people to do.

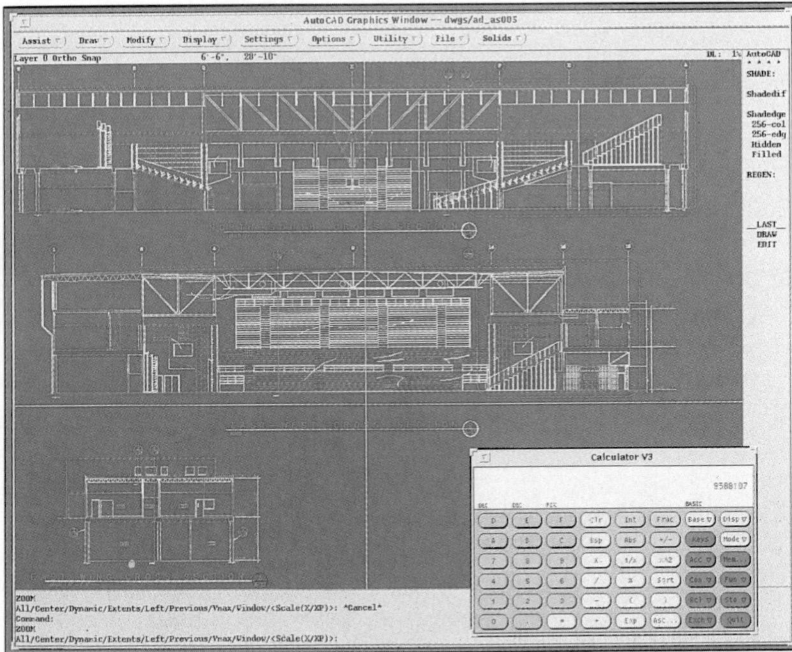

FIGURE 1.1
Computer-aided design helps architects and engineers simulate ideas at very early stages of design.

People who use computers can concentrate on solving major problems without worrying about all the minor details. Previously, people were mainly involved in solving mathematical equations, or "crunching numbers." By doing the routine calculations for people, computers have allowed human creativity and productivity to increase.

By linking computers and communications technology, information and ideas fly between computer users at the speed of light. Delays that could handicap project coordination are minimized. Furthermore, this technology promotes critical communication between people even when they are separated by large distances.

Computers perform a variety of jobs. In John and Sally's office, secretaries and architectural assistants use word processing programs on computers for correspondence, to list structural specifications, to write proposals to clients, and for other jobs.

Impact on Critical Thinking

Since the 1940s people have turned to the computer for help in solving problems. A **computer** is a machine that processes facts and figures to produce useful information. Through the years computers have become smaller, more powerful, and less expensive. As more organizations bring computers into the workplace, more people become exposed to what computers can do and acquire more computer skills. As early as elementary school, children are using computers to write stories and do math. As a result, computers influence the way many people think about and approach problems. The average person depends on, is served by, or actually operates some type of computer several times each day.

It is obvious, then, that computers will be a part of everyone's life. Your future success will require a basic level of knowledge about computers and skill in using them. This book is designed to help you attain these goals. As you read and complete assignments in this text, you will learn to involve computers in your critical thinking. You should understand how computers affect your life and how they are used to solve everyday problems. You should be able to talk intelligently about computers. Equally important, you should be prepared for the changes computers will bring into your life.

Computers are installed in cars, toys, and appliances. They are used by musicians, waitresses, artists, bank tellers, and teachers. Computers collect meteorological data, transmit it to other computers for processing, forecast the weather, and support the television and radio broadcasts of this forecast (Figure 1.2). People research, write, and edit books with the aid of computers. Then, with assistance from computers, they instantly print out the words many miles away. Doctors, lawyers, pilots, auto mechanics, and sales clerks all depend upon computers. Computers help people to organize and save their thoughts. Thought itself can be stimulated by computers that serve as storehouses of facts and figures. These facts and figures about people, things, ideas, and events are called **data.**

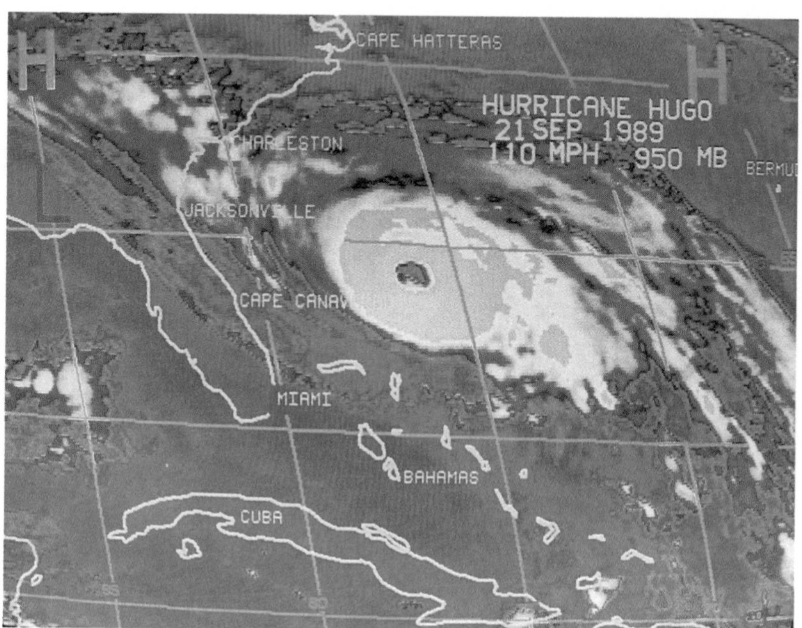

FIGURE 1.2
The speed with which computers collect and process data into useful information helps us to track and forecast weather patterns.

Promoting the Competitive Edge

With each passing year, computers become more powerful and less expensive. As more people use computers, new technological advances are introduced. Many of these improvements are intended to make computers easier to use, or more **user friendly.** Computers will allow you to become more competitive in the workplace and more efficient at home.

At home, computers are responsible for many comforts and conveniences. Microwave ovens, using computers and meat probes, turn themselves off when the proper internal temperature is reached. Computerized clothes dryers continually monitor the moisture level of clothes and shut off when a preset level of dryness has been reached. These situations are examples of **process control,** where computers constantly monitor and adjust an activity without direct human intervention. Process control is just one of several labor-saving tasks computers perform.

Many forms of recreation also depend on computers. Some people spend their leisure time at video arcades filled with computer-driven games. Computer **simulations** generate images that imitate real life or imaginary situations such as high-speed race tracks, jungle obstacle courses, or intergalactic battlefields. Animators use computers to produce the lifelike graphics found in movies, advertisements, and television shows. Architects, like John and Sally, simulate stresses caused by earthquakes or high winds on new building designs. Engineers simulate the performance of new aircraft and automotive designs before the products are actually built.

FIGURE 1.3
Information technology links students in remote classrooms together to exchange ideas and conserve resources.

With the aid of computers, scientists perform **data storage and retrieval.** Data from current research can be stored on a computer, and computerized data libraries can be searched to find relevant reference materials. Sources of information often exist in different geographic locations and are accessed through standard telephone lines. Data is usually organized and cross-referenced in large collections called **databases.** With computers, this kind of data retrieval takes a fraction of the time required to find the same information by hand. Computers also can control scientific experiments, monitor instruments used in lab tests, and analyze collected data.

In health care, computers assist physicians in diagnosing illnesses by relating symptoms to information in a medical database. Computer-controlled surgical devices aid in delicate operations. Computers monitor the vital signs, such as heart rate, of critically ill patients. Other computers maintain a patient's medical history for attending health professionals. Computer technology has generated many new medical techniques.

The competitive business world requires successful people to use a computer's speed and accuracy for **data processing.** By utilizing

Who's Who

Blaise Pascal (1632–1662)

From his earliest days, Blaise Pascal showed mathematical promise. By age 16 he had written an important book on geometry. In order to help his father, a tax commissioner, with a barrage of calculations, 18-year-old Pascal built a mechanical adding machine. Called "la Pascaline," it used cogged wheels to add and subtract up to 8-digit numbers. Its design was tailored to handle data in the form of the French monetary system.

Pascal's goal was to see his machine in every business and upper-class house of France. Unfortunately, it did not get the welcome he thought it deserved. La Pascaline was too expensive to be practical, although over 500 models were made. Depressed by his lack of success, Pascal turned his life to religion. Sporadic forays into physics and mathematics left a legacy to the scientific community. He died young, still upset by the failure of his invention.

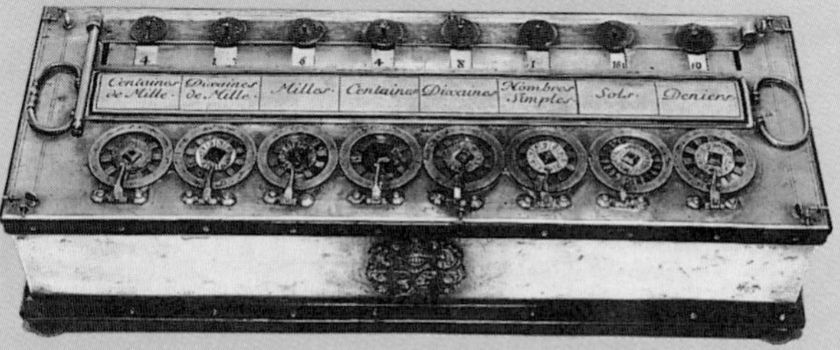

computers to convert facts and figures into useful information, businesspeople can keep track of their inventory, have immediate access to sales information, and quickly identify potential customers.

Computers can meet the individual needs of a classroom full of students. Computers can be tutors by presenting materials to students and quizzing them later. These machines also are a tool for students; they help them retrieve information for papers, type and edit the papers, produce graphs and drawings, compute answers to problems, and simulate dangerous lab experiments or historical battles. Behind the scenes, teachers are using computers to grade tests and keep student records. As shown in Figure 1.3, computers even link together classrooms from remote locations to support the exchange of ideas and values.

Computers, then, touch every aspect of your life. Understanding computers and learning how to use them is necessary both now and in the future.

TURNING DATA INTO USEFUL INFORMATION

omputers help people save time and solve problems. As a problem-solving tool the computer has much in common with other tools you use regularly. To illustrate, you have just enjoyed a delicious dinner and have a problem: dirty dishes.

The IPOS Cycle

You have some options in deciding how to solve this problem. You can use a tool—a dishwasher—or do the dishes by hand. Prospective computer users often face the same kind of decision. They can use a computer to do a job or can do it by hand.

Using the dishwasher and other tools involves four basic steps:

1. **Input.** You put something into the device.
2. **Processing.** The device changes the input in some way.
3. **Output.** You take results out.
4. **Storage.** You may save any results that have future value.

Assume you decide to use the dishwasher. You know the result you want. You also know the pattern of events that has to take place. Your solution is easy:

1. **Input.** You put dirty dishes and soap into a dishwasher. You press a button, and the dishwasher inputs the right amount of hot water.
2. **Processing.** The dishwasher increases the water temperature, washes and rinses the dishes, changing them from dirty to clean.
3. **Output.** You have the result you wanted—clean dishes.
4. **Storage.** You complete the job by stacking the dishes in the cupboard.

This four-step process, diagrammed in Figure 1.4, often is identified by its initials: *IPOS.* All uses for a computer, called **computer applications,** conform to the first three steps (IPO) of the cycle. The last step, storage, is included in many applications.

An activity as simple as ordering a cheeseburger at a fast-food outlet follows the IPOS cycle. As you place the order, the data is entered into a keyboard. The **keyboard** is an example of input equipment. Keyboards in fast-food outlets often have pictures of items on the menu. Pictures that represent data or a computer operation are known as **icons.** When the icon for a menu item on the

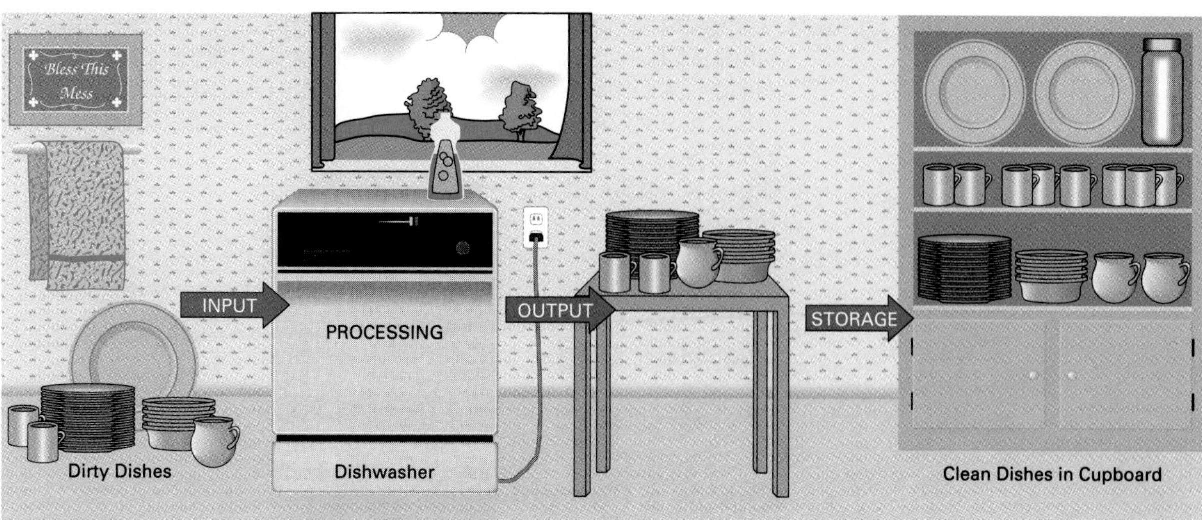

FIGURE 1.4
The IPOS cycle defines the steps common to many systems: input, processing, output, and storage.

keyboard is pressed, the computer retrieves the stored description and pricing information for that item. This immediate response of the computer to the user's request makes a computer application **interactive.** After all items have been ordered, the processing step begins.

The computer uses information input previously to calculate and print a receipt. This is done on a **printer,** output equipment that puts information on paper. The receipt includes descriptions and prices for all entered items. At the same time the item descriptions and quantities are output in the kitchen, where cooks prepare the food. The computer also stores information on the order for later use. This completes the IPOS cycle.

By exchanging your money for the food, you have participated in a **transaction,** or exchange of value. At the end of the day the computer processes all sales transactions to produce a sales report the manager can use. The report helps the manager to order more supplies and to schedule employees to match customer buying patterns.

The IPOS cycle for this system is easily identified:

1. **Input.** The counterperson presses keys to identify ordered items and quantities (Figure 1.5).
2. **Processing.** The computer multiplies quantities by prices, calculates tax amounts, and determines a total.
3. **Output.** Items and totals are printed in the kitchen and at the counter. This information is used by cooks and customers.
4. **Storage.** Data on sales, by product and time of day, is stored for later use.

FIGURE 1.5
Data entered as a food order starts an IPOS cycle, resulting in food for you and information for employees and management.

Keyboards commonly are used to type data directly into the computer. However, dialing a telephone or activating a sensor with light or sound are also ways to input data. Processing may involve sorting names into alphabetical order or applying mathematical operations to sets of numbers. When processing is complete, information is output in the form of a screen display or a printed report. Output also takes several other forms. The action of a mechanical arm as it swings into place to tighten a bolt on a new motorcycle is another example of output. The processed data is then stored until needed on special computer-operated devices. Stored information may be used as input in other applications, putting the IPOS cycle into motion again.

What Is a Computer?

For a computer to complete a job requires more than just the actual equipment, or **hardware** we see and touch. A keyboard and printer help with the input and output steps of an IPOS cycle. Other hardware, the computer, does the processing.

Much of the processing computers do can be divided into two general types of operation. **Arithmetic operations** are computations with numbers such as addition, subtraction, and other mathematical procedures. Early computers performed mostly arithmetic operations, which gave the false impression that only engineers and scientists could benefit from computers. Of equal importance is the

In the News...

COMPUTER LITERACY

A recent survey of 1,481 MIS executives found that the need for computer literacy in all levels of an organization has grown considerably in the past three years. "Managing Today's Automated Workplace," conducted by The Olsten Corp., found that 71% of companies now require computer literacy for their managers and supervisors, up from 36% three years ago. Seventy-five percent of the companies require other professionals to have computer skills; that's up from 42%.

"71% of companies now require computer literacy"

Of the executives surveyed, 86% rated employee productivity as the most critical reason for buying computers.

computer's ability to compare two values to determine if one is larger than, smaller than, or equal to the other. This is called a **logical operation.** The comparison may take place between numbers, letters, sounds, or even drawings. The processing step in the IPOS cycle is built around the computer's ability to perform logical and arithmetic operations.

Computer Software

However, instructions must be given to the computer to tell it how to process the data it receives and the format needed for output and storage.

For example, suppose a chemistry student needs to convert a series of temperatures from Fahrenheit to Celsius. With an inexpensive calculator, the following formula would have to be entered repeatedly and new values keyed each time:

$$\text{Celsius} = (\text{Fahrenheit} - 32) \times (5/9)$$

With this amount of repetition, the risk of error is high. With a computer, the equation, along with input and output steps, can be captured in a **computer program.** This program, also called **software,** provides a series of instructions followed in sequence to control the input, processing, output, and storage performed by the computer. Figure 1.6 shows a program that a chemistry student could use to complete the computation.

```
10  REM: PROGRAM TO CONVERT FAHRENHEIT TEMPERATURES
20  REM: TO CELSIUS
30  REM: ***** INPUT ROUTINE *****
40  INPUT "ENTER FAHRENHEIT TEMPERATURE: ": F
50  REM *****PROCESSING ROUTINE *****
60  C = (F - 32) * (5/9)
70  REM ***** OUTPUT ROUTINE *****
80  PRINT "CELSIUS:": C
90  INPUT "ANOTHER CONVERSION (Y/N) "; ANSWER$
100 IF ANSWER$ = "Y" THEN GO TO 40
110 END
```

FIGURE 1.6
Computer programs make it possible for people to communicate with computers in statements understandable to both humans and machines.

When the program is in place, the student enters only the Fahrenheit temperature for each conversion. The resulting information is displayed on a screen. Output also could be printed on paper or stored for later use. In either case, if the hardware is directly connected to the computer it is said to be **online.**

The ability to follow a program sets computers apart from most tools. However, new tools ranging from typewriters to electronic ovens have *embedded computers*, or built-in computers. An embedded computer can accept data to use several options in its program; however, the program itself cannot be changed. This makes the tools flexible but not computers themselves.

Types of Data

Historically, both computers and calculators used numbers as the primary form of input data. With the advent of new computing applications and hardware, the definition of data has expanded to include many types (Figure 1.7).

Numeric. **Numeric data** consists of numbers and decimal points, as well as the plus (+) and minus (−) signs. Both arithmetic operations and logical operations are performed on numeric data. This means that the numbers can be used for calculations as well as sorted and compared to each other.

Text. **Text,** or **textual data,** can contain any combination of letters, numbers, and special characters. Sometimes textual data is known as *alphanumeric* data. Usually, text is organized into words, sentences, and paragraphs. Term papers, labels, books, and correspondence are examples of textual data.

Audio-Visual. Various forms of data that we can hear or see make up **audio-visual data.** Although computers have contained speakers for many years, recently we have seen the advent of data in the form of voices and music. The computer can produce spoken output as well as accept a human voice as input. Data can also take the forms of graphs and drawings generated by both users and software. Existing visual images, such as photographs and video sequences, can be input into the computer and manipulated as data.

Physical. **Physical data** is captured from the environment. For example, light, temperature, and pressure all are types of physical data. The temperature of the room in which you are sitting may be controlled by a computer. A thermostat is set to sense the air temperature. When the temperature exceeds a specified level, a cooling

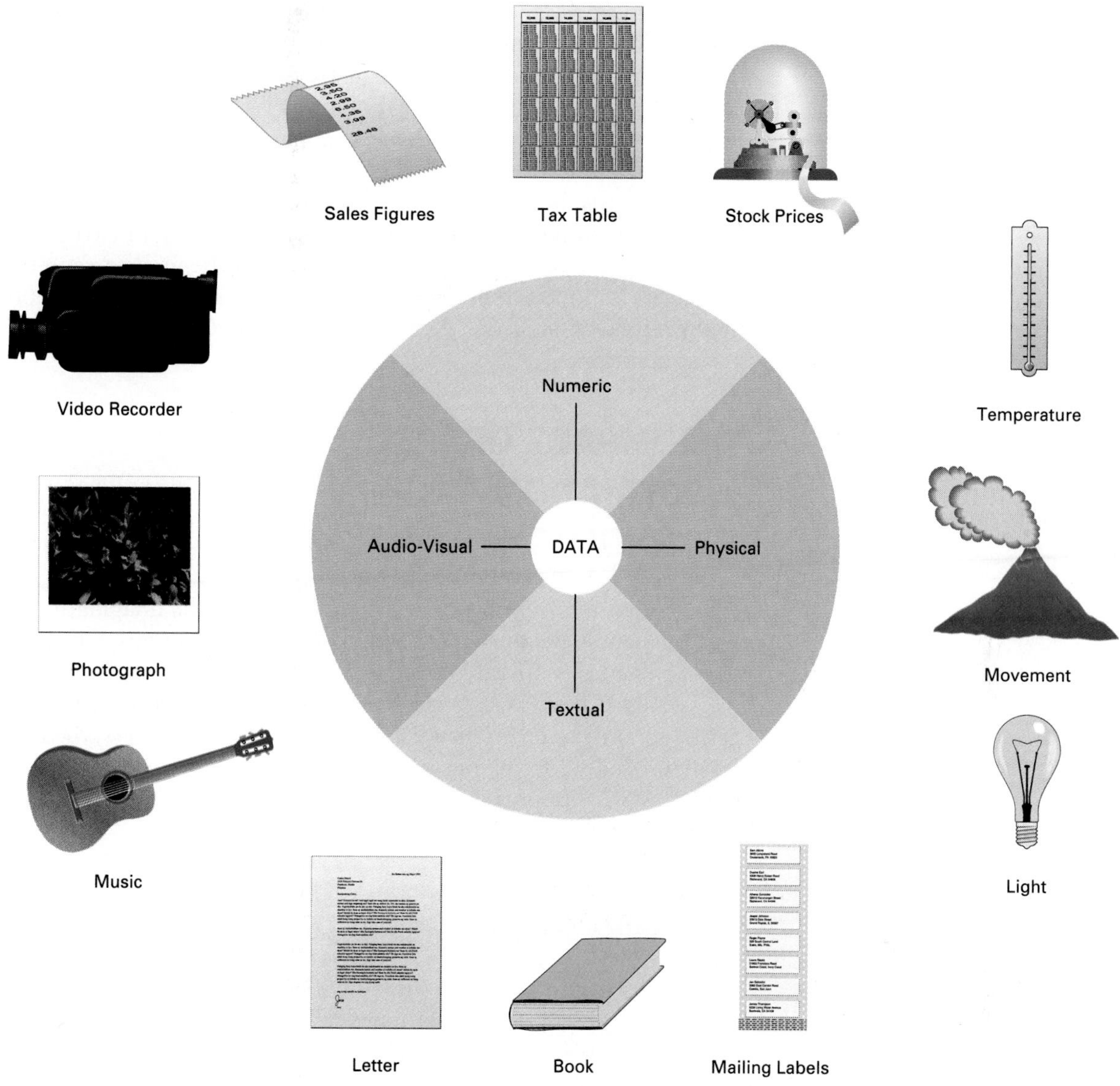

FIGURE 1.7
Data comes in different forms to accommodate a variety of input and applications.

system is turned on. The warmth of the air is used as physical data input into a thermostat to regulate room temperature. In many large buildings, computer systems process several kinds of physical data to regulate operations. Computers can set off security alarms, control temperature and humidity, or turn lights on and off, all in response to physical data. These applications increase people's safety and save them time and money.

As you can see, all types of data are stored and processed in the computer. Because computers run on electricity, the data is stored as a series of on and off patterns. Think of a row of light bulbs. Each bulb can be in only one of two states, on or off. By using different patterns of on and off bulbs, many unique combinations can be obtained. Each individual computer circuit also functions in one of two states: on (represented as 1) or off (represented as 0). These two values are *binary digits,* or **bits.** They are the building blocks for the **binary code** used to represent data and program instructions for computers. Binary means "consisting of two parts." Different patterns of bits in a binary code can be used to represent characters or operations. For example, the bit pattern 01000001 might represent the letter A, while 10111110 00100001 might represent addition.

THE IMPACT OF INFORMATION TECHNOLOGY

Information technology is limited chiefly by the imaginations of the people who program and operate the computers. Computer applications already cover a wide range of human needs and wants. These uses range from optimizing cattle feed to navigating aircraft to customizing car production. Computers, then, are powerful tools for solving problems and meeting needs in today's world. With support from human intelligence, computers can expand human capabilities.

Expanding Your Capabilities

Computers generally are equipped with vast storage capacities that permit easy access to great volumes of knowledge. Suppose a doctor receives a call from an anguished mother about a child who has swallowed a poisonous substance. The physician can be connected immediately to a computer database in Atlanta that provides exact information on antidotes, their dosages, and other treatment information. No matter how experienced a physician might be, it would be impossible for him or her to memorize such volumes of information and recall it instantly.

Fast processing speeds enable computers to perform lengthy computations or establish relationships among large amounts of data within seconds. Such speeds reduce the time people spend in routine tasks. The ability of a computer to process data quickly and accurately is invaluable for monitoring physical activity. Changes in a patient's pulse rate or in the radiation level at a nuclear power plant can be detected and reported immediately by a computer. If the correct instructions have been entered, the computer also can react automatically. For example, the computer can sound an alarm if a patient's health is endangered. If a nuclear reactor shows danger signs, the computer can initiate a shutdown sequence.

Computers also go where people cannot. In space, under the sea, and inside volcanoes, nuclear reactors, and oil refineries, computers monitor conditions and warn people when dangerous situations arise. Inside people, computers monitor body functions; inside machines, such as car ignitions or microwave ovens, computers control operations. By connecting computers together, **networks** are created that allow exchange of data and software over many locations simultaneously. Networks can link many users to the information provided by strategically placed computers.

Further, some computers can simulate, or imitate, human performance: Voice synthesizers, computer-operated limbs, and Braille printers increase the ability of physically challenged people to move about or to communicate. Computers increase the capacity of people to control their environment (Figure 1.8).

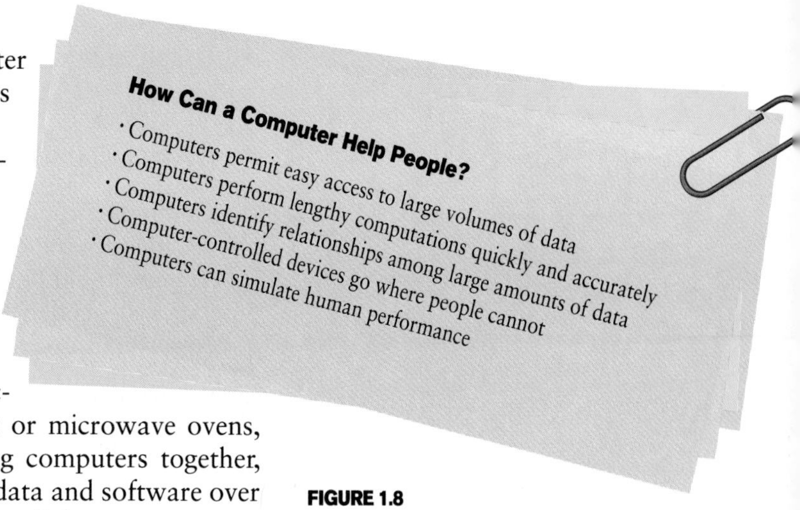

How Can a Computer Help People?
· Computers permit easy access to large volumes of data
· Computers perform lengthy computations quickly and accurately
· Computers identify relationships among large amounts of data
· Computer-controlled devices go where people cannot
· Computers can simulate human performance

FIGURE 1.8
Computers increase our capacity to control the environment in many ways.

What Computers Can, Cannot, and Should Not Do

Since computers are products of advanced technology, they tend to be regarded as mysterious. People have attributed human, even superhuman, qualities to computers. This simply is not warranted. Computers are merely tools, designed by people, programmed by people, and used by people. A computer's most basic limitation is that it cannot think; nor can it solve problems or make decisions by itself.

Computers are, however, useful in organizing information to expedite problem solving and decision making by people. By following well-written programs, computers can do amazing things. But people must do the thinking necessary to write the software.

Computers exist to benefit and assist people, not to replace them. Computers cannot, for example, make emotional judgments, disobey instructions entered by humans, or replace interpersonal relationships. On the contrary, people must be extremely explicit when instructing a computer to perform even the simplest commands. What computers can do, however, is extremely helpful. They can

- Store data in vast amounts.
- Process data quickly and accurately.

- Graphically represent numbers.
- Simulate possible outcomes based on a given set of conditions.
- Recommend or take action based on output.

Computers cannot be effective unless the people using them are able to identify the output they need, the input required, and what processing should be used to achieve those results. Ultimately, computers are dependent upon people.

Accordingly, people should not relinquish their decision-making responsibilities to computers. Humans need to be on hand to interpret conditions reported by computers, particularly if medical treatment, national defense, air traffic control, or even loan processing

In the News...

FIGHTING FEAR OF CHANGE

Experts and veterans of re-engineering projects say the biggest problem you may face is not mastering the big management principles or implementing new technology; it's probably sitting in the next office.

The human factor—more specifically, near universal dislike of change—drags down most re-engineering projects.

And experts say people are very resourceful when it comes to acting on their fear of the unknown. Their behavior can take the form of passive aggression, such as not bothering to attend an important meeting, or surface as guerrilla warfare, such as publicly proclaiming that a proposed new process has all sorts of flaws and will bomb.

The key, experts add, is to expect these reactions and continually work to manage them.

"The really hard part (of re-engineering) is in making an organization change that doesn't want to change," says Steven Stanton, a vice president at CSC Index in Cambridge, Mass.

> *"Communicate, communicate, communicate"*

Here are ideas from veterans and consultants:

Communicate, communicate, communicate. Try newsletters, videos, informal powwows, etc. The more management talks, the more quickly staff members grow comfortable with change. "If there's a chance people are going to lose their jobs, you can't keep them in the dark about it," says Mark Klein, a senior vice president and managing director at Gateway Management Consulting.

Staff re-engineering committees with the best and brightest. It sends a message through the ranks that the company considers the project crucial.

Make sure senior management stays with the project. "In large part, senior executives make pronouncements and then delegate," said Bradford Power, a principal at CSC Index and director of Index Quantum, a research and advisory service. "In re-engineering, they have to stay involved, and they aren't used to that."

are involved. Nonprogrammable, human factors must complement computer read-outs for a complete and fair analysis.

At times computers may appear to make decisions. In monitoring a building's temperature, for example, a computer might trigger a fire extinguishing system. Another computer, used for monitoring vital signs, might regulate the flow of oxygen to a patient. More complex programs that simulate human responses and decision making are said to have **artificial intelligence.** In all these cases, however, although the computer initiates action, it does not make a decision. Rather, the decisions of these process control systems were made by the human beings who programmed the machines to respond to a particular set of conditions. Therefore *people must take complete responsibility for a computer's actions.* They must anticipate all potential problems and direct computers to avoid them.

While computers may be able to enhance a person's capabilities, they can never adequately replace interpersonal relationships. Even the most sophisticated computing machinery cannot supplant parent-to-child and teacher-to-student relationships. Similarly, the rapport between physician and patient is essential for successful treatment.

People, then, are an integral part of any computer system that accepts input, processes it, and delivers output. People control computer systems through program design, by monitoring operations, and by making final decisions based upon computer output. They should not give up decision-making responsibilities because the human qualities of analysis, reasoning, and compassion are required to interpret computer-delivered results. Computers cannot operate independently. Humans are the driving force behind computer processing.

FIGURE 1.9
Computers can help hearing-impaired people to speak. However, computers cannot replace a teacher's smile or a child's look of joy.

Who's Who

Steve Jobs (b. 1955)
Steve Wozniak (b. 1950)

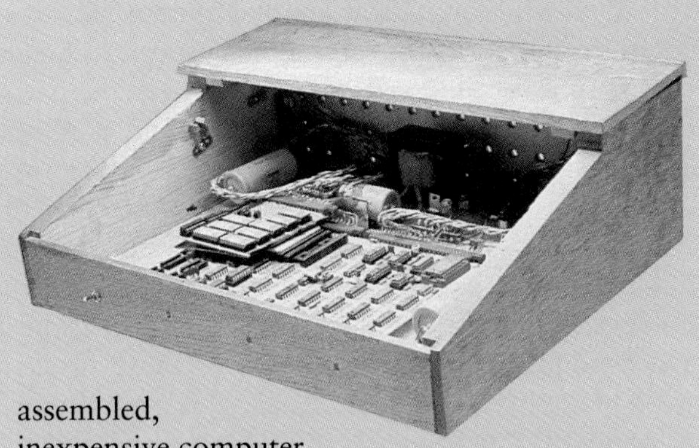

When Steve Wozniak was 13, he won first prize at a local science fair for a transistor-based calculator. Taught about electronics at an early age by his engineer father, Wozniak always wanted to be an engineer. While Wozniak was still a teenager, circuitry became available to build computers at home. He and other computer hobbyists formed the Homebrew Computer Club. In 1971 Wozniak met Steve Jobs, then 16. They found a mutual interest in computing and guessed that a completely assembled, inexpensive computer would be in demand. Using money raised from selling personal possessions, Jobs and Wozniak formed a partnership in 1975 to make the computers in Jobs' attic. The computer was somewhat primitive; it had a little keyboard and no case. Yet, at the time, people were impressed. The Apple I contained a $25 microprocessor and sold for $500. Only 175 of them were sold. By the end of 1977 the Apple II was announced, and it was highly successful. The partnership went on to become the Apple Computer Corporation. Wozniak left Apple in 1985 to start the CL9 (Cloud 9) Company. He later earned a degree in computer science under an alias. Presently he runs a company that specializes in developing universal remote controls and other technological devices. Jobs resigned from Apple also in 1985 and formed the NeXT Corporation, a firm that designs sophisticated computer programs.

Mastering Change

Change is a way of life for people in today's society. The average adult, according to some estimates, will change jobs four to seven times. To cope successfully with a changing world, the individual must recognize that change can be constructive. People who resist change because they fear new technology undermine their potential to become more effective. Still, people fear computers for many reasons:

- Some people don't understand how computers work. The "magical box" that performs seemingly amazing operations is viewed as mysterious and terrifying. However, the qualities of the computer are not mystical. Computers should be regarded as tools to be manipulated by people. The more a person understands about a computer, the more comfortable the person is with it.

- People think computers will take away their jobs. The computer is more predictable and more efficient than humans. Often it is responsible for employee displacement. Actually, the introduction of computers and automation can increase the number of jobs within a company—but the new jobs often require computer knowledge. Since this trend is likely to continue, people should learn to make computers work for them. Few benefits can be gained by rejecting computers out of fear or resentment.
- People think computers will replace free will and decision making. Fears that a machine can assume control of human thinking are unfounded. At all times people instruct computers. When computers provide information and advise decision makers, they do so according to criteria specified by people. However, computers do identify and assemble decision-related information quickly and efficiently. By using computers, decision makers can be more efficient.
- Humans are reluctant to give up old habits. Some people think change is bad. Often using new computer technology requires learning new procedures. This requirement can disrupt the "comfort level" in a job. Once people are willing to discard outdated procedures, they can promote progress. They increase their productivity, and may be able to make their lives easier, by allowing computers to take up some of their work load.

FIGURE 1.10
Keeping up with change is a necessary part of living in modern society.

By overcoming the urge to cling to the status quo, people can accept computers as an integral part of their lives. Many opportunities follow such acceptance. Computers provide people with more information in less time. Databases can be changed immediately, allowing people to act on the most current information. With fast feedback, problems can be identified and dealt with promptly. The efficiency of any operation can be enhanced with increased access to information—the primary output of computers.

Computers provide access to hundreds of information sources. Tapping these resources can provide new insights, or even prevent the waste of time and effort involved in duplicating work. For example, during the early days of the U.S. space exploration program, $250,000 was spent on a metallurgic study. It was then discovered that the same research already had been conducted by Soviet scientists and reported in a Soviet journal. Had the U.S. scientists been aware of Soviet contributions in the field, they might have built upon the available knowledge. Instead, they duplicated it, an action that resulted in wasted money, effort, and time. In cases such as this, access to diverse sources of information is extremely valuable.

A Closer Look...

Personal Computing

You may be asking yourself "What does this mean to me?" It means you should try to become a proficient end-user. In the broadest sense an **end-user** is a person who knows how to use a computer and communication technology to organize data, stimulate new ideas, solve problems, and communicate the results to others. At a personal level a wide variety of activities fit into this description. As end-users, teachers and students employ a different mix of computer skills, equipment, programs, and data than is required for users in law, medicine, business, and government. The following questions are often asked by people as they learn how to become proficient end-users.

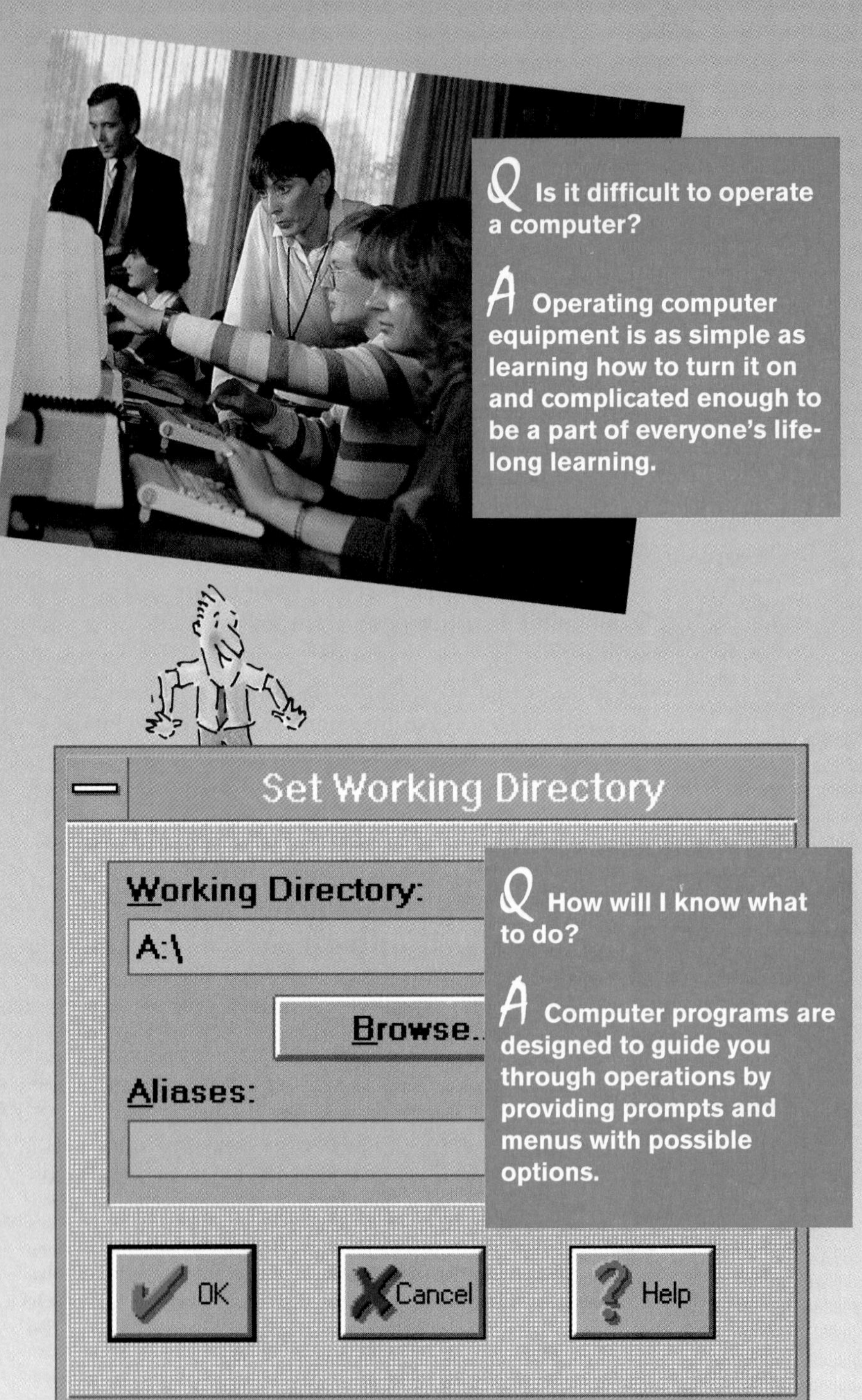

Q Is it difficult to operate a computer?

A Operating computer equipment is as simple as learning how to turn it on and complicated enough to be a part of everyone's life-long learning.

Q How will I know what to do?

A Computer programs are designed to guide you through operations by providing prompts and menus with possible options.

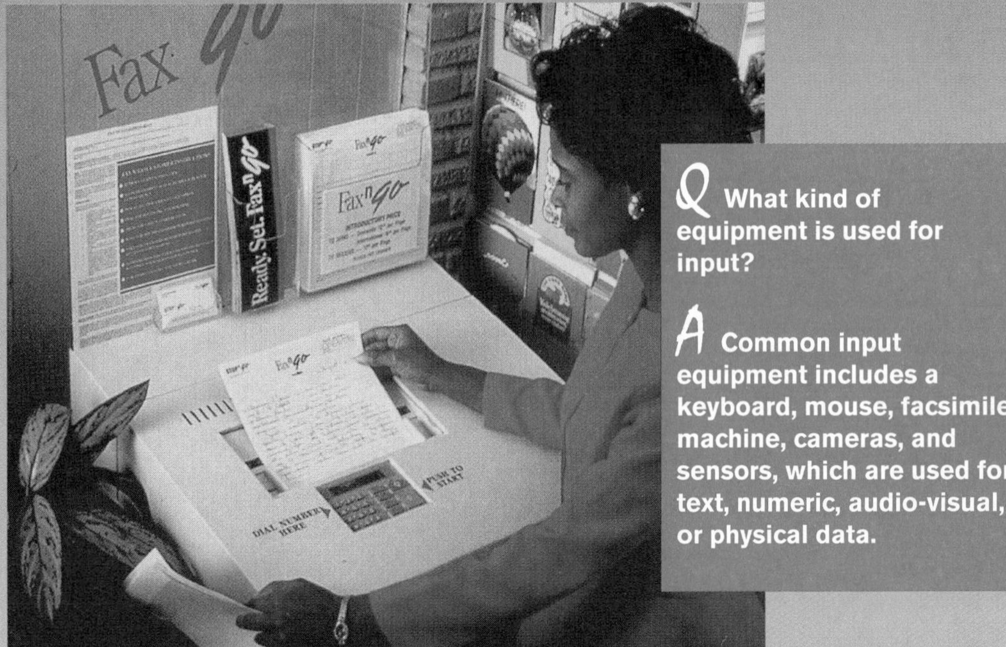

Q What kind of equipment is used for input?

A Common input equipment includes a keyboard, mouse, facsimile machine, cameras, and sensors, which are used for text, numeric, audio-visual, or physical data.

Q Why do computer keyboards use extra keys besides those found on a typewriter?

A Special keys on a computer's keyboard give you control over many computer actions. For example, there are keys that let you correct mistakes (Delete or Del), print screen displays (Print Screen or PrtSc), and in the worst case, reset the computer (ask your teacher).

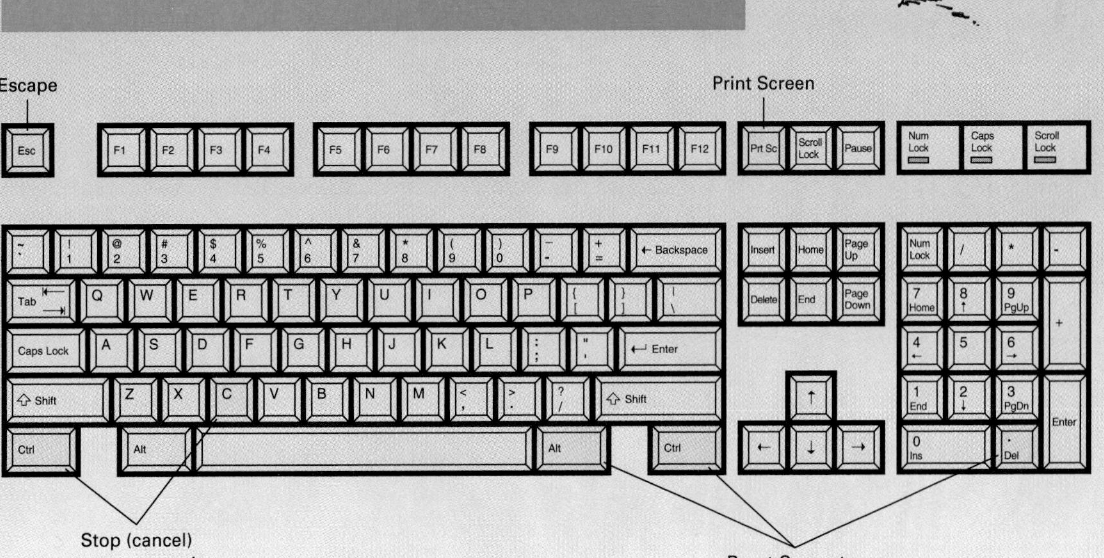

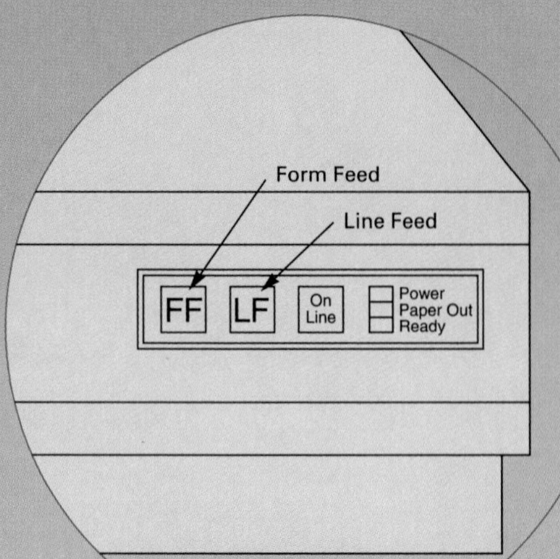

Q What do I do with the disks when they are not being used by the computer?

A Disks and other storage media must be kept in cool, dry, static-free cases that are stored away from direct sunlight and magnetic sources.

Q How do I get paper out of the printer?

A Users feed paper one line at a time (line feed) or a whole page at a time (form feed) when a printer is **offline**–not communicating with the computer.

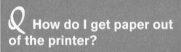

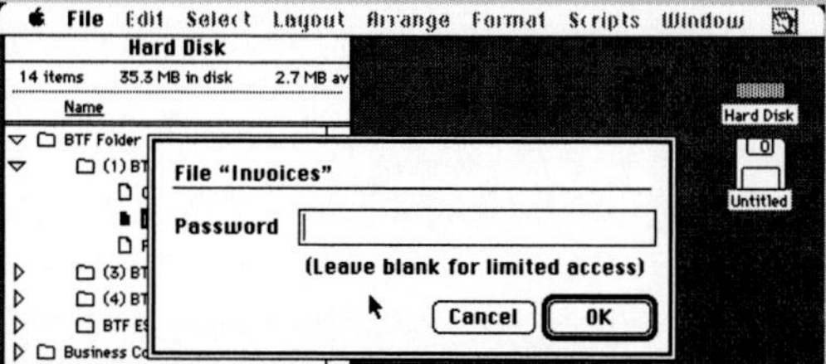

Q How can I guard computer equipment from physical harm or theft and protect myself from loss of data or electronic invasions?

A Common sense goes a long way in protecting your computer resources. In particular, do not leave your equipment unattended or share your password with others.

Q Where do I go to get answers to problems?

A Manuals, telephone help lines, and knowledgeable friends or colleagues can help answer questions.

Chapter Facts

- Computers process facts, figures, and images. They have been used as problem-solving tools since the 1940s. As computers have become more user friendly, they have been adapted for a variety of applications by many levels of users.
- The facts, figures, and images a computer uses to solve problems are called data.
- Many computer applications take the form of process control, simulations, data storage and retrieval, and data processing.
- Computers and other tools operate under the four-step IPOS cycle: Input, Processing, Output, and Storage. Once it is completed, the cycle can be repeated with different input data.
- When a user's request from a computer is immediately acted upon it is considered interactive.
- Data can be input into a computer through such hardware as a keyboard, a telephone, or a mouse, through a camera, and through sensors. Any transaction can produce useful data.
- Computer output can be a screen display, printed report, action of a mechanical arm, sounds, and visual images.
- Computers perform both arithmetic and logical operations in the IPOS cycle. Arithmetic operations involve computations while logical operations do comparisons of data.
- A computer program or software is a set of instructions that is followed to produce a desired result.
- Data can be numeric, textual, audio-visual, or physical. All four types of data may be input or output.
- The chief limitation of computers is that they cannot think. They cannot replace the decision-making power of people, make emotional judgments, or disobey their programming.
- Computers effectively store large amounts of data, perform processing quickly and accurately, simulate outcomes on the basis of given conditions, and recommend actions.
- Computers depend upon people to provide correct data and instructions. Computer output must be interpreted by people as a basis for making decisions.
- Some misunderstandings arise when people don't realize how computers work. People may feel computers will replace them on the job or make decisions previously made by humans. Also, some people are reluctant to change to new technology.
- Proficient computer end-users can perform common tasks with their computers.

Terms to Remember

a. arithmetic operations
b. artificial intelligence
c. audio-visual data
d. binary code
e. bit
f. computer
g. computer application
h. computer program
i. data
j. data processing
k. data storage and retrieval
l. database
m. end-user
n. hardware
o. icon
p. interactive
q. keyboard
r. logical operations
s. network
t. numeric data
u. offline
v. online
w. physical data
x. printer
y. process control
z. simulation
aa. software
bb. text
cc. textual data
dd. transaction
ee. user friendly

Mix and Match

Match the following definitions to the Terms to Remember.

1. _____ any use for a computer.
2. _____ organized collections of data that can be retrieved and cross-referenced by a computer.
3. _____ direct communication with a computer wherein every request is immediately acted upon.
4. _____ the set of instructions a computer follows in sequence to control the input, processing, output, and storage it is to perform.
5. _____ ability of a computer to do mathematical functions, like addition and subtraction, with numerical data.
6. _____ a system of computers and hardware sharing data and software over communication lines.
7. _____ capability of computers to store vast amounts of data and later search the data for related information.
8. _____ situation wherein a computer constantly monitors and adjusts an activity.

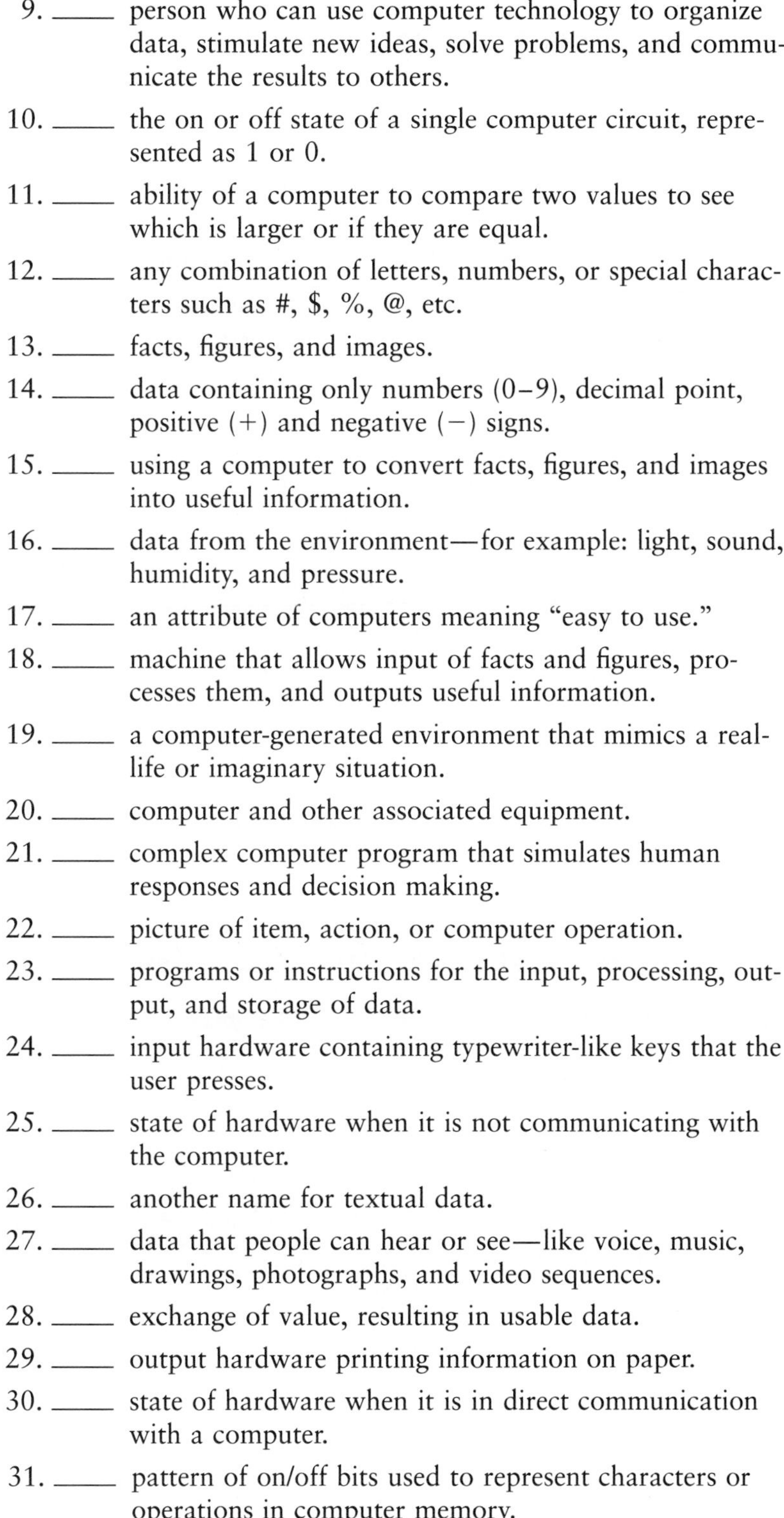

9. ____ person who can use computer technology to organize data, stimulate new ideas, solve problems, and communicate the results to others.
10. ____ the on or off state of a single computer circuit, represented as 1 or 0.
11. ____ ability of a computer to compare two values to see which is larger or if they are equal.
12. ____ any combination of letters, numbers, or special characters such as #, $, %, @, etc.
13. ____ facts, figures, and images.
14. ____ data containing only numbers (0–9), decimal point, positive (+) and negative (−) signs.
15. ____ using a computer to convert facts, figures, and images into useful information.
16. ____ data from the environment—for example: light, sound, humidity, and pressure.
17. ____ an attribute of computers meaning "easy to use."
18. ____ machine that allows input of facts and figures, processes them, and outputs useful information.
19. ____ a computer-generated environment that mimics a real-life or imaginary situation.
20. ____ computer and other associated equipment.
21. ____ complex computer program that simulates human responses and decision making.
22. ____ picture of item, action, or computer operation.
23. ____ programs or instructions for the input, processing, output, and storage of data.
24. ____ input hardware containing typewriter-like keys that the user presses.
25. ____ state of hardware when it is not communicating with the computer.
26. ____ another name for textual data.
27. ____ data that people can hear or see—like voice, music, drawings, photographs, and video sequences.
28. ____ exchange of value, resulting in usable data.
29. ____ output hardware printing information on paper.
30. ____ state of hardware when it is in direct communication with a computer.
31. ____ pattern of on/off bits used to represent characters or operations in computer memory.

Review Questions

1. Provide an example of each of the following tasks computers perform everyday: process control, simulations, data storage and retrieval, and data processing.
2. What is the four-step cycle used by computers and other tools?
3. Describe two processing operations that computers perform.
4. Why do embedded computers make tools more flexible?
5. What are four types of data computers can use as input?
6. What are five ways in which computers increase the capacity of people to control their environment?
7. What is the chief limitation of computer technology?
8. List three activities that computers cannot perform.
9. List five general activities that computers can do well.
10. Why should people avoid giving up decision-making responsibilities to computers?
11. What are four misunderstandings that people have about computer technology?
12. Identify eight questions and the associated answers new end-users often ask.

Applying What You've Learned

1. Computers are being used as tools in many jobs. In fact, few areas of work are untouched by computer technology. How could computers be used in your future career? If you don't think computers could be involved, why not?
2. Identify the input, processing, output, and storage (if relevant) steps in each of these situations:
   a. making a chocolate milk shake
   b. operating a car or motorcycle
   c. studying for and taking an exam
   d. using a solar-powered generator
   e. testing a building's security system
3. The IPOS cycle is found in the application of many tools. Pick a tool not mentioned in the text and identify the four steps in its IPOS cycle. What types of data are used? How is data input? What form does the output take?

4. Two common forms of output are reports and screen displays. Describe three situations in which a printed report is more useful than a display. Describe three situations in which a screen display is more useful.
5. Identify which type(s) of data (numeric, textual, audio-visual, or physical) would be used in these situations:
   a. writing a term paper on a computer
   b. monitoring a baby for continuous breathing
   c. playing a video game
   d. sensing earthquake tremors
   e. providing computerized telephone directory assistance
   f. mixing voices, instruments, and recorded dancing on a music video
   g. calculating income tax through use of a computer
6. Embedded computers are found in many devices you use each day. Name a tool you use that could be improved by embedding a computer. What type of data would the computer use? What kind of processing would it do?
7. Despite the many applications for computers, they are not the solution to all problems. Name three situations in which use of a computer would be unethical, impractical, or pointless. What could be done to prevent computer use in these situations?

Answers to Mix and Match

1. g 2. l 3. p 4. h 5. a 6. s 7. k 8. y 9. m 10. e
11. r 12. cc 13. i 14. t 15. j 16. w 17. ee 18. f
19. z 20. n 21. b 22. o 23. aa 24. q 25. u 26. bb
27. c 28. dd 29. x 30. v 31. d

2

Computer Information Systems

- From the User's Point of View
- System Components
- People
  - Computer users
  - Computer professionals
  - Systems development
  - Operations
  - Management
- Data
  - Organizing data
  - Data versus information
- Procedures
  - Operating procedures
  - Emergency procedures
- Hardware
  - Input hardware
  - Processing hardware
  - Output hardware
  - Storage hardware
- Software
  - Applications software
  - Systems software
- *A Closer Look . . . Buying a Computer System*

FROM THE USER'S POINT OF VIEW

It is easy to be overwhelmed by new technology and all the terms and concepts that come with it. To make sense out of new ideas, it helps to have a logical framework to organize related facts. The five components of a computer information system (people, data, procedures, hardware, and software) form such a framework. Every term and concept discussed in this text is associated with one or more of these components.

SYSTEM COMPONENTS

Computers come in many makes, models, and sizes—from those the size of your fingernail, to laptop computers, to computers that occupy entire rooms. It may be surprising to discover that computer hardware is only one part of a **computer system.** A system is a collection of elements that work together to solve a specific problem. Regardless of size, every computer needs other components to produce results. The components of a computer system are:

- People
- Data
- Procedures
- Hardware
- Software

These components are integral to every computer system (Figure 2.1). Every time you use a computer to generate information, you become one of the five system components.

PEOPLE

Computer systems are developed for and by people. People build and control computer systems to help them make decisions and solve problems. The components of a computer system are brought together by people. These people fall into two categories:

- Computer users
- Computer professionals

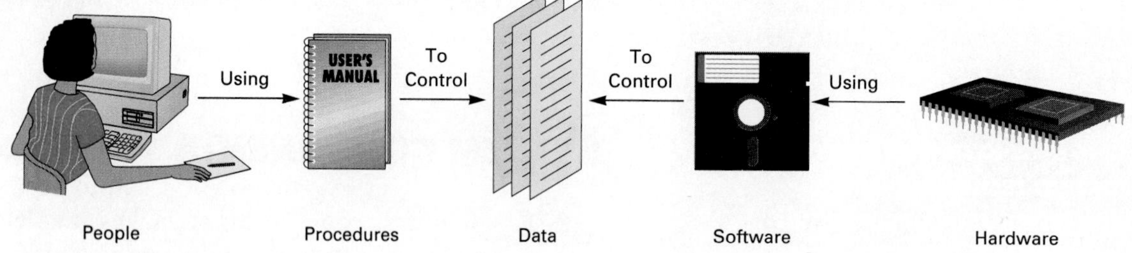

FIGURE 2.1
People use procedures to control data that is processed by hardware following detailed software instructions. These are the five components of every computer system.

Computer Users

Users are the driving force behind the development of computer systems. The user must identify a problem, then direct the computer system to produce information that supports a solution. People's demands for answers and assistance push forward the development of technology.

A computer user applies the information produced by a computer. Users include anyone who requests a phone number from directory assistance, withdraws money through an automatic teller machine, or watches an animated commercial. At times, you may become a computer user by circumstance rather than by choice. For

In the News...

COMPUTER CHIPS

It seems that whenever there is talk of "reaching the limits" of chip technology, a new breakthrough shows there is still no end in sight. Chips—the building blocks of computers—have been doubling in speed and quadrupling in capacity every three years. Today, a tiny 4-million-bit chip contained in a piece of silicon no larger than a pencil eraser can store the equivalent of five IBM annual reports. A 16-million-bit chip can store the equivalent of 1,600 double-spaced, typed pages of text and "read" all of it in 1/25th of a second. This power will significantly boost the performance levels of future computers.

"Today, a tiny 4-million bit chip...can store...five IBM annual reports"

example, choosing an outside activity according to the weather report is an action that depends on a computer. Weather forecasts result from computer analysis of weather data. Indirectly, the information a computer provides influences your decision. In many situations like this you are a user, but not by direct choice. However, you can choose whether or not you will be an *informed user* (Figure 2.2).

FIGURE 2.2
An informed user takes responsibility for all aspects of the IPOS cycle, gaining total control over the information produced.

Informed users understand how the components of a computer system work together to perform a task. They know what a computer can and cannot do. Most important, informed users can employ computer output for their benefit, and for the benefit of others.

Increasingly, however, users in all types of jobs are satisfying their computer needs on their own through *end-user computing.* This implies that the end-user is responsible for data entry, computer operations, and application of the resulting output. Many of these people go on to become *user-developers* who design and test their own computer applications. As a result, they have been able to meet their own processing needs with minimal aid from computer professionals.

Computer Professionals

People who work directly with the development and operation of computer technology are called *computer professionals.* Some help users design computer-assisted solutions. Others operate and repair the computer equipment. Still other computer professionals manage data, end-user training, and all computer acquisitions in an organization. Interesting computer-oriented career opportunities are found in systems development, operations, and management.

Systems Development

Components of a computer system are brought together in various ways. Local stores provide knowledgeable *computer salespeople* to help new users decide which software and hardware best meet their needs. The Closer Look at the end of this chapter details several questions you should ask when shopping for a new computer system.

Larger organizations employ *systems analysts* who work with users to develop computer systems that satisfy specific requirements. The analyst is the link between users and new technological innovations that improve personal productivity. Users describe what they need to an analyst, who coordinates the development of a new system. This could involve purchasing new computer software and

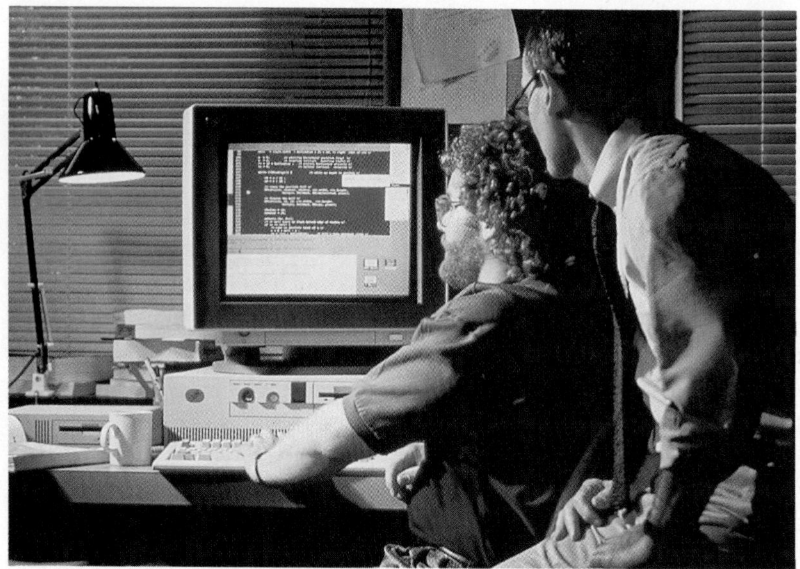

FIGURE 2.3
Programmers write and review system documentation as a basis for their work in creating new software or modifying existing programs.

equipment. Other times, it means linking existing hardware into a computer network. In this way users and systems analysts work together to build productive computer systems.

When new information is needed, *programmers* translate program specifications, written by a team of analysts and users, into computer programs. Their duties include writing and testing instructions used by the computer (Figure 2.3). To accomplish this, they first determine which processing functions must be performed. Then they construct a sequence of computer operations that fulfill those functions, and code the operations in a programming language. Finally, they run tests to check the program for errors in logic or coding.

Sometimes, instead of generating new programs, programmers adapt existing programs to meet new needs. *Program revisions* are often made to improve applications or to bring them into compliance with changing laws or company policies. In fact, 50 to 75 percent of the life-long cost of a program occurs in keeping it up-to-date.

Operations

To support end-user computer operations, many organizations have **help desks** staffed by computer professionals. These professionals answer questions about computer operations, software applications, and hardware problems. Job responsibilities also include knowing how to respond to emergencies.

Some organizations centralize computer professionals and hardware resources into a **computer center.** Computer centers employ a variety of specialized operations personnel to oversee the daily IPOS cycles (Figure 2.4). Larger computer centers also have *service technicians* on staff to perform repairs and preventive maintenance. Operations personnel work at several different levels of responsibility: data entry, computer operations, and control of computer center equipment and output.

The work performed within a computer center follows the IPOS cycle common to all computer systems. Clerks supply data to *data entry operators*, who input the data into the computer. *Computer operators* ensure that all equipment is functioning properly and set up storage devices and printers. They also make sure the computer has programs scheduled to run when needed. Output is given back to the *control clerk*, who schedules when programs are run and delivers the information to the appropriate users. Finally, *data librarians* catalog and store important tapes and disks in fireproof tape/disk libraries when not in use. Thus, the IPOS cycle is reflected in the tasks of operations personnel.

Management

The *information systems manager* is ultimately responsible for ensuring that the computer resources of an organization are used effectively (Figure 2.4). This means coordinating employees so that computing jobs are completed on schedule and within budget. Managers also analyze computer operations to detect inefficiencies and illegal uses of the system, and they look at opportunities for improvement. In most organizations information systems managers

FIGURE 2.4
An information systems manager oversees an organization's computer resources.

work closely with top-level executives on plans and decisions concerning computer resources and operations throughout the organization.

Organizations manage their information technology in many ways. Unfortunately, in some cases, no one officially manages the computer technology and associated information resources. Once an information system manager is designated, other management levels are added as the organization's information system grows. Often database and network administrators are added to work with end-users to manage the sophisticated systems found in larger organizations.

People—whether they are users, analysts, programmers, operators, or managers—all work together to make a computer system function properly. At times, one person may perform several jobs. With a personal computer system one person often does everything. In larger operations several people are involved with a computer system. For the successful operation of that system, coordination of effort is imperative.

DATA

The second component of a computer system, data, represents facts about people, things, ideas, and events. For example, eye glasses, a video of a ski race, brown hair, Lincoln's Gettysburg address, and six feet tall all are items of data. Taken individually, they have little to do with each other. However, when data items are combined and processed to form information, these items have meaning for people. From the above list, eye glasses, brown hair, and six feet tall can be extracted. Combined on a driver's license, these data items could form a partial description of your father. These same pieces of data in another situation could be describing Abraham Lincoln. Lincoln's speech read while showing pictures of the Gettysburg battlefield adds meaning to a history lesson. The ski video combined with the coach's comments describing the skiers' styles could be used to teach ski racing to others.

Organizing Data

The most fundamental unit of text or numeric data is the character, represented in Figure 2.5 by a single letter, number, or symbol. A related group of characters is referred to as a **field.** A related group of fields is known as a **record.** Records that reflect a common meaning or use are grouped together to form a **file.** To understand these relationships, consider how the data on your father's driver's license is organized. The license application number, CO249615, is a field

Field
Character

Record

FIGURE 2.5
A database contains related files that are organized into records. Each record contains text and numeric data organized into fields.

made up of numeric and alphabetic characters. Sometimes a single character, such as M or F—indicating the sex of the driver—can be used as a field. A photograph of your father can be another field. Additional fields hold data about physical descriptions, including need for corrective lenses, hair color, height, and weight. When combined into a record, a driver's license, these data relationships become apparent. In this case the record provides information about the driver's identity and appearance.

When several driver's licenses are brought together, they can be analyzed to produce even more information. This collection of licenses—or records—constitutes a file. A file groups similar records that can be summarized to increase knowledge. For example, examination of all licenses in California can show how many drivers in the state are over 65 years old. Additional information can be obtained by processing related records as a file.

At times people must use several files to meet their information needs. Information contained in one file is often related to information in several other files. For example, the file of registered vehicles and the file of licensed drivers have many names and addresses in common. Using data from both files would help state agencies identify the names and addresses of drivers with vehicles that have been recalled by the manufacturer.

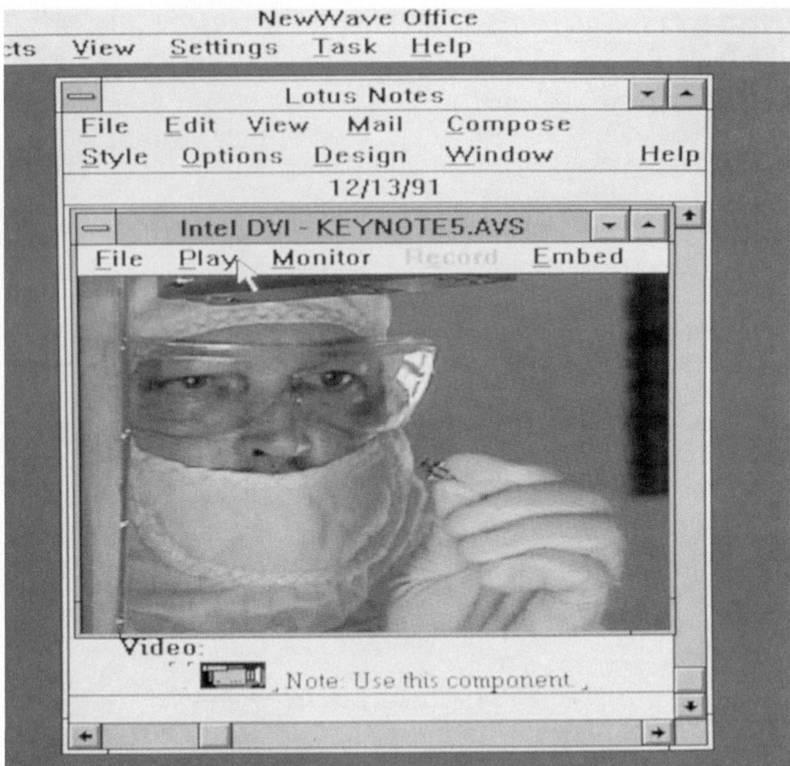

FIGURE 2.6
Movies, music videos, and other audio-visual data can be edited by using a computer and special software.

Computer systems permit access to a wide range of files. Systems allow people to share, modify, and manipulate files to increase knowledge. Cross-referencing files is made easier with the aid of a database program that integrates related files into a common database. Users of databases are able to access information selectively, on the basis of their specific needs.

However, data is not always organized into databases or even fields and records. Audio-visual data and physical data are often stored as files. Many times, further subdivision is not practical or useful. Data items that have meaning by themselves are sometimes referred to as an **object.** A photograph, song, or movie becomes an object when converted to a computer-usable format. Objects can be inserted into other objects or files. For example, photographs are inserted into a text file when writing a newspaper article.

Data versus Information

Complete, correct, and timely data is essential to the successful completion of the IPOS cycle. Computers have impressive capabilities, but they do not have the intuition or judgment to find data entry errors. Data entry personnel must check the correctness of input data. Accurate information depends on the complete and timely input of correct data. This notion is the basis for what computer professionals refer to as *GIGO*: Garbage in, garbage out.

As data is accumulated and processed, it becomes information, a valuable product in its own right. People use computers to obtain information, and the foundation of information is data. Without information, many human and organizational functions would be stymied. If your school lost all of its student records, you would have a difficult time proving you completed required courses. If your bank's data files were destroyed, there would be no record of your money holdings. All your savings could be lost. Loss of data on an airline reservation system could cause chaos all over the world. As you can see, collections of data are major assets in large organizations and for individuals. It is important that the data is kept secure.

PROCEDURES

Procedures are the third component of a computer system. They are systematic courses of action that help people use software, data, and hardware. Procedures identify what needs to be done and how to do it properly. They also help new users to understand how to work with computer systems and what to do if something goes wrong. A typical set of procedures for a session with a personal computer might include the following:

- Turning all the hardware components of a computer system on
- Formatting a new disk
- Running an application program
- Inputting text and scanning related photographs

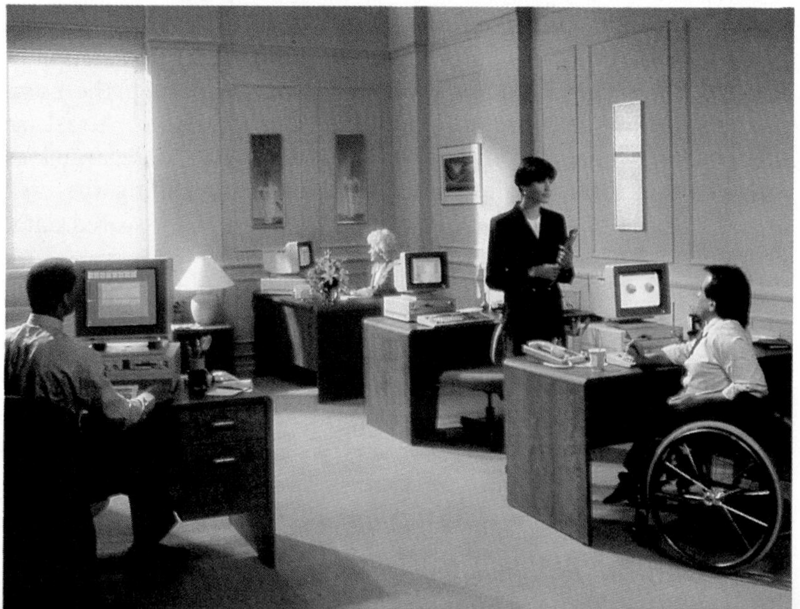

FIGURE 2.7
End-users need to be familiar with operating, data entry, backup, error recovery, and other procedures.

- Verifying the correctness and completeness of the data entered
- Saving the input on a formatted disk
- Preparing the printer for output
- Printing a document
- Copying data files onto a second disk as backup
- Turning off hardware

Operating Procedures

FIGURE 2.8
At this center a technician follows troubleshooting procedures to help users solve equipment problems.

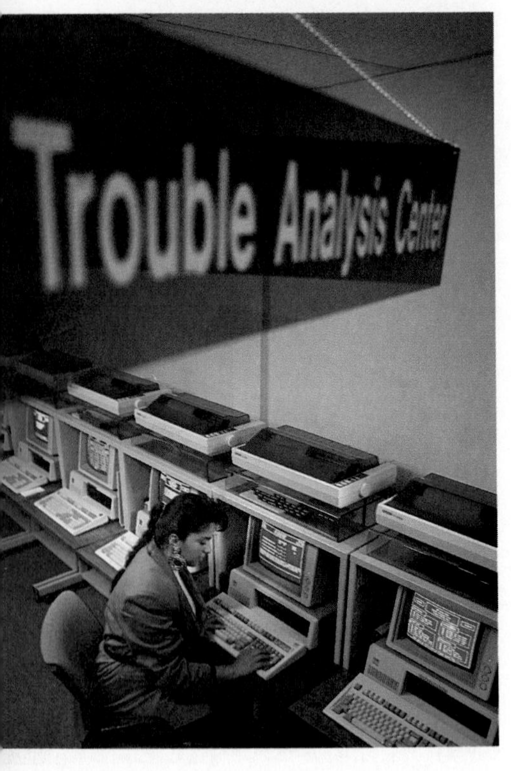

Anyone owning or operating a personal computer must follow procedures. Before a computer can be put to work, *operating procedures* are used to turn on the machine. They also include instructions on locating, copying, and erasing files on a disk. In fact, operating procedures refer to rules for using any hardware or software correctly.

Procedures exist for every computer application. Once equipment is on, users need *data entry procedures* that describe the preparation and input of data. Included in data entry procedures would be a manual check of data before entry to ensure it is accurate and complete. The term *verification* is used when the data entry operator takes responsibility for checking data for errors. Data should be verified after it is entered and before processing.

When computer programs check for errors as part of data entry procedures, this is called *error correction.* For example, the data entry operator visually verifies that every address entered is correct, while a computer program performs error correction by checking each telephone number field for nonnumeric characters. *Error recovery procedures* are used to respond to and eliminate processing errors. For example, changing a grade that was incorrectly entered is an error recovery procedure.

Service technicians and users follow *preventive maintenance procedures* for cleaning equipment and running checks on computer circuitry. Preventive maintenance procedures help keep the computer and other hardware in good operating condition. A task as simple as cleaning a computer keyboard should be regarded as important. Another maintenance procedure is cleaning the disk drive's read/write heads, which input and output disk-stored data. Printers, too, must be cleaned regularly.

In addition, informed users and operators should follow *backup procedures* to protect their computer files. By backing up, or copying, data and information onto a second disk, users minimize the possibility of losing data.

Emergency Procedures

Users handle a computer *crash*, or failure, with *emergency procedures.* These procedures may enable people to recover important data and start the system working again. Often, standardized emergency procedures are included in computer manuals. Many computer manufacturers have established emergency telephone numbers where experts answer users' questions in the event of a crash.

To locate the cause of a crash, people use *troubleshooting procedures.* One of the most important troubleshooting procedures involves using **diagnostic software** to track down malfunctioning components in a computer. With diagnostic software, a user can detect and eliminate a problem in computer circuitry or attached hardware before more damage is done.

Procedures are essential to the upkeep of any computer system. The cost of implementing these procedures is dwarfed by the potential costs of repairing neglected systems or recovering lost data.

FIGURE 2.9
The keyboard and mouse are common types of input hardware.

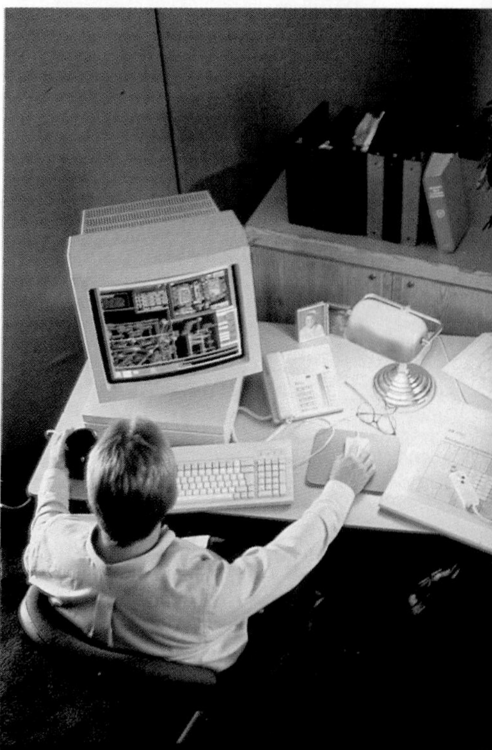

HARDWARE

The fourth computer system component, hardware, comes in many configurations, depending on what the computer system is designed to do. Hardware can fill several floors of a large office building or can fit on your lap. Different types of hardware are used for each step of the IPOS cycle.

Input Hardware

Input hardware is used to enter data into the computer. The keyboard at the ticket outlet where you reserve seats for a basketball game is a type of input hardware. The checker who slides your groceries over a scanner to record a sale uses another type of input hardware. In Figure 2.9 a draftsperson uses a **mouse** to create drawings for blueprints. A mouse is an input device users move around on a flat surface. Its movements become input and are duplicated on a screen. Users activate program options by using the mouse to point at the related screen icon. Pressing a button on the mouse initiates the desired input.

Even Ma and Pa grocery stores are using specialized input devices. A scanner enters your grocery items directly by using input hardware that is either handheld or part of a cash register. The device sends the data into a computer that prints your bill and reorders stock.

Who's Who

John Mauchly (1907–1980)

J. Presper Eckert (b. 1919)

The war effort of the early 1940s and the increase in the level of sophistication of circuitry influenced several research groups to attempt to build an electronic computer to aid the armed services. In England the war brought the need to break German military codes faster than could be done manually. The end of 1943 marked the initial operation in England of the Colossus, the world's first working electronic computer. It could decode messages 12 times faster than any previous machine.

At the same time the U.S. government signed a contract with the University of Pennsylvania to develop an electronic computer for calculating artillery trajectories. John Mauchly and J. Presper Eckert met at the University of Pennsylvania while Mauchly was a professor and Eckert a lab instructor. Together they designed and built the Electronic Numerical Integrator and Calculator (ENIAC), completed in 1946. The ENIAC weighed 30 tons and contained 17,000 vacuum tubes, 70,000 resistors, and 5 million soldered joints. ENIAC was able to perform 5,000 additions per second and used so much power it caused the lights to dim in one section of Philadelphia.

Unlike the Colossus, the ENIAC was considered a general-purpose computer because it was able to perform a wide variety of jobs very quickly. However, it was not programmable by today's definition. To change ENIAC's program, it was necessary to rewire the master program circuits, requiring much expertise and time. Their later collaboration, the UNIVAC, was used by the Census Bureau in 1951. Mauchly went on to found ACM (Association of Computing Machinery) and worked for Remington Rand. Always good at conceptualizing new ideas, he later formed his own firm, Dynatrend, which forecasted the weather and stock market trends. Eckert continued work in the electronics field, receiving 85 patents and the National Science Foundation's National Medal of Science.

John Mauchly (fourth from right) and J. Presper Eckert (far left) with ENIAC development team.

Processing Hardware

The computer itself is processing hardware. As shown in Figure 2.10, a computer is composed primarily of a memory unit and a processing unit. The memory unit, or **memory,** provides temporary storage for input data, programs, and the results of processing. The processing unit, or **processor,** interprets the program instructions in memory, controls the flow of data into and out of memory, and performs arithmetic and logic operations. The processor fetches the program instructions from memory one at a time, along with any needed data. After that instruction is followed, results are sent to memory and the next instruction is brought in. This cycle continues until the program is completed.

Processing hardware can be a small embedded computer performing a single task or a large **mainframe** working on many concurrent tasks. Describing the most powerful computers as mainframes dates back to a time when computers were filled with racks of vacuum tubes and miles of wire. This term is used today to describe very powerful machines that often house several processors and large amounts of memory. Mainframe computers handle many users performing different tasks all at the same time.

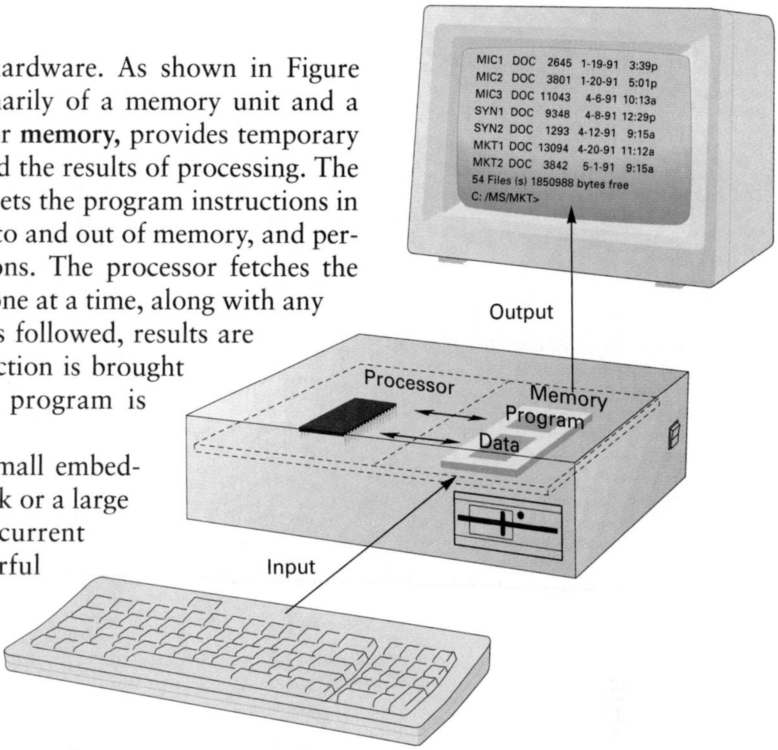

Minicomputers service a different user need. A minicomputer can handle a limited number of users and programs at the same time, using a single processor. Often this is all a small business or workgroup of users would need. Sometimes a network of minicomputers is used in place of a single mainframe.

Computer systems designed to be used by one person at a time are called **personal computers** or **PCs.** Many personal computers are portable and some even operate on rechargeable batteries. Personal computers are also referred to as *microcomputers.* Other common names for personal computers are discussed in Chapter 8: Processing Hardware.

FIGURE 2.10
A computer uses program instructions in memory to perform calculations and comparisons by an internal processor.

Output Hardware

Output hardware provides processed information to the user. The two primary forms of output hardware are monitors and printers. **Monitors** hold information on a screen for temporary use. Directory assistance operators, for instance, enter a name into a computer, which displays the telephone number on a monitor. On the other hand, printers deliver copies of output on paper for distribution or long-term use. Printed output includes report cards, bills, and junk mail.

In the News...

CARING FOR YOUR FLOPPY DISKS

Always place diskettes back into a disk envelope when you are not using them.

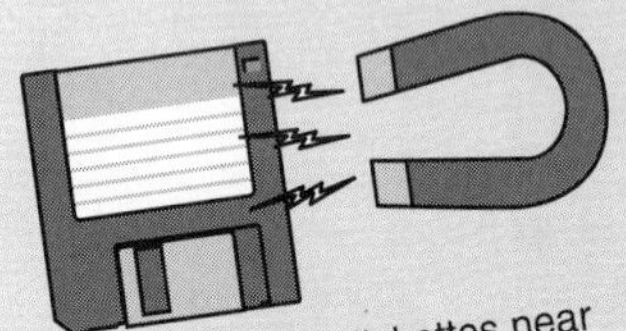

Never place diskettes near magnetic devices.

Do not use paper clips on disks.

Store and use at temperatures between 50° and 110° F.

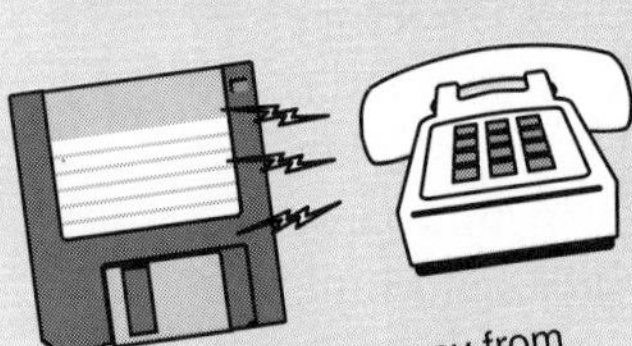

Keep diskettes away from the telephone.

Never bend floppy disks.

Never touch the floppy disk media.

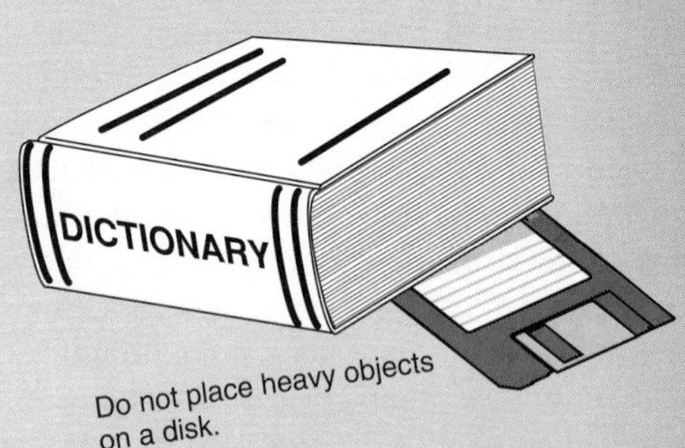

Do not place heavy objects on a disk.

Store your diskettes in a safe place.

Always make backup copies of your data.

FIGURE 2.11
Compact disks, also called CD-ROMs, store text, music, photographs, and video images.

Storage Hardware

Since the computer's memory is temporary and has only a limited capacity for holding data, storage hardware is needed. The most common types of storage hardware are **tape drives** and **disk drives.** These drives can save (write) data on a tape or disk and copy (read) it back into the computer's memory upon command. Computer systems are much like stereo systems in this regard. In both systems, when the machinery is not in use, the music or the data must be stored in a common machine-readable format for later use.

There also are similarities in the storage media. Both music and data can be stored on a **compact disk** (**CD**) as shown in Figure 2.11. However, this information is permanent and cannot be changed. When users need to save their own data, they use a tape, floppy disk, or hard disk. **Floppy disks** (**diskettes**) are removable, and a diskette drive uses any number of disks, one at a time. Hard disk drives are built inside the computer and the **hard disk** is not removable. Unlike CDs, floppy and hard disks may have data erased and recorded on them many times. Hard disks hold more data and cost more than floppy disks. In addition, hard disk drives provide faster access to the data on disk than do diskettes.

Thus, each step of the cycle—input, processing, output, and storage—has an accompanying set of hardware (Figure 2.12). Traditionally, the equipment used for processing is called the computer. Attached equipment used for storing, entering, and outputting data is generally referred to as **peripherals.**

FIGURE 2.12
A computer system includes input, processing, output, and storage hardware.

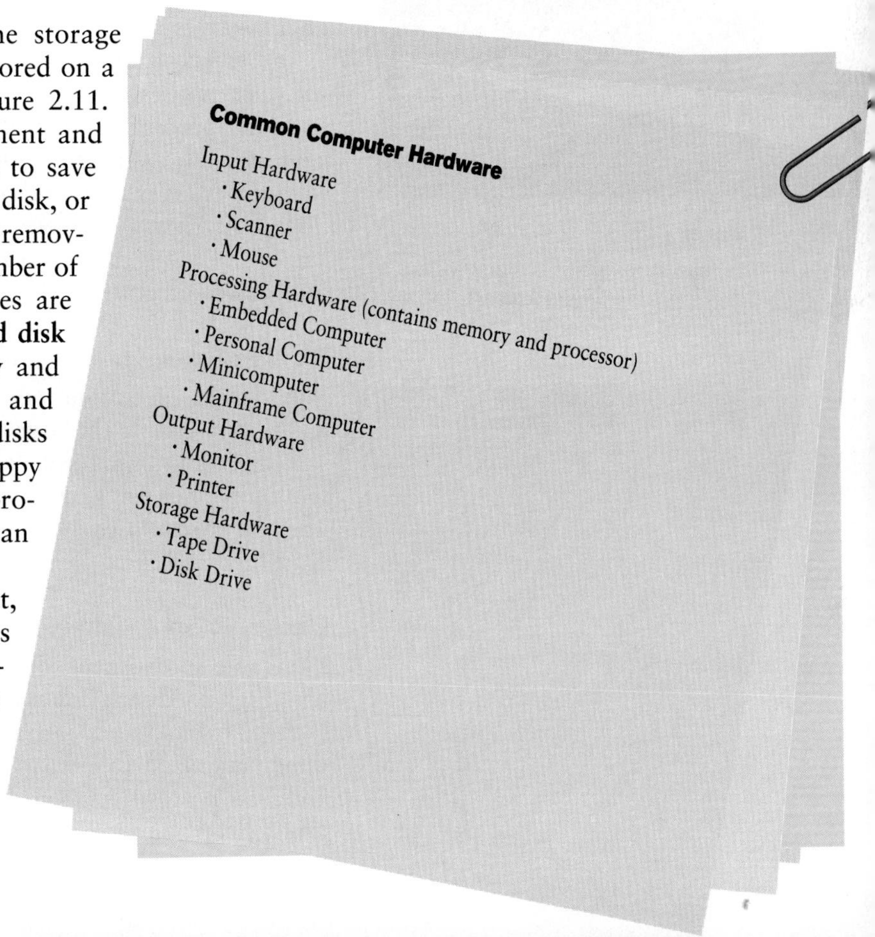

Common Computer Hardware

Input Hardware
- Keyboard
- Scanner
- Mouse

Processing Hardware (contains memory and processor)
- Embedded Computer
- Personal Computer
- Minicomputer
- Mainframe Computer

Output Hardware
- Monitor
- Printer

Storage Hardware
- Tape Drive
- Disk Drive

SOFTWARE

Software is the final computer system component. These computer programs instruct the hardware how to conduct processing. The computer is merely a general-purpose machine that requires specific software to perform a given task. Computers can input, calculate, compare, and output data as information. Software determines the order in which these operations are performed. Like data, programs are stored on tapes or disks when not in use. When needed, storage hardware reads the instructions into the computer's memory. The programs then direct processing. Programs usually fall into one of two categories:

- Applications software
- Systems software

FIGURE 2.13
A software package contains a disk or disks with the program, user manuals, copyright agreement, and operating instructions.

Applications Software

Applications software is a class of programs that solve specific user-oriented processing problems. Common business applications include payroll, accounting, inventory, budgeting, and personnel management. Closer to home, video games and checkbook balancing programs are personal applications.

Personal productivity programs are another type of applications software. This software allows the user to apply the computer to standard problems and tasks an individual may have, even if not part of an organization. Often, personal productivity software is sold in packages that contain the program itself, operating instructions, copyright agreement, and a user's manual, as shown in Figure 2.13. The most popular personal productivity programs fall into four basic categories:

Word Processing

Word processing programs expedite report and letter writing. Typically, they enable the user to insert, move, copy, and erase words, sentences, and paragraphs on a screen. Upon request, the programs will center headings, number pages, and double-space a document. The software allows the user to control the printed form of the document as well.

Electronic Spreadsheets

Electronic spreadsheet software creates documents containing numbers organized into columns and rows for processing and analysis. Financial data, such as budgets or monthly income statements, is often organized this way. The spreadsheet software formats data and also performs arithmetic operations or complicated formulas. Thus, electronic spreadsheets are valuable as a time-saving tool.

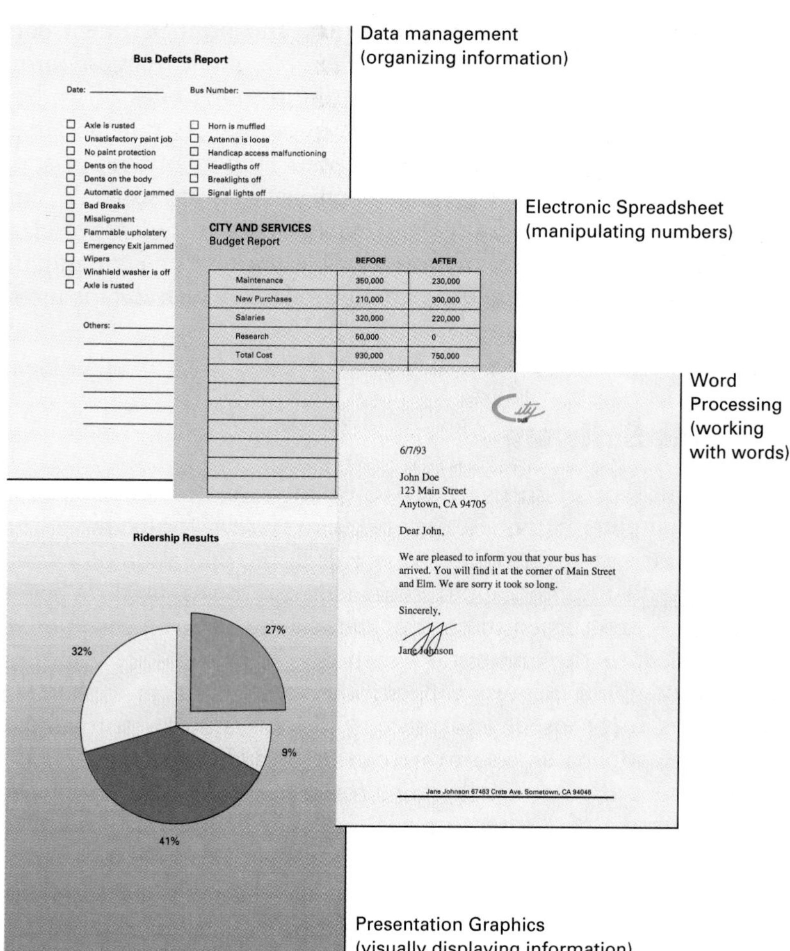

FIGURE 2.14
Personal productivity software helps people use a computer to write letters (word processing), manage budgets (electronic spreadsheet), create charts and graphs (graphics package), or organize related data (database programs).

Graphics

Graphics packages generate pictures, drawings, charts, and diagrams on a screen or on paper. Some graphics software is guided by information produced from electronic spreadsheets. Numbers from the spreadsheet can be used to draw bars on a graph, points on a diagram, or slices of a pie. Other graphics software enables users to draw pictures. The screen becomes an empty canvas, and the mouse or other input device becomes a paintbrush. Graphics software often enables users to select shades and colors for the drawings. Specially equipped printers can paint the computer-generated drawings on paper or film.

Databases

Software that sets up and maintains related data files is called a **database program.** Database programs assist users in assembling data to answer questions and solve problems. Database software provides capabilities for loading and modifying databases. These

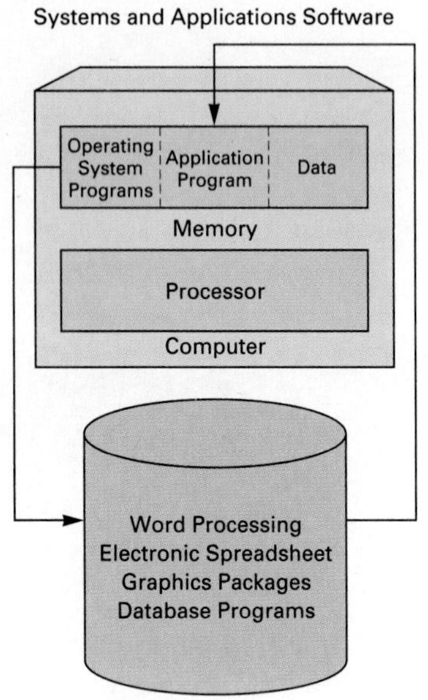

Systems software controls the flow of applications software and related data in and out of the computer's memory.

packages enable users to extract, format, and print pertinent data with ease. A school's registrar, for example, could request information from a database instead of sifting through piles of student records. The registrar might ask such questions as: Which classes filled during the first week of registration? How many out-of-state students are enrolled? Which classes still have empty seats? Within seconds, a database program could provide lists of students or classes meeting the specified conditions. Building or using a database requires an understanding of the many ways in which data is interrelated and how the data can be used.

Systems Software

The second type of software, **systems software,** controls standard internal computer activities. An *operating system,* for example, is a collection of systems programs that aids in the operation of a computer regardless of the applications software being used. When a computer is first turned on, one of the systems programs is *booted*, or loaded, into the computer's memory. This software contains information about memory capacity, the model of the processor, the disk drives to be used, and more. Once the systems software is loaded, the applications software can be brought in (Figure 2.15).

Systems programs are designed for specific pieces of hardware. These programs coordinate peripheral hardware and computer activities. For example, microcomputers primarily use disks for storing data and programs. Therefore, personal computer users initially use a disk with the **disk operating system (DOS)** to *boot* their equipment. When the computer is turned on, one system program from the DOS disk is loaded into memory. As the user works with the computer, whether it is a personal computer or mainframe, DOS will transfer input from keyboard to memory, then from memory to storage, and allocate storage space on disks for data files. Later, DOS may transfer data from memory or a disk onto a printer. Many of the services provided by DOS are transparent to users; that is, the services are performed without users being aware of this support.

Data communications within and between computers systems is handled by system software. **Communications software** transfers data from one computer system to another. These programs usually provide users with data security and error checking along with physically transferring data between the two computers' memories.

A Closer Look...

Buying a Computer System

Purchasing your first personal computer system can be a little intimidating. Approach this purchase like you would approach buying any other household appliance. First and foremost, you should have a good idea of how you would use a personal computer. If you don't know how you would use it, spend your money on something else. In addition, establish a budget and work within it. What follows are a series of questions users often ask when buying their first computer system.

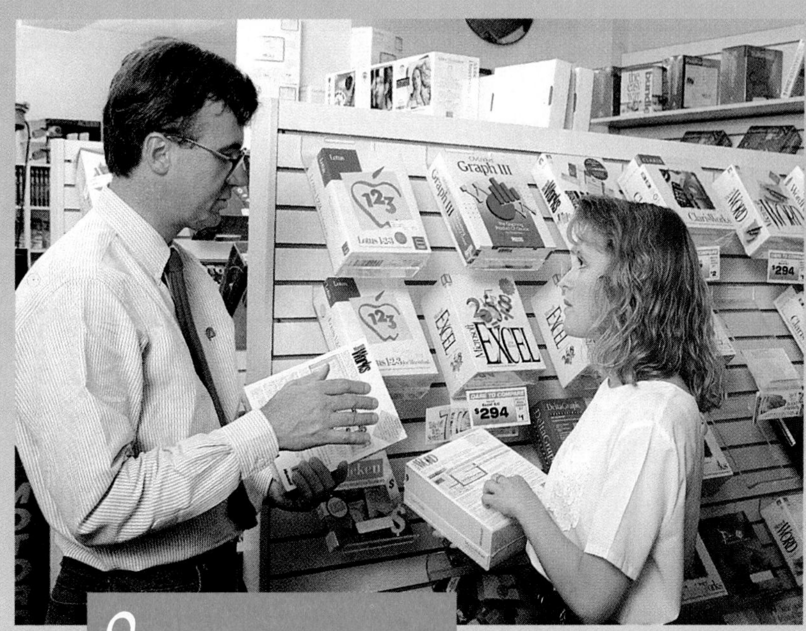

Q What comes first–hardware or software?

A Software drives hardware. Look at your application needs and talk to others about what programs work for them. Once you have decided the application packages you want, their use will dictate minimum hardware requirements.

24-Pin Dot Matrix Printers

Manufacturer	Product	Price	KEY FEATURES: Dimensions (inches)	Weight (pounds)	Draft/LQ speed (cps)	Standard/maximum buffer size (K)	Noise (db)	Quiet mode	FONTS: Resident typefaces	Scalable fonts	Maximum resolution (dpi)
Brother Int'l 800/284-4357, 908/356-4085 (fax)	M-1824L	$749	6 × 19 × 15	20	337/112	64/96	55	●	5	○	360 × 360
	M-1924L	$749	6 × 24 × 15	26	337/112	64/96	55	●	5	○	360 × 360
Citizen America 800/477-4683, 310/453-2814 (fax)	GSX-145	$599	6 × 23 × 13	17	192/64	8/40	51	●	6	○	360 × 360
	GSX-230	$399	5 × 17 × 13	11	270/90	8/136	47	●	8	○	360 × 360
	GSX-240	$519	5 × 17 × 13	11	300/99	8/136	47	●	13	●	360 × 360
Epson America 800/922-8911, 310/782-5220 (fax)	ActionPrinter 3250	$269	5 × 15 × 10	12	250/90	11/11	50	●	6	●	360 × 360
	ActionPrinter 5000	$499	6 × 17 × 15	15	315/105	8/128	47	○	10	●	360 × 360
	ActionPrinter 5500	$699	6 × 24 × 15	15	315/105	8/128	55	○	10	●	360 × 360
	LQ-570	$499	6 × 17 × 15	15	315/105	8/128	47	○	10	●	360 × 360
	LQ-870	$749	7 × 18 × 15	20	413/138	8/128	55	○	10	●	360 × 360
	LQ-1070	$699	6 × 24 × 15	19	315/105	8/128	55	○	10	●	360 × 360
NEC 800/632-4636, 800/366-0476 (fax)	Pinwriter P3200	$429	6 × 17 × 14	19	216/72	8/8	52	●	7	○	360 × 360
	Pinwriter P3300	$599	6 × 23 × 14	25	216/72	8/8	52	●	7	○	360 × 360
	Pinwriter P6200	$749	8 × 17 × 14	23	300/100	80/80	54	●	8	○	360 × 360
Okidata 800/654-3282, 609/778-4184 (fax)	Microline 590	$699	6 × 17 × 15	17	450/120	64/64	53	●	8	○[3]	360 × 360
Panasonic 800/742-8086, 201/392-4792 (fax)	KX-P2123	$419	6 × 18 × 24	19	240/80	14/46	47	●	10	○[3]	360 × 360
	KX-P2124	$549	6 × 17 × 14	19	320/106	20/52	47	●	12	○[3]	360 × 360
	KX-P2624	$649	7 × 23 × 16	34	300/100	26/58	47	●	11	○[3]	360 × 360

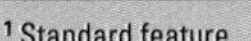

[1] Standard feature. [2] Minimum label width 2.5 inches. [3] Scalable soft fonts bundled with printer.

Q There are so many software packages and hardware manufacturers, how do I know where to start looking?

A Reading computer magazines and talking to friends can help you focus on reliable computer software and hardware. Computer magazines often contain consumer reports on selected software and hardware. These reviews identify important features and test comparable products.

PAPER HANDLING							FRONT-PANEL CONTROLS					OTHER OPTIONS		
Optional sheet feeder	Form parking	Envelopes	Labels	Maximum form width (inches)	Maximum form parts	Paper paths	Pitch	Font	Line spacing	Margins	Microline	Serial Interface	Color printing	Warranty
●	●	●	●	11	5	1	●	●	○	○	○	●[1]	●	1 year
●	●	●	●	16	5	1	●	●	○	○	○	●[1]	●	1 year
●[1]	●	●	●	16	4	3	●	●	●	●	●	●	●	2 years
●[1]	●	●	●	10	4	3	●	●	●	●	●	●	●	2 years
●[1]	●	●	●	10	4	3	●	●	●	●	●	●	●	2 years
●	○	●	●	10	2	2	○	●	●	○	●	○	○	2 years
●	●	●	●[2]	10	4	4	○	●	●	○	●	●	○	2 years
●	●	●	●[2]	16	4	4	○	●	●	○	●	●	○	2 years
●	●	●	●[2]	10	4	4	○	●	●	○	●	●	○	2 years
●	●	●	●[2]	10	4	4	○	●	●	○	●	●	○	2 years
●	●	●	●[2]	16	4	4	○	●	●	○	●	●	○	2 years
●	●	●	○	10	3	2	●	●	●	●	●	●	○	1 year
●	●	●	○	16	3	2	●	●	●	●	●	●	○	1 year
●	●	●	●	10	4	3	●	●	●	●	●	●	●	1 year
●	●	●	●	8.5	5	3	●	●	●	●	●	●	●	2 years
●	●	●	●	12	4	3	●	●	●	●	●	●	●	2 years
●	●	●	●	12	4	4	●	●	●	●	●	●	●	2 years
●	●	●	●	16	4	4	●	●	●	●	●	●	○	2 years

PC World, March, 1993, pp. 178–179.

Q Should I be concerned about compatibility?

A Yes; keep in mind the people with whom you will be sharing data, ideas, and information. Existing systems at school or work, and those belonging to friends, can influence your decisions. Compatibility concerns the sharing of programs, data, and operating procedures among hardware components.

Q Should I "test drive" a system before I buy?

A Like any other major purchase, try before you buy. Use the systems at local schools, belonging to friends, or at computer stores. Look for a system that not only fits present needs but will accommodate future expansions in memory and peripheral hardware.

Q How can I get the best deal on a system?

A When it comes time to buy, the training and service provided by a local full-service computer store must be balanced against the lower costs offered by discount stores and mail-order houses. Check to see if any system software and applications software are included in the price. Compare warranties based on length of time and whether repairs are made at your home (on-site) or by you getting the faulty hardware to a service center.

Q Do I need a special room or any extra equipment to set up the system properly?

A Most rooms with a desk and available electrical outlets can serve as your new computer center. Set up the system in a relatively clean, cool, dry place. You will want a surge protector to minimize damage due to power fluctuations. Give yourself plenty of work room, good lighting to avoid glare, and storage space for easy access to disks and manuals.

Q Once the system is set up, who will help me get started?

A Training sessions can help you learn about backup, maintenance, troubleshooting, and other procedures. Special classes may be offered in the software applications you have purchased. This training is included with some purchases. Otherwise, check local computer stores, user groups, colleges, and community education centers for classes.

Q What can I do to make sure I keep my system up-to-date?

A Turn in the warranty registration for your hardware and software; it puts you on mailing lists for updates and new product information. Join a user group for your brand of computer or in an area of interest. Read computer magazines regularly; they contain helpful reviews of new products and hints on using your present system.

Chapter Facts

- A computer system is made up of five components: people, hardware, software, data, and procedures that work together to solve specific problems.
- People can be computer users or computer professionals. A user directs the computer to produce information that can be applied to a problem. Informed users participating in end-user computing understand a computer's uses, misuses, and limitations. User-developers can set up and program their own computers.
- Computer professionals work directly with computer technology. They can be involved with systems development, operations, or management.
- Computer professionals who are a part of the systems development process include salespeople, systems analysts, and programmers.
- Operations-oriented computer professionals help end-users solve problems, answer questions through a help desk, enter data, operate equipment, control the flow of data into and out of the computer center, store unused tapes and disks in libraries, and service equipment.
- Information systems managers coordinate work and supervise personnel in a computer center to assure jobs are completed on schedule and within budget.
- Text and numeric data made up of characters are often organized into fields, which make up records. Similar records are combined into files. Related files may be organized into databases.
- Audio-visual or physical data, like video recordings or sounds, are referred to as objects when in a computer-usable format. They may be stored in files.
- Procedures are instructions to help people use data, software, and hardware correctly and efficiently. Procedures can relate to data entry, error recovery, preventive maintenance, hardware operations, backup, emergency, and troubleshooting.
- Hardware is classified by the steps of the IPOS cycle. Input hardware may be a keyboard, mouse, or scanner. Processing hardware consists of the memory unit and processing unit found within all sizes of computers. Output hardware may be a monitor or printer. Storage hardware is usually a disk drive or tape drive.

- Software is divided into two categories: applications software and systems software. Applications software solves users' specific processing problems, often through personal productivity programs. Systems software is the series of programs that control the computer's resources regardless of the application package used.
- Four common types of applications software are word processing, electronic spreadsheets, graphics packages, and database programs.
- Many personal productivity software packages come with the program, instructions, user manual, and copyright agreement.
- Disk operating systems and communications software are types of system software.

Terms to Remember

a. applications software
b. communication software
c. compact disk (CD)
d. computer center
e. computer system
f. database program
g. diagnostic software
h. disk drive
i. disk operating system (DOS)
j. diskette
k. electronic spreadsheet
l. field
m. file
n. floppy disk
o. graphics package
p. hard disk
q. help desk
r. mainframe
s. memory
t. minicomputer
u. monitor
v. mouse
w. object
x. peripheral
y. personal computer (PC)
z. procedure
aa. processor
bb. record
cc. systems software
dd. tape drive
ee. word processing program

Mix and Match

Match the following definitions to the Terms to Remember.

1. ____ collection of system software designed to control a computer system using disks for storage of programs and data files.
2. ____ another name for a diskette.
3. ____ output hardware with screen.
4. ____ centralized location for computer hardware and related professionals.
5. ____ programs that help users write reports, letters, and other documents.
6. ____ processing hardware that handles a limited number of users and programs at the same time, using a single processor.
7. ____ storage hardware that reads and writes data, using a disk.
8. ____ class of programs that solves specific user-oriented processing problems.
9. ____ collection of people, procedures, data, software, and hardware that works together to solve specific problems.
10. ____ related group of letters, numbers, and special symbols.
11. ____ storage hardware that reads and writes data, using magnetic tape.
12. ____ computer hardware that is often called a microcomputer.
13. ____ group of related records.
14. ____ group of related fields.
15. ____ computer programs that generate drawings and diagrams.
16. ____ another name for floppy disk
17. ____ system software that transfers data from one computer system to another.
18. ____ group of computer professionals that answers questions related to computer operations.

19. ____ systematic courses of action.
20. ____ computer program that organizes and maintains related data files.
21. ____ input, storage, and output equipment attached to processing hardware.
22. ____ large computer that houses several processors and large amounts of memory.
23. ____ computer programs that control internal computer activities and external resources.
24. ____ computer circuitry inside a computer that temporarily stores data and programs.
25. ____ nonremovable disk with a large storage capacity built into a disk drive.
26. ____ computer program that organizes numbers and associated text into rows and columns.
27. ____ input device that user rolls on flat service to control pointer on screen.
28. ____ circuitry inside a computer that performs arithmetic and logical operations.
29. ____ data item that has meaning by itself.
30. ____ computer program that detects operating problems in hardware.
31. ____ removable disk that permanently stores data and cannot be changed.

Review Questions

1. What are the five components of a computer system?
2. How are the skills of a user-developer different from those of an informed user?
3. What career options are available to computer professionals?
4. Why are program revisions made to working software?
5. What type of data is organized into fields and records?
6. What three characteristics must data have for successful completion of the IPOS cycle?
7. How are each of these procedures used: operating, data entry, error recovery, preventive maintenance, backup, emergency, and troubleshooting?

8. How is verification different from error correction?
9. Identify one type of input hardware, processing hardware, output hardware, and storage hardware.
10. What do you get in a personal productivity software package?
11. What are the functions and types of data used for each of these application programs: word processing, electronic spreadsheet, graphics, and database?
12. What happens when you boot a computer?
13. Why would a user want to select application software before purchasing new hardware?

Applying What You've Learned

1. Pick three examples of computer systems you have seen in action. Identify what is involved in each of the five components of every system. If you are unsure of a component or the correct term to be used, describe what is included in that component.
2. Find several ads for one of the computer professional positions mentioned in the text. Remember that the actual name of the position may be different. Summarize requirements for experience and education, as well as pay and benefits offered.
3. When incorrect output appears, or a computer system does not work properly, you'll often hear the excuse, "The computer did it!" In light of GIGO, and the need for good procedures and well-trained people, what could be some possible causes of the following situations?
   a. You get a home telephone bill for $42,450.00.
   b. Your mother's flight reservation back from Bermuda is not on the airline computer, but she has a ticket.
   c. When she applies for a loan, your sister is told she has a bad credit rating (but she's never applied for credit before).
   d. A computer-controlled heating/cooling system turns up the furnace when the temperature outside is 90 degrees.
4. Identify the content of the fields, records, and files for these applications:
   a. information about patients entering a hospital
   b. a university's collection of data about presently enrolled students
   c. the customer ordering system for a fast-food restaurant

5. Trouble comes when procedures are not written down or when they are ignored by people. Some people say, "If at first it doesn't work, then read the instructions." Make a list of essential procedures for one of these situations or one of your own choosing.
   a. using and maintaining a new car
   b. operating a special tool or piece of equipment you know how to use
   c. installing an electrical outlet or replacing a fuse
   d. cooking a complex dish such as baked Alaska
6. Find an article in a computer magazine that compares similar hardware—for example, two computers or two printers. What features or options are available? What testing procedures or comparisons were used? If several features are available, how would you rank these features from most important to least important? Which of the products would you purchase? Explain your reasoning.

Answers to Mix and Match

1. i 2. n 3. u 4. d 5. ee 6. t 7. h 8. a 9. e 10. l
11. dd 12. y 13. m 14. bb 15. o 16. j 17. b 18. q
19. z 20. f 21. x 22. r 23. cc 24. s 25. p 26. k
27. v 28. aa 29. w 30. g 31. c

3

Software Concepts

From the User's Point of View

User Interfaces
- Command-driven interfaces
- Shells
- Graphical user interfaces
- Natural language interfaces

Evaluating Software Features
- File conventions and groupware
- Windows and multitasking
- Menus and dialog boxes
- Palettes and toolboxes
- Manuals and help screens

Systems Software
- Operating systems
- Utilities
- Language translators

Where to Find Software
- Magazines
- Public domain software and shareware
- User groups and professional associations

A Closer Look . . . Comparing Popular Operating Environments

FROM THE USER'S POINT OF VIEW

Personal taste and needs are reflected in the software you purchase. Whether you like to use a mouse or keyboard for input, there are common procedures for accessing data, selecting program options, and printing results. Being familiar with the common user interfaces discussed in this chapter makes learning to operate new software packages easier. Understanding these basic software concepts also helps you minimize frustrations when recovering from mistakes.

USER INTERFACES

Software turns general-purpose computer hardware into a tool that solves specific problems. The detailed instructions of a program determine how easy a computer system is to use, what gets done, and how the final results are presented. The combination of menu options, icons, and commands you use when working with a computer program is called the **user interface.**

Experienced end-users are comfortable using several of the common user interfaces. For example, Nancy Mitchell and friend Linda Frye just purchased a new adventure game that explores a haunted house. Both friends were anxious to get the program running on their personal computers—they have a friendly competition in being the first to find the hidden key or trap door. Although their computer hardware is basically the same, the procedures Nancy and Linda use to explore the program features are quite different. They work with different user interfaces. Common user interfaces fall into one of four categories:

- Command-driven
- Shell
- Graphical
- Natural language

Command-Driven Interfaces

Nancy's computer system uses a **command-driven interface** for its system software. A special set of key words and symbols initiate program options and operations. Most command-driven interfaces employ a **screen prompt** which indicates the system is ready to accept a new command. A blinking **cursor** highlights where the computer is going to display the next

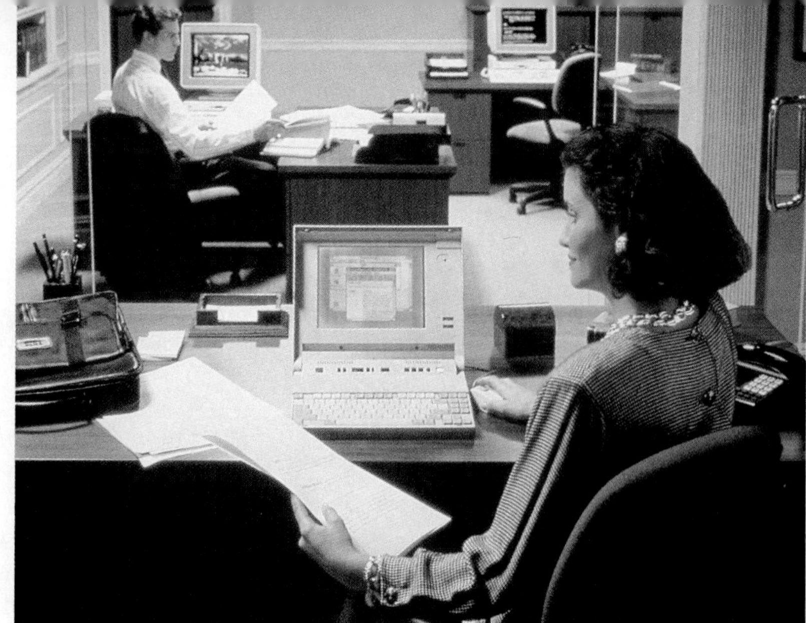

FIGURE 3.1
Users interact with a program's user interface through a keyboard by entering commands or with a mouse by selecting menu options and activating icons.

keyboard entry. Special key combinations entered through the keyboard provide control of the cursor's location on the screen (see Figure 3.2).

Figure 3.3 shows a screen display of the DOS prompt and command Nancy uses to display the directory of her Haunted House

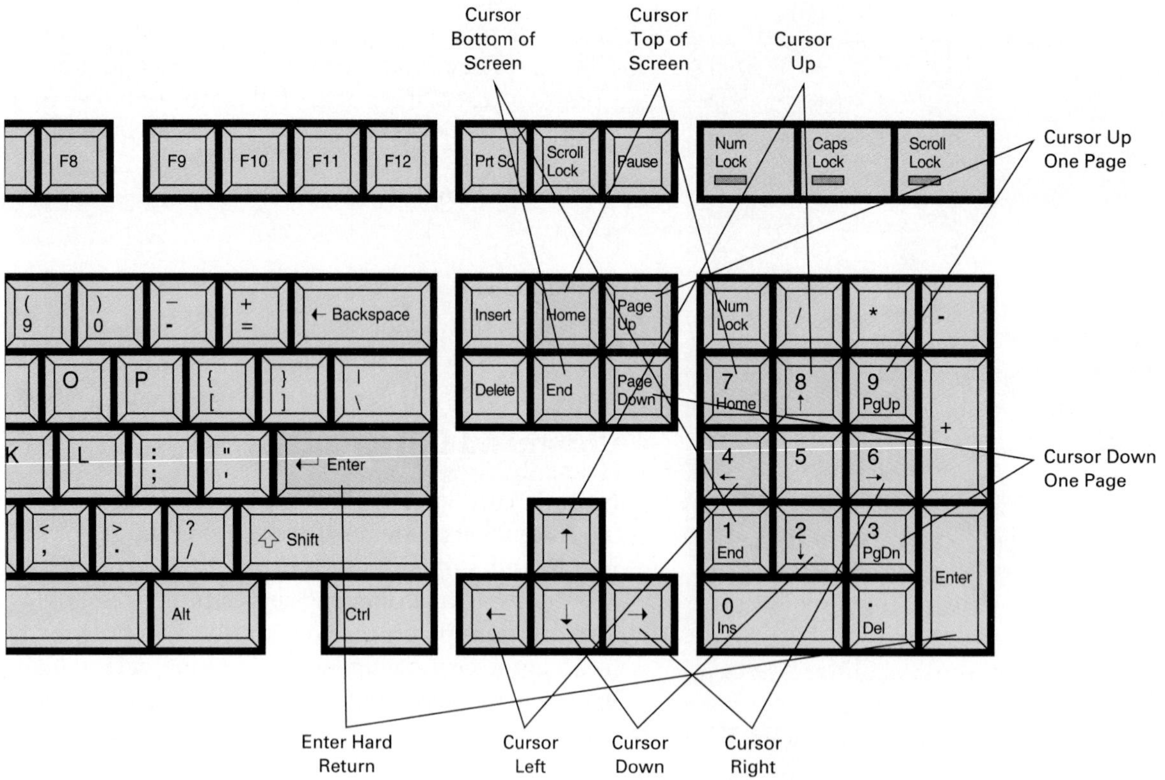

FIGURE 3.2
Several keyboard keys control the location of the cursor on the screen.

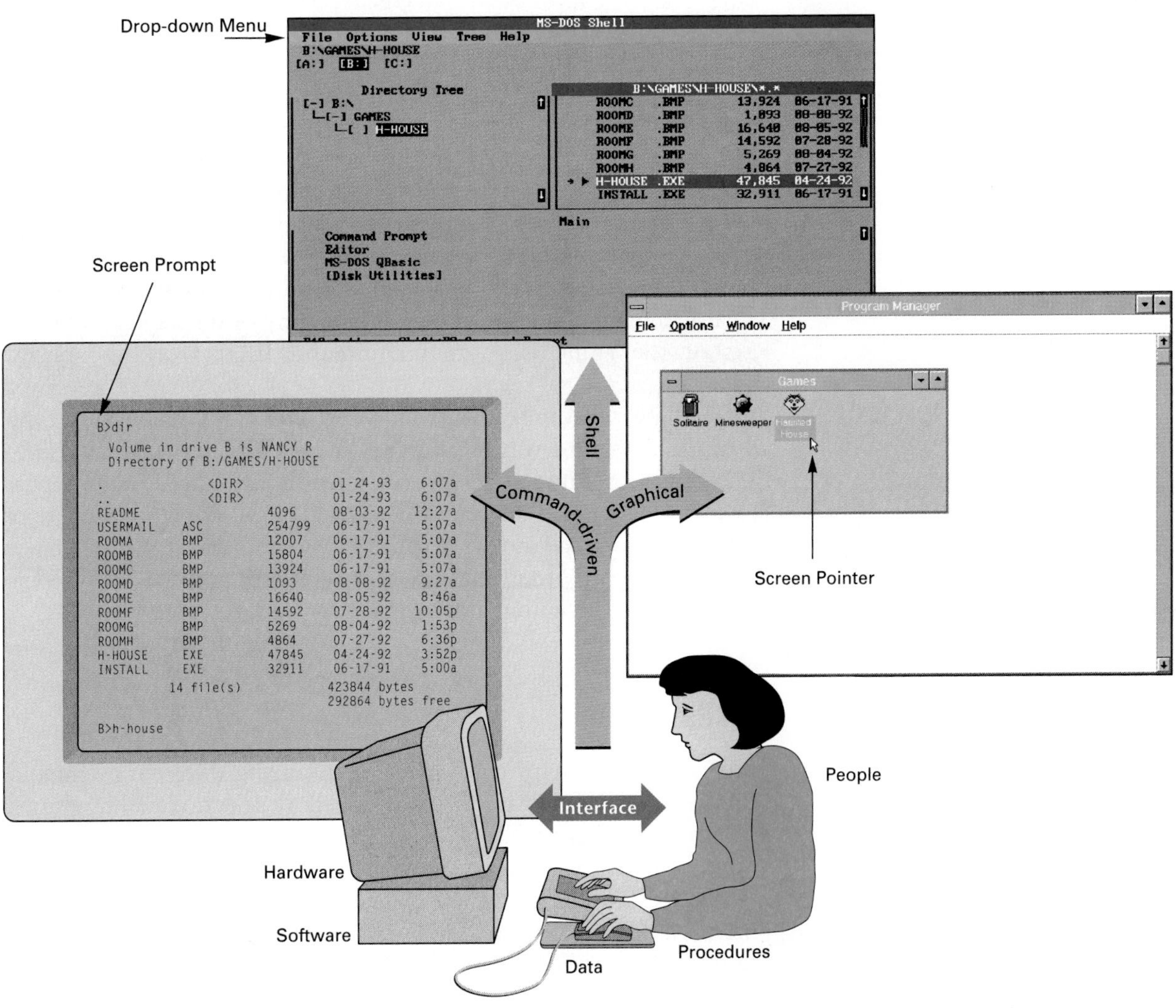

disk. A **disk directory** contains the name, size, creation date, and creation time of each data file or program saved on the disk.

To get started, Nancy could read the paper version of the user's manual or display an electronic copy on the screen. Instead she displays the *readme file* that often accompanies professionally developed software. Nancy knows the readme file shown in Figure 3.3 will provide enough instructions to get her started.

Nancy needs to install the program on her computer system. Before playing her new game, she follows (*executes*) the installation program and answers questions about her computer system. These questions include information about the printer model, screen type, mouse type, and memory capacity of the computer. Many times questions are answered with single-character input like Y (yes) or N (no).

FIGURE 3.3
User interfaces let people control their computer systems by selecting various program options, using commands, menus, or icons.

Once the game program is installed, Nancy starts Haunted House by typing the program name, H-HOUSE, after the screen prompt. Pressing the Enter key initiates program execution. An application package and the computer's system software may not use the same user interface. In this case, the system and application software each uses a different set of commands. What Nancy sees next is a series of color graphics depicting different rooms. She navigates through the rooms by entering different key words. The game accepts commands like "west" and "door" or "pickup" and "key." The user's manual and help screens list many of the key commands. Part of the game is to find commands that work in special situations.

The use of command-driven interfaces dates back to a time when the keyboard was the primary means of entering data. Experienced users became extremely proficient in using these commands. However, new users do not find memorizing commands very user friendly. This is true in part because each command-driven interface has its own word order, spacing, abbreviations, and special symbols that make up the command **syntax.**

Shells

A software **shell** helps users avoid memorizing different command syntaxes. People navigate through a shell by selecting menu options as shown in Figure 3.3. Popular command-driven systems and applications software often have compatible shells. Menu options are highlighted by using the mouse or designated keys on the keyboard. Nancy could have used the DOS shell in Figure 3.3 to display the disk directory or run the game.

Menus are often used in applications software as well. The Haunted House program has menus labeled Door and Window. Options within the Door menu include North, South, East, and West. When a menu option appears in a light color on screen, the related option is not active or available. If the room Nancy is in does not have a door in the north wall, then the option North is not highlighted in the menu. Menu options are often key commands used by the user interface.

Graphical User Interfaces

Linda's computer system uses a **graphical user interface (GUI).** This type of interface uses a mouse that controls the location of a **screen pointer.** The pointer determines which areas of the screen are used for input. To select a menu option or activate a program icon, Linda *clicks* (presses) a button on the mouse. After installing the game,

Linda runs the Haunted House program by using the mouse to position the pointer on the Haunted House icon (see Figure 3.3) and *double-clicking*—quickly pressing the mouse button twice. Users execute or *launch* programs by double-clicking on the associated icon.

Linda navigates through different rooms by using another graphical user interface. Clicking on a door knob means she wants to exit through the selected door. When Linda wants to *drag* or move an object on the screen, she uses the mouse to point at the object and holds down the mouse button while moving the icon to a new location. When Linda uncovers the skeleton key, she drags it across the screen and into her basket (icon) of goodies.

Dragging and dropping icons into new screen locations is also useful when working with system software. Linda can backup data files by duplicating the file icon and dragging one of the copies to a different disk icon. An outdated data file is removed from a disk by dragging the icon to the trash can (see Figure 3.4) or paper shredder icon. Many of the icons used with graphical user interfaces draw upon desktop analogies. Besides a trash can, you will find icons representing file folders, documents, calendars, calculators, clocks, and address books.

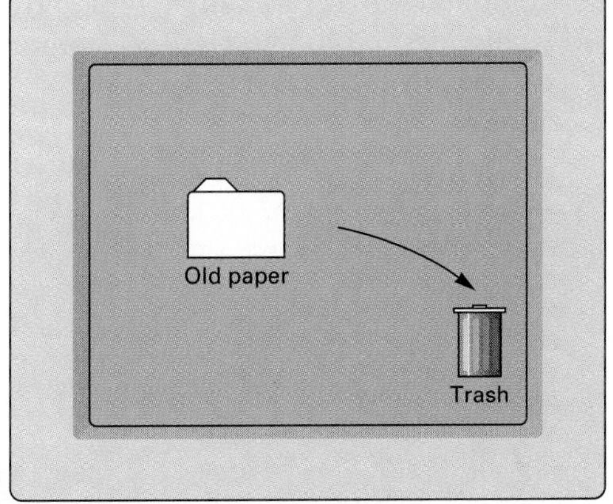

Movement of the mouse results in a corresponding movement of the pointer on the screen.

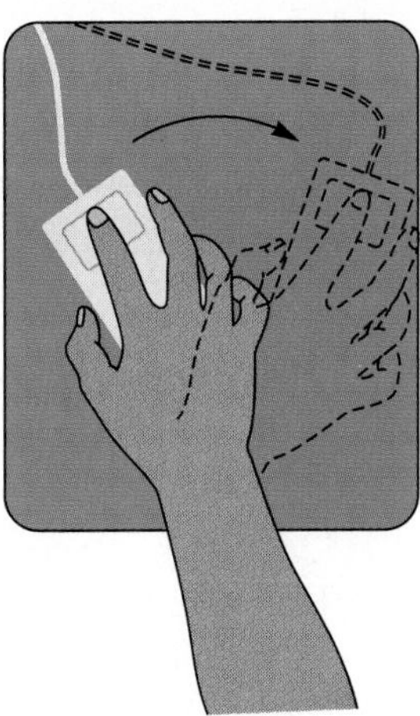

Hold mouse button down to drag icon to new screen location.

FIGURE 3.4
Icons are dragged to new screen locations or dropped onto other icons to initiate program operations.

Natural Language Interfaces

A **natural language interface** allows the user to activate program options by writing or speaking in the native language: English, Spanish, Japanese, etc. Interfaces that recognize spoken words are not widely available. However, you can find natural language interfaces that accept keyboard entries. The Haunted House program with a natural language user interface must be extremely flexible to be effective. For instance, it should accept the entry "let's see what's on the other side of that door by the lamp." Currently these systems are restricted to a specific domain, such as a haunted house, and limit the number of words they recognize.

EVALUATING SOFTWARE FEATURES

Properly designed software is user friendly because it is self-explanatory and handles situations in a comfortable, common-sense approach. You personalize your computer system by selecting software you need and feel comfortable using (Figure 3.5).

Computer programs differ with the individual job performed and results desired. Some features support specific user needs, and

In the News...

THE FUTZ FACTOR

A study released by a software company called SBT concludes that 2 percent of America's gross domestic product—$97 billion—is being "futzed away" by workers who spend too much time tinkering with their PCs. The top futzes:

Font futzing: Spending too much time prettying up copy with fancy typefaces, etc.

The network gnash: Trying to link PCs so they can "talk" to each other. Often leads to crashes in the early going.

Office block: Writing the same thing over and over because tinkering is so easy.

The spread web: Getting caught up in overly elaborate spreadsheets.

Presentation perfection: Endlessly polishing charts, graphs and other snazzy doodads.

FIGURE 3.5
People look for flexible, user-friendly software packages that can share data with other programs.

other features make the software easier to use. When evaluating different applications packages, you should ask yourself these questions:

- Are the program and associated procedures easy to use?
- Does the software work the way I desire, or will changes be necessary?
- How flexible is the program, and can I use it for more than one application?
- Can the new software access data stored by other programs and vice versa?
- Does the software come with help screens, manuals, and other forms of easy-to-read documentation?
- Is there a telephone number I can call when the manuals and other documentation do not answer a question?
- On which computers does the software work?
- Does the software require special hardware?

While problems and computer applications may differ between people, common features are easy to identify. These features help us learn how to use the software effectively, minimize frustrations, and provide insights into future applications for the package.

File Conventions and Groupware

Many applications packages stand alone. That is, they operate as single entities and are not designed to share data with other programs. Over time, demand has grown for sharing data among several applications. People discovered that spreadsheets could lend

FIGURE 3.6
Three-letter filename extensions are added to the filename to identify the file format.

Summary of Common File Extensions

Extension	Software	Description
asc	Many products	American standard of information interchange
bmp	Paintbrush	Bitmap graphic
cal	Calendar	Data - text
cbt	Many products	Computer-based training data file
chp	Ventura	Chapter
crd	Cardfile	Data - text
db	Paradox	Database file
dbf	dBASE	Database file
doc	Many products	Data - text
dot	Word (Windows)	Document template
dll	Windows	Dynamic link library
dwg	AutoCAD	Data - 3D drawing
dxf	AutoCAD	Database file
mtw	Minitab	Data - numeric

support to information presented in a textual document. Also, a bar chart can clarify figures laid out in a spreadsheet. In short, people needed the capability to combine formerly independent applications.

The need to share data led to the emergence of standards for text, database, worksheet, and graphic files. The **filename** uniquely identifies the file. A three-letter *filename extension* is added to the filename to identify the file format. Figure 3.6 identifies common file formats and their filename extensions.

Software developers have also addressed the need to share data through the development of *integrated software*. One software package provides user interfaces for word processing, spreadsheet,

Summary of Common File Extensions *(Continued)*

Extension	Software	Description
pcx	Paintbrush	Data - graphic
pic	Lotus	Data - graphic
pm5	Pagemaker	Data for version 5
pt5	Pagemaker	Template for version 5
rbf	R:base	Database file
sld	AutoCAD	Data - 2D drawing
sty	Ventura	Style sheet template
tif	Many products	Data - typeset
txt	Notepad	Data - text
wb1	Quattro Pro	Data - spreadsheet
wk1	Lotus	Data - spreadsheet
wpg	WordPerfect	Data - graphic
wri	Write	Data - text
xls	Excel	Data - spreadsheet
xlc	Excel	Data - graphic

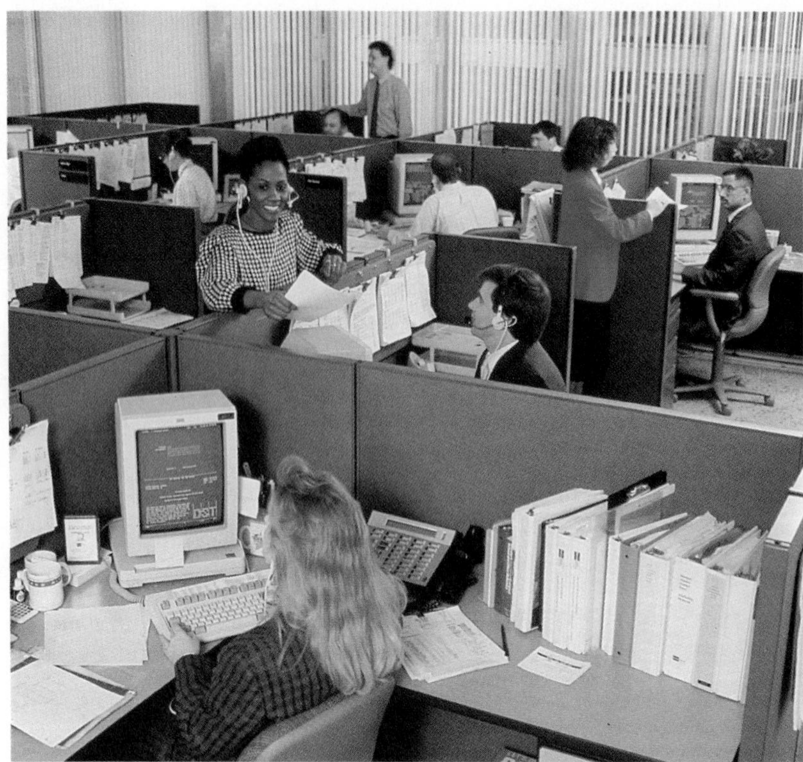

FIGURE 3.7
Personal computer users linked to a network use a groupware package to support common appointment calendars, document sharing, interactive conference calls, and group editing sessions.

and data management applications, which permits users to share data among those applications.

Compatible data and integrated software are provided by *groupware* packages that support personal computer users connected through a network. Groupware applications include common calendars, electronic mail, interactive conference calls, document sharing, and editing sessions with several users (Figure 3.7).

When people working on common tasks can share data, everyone benefits from increased productivity. A company engineer might use a popular graphics package to design a new water pump valve. Each drawing includes a list of the individual pieces and the materials from which they are made. The graphics package allows the engineer to save the same drawing in two different file formats, DXF and SLD. The DXF file can be read by an electronic spreadsheet, which uses the parts list to project materials costs and a break-even point. A tool path program uses geometry from the drawing in the SLD file to create programs that operate milling machines that make each part. A word processing program even incorporates the drawing from the SLD file to create a process control form. Technicians in the shop use the form when checking new parts for flaws.

Windows and Multitasking

Applications programs, particularly integrated software, often are powerful enough to allow users to switch between two or more activities. Other times, a computer's operating system supports **multitasking,** which enables the computer to maintain the operation of two independent programs concurrently. To track multiple operations, the computer's screen is divided into sections, or **windows.** Each window displays a menu or status report on a separate program or activity. Programs used to create a financial status report, for example, might use three windows. One would display the text of the report, generated through word processing software. The second could hold a spreadsheet. Graphics tying together the words and the numbers might occupy the third window.

Windows are used widely with **terminate stay resident (TSR)** programs. The TSR program stays inactive, but in memory, while other applications programs are in use. A desktop TSR program is a common TSR application. This program provides resources commonly found on a person's desk and might include a calendar, calculator, telephone directory, appointment schedule, and notepad. When the user needs a calendar to schedule a meeting, the desktop TSR can be accessed without exiting the active application program.

Imagine, for example, someone interrupted by a telephone call as he is trying to write a report, using word processing. The telephone caller is requesting the rescheduling of an important meeting. The user can activate the desktop TSR's calendar and appointment schedule without interfering with the work in progress (see Figure 3.8). He just presses a special combination of keys to activate the TSR program. In this situation a window appears on the screen, and

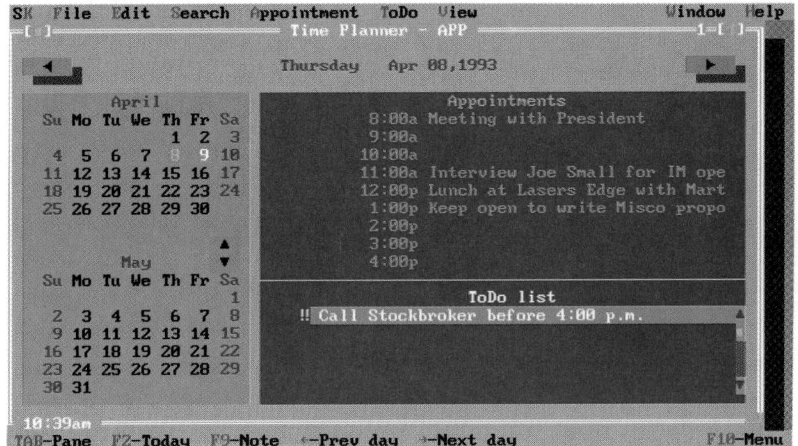

FIGURE 3.8
When activated by a special combination of keystrokes, this desktop TSR program displays program options in different windows.

the user selects the calendar and appointment scheduling options. Once the meeting time is changed on the calendar, he deactivates the desktop TSR and continues working on the report. All these activities take place within windows on the screen and do not affect the report.

Menus and Dialog Boxes

Menus are used in a variety of user interfaces. Shells use menus almost exclusively. Full-screen menus stay on the screen until the user selects a menu option. To minimize space taken by menus, some programs use *drop-down menus*, sometimes called pull-down menus. In this case the menu stays at the top of the screen, hidden in a menu bar until selected by the user. In Figure 3.10, an activated menu opens to list program options. Once an option is selected, the menu rolls back up, out of the way.

Some menu selections open a dialog box, which asks for additional data. A common convention is to add three periods, called an *ellipsis,* behind the menu option when more user input is needed. A **dialog box** prompts the user to enter text, select names from a list, or click on a *button* icon which confirms a selection or cancels the operation. Each button is labeled to identify the associated operation, such as OK, Cancel, Browse, or Help.

The dialog box in Figure 3.9 includes a text box, list box, OK button, and Cancel button. *Text boxes* accept keyboard entries. For example, the user could enter a new filename for data being saved to disk.

When a disk directory or any list of filenames is available, a *list box* is used to display the names. The *scroll arrows* roll the list up and down within the list box. Any time information is hidden from view, a window or list box can move or **scroll** the view left and right or up and down. Another way to scroll through a list is to drag the

FIGURE 3.9
A dialog box prompts user input through text boxes, list boxes, and buttons.

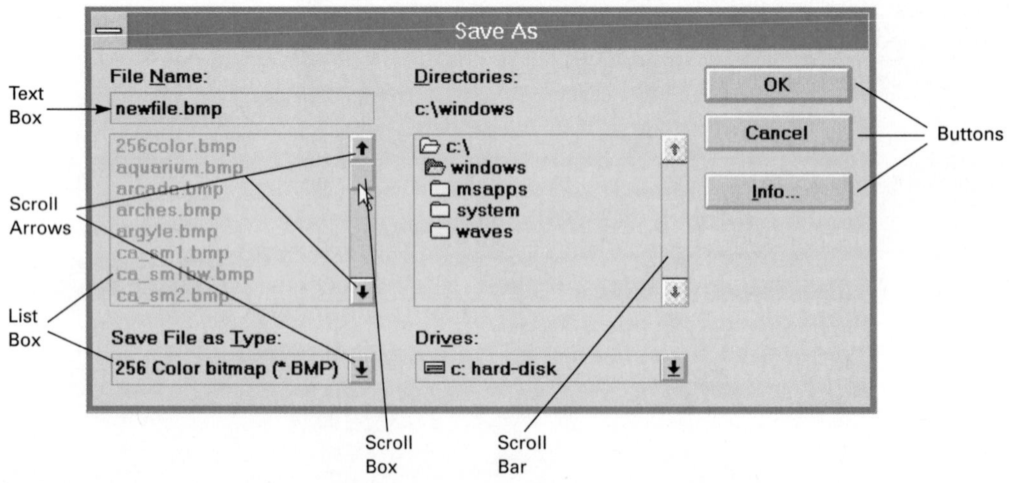

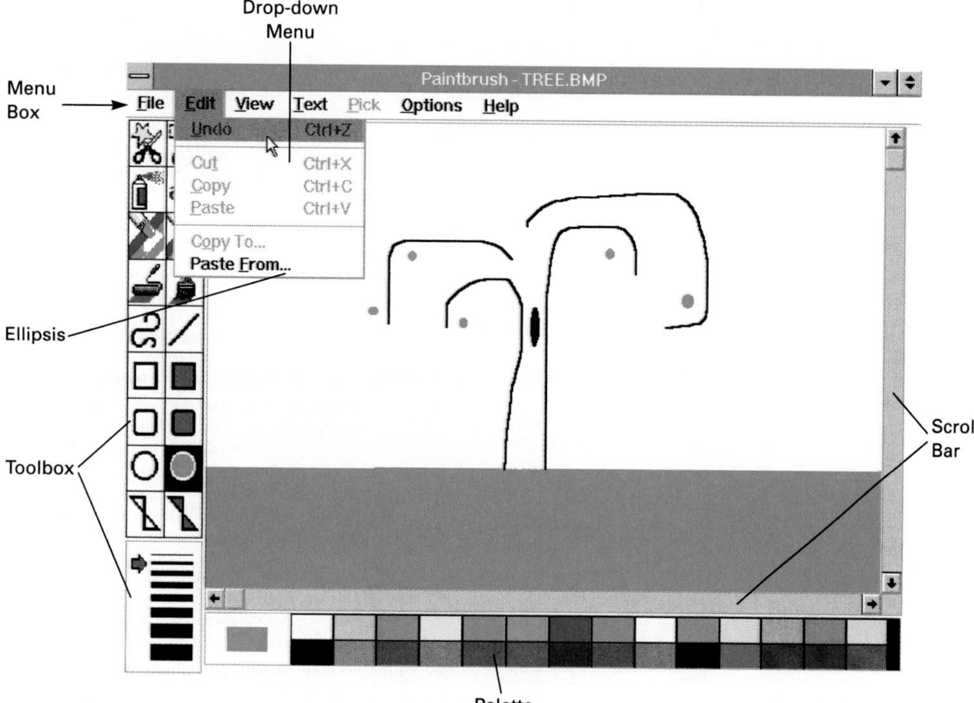

FIGURE 3.10
Artists working with a graphics package's GUI select options from drop-down menus, toolbox icons, and palette chips.

scroll box within the *scroll bar* (see Figure 3.9). The scroll box moves up and down with the list when you click on the associated scroll arrow or drag it with the mouse. To select an item, the user scrolls the desired item name into view within the list box, points the screen pointer at it, and clicks the mouse.

Palettes and Toolboxes

To support graphics applications, a *palette* and *toolbox* display options for drawing and coloring an image (see Figure 3.10). A palette usually contains icons that correspond to different screen colors. The toolbox provides icons for brush size, shape, and width along with other editing features. The user selects desired options by moving the pointer and clicking on the corresponding icons. As the user creates a screen drawing, the graphics package responds with the specified options. The final product reflects the combination of images and colors selected by the user.

Manuals and Help Screens

Learning to use a new applications program puts a new user interface in front of the user. When users of unfamiliar software face problems or uncertainty, they must look to the **user's manual** for answers. The user's manual provides information on how to operate the program, descriptions of program features, an explanation of error messages, and a telephone number for customer support ser-

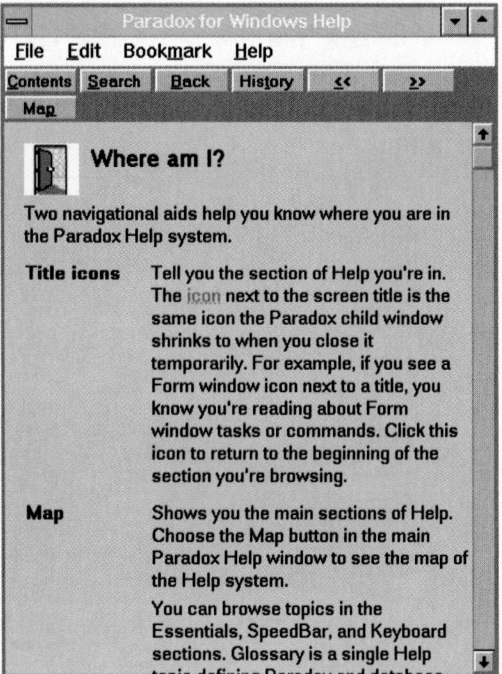

FIGURE 3.11
Context-sensitive help screens often answer user questions instead of the user's manual.

vices. This same information is also available on the **help screens** users activate through a keyboard keystroke or by clicking on a mouse button.

Help screens, like the one illustrated in Figure 3.11, put answers at users' fingertips. Some help screens are even *context-sensitive.* In these situations the help screen displays information directly related to the program options that were available when the user asked for help.

Each user interface provides a different way of accessing help screens. Some programs list a help directory on the menu, while others require use of a special function key. Still others require that users ask for assistance by typing in "help" or by clicking on a Help button. There is currently an attempt by several software developers to standardize accessing help screens by using the F1 function key.

SYSTEMS SOFTWARE

Applications software is designed to work with a computer's systems software. This relationship did not always exist. The earliest forms of applications software were executed without the assistance of systems software. Computer operators and programmers did all of the setup. They had to schedule jobs, control devices, allocate memory, and direct processing for each application. In effect, these people were responsible for system control. However, it was inefficient to require operators to prepare the computer for each job.

Soon every computer manufacturer provided systems software to minimize this problem and help people communicate more easily with their computers. Three types of systems software can be identified: operating systems, utilities, and language translators.

Users first deal with an **operating system,** a collection of systems programs that oversee the coordination and control of a computer system's resources. Another form of systems software, called **utility software,** performs special processing tasks, such as hardware optimization and transferring data by using a telephone. A **language translator** is a systems program that converts the English-like instructions used by computer programmers into the machine-readable code used by the hardware. Programs written in languages like BASIC, Pascal, C, or COBOL must be converted into the appropriate machine language.

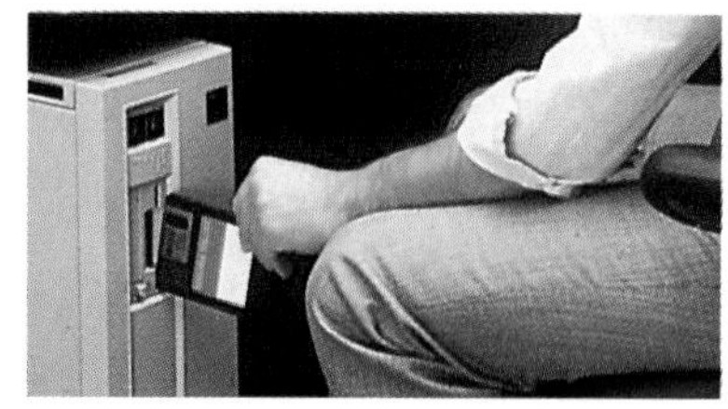

FIGURE 3.12
A supervisor program that oversees internal operations is loaded into the computer's memory when the system is turned on.

In the News...

DESKTOP OPERATING SYSTEMS

Windows NT (Microsoft)

Strengths: NT combines the power of multitasking and memory management with the intuitive interface of Windows 3.1. The DOS/Windows/NT trio is highly scalable, supporting the smallest laptop up to DEC's Alpha systems.

Weaknesses: The first release may lack the maturity and stability of its competitors. Beta-test versions require substantial memory and disk space.

OS/2 (IBM)

Strengths: Runs several processing tasks simultaneously and doesn't crash when an application crash occurs. Serves as a highly stable and reliable platform.

Weaknesses: Requires substantial memory and disk space, and it operates only on Intel-based microprocessors. There's also a dearth of native OS/2 applications.

Unix

Strengths: User-friendly interfaces are now available, which puts a familiar face on Unix's powerful but difficult to use features, such as multitasking and multiuser support.

Weaknesses: Expensive compared with other operating systems. Can be complicated to install and administer.

System 7 (Apple)

Strengths: High stability and ease of use. Applications easier to master because of the consistent interface. Exhibits the best handling of graphics applications, compared with other systems.

Weaknesses: Requires state-of-the-art Macintosh hardware. Difficult to integrate into the PC-oriented business world.

Operating Systems

As its name implies, the operating system is a collection of programs that oversee all computer operations. Before any processing can occur, the command program or **supervisor** is booted into the computer's memory. Two methods are available for booting the operating system into memory, as shown in Figure 3.13. Most computers load the operating system from a disk. When a hard disk is available, the supervisor is automatically loaded. In other situations the user/operator places the operating system disk into a floppy disk drive and turns on the computer. Without further instructions from the operator, the computer transfers the operating system into memory, preparing the machine to begin processing. In larger computer systems this booting process may require several steps to identify each attached peripheral. Mainframe operators often refer to the booting process as the initial program load (IPL).

The second method of booting the operating system requires even less user intervention. The operator need only switch on the computer, and a built-in operating system is activated. Such systems are hardwired into permanent memory. Hardwired operating systems need not be loaded physically into the computer because they are permanently within it.

Once the supervisor program is loaded into memory, it activates other programs from the operating system to oversee resources, manage files, and control tasks.

FIGURE 3.13
While most computer systems boot the operating system's supervisor program from disk, a few computers have it hardwired into memory.

Two Methods for Booting an Operating System

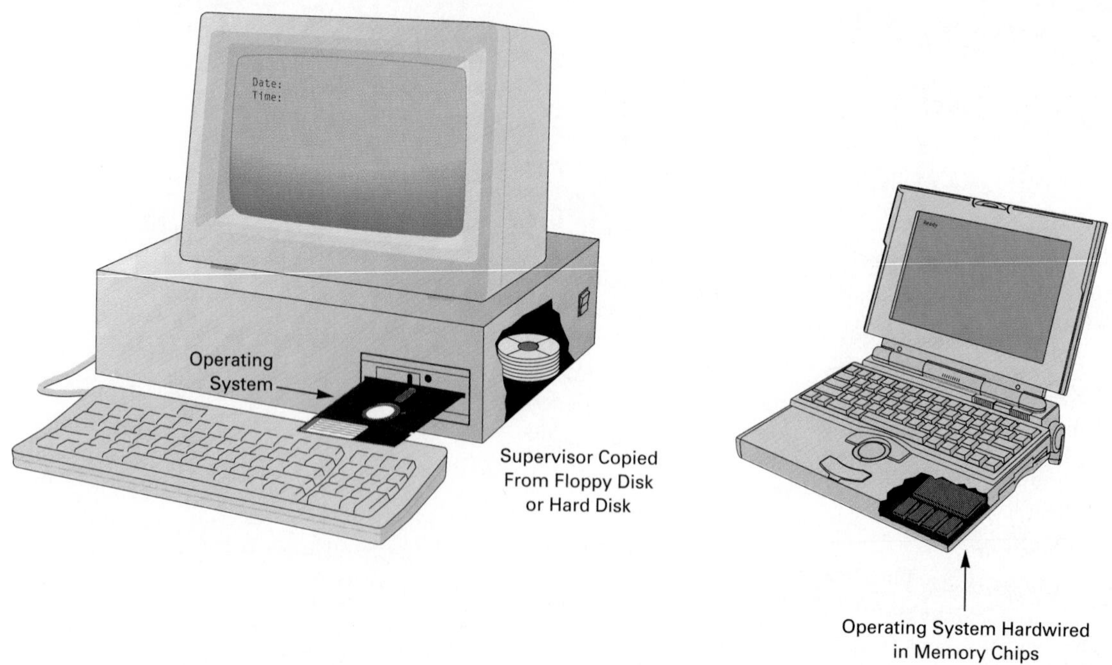

Resource Management

A major responsibility of any operating system is to make sure each hardware component is receiving and sending data and software in an error-free method. Resource management would include formatting new disks, system security, transferring error-free data between system components, and displaying error messages when problems occur. An operating system even detects such "error" conditions as an open disk drive door or a printer that has run out of paper.

The operating system also sets up system **defaults,** or standard hardware connections and formats the computer uses unless otherwise instructed. Default values save the user's time by preparing computer resources to operate in a predetermined fashion. Many defaults get set up by special system files. During booting the supervisor reads different device drivers from disk. When users connect equipment to the system, they copy the related device driver file to the boot disk. The *device driver* file identifies operating characteristics of such peripherals as a mouse, printer, or scanner.

One of the most important resources an operating system manages is the computer's memory. Data and programs reside in memory during processing. When multitasking is possible, the operating system must keep track of several programs and associated data at the same time. To make sure programs and data run properly, the operating system also checks everything coming into the memory for transmission and storage errors. When errors are found, the operating system reads the data or program again from the input device, asks the user to re-enter it, or displays an error message.

In the News...

OPERATING SYSTEMS: TOP 10 USER PRIORITIES

IS professionals asked to rate the most important qualities of a desktop operating system said:

9.1 Stability
8.7 Compatibility
8.4 Ease of use
8.4 Value for the dollar
8.2 Local-area network capability
8.1 Available third-party applications
8.1 Speed
7.9 Memory management
7.9 Service and support
7.7 High-quality documentation

Based on Buyers' Scorecard survey of 180 IS professionals, who ranked the importance of each area based on a 1-to-10 scale, where 10 is most important.

Computers with limited amounts of memory cannot store large computer programs. Since only a small portion of a program can be processed at any given moment, most of the program and memory are unused. Yet the entire program takes up space in memory during processing. Some operating systems support **virtual memory** as a way of getting around this resource limitation. The operating system uses disk storage as an extension of memory. In other words, the processor treats storage on a disk drive as part of memory. Figure 3.14 depicts a large program that is broken down into sections, called *pages*. Pages that are not currently being used by the processor are stored on disk. When a page is needed, the operating system swaps it into memory by replacing a completed page. One drawback is slower processing speeds because of the time it takes to transfer pages between the disk drive and memory. However, virtual memory increases the versatility of the processor by letting it handle programs that exceed its memory capacity.

File Management

When storing programs and data on tape or disk, the operating system prompts the user to enter a unique filename. It then adds the filename along with the current date and time to a disk directory or tape label. File management means keeping track of these files and being able to move them from storage into memory and back again.

FIGURE 3.14
Virtual memory operations use disk drives as extensions of the computer's memory.

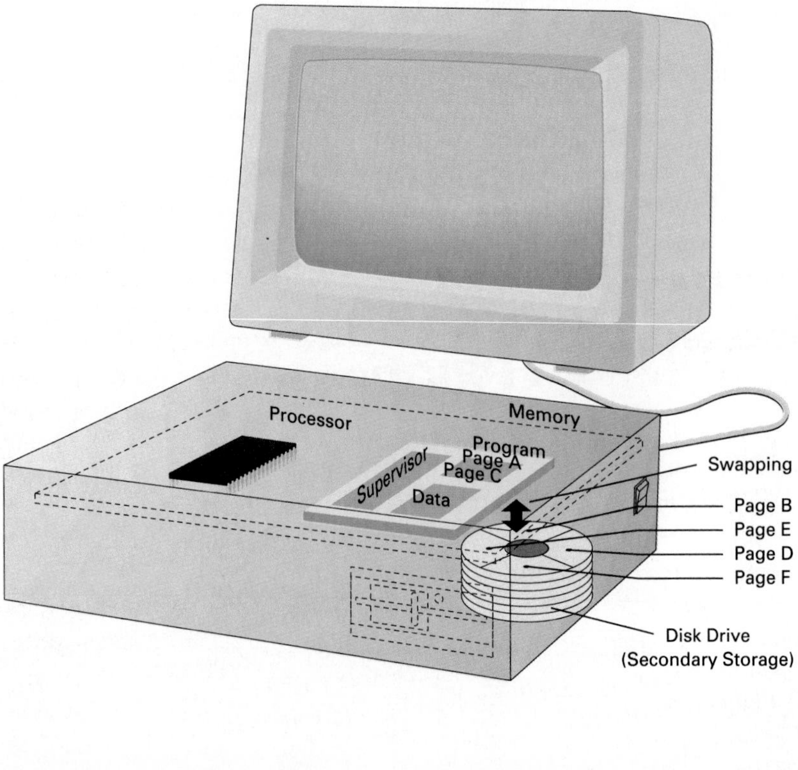

William (Bill) Gates (b. 1955)

Bill Gates taught himself programming at age 13. As Seattle teenagers, he and his friends would ride their bicycles to a local computer company to help them look for programming errors. In 1962 he took a leave from high school when TRW offered him a job at $20,000. With a friend, Paul Allen, he did system programming for Honeywell Corp. Together they wrote a BASIC interpreter for Altair microcomputers based on the Intel 8008 processor. In 1975 he formed Microsoft Corporation, which wrote systems programs for Altair and Apple microcomputers and expanded BASIC for others. IBM asked Gates to develop an operating system for its new PC machine. The result was MS-DOS, one of the largest-selling operating systems in the world. Gates also directed software development for the Macintosh and Radio Shack Model 100 of the TRS-80 microcomputers. Microsoft kept producing winning software like Word, Works, and Flight Simulator. In 1987 IBM chose Microsoft's Windows operating environment for PS/2, and Windows has become a new standard. Bill Gates is considered one of the richest men in America.

Users interact with the operating system to change a filename in the disk directory, copy it to another disk, delete it, or protect it from accidental deletion. When the operating system designates a file as *protected* or *read-only*, the file can be used and copied, but not altered or erased. The user must turn off the file protection before the operating system removes a file from disk.

People also use an operating system's file management features to organize their data. Files are stored sequentially one after another on tape. Disk files are independently accessed and stored in different disk directories. It is recommended that you store applications programs with their associated data files in separate disk directories. By doing so you make it easier to backup files in the data directory on a regular basis. Files in the program directory get copied to another disk as backup and protected to prevent accidental erasure. When program revisions occur, you unprotect the old program files, erase the directory, and install the new program while leaving the data files alone.

System software using a graphical user interface displays disk directories as file folders. In this case, programs and data are kept in separate file folders. In addition, file folders can be stored inside other folders. For instance, Linda has a Games file folder on her hard disk. When she installed the Haunted House program, she cre-

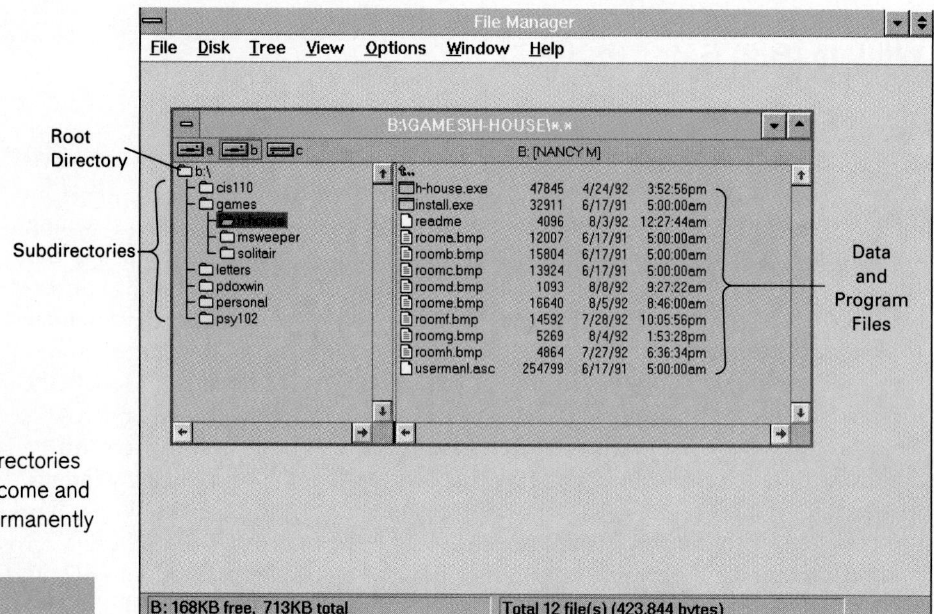

FIGURE 3.15
Users make or remove subdirectories as computer-based projects come and go. Only the root directory permanently remains on the disk.

ated a new file folder, Haunted House, in the Games folder. Linda's Games folder has two other file folders: Solitaire and Mine Sweeper.

Nancy's system works the same way. When installing the Haunted House game she added a directory labeled H-HOUSE to the Games directory. Figure 3.15 shows the relationship between the Games directory, H-House directory, and other related directories. These directories are called *subdirectories* because they are added after a disk is formatted and are subordinate to the original disk directory known as the *root directory*.

Task Management

A **task** is any operation performed by a computer system. Printing a document, copying a file, or computing the volume of concrete needed for a bridge footing are examples of tasks. A single-task operating system can handle only one operation at a time. Early computer systems and many personal computers use single-task operating systems.

Mainframe and minicomputer systems are often asked to perform several processing jobs at one time. Since modern computers perform operations for most applications with time to spare, the operating system can divide the computer's processing power among different applications and users. As a result, multitasking and timesharing are two features that allow more than one user to take advantage of the computer's power.

As you may recall, multitasking is the ability of a computer system to handle several programs concurrently. Actually, each program is given a priority. The program with top priority is processed until the computer has to wait for input or output. Instead of standing idle, operating systems with multitasking capabilities shift to the program with the next highest priority. When the input or output for the first program is complete, the computer resumes processing of the instructions from the top priority program.

For example, a mail-order business with a minicomputer may find that the computer is not utilized to its full capacity when order clerks enter phone orders on it. However, with multitasking capabilities, the computer can work on weekly sales reports when no orders are being taken. Since the order entry program has top priority, the operating system will interrupt the report program and return to order entry when an operator begins to enter a new order.

Timesharing is a special type of task management. Instead of one program getting special priority over others, timesharing assigns each program a slice of time. The programs are then processed in a round-robin pattern. However, each user is served individually and is unaware that others are being served at the same time. Students using a university's mainframe computer system find themselves in a room timesharing the computer with dozens of other students. Since each student is given a time slice, it seems as if each has the computer to himself or herself (Figure 3.16).

FIGURE 3.16
Timesharing is a special type of multitasking where the computer system skips between different application programs and gives each user roughly the same amount of processing time.

Utilities

Utility software performs jobs the operating system does not automatically handle (Figure 3.17). For example, a variety of file conversion utilities exist to convert data into another format. Users might run a file conversion utility to convert a database file into a text file or to change drawings from one graphic format to another.

Some utility programs help users optimize their computer hardware. Data compression utilities reduce the amount of disk space a file uses by stripping out unnecessary spaces and by performing other data compaction tricks. The same software restores the file to its original form when the data is read from the disk. Other utility programs reorganize files on disk to optimize data access and retrieval times.

Another common utility program is used to save time when printing large documents. A *SPOOLer* (*S*imultaneous *P*eripheral *O*peration *O*n*L*ine) utility coordinates the transfer of data between the computer and other peripherals, in this case the disk drive and printer. Instead of waiting for the document to be printed, the user can work with other programs and files. The spooler transfers the document from the computer to the disk drive and handles the printing of the document.

Communication software that allows users to link their computers with other computers by using the telephone is a popular type of utility program. Once the user stores the appropriate data

Jobs Performed by Utility Programs

- File conversions
- Data compressions
- Disk optimization
- Spool data between peripheral hardware
- Data communications with other computers
- Emulation of other equipment

formats and telephone numbers, the communication software oversees the telephone call, linkage between computers, and transmission of data.

Sometimes situations arise where a user wants one piece of equipment to act like another. Take, for instance, a document saved in a file format used by an out-of-date printer. By using a printer emulation utility on your computer, a different printer can still output the file. *Emulation* programs mimic the operation of other equipment.

FIGURE 3.17
Utility programs perform jobs the operating system does not automatically handle.

Language Translators

In its simplest form, a computer program indicates which switches inside the computer are on and off, which circuits flow with electricity, and those that do not. However, it is not very efficient for a programmer to write programs in this **machine language.** Programmers are most efficient when they can work with discrete operations, like sorting, adding, or copying. Data structures are easier to organize when expressed as fields, records, and files instead of binary codes comprised of 1s and 0s.

Computer professionals realized in the 1950s that they needed to develop their own computer programming languages. Different **high-level languages** have developed over the years. The command syntax of these languages resembles human languages. High-level languages eliminated the need for programmers to memorize unique codes for different computer operations or memory locations. IBM's FORTRAN, or FORmula TRANslator, language uses words such as READ, WRITE, and STOP as programming statements, as seen in Figure 3.18. FORTRAN also is capable of dealing with complex mathematical equations. This language was introduced in 1957 and came into widespread use during the 1960s. Because FORTRAN eases the transition from mathematical notation to computer programming, it is still used today for engineering and graphics appli-

FIGURE 3.18
This high-level program is written in the FORTRAN programming language. After it is translated into the computer's machine language, it will accept two numbers as data and add them together.

FORTRAN

```
   INTEGER NUM1, NUM2, SUM
   READ ( 5,10) NUM1, NUM2
10 FORMAT (I4, I4)
   SUM = NUM1 + NUM2
   WRITE (6,20) NUM1, NUM2, SUM
20 FORMAT (10X, 'THE SUM OF', I4, '+', I4, 'IS', I5)
   STOP
   END
```

cations. Other popular high-level languages are BASIC (see Figure 1.6), COBOL, Pascal, C, and Logo.

Each program written in a high-level programming language must be translated into the computer's machine language before it can run. To write a FORTRAN program that works on a personal computer, you need a systems program that translates FORTRAN instructions. The FORTRAN translator converts the English-like FORTRAN into the personal computer's own machine language.

WHERE TO FIND SOFTWARE

Software can be developed by employees, leased, bought, or shared. With the abundance of prepackaged software on the market, development by computer professionals is usually reserved for customized programs. New system and application packages are announced every week, and rumors abound about others that are not yet available to consumers. Software associated with these rumors becomes *vaporware* if it is never released or becomes delayed due to programming problems.

For general applications, leased or purchased software provides needed capabilities at minimum cost. Inexpensive or free software is distributed through networks and among users with similar interests. The most popular software sources are described below.

Retail Stores and Computer Manufacturers

Most users purchase off-the-shelf software packages at retail computer stores. These outlets provide hardware, supplies, magazines, and manuals—in addition to vast selections of software. Purchasing software through retail stores has a distinct advantage. Most retailers will permit you to test applications programs before you purchase them. Also, salespeople usually are on hand to describe software features and review users' manuals.

Before you buy a software package, you should use it. This gives you a chance to see if a software package meets your needs. Friends and family members with their own computer systems can often help by letting you try computer programs they use and like.

Manufacturers of computer hardware usually provide compatible systems software. In addition, some hardware manufacturers make applications programs available to customers. Since many users base their hardware decisions on availability of a specific software package, computer manufacturers often package personal productivity software with their hardware as a sales incentive. For example, a new user might be purchasing a personal computer specifically for its word processing ability. If he or she is working with a limited budget, hardware packaged with a compatible operating system and word processing program could be highly desirable.

Magazines

Computer trade magazines are an inexpensive source of information on programs. Often these magazines review competing software packages and provide readers with feature-by-feature comparisons, as shown in Figure 3.19. Hundreds of magazines and newsletters publish articles geared toward personal computer use. Many magazines specialize in reviewing software compatible with one or two brands of computers. Also, special-interest magazines, such as periodicals about sports, music, or entertainment, may review technology and software of interest to their readers.

FIGURE 3.19
Computer magazines provide readers with comprehensive software reviews. This review compares popular vacation planning programs that display maps and provide related hotel and restaurant information.

Navigation and Travel

● = Yes ○ = No
n/a = not applicable

Company	Product	Price	MAPS: U.S. highways	U.S. towns	U.S. cities	Foreign countries	Foreign cities	SEARCH BY: Place name	Address	ZIP code	Area code	Phonetic searching
Adept Computer Solutions 800/578-6277	Street Wizard (W)	$99	●	●	●	○	○	●	●	○	○	●
Automap 602/893-2400	Automap for Windows (W)	$99.75	●	●	●	●	●	●	○	○	○	●
Axxis Software 800/394-3549	Zagat-Axxis City Guide	$99 per city, $249 for three cities	●	●	●	○	○	●	●	○	○	●
Brøderbund Software 800/521-6263	PC Globe (W)	$59.95	○	○	○	●	●	●	○	○	○	●
DeLorme Mapping 207/865-1234	Street Atlas USA	$169	●	●	●	○	○	●	●	●	●	●
IntraCorp 800/468-7226	Travel Partner	$79.95	○	○	●	○	○	●	○	○	○	○
Personal Travel Technologies 516/877-1234	Personal Travel Guide	$299.95	○	●	●	○	○	●	●	○	○	●
Road Scholar 713/266-7623	City Streets (formerly PC Maps)	$99.95[1]	●	○	●	●	●	●	●	●	○	●
Softkey Software Products 800/377-6567	Key Map (W)	$59.95	●	○	●	○	○	●	●	○	○	●
Strategic Mapping 408/970-9600	Local Expert	$99[1]	●	○	●	●	●	●	●	●	●	○
The Software Toolworks 415/883-3000	Travel Companion	$79	○	○	●	○	○	●	●	○	○	○
	U.S. Atlas With Automap (W)	$99.95	●	●	●	○	○	●	○	○	○	○
	World Atlas (W)	$79.95 ($99.95 on CD ROM)	●	●	●	●	●	●	○	○	○	○

(W) Windows product

[1] One city free (user's choice).

Magazines also contain advertisements for software. Computer programs available through mail-order may seem like a convenient way to acquire software. However, ordering anything sight unseen has its risks. Mail-order customers should try to get permission to review the software before buying it. Promotional copies sometimes are available. *Promotional software* allows people to try out programs with limited amounts of data. For example, a promotional database program might limit the user to 30 records. Thus, promotional copies are not useful for regular workloads. They do, however, allow the user to become familiar with the program before buying the package.

INFORMATION									SYSTEM REQUIREMENTS			
Hotels	Restaurants	Entertainment	Reviews	Pop-up Information on areas	Interactive editing (personalized map information)	Displays route on map	Prints directions	Provides geopolitical information	RAM	Disk space	CD ROM drive required	Update schedule
○	○	○	○	●	●	●	●	○	2MB	5MB	○	yearly
●	○	○	○	●	○	●	●	○	512K	4MB	○	yearly
●	●	●	●	●	●	●	●	○	2MB	5MB–9MB	○	yearly (planned)
○	○	○	○	●	○	○	○	●	640K	3MB	○	yearly
○	○	○	○	○	○	○	○	○	2MB	n/a	●	yearly (planned)
●	●	●	○	○	○	○	○	○	640K	3MB	○	yearly
●	●	●	●	●	●	●	●	●	4MB	4MB–8MB	○	quarterly
○	○	○	○	●	●	○	○	○	640K	2MB–12MB	○	monthly (planned)
○	○	○	○	●	●	●	●	○	640K	5MB	○	semi-annually
●	●	●	●	●	●	○	●	○	500K	750K per city	○	monthly
●	●	●	●	●	●	○	○	○	640K	2.5MB–3MB	○	yearly
○	○	○	○	●	●	●	●	●	640K	4MB	●	yearly
○	○	○	○	●	○	○	○	●	2MB	5.7MB	○	yearly

Infoworld (This is an update of 3d edition p. 111.)

Public Domain Software and Shareware

Some very good software, and many marginal programs, are available to interested computer users free of charge. This **public domain software** is distributed through networks and by trading software with other computer users. Several magazines even operate reader services that provide lengthy catalogs of public domain listings. Pages full of utility and applications software are made available to anyone who requests it.

Great care should be taken when using public domain software. Free software comes with no guarantees concerning reliability. In some cases public domain software harbors a "virus" or "worm" that can erase data or damage equipment. To protect yourself, try to acquire public domain software from reliable sources, such as friends or local user groups. Special utility programs are also available that check for and neutralize infected software before it causes any problems.

Public domain software is a "take it as it is" proposition. However, several public domain software programmers continue to make improvements on their programs. To support this work, they ask for a small contribution from people who find their programs useful. Typically, this request is included in a message preceding the program. The message also asks people to pass copies to others. As a result, this special type of "try before you buy" software is known as **shareware.** People who support shareware programmers with a monetary donation usually receive a manual, as well as the next version of the program when it is ready.

User Groups and Professional Associations

User groups provide fellowship among users who share an interest in computers. They also are good sources for public domain software, shareware, and programs developed by users themselves. Usually, user groups consist of people interested in the same brand of computers. They meet to discuss shared problems and new ideas. New users who join these groups can learn about the latest software and hardware developments for their machines.

User groups develop around many types and sizes of computers. Personal computer users generally form local groups. National user groups bring together users of large systems. In both cases computer interests spawn homemade programs that can be shared by all members of the group. Some programs are circulated among club members free of charge. Others are sold for the cost of the tape or disk. In general, the distribution of software by user/developers is not for profit.

A Closer Look...

Comparing Popular Operating Environments

The wide variety of user interfaces has created a demand for a common standard. New users find it frustrating to have to learn different menus and the meaning of new icons every time they launch another software package. Informed users want to use skills they have mastered with one application package on others. In both cases, having a common user interface reduces the amount of time it takes to learn new applications.

Q How do you display the active directory of disk A (disk in drive A)?

A DOS command:

dir a: (press Enter key)

A Windows: Launch the File Manager from the Main group and click on the drive A icon.

A Macintosh: Double-click on disk A icon.

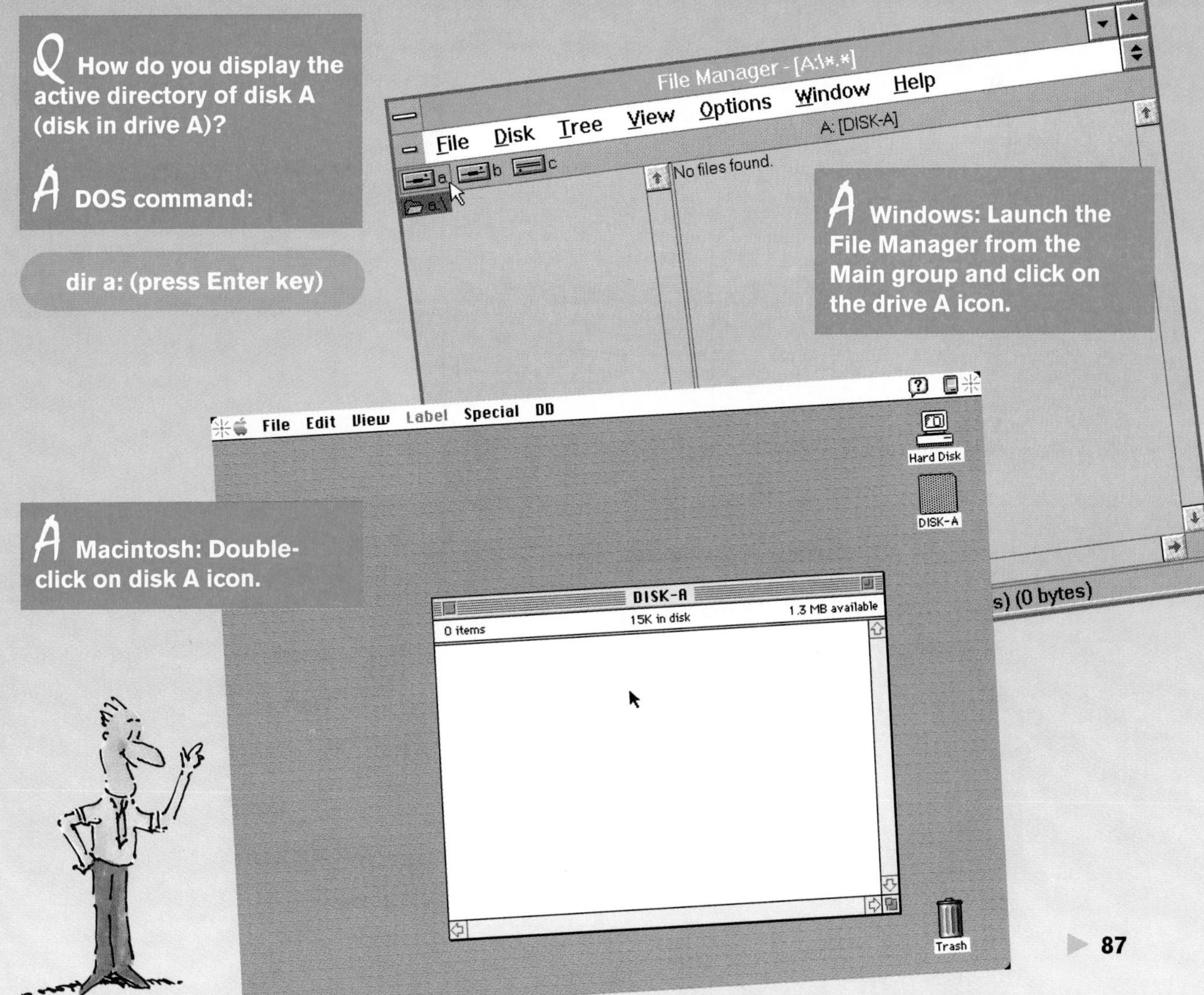

Three user interfaces for system software have emerged as de facto standards. Microsoft's Windows graphical user interface is a popular alternative to the command-driven DOS interface used by IBM and compatible personal computers. The graphical user interface used by the Apple Macintosh has set a standard for user-friendliness. The design and layout of these interfaces have in turn established a look and feel that many application packages use. By standardizing on common menus and screen layouts, users spend less time learning the user interface and more time exploring software options. What follows are screen displays of each interface handling common file management tasks.

Q How do you make a file folder (subdirectory) called PROJECTS on the active disk?

A DOS command:

md \projects (press Enter key)

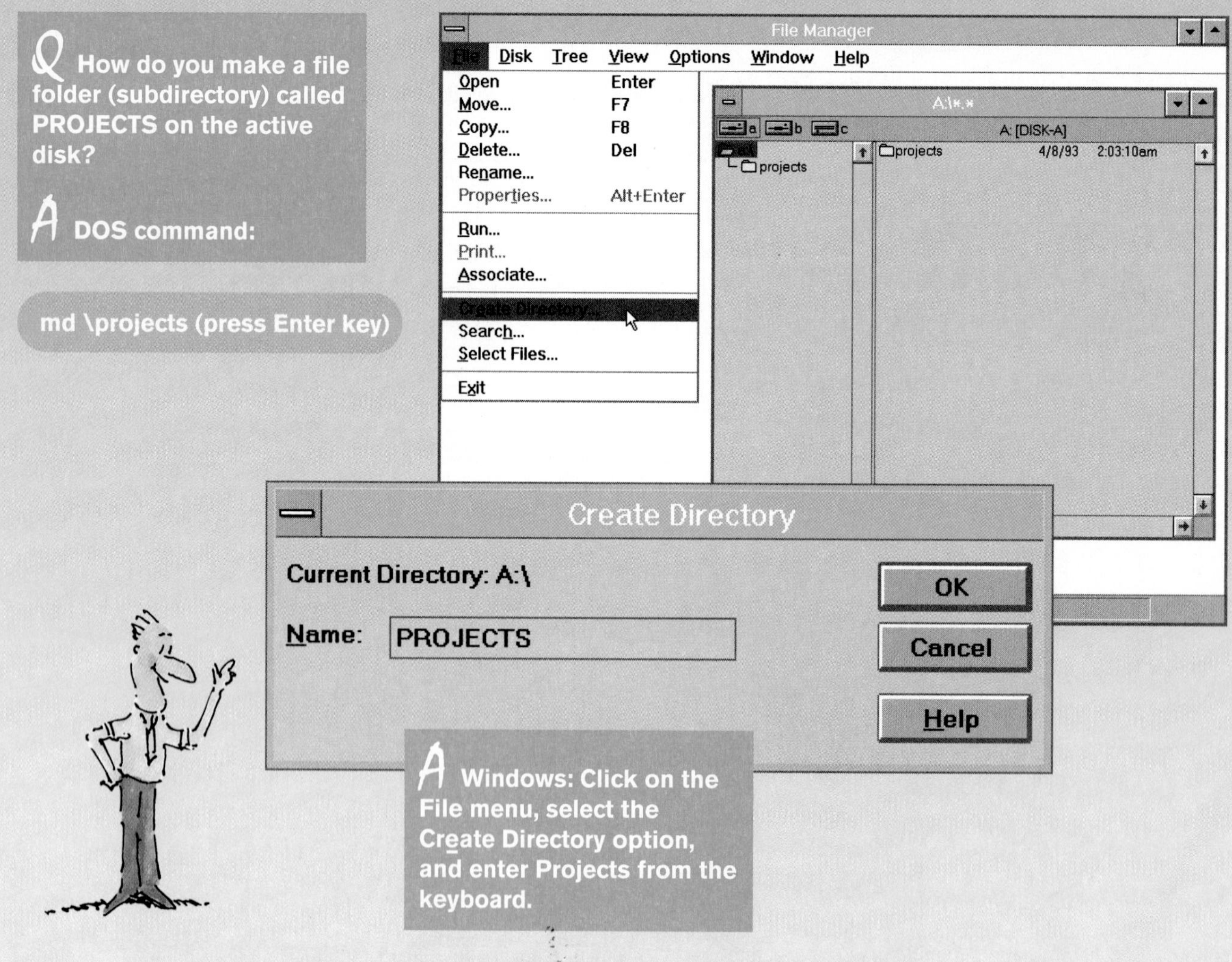

A Windows: Click on the File menu, select the Create Directory option, and enter Projects from the keyboard.

A Macintosh: Click on File menu and select New Folder to display untitled file folder. Entering Projects from the keyboard creates a new file folder title.

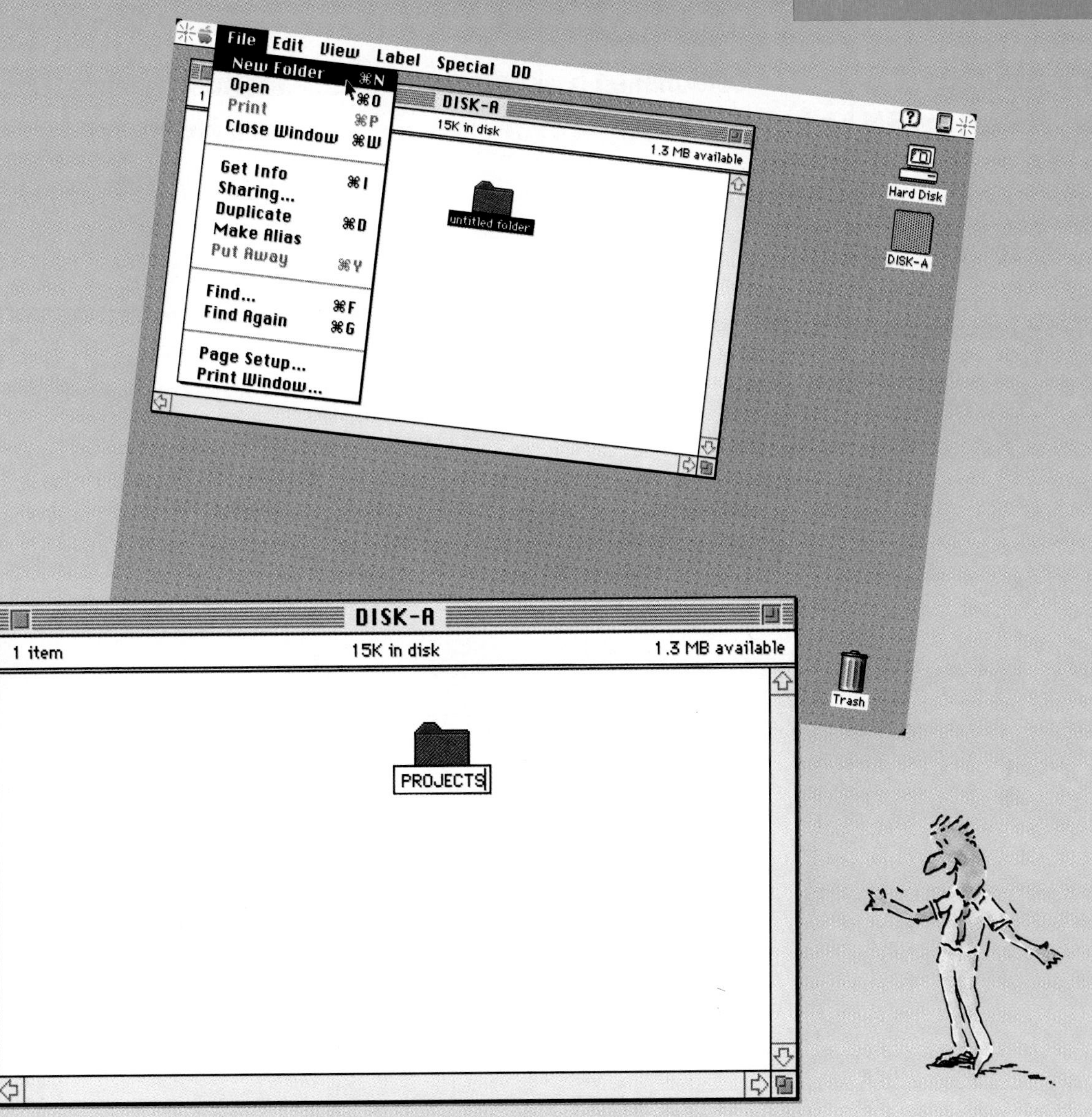

Q How do you copy the document file named HOMEWORK from the active disk to the Projects subdirectory on disk A?

A DOS command:

copy homework a: \projects (press Enter key)

A Windows: Drag the Homework icon to the Projects directory windows and release the mouse button.

File Manager
File Disk Tree View Options Window Help
A:*.*
a b c
A: [DISK-A]
a:\
projects
projects 4/8/93 2:03:10am

Copying...
Copying: B:\HOMEWORK
To: A:\PROJECTS\HOMEWORK
Cancel

B: [NANCY M]
2:34:50am
6:06:58am
2:34:42am
letters
pdoxwin
personal
psy102
pdoxwin 2/16/93 10:15:54am
personal 9/30/92 2:35:44am
psy102 1/31/93 2:34:34am
homework 4224 1/5/93 12:02:22pm
Selected 1 file(s) (4,224 bytes)
Total 7 file(s) (4,224 bytes)

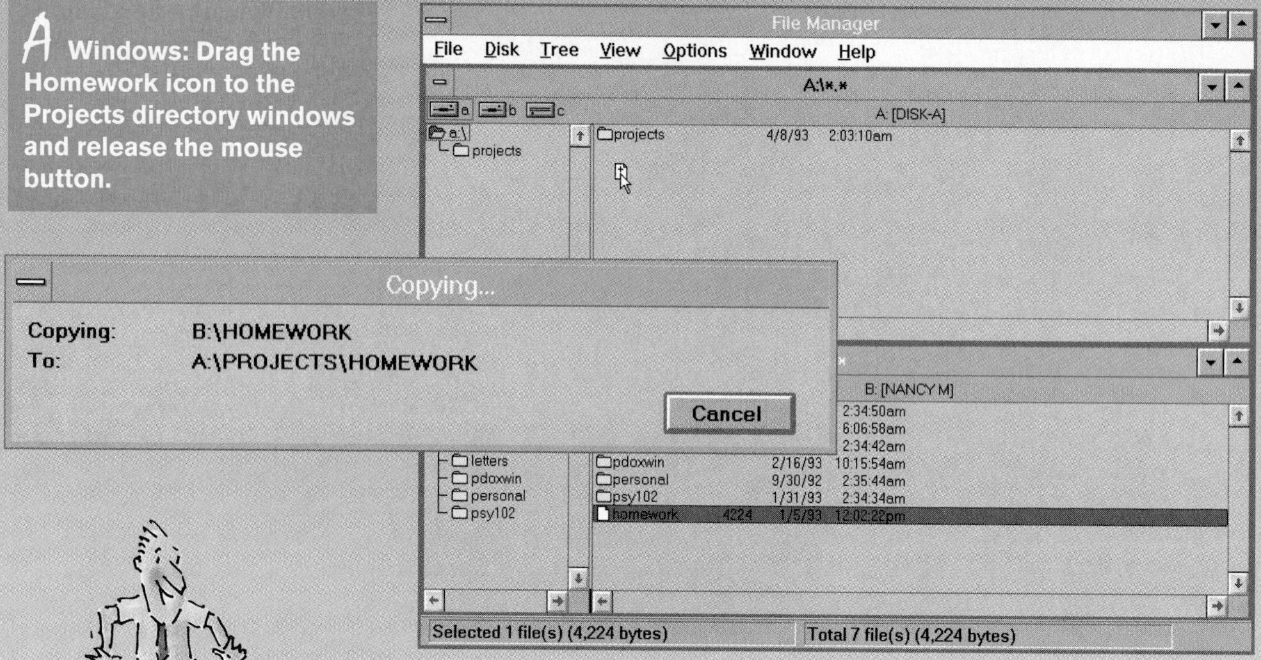

A Macintosh: Drag the Homework icon to the Projects file folder and release the mouse button.

File Edit View Label Special DD
Hard Disk
12 items 24.9 MB in disk 13.4 MB available
HOMEWORK
Hard Disk
DISK-A
DISK-A
1 item 15K in disk 1.3 MB availal
PROJECTS
Trash

Copy
Items remaining to be copied: 1
Writing: HOMEWORK
Stop

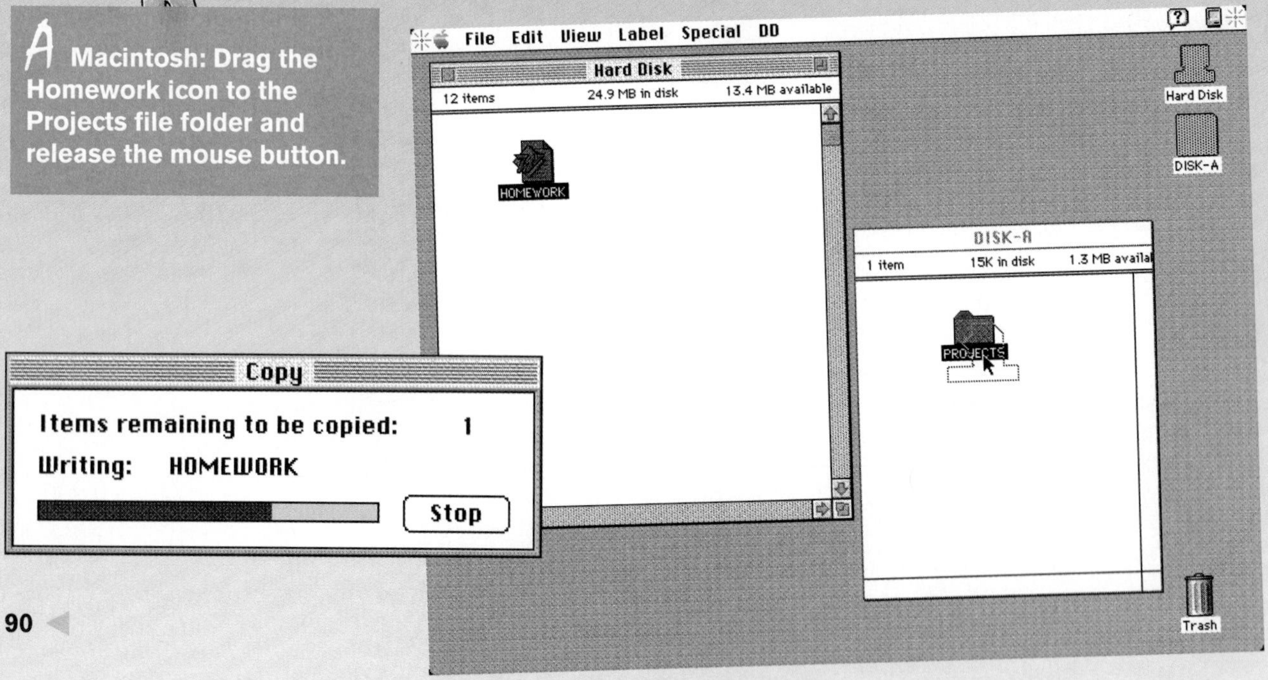

Q How do you change the HOMEWORK filename in Projects to OLDWORK?

A DOS Command:

rename \projects\homework oldwork (press Enter key)

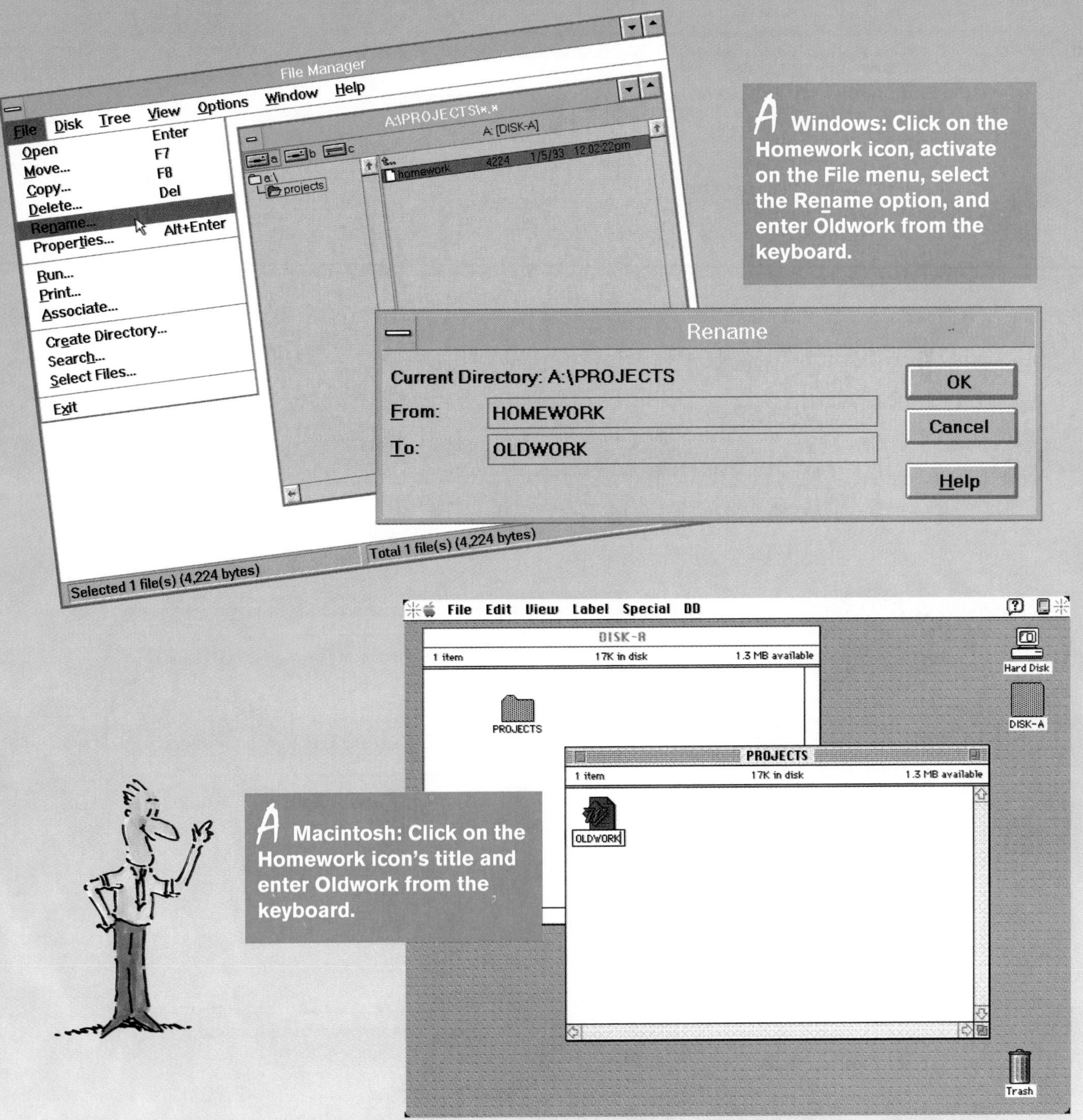

A Windows: Click on the Homework icon, activate on the File menu, select the Rename option, and enter Oldwork from the keyboard.

A Macintosh: Click on the Homework icon's title and enter Oldwork from the keyboard.

Q How do you delete the file OLDWORK from the disk?

A DOS Command:

del \projects\oldwork (press Enter key)

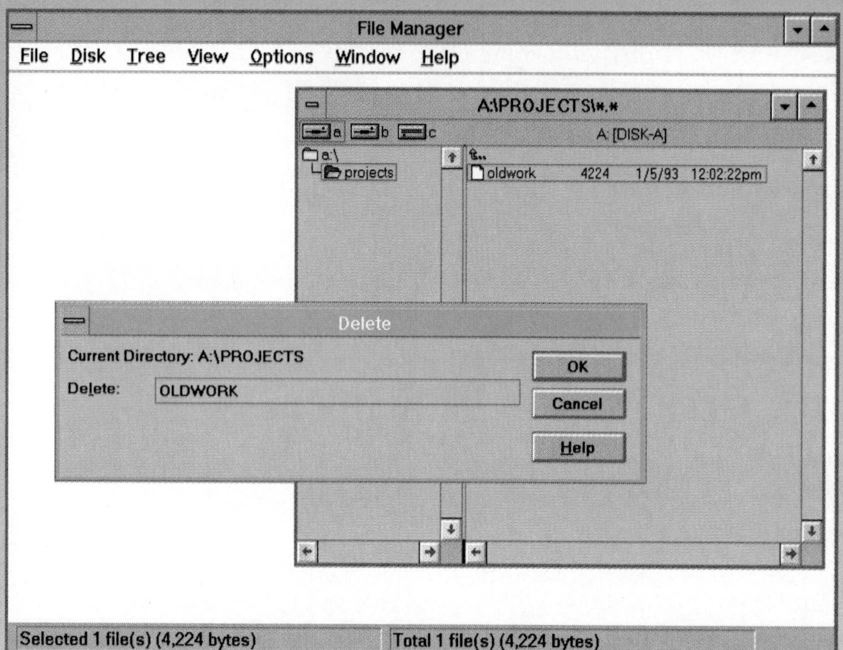

A Windows: Click on the Oldwork icon, press the Delete key, and confirm deletion by clicking on the OK button.

A Macintosh: Drag Oldwork icon over Trash Can icon and release mouse button.

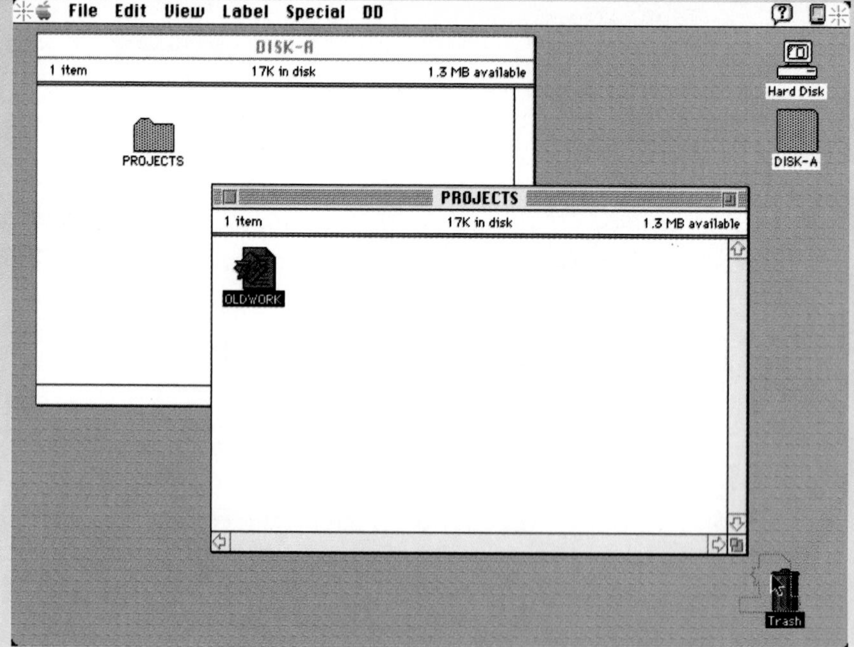

Chapter Facts

- User interfaces include features such as windows, menus, icons, dialog boxes, and help screens to increase user-friendliness.
- User interfaces can be categorized as command-driven, shell, graphical, or natural language.
- Command-driven interfaces rely on key words and common syntax to initiate computer processing.
- Software shells display program options as menu options. Users choose the options through a mouse or keyboard.
- Graphical user interfaces with icons and menus are designed to use a mouse as the primary input device.
- Clicking, double-clicking, and dragging are all input operations performed by a mouse.
- Natural language interfaces accept spoken or typed instructions in the user's native tongue.
- Software drives hardware, and as a result users should evaluate programs and determine software needs before making hardware decisions.
- The ability to share data with other software, work concurrently with other programs, and contain easy-to-understand user interfaces and manuals are all desirable features of a software package.
- Systems software monitors the computer's internal operations. Operating systems, language translators, and utilities represent different kinds of system software.
- An operating system is a collection of programs, coordinated by the supervisor, that controls hardware and memory resources, manages files using peripherals, and coordinates task processing.
- An operating system may support multitasking, the concurrent operation of two programs.
- Utility software performs such standard processing tasks as file conversions, spooling, emulations, disk optimization, and data compression.
- Language translators convert high-level languages understandable to people into machine language, usable by computer circuitry.
- Software is available from retail computer stores, manufacturers, magazines, networks, and user groups.

Terms to Remember

a. command-driven interface
b. cursor
c. default
d. dialog box
e. disk directory
f. filename
g. graphical user interface (GUI)
h. help screen
i. high-level language
j. language translator
k. machine language
l. multitasking
m. natural language interface
n. operating system
o. public domain software
p. screen pointer
q. screen prompt
r. scroll
s. shareware
t. shell
u. supervisor
v. syntax
w. task
x. terminate stay resident (TSR)
y. timesharing
z. user's manual
aa. user interface
bb. utility software
cc. virtual memory
dd. window

Mix and Match

Match the following definitions to the Terms to Remember.

1. ____ type of public domain software that is shared by users who are asked to pay a nominal fee to the author.
2. ____ screen icon that is controlled by the movement of a mouse or some other pointer device.
3. ____ system program that is loaded into a computer's memory from the start to coordinate all processing activities within a computer system.
4. ____ special window that prompts the user to enter text, select names, or click on an icon to initiate or cancel a program option.
5. ____ programs that are distributed free of charge.
6. ____ word order, spacing, abbreviations, and special symbols used by a command-driven interface or programming language.
7. ____ interface that relies on mouse or keyboard input to select menus or icons.
8. ____ unique set of letters, numbers, and symbols that identifies a data file or program.

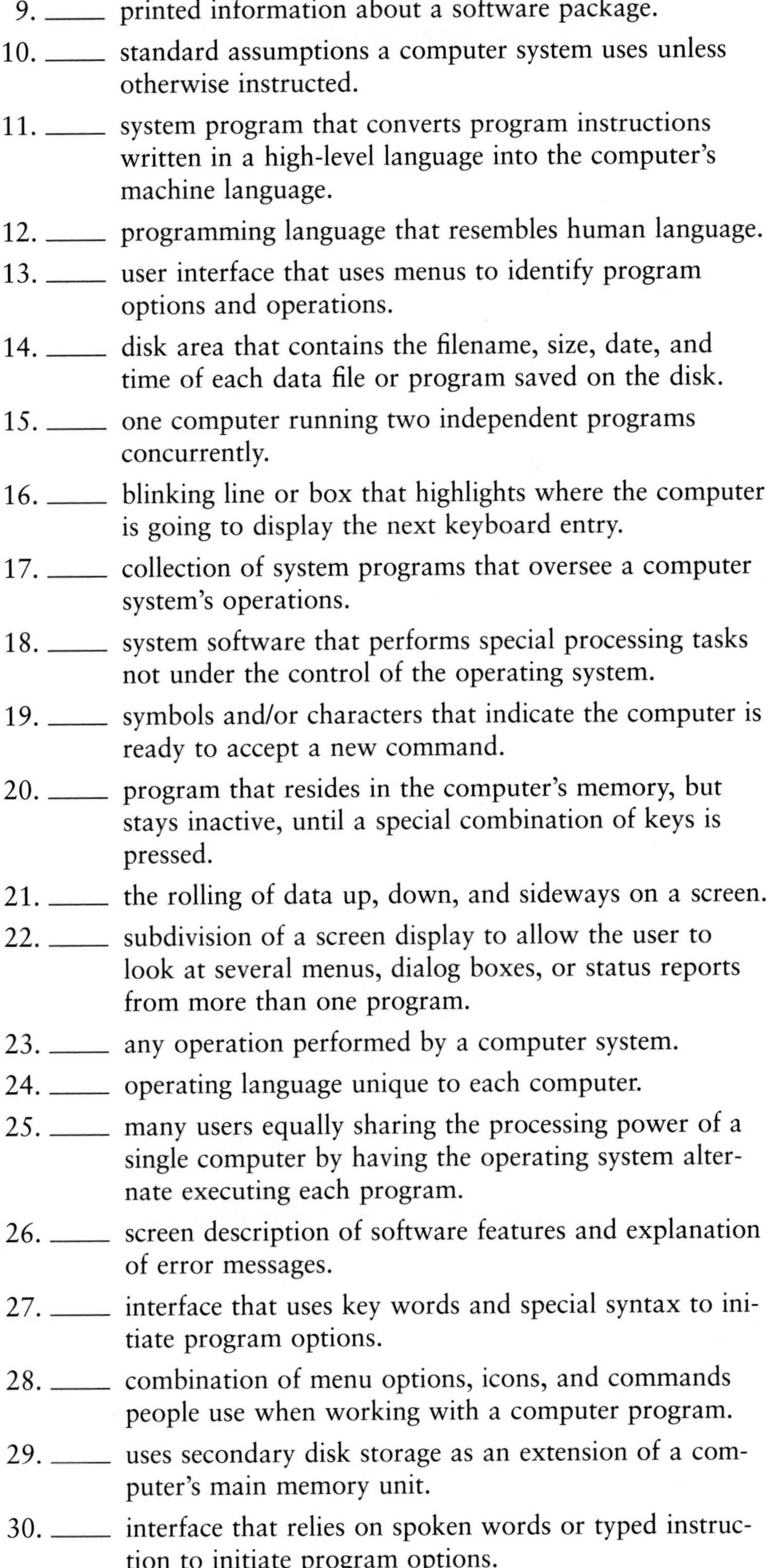

9. ____ printed information about a software package.
10. ____ standard assumptions a computer system uses unless otherwise instructed.
11. ____ system program that converts program instructions written in a high-level language into the computer's machine language.
12. ____ programming language that resembles human language.
13. ____ user interface that uses menus to identify program options and operations.
14. ____ disk area that contains the filename, size, date, and time of each data file or program saved on the disk.
15. ____ one computer running two independent programs concurrently.
16. ____ blinking line or box that highlights where the computer is going to display the next keyboard entry.
17. ____ collection of system programs that oversee a computer system's operations.
18. ____ system software that performs special processing tasks not under the control of the operating system.
19. ____ symbols and/or characters that indicate the computer is ready to accept a new command.
20. ____ program that resides in the computer's memory, but stays inactive, until a special combination of keys is pressed.
21. ____ the rolling of data up, down, and sideways on a screen.
22. ____ subdivision of a screen display to allow the user to look at several menus, dialog boxes, or status reports from more than one program.
23. ____ any operation performed by a computer system.
24. ____ operating language unique to each computer.
25. ____ many users equally sharing the processing power of a single computer by having the operating system alternate executing each program.
26. ____ screen description of software features and explanation of error messages.
27. ____ interface that uses key words and special syntax to initiate program options.
28. ____ combination of menu options, icons, and commands people use when working with a computer program.
29. ____ uses secondary disk storage as an extension of a computer's main memory unit.
30. ____ interface that relies on spoken words or typed instruction to initiate program options.

Review Questions

1. What are the four basic categories of user interfaces?
2. What determines where input commands and data are located on the screen when using a command-driven interface?
3. What type of data does an installation program accept from the user?
4. What does it mean when a menu option appears as a light color (unhighlighted) or with an ellipsis behind it?
5. How are the procedures for getting a program up and running different between command-driven system software and software using a graphical user interface?
6. What makes software user friendly?
7. Identify eight questions users should ask when evaluating new software.
8. How can a user tell if a file is in one of the standard formats?
9. What are three different methods a dialog box uses to prompt user input?
10. How are the scroll arrows used when selecting an item from a list box?
11. Explain how a palette and toolbox are used by a graphics package.
12. What type of information is found in a user's manual?
13. What are the two methods for booting an operating system into memory?
14. Describe three responsibilities of an operating system.
15. What are six jobs performed by utility software?
16. How can you try software before purchasing it?
17. How do you protect yourself from problems associated with public domain software?
18. What are six sources for computer software?

Applying What You've Learned

1. Try one of the applications packages available to you at school or home. What type of user interface does it use? What came with the package (user's guide, etc.) besides the software itself? List the features that make it user friendly to you.
2. The price of a software package may vary greatly depending upon its source. Choose a popular applications package, such as a word processing or graphics program. Find out its current price by checking several computer stores and looking for mail-order advertisements in magazines. From whom would you order the software if money was not a problem? Why wouldn't you patronize the other sources?
3. Look at the user's manual for the operating system used on a school or home computer. What type of user interface is used? Are help screens available? How do you initiate the file management options displaying a disk directory and for copying, renaming, and deleting a file? What type of device drivers come with the operating system? Is multitasking available?
4. A wide variety of utility programs are available for popular personal computers. Research one type of utility program to find out where you can get it, what it does, and how much it costs.
5. Find out what language translators are available for computers at your school. For what type of applications is each language used?
6. Find three advertisements for programmers in the newspaper. Can you tell what types of programs (systems or applications) they write? How do the positions compare in salary, experience required, and high-level programming language used?

Answers to Mix and Match

1. s 2. p 3. u 4. d 5. o 6. v 7. g 8. f 9. z 10. c
11. j 12. i 13. t 14. e 15. l 16. b 17. n 18. bb
19. q 20. x 21. r 22. dd 23. w 24. k 25. y 26. h
27. a 28. aa 29. cc 30. m

UNIT TWO

Personal Productivity Tools

Computer software turns a general-purpose system into a specialized problem-solving tool. Chapter 4 provides an in-depth look at word processing and desktop publishing software. Applications for these popular personal productivity tools are highlighted throughout the chapter. In addition, the features users need to create and edit documents are explained in detail. The chapter concludes with a discussion of questions to ask when purchasing a word processor.

The manipulation of numeric data through electronic spreadsheets is the focus of Chapter 5. The standard procedures for entering and organizing data in a spreadsheet's row-and-column format are discussed at length. Common applications are presented throughout the chapter to illustrate the versatility of this personal productivity package. A review of good design features for worksheets concludes the chapter.

Computers can help users create spectacular drawings and graphics. They can also let a nonprofessional integrate textual, audio, and video data. Chapter 6 overviews graphics packages that support the development of graphs and charts using a four-step process. Free-drawing graphics software turns the computer monitor into an electronic canvas. Integration of different types of data is made possible with the features of multimedia software. The broad nature of visual and audio data is seen through the chapter examples. Common questions about presentation software are answered as well.

The file and database management programs discussed in Chapter 7 represent some of the most powerful applications of computers. This chapter shows how data is organized and cross-referenced to provide useful information to users. The merging of multimedia techniques with data management into hypermedia applications is examined in detail.

4

Word Processing and Desktop Publishing

- **From the User's Point of View**
- **Word Processing**
  - Editing
  - Formatting
  - Integrated services
- **Desktop Publishing**
  - Page composition
  - Typography
  - File integration
- **Automating the Office**
  - Electronic offices
  - Advertising
  - Journalism
  - Electronic classrooms
- *A Closer Look . . . Selecting a Word Processing Package*

FROM THE USER'S POINT OF VIEW

Word processing can have a profound effect on your writing. Whether you produce a letter, research papers, newsletters, or an occasional poem, word processing simplifies the process of writing and editing. A hidden benefit is that the ease with which text can be changed makes users better writers. Since a document no longer has to be completely retyped to produce an error-free copy, you do not have to hesitate when it needs to be modified. Once the words look right, you can add graphics and special accents by using sophisticated word processing or desktop publishing software. The final result can be a professional-looking document that effectively delivers your ideas.

WORD PROCESSING

Nearly every occupation relies, to some extent, on written documents. The movie industry, for example, requires many written documents, including scripts, contracts, even press kits. These documents are not seen on screen, yet they are integral to the production of the film. Every day, in homes, schools, and offices, millions of documents are exchanged (Fig. 4.1).

Creating documents has become a huge part of the operation of most organizations. Each document needs to clearly communicate ideas and information to the reader in a professional way. Word processing software facilitates this process by making it easier for people to write. This software also helps writers edit, store, and print their words. The finished documents would include letters, manuals, reports, memos, and articles.

Devices used for word processing include a special electronic typewriter, printer, screen, keyboard, scanner, and mouse, as well as a computer. Sometimes this hardware is combined into dedicated office equipment, called standalone word processors, which create and edit text documents exclusively. In other environments personal computers running word processing software perform text processing along with data processing. Software operations involved in word processing fall under two broad categories:

- Editing
- Formatting

Lee Butterfield is a psychology student who is preparing a report for class. While doing this on his personal computer, Lee uses many of the word processing operations available. The precise operating procedures for word processing operations vary from package to package, but Lee's software contains some of the most common features.

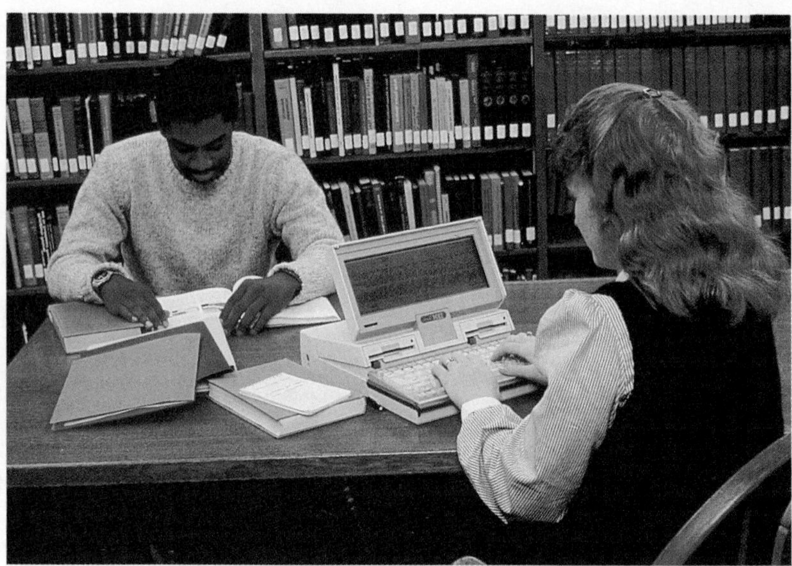

FIGURE 4.1
Word processing increases everyone's personal productivity.

Before he starts to work on his report, Lee boots the computer with system software. This procedure, explained in Chapter 3, prepares the computer to begin processing. Once the operating system is booted, Lee loads word processing software from a diskette or hard disk (see Figure 4.2). The word processing software helps him create, edit, and save documents through the use of menus, help screens, and *keyboard overlays.* Menus and help screens appear directly on a monitor; keyboard overlays are paper or plastic forms cut to fit around a keyboard, showing which keys to press for certain commands. The following sections review the editing and format operations Lee uses to complete the document.

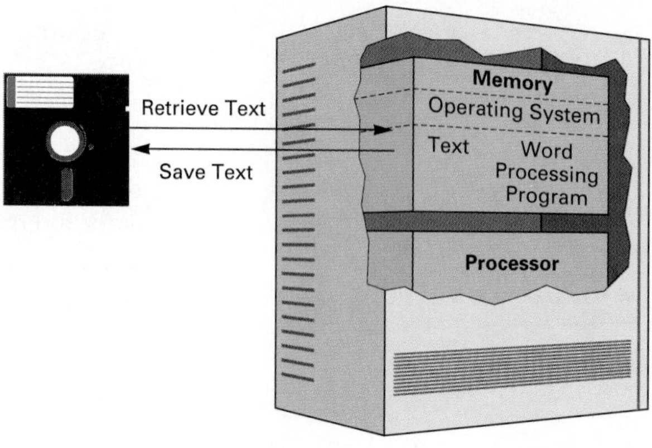

FIGURE 4.2
A disk operating system works with the word processing program to create, edit, print, and store documents.

Editing

Lee uses a computer keyboard much as he would use a typewriter to create the original report. The word processing software, however, accommodates operations that make **editing** or revising the text easier and more efficient.

Word Wrap and Cursor Control

The **word wrap** operation enables Lee to write in a continuous flow of sentences, uninterrupted by carriage returns. When Lee types a word that goes past the right margin (see Figure 4.3), the software enters a **soft return** character, which automatically moves the cursor and word being typed to the next line. Soft returns are carriage returns added or deleted by the word processing software to keep text within specified left and right margins.

Since word wrap is a default operation, Lee can concentrate on the logical organization of his report, rather than the physical placement of words on the screen. The Return or Enter key on the computer's keyboard is used primarily to mark the end of a paragraph

FIGURE 4.3
With the word wrap feature on, word processing software automatically moves "around" to the next line when it does not fit on the current line, inserting a soft return. A hard return is inserted when the user presses the Enter key.

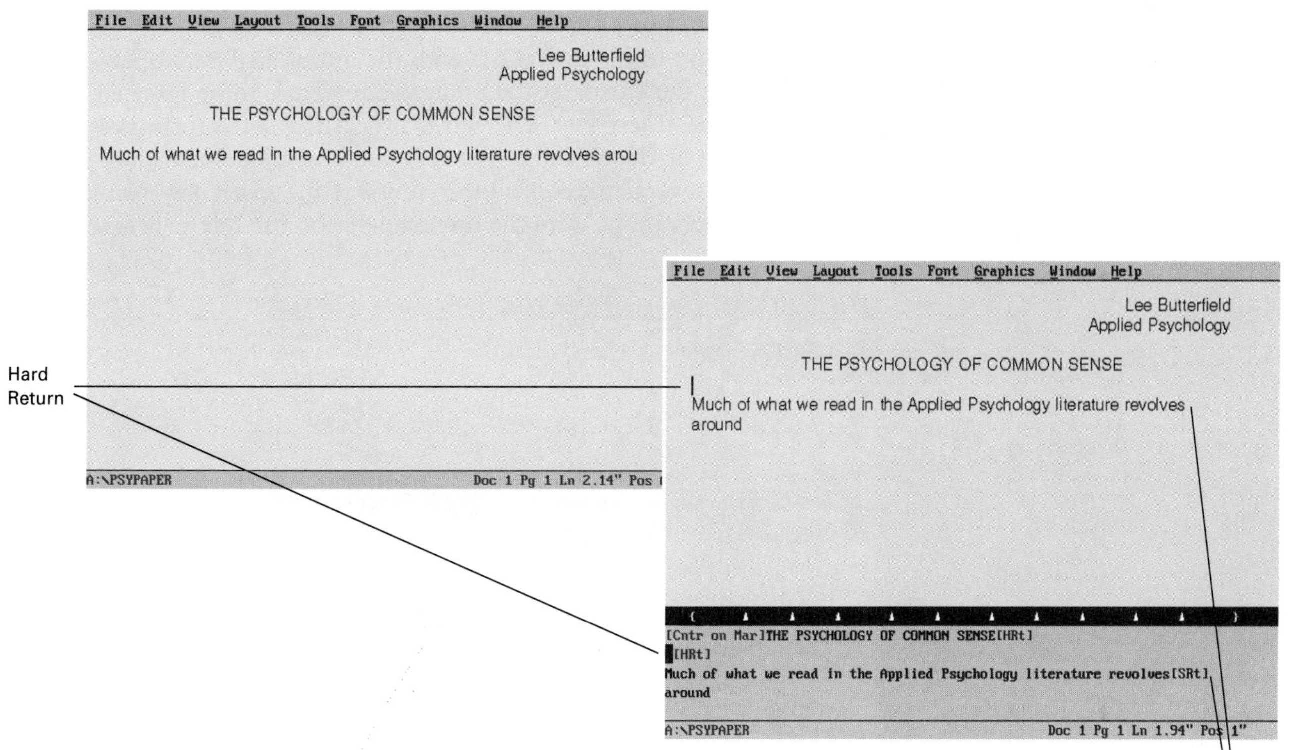

with a **hard return** character. Hard returns are entered by the user and are not subject to change by the software. They are also used to insert blank lines.

Once Lee has completed his first draft, he scrolls through the report, correcting typographical errors and making content changes. By using the cursor control keys, Lee can move the cursor to the next word, paragraph, or page. Other operations send the cursor to the beginning or end of a line, page, or document. Lee manipulates these operations to move quickly to sections of his document needing review.

Delete and Insert

The *Delete* operation enables Lee to erase text within the document. He has the choice of deleting a character, word, paragraph, or several paragraphs. Lee places the cursor at the point where the delete is to begin, then presses the Delete key for each character he wants to erase. When several lines need to be removed, Lee selects the **block** or group of text. The block is defined by *highlighting*, a change in the intensity of the characters on the screen (see Figure 4.4). Lee then deletes the block by pressing a special combination of keys at the same time. A block of text can be deleted, moved, copied, or printed in a special format at Lee's discretion.

Lee adds text to his document with the aid of an *Insert* operation. He places the cursor at the point where text is to be inserted, then presses the Insert key. The word processing software makes space available at this point in the text for a new character, line, paragraph, or several pages. Another press of the Insert key turns off the insert operation. With the insert operation off, any new text

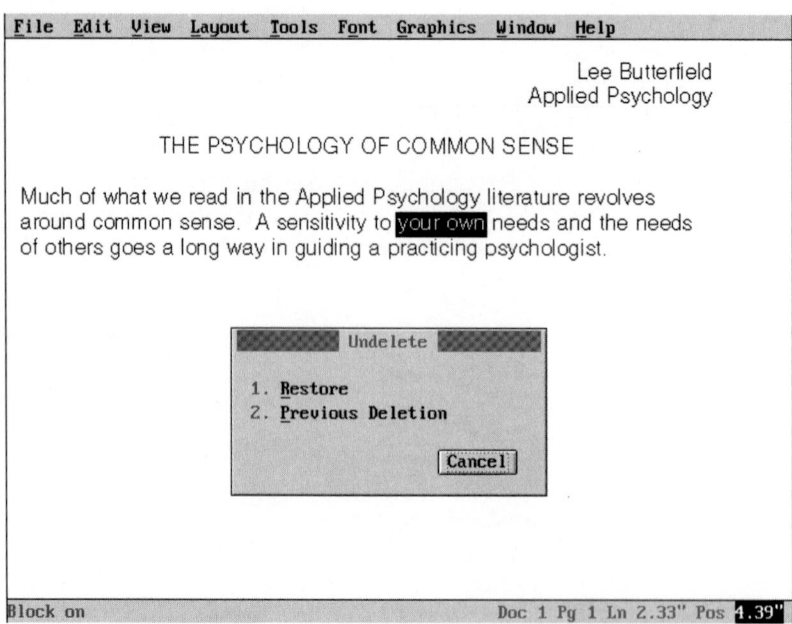

FIGURE 4.4
The highlighted words "your own" were deleted from the text. A user can restore the words by undoing the previous command.

entered *overwrites* or types over text currently on the screen. In some word processing packages, word wrap automatically adjusts margins to make the inserted text fit properly.

Undo

Deleting blocks of text in a document takes only a few keystrokes. While Lee was modifying the beginning of his paper, he decided to delete the phrase "your own" in the second line of text. Lee changed his mind and wanted to retain those words, but he had already pressed the delete key. Fortunately, Lee's word processing package has an *undo* feature. By pressing another combination of keys, Lee was able to recall or undo the previous command that had deleted the words (see Figure 4.4). For a word processing package to undo a command, however, action must be taken directly after an error is made. If a serious mistake is found much later, the user may have to exit the document without saving it and reload the backup version of the document to start again.

Move and Copy

Lee uses the *Move* operation to move blocks of text from one location to another. The Move operation enables him to rearrange paragraphs, move sentences within a paragraph, and switch words within a sentence. This operation is sometimes referred to as cutting and pasting because these tasks were explicitly performed before word processors became available. Now users "cut" text from one part of a document and "paste" it into a new location.

Similarly, Lee can duplicate portions of his document with the aid of the *Copy* operation. A block highlighted within the document can be copied to another location in the same file, or it may be copied as a separate file onto disk, and then later into a different document. This latter procedure is called an **external copy.** As he gathered background material for his paper, Lee stored quoted material in a document called PSYNOTES and the references in PSYREFS. He **imports** the quotations in PSYNOTES into appropriate places within his PSYPAPER document by copying them from disk into the document. The PSYREFS file was imported at the end of his report. He is spared the trouble of retyping material he collected while researching the paper.

Find

When Lee uses the *Find* option on his word processor, he is able to locate a single symbol or a group of symbols anywhere in the document. In reviewing his paper, Lee wanted to locate where he first used the word "motivation." After requesting the Find function, Lee is prompted for the phrase. After he enters "motivation," the word processor looks through the text from the beginning and sets the cursor at the point where the word is found in the text. Subsequent Find requests result in locating further occurrences of the word.

Search and Replace

The *Search and Replace* operation enables Lee to make changes in selected words or phrases. As Lee proofreads his report, he discovers that he has misspelled the name "MacArthur," in several quotations. Throughout his report the name is spelled "McArthur." Instead of scanning the report line by line to change each misspelling manually, Lee calls on the search and replace operation.

First, Lee requests the search and replace operation by pressing appropriate keys. As shown in Figure 4.5, the software prompts for the text to be searched and he enters "McArthur." Lee is then prompted for the replacement text and types in "MacArthur." The computer then locates every instance of the misspelled word and replaces it with the correct spelling. In a *global replace* the computer automatically takes care of all word substitutions. In a *discretionary replace* the computer finds the misspellings, and waits for user approval before making each replacement. Lee is careful when using the global replace feature. Changing "tha" to "the" throughout a text could result in "that" being changed to "thet" as well.

Save and Retrieve

Before the computer can save a document, the user must assign a unique filename to it. Responding to a screen prompt for a filename, Lee enters PSYPAPER. When Lee *saves* a new document, the word processing software assigns a disk storage area to it. If a file by the same name already exists on disk, the software asks if the file should be replaced. Answering Yes means the disk file will be overwritten by the text currently being edited. The long-term storage of documents is an important capability of word processing software, since stored documents can be edited and printed at a later time.

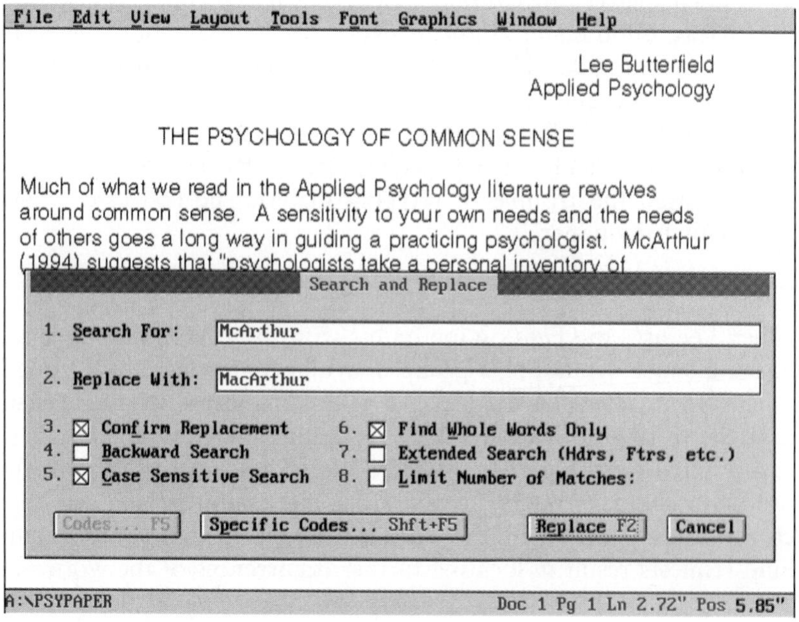

FIGURE 4.5
By using a search and replace feature, users can locate and change all occurrences of a block of text in a document.

After saving PSYPAPER, Lee can *retrieve* this document as many times as he wishes. Each time he retrieves the document, the word processing software copies the document back into the computer's memory for further editing. In this way Lee's writing of the report is an ongoing process.

Formatting

While editing operations enable Lee to revise the contents of his report, **formatting** operations allow him to manipulate the report's appearance. With formatting operations Lee can create a document that is single-spaced, double-spaced, or triple-spaced. Line lengths and tab spacing, as well as the number of lines per document page, are determined through formatting operations. Lee uses another formatting operation—centering text on a line—to center the title of his report. Figure 4.6 outlines a number of other formatting operations found in word processing applications packages. The following are some of the most common.

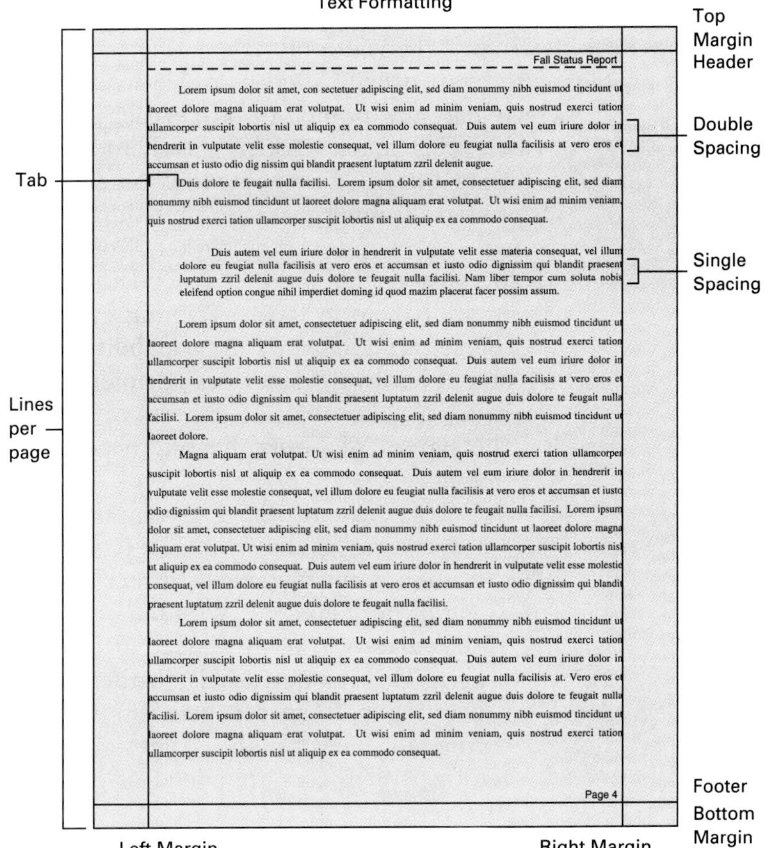

FIGURE 4.6
Word processing software has a lot of control over a document's final printed format. Style sheets often provide the format specifications identified in this figure.

Header and Footer

A *header* is one or more lines of text that appear at the top of each page in a document. The header often holds a document title, date, or page number. The header is entered only once, at the beginning of a document. The computer instructs the printer to duplicate the header at the top of each page.

Footers are similar to headers; they are lines of text repeated at the bottom of each page. Most headers and footers offer special control of the beginning and ending of each page and the page numbering (Figure 4.7). This feature is called **pagination.** Lee, for example, wishes to print a page number at the top of each page. A special symbol is included in the header, and the computer automatically tallies and prints the appropriate page numbers. He also has the option of starting the page numbers at any value or omitting page numbers altogether.

Print Options

The print options of a word processing package let users output selected pages of a document. Through these options the user can also control the size, style, spacing, and density of characters. For example, the print menu might offer **font** options, which determine the type style, size, and weight of printed characters (see Figure 4.8). These options are explored in more detail in the section on desktop publishing. **Pitch** determines the width of each character.

Word processing software usually offers a double-strike feature, which tells the printer to strike each character twice. This action darkens the characters, producing a near letter-quality look on dot-matrix printers. Printing characters in boldface would make them appear even darker. Word processors also enable the user to underline words or print them in italics. Printing options, of course, are limited to the capabilities of the output hardware. Since Lee's printer does not have an italics font, he chooses to underline the names of books he references in the report.

Users can also have a computer justify a document as shown in Figure 4.8. **Justification** is the alignment of text along the left or right margins. With *full justification* the edges of text are aligned at both margins. The computer fully justifies text by inserting **soft spaces** between words to bring all lines to one length. Like soft returns, soft spaces are added or deleted by

FIGURE 4.7
These formatting operations are common to most word processing packages.

Common Formatting Operations

1. Line spacing (single, double, triple, etc.)
2. Line length (characters per line)
3. Tabulation
4. Lines per page
5. Centering text in line
6. Set headers
7. Set footers
8. Pagination
9. Select font
10. Select pitch
11. Double strike
12. Justification

Right Justification
Lee Butterfield
Applied Psychology
Sans-serif Font 8 point
Centered
THE PSYCHOLOGY OF COMMON SENSE
Sans-serif Font 14 point
Left Justification
Much of what we read in Applied Psychology literature revolves around common sense. A sensitivity to personal needs and the needs of others goes a long way in guiding a practicing psychologist.
Serif Font 11 point
Full Justification
Much •of what we read in Applied Psychology •literature •revolves around •common •sense. A sensitivity to personal needs •and •the needs ••of •others •goes •a •long •way •in •guiding •a ••practicing psychologist.
Sans-serif Font 11 point
Soft Spaces

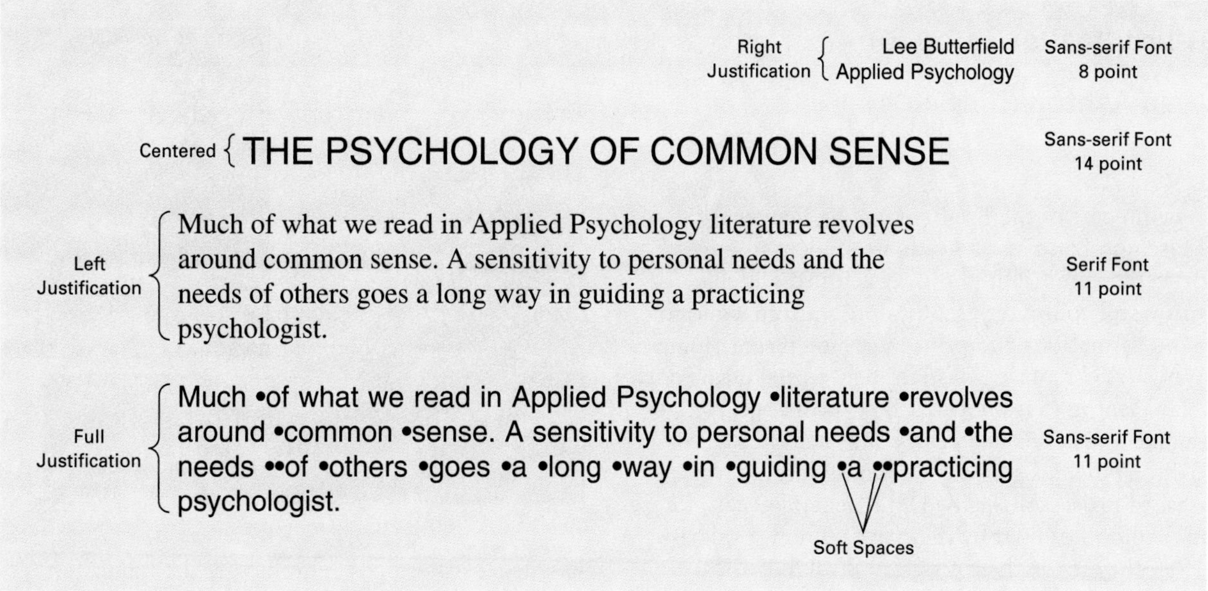

FIGURE 4.8
Word processing users select fonts and determine how text is justified.

the word processing software as needed. Text with *left justification* all starts in the same column of the page, and no soft spaces are added, leaving a ragged right margin. *Right justification* is just the opposite, with the text aligned along the right margin with a ragged left margin. Most documents are left-justified.

Integrated Services

Many word processing packages have expanded their capabilities beyond the editing and formatting features just discussed. These packages are able to save commonly used formatting options or to read in text created on other word processors. Other integrated services can create personalized form letters, check for spelling errors, and even suggest alternative words.

Online References

With his paper written, edited, and formatted, Lee calls upon several software tools that check the spelling, grammar, and writing style. His word processing package allows Lee to access several other features online without exiting the document being processed. As a result these special procedures can be performed while the document is still on the screen. Word processing software frequently includes a dictionary and thesaurus. With a few keystrokes these online reference materials are at Lee's disposal. Looking up the spelling and meaning of words, or finding a suitable synonym, becomes an online procedure.

Who's Who

Bruce Bastian (b. 1949)

Alan Ashton (b. 1943)

As director of the Brigham Young University Marching Band and a graduate student in music, Bruce Bastian (right photo) developed a highly successful computer graphics program to simulate band formations and print marching instructions. When BYU replaced Bastian, he was encouraged by Alan Ashton (left photo), a BYU professor, to pursue a master's degree in computer science, Ashton's field. Later Bastian and Ashton developed a word processor for the Data General minicomputer used by the city of Orem, Utah. By 1980 they made their program available to other users. Soon after the IBM PC came out in 1981, they rewrote the word processing package for it and named the package WordPerfect.

Since its public introduction in 1982, WordPerfect has become the most widely used word processing software. It is available in over 15 languages, can import graphics, and contains an editor for mathematical equations. In the early days, Bastian or Ashton would stop work to help anyone who called into WordPerfect's telephone help service. Today, the WordPerfect help line alone involves 500 people and over 10,000 calls a day.

After proofreading his report Lee realizes the word "sensitivity" does not sound right in the report. The *online thesaurus* helps Lee identify synonyms by displaying them in a window within the text (see Figure 4.9). Lee moves the cursor to the alternative of his choice, and the thesaurus automatically replaces the highlighted word with the selected synonym.

Related software is the *spelling checker* (see A Closer Look) offered with most word processing packages. Special processing routines match each word in a document with words in an electronic dictionary. Any word not found in the dictionary is highlighted. The user then reviews the highlighted word, correcting errors or leaving the words as they are. Users can add unusual words and names to the dictionary to prevent the dictionary from marking those words that are spelled correctly.

Some word processors are even equipped with online *hyphenation help* routines. This software consults a dictionary to look up words that are too long to fit at the end of a line. The dictionary contains information about where a word may be broken. As an optional part of the word wrapping operation, the computer breaks the word between syllables and inserts a hyphen.

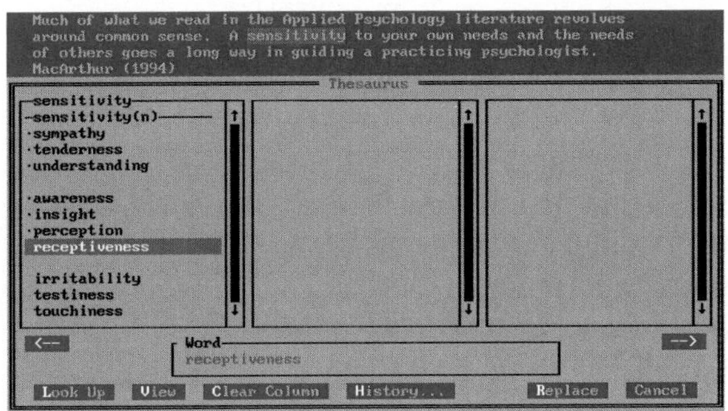

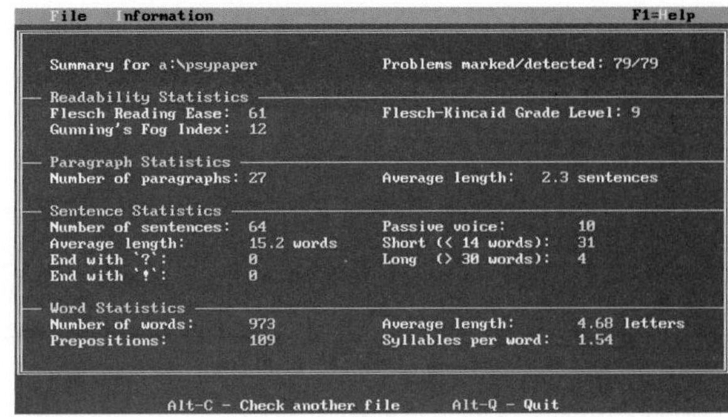

FIGURE 4.9
This online thesaurus suggests alternatives to using the word "sensitivity."

FIGURE 4.10
Writing analyzers help authors to improve the quality of their written work.

Writing Analyzer

Other support packages critique Lee's writing style. The *writing analyzer* in Figure 4.10 works independently from Lee's word processing software. When he runs this program, it asks for a document's filename and its disk location. The writing analyzer makes a copy of the text before it computes a reading level for Lee's paper. In other words, it indicates what grade level of education is assumed for the reader to understand this report. The writing analyzer also identifies the use of passive voice, flags long or complex sentences, highlights jargon, and provides a list of frequently used words.

Style Sheets

The ability to create documents by using any combination of formatting options has led to the development of style sheets. **Style sheets** allow word processing users to save the formatting options they established for a particular report, letter, memo, or any text file. These options could include the following:

- Margin settings
- Tab locations
- Full, left, or right justification
- Line spacing
- Number of lines per page
- Headers or footers
- Fonts

When users need to create a similar document, they load the style sheet, and the word processing software automatically uses the desired formatting options. For example, if the psychology department of Lee's school required certain margins and indentation on all reports, a copy of the report style sheet may be available to Lee on disk. This eliminates having to reset formatting specifications for each new report. Style sheets may also be available for printing such special forms as labels or envelopes.

Merging Files

The use of style sheets also helps people standardize commonly prepared documents, such as a form letter. Many word processing packages support *file merging* the letter with data files containing names and addresses of the people who will receive it. This letter contains a *boilerplate,* a document made up of standard or frequently used paragraphs and spaces or special codes left for specific details. Figure 4.11 illustrates how special codes can be added to a letter to merge a data file into the letter at specified locations.

The quality of a word processed document can be improved by integrating a spelling checker, online thesaurus, and writing analyzer. In turn, documents created by word processing software can be integrated with other data files as seen with file merging applications. Desktop publishing software improves the appearance of the finished text to an even higher level.

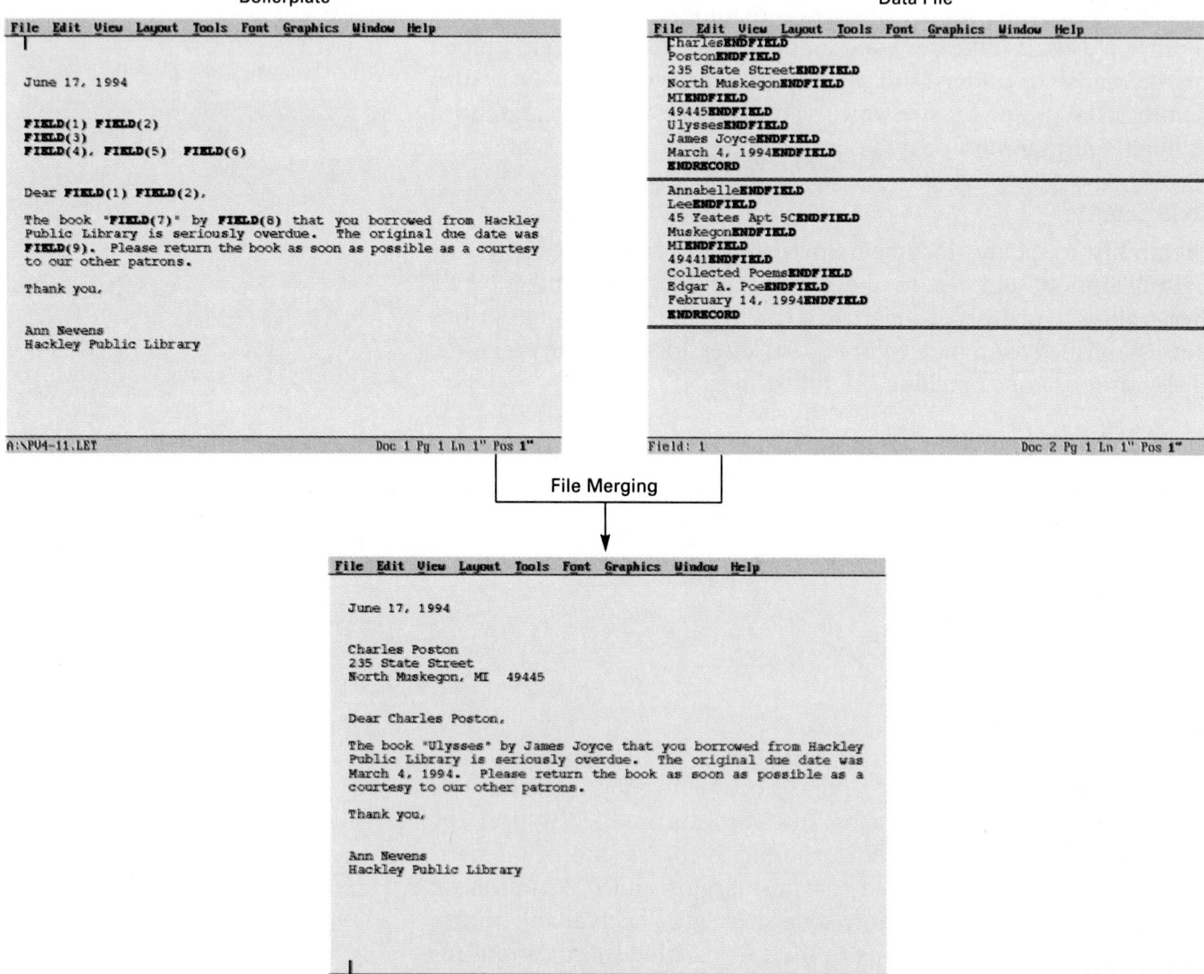

FIGURE 4.11
A form letter file can be merged with a data file containing names and addresses by using a word processor.

Desktop Publishing

Many users of word processing packages need to go beyond the formatting features previously described. Some want to integrate graphics. Others must manipulate the text into columns, banners, and headlines like a newspaper. Still others require a variety of fonts commonly found in professionally published material. Until recently, people who wanted sophisticated document designs for advertisements, newsletters, brochures, and other customer-oriented documents had to hire professional typesetters and designers. Now they can do this work on their personal computer with a desktop publishing package.

The hardware components of a desktop publishing system include a personal computer, scanner, mouse, high-quality monitor, laser printer, and desktop publishing software (see Figure 4.12). *Scanners* capture and save text, photographic images, and graphics on disk. A *full-page monitor* displays what would be printed on an entire page of a document. Any special typefaces, graphics, or formats would appear on the monitor exactly as they would be printed. This feature is called **WYSIWYG** (What You See Is What You Get). *Laser printers,* which print six or more pages a minute, can reproduce the WYSIWYG display on paper by using a method similar to a copy machine.

FIGURE 4.12
Desktop publishing software works on a personal computer with access to a scanner, mouse, high-quality screen, and laser printer.

Until recently, a user had to employ two different types of software to produce professional-looking output. A document was created and edited in a word processing package with limited formatting available. The document was saved and imported into a desktop publishing package. Then the user was able to insert graphics, change typefaces, and rearrange text into columns on the page. However, the editing capabilities of desktop publishers were limited.

Presently, the distinction between word processing and desktop publishing software has blurred. Many word processing packages contain features to produce *camera-ready copy,* a printed document in final form. This version is ready to be photographed for traditional plate printing or professionally copied. Adding to the confusion, desktop publishing software now contains full-featured editors. However, it is generally accepted that desktop publishing brings to the user three additional levels of control over a document's design and layout. These levels of control include

- Page composition
- Typography
- File integration

Page Composition

The best printing technology in the world cannot make a poorly designed document look professional. On the other hand, a desktop publishing system can enhance a document put together by using basic design principles. For example, the "three easy pieces" principle employed by photographers, artists, architects, and other professional designers advocates breaking a page design into thirds. As shown in Figure 4.13, it does not matter if it is sectioned off hori zontally (**landscape**) or vertically (**portrait.**) By using the three easy pieces principle, designers avoid drawing the reader's eye to the middle of the page. If anything, they want to draw the eye up to the top left corner since we usually read from left to right and top to bottom.

White Space

With the three easy pieces principle governing the basic page composition, the designer's objective is to fill the page with text, graphs, and images without it appearing cluttered. Therefore, unused areas of the document, called *white space,* are very important. Good designs use a lot of white space. Usually designs with plenty of white space are more eye appealing than those that overpower the reader with too many design elements. Nothing intimidates readers more than turning the page and finding many closely printed words to read or complex graphs to decipher.

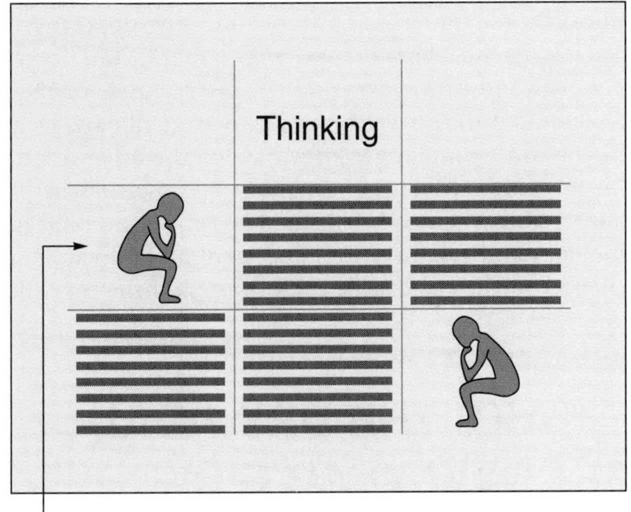

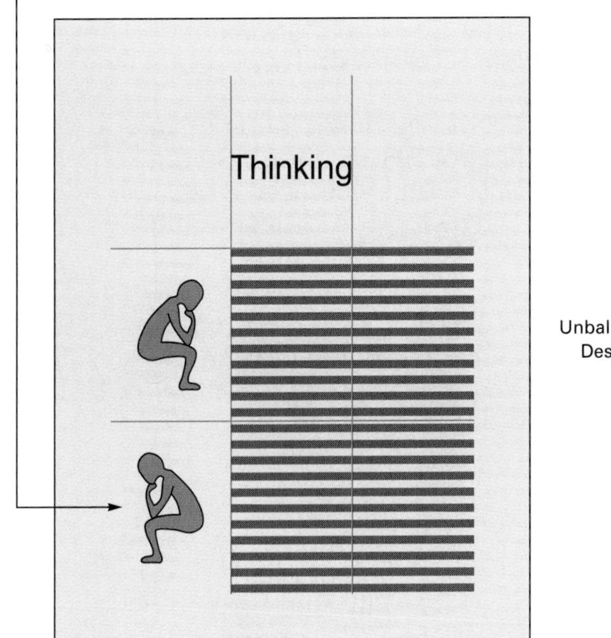

FIGURE 4.13
Designers can lay out a document in thirds horizontally (landscape) or vertically (portrait) and need to balance design elements with each other on the page.

Adding Emphasis

A document that catches our eye causes us to pay attention. Words such as love, money, easy, or save serve this purpose. Figure 4.14 uses the word "free" as a design element. For added emphasis, designers change the weight of the font to bold (**free**) or italics (*free*). Other options include underlining (<u>free</u>) and using uppercase letters (FREE). Such graphic elements as boxes, bars, and icons also emphasize words and draw attention to specific areas of the document. The secret is not to overemphasize. A page filled with arrows or underlined words is no longer effective. On the other hand, what separates a professional from an amateur is knowing when to use these principles and when to break the rules for additional impact.

When images and graphics are integrated into a document, they need to balance on the page with each other and the text. Balance

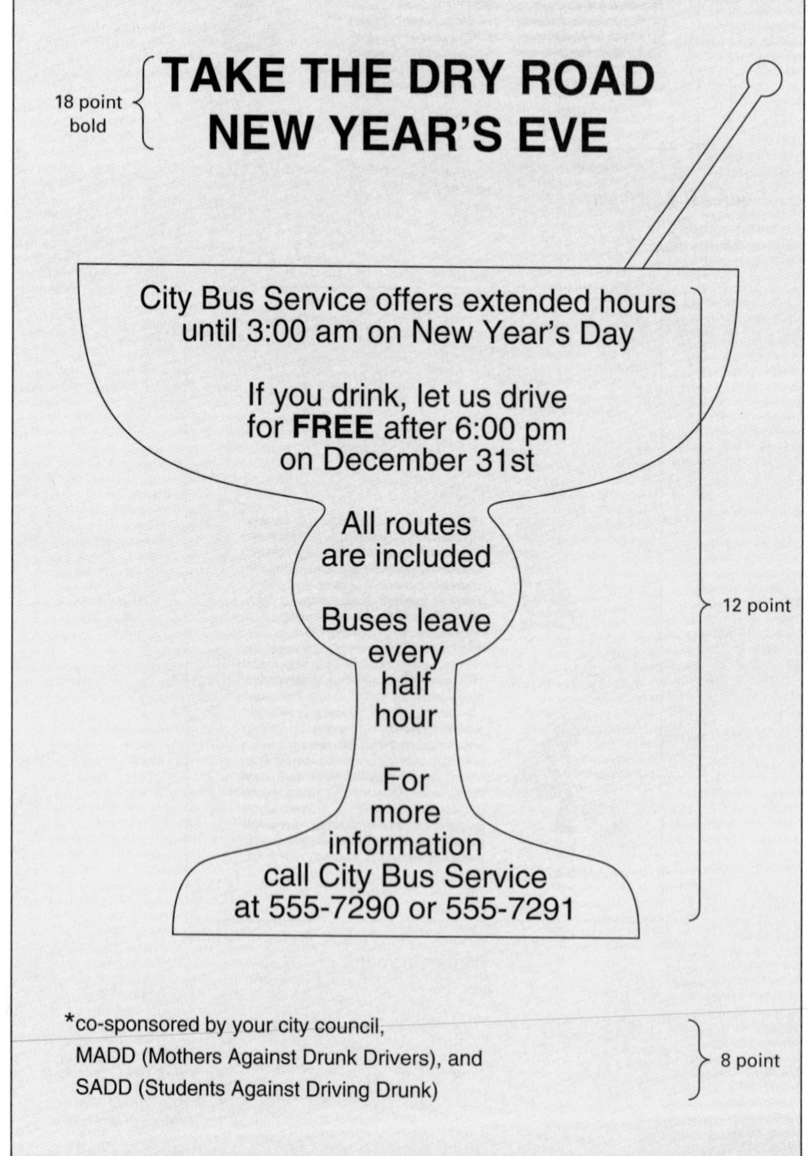

FIGURE 4.14
Attention-grabbing words, such as free, catch the reader's eye.

includes maintaining even margins on all four sides of the page. Figure 4.13 shows examples of both balanced and unbalanced placement. In addition, designers place images so they draw the reader's eye into the page, not toward the margins (Figure 4.15).

Design and Layout

- Lay out document in thirds
- Avoid centering text or images in the middle of the page
- Balance graphs, illustrations, and text on the page
- Position images to draw eye into page
- Use plenty of white space
- Do not overuse emphasized words in:
  —bold
  —italics
  —underlining
  —uppercase

FIGURE 4.15
General rules for good document design.

Typography

Part of page composition is selecting fonts for headings, captions, and other design elements in the document. For a commonly used application, like a newsletter, a style sheet can determine which fonts and how many columns are used. In selecting a font, the designer decides on a weight, size, and typeface. Text is usually printed at a roman (standard) weight. As mentioned earlier, bold and italic weights are used for emphasis.

Professional printers measure type size in *points*. One point equals 1/72 of an inch. Figures 4.8 and 4.14 illustrate several sizes of type. The words you are reading are printed in $10\frac{1}{2}$-point type. Textbooks, reports, and most documents use 10- to 12-point type as a standard. Six-point type is considered fine print. Chapter headings and headlines range from 14 to 24 points. Only very special headlines or ads use type larger than 24 points (see Figure 4.16).

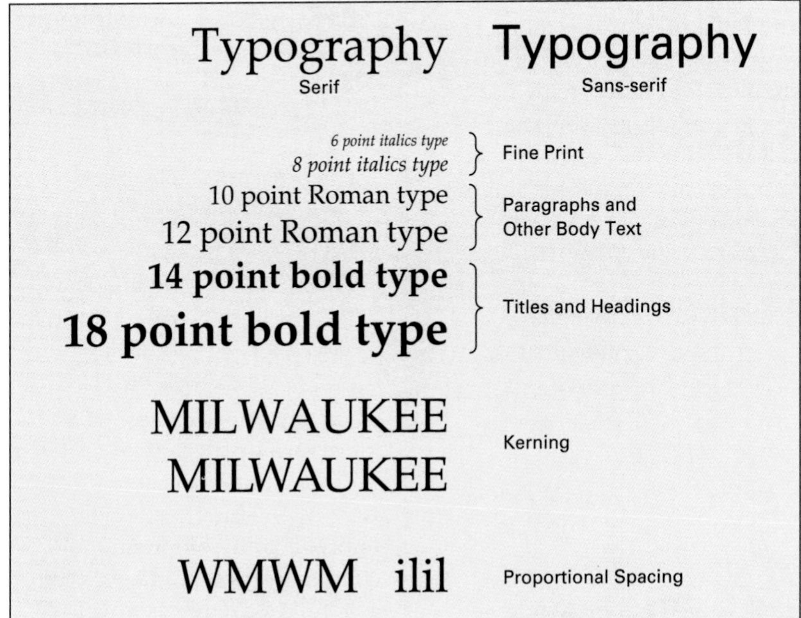

FIGURE 4.16
Typography concerns the size, style, and spacing of characters in a document.

As you would expect, type size affects the pitch (characters per inch). The smaller the type size, the greater the pitch, that is, the more words fit on a line. Another way of increasing the number of characters on a line is through *kerning*—using the shapes of the characters themselves to fit them closer to each other (see Figure 4.16).

Proportional spacing is a way of naturally fitting letters together. Letters and symbols are given different spacing depending on their widths rather than equal space for each symbol as is found

In the News...

HOW TO IMPROVE YOUR COMPUTER COMMUNICATION

Scenario #1: "Oh no, I'm not busy, not at all," she said lightly, motioning me into her office.

Scenario #2: "Oh no, I'm not busy, not at all," she said sarcastically. I could almost see the obstacles hanging from her words as she slammed her office door in my face.

"based on the ubiquitous smiling face"

Tone of voice and body language can be as important as the words we use. Computer-to-computer communication, however, is limited to what we can keyboard. This limitation can cause misunderstandings, sometimes serious ones.

Over the last few years an interesting solution has evolved among users of electronic mail and bulletin board systems. They employ a series of symbols to supplement the written word. These symbols are sometimes called "Smileys," since they are based on the ubiquitous smiling face drawing, placed sideways. Here are some examples:

Symbol	*Meaning*
:) or :-)	smile; happy
:(or :-(	frown; sad
;) or ;-)	wink; shyness; sarcasm
;-O	surprise; shock; boredom
:*	kiss

Smileys also can be supplemented by abbreviations. Some of these also express emotions, while others are merely a form of shorthand.

Abbreviation	*Meaning*
AFK	away from the keyboard
BAK	back at the keyboard
B4	before
CUL8R	see you later
<g>	grin
ILU	I love you
NBD	no big deal
ROFL	rolling on the floor laughing

These are only a sampling, and more turn up all the time. Watch for them, adopt them and invent your own. Using them will improve your computer communication, and mark you as a full-fledged E-mail or BBS aficionado.

on a typewriter. For example, the letters M and W require more space than the letters i and l.

Professional printers first used the terms serif and sans-serif to describe typefaces. Typeface describes the design of the characters in a font. A typeface with *serifs* has short line segments or extensions projecting from upper or lower ends of a character, for example, the leg of an upper case L or R. As also shown in Figure 4.8, *sans-serif* (without serif) type does not include these short lines.

Some professional printers argue that serif type is easier to read. They say that serifs draw the reader across the printed line, which allows the eyes to flow over words. These typefaces are considered more traditional. Reports and books written in the United States often use serif type for standard text. Sans-serif type is reserved for titles, headings, and captions. Europeans are more liberal in their application of sans-serif typefaces and use them in a wider range of situations.

The variety of fonts and other design features need to be translated for accurate reproduction through a laser printer or even a typesetter. The **page definition language (PDL)** of a desktop publishing package codes document files for this purpose. Each output device used with a desktop publisher contains an embedded computer with instructions for understanding the PDL. PostScript is a popular PDL.

File Integration

Pictures, graphs, illustrations, and photographs add interest and clarify written descriptions. This is one reason why desktop publishing software imports a wide variety of file formats, including those images captured by a scanner. These file formats generally fall into three categories: text, graphics, and images. Since the popular word processing packages save text in different formats, a desktop publisher must be flexible enough to accept them all (see Figure 4.17).

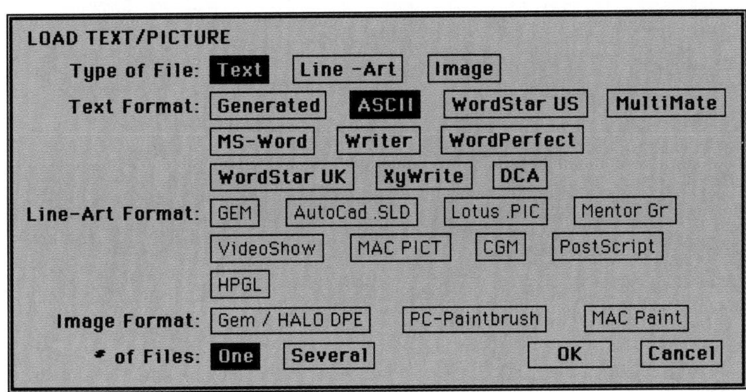

FIGURE 4.17
Desktop publishing software imports text, graphics, and images created by other software packages.

Distinguishing between images and graphics presents another problem. Look at the differences between Figures 4.1 and 4.2. One is an image and the other a graphic. They are created or reproduced by different types of software packages and are stored in different file formats. Basically, anything you can create with pencil on paper is a graphic like Figure 4.2. A graphic may be purchased or produced by the user with drawing software. The demand for ready-to-go art is so high that designers can purchase **clip art.** Figure 4.18 illustrates just a few of the thousands of graphics that are available in a clip art set. Clip art is available on paper, which may be scanned, or on a disk, which can be directly imported.

If you need a camera or scanner to capture an object, then it is considered an image like Figure 4.1. Desktop publishing packages can accept scanned photographs, but their quality of reproduction depends on the scanner and printer. The grays found in the "black and white" photographs in newspapers are produced in *halftones.* The image is made up of various sizes and placement of black dots on a white background, which tricks the eye into seeing varying

FIGURE 4.18
Clip art is packaged and sold to designers as ready-to-use graphics.

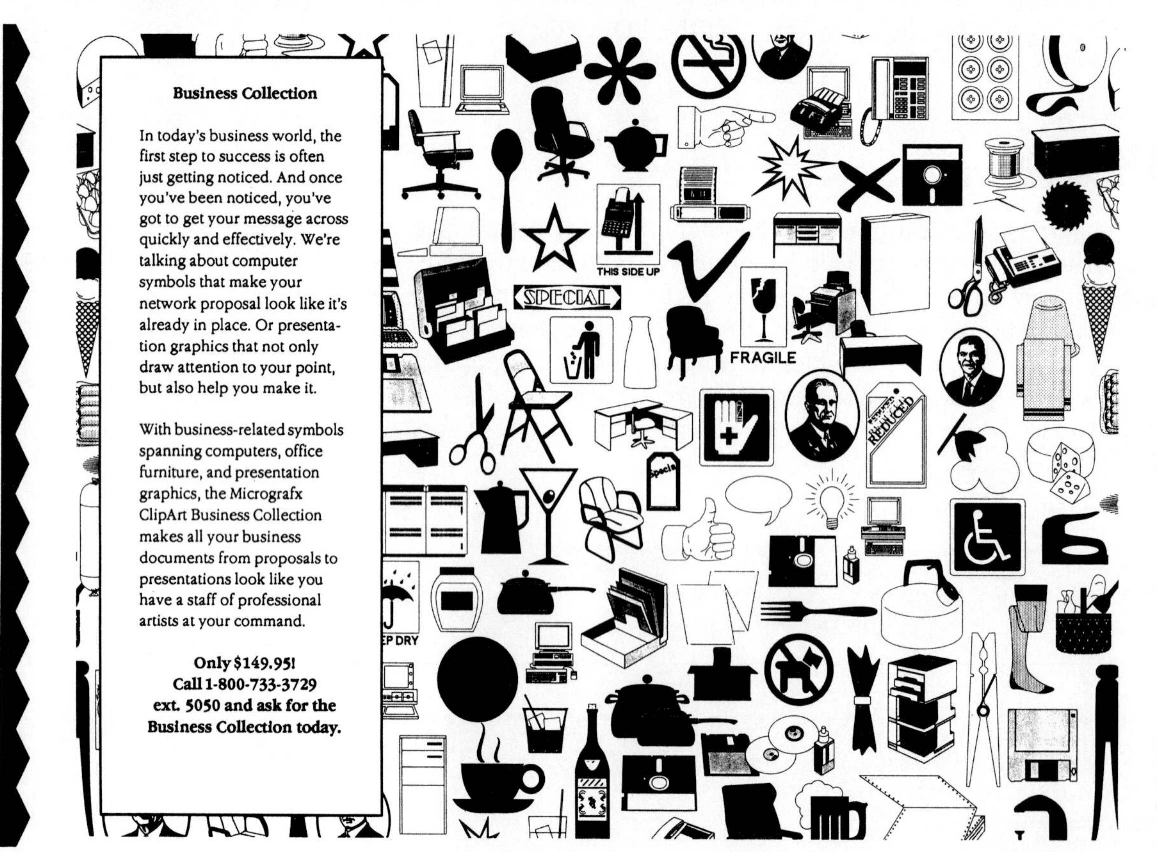

FOUR COLOR PROCESS PRINTING

BLUE FILTER / YELLOW PRINTER

GREEN FILTER / MAGENTA PRINTER

RED FILTER / CYAN PRINTER

MODIFIED FILTER / BLACK PRINTER

ROTATION OF COLORS

YELLOW

YELLOW & MAGENTA

YELLOW, MAGENTA & CYAN

YELLOW, MAGENTA, CYAN & BLACK

FIGURE 4.19
In color separation, a master copy of each color is produced to print four-color images.

shades of gray. It requires a very high-quality laser printer to produce halftone images of photographic quality. Multicolor images can be accurately reproduced after they are scanned by using *color separation* available on some desktop publishing systems. As seen in Figure 4.19, each page is printed in four different colors. When printed on top of one another, they produce the full-color images you see in this book.

Desktop publishing can never be a substitute for clear, concise, and imaginative writing. It can make a well-written document look better, but does little to hide incomplete sentences, misspellings, and overused words. In the final analysis, the words used when composing a document still come from you. Selection of the type size and style of text is your choice. Human hands and minds determine the final placement of graphs and pictures in the document.

AUTOMATING THE OFFICE

Everyone has a place where he or she writes letters, pays bills, and keeps personal records. The work varies, but several activities are common: reading correspondence and reports, filing important data, and organizing ideas and data into words, graphics, and images. These places of work, our offices, are changing as computers replace such office tools as typewriters. Desktop TSR software reduces the need for address books, calculators, and calendars. Letters, reports, and memos are created online, instead of on paper, and stored on disks.

Electronic Offices

In businesses, computers have increased office efficiency when they are connected with other office equipment. This development, known as **office automation,** replaces manual office procedures and encompasses:

- Word processing
- Desktop publishing
- Electronic mail
- Electronic filing
- Voice mail

In automated offices, transactions are completed with increasing speed. As a result, automated office techniques have stimulated the very business demands they are helping to meet.

By using word processing and desktop publishing in the automated office, attractive and correct documents are output at high speeds. The result is a rise in productivity. Accuracy and attractiveness are necessary for all formal documents, particularly in business. A letter, for example, represents the sender. In addition to conveying information, the letter forms an image. The appearance of the letter makes a statement about the sender just as clothes reveal a person's tastes and preferences. To promote a positive image, correspondence should be appealing to the eye, as well as easy to read and accurate. When an office sends out advertising or sales literature, the design is especially important.

In the News...

10 WAYS TO MAKE YOUR OFFICE ENVIRONMENT-FRIENDLY

When personal computers exploded into the scene, environmentalists rejoiced. The small computer promised an ecological utopia: the paperless office.

But today many of our computerized offices are anything but paperless. But if we recycle paper, reduce the amount of disposables we use, and avoid using office products containing compounds that harm the ozone layer, we can create a clutter-free office and a cleaner, healthier environment. Here are 10 ways to get started:

1. Don't print. Edit your documents onscreen. If you use e-mail or a fax board, print documents to disk rather than paper.

2. Use both sides of the page. Photocopies and printer test runs gobble paper. Print test runs on the backs of old drafts. Use fresh paper for final printouts only.

3. Reuse printer ribbons, so you will throw away fewer plastic cartridges. Keep an old ribbon for test prints and a new one for final copies.

4. Stop cleaning your computer with canned air. Or find a brand without chlorofluorocarbons (CFCs), which destroy the ozone layer. Use a mini vacuum cleaner instead.

5. Use rechargeable batteries. You'll save money and reduce the level of toxic metals in our landfills.

"Printed on Recycled Paper"

6. Recycle junk mail. Instead of reaching for the trash can, sort mail first and recycle all the high-grade white paper. Make sure it's free of foreign materials, such as plastic paper clips or address windows, which are not recyclable.

7. Use recycled products. Let customers know you care about the environment by including a discreet notation that says "Printed on Recycled Paper" on your brochures.

8. Dispose of disposables. Use up your supply of disposable pens, mechanical pencils, lighters—anything meant to be used once and tossed. Replace them with refillables and reusables and buy bulk refills.

9. Replace incandescent light bulbs with compact fluorescents. According to *Fifty Simple Things You Can Do to Save the Earth* by The Earth Works Group, compact fluorescents cost more, but they last more that 100 times longer and use a quarter of the electricity.

10. Keep your eyes open. You know your business better than anyone. Examine how you do things with an eye toward finding environment-friendly improvements.

If you'd like more tips, look in the ecology section of your local library or bookstore. Or contact the Environmental Defense Fund by calling (800) CALL-ED

—JOHN PIVOVARNICK

In an automated office, personal computers are linked to other office equipment. Geographically dispersed offices use telephones to interconnect equipment. In a small office, the equipment is usually directly linked by cable. For example, a word processor might be connected to a nearby intelligent copier to reproduce a text document. A secretary using a word processor would issue a command to make 100 copies of a report. Without further intervention from the secretary, the word processor would retrieve the report from disk and send it to the copier. The copier would translate the commands, making the requested copies in collated order. This method is more efficient than producing 100 copies on a regular printer. The copier is faster and quieter than the letter-quality printers normally attached to word processors. Furthermore, the file could be reproduced on copiers around the country as easily as in the same office.

Networks of personal computers in automated offices often use **electronic mail (E-mail)** to replace or enhance the traditional interoffice mail system. A memo can be sent to one person, several people, or everyone connected to the network. Some systems assign a personal disk file or *electronic mailbox* to each user. The originator prepares a list of recipients for each word-processed document. The electronic mail program uses the list to identify the mailbox destinations to a computer. The computer delivers the memo by copying it into the specified mailbox files. People can read their electronic messages each time they check their electronic mailboxes. They can use E-mail to respond immediately to the memo if necessary.

Some electronic mail systems will even let users leave voice messages along with written documents. These **voice mail** systems play a prerecorded answer and record any messages like a home telephone answering machine. However, instead of tape recording the message, the voice mail system handles the message just like other data and saves it on disk. The recipient can then play back the voice mail messages by accessing the system from any public telephone and entering a personal identification code. Handling interoffice correspondence through E-mail or voice mail is quicker than typing, copying, and routing it through the regular or express mail.

Electronic filing methods replace the tedious and error-prone task of maintaining paper records in metal filing cabinets. The computer keeps an index of the names of documents and the dates they are stored. To access a file, the user need only enter a name. The computer then consults the index, locates, and retrieves the desired document. Automatic filing directed by the computer prevents carelessness and misfiling in handling documents.

Automated offices may evolve into *paperless offices.* In such an office, word processors, desktop publishing software, E-mail, and electronic filing systems are combined. Documents exist only within the computer system; fewer paper copies are stored. Documents held on system storage media can be accessed by users at any time. Further, files can be shared by users more readily. The original version of a document remains in storage, so that several users may request a copy at the same time. Documents are printed only when they need to be sent to someone outside the office. The result is less paper in the paperless office. Paper is not eliminated, but significantly decreased.

Advertising

One of the fringe benefits of automating an office is that it promotes the exchange of ideas and information. An advertising agency serves as a good example of how increased communication supports creative thinking. Making people aware of the goods or services to be sold is crucial to an effective advertising campaign. In this age of multimedia television and four-color print, a great deal of effort goes into making a new (or old) product appear desirable to potential customers. An idea started as an E-mail memo could evolve through a barrage of follow-up memos into a new advertising campaign. The personnel in an automated office could then coordinate writing and publishing the proposal, scheduling meetings, printing contracts, and even creating the sales literature using computer technology.

Attractive sales literature can be personalized in another automated office by an informed salesperson. By using word processing software to merge data from customer data files, a salesperson can produce attractive personalized brochures for prospective customers. An attached individualized letter would also include the customer's name and address along with a reference to past purchases and specific information about an upcoming sale.

Journalism

Over the last 20 years automated offices have dramatically changed journalism. The image of a reporter sweeping the last page out of the typewriter while shouting for the copyboy to pick up the work is no longer accurate. Now journalists pound on personal computer keyboards. Their PCs link them electronically through a network to the desk editor. With the press of a few keys, stories are transferred to the editor for online review and revision.

Increasingly smaller portable computers are even letting reporters take computers into the field. With a battery-operated portable computer, a reporter can write and store a story at the scene of news or while attending a sporting event. A nearby telephone links the portable to the newspaper's main computer for data transfer.

The factory-like atmosphere that once prevailed in the typesetting department before a newspaper went to press is also changing. Small foundries with molten lead used for setting type have become obsolete. Now many newspapers employ sophisticated **electronic publishing** systems that run high-speed printing presses and control page composition, typography, and file integration just like desktop publishing software. The masthead, stories, headlines, and photos can be positioned on screen as shown in Figure 4.20. When each element of the page is in place, the computer produces a film on the page, which is used to make copies of the paper. As a result, news stories composed on a computer and stored on disk need not be retyped into a typesetter. The electronic publishing system just incorporates the files with graphics and images to produce the final plates used by the printing presses.

Many newspapers have established communication links to large news-gathering services such as the Associated Press (AP). As these news services constantly update their databases, local newspapers receive instant notification on computers dedicated to receiving wire copy. Late-breaking news reports can be shared immediately with all subscribers to the news service network. Similarly, syndicated columns and features are sent like electronic mail over communication lines.

The need for electronic offices is not confined to print journalism. Broadcasters also convey the news with the help of word processors. Anchorpersons appear to stare directly into your living room as you watch the news. However, the newscaster actually is reading a script displayed on a teleprompter placed right over the lens of the camera. The script is prepared by word processing software and displayed onto the teleprompter.

Electronic Classrooms

As word processing, networks of personal computers, and other features of the automated office gradually become part of education, an electronic classroom has evolved. Computers are found in grade schools, high schools, and colleges, as computer literacy becomes a graduation requirement (Figure 4.21). While computer use on campus encompasses many computer applications, one of the most widespread for schools is word processing.

A teacher can generate bulletins, written assignments, tests, and syllabi with a word processor. The documents can be stored and revised easily. Generating a make-up test, for example, is accomplished quickly with the aid of online editing techniques. The teacher decides to retain or replace questions, then makes the changes quickly on screen.

Students, of course, use word processing to complete written assignments. Using manual typewriters, a student might retype several drafts of a report before the document is completed. However,

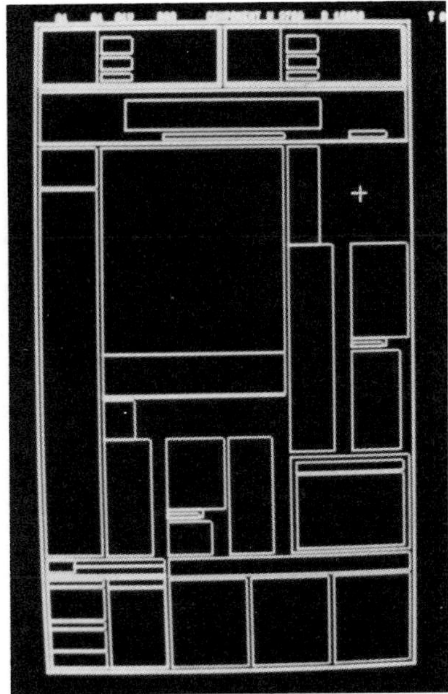

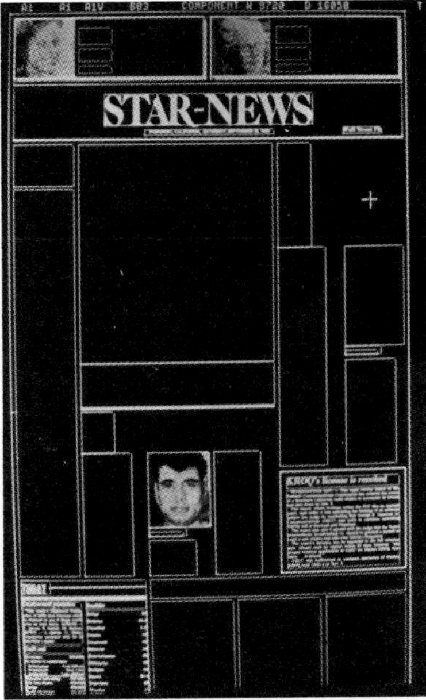

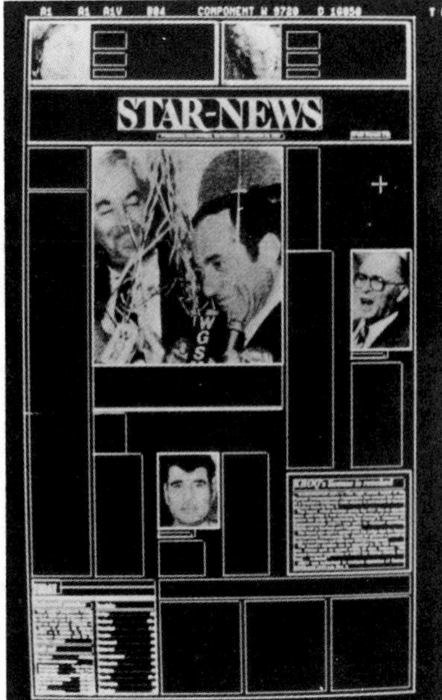

FIGURE 4.20

Electronic publishing supports the on-line development of each newspaper page.

FIGURE 4.21
Students and teachers use information technology as tutors and to support communication.

with the help of computers and word processing software, the student can move from first to final draft with little duplication of effort. Personal computers and word processing software are a boon to creative writers, especially those with poor typing skills.

Desktop publishing is also being used in schools to produce newsletters, posters, and yearbooks. Some high schools even have printing classes where students use desktop publishing to learn the printing business.

Many elementary schools use *banner programs* to help produce displays and awards. These programs contain their own clip art with many designs useful in printing birthday banners, special certificates, or designs for a bulletin board. The designs in a banner program can be personalized and edited similarly to a word processing document.

Some college campuses have even incorporated electronic mail systems for students and faculty. The E-mail system helps the faculty distribute assignments and allows students to submit homework electronically. It even allows students and faculty to participate in questions and answers through the exchange of E-mail during "electronic" office hours.

A Closer Look...

Selecting a Word Processing Package

A prospective buyer of a word processor would be wise to learn as much as possible about the vast selection of packages on the market. The first step in the selection process is identifying your needs and the nature of the applications that will meet those needs. Some users might need a word processor to create one-page business letters or brief reports. Others may wish to create technical documents that are several pages in length.

Software preferences depend largely on individual tastes. Methods for creating, formatting, editing, and printing a document may differ slightly or substantially from package to package. Hands-on testing of several packages enables users to evaluate features. In the final analysis, the price of a package should be balanced against its overall performance in determining the real value of the software. Here are some questions you should consider when purchasing a word processing package.

Q Do you have any special formatting or printing requirements?

A Documents containing foreign languages or scientific/technical symbols may require special word processing features. Some general-purpose word processors allow the user to create symbols. Special utility programs that provide specialized characters and symbols are also available.

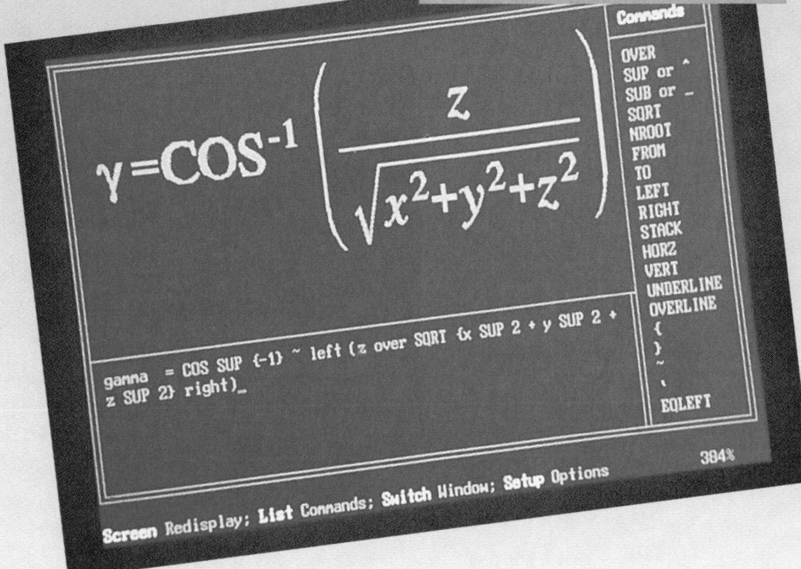

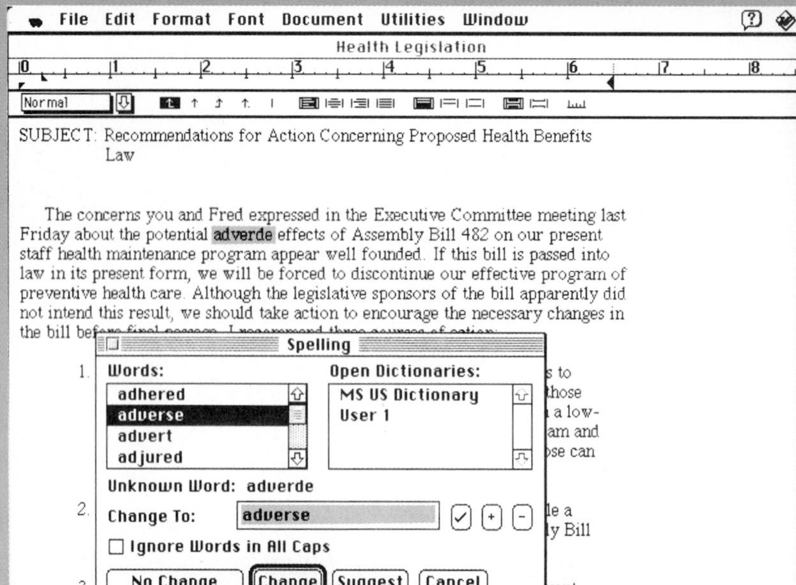

Q Which online services are important to you?

A Personal preference comes into play when evaluating spelling checkers, online thesaurus, style sheet procedures, or file merging capabilities.

Q Will your word processing requirements include special hardware?

A Some word processing packages are designed to take advantage of high-quality screens for WYSIWYG displays or use a mouse to highlight blocks of text. Potential desktop publishing users will probably use a scanner and laser printer.

Q What type of support materials will you need?

A Support materials such as tutorials are geared toward new users while manuals, screens, easy-to-understand menus or prompts, online help, and easy-to-use prompts serve everyone.

Q **Is the software compatible with hardware available to you at work, school, or through friends?**

A **People interested in sharing electronic documents with others need to know what file formats and formatting codes will be used in common.**

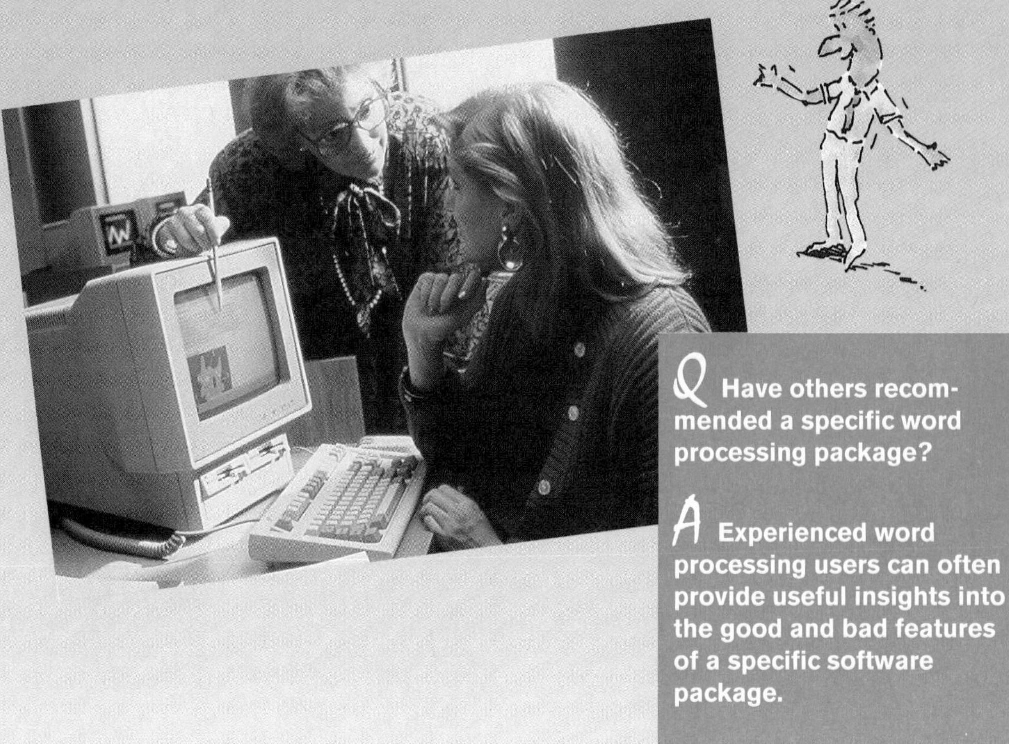

Q **Have others recommended a specific word processing package?**

A **Experienced word processing users can often provide useful insights into the good and bad features of a specific software package.**

WINDOWS WORD PROCESSORS: SUMMARY OF FEATURES

Products listed in alphabetical order
PC—Editors' Choice   N/A—Not applicable: The product does not have this feature.
■ Yes   □ No

	PC Ami Pro	PC Microsoft Word for Windows	WordPerfect 5.1 for Windows
	$495	$495	$495
Ready	■	■	■
Additional user on network	$395	$395	$395
TEXT-FORMATTING FEATURES			
Broken underline	■	■	■
Double underline	■	■	■
Strikethrough	■	■	■
Small capitals	■	■	■
Variable page length within document	■	■	■
Automatic renumbering of pages after formatting	■	■	■
Vertical centering	■	■	■
Conditional page breaks	■	■	■
Paragraph linking	■	■	■
Sorting	■	■	■
Line numbering	■	■	■
Portrait and landscape pages within single document	■	■	■
TEXT ENTRY AND EDITING FEATURES			
User can adjust margins on ruler	■	■	■
User can adjust columns on ruler	■	■	■
Paragraph marker display option	■	■	■
Format code display option	□	□	■
Maximum number of undelete levels	4	1	3
Widow and orphan control	■	■	■
Zoom feature	■	■	■
User-adjustable zoom levels	10–400%	25–200%	Unlimited
Appends block to file on-disk	□	■	■
Search-and-replace:			
Searches forward and backward	■	■	■
Searches within other files	■	□	■
Performs case-sensitive searches	■	■	□
Recognizes whole words	■	■	■
Uses wildcards in search	■	■	■
Uses wildcards in replace	■	■	□
Searches and replaces format codes	■	■	■
Maximum number of documents open simultaneously	9	9	9
Maximum number of text windows in one document without opening second copy of program	9	9	9
PRINTING FEATURES			
Prints in background	■	■	□
Prints blocks	■	■	■
Prints discontinuous range of pages	■	□	■
Prints current page	□	■	■
Prints landscape printer setup change	■	■	■
Prints with crop marks	■	□	□
Prints in reverse order	■	■	■
Collates print job	■	■	■
Controls printer bin for first page	■	■	■
Supports non-Microsoft Windows character set	■	■	■
Automatic envelope formatting and printing	□	■	□

PC Magazine, February 25, 1992, pp. 146–147.

Products listed in alphabetical order
PC - Editors' Choice   N/A—Not applicable: The product does not have this feature.
■ Yes   □ No

	PC Ami Pro	PC Microsoft Word for Windows	WordPerfect 5.1 for Windows
FILE-HANDLING FEATURES			
Maximum number of documents open simultaneously	9	9	9
Performs backup at user selected time intervals	■	■	■
Includes file management functions	■	■	■
Searches disk for filenames	□	■	■
Searches disk for text within files	■	■	■
File import/export format:			
Ami Pro	■/■	□/□	■/■
Microsoft Word	■/■	■/■	■/■
Microsoft Word for Windows	■/■	■/■	■/■
MultiMate	■/■	■/■	■/■
WordPerfect	■/■	■/■	■/■
WordStar	■/■	■/■	■/■
HYPHENATION AND GRAMMAR FEATURES			
Hyphenation	■	■	■
Customizable hyphenation dictionary	□	■	■
User can enter soft hyphens from keyboard	■	■	■
Hyphenation on a paragraph level	■	■	■
Limits number of consecutive hyphens at end of columns	■	■	□
Spell-checker:			
Number of words in standard dictionary	130,000	130,000	115,000
Spell-checks defined block	■	■	■
Spell-checks document with one command	■	■	■
Specialized spell-checkers:			
Legal	□	■	□
Medical	□	■	□
Foreign-language	■	■	■
Thesaurus	□	□	■
Antonyms provided	N/A	N/A	■
Grammar checker	□	■	□
Customizable rules	N/A	■	N/A
MANUSCRIPT PREPARATION FEATURES			
Generates table of contents	■	■	■
Generates index	■	■	■
Footnotes	■	■	■
Endnotes	■	■	■
Cross-referencing	■	■	■
Collapsible outlines	■	■	□
Allows user defined numbering schemes	■	□	■
Allows military-style numbering	■	■	■
Bookmarks	■	■	□
DESKTOP PUBLISHING			
Includes stylesheets			
User can modify default styl			
User can apply different sty document			
Maximum number of colum			
Column snaking			
Automatically balances tex multiple columns			
Adjustable gutter width			
User can define column w			
User can draw lines with c			
Expandable box around te			
Irregular nonrectangular b			

Q **What do the software reviews in the computer magazines have to say about the packages you like?**

A **Software reviews performed by computer magazines list features, give retail prices, and often provide information on several comparative packages.**

Chapter Facts

- Word processing is the writing, editing, formatting, storing, and printing of documents.
- Word processing operations consist of editing and formatting a document.
- Editing is the creation, storage, and revision of text.
- Specific editing features include word wrap, cursor control, insertion, deletion, move, copy, undo, find, search, and replace.
- Formatting is the manipulation of a document's appearance.
- Specific formatting features include line space and length, tabulation, centering, headers and footers, pagination and page length, print font and pitch, double-striking, and justification.
- Word processing packages can be integrated with other online services to increase user productivity. These include a spelling checker, online thesaurus, style sheets, writing analyzer, hyphenation help routines, and file merging.
- Desktop publishing software controls page composition, typography, and the integration of files created by other software. The result is camera-ready output.
- Hardware components of a desktop publishing system include personal computer, scanner, mouse, full-page monitor, laser printer, and software.
- To avoid centering the reader's eye in the middle of the page, subdivide a page into thirds when laying out text and graphics.
- Good designs use plenty of white space.
- Serif typefaces are most often used with blocks of text, while sans-serif typefaces are used when printing headings and titles.
- Office automation, including word processing, desktop publishing, electronic mail, and electronic filing, has increased office productivity.
- Electronic filing involves storing and retrieving documents on disk. When used with word processors and other online data processing systems, electronic mail can replace an organization's internal mail service.
- Personalized advertising literature is created by merging files of customer information with a word-processed letter.
- Journalists work in automated offices for writing stories, accessing online news services, and electronically publishing books, newspapers, newsletters, and articles. Teleprompters and word processing aid in television broadcasting.

- Teachers prepare tests, syllabi, and assignments in electronic classrooms where students also write and edit assignments.
- Word processing software should be evaluated on how well it fits the user's needs, the features it contains, its aids to new users, and its integration with other software.

Terms to Remember

a. block
b. clip art
c. editing
d. electronic mail (E-mail)
e. electronic filing
f. electronic publishing
g. external copy
h. font
i. formatting
j. hard return
k. import
l. justification
m. landscape
n. office automation
o. page definition language (PDL)
p. pagination
q. pitch
r. portrait
s. soft return
t. soft space
u. style sheet
v. voice mail
w. word wrap
x. WYSIWYG

Mix and Match

Match the following definitions to the Terms to Remember.

1. ____ networking document processing equipment together in an office.
2. ____ storing documents on disk instead of a filing cabinet.
3. ____ coding of graphics, images, and text for use by laser printers.
4. ____ printing technology that runs high-speed printing presses and controls page composition, typography, and file integration.
5. ____ word processing feature that includes counting pages and printing page numbers.
6. ____ style, weight, and size of a printed character.
7. ____ number of characters printed per inch in a document.
8. ____ a carriage return entered into the text when the user presses the Return or Enter key.

9. _____ sending and receiving memos, reports, and personal messages through a computer network.
10. _____ vertical layout of a document page.
11. _____ graphics and images on paper or disk that are purchased for use by designers.
12. _____ copying a block of text from a document to an outside file.
13. _____ adding graphics, images, or text created by other software to a document.
14. _____ a carriage return entered into the document by the word wrap operation.
15. _____ controlling the final appearance of a document.
16. _____ horizontal layout of a document page.
17. _____ blank spaces added between words to fully justify text within the left and right margins.
18. _____ selected text within a document that can be independently moved, copied, or deleted.
19. _____ document containing the margin settings, tab locations, justification instructions, line spacing, as well as other formatting specifications a user wants for an application.
20. _____ computer system that answers telephone calls with a pre-recorded message and saves callers' messages on disk for later playback.
21. _____ when a document is entered without carriage returns, the word processor senses the margins and moves words to the next line as needed.
22. _____ the alignment of text along the margins.
23. _____ the feature of a word processing or desktop publishing package to show on the monitor exactly how a document will look when printed.
24. _____ revising text in a document.

Review Questions

1. How do the following editing operations work?

insert	find
delete	search and replace
move and copy	save
undo	retrieve

2. What are twelve formatting operations common to most word processing software?

3. How is a left-justified document different from one with full or right justification?
4. Identify and describe six services that can be integrated with word processing.
5. What formatting operations are controlled by style sheets?
6. How is a boilerplate used?
7. When compared to word processing software, what additional levels of control are available with desktop publishing?
8. Explain six features of good document design and layout.
9. What sizes of type are associated with fine print, standard text, and headings or titles?
10. Identify situations when serif and sans-serif type is used.
11. Briefly describe the three basic file types desktop publishing software imports from other software packages.
12. Describe five operations of an automated office.
13. When is a paper copy necessary in a paperless office?
14. Explain how a business can use word processing software to create personalized advertising.
15. Describe six ways the electronic office has changed journalism.
16. How do teachers and students use an electronic classroom?
17. What seven steps should be a part of the evaluation process when purchasing a new word processing package?

Applying What You've Learned

1. All computer systems are made up of these five components: people, procedures, data, programs, and hardware. For each of the following systems name or describe what makes up each component.
   a. desktop publishing an advertisement
   b. sending an electronic mail message
   c. editing a report in a paperless office
   d. filing a letter by using electronic filing
   e. writing a term paper on a word processor
2. Keep track of mail to your household for a week. What type of correspondence has been done (or could have been done) with a word processor? Do you think the use of a word processor enhances or detracts from the quality and "personalized" nature of the correspondence?

3. Make a list of the features you would require in a word processor. Assume that money is not a limiting factor. Include any special character types, related software, and printing options. Also list the user aids (help screens, prompts, etc.) you would like to have now and in the future.
4. The text mentions the use of automated offices in journalism, education, business, law, and government. List the ways information technology might be useful in these occupations:
   a. manager for a professional sport team
   b. hospital administrator
   c. regional manager for a charitable organization such as the Red Cross or United Foundation
   d. director for a state lottery
   e. museum curator
5. Writers can use spelling checkers, writing analyzers, and an online thesaurus to aid in creative or technical writing. Other available related software includes gender checkers (for nonsexist writing) and grammar checkers. Do you feel such software helps to increase writing skills of, or acts as a crutch to, writers lacking good writing skills? Is using a word processor unfair to those who do not have one?
6. Investigate a desktop publishing package that could be useful to you in school, in an organization, or in a job situation. Use information from sales literature, retail store salespeople, or magazines to determine the following:
   a. What type of user interface does it use?
   b. What editing options does it offer?
   c. On what kinds of computers does it work?
   d. What kind of printer is required?
   e. Does it handle color graphics?
   f. Can it be used with other software packages?
   g. What special input hardware is needed?
   h. What training manuals or tutorials are included?
   i. What are the memory and disk space requirements?
   j. How much does the package cost?
7. Designing an interesting page layout and desktop publishing a document takes time. Identify three types of documents that should be and three that should not be desktop published.

Answers to Mix and Match

1. n 2. e 3. o 4. f 5. p 6. h 7. q 8. j 9. d 10. r
11. b 12. g 13. k 14. s 15. i 16. m 17. t 18. a
19. u 20. v 21. w 22. l 23. x 24. c

5

Electronic Spreadsheets

- From the User's Point of View
- Presenting and Processing Numbers
  - Manual worksheets
  - Electronic spreadsheets
- Electronic Spreadsheets: Features and Functions
  - Worksheet layout
  - Common spreadsheet operations
  - Combining operations with macros
  - Expanded uses of worksheet data
- Spreadsheets as a Tool
  - Personal applications
  - Volunteer activities
  - Education
  - Athletics
  - Science
  - Manufacturing
- *A Closer Look . . . Designing a Better Worksheet*

FROM THE USER'S POINT OF VIEW

If you work at organizing and manipulating numbers, you will want to know about electronic spreadsheets. It does not matter if you are handling the accounts of a large multinational corporation, the grades for a composition class, or the operating expenses for your club. Electronic spreadsheet packages help you total a column of numbers in the blink of an eye. Averages and other statistics are easily performed on whole tables of numbers. This personal productivity software will get the job done with fewer errors and headaches.

PRESENTING AND PROCESSING NUMBERS

Numbers are used to make decisions and evaluate performance. The results of many activities are expressed as numbers. The profit from the sale of a house is expressed numerically as money. Performance in school often is measured as a grade point average, which involves numbers to indicate academic success. Film critics often convey their opinion of a movie by placing it on a scale of 1 to 10. Numbers have become an inescapable part of modern living (Figure 5.1).

Money, in particular, affects nearly every activity in our lives. Many of the functions of individuals, families, businesses, and governments revolve around the earning and spending of money. The fundamental premise of operating within a monetary system is to acquire at least enough income to cover expenses.

Expenses can be either fixed or variable. *Fixed expenses* might include rent, mortgage payments, car payments, bus fare to work, or any other predictable, regular expense. Expenses over which you have more control are known as *variable expenses.* These expenses might include the purchase of either needed or luxury items. Food, for example, is an essential, variable expense. Buying some food is necessary for survival, but people can control the amount and cost of what they buy. Variable expenses that are discretionary, or nonessential, might include movie tickets, magazines, vacations, sports events, and other forms of entertainment.

FIGURE 5.1
Electronic spreadsheets organize data into rows and columns.

Manual Worksheets

Controlling activities involving numbers often requires planning and processing. These activities can be performed on a worksheet like the one in Figure 5.2. A **worksheet** organizes related numbers and labels into rows and columns. This easy-to-read format allows users to compare numbers for different activities and for different periods of time. With this information you could analyze present conditions and use the analysis to influence future plans.

For decades business managers created worksheets to evaluate performance and predict trends. Although used primarily in financial applications, this method of organizing data has expanded to encompass such areas as scoring sporting events, keeping class gradebooks, doing statistical analysis, and tracking cultural trends. In each case people have used worksheets to support decision making with data.

Basically, worksheets are tables that organize data for easy comparison. Comprised of horizontal rows and vertical columns, worksheets resemble a grid. In financial applications rows typically are

CITY BUS SERVICE	Annual operating budget	JAN Actual	FEB Actual	MAR Actual
Administration	$215,749	$17,979	$17,979	
Facility rental	21,120	1,760	1,760	
Wage & benefit, Operator	476,000	39,528	38,997	
Fuel	62,416	5,386	4,721	
Maintenance	431,952	31,994	38,584	
Insurance	125,384	10,449	10,449	
Public Information	15,064	1,045	976	
Depreciation of Busses	195,000	16,250	16,250	
Total costs	$1,542,685	$124,391	$129,716	$0
Total miles	421,991	35,219	32,461	
Cost per mile	$3.6557	$3.5319	$3.9961	

FIGURE 5.2
Manually prepared worksheets like this one have been around for hundreds of years. This work is now performed by electronic spreadsheets that help computer users to quickly and accurately manipulate worksheet numbers.

used to distinguish items to be evaluated, while columns represent different periods of time. A worksheet for figuring monthly income and expenses, then, might include thirteen columns, one for each month of the year and an additional column for year-end totals.

Each unit, or **cell,** on the grid is the intersection of a column and a row. Cells contain items of data or special instructions for processing the data. On manual worksheets the content of each cell is usually written in pencil. To change a cell value, the pencil marks are erased. This method often produces somewhat sloppy worksheets. However, it spares people from having to create an entirely new worksheet when data changes.

Another drawback to using manual worksheets is the time it takes to change data values. Quite often, changing one value requires recalculation of several other worksheet values. Recalculating totals and averages are examples. This task becomes frustrating and tiresome when using worksheets designed for "What if?" speculations. "What if?" questions allow people to determine the probable results from a given set of conditions. For example, how would the budget in Figure 5.2 change if insurance rates went up starting in March?

Usually, several worksheets are required to assess all the alternatives in "What if?" situations. A store manager might wish to determine quarterly profits given a 5, 6, or 7 percent increase in sales. Three manual worksheets would be created, requiring three different sets of calculations. Producing complete "What if?" analyses can require a good deal of time and energy.

Electronic Spreadsheets

The late 1970s brought a breakthrough in worksheet analysis with the introduction of VisiCalc electronic spreadsheet software, which teamed worksheets with computers. For more information about VisiCalc's inventors, Daniel Bricklin and Robert Frankston, see the Who's Who in this chapter. An electronic spreadsheet program displays a worksheet on the computer's screen. Cells are filled with text, numbers, and formulas entered through the computer's keyboard. Moving or copying data is accomplished with a few keystrokes. With electronic spreadsheet software, people can edit a worksheet without making messy erasures.

One of the most valuable features of electronic spreadsheets is its ability to perform calculations. Cells can contain arithmetic symbols that instruct the computer to add, subtract, multiply, or divide values from other cells. Upon entry of a single instruction, the computer performs these calculations with both speed and accuracy.

People can ask any number of "What if?" questions by changing numbers or formulas, and the spreadsheet then quickly recalculates new answers. Thus, armed with a computer and electronic spreadsheet software, people interested in forecasting no longer need to spend long hours with a calculator to develop a complete "What if?" analysis.

The primary value of electronic spreadsheets lies in the ease of making and processing changes. People can create large worksheets—a thousand rows by several hundred columns—with greater accuracy and in less time than with manual methods. As a result, people can test data under many circumstances to build a broader base of information from which to make decisions.

ELECTRONIC SPREADSHEETS: FEATURES AND FUNCTIONS

Electronic spreadsheets are useful for all types of personal and business applications. Figure 5.3 shows a worksheet created by Terri LaFriend, the administrative assistant at City Bus Service. Mike Rodriguez, her supervisor and manager of the bus company, helped her plan the worksheet organization.

Terri included rows for eight expense items, along with two rows for computing total miles driven and cost per mile. As shown in Figure 5.3, the first column contains identifying labels or text for each row. An additional row holds total costs. Terri's complete spreadsheet data includes columns for monthly actual expenses as well as columns for the annual operating budget and actual yearly totals. The final column on the right contains the difference between actual and budgeted totals for the year.

Terri followed a number of steps to create this worksheet. First, she identified the purpose of the worksheet. In this case she wanted

FIGURE 5.3
The City Bus Service budget worksheet is designed to store financial data for an entire year and to identify accounts that are under or over budget.

CITY BUS SERVICE
1994 Annual Budget

	Annual operating budget	JAN Actual	FEB Actual	MAR Actual	APR Actual	MAY Actual	JUN Actual	JUL Actual	AUG Actual	SEP Actual	OCT Actual	NOV Actual	DEC Actual	TOTAL	(Over) under budget
Administration	$215,749	$17,979	$17,979											$35,958	($0)
Facility rental	21,120	1,760	1,760											3,520	0
Wage & benefit, Operator	476,000	39,528	38,997											78,525	809
Fuel	62,416	5,386	4,721											10,107	296
Maintenance	431,952	3,195	38,584											70,578	1,414
Insurance	125,384	10,449	10,449											20,898	(1)
Public Information	15,064	1,045	976											2,021	490
Depreciation of Busses	195,000	16,250	16,250											32,500	0
Total costs	$1,542.685	$124,391	$129,716	$0	$0	$0	$0	$0	$0	$0	$0	$0	$0	$254,107	$3,007
Total miles	421,991	35,219	32,461											$67,680	$2,652
Cost per mile	$3.6557	$3.5319	$3.9961												

to keep track of all expenses to help City Bus Service stay within a budget. By maintaining a worksheet, she could pinpoint areas in which the company was overspending.

Next, Terri made a list of both fixed and variable expenses, which became the spreadsheet data. She also determined her processing requirements: In this case she needed a mathematical routine to determine the difference between budgeted and actual expenses. She sketched a layout of an empty worksheet, to identify how the data and formulas were to be presented, then estimated the space needed for each column. With these specifications in hand, Terri created and formatted her electronic worksheet.

Terri entered numbers and formulas into appropriate worksheet cells. Each cell is identified by its **cell address,** which is the associated column letter and row number. She instructed the computer to calculate the cost per mile seen in Figure 5.4 by entering a formula in cell B20. Other computations help Terri see that City Bus Company was under budget in wages, fuel, maintenance, and public information. Also, insurance costs were only one dollar over budget. These figures would help her boss decide if the company could afford to start additional bus routes.

In the News...

SELECTING SOFTWARE

Computer lore is filled with stories about people who buy software, use it for a week, and then delete it from their hard drives because the package is too complicated to use, and just doesn't make life any easier. Here are some tips on selecting the right software and how to avoid buying programs that you won't use.

■ Expensive programs aren't always the best. Keep in mind exactly what functions you want performed.

■ Invest in software that will remain useful as your business grows and evolves.

■ Gauge how much technical expertise you need to use any package you purchase.

■ Stick to products that will make you productive immediately. The less time you spend learning a package, the more time you will have to work.

■ Look for software that's intuitive—that adapts to the way you work rather than making you adapt to it.

■ Once you start using your software, back up your data. Do it daily, just like brushing your teeth. You'll be glad you did when that file you were working on disappears from your screen.

■ Retain all the documentation that comes with the software. If something goes wrong, you'll need a serial number to get help and service.

Data Entry Line

Lotus 1-2-3 Release 4 - [CITYBUS.WK3]

File Edit View Style Tools Range Window Help — Command Menu

A:A1 'CITY BUS SERVICE

Icon Bar

ACTUAL EXPECTED C D E New Sheet

Active Cell

	A	B	C	D	E
1	CITY BUS SERVICE				
2	Annual Budget				
3		Annual			
4		operating	JAN	FEB	MAR
5		budget	Actual	Actual	Actual
6					
7	Administration	215,749	17,979	17,979	17,979
8	Facility rental	21,120	1,760	1,760	1,760
9	Wage & Benefit, Operator	476,000	39,528	38,997	38,968
10	Fuel	62,416	5,386	4,721	5,097
11	Maintenance	431,952	31,994	38,584	37,073
12	Insurance	125,384	10,449	10,449	10,449
13	Public Information	15,064	1,045	976	2,059
14	Depreciation of Buses	195,000	16,250	16,250	16,250
15		----------	----------	----------	----------
16	Total Costs	1,542,685	124,391	129,716	129,635
17		==========	==========	==========	==========
18					
19	Total miles	421,991	35,219	32,461	36,023
20	Cost per mile	$3.656	$3.532	$3.996	$3.599

, Comma 0 Arial 14 04/29/94 11:44 AM Ready — Status Line

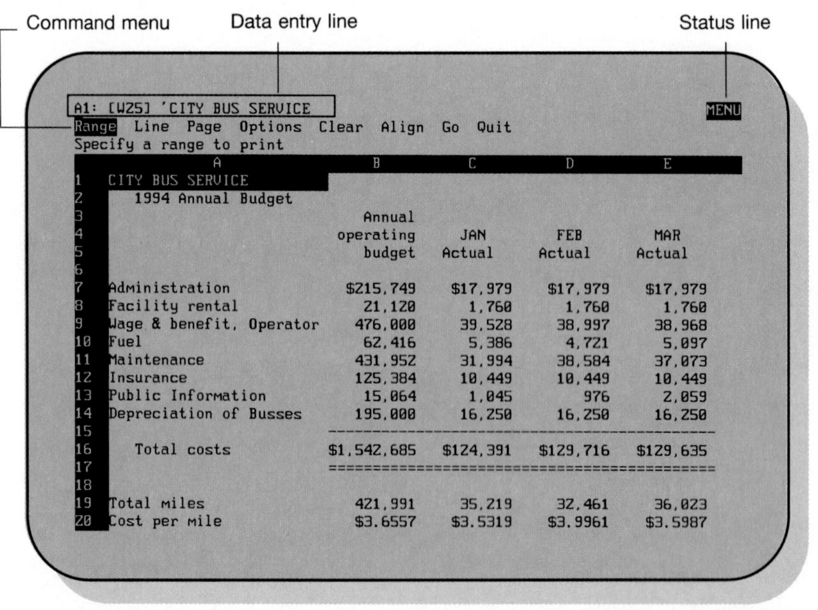

	A	B	C	D	E
1	CITY BUS SERVICE				
2	1994 Annual Budget				
3		Annual			
4		operating	JAN	FEB	MAR
5		budget	Actual	Actual	Actual
6					
7	Administration	$215,749	$17,979	$17,979	$17,979
8	Facility rental	21,120	1,760	1,760	1,760
9	Wage & benefit, Operator	476,000	39,528	38,997	38,968
10	Fuel	62,416	5,386	4,721	5,097
11	Maintenance	431,952	31,994	38,584	37,073
12	Insurance	125,384	10,449	10,449	10,449
13	Public Information	15,064	1,045	976	2,059
14	Depreciation of Busses	195,000	16,250	16,250	16,250
15		----------	----------	----------	----------
16	Total costs	$1,542,685	$124,391	$129,716	$129,635
17		==========	==========	==========	==========
18					
19	Total miles	421,991	35,219	32,461	36,023
20	Cost per mile	$3.6557	$3.5319	$3.9961	$3.5987

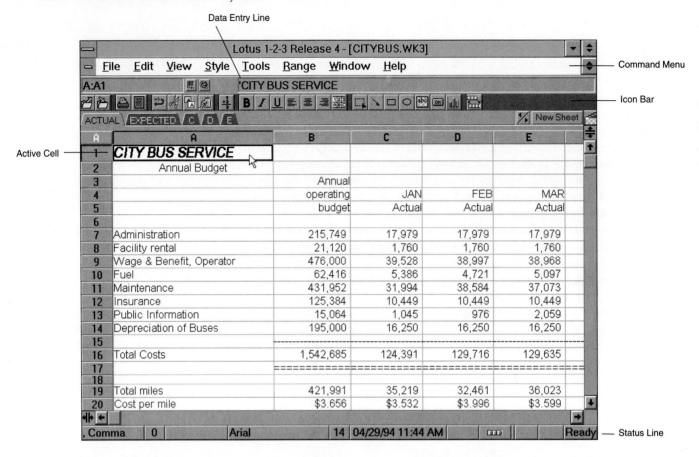

FIGURE 5.4
Electronic spreadsheets use a command menu to initiate program operations, a status line to indicate the current operating mode, and a data entry line for input. GUI spreadsheets also employ an icon bar as an alternative to the command menu.

Worksheet Layout

Electronic spreadsheets use rows and columns that intersect to form cells, just like manual worksheets. However, they also provide menus that give users control of data entry and processing activities. Typically, spreadsheets use three types of control lines: command, status, and data entry.

The **command menu** is the menu of spreadsheet features often listed in a row across the top or bottom of the spreadsheet, as shown in Figure 5.4. Selections included on the command menu enable the user to create and format worksheets, load them with data, then process and print reports. Spreadsheets that employ a graphical user interface (GUI) replace the command menu with drop-down menus and an **icon bar** (also shown in Figure 5.4). Common program operations are represented by different icons on the bar.

The **status line** indicates which operation currently is being used on the worksheet. Status lines often are located at the upper right or bottom right corner of the spreadsheet display. Different operating states (modes) would include Ready mode for data entry or menu selections, Edit mode to change data in the worksheet, and Error mode when the spreadsheet software encounters a processing problem. Other operating modes are discussed in the user manual.

Some spreadsheet packages enter data directly into the worksheet. In other packages, numbers, labels, and formulas are displayed in a **data entry line** before they are transferred to the *active cell.* Users identify the active cell by moving the screen pointer to a specific cell and clicking the mouse button. Cursor control keys are also used to highlight the active cell. If the data has not been entered into the active cell, the user can press the Esc (escape) key to cancel the operation. Pressing the Esc key closes the data entry line and clears any data already entered. Menu options and dialog boxes can be closed in the same way.

A standard screen display usually holds about 20 rows of a worksheet, but worksheets with more rows may, of course, be built. The character size (font) selected by the user determines the number of rows displayed on the screen. Scrolling the worksheet up and down enables the user to view different sections of it when a large number of rows are involved.

Similarly, the screen may not accommodate viewing all columns in a worksheet. Usually, fewer than ten columns may be displayed at one time, depending on the column width. Cursor control can instruct the computer to scroll the display from side to side to permit viewing of different column sections. For example, since Terri wanted to include actual expenses for each month, the entire worksheet will not fit on the screen. To view different sections, she would use the cursor control keys or mouse to scroll to the left and right.

In addition to horizontal and vertical scrolling, spreadsheet packages provide windowing capabilities. *Windows* display two or more separate sections of a worksheet on a single screen (see Figure 5.5). In other words, columns or rows that are not adjoined can be viewed at once. Spreadsheet users can work in either window to change cell values or to enter new formulas.

Sometimes the user needs to freeze a row or column of labels on the screen. For example, Terri locks column A in the Budget worksheet to keep the row labels (Administration, Facility Rental, etc.) on the screen when she scrolls to the right. This feature is called **title locking.** Like the windowing feature, title locking allows the user to display nonadjoining columns and rows on the screen. It is different from windowing because the user cannot make changes in the locked columns or rows.

When a worksheet fills hundreds of columns and rows, it becomes difficult to manage. Many spreadsheet packages offer **three-dimensional worksheets** as an alternative to organizing data in a single worksheet. Think of a three-dimensional worksheet as an address book with multiple pages, each with its own tab as shown in Figure 5.7. Each page contains a complete worksheet. The user now organizes related data on different pages instead of in different locations within the same worksheet. Terri enters the operating budget approved by the board of directors on page A and changes the page tab to ACTUAL. She copies this information to page B for use in "What if?" budget scenarios and labels the page tab EXPECTED (see Figure 5.7). With this multidimensional worksheet she can easily switch between the two pages to compare actual with expected costs.

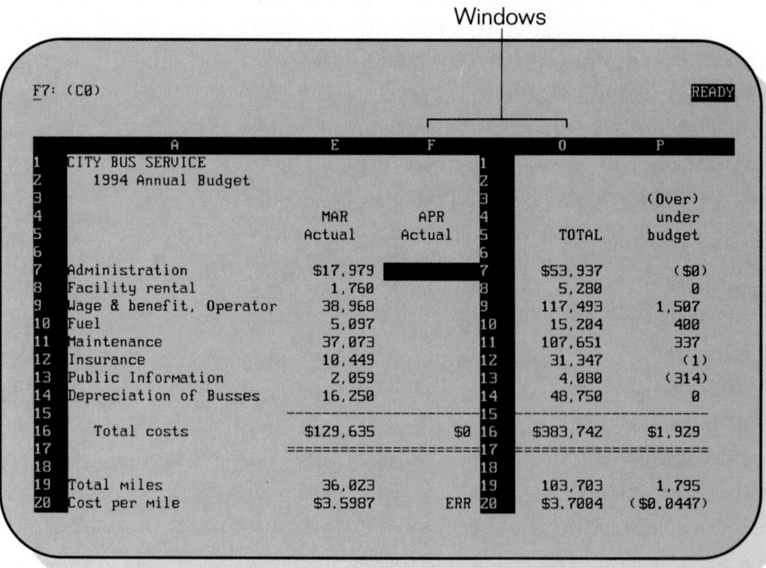

FIGURE 5.5
Since the entire annual budget cannot fit on the screen, windows are used to display nonadjoining columns.

Common Spreadsheet Operations

The software Terri is using has many options available to help her build a worksheet. With these operations she designs a worksheet format, puts values into the cells, makes changes, and prints the results. Commands and operations used to conduct these spreadsheet activities are listed in Figure 5.6.

Common Spreadsheet Operations

COPY (AND PASTE)	Duplicate contents of selected cells into other worksheet columns or rows
DATA ENTRY	Input data and formula into an active cell
DELETE	Remove a row or column along with associated data and formulas
ERASE	Remove a designated worksheet from disk
FIND	Locate a designated label, value, or cell reference
FORMAT	Format column widths, fonts, and other worksheet display features
INSERT	Add new rows or columns
MOVE (CUT AND PASTE)	Change location of data or formula within a worksheet
PRINT	Output a worksheet to printer
PROTECT	Designate a worksheet or selected cells as read-only
QUIT	Return software control to the operating system
RETRIEVE	Copy a designated worksheet from disk into the computer's memory
SAVE	Store a worksheet on disk, using designated file-name
SEARCH & REPLACE	Locate and change designated data or formula
UNDO	Cancel last deletion

FIGURE 5.6
Every electronic spreadsheet performs these common operations.

Input

In building her worksheet, Terri inputs three types of information in the cells: labels, values, and formulas. Initially, the labels were on rows and columns to help Terri know where to put numeric values and formulas. In many spreadsheet packages any data that starts with a letter is considered a **label.** Labels are not used in calculations. If a user wanted a label containing just numbers, a special **label prefix** symbol (", ', or ^) would have to precede the numeric data. These label prefixes also determine the label's placement within the cell as shown in Figure 5.7.

Numeric data or **values** can be entered into any cell. As with numeric data, only minus signs and decimal points can be included with the numbers. Other symbols, such as dollar signs and commas, are controlled by the format feature explained later.

Dates are also treated as values. Each spreadsheet has assigned some date in the past the number 1 and sequentially numbers each day since then. January 1, 1994, might be assigned the number 16000. In this case, 16001 is January 2, 1994. The worksheet displays January 1, 1994, or 1/1/94, but internally the date is stored as 16000. This technique allows the spreadsheet to easily account for leap years. Furthermore, it simplifies the situation in which the spreadsheet must determine a date for 30 days past some due date. Libraries and many businesses use dates in this way for their accounting and inventory control systems.

When Terri wanted to find the total cost of the 1994 budget, she entered a formula into cell B16. Typically, formulas allow the user to add, subtract, multiply, or divide any values found in the spreadsheet, as shown in Figure 5.7. Symbols that commonly are

Formula with @SUM Function

Lotus 1-2-3 Release 4 - [CITYBUS.WK3]

File Edit View Style Tools Range Window Help

B:B16 @SUM(B7..B14)

Tabs for worksheets — ACTUAL EXPECTED C D E New Sheet

A2: ^Expected Budget

F4: "APR

A16: 'Total Costs

B	A	B	C	D	E	F
1	*CITY BUS SERVICE*					
2	Expected Budget					
3		Annual				
4		operating	JAN	FEB	MAR	APR
5		budget	Expected	Expected	Expected	Expected
6						
7	Administration	215,749	17,979	17,979	17,979	17,979
8	Facility rental	21,120	1,760	1,760	1,760	1,760
9	Wage & Benefit, Operator	476,000	40,427	36,515	40,427	39,123
10	Fuel	62,416	ERR	ERR	ERR	ERR
11	Maintenance	431,952	36,686	33,136	36,686	35,503
12	Insurance	125,384	ERR	ERR	ERR	ERR
13	Public Information	15,064	1,255	1,255	1,255	1,255
14	Depreciation of Buses	195,000	16,250	16,250	16,250	16,250
15						
16	Total Costs	1,542,685	ERR	124,461	ERR	ERR
17						
18	***Cost Adjustments***					
19	*Fuel:*	5%				
20	*Insurance:*	20%				

, Comma 0 Arial 12 04/29/94 11:52 AM Ready

FIGURE 5.7
Three-dimensional worksheets layer several hundred worksheets on top of one another. Users display different worksheet pages by selecting the associated page tab.

used to signify these arithmetic operations include the plus sign (+) indicating addition, the minus sign (−) indicating substraction, the asterisk (*) indicating multiplication, and the slash mark (/) indicating division. Formulas start with either a number or an arithmetic operator. One way to display the total annual operating budget would be to enter this formula into cell B16:

$$+ B7 + B8 + B9 + B10 + B11 + B12 + B13 + B14$$

Once the formula is entered into the cell, the spreadsheet displays the results in the worksheet. While the worksheet displays the numeric value $1,542,685, the content of the cell is still a formula. If Terri changes the value in B7, the displayed value in B16 is automatically recalculated because it is based on a formula that uses B7.

Another symbol used by most spreadsheets is the "at" mark (@). Depending on the particular software package, the @ symbol identifies a built-in **function** that performs a common mathematical operation like summing or averaging a column of numbers. In Figure 5.7, Terri totals the expenses in column B by using this function: @SUM(B7..B14).

In this example a common notation is used to identify the cells to use in column B (B7..B14). A **range** or block of cells is defined by the first and last cells in the group. In this case the range is defined by the first cell in the column to be used (Administration costs in cell B7) and the last cell in the group (Depreciation of Buses in cell B14). Depending on the spreadsheet package, one period, two periods, or a colon separates the cell addresses. Using a range in a formula keeps it from becoming long and complicated. A range of cells in a worksheet can even be given its own unique *range name*. For example, Total-costs for the range B7..B17 and Jan-Costs for the range C7..C14 would be acceptable range names. Range names help users identify common blocks of data and minimize mistakes created by leaving out cells when copying or moving data ranges.

Most spreadsheets are equipped with functions that perform common statistical computations like averages (@AVG) or a count of the number of entries within a range of cells (@COUNT). These packages also include advanced mathematical or statistical calculations such as finding trigonometric values, square roots, and standard deviations (see Figure 5.8). Other spreadsheet functions are used to identify maximum and minimum values or to generate random numbers.

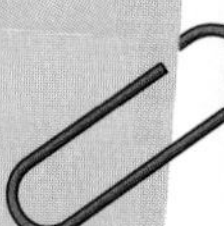

Advanced Mathematical Functions

Function	Description
@ABS	Absolute value
@AVG	Average of a set of numbers
@COS	Cosine of number
@COUNT	Count of the numbers in list
@EXP	Exponent of number
@FV	Future value of payment
@INT	Integer component of number
@IRR	Internal rate of return
@LN	Base x log of number
@LOG	Base 10 log of number
@MAX	Maximun value in list of numbers
@MIN	Minimum value in list of numbers
@RAND	Random number generator
@NPV	Net present value
@PMT	Monthly mortgage payment
@PV	Present values
@SIN	Sine of number
@SQR	Square root of number
@STD	Standard deviation of list of numbers
@TAN	Tangent of number
@VAR	Variance between list of numbers

FIGURE 5.8
Electronic spreadsheet programs have a variety of advanced mathematical functions available to the user.

Format

Most spreadsheet programs have a default format consisting of a certain number of rows and columns, and set column widths. The spreadsheet will use this standard format form unless the user requests a change. Typically, the user requests the *Format* feature to change these default display values. For example, in Figure 5.3 Terri prepared her worksheet for a 12-month period. In it she used 16 columns: one for row labels, one for each of the 12 months, two for totals, and one for the amount over/under budget. The size of each cell differs with the type of data it contains. Terri increased the default size for cells that contain labels. Since the default column width allows only nine characters, Terri increased the width in the first column. This lets her use longer labels like "Administration" and "Depreciation of Buses".

A new generation of spreadsheets now incorporates many of the text formatting features found in word processing and desktop publishing. The user can control the type size and style along with accenting important data in bold, italics, or through underlining. In Terri's case all of the worksheet columns contain numbers, except the first, which contains labels. The numbers throughout this worksheet reflect money. Terri uses the spreadsheet's global format feature to override the default format to display all numbers rounded to the nearest dollar, that is, no decimal places. Global in this case means the format is changed for all worksheet cells. She also selectively changes how values are displayed in the Total cost row (row 16). By using the range format feature, she changes the display for row 16 to the currency format. As shown in Figure 5.7, this display format precedes each number with a dollar sign ($). A partial list of the display formats for labels and values is shown in Figure 5.9.

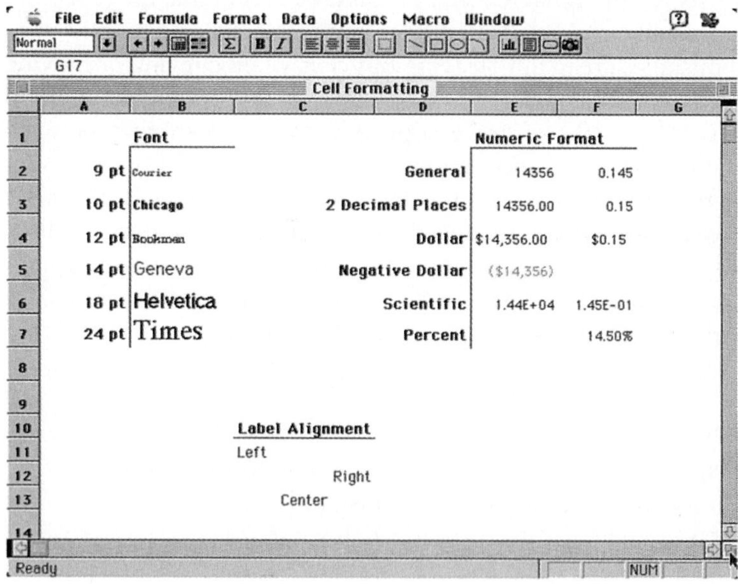

FIGURE 5.9
A spreadsheet's formatting feature allows users a great deal of control over the look of worksheet labels and values.

Move and Copy

Flexibility is a key feature of spreadsheets. For this reason most spreadsheets provide features that transfer data. The *Move* operation, as its name indicates, allows the user to change the location of data or a formula to another spreadsheet cell. Some spreadsheets use the term *Cut and Paste* instead of Move.

The *Copy* operation duplicates the contents of a single cell, row, or column at another position in the worksheet. Each of these operations spares the user the trouble—and the risk of error—involved in re-entering data and formulas. Both the Move and Copy commands can work with ranges of cells. For example, Terri wants to make a copy of the entire annual budget and rework it to reflect the expected budget. This range of cells, with all data, labels, and formulas, is then copied to the next worksheet page. The copy is now available for her to modify.

Copying a cell or range of cells creates a problem. When a cell reference is copied, should cell addresses in a formula stay the same or reflect the change in worksheet location? The solution has been to create two types of cell references. An *absolute cell reference* does not change when moved to a new cell address. When a *relative cell reference* is used, the cell address does change to maintain the relationship represented in the original formula.

To clarify the distinction between absolute and relative cell references, take a close look at the City Bus Service worksheet in Figure 5.7. To compute the bus company's expected January costs, Terri entered the formula @sum(C7..C14) into cell C16. In other words, all of the cells in column C associated with Administration, Facility Rentals, etc., are added together and put into the row for Total Costs (row 16). To save time, Terri copies this formula to the other Total cost cells in row 16. She uses the relative cell reference @sum (*C7..C14*) because the copy should change to reflect the column in which it is located. Therefore, the copy in cell D16 is @sum(D7..D14), which displays the Total costs for February.

Absolute cell references are used when the same cell needs to be used no matter where a formula is copied. The formulas for expected costs all use the budgeted amount for annual operations in column B. To figure expected Administration costs, the annual budget in B7 is divided by 12. The formula +$B$7/12 is entered into cell C7 to reflect administration costs for January. Terri saves time by copying this formula to the remaining cells for February to December. However, she does not want the reference to cell B7 to change and uses a dollar sign to identify the cell row ($B) and column ($7) as absolute. The formula Terri enters into cell C7 and copies to D7..N7 includes the absolute cell address $B$7.

Insert, Delete, and Undo

As the uses for a worksheet expand, row and column requirements are likely to change. The Insert and Delete operations enable the user to modify a worksheet without re-entering the entire file. The *Insert* operation allows the user to place a blank row or column at any point in the worksheet. The *Delete* operation removes rows or columns from an existing worksheet. For example, as Terri modifies the expected budget worksheet she recently copied from the annual budget, she may want to delete the last columns (Total and Over/Under Budget), now inappropriate (Figure 5.10).

Electronic spreadsheets also offer users an *Undo* feature. This feature allows users to recall data that was erased when deleting a cell, row, column, or range of data. To support this feature, the electronic spreadsheet temporarily stores deleted data in memory. The user can recall this data by selecting the appropriate menu option. However, this data is permanently lost when other data is deleted and takes its place in temporary memory.

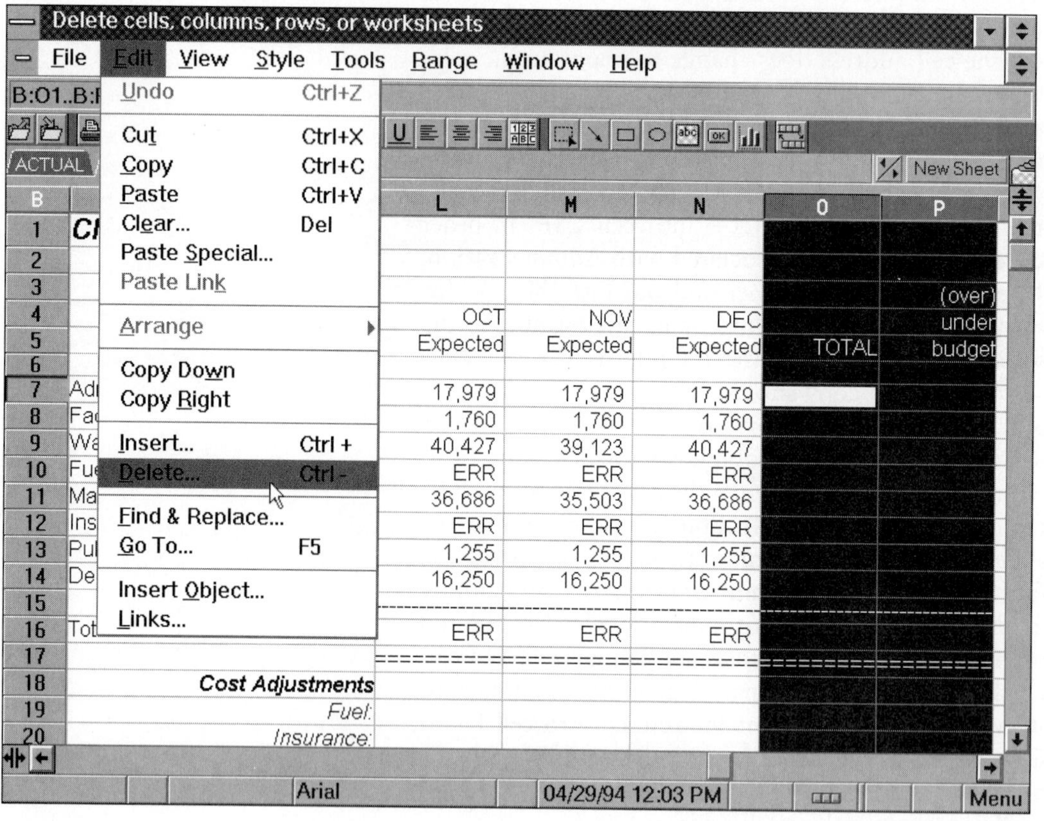

FIGURE 5.10
Spreadsheet users can easily delete selected rows or columns.

Find and Search/Replace

When large worksheets need to be modified, users can locate specific labels, values, or cell references with the *Find* feature. The *Search and Replace* feature is used when data values or formula entries need to be changed. Search and replace features offer global and discretionary replaces. Users are asked to confirm each replacement when a discretionary replace is activated. Global replaces automatically change values without further user involvement.

Save and Retrieve

Worksheets are stored on disk as part of an electronic spreadsheet's *Save* feature. This feature is sometimes referred to as filing a worksheet. Stored spreadsheet files can be recalled at a later date for further use. This procedure—bringing a saved file to the screen for revision and processing—is accomplished with the *Retrieve* feature. A saved worksheet can be retrieved, changed, and saved under the original filename.

Sometimes a modified worksheet is saved under a new filename. Users then retain both the original and the changed versions of the worksheet file. This is one method for creating several "What if?" scenarios. A worksheet that is similar in format to an existing worksheet is modified to examine a specific "What if?" condition and saved under a new name. The new version can then be modified in different ways, leaving the original intact for comparisons.

Electronic spreadsheet users often become so involved with their work, they forget to save their worksheets. Forgetting to periodically save their work to disk leaves them vulnerable to losing their data if the system crashes or a power failure occurs. As a result, many spreadsheet packages offer a **timed backup** feature. This feature automatically saves the active worksheet to disk after a specific amount of time has passed. The user can turn this feature off or adjust the amount of time that elapses before the worksheet is saved again.

Print

Printouts can be useful in examining expansive worksheets that extend beyond the screen's limits. Instead of scrolling the worksheet from section to section, the City Bus manager can have a printed version of the entire worksheet to take home for late night work.

A hard copy of the worksheet can be obtained by initiating the *Print* operation. Terri LaFriend has two printing orientations to select from: portrait (vertical) and landscape (horizontal). She can request a printout of a spreadsheet file that has been saved to disk, or she can print the spreadsheet currently in main memory.

Users have the option of adding headings, footings, and borders to a worksheet as it is printed. The report title, current date, page number, or worksheet filename could be added to a heading or footing to help organize multiple-page reports. A *border* is a row or column from the worksheet that needs to be printed on every page. Terri creates a border by using the labels in column A. These labels (Administration, Facility rental, etc.) and the heading (First Quarter) are then printed on each page of the budget as shown in Figure 5.11.

Protect

To prevent accidental erasure of data, many spreadsheet packages include a *Protect* function. Data from protected worksheet cells can be accessed, but not overwritten. A user/developer might protect specific labels and numeric constants, while leaving other cells unprotected. Fellow workers and friends can then use the worksheet, but are limited to entering data into the unprotected cells.

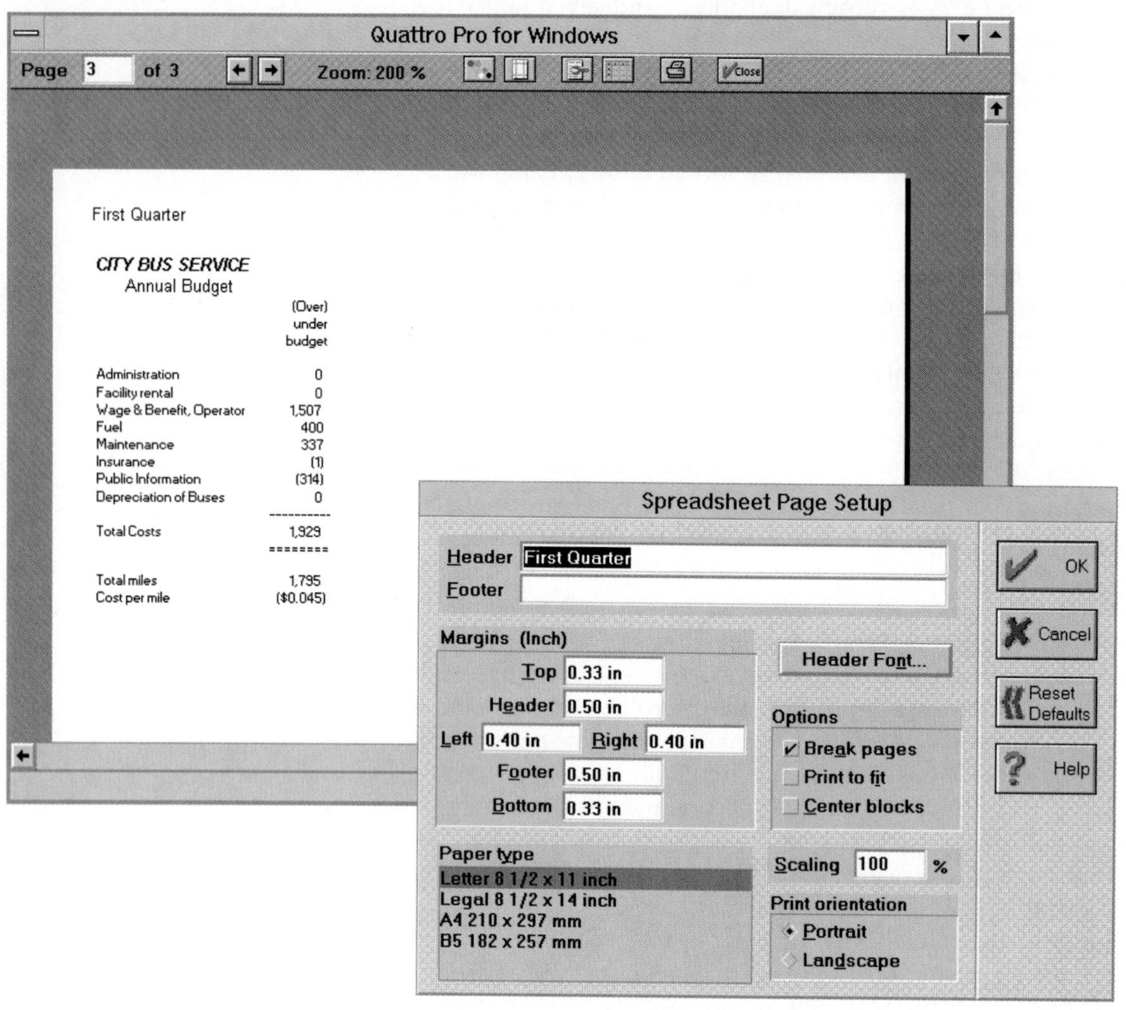

FIGURE 5.11
In this WYSIWYG preview of the printed worksheet, the border (column A labels) and the heading (First Quarter) print on every page.

Users can also *password-protect* a worksheet file. When anyone tries to retrieve a password-protected file, the spreadsheet asks for the unique password. If the user cannot provide the password, then the spreadsheet denies access to the worksheet file.

Erase

When a worksheet is no longer needed, the user may wish to erase the file from disk or tape. The *Erase* operation is used to remove the entire file. Usually, spreadsheet software requires a double-check before erasing a file. That is, once the user requests removal of a worksheet, the system generates a prompt, asking for verification of the request. This confirmation feature helps prevent the accidental deletion of a worksheet due to mistyping.

Terri updates the budget worksheet at the end of each month, then stores both the old and new versions on disk, using different filenames. After a few months several versions of a single worksheet will accumulate in storage. To rid storage space of this clutter, she retains only the two most recent copies of a worksheet. The rest are eliminated with the Erase feature.

Quit

To exit a spreadsheet program after a processing session, the *Quit* command is used. Quitting is sometimes referred to as Exiting. This spreadsheet operation usually returns computer control back to the operating system. In integrated software, however, the Quit function may produce a menu listing all available programs in the package. From there the user may begin another processing task or return to the operating system.

Combining Operations with Macros

The operations described previously can be combined to create extremely complex worksheets. Furthermore, in developing large spreadsheets users often need to repeat the same combination of operations. As a result, many electronic spreadsheets allow users to create **macros** that recall a series of related operations by using a menu or through a few simple keystrokes. Macros are like small programs that users build into their worksheets. When the user presses the designated keys, the electronic spreadsheet activates the macro and executes the associated operations.

Macros can be used for a wide variety of purposes. For example, users can create macros that add and average numbers in any given set of cells or print selected parts of the worksheet on the printer. To activate these functions could require the user to enter a dozen or more keystrokes. However, once installed as macros, a few keystrokes such as /XA or Ctrl + Alt + P can call them into action.

Expanded Uses of Worksheet Data

As part of an integrated software package, the electronic spreadsheet becomes an extremely powerful processing tool. Teamed with word processing, database, graphics programs, and networks, spreadsheets give and receive a boost in processing power. With word processing, for example, Terri does not have to re-enter the budget data because she can easily insert part of the budget worksheet into the Quarterly Budget report.

Developing the worksheet itself can be an automated process with certain spreadsheet-database linkups. Users can instruct the computer to import data from a database into specified worksheet locations. The computer reads the database file, finds the selected data fields, and duplicates them into worksheet cells. This capability increases personal productivity because the user is spared from re-entering data.

With connections to a network, worksheets can be built with data from distant files and databases. Additionally, completed worksheets can be transmitted over communication lines between users at multiple locations. For example, local branch offices of a bank would prepare their budgets on a personal computer-based spreadsheet program and send them electronically to the main office. The budget director would check them with a compatible mainframe-based spreadsheet and transmit the budget worksheets back to the branches with suggestions. One advantage is that all branch budgets are in the same format and can easily be compared to one another. Budgets prepared in the morning can be in the director's hands before lunch.

Completed worksheets also can be used to generate graphics. Many spreadsheet programs allow spreadsheet data to be displayed as presentation graphics, such as bar graphs or pie charts. The worksheet data can also be **exported** to a separate graphics program. Exporting is the opposite of importing. It describes a situation in which data is saved in file format that other software packages can use. In either case the user selects the option desired, then specifies which cells are to be reflected in the graphic. For example, the analysis of voters in a local election shown in Figure 5.12 was used to produce the pie chart. As pictured, the voters were broken into groups by age:

- 12 of the voters are between the ages of 18–30, inclusive.
- 28 of the voters are between the ages of 31–45, inclusive.
- 21 of the voters are between the ages of 46–60, inclusive.
- 39 of the voters are over the age of 60.

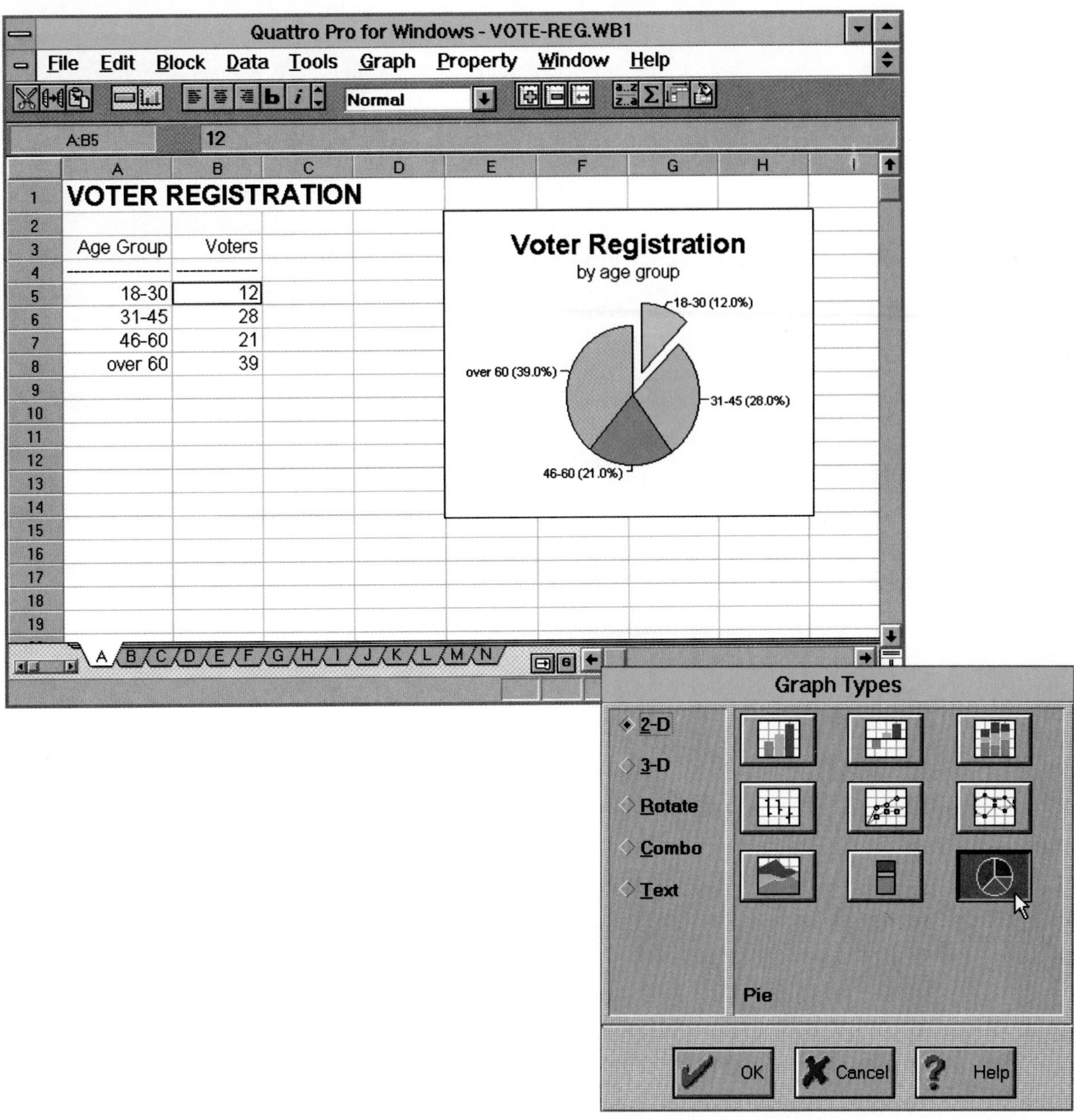

FIGURE 5.12
Presentation graphics, such as this pie chart, add visual interest to a worksheet.

As Figure 5.12 illustrates, these numbers were translated into percentages and presented in graphic form. Each slice of the pie chart is proportional in size to the percentage it represents. The graphics generated with spreadsheet software may even be more accurate than hand-produced charts.

Who's Who

Daniel Bricklin (b. 1951)

Robert Frankston

Daniel Bricklin was in the Electrical Engineering/Computer Science Department at MIT when he met Robert Frankston in 1973. Together they worked on an early word processing program, WPS-8. While attending Harvard Graduate School of Business, Bricklin and Frankston were looking for a way to do accounting procedures on a computer. After a long search, they decided to arrange a grid of cells into rows and columns. Cells at the intersection of each row and column took on the column letter and row number as a reference. Their product, written in Frankston's attic and called Visicalc, was not, at first, a popular program. The two joined with publisher Dan Fylstra of Personal Software to form Visicorp. The group was unsuccessful in trying to sell Visicalc to large microcomputer manufacturers like Apple and Altair. However, after placing an advertisement in the May 1979 issue of BYTE magazine, the software gained prominence. Legal issues led to the split-up of Visicorp. However, the ideas Visicalc represented became a standard for later spreadsheets like Lotus 1-2-3. Bricklin later worked for a time at Lotus Corporation.

SPREADSHEETS AS A TOOL

Many uses exist for spreadsheets besides business applications. Any situation where groups of numbers must be organized and analyzed would be a good place for a spreadsheet. A variety of electronic spreadsheet packages are available. Most of them use either a shell or a graphical user interface. Figure 5.13 overviews software features you should look for when purchasing an electronic spreadsheet.

Personal Applications

Budgets are not the only application in the home for spreadsheets. Financial planning—including mortgages, insurance, and purchase of stocks—can be assisted by worksheet manipulation. People interested in retirement or vacation planning can ask "What if?" ques-

User Needs

Expected size of largest worksheets
- ___ rows ___ columns

File integration
- ___ imports different file formats: ___ exports different file formats:

___ Three-dimensional (3D) worksheets
___ Find and Search/Replace operations
___ Support macros
___ Presentation graphics
- ___ 2D and 3D ___ drawing features
- ___ allows special annotations ___ others:

Special formats
- ___ foreign currency symbols: ___ different date presentations:
- ___ mathematics symbols: ___ others:

User interface
- ___ command-driven ___ shell (menus) ___ graphical

___ Timed backups
___ Worksheets with password protection
___ Title locking and windows
___ Turn off/on automatic recalulation operation

Technical Support	**Hardware Requirements**
___ Local training available	___ Compatible with your computer
___ schools:	Minimums
___ computer stores:	___ memory
___ users groups:	___ disk space
___ other:	Peripheral support
___ Context-sensitive help screens	___ mouse
___ Easy-to-read manual	___ printer
___ Tutorials for beginners	___ color monitor
___ Telephone support	
___ toll free	
___ at your expense	

FIGURE 5.13
Hardware requirements and personal needs must both be considered when purchasing an electronic spreadsheet package.

tions on the computer. The results can help them to determine how present activities will affect their retirement income or vacation.

Electronic spreadsheets also can be used to itemize home inventories for insurance purposes. Hobbyists with large collections also can maintain current inventories of items and compute their collection's present and future values. People watching their weight can use a spreadsheet to count calories and help with menu planning.

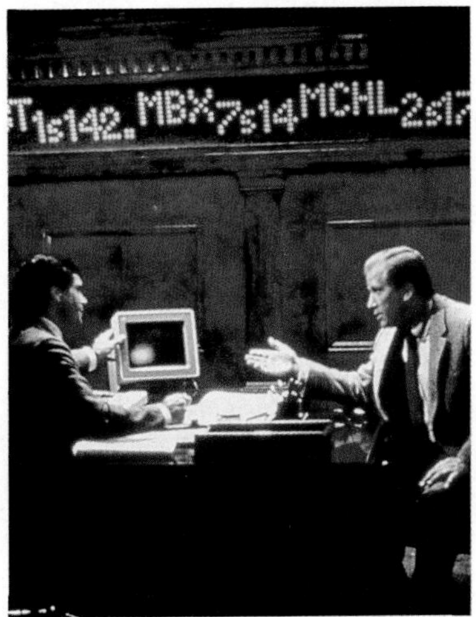

FIGURE 5.14
Electronic spreadsheets support such personal applications as financial planning.

Volunteer Activities

Many of the spreadsheet applications in business also can apply to volunteer activities. Budgets, membership dues, and hours of volunteer time contributed by members can be tracked and analyzed on a worksheet. What was once one of the most difficult duties of a club secretary or treasurer can be streamlined with the help of a personal computer and electronic spreadsheet.

Education

At schools, a large number of students must be enrolled, educated, and evaluated by relatively few teachers and administrators. Spreadsheets can be used to expedite these activities. Admissions personnel can use spreadsheets to keep track of the number of students in different majors or ethnic categories. This can aid in recruiting students. Financial aid available to a student can be calculated on a worksheet that contains the student's income and expenses, as well as money available from scholarships and loans.

Teachers can keep attendance records and grades by using a spreadsheet. The computation functions available on spreadsheets make weighting certain tests and dropping the lowest scores easy. They also aid in determining final grades.

Another advantage to using spreadsheets in education and other applications involves creating templates. A **template** is a predefined worksheet format containing labels and formulas but without data. It can be re-used many times to create worksheets for similar applications. For example, once a teacher establishes grading procedures for a course, a template can be created. This template is used each time the course is offered. The template is retrieved, individualized for a specific class, then saved under a different name. As a result the template remains unchanged and can be used again.

Athletics

Scoring any event from a local kids' soccer game to professional baseball can be enhanced by using a spreadsheet. Professionals and amateurs alike can benefit from the analysis of personal and team statistics. If you are in a bowling league, a computer with the help of a spreadsheet can figure your handicap, record pin totals over the season, and even compute league standings. In other sports, knowing what an individual has done in the past helps a coach anticipate what the athlete can do today. Spreadsheets also can be used to analyze opponents' performances for potential weaknesses.

Science

Scientists working in a variety of areas use electronic spreadsheets as a tool to help organize and analyze research data. For example, botanists interested in the effects of acid rain on local forests can take portable computers running electronic spreadsheets into the field. Data from randomly selected trees is entered and analyzed, using the advanced mathematical functions provided by the spreadsheet. These completed worksheets can then be shared with researchers from around the country through a network.

Electronic spreadsheets can be of special benefit to large research projects because of the standard row/column format. Once scientists have decided on the data they wish to collect, spreadsheets provide a common means of organizing and sharing the results. For example, public health officials monitoring a measles outbreak can use identical forms throughout the country to report data. It would then be easy to assemble and analyze the data on a regional basis.

Manufacturing

Spreadsheet programs will import data from almost any other application package as long as it is organized in a usable file format. Specialized design and manufacturing programs take advantage of a spreadsheet's versatility. An engineer may now use a graphics package to draw a three-dimensional part (see Figure 5.15). The design program partitions the drawing into small areas and stores relevant measurements of size in a file. When this data is put into a worksheet along with the prices of materials, the engineer can calculate the cost of the part very accurately. If the price of a particular raw material increases, the spreadsheet program allows easy updating of total costs.

FIGURE 5.15
Electronic spreadsheets can import materials lists from a graphic design file to compute cost of materials and break-even points.

A Closer Look...

Designing a Better Worksheet

Rows and columns of numbers can boggle the mind if not laid out in an easy-to-read manner. Furthermore, information presented in a worksheet is only as good as the numbers entered by the user. Good worksheet design draws the reader's eye to critical numbers.

Spreadsheets support decisions by making it easy to change critical variables to answer "What if?" questions. Good design also employs error checking for data entry mistakes. What follows are a few tips that will help you get the most from your electronic spreadsheet.

Q Are the headings and labels easy to understand?

A Do not use abbreviations. Complete words used as labels are easier to read and help new users understand worksheet dynamics.

C B SERVICES						
Expected						
		Month				
	ITEMS	1	2	3	4	5
Adm.	215749.00	17979.08	17979.08	17979.08	17979.08	17979.08
Facil. rent	21120.00	1760.00	1760.00	1760.00	1760.00	1760.00
W & B - Drivers	476000.00	40427.40	36515.07	40427.40	39123.29	40427.40
Fuel	62416.00	5301.08	4788.08	5301.08	5130.08	5301.08
Main.	431952.00	36686.33	33136.04	36686.33	35502.90	36686.33
Insur.	125384.00	10448.67	10448.67	10448.67	10448.67	10448.67
P R	15064.00	1255.33	1255.33	1255.33	1255.33	1255.33
Bus Deprec.	195000.00	16250.00	16250.00	16250.00	16250.00	16250.00
	----------	----------	----------	----------	----------	----------
Total:	1542685.00	130107.90	122132.27	130107.90	127449.36	130107.90
	==========	==========	==========	==========	==========	==========

Range name

JAN-COSTS

EXPECTED:C16	@SUM(JAN-COSTS)				
	A	B	C	D	E
1	***CITY BUS SERVICE***				
2	Expected Budget				
3		Annual			
4		operating	JAN	FEB	MAR
5		budget	Expected	Expected	Expected
6					
7	Administration	$215,749	$17,979	$17,979	$17,979
8	Facility rental	21,120	1,760	1,760	1,760
9	Wage & Benefit, Operator	476,000	40,427	36,515	40,427
10	Fuel	62,416	5,566	5,027	5,566
11	Maintenance	431,952	36,686	33,136	36,686
12	Insurance	125,384	12,538	12,538	12,538
13	Public Information	15,064	1,255	1,255	1,255
14	Depreciation of Buses	195,000	16,250	16,250	16,250
15		----------------------	--------------	--------------	--------------
16	Total Costs	$1,542,685	$132,463	$124,461	$132,463
17		=============	========	=========	=========
18	***Cost Adjustments***				
19	*Fuel:*	5%			
20	*Insurance:*	20%			

Isolated variables critical to "What if" questions

Q Did you isolate critical variables?

A Values that periodically change should be grouped into a specific area of the worksheet. This simplifies changes, reduces errors, and makes "What if?" questions easier to answer.

Q Did you use range names whenever possible?

A Range names help end-users identify related data and minimize copy or move errors involving large sets of data.

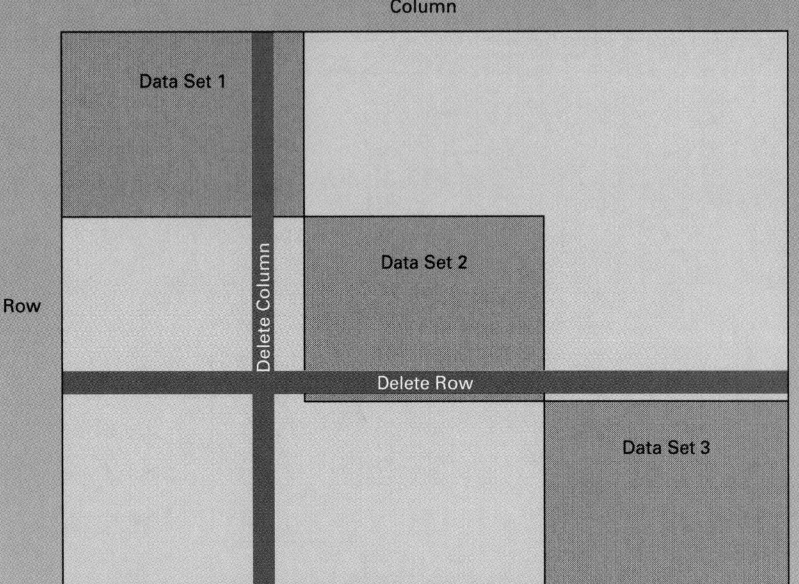

Diamond Design for Two-dimensional Worksheet

Q **Would deleting a row or column accidentally delete other data?**

A **Protecting critical formulas by making them read-only minimizes accidental deletions. Two-dimensional worksheet users arrange data into a diamond design to protect against this problem. This design principle states that data should not overlap the row or column of another data set.**

Checks for entries <0% or>100%

EXPECTED:C19 `@IF(B19>=0#AND#B19<=1," ","Error?")`

	A	B	C	D	E
7	Administration	$215,749	$17,979	$17,979	$17,979
8	Facility rental	21,120	1,760	1,760	1,760
9	Wage & Benefit, Operator	476,000	40,427	36,515	40,427
10	Fuel	62,416	37,108	33,517	37,108
11	Maintenance	431,952	36,686	33,136	36,686
12	Insurance	125,384	12,538	12,538	12,538
13	Public Information	15,064	1,255	1,255	1,255
14	Depreciation of Buses	195,000	16,250	16,250	16,250
15		----------------------	---------------	---------------	---------------
16	Total Costs	$1,542,685	$164,004	$152,950	$164,004
17		=============	=========		
18	**Cost Adjustments**				
19	*Fuel:*	600%	Erro		
20	*Insurance:*	20%			
21					

Q **Did you include error checks on input data?**

A **Every spreadsheet program can perform logical operations. In this example, an error message displays if data less than 0% or greater than 100% is entered. Error checks of this type help reduce data entry errors.**

EXPECTED:A1 'CITY BUS SERVICE

	A	B	C	D
1	***CITY BUS SERVICE***			
2	Expected Budget			
3		Annual		
4		operating	JAN	F
5		budget	Expected	Expec
6				
7	Administration	215749	+$B$7/12	+$B7/12
8	Facility rental	21120	+$B8/12	+$B8/12
9	Wage & Benefit, Operator	476000	+$B9/365*31	+$B9/365*28
10	Fuel	62416	(+$B10/365*31)*(1+$B$19)	(+$B10/365*28)*(1+$B$
11	Maintenance	431952	+$B11/365*31	+$B11/365*28
12	Insurance	125384	(+$B12/12)*(1+$B$20)	(+$B12/12)*(1+$B$20)
13	Public Information	15064	+$B13/12	+$B13/12
14	Depreciation of Buses	195000	+$B14/12	+$B14/12
15		-------------------	-------------------------------	-------------------------------
16	Total Costs	@SUM(B7..B14)	@SUM(JAN-COSTS)	@SUM(FEB-COSTS)
17		============	====================	==================
18	***Cost Adjustments***			
19	*Fuel:*	0.05	@IF(B19>=0#AND#	

ACTUAL / EXPECTED / C / D / E / F / G / H / I / J

Q **Did you have someone else audit the worksheet formulas?**

A **Spreadsheets will print cell/formula data as one of the printer or display options. Show this output to someone who can check it for errors.**

Q **Did you identify the author?**

A **Giving yourself credit covers several bets. First, it never hurts to have your name associated with a useful tool. Second, other users might benefit from knowing whom to contact for further clarifications. Adding the current date whenever changes are made is also recommended.**

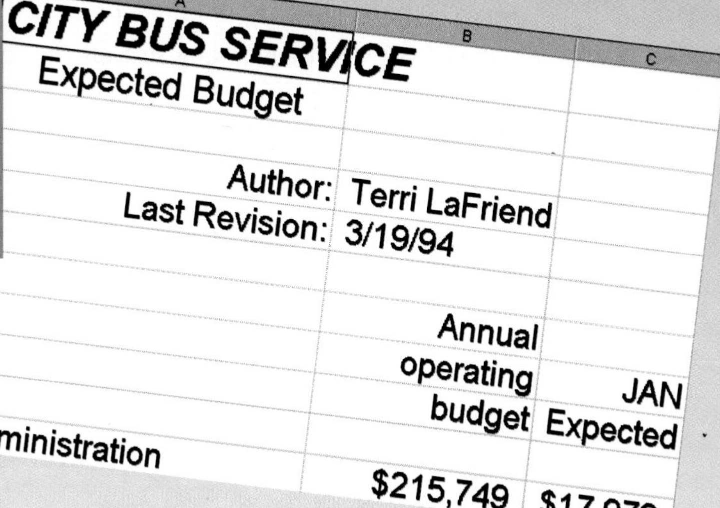

A
B
C
CITY BUS SERVICE
Expected Budget
Author: Terri LaFriend
Last Revision: 3/19/94
Annual
operating
budget
JAN
Expected
Administration
$215,749
$17,979

Chapter Facts

- An electronic spreadsheet is a tool for financial planning. For years managers have used worksheets in a paper-and-pencil form. The electronic spreadsheet allows easy alteration of data and uses the computer to perform calculations.
- An electronic worksheet is made up of horizontal rows and vertical columns, whose intersections are cells. The contents of cells can be labels, numeric values, and formulas.
- Each spreadsheet displays commands in a menu or icon bar, contains a status line to display the current operating mode, and has a data entry line to display the data before it is entered into the active cell.
- A worksheet can be subdivided into windows to display non-adjoining columns or rows. Users can freeze labels on the screen with the title-locking feature.
- Three-dimensional worksheets are stacked on top of one another like pages in an address book.
- Worksheets can be manipulated by using the variety of operations available with the spreadsheet software. They include data input, format, move, copy, insert, delete, undo, find, search and replace, save, retrieve, print, protect, erase, and quit.
- Built-in functions automatically compute a variety of financial and mathematical operations such as averages, sums, or loan payments. An @ symbol usually precedes the function name.
- Absolute references do not change when moved or copied. Relative references maintain the relationship represented in the original formula.
- Users create macros, which automatically initiate spreadsheet operations and functions.
- Data from many spreadsheets can be integrated with other software packages. It can be used with databases for easy data entry, with networks to send worksheets to remote users, and with graphics packages to display picture representations of the data.
- Applications for spreadsheets include uses in business, the home, schools, sports, volunteer activities, scientific research, manufacturing, and cost accounting.
- Good worksheet designs include descriptive labels, isolation of critical variables, use of range names, cross-checking of totals, and incorporation of error checking whenever possible.

Terms to Remember

a. cell
b. cell address
c. command menu
d. data entry line
e. export
f. functions
g. icon bar
h. label
i. label prefix
j. macro
k. range
l. status line
m. three-dimensional worksheets
n. timed backup
o. template
p. title locking
q. value
r. worksheet

Mix and Match

Match the following definitions to the Terms to Remember.

1. _____ a stored series of spreadsheet operations a user can activate by using a menu or by pressing a few keys.
2. _____ text that is used to describe a worksheet or worksheet data.
3. _____ freezing selected worksheet columns and/or rows on the screen.
4. _____ predefined formulas that perform common mathematical, financial, and logical operations.
5. _____ area of a worksheet where data and formulas are input.
6. _____ selection of icons that represent different electronic spreadsheet operations.
7. _____ a worksheet with labels and formulas, but no values.
8. _____ the column letter and row number of a specific worksheet cell.
9. _____ automatic saving of a file to disk after a designated amount of time has passed.
10. _____ special symbol (', ", ^, or \) that determines label's placement within a cell.
11. _____ related data organized into a row/column format.
12. _____ group of cells within a worksheet that are defined by the first and last cells in the block.

13. ____ saves data in a file format that enables other software packages to use it.
14. ____ series of worksheets visually stacked on top of one another.
15. ____ intersection of a single column and row on a worksheet.
16. ____ lists operations performed by an electronic spreadsheet.
17. ____ area of a worksheet that displays which operation is currently being performed by spreadsheet.
18. ____ numeric data within a worksheet.

Review Questions

1. What are two disadvantages to using paper-and-pencil worksheets?
2. What are two advantages to using electronic spreadsheets?
3. How does an electronic spreadsheet user change the active cell?
4. What keyboard key cancels the current spreadsheet operation?
5. How are windows used with an electronic spreadsheet?
6. Identify and briefly describe 15 common spreadsheet operations.
7. What three types of information are used by an electronic spreadsheet?
8. How are dates stored by an electronic spreadsheet?
9. How are range names used within a worksheet?
10. What is the difference between an electronic spreadsheet's global and range formatting features?
11. How is an absolute cell reference different from a relative cell reference?
12. What are two ways an electronic spreadsheet user can protect a worksheet?
13. What are the advantages to integrating worksheet data with a word-processed document, databases, network, or graphics programs?
14. What are the applications for electronic spreadsheets at home, with volunteer organizations, in school, in sports, as part of scientific analysis, and in manufacturing/design?
15. What are six features of good worksheet design?

Applying What You've Learned

1. Design a personal budget for a spreadsheet, using a template or graph paper. Include the number of rows and columns you will need, how each column will be labeled, and any formula required. List five "What if?" questions you would like to ask.
2. Use an actual spreadsheet to enter the budget you have designed in #1. Enter the proposed budget figures for the year. Enter the actual figures for last month (or an estimate). Save and print the worksheet. Then answer one of the "What if?" questions you listed. Print the modified worksheet.
3. For the following spreadsheet applications, list the labels that would appear on the rows and columns. Name three "What if?" questions for each that could be useful to the user.
   a. attendance records for a grade school class
   b. budget for the school computer center
   c. scoring a little league baseball game (or other sport)
   d. monitoring volunteers' hours at a local soup kitchen
   e. grades for your entire computer class
4. Examine a spreadsheet package in depth. Find the user's manual or description of one used in school, available in a retail store, or described in a magazine.
   a. Does it support three-dimensional worksheets? What is the maximum number of rows and columns allowed?
   b. What common file formats can it import and export?
   c. What functions can be used on the spreadsheet?
   d. How much memory and disk space does it require?
   e. With what kind of operating system does it work?
   f. What is its cost?
5. Applications for spreadsheets abound in many careers. Name five uses for a spreadsheet (not already mentioned in the text) that you would find useful now or in your future career.
6. Not all financial and numerical problems can be solved with a spreadsheet. Name three types of problems concerning numbers that would not be solved efficiently with a spreadsheet.

Answers to Mix and Match

1. j 2. h 3. p 4. f 5. d 6. g 7. o 8. b 9. n 10. i
11. r 12. k 13. e 14. m 15. a 16. c 17. l 18. q

6

Graphics and Multimedia

- From the User's Point of View
- Graphical Tools
  - Representing graphics and images
  - Types of computer graphics
- Presentation Graphics
  - Pie charts
  - Bar graphs
  - Line graphs
  - Area graphs
  - Symbol charts
  - Enhancing a graph
  - Creating presentation graphics
- Free-Drawing Graphics
  - The palette
  - The toolbox
  - Free-drawing utilities
- Multimedia
  - Visual data
  - Audio data
  - Animation
- Graphics and Multimedia Applications
  - Business/scientific presentations
  - Computer-aided design (CAD)
  - Computer imaging
  - Athletics and the perfoming arts
  - MIDI
  - Space exploration
- *A Closer Look . . . Presentation Software*

FROM THE USER'S POINT OF VIEW

Audio or visual features enhance the impact your ideas or information have when presenting them to others. In a competitive world, your work needs every edge it can get. The charts and diagrams of presentation graphics and the artistic results of free-drawing graphics can make a fact or idea more interesting to an audience. If you add the powerful tools of sound, music, voice, animation, and video, you have a **multimedia** presentation. Multimedia has revolutionized graphic arts, business presentations, educational technology, and the media. Knowing what graphics and multimedia tools are available and how to use them could make new opportunities available to you.

GRAPHICAL TOOLS

Pictures convey both information and ideas. Images provide a powerful source of information for many people and clearly communicate ideas that would be difficult or impossible to portray in words. For example:

- You can find your way far more easily with a road map than if you were given written directions.
- The popularity of educational TV reflects that people can use images to learn.
- Art collectors make paintings valuable by paying millions of dollars for selected works.
- An instant replay is more vivid and telling than thousands of words of narration by sportscasters.

Pictures have been used for communication ever since prehistoric people created drawings on cave walls in southern France. In recent years computers have been adopted as tools for graphic communication.

Representing Graphics and Images

As mentioned in Chapter 4, computer graphics are those drawings or charts that could be produced with a pen (and a lot of patience) on paper. They can be developed internally by using a spreadsheet or other software, or input with hardware like a mouse, joy stick, or keyboard. Images consist of visual data that is converted from another media, for example, film or video. Two approaches are used to display the graphics and images we see on a monitor.

Bit mapping, also called pixel graphics, treats a video screen, paper, or film as a pattern of tightly packed dots. Bit mapping means that each **pixel,** or picture element, has a separate memory position that is represented by a color or shade of gray, as seen in Figure 6.1. The total pattern of digitized pixels makes up a black-and-white or color illustration.

Vector graphics use a different type of software that allows continuous lines to be drawn between points on the screen. The graphics are stored as mathematical formulas. Connections are displayed as lines or curves, as in Figure 6.2. Vector graphic output is known as a line drawing. You will find vector graphics used in some video games. Engineers, architects, draftspeople, scientists, and others use vector graphics to create precise designs.

Computers actually recreate graphics and images through techniques that **digitize** the data. Digitizing is breaking an image into a binary code. Specialized input hardware, such as a *scanner,* digitizes an image by converting each pixel into a binary code that can be located on a row/column (x-y) coordinate scale.

Computer-generated images are everywhere. You are a user of computer graphics when you play a video game, watch a scoreboard at a stadium, or view an animated TV commercial. Blueprints, sales charts, and maps may be the result of computer-based processing. Computer graphics is a rapidly growing application area that will have a major impact on application and system software for some time to come.

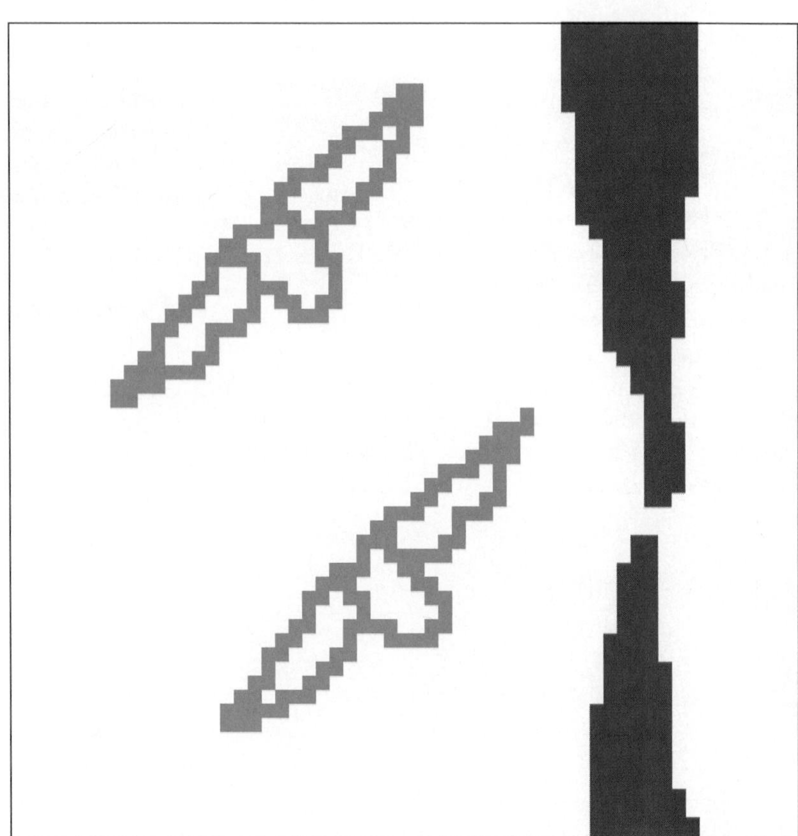

FIGURE 6.1
Bit-mapped graphics use thousands of pixels of varying colors to create an image.

FIGURE 6.2
The engineer is using a monitor that supports vector graphics to create a design for an oil-drilling platform.

Types of Computer Graphics

Many organizations make extensive use of **presentation graphics.** Business applications provide opportunities to use presentation graphics techniques to represent numeric data in standard formats. Bar graphs, pie charts, and other examples of presentation graphics are shown in Figures 6.4 through 6.7.

Computer graphics can also be used in a more artistic fashion. The computer can be viewed as a tool for drawing or creating graphics in much the same way as an artist uses canvas (Figure 6.9) or an architect uses a drafting table. These applications require **free-drawing graphics,** where the shapes, colors, and patterns are under the control of the user.

PRESENTATION GRAPHICS

Graphics are often used to produce visual support for written reports. In many cases information contained in large reports, taking hours to read, can be charted or graphed for better comprehension. The full, textual reports are still needed. By adding computer-produced graphics, you can make the important points of the report more apparent. Experience has shown that information presented through graphics is remembered better than written explanations.

Presentation graphics come in several forms. An architect might show projected costs over the lifetime of a building with a bar graph, while a researcher might show ethnic makeup of a city with a pie chart. However, most presentation graphics fall under one of five categories:

- Pie charts
- Bar graphs
- Line graphs
- Area graphs
- Symbol charts

Graphics provide a clear way of viewing individual and grouped statistics. The Panorama Music Company records and distributes tapes and compact disks for just a few recording artists. The sales manager, Stephanie Reboy, uses presentation graphics to show how

In the News...

TRENDS IN COMPUTER GRAPHICS MARKET

The computer graphics market is benefitting from several favorable trends:

■ **Graphical User Interfaces (GUIs)** With Microsoft and Apple shipping millions of GUIs each year, most major software vendors have introduced applications for use with GUIs. In turn, computer graphics is becoming a mainstream component technology.

■ **Multimedia** With the increased availability of GUIs, multimedia applications are finally becoming a reality. Most PCs shipped today are multimedia-ready, and authoring software is finally robust enough to support the growing demand.

■ **Imaging** Imaging is taking on a new life as multimedia applications create demand at the low end of the market and software enhancements create it at the high end. Companies are finally using imaging to gain a competitive advantage.

> *"Computer graphics is becoming a main-stream technology"*

■ **Color** As more and more computers come with color displays, and as digital color proofing and separation systems cut expensive steps out of the process of producing color output, colorization of more and more applications is inevitable.

ANNUAL SALES REPORT BY ARTIST AND AGE GROUP
(IN MILLION DOLLARS)

	AGE GROUP (YEARS)					
ARTIST	UNDER 17	17-25	26-35	36-50	OVER 50	TOTAL
LOOK 2 ME	22.2	25.3	9.5	3.7	0.2	60.9
ALBERTO MAVANI	0.1	0.3	1.3	14.6	37.3	53.6
FEATHERS	11.2	0.2	5.6	6.8	8.2	32.0
C. T. JONES	0.3	2.1	15.6	25.7	23.8	67.5
SEASONS	0.2	1.2	7.9	26.7	12.8	48.8
NEW TIMES	1.3	0.4	15.4	25.4	18.9	61.4
TOTAL	35.3	29.5	55.3	102.9	101.2	324.2

FIGURE 6.3
Presentation graphics software often uses data originally stored in spreadsheets or databases. The following figures use data from this spreadsheet.

individual artists contributed to total sales last year. A further breakdown of sales by age of customer explains the sources of income. Although data is kept on a spreadsheet (see Figure 6.3), Stephanie uses an integrated graphics package to create the graphics needed.

Pie Charts

The relative sizes of parts to a whole are illustrated in a **pie chart.** Pie charts derive their name from their shape, circles divided into wedges, like slices of a pie. Pie charts show percentages, proportions, or ratios of a total. Each wedge of the pie represents a certain portion of the whole. The sum of all the wedges is 100 percent.

After yearly sales figures were in, Stephanie used a pie chart to show each artist's contribution to the company's total sales, as seen in Figure 6.4 (left). Using another technique, slices of the pie can be separated from the main circle to create an **exploded pie chart.** Stephanie highlighted the sales of Look 2 Me, a pop music group, by using the exploded pie chart in Figure 6.4 (right).

FIGURE 6.4
These pie charts are derived from the annual sales spreadsheet in Figure 6.3. The pie chart on the right has been exploded to show one artist's sales in relation to the others.

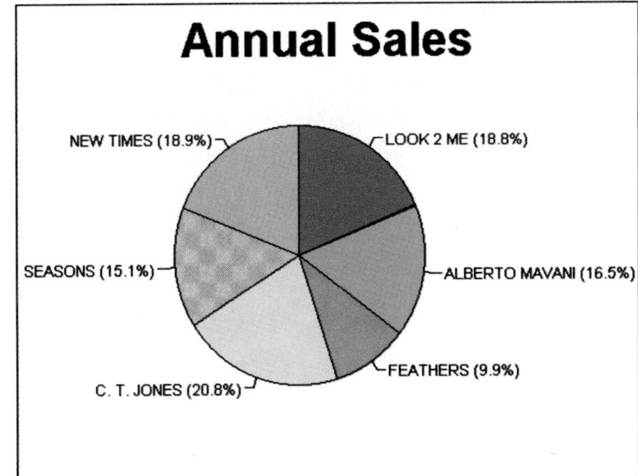

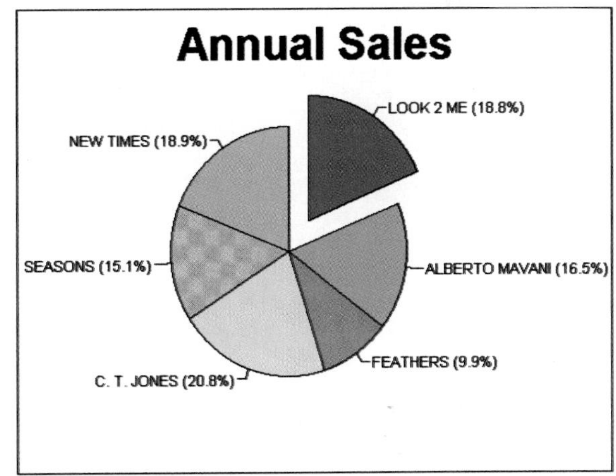

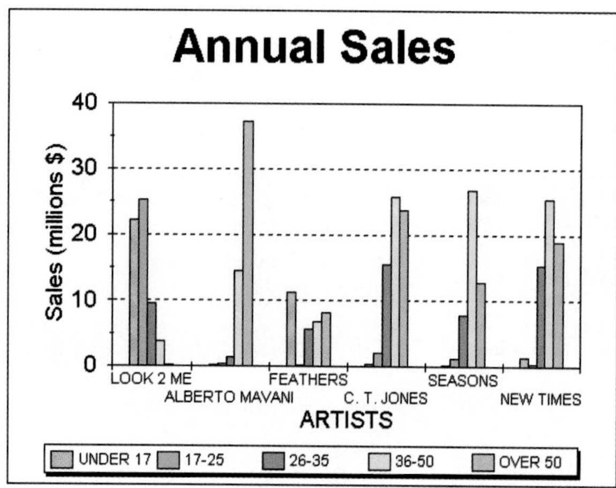

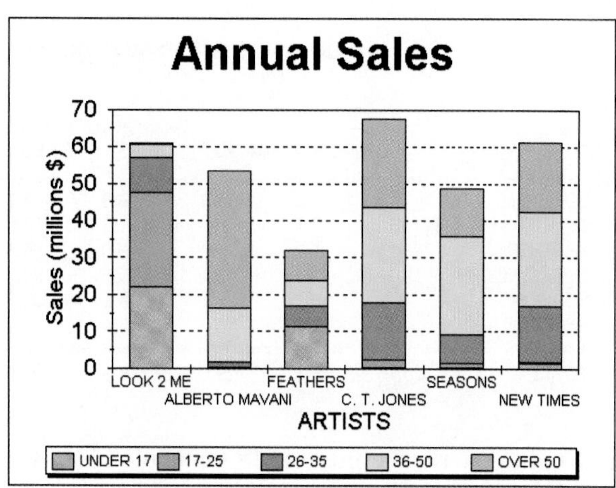

FIGURE 6.5
Bar charts provide a graphic basis for a direct comparison of values, like annual sales for each artist in each age group. Stacked bar charts show the composition of each bar's value.

Bar Graphs

Stephanie decided to present the sales of each recording artist, as compared to customer age group, with a **bar graph.** Bar charts, as bar graphs are also known, display numeric data as lines or bars of representative length. A bar chart conveys meaning through use of scales, or marked values, at the bottom or side of the graphic. For example, the bar graph in Figure 6.5 (left) shows how all artists compared in record sales by age groups. This bar graph is based on the same spreadsheet as the pie chart. From this graphic it is easy to see that Alberto Mavani is most popular with the over-50 age group while Look 2 Me had the majority of its sales in customer groups under age 25. The bottom scale, or set of labels for this bar chart, identifies the age groups. The scale at the left indicates the amount of sales in millions of dollars. Different shading helps to distinguish age groups.

When a bar graph shows the subcategories of a total within a single bar, it is known as a **stacked bar graph.** This type of graph is used when the data represented by each bar must be further divided. A pie chart can be represented as a single stacked bar graph. Figure 6.5 (right) also depicts a stacked bar graph, displaying the breakdown of each recording artist's sales by age group of customer. While the data is the same for both bar charts, the stacked bar graph clearly shows the accumulated sales for each artist, while the regular bar chart does not.

Line Graphs

Line graphs often show trends tracked over a period of time. Like bar charts, line graphs have two sets of scales, at the top or bottom and on one side. Traditionally, the horizontal scale reflects related categories or changes in time. For example, Figure 6.6 illustrates the

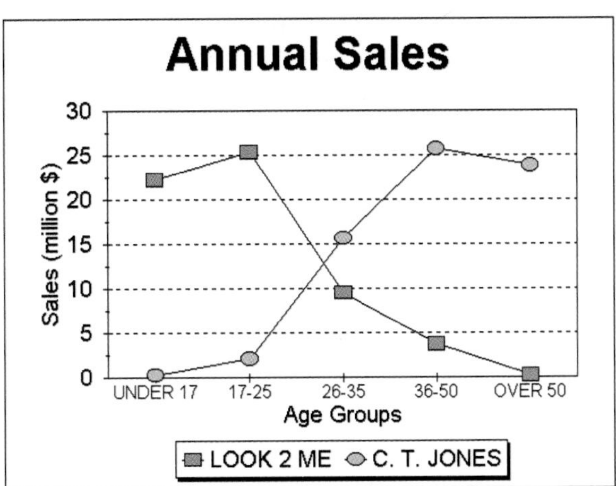

FIGURE 6.6
Line graphs are used to trace performance over time or to chart statistical trends.

sales for two recording artists, Look 2 Me and C. T. Jones, over the age groups. The data for each artist is indicated by a separate line containing a unique symbol or color. The legend at the bottom of the graph explains which artist's sales the symbol represents.

In the News...

PRESENTATION RULES OF THUMB

■ **Choose Your Medium Based on Audience Size** Use 35-mm slides for audiences of 20 or more, overhead transparencies for smaller groups.

■ **Use Handouts** Distribute copies of your visuals before beginning your presentation so your audience can follow along and leave with organized notes.

■ **Keep It Simple** Limit each page/slide to 50 words or two graphics. Label charts simply and clearly.

■ **Maintain Contrast** For example, dark text and brightly colored graphics set against a light background.

■ **Be Careful with Type** Limit your fonts to two; one for titles, another for subtitles and text. Lean toward sans serif fonts; they're more readable than serif fonts. Never use type smaller than 24 points.

■ **Double-Check Details** Save yourself a lot of time and grief and money by identifying problems while they're still easy and inexpensive to correct.

Good luck!

Some line graphs are also known as *x-y* graphs. In an *x-y* graph the horizontal and vertical scales represent continuous measurements, such as weight or time, rather than distinct categories like political parties or ethnic backgrounds. Since line graphs are used to show trends, the user must avoid showing too many lines on one graph because multiple lines might mask differences in the data.

Area Graphs

In an **area graph,** the space beneath a single-line graph is shaded in, showing a volume. In some fields, such as economics and mathematics, the actual value of this area may be significant. At other times the area is shown just for emphasis. An area graph can be seen in Figure 6.7.

Symbol Charts

A variety of other presentation graphics exist to help clarify data. *Symbol charts,* as shown in Figure 6.7, use colors and symbols to highlight data values. Maps with color-coded areas or exploded regions display a geographical arrangement of information. Flowcharts, hierarchy charts, and scatter diagrams are graphics for such specialized audiences as management or system analysts.

Enhancing a Graph

The five basic categories of presentation graphics can be presented in a variety of formats:

- Two-dimensional (2D)
- Three-dimensional (3D)
- Rotated
- Combined with other graphics

All of the graphic categories illustrated above were in two-dimensional format, usually involving horizontal and vertical scales. Three-dimensional pie charts are available to summarize a group of data. Like pie charts, bar graphs can be presented in a three-dimensional format to represent three levels of data, as seen in Figure 6.7. Bar graphs, traditionally presented as vertical columns, can be rotated into horizontal form. Many types of graphics can be combined to compare data in different formats.

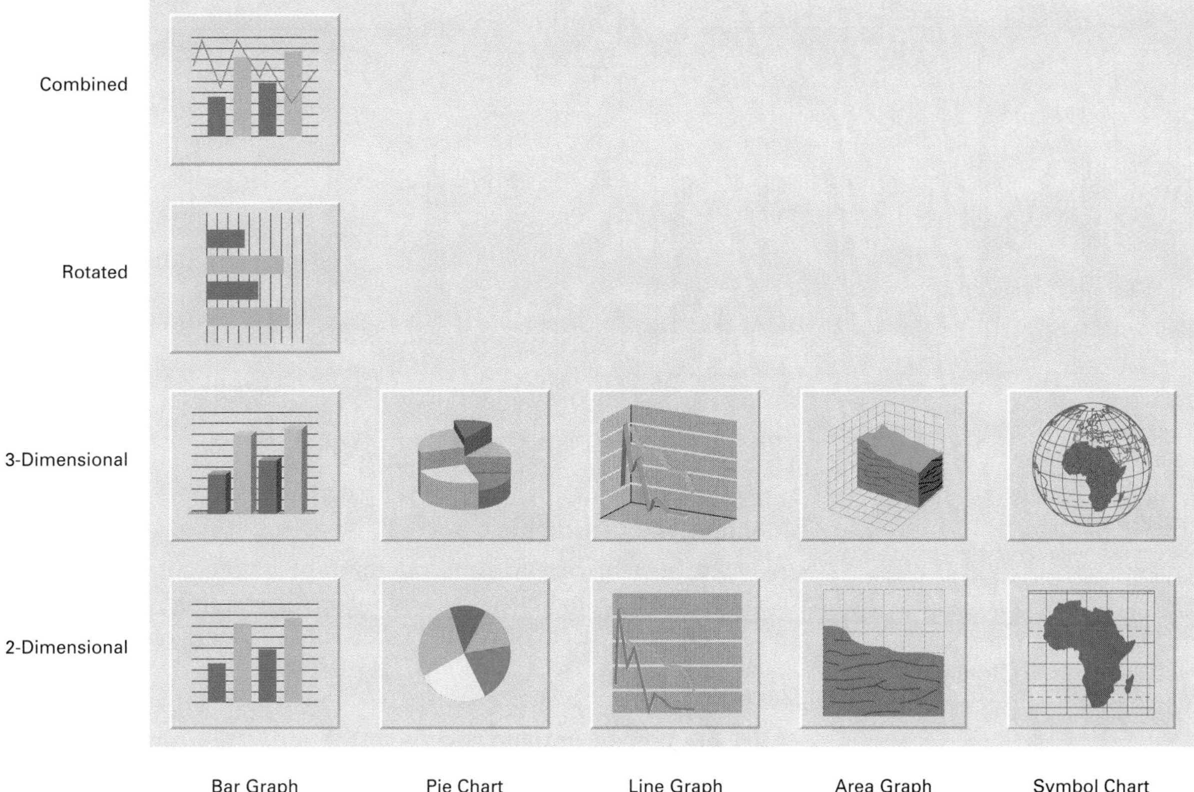

FIGURE 6.7
A variety of formats are available for presenting data accurately and in an interesting manner.

Care must be taken when combining graphics or using 3D formats. First, including too much data or creating too complex a graphic can reduce, not increase, the viewer's understanding. Also, it is possible when using 3D bar graphs to have lower values of a bar hidden behind higher bars. This unintentional but significant misrepresentation of the data relationships is also a potential problem with 3D line and area graphs.

Creating Presentation Graphics

Graphics software converts data values to points on a pattern or grid. Then it creates the digital patterns to produce output. Many application packages—such as desktop publishers, spreadsheets, statistical packages, and database programs—contain options that produce graphic output. Some graphics software will read files created by other software. Regardless of the software package and type of graphic, four levels of information are required to create presentation graphics.

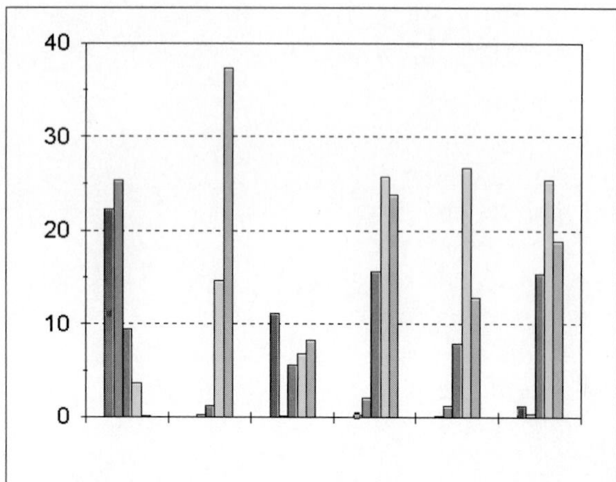

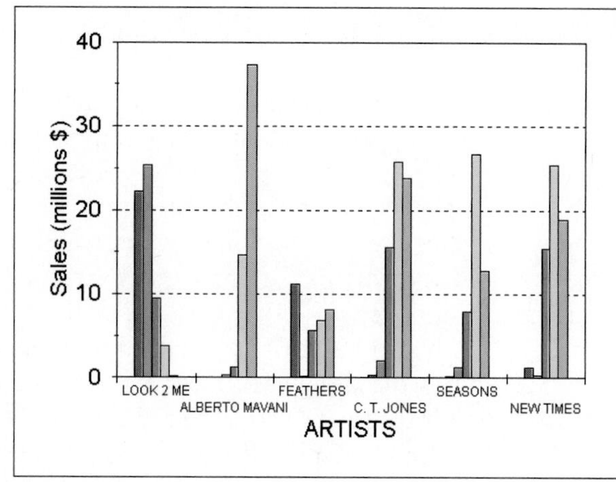

FIGURE 6.8
Care must be taken in designing and labeling images. The first bar graph, without labels and a meaningful scale, is difficult to read. The second graph, with labels, is easier to understand.

Identify Type of Graphic

A menu or icon is used to select the type of presentation graphic needed. When a pie chart is requested, for example, the program will prompt the user for related labels and the location of the data.

Identify Data

After the type of graphic is chosen, the software prompts the user for data. Sometimes this can be entered manually at the keyboard. If the data has been previously stored, the user does not need to re-enter it. Instead, the name of the file containing the data is entered. When only selected data from the file is needed, the user must specify which fields or records are included and how they are organized. At this point a graphic can be output. However, as shown in Figure 6.8 (left), there is little information to identify what the graphic represents.

Identify Labels

To clarify the meaning of the graphic, each scale must be labeled. These labels can be taken from the data file or entered by the user. In Figure 6.8 (right) the bottom scale came from the first column of the spreadsheet (Figure 6.3), containing names of the performing artists. The side scale, Sales (millions $), was entered by the user. In both cases the software sets scales based on the range of data values used. The user can manually reset these scales when necessary.

Create Titles and Legend

To complete the graphic, a title and legend may be included as shown in Figure 6.5. A title provides a general description of the output (like Annual Sales). Legends explain the specific meaning of any special symbols, colors, or shading found on the graphic. Titles and legends usually are prompted by the software and manually entered at the keyboard.

FREE-DRAWING GRAPHICS

Free-drawing graphics software aids the creative artist or engineer in producing high-quality, complex drawings. Although each free-drawing graphics package has unique capabilities to help the user, most have some features in common. After the free-drawing software is loaded, the user defines the work area, or canvas. In many packages this is done through an icon or menu selection. Usually, initial designs and menu selections are input with a mouse or a specialized drawing board called a tablet. Sometimes the design is imported from an external file. If the design extends longer or wider than the screen, scrolling takes place to move the screen display from position to position.

A variety of features are available for the large number of free-drawing graphics applications. Drawing options are displayed as icons in the palette and tool box (see Figure 6.9). Utility options are activated from drop-down menus.

Panorama Music Co. was pleased to hear that one of their clients, Look 2 Me, was selected to write and perform the theme song for a big-budget animated film, *Under the Earth*. They immediately subcontracted a graphic artist to create a design to be used in posters, advertisements, and the cover of the CD and tape releasing the song.

Rob Merrill is a graphics artist who uses free-drawing graphics for much of his work. By using a graphics package, Rob can easily change his design and store it in a file. After Rob has made some initial sketches, he loads an icon-driven graphics package into his personal computer.

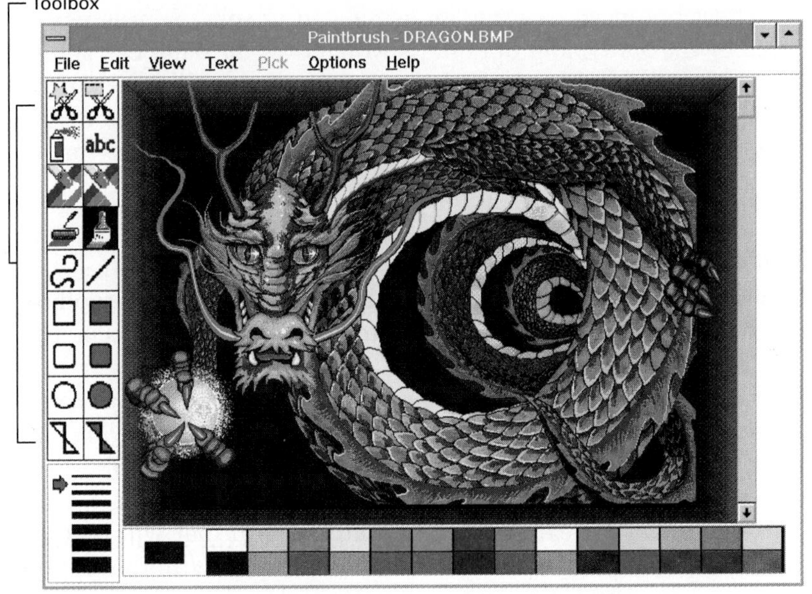

FIGURE 6.9
A graphic artist uses the palette and toolbox when drawing and selecting program options.

The Palette

The palette provides an opportunity for Rob to choose the colors, patterns, and shading needed in the design. Basic graphics palettes for color output may offer as few as three colors, but sophisticated packages can provide thousands of color choices. The palette may include patterns of dots, stripes, or lattices. The palette can also provide a variety of simulated textures (brush strokes, paint roller marks, gritty, smooth, etc.) from which Rob can choose. These textures give the design an almost three-dimensional quality.

The Toolbox

The icon menu of free-drawing software provides a series of drawing choices known as a toolbox. By using a *toolbox* option, Rob selects the type of drawing tool he will use on the electronic canvas.

Paintbrush

The *Paintbrush* enables Rob to create visual patterns using different line widths and shapes. Paintbrushes can be large or small, round or flat, straight or tapered. In addition, Rob can select the color of "paint" to be used from the palette. To outline the crystal formations, caves, and bats of Figure 6.10, Rob uses the paintbrush like a pencil by selecting a thin line from the toolbox. As Rob rolls the mouse on a flat surface, the movement is echoed on the screen, drawing the figures.

Spraypaint

The effect produced by using an actual can of spraypaint is reproduced by the *Spraypaint* option. As Rob moves the paint can across the screen very quickly, a light spattering of the selected pattern appears. To produce varying depths of color on the walls of the cave, Rob lingers at a particular place on the screen and the "spray" becomes denser, more pronounced.

Shapes

Circles, ovals, rectangles, and other geometric *Shapes* are toolbox selections that can be reproduced automatically on the screen. The shapes may be filled or left unfilled. That is, they will appear as a solid shape or as an outline. The *Stretch* command, as its name implies, widens and distorts these geometric figures, giving the impression that the shape is being stretched. For example, Rob moves the cursor to the circle shape in the toolbox, drags a copy onto the drawing area, then pulls it into an oval that will become the bat's body. He repeats this action as necessary. With this option Rob also can stretch a square into a rectangle.

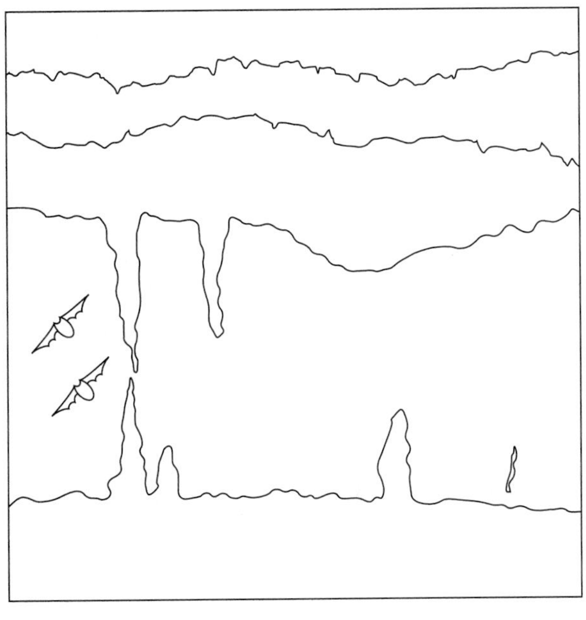

(a)

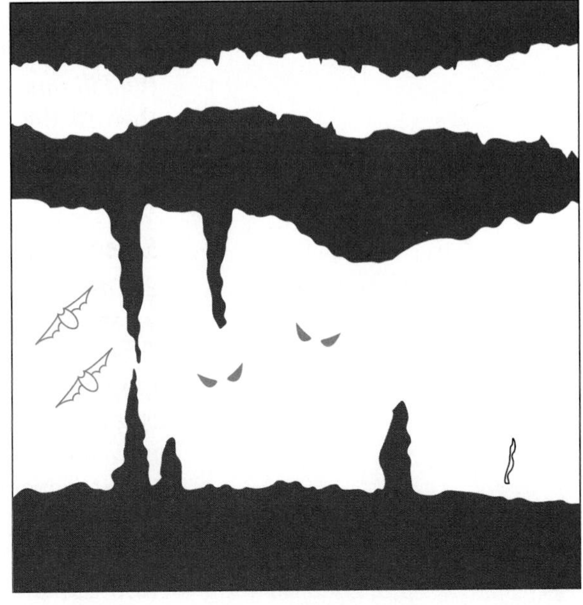

(b)

(c)

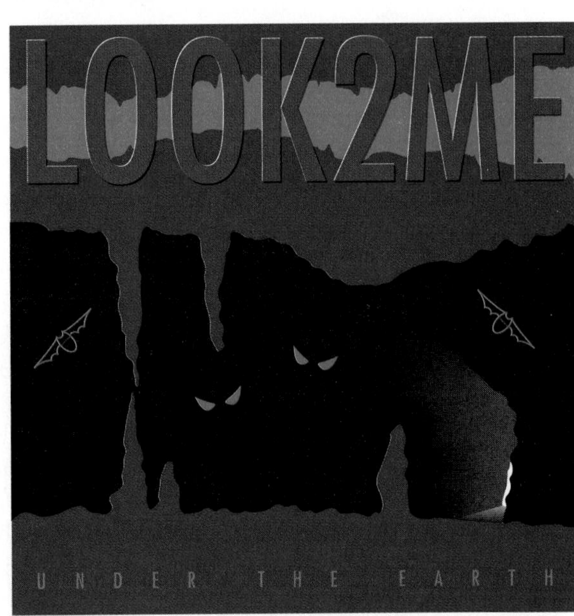

(d)

FIGURE 6.10
Free-drawing software helped to create this CD cover. The paintbrush option drew the cave walls (a). Spray-paint shaded the cave walls, and the shape and stretch options created the outline of the bats' bodies (b). The fill bucket option was used to darken the cave entrance and the eyes. The bats were lassoed and moved to different positions (c). Text was then added to the finished graphic shown in the last figure (d).

Fill Bucket

Any enclosed shape can be filled with a pattern or color by using the *Fill bucket* option. Rob moves the cursor to the fill bucket icon, then to the desired pattern, and finally to the cave outline at the right of the design. The pattern or color automatically fills the entire area within a cave shadow or the center of the eyes.

Lasso

A *Lasso* enables Rob to copy or move parts of the graphic from one location to another. After drawing several bats, Rob realizes they should be repositioned around the center of the design. He draws a loop around, or "lassoes," the bat graphic to be relocated. He relocates it by dragging the lassoed graphic to a position. The bat is moved to the current location of his cursor. This option enables Rob to experiment with the placement of elements in the graphic design.

Fatbits

Rob can zoom into a specific section of a graphic to view a pixel-by-pixel enlargement by using the *Fatbits* option. For example, he can refine the drawing of the bat by inspecting the magnified portion, turning pixels on or off to change lines and patterns. Figure 6.1 at the beginning of the chapter shows a fatbits representation of the bats.

Eraser

The *Eraser* works much like a chalkboard eraser. With a mouse Rob moves the eraser across the screen. The areas covered by the eraser are cleared of colors and patterns.

Text Options

To type text onto the screen, Rob uses a keyboard. Many free-drawing packages allow users to select fonts and type size, similar to those found in a desktop publishing package. These features are available from a drop-down menu or window. Rob uses the text option to add the group's name and the title of the film to the design. Another menu gives Rob the opportunity to try plain, bold, italic, underlined, outlined, justified, and centered text.

Free-Drawing Utilities

Other drop-down menus contain standard utilities, some as simple as clearing the screen. Utilities are also available for saving a graphic file and for loading a file from storage. A special utility is used to undo the last request made by a user in creating a graphic. Rob can experiment with different visual effects, then use this utility to

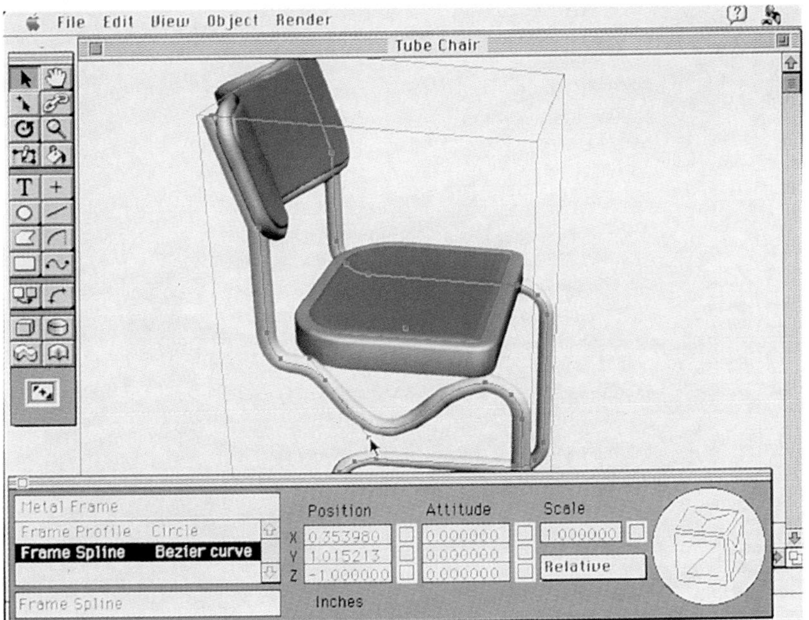

FIGURE 6.11
Free-drawn, three-dimensional images can be tilted, rotated, and viewed from all sides.

remove the last change. Special editing utilities enable Rob to rearrange different parts of a graphics file with cut, copy, and paste routines. These utilities make it easy to try different designs.

Graphics produced by inputting dimensions and mathematical relationships into the computer also make use of special utilities. With this information the computer draws a three-dimensional view of an object. The object can be tilted, rotated, and viewed from all sides with use of these special utilities (see Figure 6.11).

MULTIMEDIA

Recent advances in both hardware and software now allow a developer to go beyond static presentation and free-drawing graphics. Text and graphics can be enhanced with audio, video, and animation by using the techniques of **multimedia** production.

While the poster/CD jacket design was being developed for the theme song from *Under the Earth,* Panorama Music hired an independent video firm to create a music video to accompany the release of the song and movie. To be competitive, the video company relies heavily on multimedia hardware and software.

The hardware required to produce multimedia varies with the sophistication of its users. Professional production studios may use complex audio and video capture equipment along with having film

FIGURE 6.12
Many of the tools for editing visual data are similar to those for creating free-drawing graphics.

processing and editing capabilities. This hardware may come from different vendors, and create compatibility problems. Even for the novice multimedia user, equipment standards are of concern. In 1990 Microsoft, Tandy, AT&T, and eight other computer hardware and software manufacturers announced the *MPC (Multimedia PC)* standard. A system considered meeting MPC standards has, at a minimum, a CD-ROM drive, sound board, and multimedia extensions to Microsoft's Windows graphical interface. Upgrading kits exist to bring older computers to MPC standards. Qualifying new computers will carry an MPC label.

Visual Data

As stated previously, data used in a graphics package is digitized for storage and processing by a computer. This same action takes place when other sources of visual data are used. If the video firm wishes to use a photograph in the music video, it can be input by using a scanner and saved on disk. The scanner digitizes the image, making it computer compatible.

More likely, film clips, perhaps of the band playing the song, will be included. This form of data, as well as visual data from television and video tape, is converted into a series of **frames** to be stored on disk in a computer-usable format.

Although each frame is a still picture or image, a series of frames shown in quick succession give the impression of moving pictures. Special conversion hardware can connect a video recorder or television directly to a computer. As the visual data is input, each frame is numbered.

A toolbox in multimedia software allows a developer at the video firm to examine and edit, frame by frame, a video of the band. All of the tools available in free-drawing software are also available in the multimedia toolbox. Additional options include:

Frame Selection

The *frame selection* options available in a multimedia toolbox are quite similar to those on a video recorder/player. They include forward, fast forward, reverse, stop, play, and pause. In fact, as seen in Figure 6.13, these options are used when the developer moves a mouse pointer over a small button on the screen, like that of a VCR player. A search option also allows a user to find a specific frame number.

Speed Control

While icons control basic movement through the visual data, its display speed is measured in frames per second (fps). Some multimedia packages allow the developer to use *speed control* to change the fps value, the speed at which the video is displayed. This feature can be used to help synchronize audio data with visual data, like the music with the movements of the band. Also, unique effects can be produced by slowing or speeding up a video sequence.

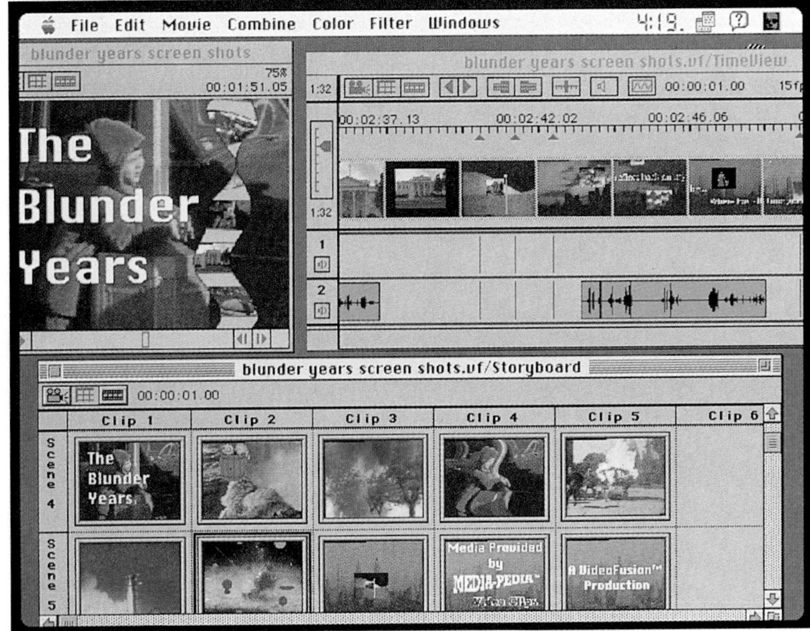

FIGURE 6.13
A toolbox and other control options allow imported visual data to be edited frame by frame.

Color/Contrast Control

Within a single frame, the developer can use *color and contrast control* to add color or change emphasis. Special software is required to realistically colorize a black-and-white video sequence (Figure 6.14). This software not only controls color quality but aids the user in the subtleties of shading and other techniques to improve realism. At the other extreme, unusual colors could be introduced to grab the viewers' attention.

FIGURE 6.14
Special software is used to realistically colorize a black-and-white movie.

Object Integration

By using frame reference numbers, the *object integration* feature allows a new video or audio sequence to be overlayed anywhere into the music video. This ability to integrate data from different sources could result in a scene where the human band is interacting with an animated character from the movie.

Image Exporting

Once completed, a multimedia package can present several options for image exporting. The visual data can be stored as a series of files, each containing one or more frames. The files themselves can be output frame by frame onto paper, slides, videotape, or traditional film. Also, images can be saved for later importation into other types of software, like free-drawing or desktop publishing. Since the images are digitized, related files can require a lot of computer memory and disk storage space.

Audio Data

By using multimedia tools that manipulate audio data, a movie soundtrack and a recording of the band's music can be integrated. Audio data also includes voices and sound effects. Special features are needed to allow maximum control by the developer over audio data.

Measure Selection

One way multimedia software helps the developer control audio data is by breaking the recording into measures, based on timing. By using the *measure selection* option, a developer can edit the sounds within each measure. Editing can include adding, deleting, or changing the timing and pitch of sounds within a measure.

Channel Separation

When recording music or voice, it is possible to create harmonies by simultaneously playing back sounds that were recorded separately. Each individual source of sound is recorded on a separate **audio channel.** The channels can then be individually controlled for volume and playback speed. For example, each band member can be recorded on different days and mixed into the final version at a later date.

Playback Control

The *playback control* feature of a multimedia package not only enables the developer to control the volume of audio data on each separate channel, but can include fade in/out, echoing, and other special audio effects. Several of these techniques are used to refine the music video.

Synchronization

The ability to control the quality of audio data on individual channels would be incomplete without the power to integrate those channels. Multimedia software contains features to *synchronize* the sounds on different channels as well as import other forms of audio data. By using synchronization features, the developer of the music video can integrate the band's performance of the title song for *Under the Earth* with the video of the band's performance and clips from the movie itself.

FIGURE 6.15
Each separate channel of an audio file can be analyzed and edited. Many of the buttons are similar to those found on a tape recorder/player.

Animation

Graphic artists can combine output from free-drawing software with multimedia production techniques to develop animated films and cartoons. **Animation** is the sequencing of single drawings, or frames, resulting in motion. Traditional animation was costly and complex. In the first animated productions, each second of an animated film required 36 hand-drawn graphics. Today television requires only 30 frames a second for broadcast, and animators employ computers both to create the drawings and to sequence their movement.

Computer-animated graphics initially require sophisticated application generators. Once a drawing is made, instructions have to be input as to the type of movement required. However, once the instructions have been entered, creating motion of animated characters and objects is relatively quick and easy. Animators use free-drawing software and special programs to manipulate motion sequences. As video images are created one frame at a time (see Figure 6.16), a motion picture camera or videotape records the sequence of images. These techniques are used not only in producing commercials and cartoons, but for a variety of applications in other areas as well.

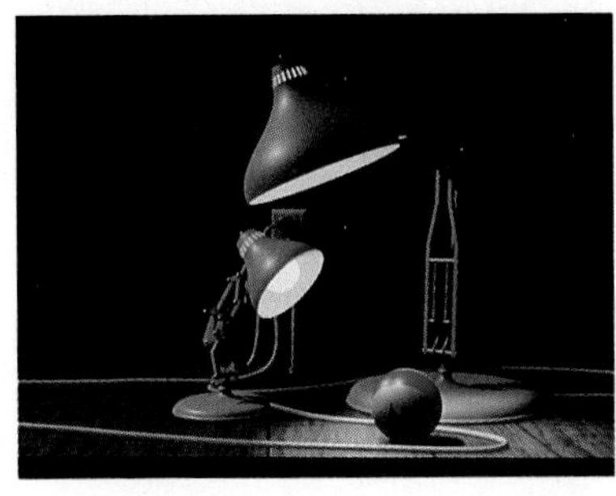

FIGURE 6.16
The frame of an animated feature film uses special shading features of an animation system to give it a near-photo quality.

Animation goes well beyond the cartoons we see on Saturday mornings. Computer-generated images of such things as cars, animals, and people, combined with the realistic movement of those objects can make the seemingly impossible exist. Several movies and music videos contain images of one object, say a person's arm, turning into another, such as a metallic weapon. Or a face seamlessly changes into that of another person. This smooth transition from one image to another, called morphing, is made possible with computers and animation software.

GRAPHICS AND MULTIMEDIA APPLICATIONS

Some graphics and multimedia applications are purely for artistic purposes. In different situations, the computer is used only in the design phase. An artist might produce the initial design for a weaving pattern, sculpture, or still life on the computer but create the piece by hand. In other cases the computer graphic, enhanced with audio, is the finished product. Magazine ads and television commercials often use images produced with computer graphics. Computer-constructed images also become the background shots in motion pictures, as in a futuristic film where a set may be difficult to build. Other designs are put to more practical uses. Engineers and architects, for example, use graphics applications to design machines and buildings. Multimedia software can be used to present the design in a format that includes movement and sound. In the hands of creative and informed users, graphics and multimedia software are powerful tools.

Business/Scientific Presentations

When the bottom line counts, businesspeople and scientists turn to graphics and multimedia to make their point. They have found that reports with a lot of detailed information can be clearly summarized by a pie chart or other form of presentation graphic. A dry analysis of data can be enlivened with colorful slides or animation. A University of Minnesota/3M study concluded that presentations with visual aids were 43% more persuasive than those without. Furthermore, research at the Wharton School of Business found that business meetings involving graphics were shorter and consensus was reached more quickly. As shown in Figure 6.17, scientific information can be shared in an interesting manner. In short, graphics and multimedia help businesspeople and scientists present a professional image while keeping people awake during long or otherwise dry meetings.

Computer-Aided Design (CAD)

Development of a major new product, such as an aircraft or automobile, formerly involved a cycle of activities that ran five to nine years. Well over half of this time was spent in research and design. Before construction work could start on the product, designers had to figure out how the new product would look and how it would meet performance and safety goals. The same was true for development of a major building; skilled architects had to draw and redraw many sets of pictures and detailed plans. Once the drawing

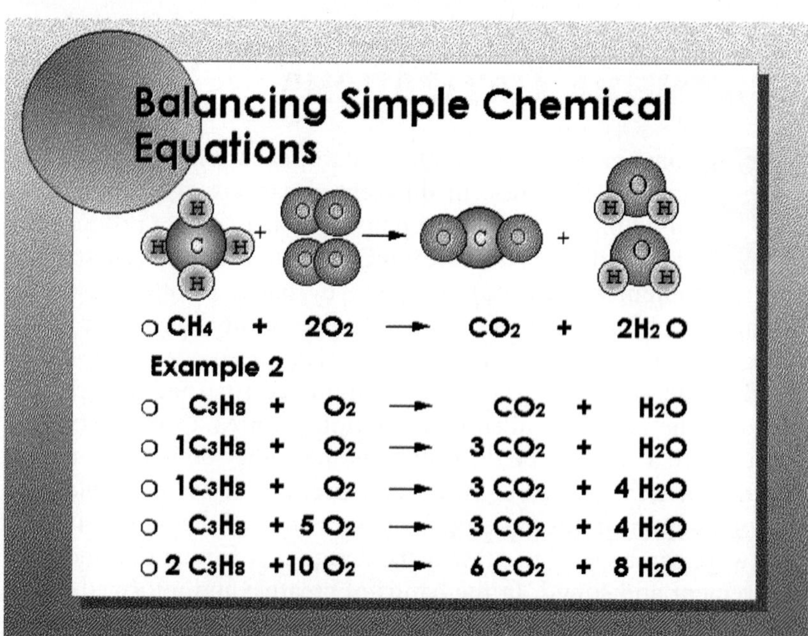

FIGURE 6.17
Multimedia software can be used to organize scientific data, enhance its presentation, then export it to a slide for later use.

Who's Who

Marshall McLuhan (1911–1980)

To many people in the 1960s the advent of technology was frightening. To Marshall McLuhan it represented an opportunity. McLuhan was a Ph.D. in English Literature and a professor when he started to write about connections between technology and culture. Writing in a society where television was gaining popularity, he saw technology as an extension of our bodies. He also anticipated the increased need for interdependency on other cultures to maintain our own. His term *global village* predicted societies coming closer to each other through technology. It brought a commonalty that printed literature could not.

To some people McLuhan seemed out of touch. Despite his fascination with technology, he hesitated to immerse himself in it. He delayed buying a television because he felt it had a bad influence on people. In fact, he asked Jerry Brown, then governor of California, to legally ration TV for the good of the people. Critics claimed that his theories, expounded publicly and through several books, contained illogical reasoning and had little research to back them up. However, one of his books, *Understanding Media: The Extensions of Man*, became quite popular and served as a springboard for contemporary scholars to examine the effects technology has on us as individuals and members of society. In any case, McLuhan's ideas have seen fruit in data communications, remote controls, and the intermingling of sound, visual images, and numerical information in present-day multimedia software. Today, McLuhan is often credited with the phrase "the media is the message." Although this phrase is a corruption of his book title *Medium is the Massage*, both phrases can be applied to the latest multimedia applications.

was finalized, cameras mounted on special stands photographed the image to produce color slides.

The design, analysis, and simulation of new products, utilizing computers, is known collectively as **computer-aided design (CAD)**. A designer inputs data by using a keyboard, mouse, or special input hardware, making it possible to draw directly on computer screens, using many of the features of free-drawing packages. The computer forms images by digitizing entered data. These images can be rotated on the screen for close evaluation of appearance and prospective performance before products are made. Some software will graphically show the effects of wind, earthquakes, or other environmental factors upon the design. Computer simulations, in effect, drive cars or fly aircraft long before the vehicles actually are built.

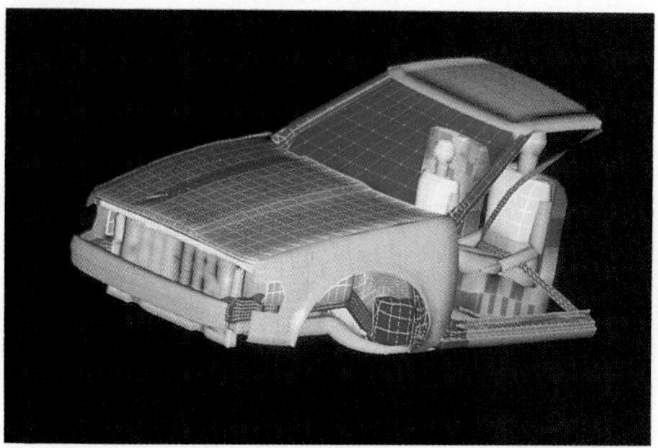

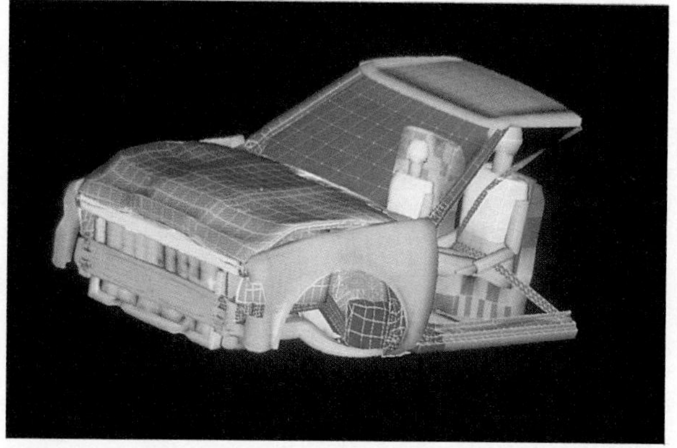

FIGURE 6.18
With a computer-aided design (CAD) system, engineers can design new products as well as test to see if they meet safety standards.

When CAD techniques are used for product or structural design, computations are used to predict how the design will react under different situations. Mathematical equations representing environmental stresses are put into the computer. The computer then runs the design through the equations, sometimes showing the effects with animation (see Figure 6.18). This process enables a designer to observe weaknesses in the design before the actual product is made.

Computer Imaging

Having a computer process data, mathematics, and graphics to see what is normally difficult or impossible for a person to observe is called **computer imaging.** Medical researchers use computer imaging to graphically display the expected results of a specific procedure. As seen in Figure 6.19, doctors can combine data and images

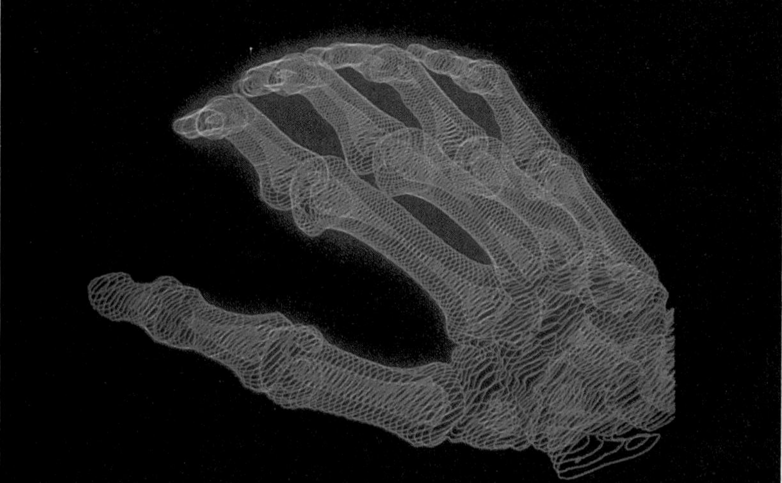

FIGURE 6.19
Computer imaging was used to create this 3D visualization of human hand bone structure. It can be used to diagnose problems as well as develop a plan for treatment.

into a three-dimensional graphic. This can aid doctors in determining the best procedures to use in a delicate surgery.

Computer imaging is used to reconstruct what no longer exists. It can also simulate what might be. Pictures of long-missing children are computer aged to suggest what they might look like now. Lawyer-artist teams use graphics software to reconstruct an accident or scene of the crime for a trial. Prospective cosmetic surgery patients can see what they will look like after the work is done. Some hair salons can even show you how a new hair color or style will affect your looks.

Athletics and the Performing Arts

Coaches can analyze an athlete's performance with a special type of graphics software. For example, a computer loaded with this software might record the motion of a runner. Body movements are input into the computer through specialized scanners. Or the computer might digitize films of the athlete in action. The body movements are reproduced graphically, as in Figure 6.20, then compared with computer models representing desired form. Sometimes the computer can identify subtle variations in an athlete's form that could hurt his or her performance. Coaches and athletes work together to use computer graphics to improve form and performance.

Like a coach, a dance choreographer can also use computer graphics to analyze a dancer's movement. Another important graphics application is in dance notation. Since a film record of a dance cannot show all of the dancers' movements in detail, dance notators are using the computer to create a graphic record of a performance. In one notation system an animated stick figure is used to represent each dancer, and movements are stored as data. Multimedia software can integrate the musical score with the dancers' movements. Choreographers and play directors are also using graphic software

FIGURE 6.20
Medical researchers at the Olympic training center in Colorado use computer-generated graphics to analyze a runner's form and performance.

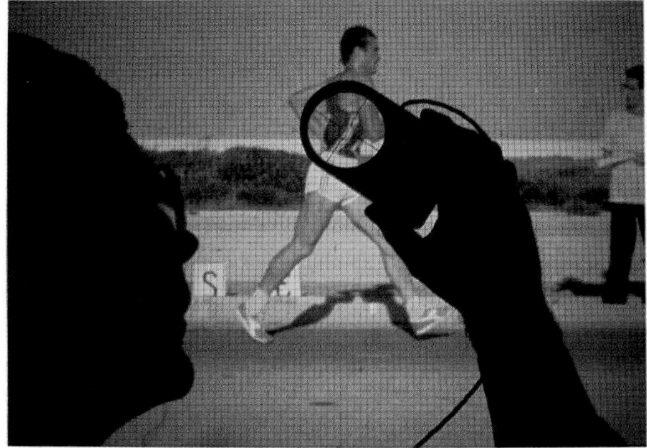

to design character movement, sets, and lighting. Multimedia software was used to choreograph the Look 2 Me video with the *Under the Earth* theme song. Like engineers using CAD, these designers can experiment with different effects and see the total picture before having to work with the actual production.

MIDI

For over a decade, musicians have been using electronics to enhance and distort the sounds created by traditional musical instruments. Electric guitars and pianos have been joined with enhanced wind, brass, and percussion instruments to create new sounds. A standard has been developed within the music industry for connecting electrical instruments to each other and to computers. The standard is called *MIDI,* which stands for Musical Instrument Digital Interface. As the name suggests, MIDI provides a system for sending signals that represent musical notes (Figure 6.21).

The actual sound is not sent by using a MIDI. Instead, a series of digital codes are transmitted by the instrument to the computer. These codes represent three characteristics: whether a note is to be switched on or off, the code for the note (such as 3C for middle C), and a velocity code.

The digital codes are sent through the cable to a synthesizer that plays (or stops playing) the note at a certain volume. By using a

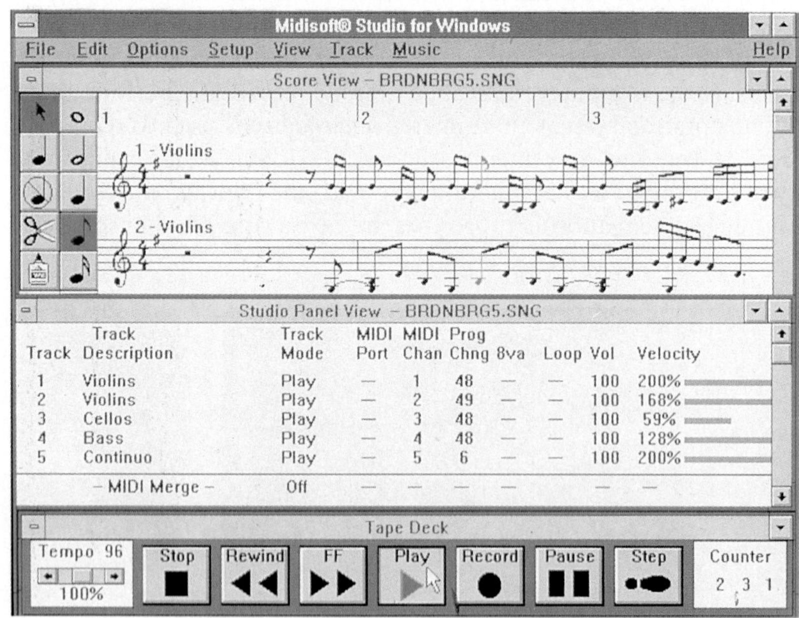

FIGURE 6.21
MIDI allows a musician to create and synchronize sound volume and speed for each channel in a musical piece.

combination of voices (or sounds) controlled by a program, MIDI allows a musician to use a keyboard to generate the sounds of many different instruments. When recorded on different tracks and played simultaneously, the result can sound like a small group of musicians or an entire orchestra. An additional advantage is that the developer need not know how to play all the instruments he or she can generate using the MIDI. As MIDI technology is perfected, it gets more difficult to distinguish synthesized output from a recording of a live human performance.

Space Exploration

Graphics applications extend beyond earthly uses. Computer-controlled space probes record images of Mars, Venus, the Moon, and other galactic bodies as streams of digital data. The images are sent back to an Earth base and converted into graphics. Specialists analyze the graphics, then use image enhancement techniques to adjust the pictures to indicate surface conditions (Figure 6.22).

These image-enhancement techniques can fill in missing data by checking surrounding pixels and estimating the likely content of an unknown pixel value. The contrast in images is improved by using temperatures, air densities, and other conditions on the celestial body as data. These image-enhancement techniques change the pictures from shades of gray to various intensities of color.

FIGURE 6.22
NASA's Jet Propulsion Laboratory uses computers to enhance digitized pictures from space probes.

A Closer Look...

Presentation Software

Anyone who gives a presentation knows the importance of getting and keeping the audience's interest. Presentation software—a combination of word processing, graphics, and multimedia software—helps the speaker make a professional presentation with coordinated electronic slide shows, transparencies, and handouts. For example, a science teacher could use presentation software in preparing a lab demonstration. Sales-people, teachers, ministers, business-people—in fact, anyone who gives presentations or lectures in front of an audience—can use this tool.

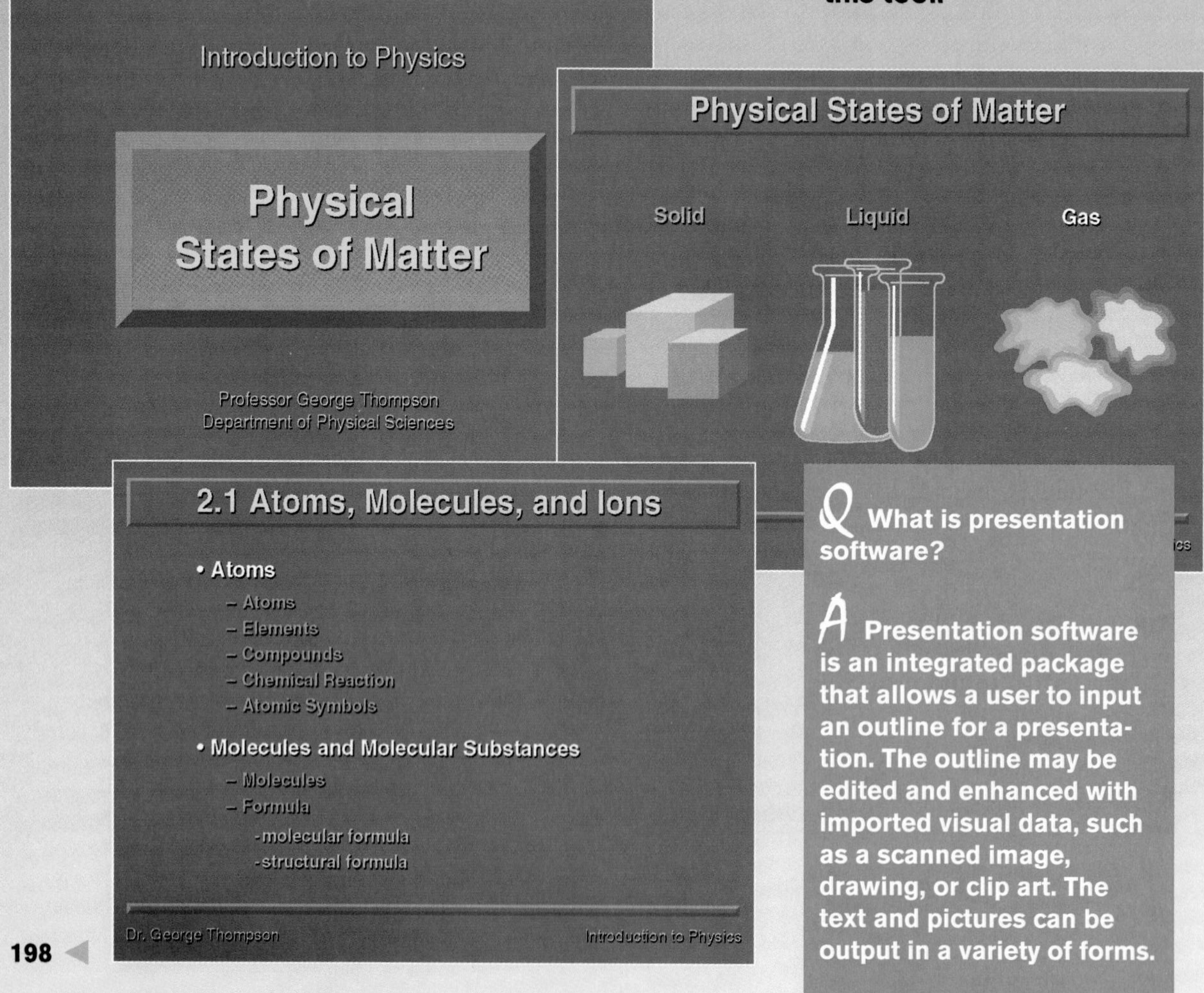

Q What is presentation software?

A Presentation software is an integrated package that allows a user to input an outline for a presentation. The outline may be edited and enhanced with imported visual data, such as a scanned image, drawing, or clip art. The text and pictures can be output in a variety of forms.

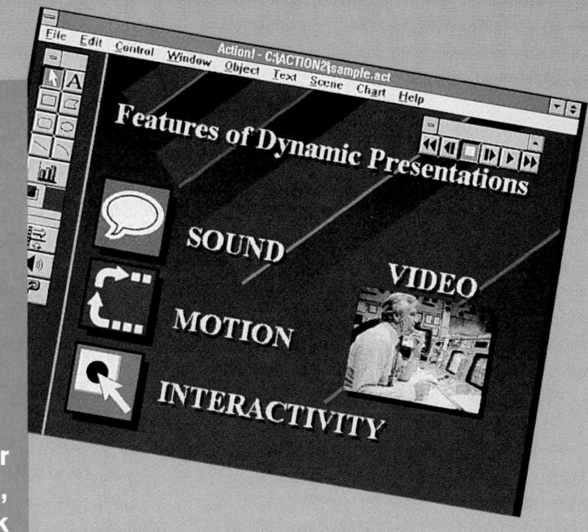

Q Why use presentation software?

A There are a number of advantages. The major points of a lecture or presentation can be covered without using a chalkboard or overhead transparency. If a computer is used in the presentation, important points in the talk can be reviewed or topics skipped at will. The speaker has increased control over the presentation of the information.

Q What kinds of graphics can be incorporated into a presentation?

A Usually, a presentation graphics package includes clip art. The user can purchase additional clip art, increase the images available by scanning photographs, or create original graphics with free-drawing software.

Q What kind of hardware is needed?

A Aside from the computer and software, a *projection plate* fitting on an overhead projector to show the output on a wall screen, large screen monitor, or slide projector is needed to display the output. A scanner or camera, which stores images on disk rather than film, will increase the types of visual images that may be imported.

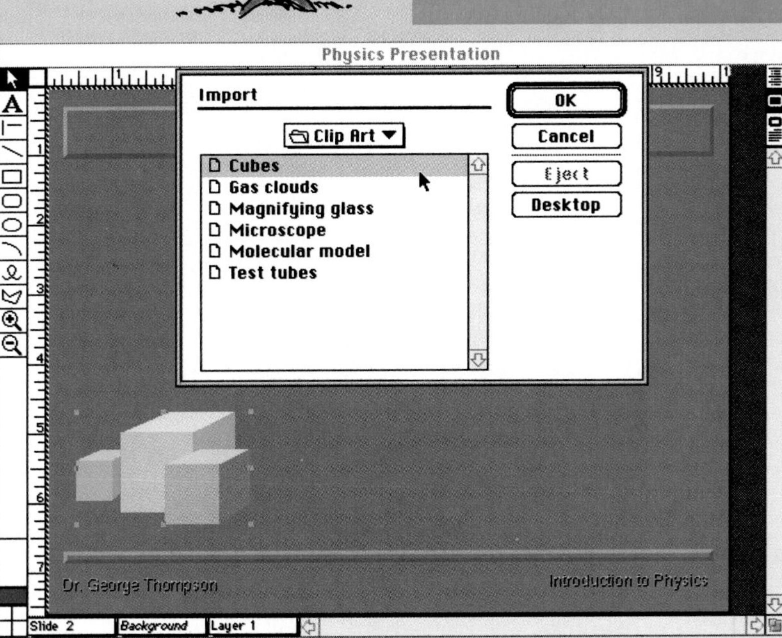

Q Is the presentation difficult to lay out and edit?

A Like spreadsheets, presentation software includes templates that contain the basic design elements of a presentation. These include background graphics, color scheme, and text formats. By using a toolbox and palette, editing is easily done.

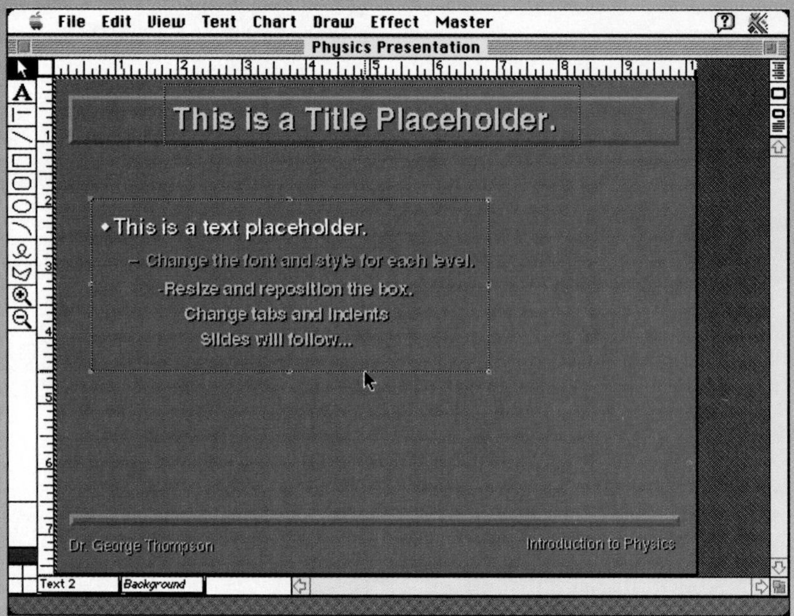

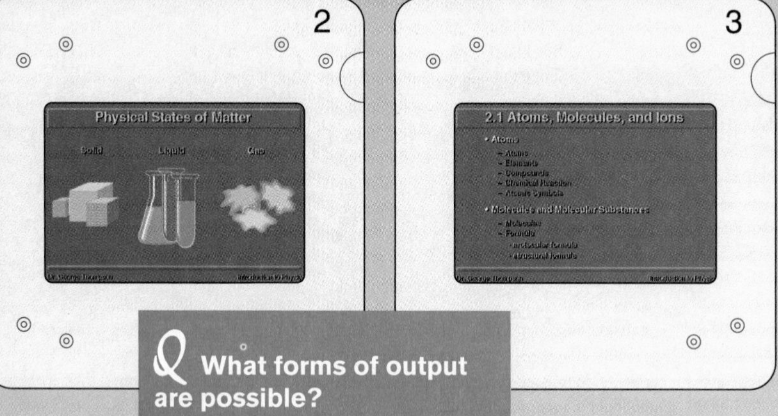

Q What forms of output are possible?

A If the presenter has a computer available, the outline and accompanying images can be shown directly on a screen, one frame at a time. Paper copies or transparencies of an outline can be generated on a laser printer. The outline can also be transmitted over a phone line to a professional service, which will convert it to color slides.

PRESENTATION SOFTWARE PACKAGES

	Action! 2.5	DeltaGraph Professional 2.02	Harvard Graphics 1.01	Persuasion 2.1	PowerPoint 3.0
Platform	Windows	Macintosh	Windows	Macintosh	Windows
Company	Macromedia Inc.	DeltaPoint Inc.	Software Publishing Corp.	Aldus Corp.	Microsoft Corp.
Media Creation					
Word Processor (full/limited/none)	full	limited	limited	full	limited
Spelling checker	no	yes	yes	yes	yes
Drawing tools	12	8	6	11	6
Paint module	no	no	no	no	no
Internal spreadsheet	yes	yes	yes	yes	yes
Charts	yes	yes	yes	yes	yes
Sound recording &/or editing	editing	thru QT only	no	thru QT only	no
Media Integration					
Outliner	no	yes	yes	yes	yes
Visual slide sorter	no	no	yes	yes	yes
Automated templates	yes	no	yes	yes	yes
Animation capabilities	basic	none	none	none	none
Sound playback/ volume control	yes/no	no	thru VFW/yes	thru QT	no
Movie support	AVI, DVI, QT	QT	AVI	QT	AVI
Speaker notes & audience handouts	no	yes	yes	yes	yes
Output to videotape	yes	no	no	no	no
Clip media included (graphics/sound/video?)	all	graphics	graphics	graphics	graphics

New Media, March, 1993, pp. 62–63.

Q How can I compare the features of presentation software packages?

A Magazines and computer journals contain reviews of the newest software and comparison lists. Of course, it is best to talk to current users and try the software yourself before you buy.

Chapter Facts

- Graphic images can be produced through bit mapping (also called pixel graphics) or vector graphics.
- Presentation graphics can be pie charts, exploded pie charts, bar charts, stacked bar graphs, line graphs, area graphs, or symbol charts.
- Pie charts show how components proportionally make up a whole total. Each slice represents a single component.
- Bar charts display data as varying lengths of bars, each showing the relative quantity or measurement of a value.
- Line graphs show the trends found in a group of data over time.
- Area charts contain a shaded area below a single line graph.
- Symbol charts use colors and symbols to accentuate data values.
- Enhancements to presentation graphics include two- and three-dimensional graphs, rotation, and combination graphs.
- Presentation graphics are created by identifying the type of graphic, the data to be included, and labels for the graphic, and by stating the graphic title and legends.
- Free-drawing graphics software includes a palette, toolbox, and drop-down menus to aid the user.
- The palette allows the user to choose colors and shading for the graphic.
- The toolbox includes tools for creating the graphic. These include paintbrush, spraypaint, shapes, fill bucket, lasso, fatbits, eraser, and text options.
- Drop-down menus contain standard utilities for clearing the screen, saving a graphic file, and editing the graphic.
- Multimedia is the coordination of text, visual images, and audio data into a single presentation.
- Visual data is stored and edited in frames that can be edited by using frame selection, speed control, color/contrast control, integration, and exporting.
- The measures in audio data can be selectively edited for volume, channel separation, and synchronization.
- Graphics applications include animation for film and videotape, business and scientific presentations, computer-aided design, computer imaging, analysis of body movement for athletics and performing arts, and space exploration.

- MIDI (Musical Instrument Digital Interface) allows a musician to synthesize audio signals and control their volume, duration, and type of instrument they represent.
- Presentation software allows the integration of video images into text for more informative lectures. Output can be on a screen, slides or transparencies, and by printed handouts.

Terms to Remember

a. animation
b. area graph
c. audio channel
d. bar graph
e. bit mapping
f. computer-aided design (CAD)
g. computer imaging
h. digitize
i. exploded pie chart
j. frame
k. free-drawing graphics
l. line graph
m. multimedia
n. pie chart
o. pixel
p. presentation graphics
q. stacked bar graph

Mix and Match

Match the following definitions to the Terms to Remember.

1. ____ information technology application wherein computers are used to create two- or three-dimensional drawings.
2. ____ the combination of textual, audio, and visual data under software control for importing, editing, and exporting.
3. ____ a bar graph in which each bar is broken down to show its components.
4. ____ graphic showing trends in data with a continuous line.
5. ____ division of audio data, representing a single voice or instrument.
6. ____ graphic showing data as different lengths of bars.
7. ____ using the computer to create drawings of a screen much as an artist uses a canvas.
8. ____ visual images of motions produced by rapid presentation of drawn or computer-generated graphics.
9. ____ a pie chart wherein one slice is emphasized by separating it from the rest.

10. ____ line graph with the area below the line shaded.
11. ____ picture element that is one component of an array or matrix of dots that makes up a visual image.
12. ____ conversion of a point on a drawing into mathematical coordinates.
13. ____ pattern of pixels making up a graphic image.
14. ____ division of visual data such as film or video.
15. ____ common graphics, including pie charts, bar graphs, line graphs, area graphs, and symbol charts, used in business and other applications.
16. ____ using data, graphics, and mathematics to display complex images.
17. ____ a circle divided into slices, each representing the proportion one component has when related to the whole. Each slice is labeled with the component name and the actual percentage. Percentages for the entire chart total 100.

Review Questions

1. What types of information are associated with each pixel in bit mapping?
2. Describe two ways to create a graphic image.
3. What are the four levels of information needed by graphics software to produce presentation graphics?
4. What options do the palette, toolbox, and drop-down menus provide for free-drawing graphics software?
5. How do the paintbrush, spraypaint, shapes, stretch, fill bucket, lasso, fatbits, eraser, and text options work?
6. Briefly explain how these multimedia options work: frame selection, speed control, color/contrast control, object integration, and image exporting.
7. What are four ways audio data can be controlled and edited?
8. How do animators use computers in their work?
9. How are computer-generated graphics or multimedia used in business or scientific presentations, computer-aided design, computer imaging, athletics and performing arts, and space exploration?
10. What is MIDI and how is it used?
11. What are the answers to the seven questions frequently asked about presentation software?

Applying What You've Learned

1. Applications for both presentation and free-drawing graphics exist in most career areas. Name three uses for graphics software in your chosen field (other than those mentioned in the text). Will the graphics be presentation or free drawings?
2. Find or describe six examples of computerized graphics output. If it is a presentation graphic, identify its type, pointing out the labels, title, and legend. If it is a freehand drawing, what drawing tools and colors were used? Television, magazines, and films are possible sources of graphic output.
3. Explain how graphics software can enhance user understanding in these situations:
   a. presentation of the racial groups that make up the faculty of your school.
   b. advertising the opening of a new video rental store.
   c. showing how to assemble a bicycle from a kit.
   d. displaying the change in Pentagon spending over the last twenty years.
   e. demonstrating how renovation of a historical building may change its appearance.
4. Use a graphics package to produce and print a presentation graphic reflecting a simple collection of data. This could be your personal budget, grade point average over time, or another application. Be sure that the graphic is clearly labeled and contains a legend.
5. Use a graphics package to produce a simple freehand drawing. Make use of the palette and toolbox to show a variety of shapes and patterns. Save the graphic and print it out.
6. Use a multimedia package to learn about a new subject or review an old one. What features of multimedia learning do you like the best? Which ones do you like the least?

Answers to Mix and Match

1. f 2. m 3. q 4. l 5. c 6. d 7. k 8. a 9. i 10. b
11. o 12. h 13. e 14. j 15. p 16. g 17. n

7

File and Database Management

- From the User's Point of View
- Data Processing
  - Sequential access
  - Direct access
- File Management
  - Data definition
  - Data manipulation
  - Application generators
- Database Management
  - Database designs
  - Hierarchical model
  - Network model
  - Relational model
  - Pros and cons of database processing
- Applications for Data Management Software
  - Hypermedia
  - Education
  - Public health
  - Law enforcement
  - Automotive repair
  - Libraries
  - Agriculture
- *A Closer Look . . . Hypermedia*

FROM THE USER'S POINT OF VIEW

Computer information systems allow you access to vast amounts of information. You might wonder why anyone would need to work with so much data. However, you probably now have files or different lists, perhaps in overcrowded file cabinets, that could be arranged into personal databases. You need to know how to organize this data, thereby reducing clutter and promoting better access to important information.

Not only is there a place for personal information systems in your future, but you already have access to a wide variety of public data. Airline schedules, library card catalogs, and sports statistics are organized into databases available to the knowledgeable consumer. Understanding how data management software organizes and retrieves information can increase your productivity when electronically accessing consumer and public data.

DATA PROCESSING

Stored data is an extremely valuable asset for any person or organization using a computer system. Individuals, schools, businesses, and other users rely on data to conduct their daily activities (Figure 7.1). Even without computers, people organize data for storage and use. Computers just make it easier. Take, for instance, the different collections of data used by your local video store.

As a customer, your name, address, and telephone number are collected into a record. The records are organized by a unique customer number given to every customer. Together, these records become the customer file. Data from your record is on a plastic video store identification card like the one shown in Figure 7.2. Your customer number appears as a bar code on this card. The store also maintains an inventory file on every video tape the store rents. Each tape has a unique tape number that is bar coded on it.

FIGURE 7.1
Every business transaction creates valuable data. Computer information systems maintained by the New York Stock Exchange process millions of transactions every business day.

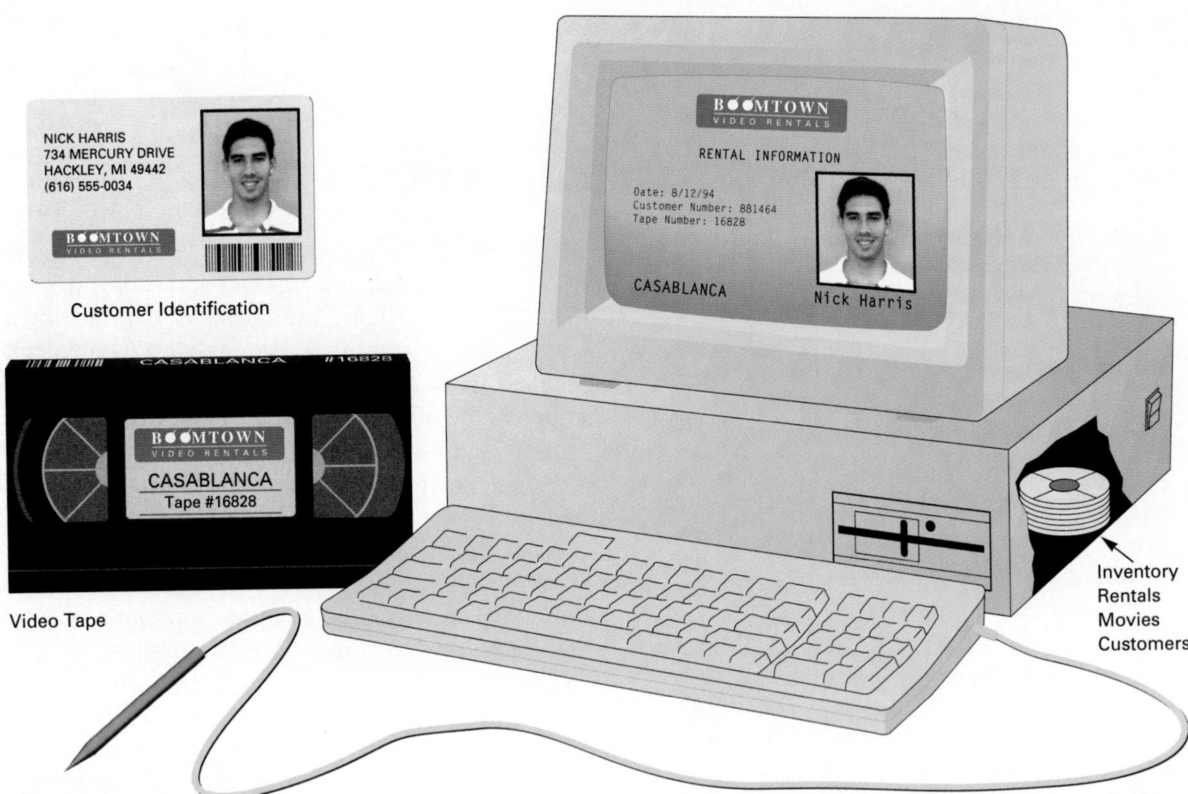

FIGURE 7.2
Integrating data from the customer and inventory data files provides complete access to information related to video tape rentals.

Sometimes data files are processed independently. The store manager can access the video tape inventory file to see if a specific tape is rented. When data is integrated with other data files, even more information is available. For example, combining data from the customer file with the inventory file allows the manager to find which customer rented a specific tape. By relating files within a database, it is possible to allow easy access to a variety of data items.

If the video store's data is properly organized, customers and employees can get different types of information. For instance, one customer might want a list of all the available adventure movies that run over two hours. Also, the store manager could list overdue tapes or compute the store's income.

However, stored data must be organized according to its intended use. Different file and database schemes exist for different applications. Computer systems, under user control, then retrieve, or access, data from the storage medium, usually a disk. Different access methods fit varying data processing requirements. In turn, these access methods determine the physical arrangement of data on storage media. Two basic types of file access methods are available:

- Sequential
- Direct

Edgar F. Codd

The interrelated nature of data had been recognized from the beginning of computing. Before 1970 the most advanced forms of data organization were hierarchies. Through a series of articles in the 1970s Dr. Edgar F. Codd presented a new organization—the relational database. Codd's theories had a basis in mathematics. His ideas were so radical for the time that they were met with skepticism. The simplicity of the relational model won over software designers, and relational database management systems (RDBMS) were made available. In 1985 Codd wrote the guidelines for RDBMS in the form of 12 rules. They are, in simple terms:

1. Data should be presented to the user in table form.
2. Every data element should be accessible without ambiguity.
3. A field should be allowed to remain empty for future use.
4. The description of a database should be accessible to the user.
5. A database must support a clearly defined language to define a database, view the definition, manipulate the data, and restrict some data values to maintain integrity.
6. Data should be able to be changed through any view available to the user.
7. All records in a file must be able to be added, deleted, or changed with a single command.
8. Changes in how data is stored or retrieved should not affect how a user accesses the data.
9. The users' view of the data should be unaffected by its actual form in files.
10. Constraints on user input should exist to maintain data integrity.
11. A database design should allow for distribution of data over several computer sites.
12. Data fields cannot be changed in any way that affects the organization of the database.

Sequential Access

To find a specific record by using **sequential access** means starting with the first record and looking at each consecutive record in the file, one at a time, until the specific record is found. Sequential access methods work equally well with tape or disk storage. Records are retrieved in the sequence in which they were originally stored. As an example, songs on a commercially produced music tape are organized for sequential access. When you play a tape, the songs are heard in a predetermined order. Once the songs are stored on the tape, they cannot easily be rearranged.

If you wish to hear the sixth song on a prerecorded tape, you must listen to the first five, or fast forward past them. In either case the first five songs must be run through the tape player in sequence. Similarly, a computer that uses sequential access methods reads one record at a time to locate the desired record. To retrieve the fifty-fifth record in a data file, the first 54 must be read by the tape or disk drive.

Each record in a file should have at least one **key** or key field that makes the record unique. Keys serve to identify and organize records in a file. Locating a specific record by using sequential access methods means the key from each record is examined until a match is found or the last record is processed. For instance, in the video store's inventory file, the key field is the unique tape number the store assigns to every video tape. When the file is initially stored on disk, the records are placed in order by tape number. This arrangement establishes a logical organization of the data in the file. Thus, for sequential access, records are arranged in order by a key field prior to being saved on tape or disk as shown in Figure 7.3.

Sequential access methods are best in situations where every record must be read and processed. Printing weekly paychecks is a good example of using sequential access for **batch processing.** When results are not needed on an immediate basis, records can be collected into groups (batches) and processed all at once. In the case of payroll processing, this approach affords a greater level of security, because all the paychecks are printed at one time.

Every week the computer system batch processes records in the employee file to print paychecks and change (**update**) federal and state tax records. Updating involves adding or deleting records to or from a file or modifying existing records. During payroll processing every employee's record is updated in some way. Either wages and taxes are added to yearly totals or time is subtracted from sick leave or vacation time.

Sequential access is often impractical when users cannot predict the order in which records need to be accessed. For instance, video store employees must be able to process video tape rental requests one at a time, in any order. If the video store employees sequentially accessed video tape and customer records, it could take an unacceptably long time to find records near the end of the file.

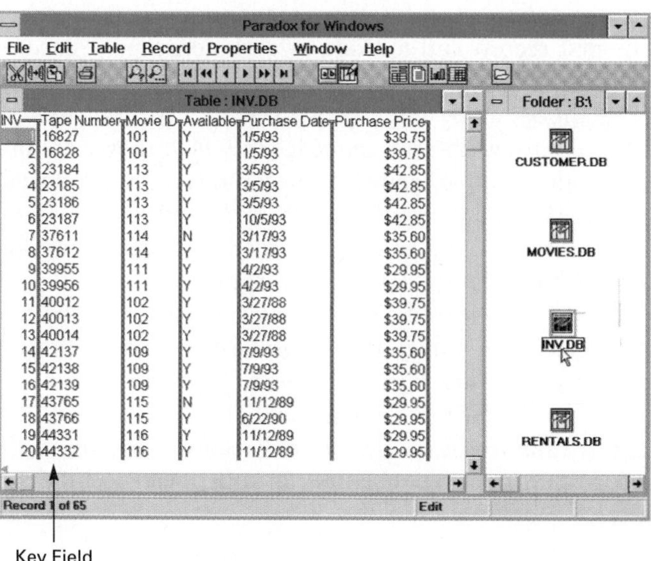

INV	Tape Number	Movie ID	Available	Purchase Date	Purchase Price
1	16827	101	Y	1/5/93	$39.75
2	16828	101	Y	1/5/93	$39.75
3	23184	113	Y	3/5/93	$42.85
4	23185	113	Y	3/5/93	$42.85
5	23186	113	Y	3/5/93	$42.85
6	23187	113	Y	10/5/93	$42.85
7	37611	114	N	3/17/93	$35.60
8	37612	114	Y	3/17/93	$35.60
9	39955	111	Y	4/2/93	$29.95
10	39956	111	Y	4/2/93	$29.95
11	40012	102	Y	3/27/88	$39.75
12	40013	102	Y	3/27/88	$39.75
13	40014	102	Y	3/27/88	$39.75
14	42137	109	Y	7/9/93	$35.60
15	42138	109	Y	7/9/93	$35.60
16	42139	109	Y	7/9/93	$35.60
17	43765	115	N	11/12/89	$29.95
18	43766	115	Y	6/22/90	$29.95
19	44331	116	Y	11/12/89	$29.95
20	44332	116	Y	11/12/89	$29.95

FIGURE 7.3
The video tape inventory file is organized for sequential access by video tape number.

Direct Access

Direct access, also called random access, is possible when data is stored on disk. The computer system uses an index or other technique to identify a record's location within a file and can directly access an individual record without processing other records. This access method uses a key field to identify the record, and disk storage provides fast access to individual records, especially when the order of retrieval cannot be predicted. To support direct access, an **index** or index file is created. The index is based on a specific key field and contains a separate directory that identifies where each record is located within the file (see Figure 7.4). To find any record, the computer consults the index, looks up the disk location, then performs a direct access operation.

Using an index to access data cuts down on the number of records that are looked at when searching for a record. It is like using the index at the back of this book. When looking up the definition to a "term to remember," the index sends you to a specific page within the book. This allows you to skip over the other pages. Once you get to the page in question, a quick scan of the page reveals the definition. Sequentially searching one page at a time from the beginning of the book would be a lot slower in most cases.

FIGURE 7.4
Indexes allow a record to be directly accessed from a file on disk.

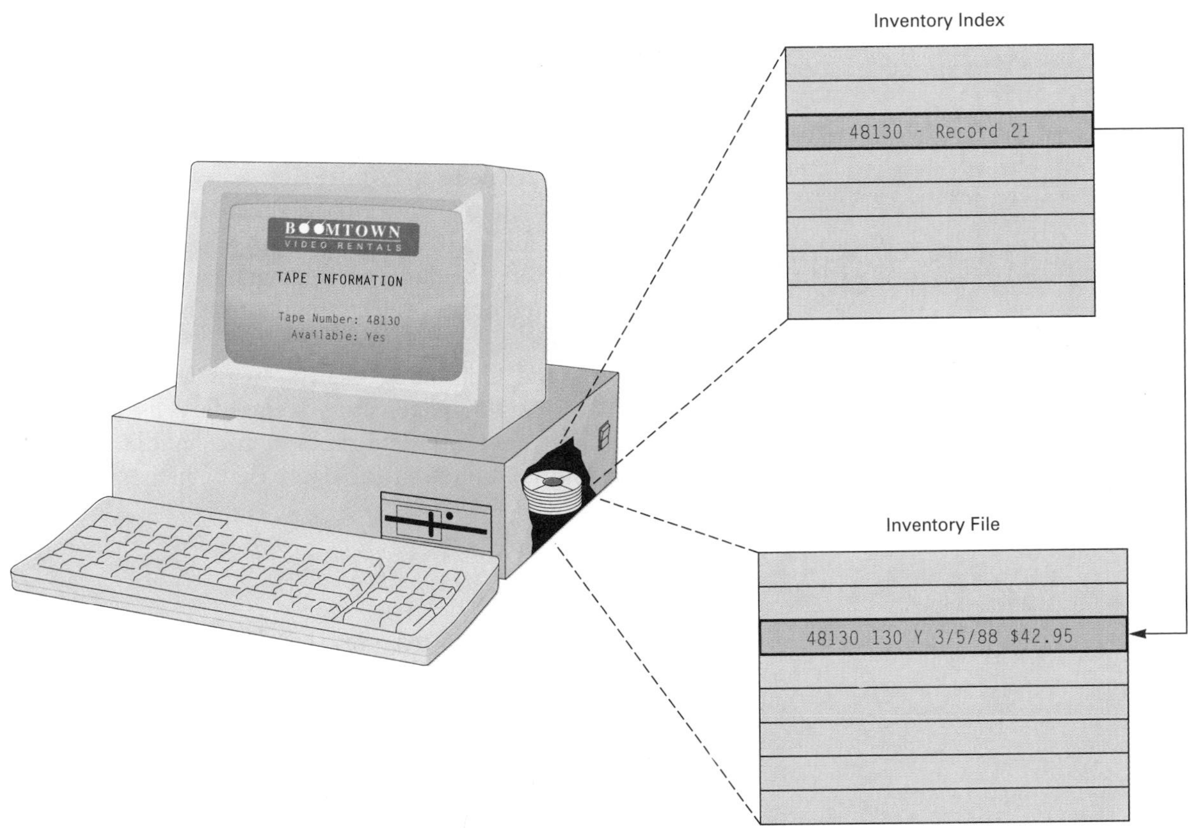

Furthermore, creating an index does not eliminate sequential access to data, but provides users with the option of directly accessing data when necessary. This versatility is the primary advantage to creating an index. The method of accessing data can be altered according to a user's needs. For example, the video inventory file would be a prime candidate for an index. Direct access by video tape number would expedite individual customer rentals as they occur. But sequential access by tape number would be preferred in preparing monthly inventory reports for the store manager. Thus, indexed files provide the flexibility to meet a wide range of accessing and processing needs.

Direct access supports **real-time processing.** As the name implies, real-time processing means the computer system processes a user request as soon as it is input. The user waits only as long as it takes the computer to process the input and to output the results. The time between the user's request and the output is referred to as the *response time.* Research has shown that users become impatient with real-time processing when the response time is longer than three seconds. Therefore, computer professionals almost always use direct access techniques when designing systems that require real-time processing.

FILE MANAGEMENT

Different data processing abilities distinguish file management and database management software. **File management software** helps maximize user access to a single data file. Files used by a file management system are often called *flat files.* A flat file is not designed to integrate with other data files. File integration is left to **database management software.** These software packages interconnect the contents of several files for flexible storage and retrieval.

Both database and file management systems have many common features. These data management systems allow users to define field types, manipulate data, create reports, and handle individual inquiries about data contained in the database or file.

Data Definition

A data management program oversees the physical organization of files on disk, as well as input and output operations. Well-designed software enables users to define, add, delete, and change records efficiently. Normally, users start by using a *data definition language* to identify fields and organize related records.

Teresa Romero is responsible for Boomtown Video Rental's data. In some organizations she would be called a **data administra-**

tor. Her duties include designing files and databases, setting up the rights and responsibilities for accessing data, training employees in proper backup procedures, and evaluating the performance of the store's data management systems.

Teresa uses the data definition language's *Create* operation to identify the fields associated with the Customer file shown in Figure 7.5. In doing so, each field is given an *attribute name* like Customer Number, First Name, Last Name, Address, Photo ID (identification), etc. The attribute name refers to the data, but is not data

FIGURE 7.5
Attribute names, data types, and data sizes associated with customer records are all identified when using the data definition language's Create operation.

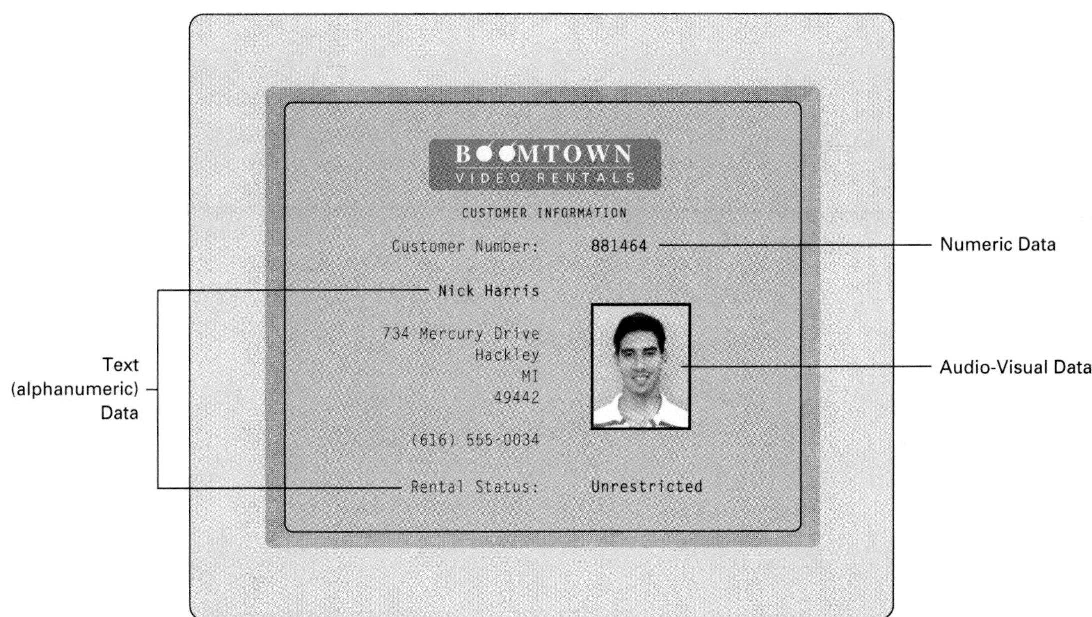

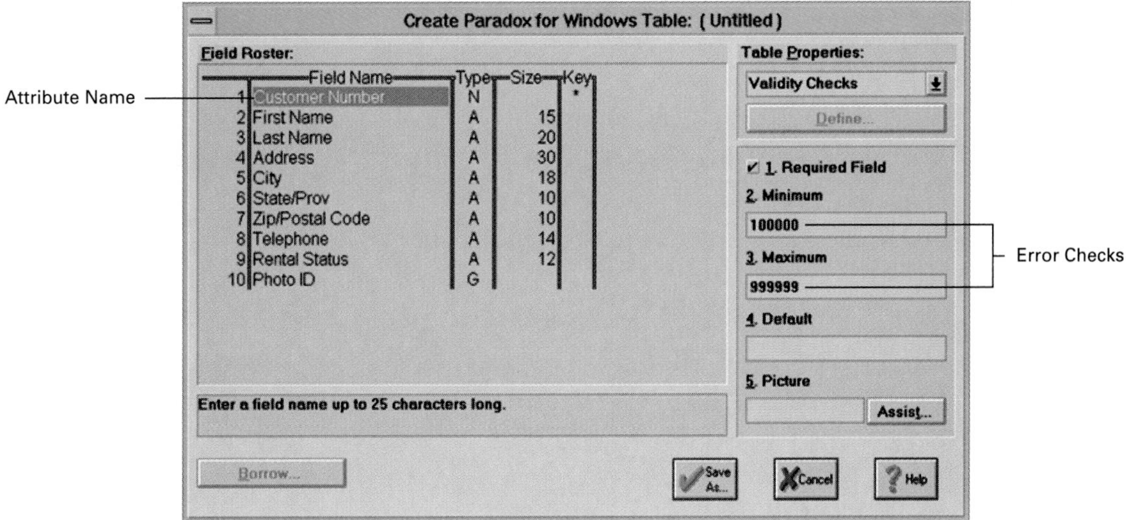

itself. It identifies specific data and is useful when designing data entry forms or report formats. The expected size (number of characters or digits) and type (text, numeric, audio-visual) of data are entered as part of data definition. At this time Teresa can also establish error checks and passwords to protect the data.

Figure 7.5 shows how common data types could be used within a customer record. The customer number is numeric, with name and address data typed as text. Audio-visual data could be in the form of a photograph of the customer.

Data Manipulation

Teresa is also supervising the training of new store managers in using Boomtown's data. They are learning a command syntax known as the *data manipulation language.* By training store managers to use the data manipulation language, Teresa is placing a great deal of control back into the end-users' hands. In addition, she is relieving the store's computer professionals of day-to-day responsibility for maintaining the data. During the training session, Teresa explains how each command performs a critical role in data access, maintenance, and protection.

Select

The data management program can retrieve records that fit certain logical conditions under the *Select* operation. The store manager might want a list of all tapes that are currently rented (see Figure

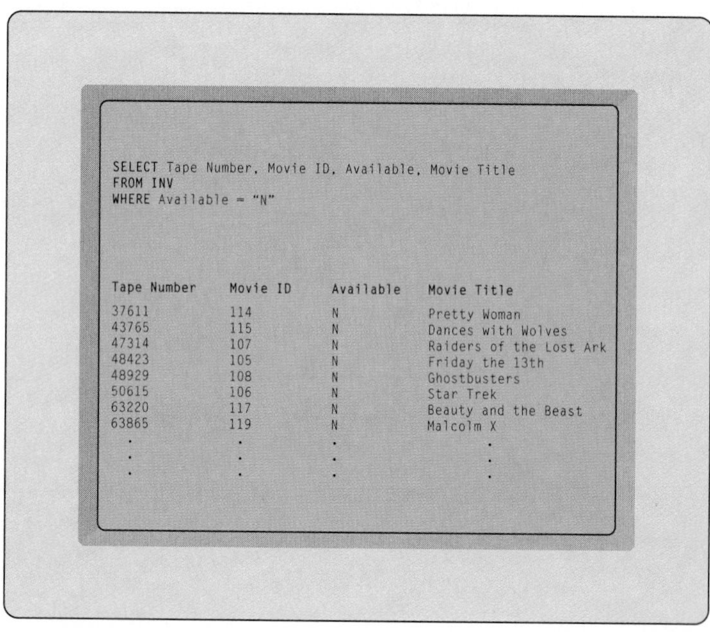

SELECT Tape Number, Movie ID, Available, Movie Title
FROM INV
WHERE Available = "N"
Tape Number
Movie ID
Available
Movie Title
37611 114 N Pretty Woman
43765 115 N Dances with Wolves
47314 107 N Raiders of the Lost Ark
48423 105 N Friday the 13th
48929 108 N Ghostbusters
50615 106 N Star Trek
63220 117 N Beauty and the Beast
63865 119 N Malcolm X

FIGURE 7.6
The data manipulation language's Select operation allows users to locate records that meet specific conditions. In this case the monitor displays all video tapes that are not currently available.

7.6). By looking for the letter N in the Available field, the data management program selects all records that fit the criterion and displays them on the screen or copies them to a new file. Select is used only to view data and cannot be used to update data.

Append

The *Append* operation allows the user to load data into a record defined by the data definition language. Most data management packages will provide a data entry screen, like the one in Figure 7.7, which shows the designated fields. These screens can be customized when necessary. Store managers will instruct their staff on the procedures for entering new movie data into the appropriate field positions as new movies are purchased and rented through the store.

Update

The staff will change data entries in records with the *Update* operation. This operation, for instance, is needed to keep customer data current. Staff members update the records of recently moved customers with new addresses and telephone numbers.

FIGURE 7.7
New data is appended to a file by using a data entry screen, which prompts the user for specific input. These data entry screens are automatically generated by the data management program or created by a user/developer.

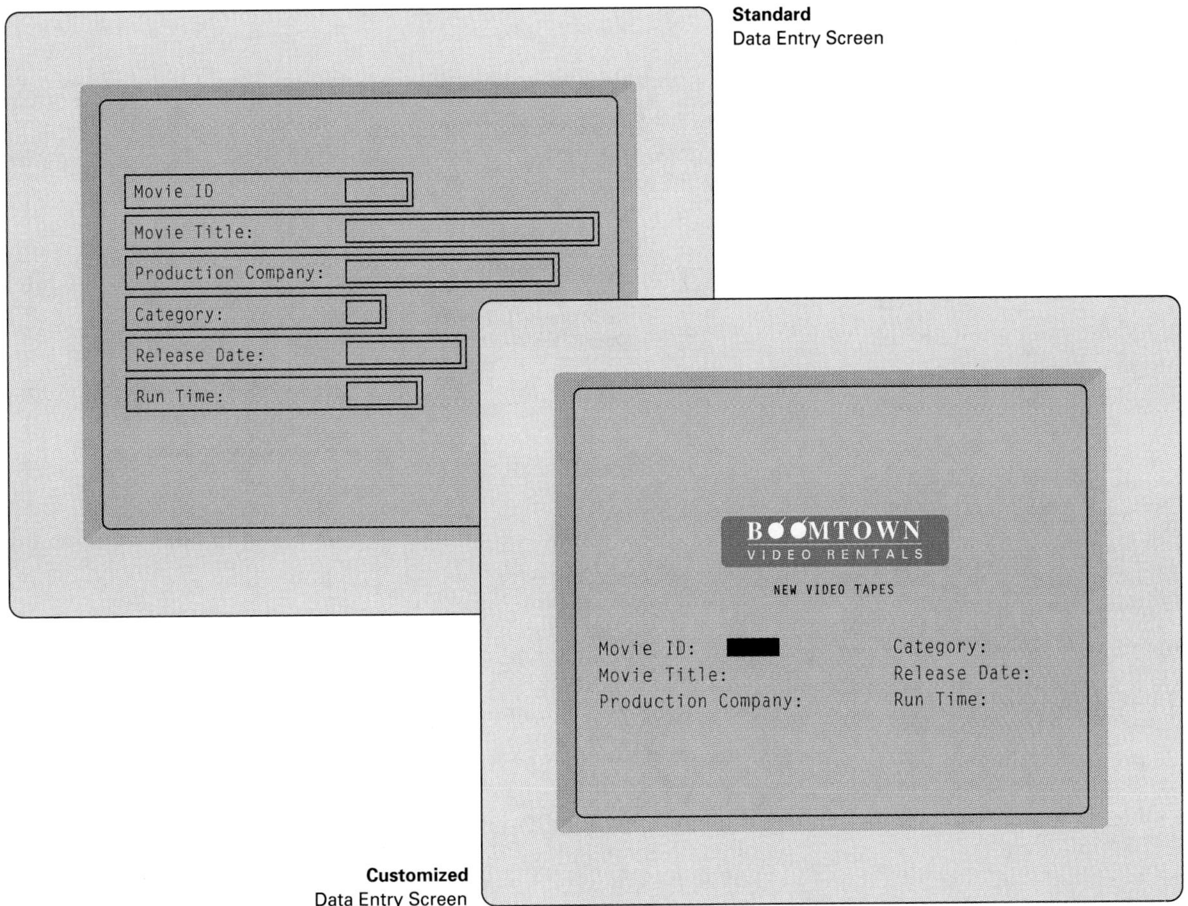

Sort

The *Sort* operation physically reorders the records in a file by placing data into a sequence defined by the user. The operation is conducted through use of a sort field. This sort field is part of the record and serves as the basis for the sort. For example, movie titles would be a suitable sort field for creating a viewing guide as shown in Figure 7.8. The sorted file could be used for printing a complete list of movies carried by the store in alphabetical order by title.

Index

The *Index* operation allows users to access records in different key field order while maintaining a file's original record sequencing. This task is accomplished by creating an index file that uses the key field to identify a disk address for each record. For example, the original customer file might be maintained in customer number order and indexed by last name and zip code. Since the postal service requires bulk mail to be organized by postal code (zip code), this index is used when printing personalized advertisements. As a result, customer records are processed and mailing labels output in postal code order.

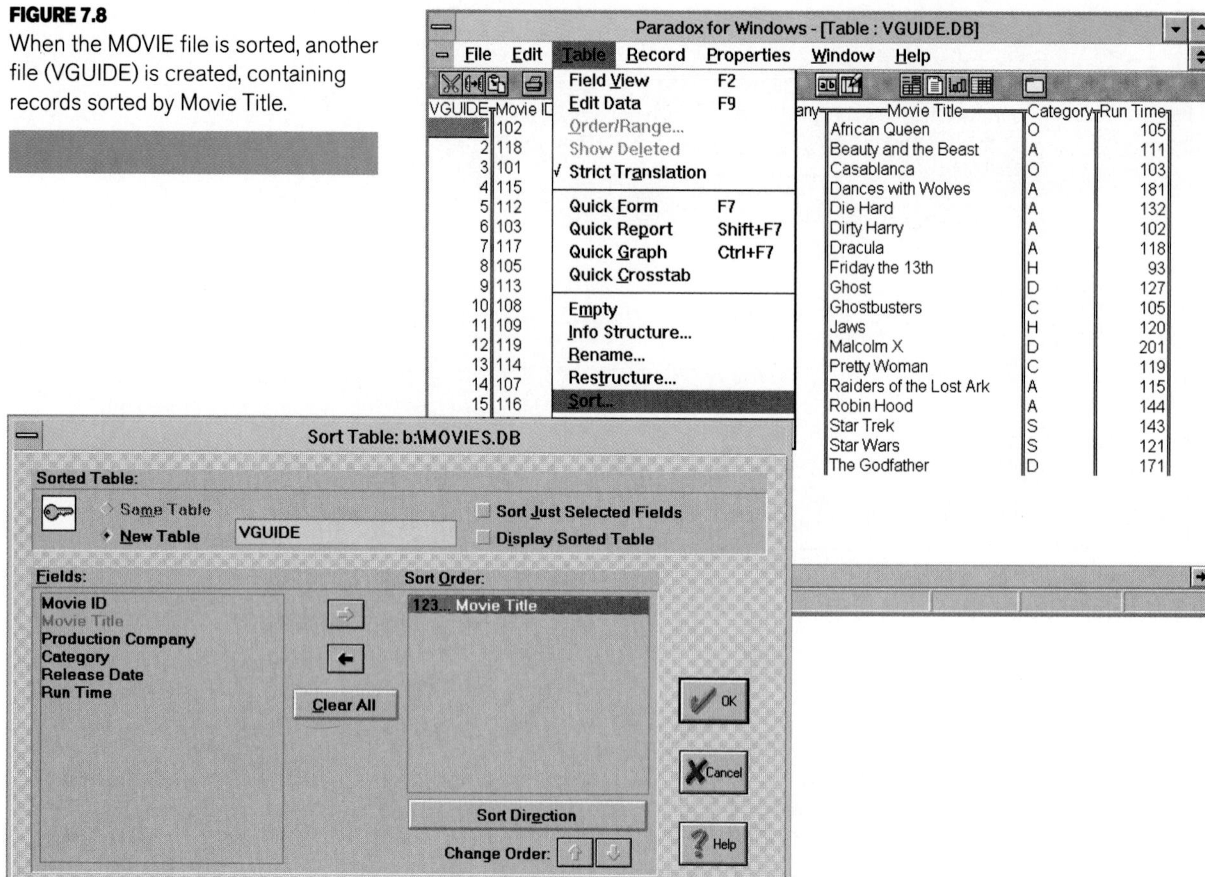

FIGURE 7.8
When the MOVIE file is sorted, another file (VGUIDE) is created, containing records sorted by Movie Title.

Application Generators

After the data administrator has defined and created critical files, a customized user interface is developed. Special software packages called **application generators** are purchased or provided with the data management system to support this development. Through various menus and graphical tools, a user/developer can design data entry requests, informational screens, and printed reports.

Teresa uses an application generator to develop a user-friendly interface to answer customer questions about movies carried by the video store. The application generator helps her create the icons and data entry prompts the data management system uses to access desired information. Customers will use a touch-sensitive screen to select movie titles by name, category, run time, or release date.

Queries

These requests for movie information are known as queries. A **query** is a user request to a data management system for information. Queries allow users to access, but not change, data. Each screen option created by the video store's application generator activates different predefined queries. Like other user interfaces, queries come in many formats.

SQL (Structured Query Language) is a popular command-driven interface. It is a data manipulation language consisting of designated key words. For example, a user who wished to print all customer names from records with a specific zip code field might enter:

```
SELECT LAST NAME, FIRST NAME
FROM CUSTOMER
WHERE ZIPCODE = 49442
```

These commands would direct the data management system to search the CUSTOMER file for records with the value of "49442" in the ZIPCODE field, then display the customer names held in those selected records.

Some packages enable the user to enter a query in ordinary English. The data management program deciphers the request to initiate processing through use of a natural language interface. For example, a video store manager might make the following natural language (English) request:

- Find all customers who have a tape overdue by more than 5 days.
- Print customer names and telephone numbers in sorted order based on the telephone number.

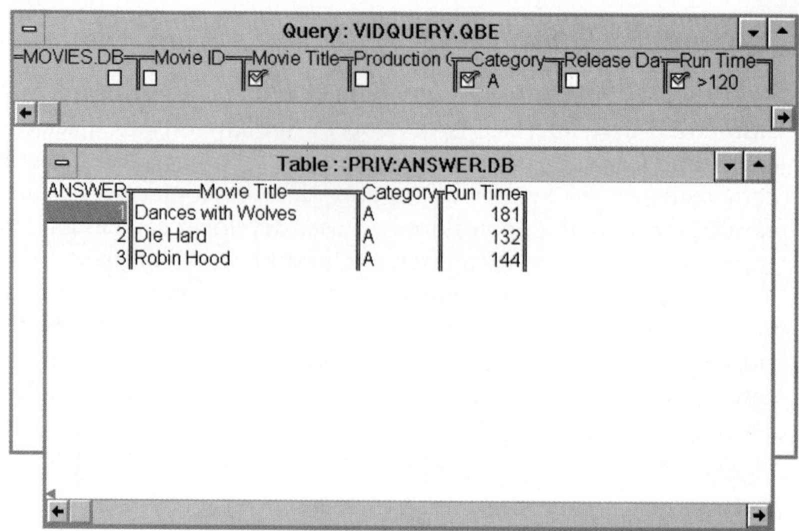

FIGURE 7.9
Queries by example employ a graphical interface that lets users identify specific fields and conditions. This query lists all movie titles with associated category and run time that are adventures (A) that run more than 120 minutes.

The data management system would translate these requests into computer-executable actions.

Data management software with a graphical user interface often employs *Query By Example (QBE)* as illustrated in Figure 7.9. In this case, the user is requesting a list of all adventure movies with a run time more than 2 hours (120 minutes) long. Check marks identify fields the user wants displayed. Conditions next to the field stipulate search conditions, for example, run times more than 120 minutes and movie category equal to A (Adventure).

In the News...

CHARACTERISTICS OF GOOD INFORMATION

The value of information is rooted in the validity of the underlying data and how accurately it is manipulated. To be effective, information must be:

- Current
- Timely
- Relevant
- Consistent
- Presented in a usable form

Report Generators

Every data management package and associated application generator should be equipped with capabilities to create hard copy output. These interfaces are called **report generators.** A report generator interface lets the user modify and design printed documents. Typically, report generators allow users to establish headings, footings, margin widths, pagination, page lengths, and line spacing. Additional report writing capabilities include printing mailing labels, arranging fields, and making calculations used for report subtotals, totals, and averages.

DATABASE MANAGEMENT

Many processing activities in an organization are integrated. Data processed in one application might well affect several other applications. Instead of building a file to meet the requirements of a single application, databases are organized for use in multiple applications. A database consists of several related files. Data held in databases appears only once. Key fields are repeated in multiple locations as links to related data items. For each processing job the data fields needed are identified and accessed through these key field links. This is accomplished with database management software.

Users define data needed for a processing job, and the database program manipulates and controls access to the needed data. The database software also maintains an extensive set of indexes that reflect the interrelationships among data fields.

Duplication of data is avoided in databases, except for keys that tie data fields together. If the video store uses a database program, a movie title, category, movie's run time, and release date would not be repeated for every copy of the movie maintained by the video store. Instead, each movie would have its own ID (identification) and every tape copy a unique tape number. As shown in Figure 7.10, a database management system would integrate the data from two files (tape inventory and movies) in order to avoid data redundancy.

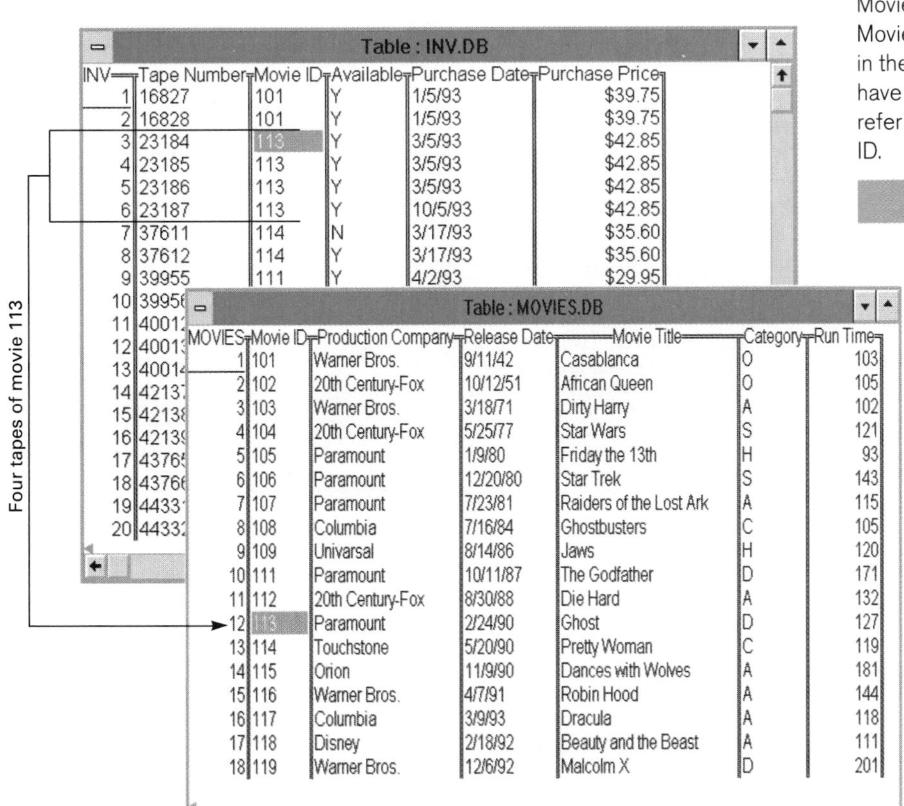

Table : INV.DB

INV	Tape Number	Movie ID	Available	Purchase Date	Purchase Price
1	16827	101	Y	1/5/93	$39.75
2	16828	101	Y	1/5/93	$39.75
3	23184	113	Y	3/5/93	$42.85
4	23185	113	Y	3/5/93	$42.85
5	23186	113	Y	3/5/93	$42.85
6	23187	113	Y	10/5/93	$42.85
7	37611	114	N	3/17/93	$35.60
8	37612	114	Y	3/17/93	$35.60
9	39955	111	Y	4/2/93	$29.95
10	3995				
11	4001				
12	4001				
13	4001				
14	4213				
15	4213				
16	4213				
17	4376				
18	4376				
19	4433				
20	4433				

Table : MOVIES.DB

MOVIES	Movie ID	Production Company	Release Date	Movie Title	Category	Run Time
1	101	Warner Bros.	9/11/42	Casablanca	O	103
2	102	20th Century-Fox	10/12/51	African Queen	O	105
3	103	Warner Bros.	3/18/71	Dirty Harry	A	102
4	104	20th Century-Fox	5/25/77	Star Wars	S	121
5	105	Paramount	1/9/80	Friday the 13th	H	93
6	106	Paramount	12/20/80	Star Trek	S	143
7	107	Paramount	7/23/81	Raiders of the Lost Ark	A	115
8	108	Columbia	7/16/84	Ghostbusters	C	105
9	109	Univarsal	8/14/86	Jaws	H	120
10	111	Paramount	10/11/87	The Godfather	D	171
11	112	20th Century-Fox	8/30/88	Die Hard	A	132
12	113	Paramount	2/24/90	Ghost	D	127
13	114	Touchstone	5/20/90	Pretty Woman	C	119
14	115	Orion	11/9/90	Dances with Wolves	A	181
15	116	Warner Bros.	4/7/91	Robin Hood	A	144
16	117	Columbia	3/9/93	Dracula	A	118
17	118	Disney	2/18/92	Beauty and the Beast	A	111
18	119	Warner Bros.	12/6/92	Malcolm X	D	201

FIGURE 7.10
The video store created two files (Inventory and Movies) to promote data integrity within the video tape data. A Tape Number identifies each tape, and Movie ID distinguishes each movie. Movie information appears only once in the Movies file. Related tapes each have a different Tape Number and refer to movie data by using the Movie ID.

This would not be the case for stores using a file management system. Without file integration every tape record would have to include the movie title and other information, even if the store had four copies (records) of the same movie.

The same is true for rental records within a file management system. Any customer renting several video tapes would have basic information, such as name and telephone number, repeated for each rental. This redundancy of data means that storage space is wasted and the updating of records is difficult. If a customer moves, the telephone number could be incorrect in several records.

As a result **data integrity** is critical when redundant data is possible. A data management system loses its data integrity when one field in one record is updated while related fields in other records remain unchanged. Maintaining data integrity is just one of several problems associated with file processing. Another problem centers on the difficulty in cross-referencing information among the files. Special requests for information residing across several files require the development of new programs or depend on manual processing. As a result, people have come to appreciate the potential knowledge they can gain from integrated data and have begun to demand more sophisticated data management software (see Figure 7.11).

FIGURE 7.11
User needs, technical support, and hardware requirements must be considered when purchasing data management software.

User Needs

___ Need to integrate files into a database
___ Expected maximums in most sophisticated application
  ___ fields/record ___ records/file ___ files/database
___ File Formats
  ___ imports different file formats ___ exports different file formats
___ Preferred user interface
  ___ command-driven ___ graphical
  ___ shell (menus) ___ natural language
___ Data formats
  ___ text ___ graphics ___ sounds
  ___ numbers ___ images ___ others
___ Special utilities
  ___ application generator ___ queries ___ report generator
___ Option to save queries and report formats
___ Error correction
  ___ checks data integrity of designated fields ___ customized error checks
___ Data security and password protection
___ Works within network operating environments

Technical Support

___ Local training available
  ___ schools
  ___ computer stores
  ___ users groups
  ___ other
___ Context-sensitive help screens
___ Easy-to-read manual
___ Tutorials for beginners
___ Telephone support
  ___ toll free
  ___ at your expense

Hardware Requirements

___ Compatible with your computer
___ Maximum number of files in use at same time
___ Minimums
  ___ memory
  ___ disk space
___ Peripheral support
  ___ mouse
  ___ printer
  ___ color monitor

Database Designs

As people became more experienced in using computer systems, they recognized that relationships existed among all data files connected to the operation of an organization. In all types of organizations—businesses, governments, schools, churches, and volunteer agencies—a global view of data's value and its many relationships began to take shape. It was seen that each data file represented a small part of an organization's operating cycle. Combined, the data and the relationships among the data items presented a model of the organization, its operations, its status, and its potential.

An integrated set of data files, a database, allows easy cross-referencing of related data items, promotes data integrity, and minimizes data redundancy. Databases are formed, in simple terms, by creating links between files. Sometimes these links are provided by indexes that locate related data in other files. Linked lists and other techniques are also used to integrate data files into a single database.

A database is seen as a useful, interrelated set of files within which individual records and fields are identified and located through the use of data manipulation language queries. Each database, in turn, is built upon a **data model,** or a plan the computer uses for storing and accessing data items. Data models used in building databases fall within three main categories:

- Hierarchical
- Network
- Relational

Hierarchical Model

A hierarchy is an organization that follows a top-down structure. A typical organization chart for a company presents a hierarchical structure. The highest-ranking executives are placed at the top of the chart, and relationships with subordinates are shown on a top-down basis.

A *hierarchical model* for a database follows the same principle. Data items and references to those items are related in a top-down structure. For example, the video store might structure a database as shown in Figure 7.12. At the top of this hierarchical model are the customers, at the next level are video tapes rented by the store, followed by tape rentals that connect a customer to specific tapes.

In this instance a hierarchical model makes possible orderly navigation of paths to the desired information through a series of related items. A potential disadvantage is that the same path must be followed for each access operation. Data access operations

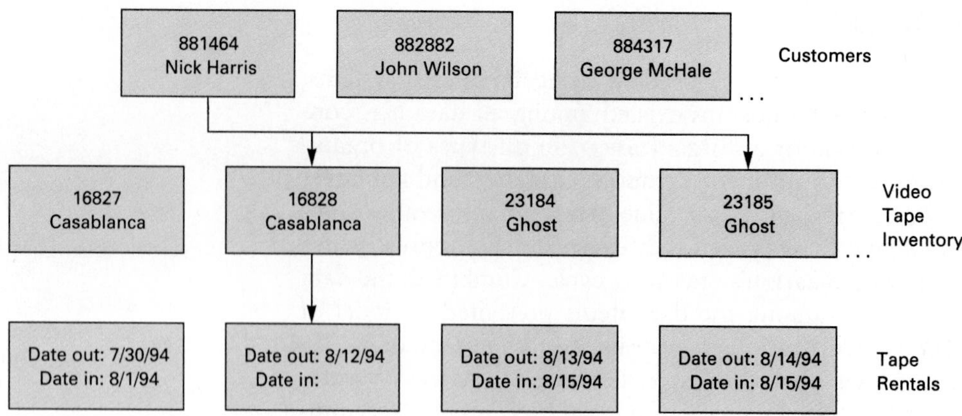

FIGURE 7.12
Hierarchical database models are characterized by a top-down design and structured access paths.

always begin, in this instance, with the customer. This design is useful if you want to know which tapes a customer has rented. It is less useful if someone wants to find out how many times a specific tape has been rented.

Network Model

A network model resembles a hierarchy in that both contain structured access paths. With a network, however, it is not necessary to follow a top-down order for each access of the database, and multiple access paths are possible between records. Networks can be entered at different points, with access routes leading in many directions. In the video store example, a network model makes it possible to access video rental data by either customer number or video tape number, as shown in Figure 7.13. Unlike a hierarchical data model, a network model supports a situation wherein the store can find out which customer rented a specific tape, along with how many times that tape has been rented.

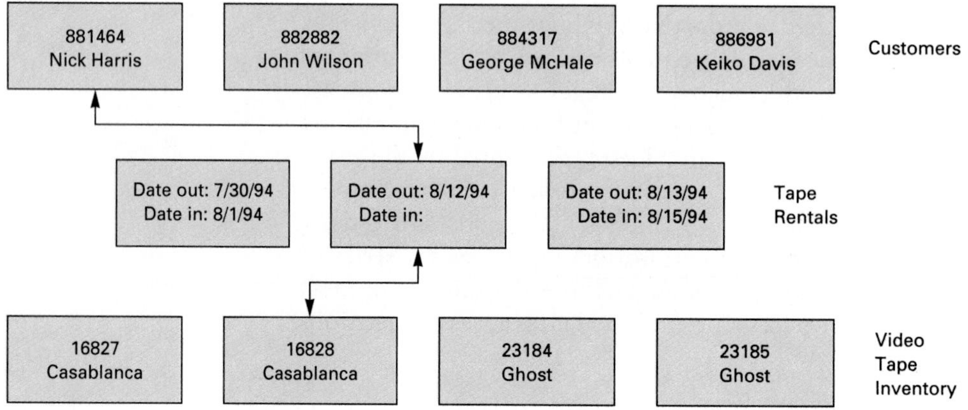

FIGURE 7.13
Network database models can access data a variety of ways by using preset access paths.

Relational Model

The success of the relational model has revolutionized the design and development of database management systems. As mentioned in this chapter's Who's Who, E. F. Codd's model employs a series of files organized as data tables. A **table** consists of a matrix of columns (vertical) and rows (horizontal) into which data can be placed. The example in Figure 7.14 contains the tables used by Boomtown Video Rentals. Each table is divided into a series of columns that represent data fields and rows that represent records.

To implement a relational model, a series of relations or tables would be established for each of two or more sets of data. Common fields establish relations between two tables. To support video tape rentals, for example, there would be relations for each movie, tape, customer, and rental. These tables would interconnect, using the Movie ID, Tape Number, and Customer Number to form multiple relations, as illustrated in Figure 7.14.

FIGURE 7.14
Relational database models allow flexible access to data by integrating data tables (files) using common data fields. In this model the Customer Number links data from the Customer and Rentals tables. Video Number links the Rentals and Inventory tables, while Movie ID links the Inventory and Movies tables.

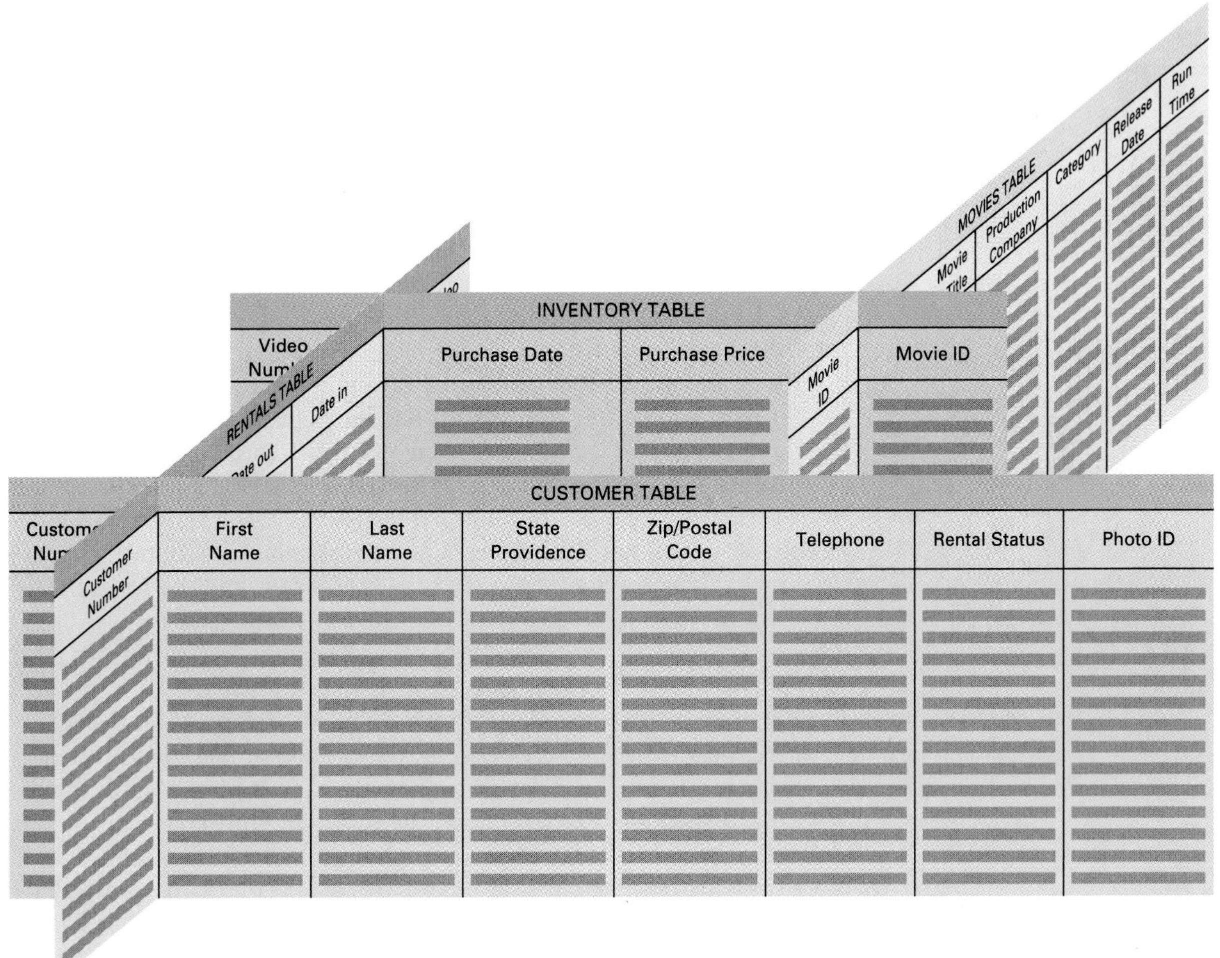

MOVIES TABLE

Movie ID	Movie Title	Production Company	Category	Release Date	Run Time
101	Casablanca	Warner Bros.	O	9/11/42	103
102	African Queen	20th Century-Fox	O	10/12/51	105
103	Dirty Harry	Warner Bros.	A	3/18/71	102
104	Star Wars	20th Century-Fox	S	5/25/77	121
105	Friday the 13th	Paramount	H	1/9/80	93
106	Star Trek	Paramount	S	12/20/80	143
107	Raiders of the Lost Ark	Paramount	A	[illegible]	115
108	Ghostbusters	Columbia	C		
109	Jaws	Univarsal	H		
111	The Godfather	Paramount	D		
112	Die Hard	20th Century-Fox	A		
113	Ghost	Paramount	D		
114	Pretty Woman	Touchstone	C		
115	Dances with Wolves	Orion	A		
116	Robin Hood	Warner Bros.	A		
117	Dracula	Columbia	A		
118	Beauty and the Beast	Disney	A		
119	Malcolm X	Warner Bros.	D		

ADVENTURES TABLE

Movie ID	Movie Title	Category	Run Time
103	Dirty Harry	A	102
107	Raiders of the Lost Ark	A	115
112	Die Hard	A	132
115	Dances with Wolves	A	181
116	Robin Hood	A	144
117	Dracula	A	118
118	Beauty and the Beast	A	111

FIGURE 7.15
A table just listing adventure movies is created by projecting selected data from the Movies table.

Relational database programs and related application generators have additional capabilities beyond those available to file management packages. These operations create new relationships by combining data into new tables.

Project

The *Project* operation is used to create an abbreviated version of an existing database table. In a relational database certain columns of a data table are copied, or projected, into a new table. In Figure 7.15 data related to movies within the adventure category is projected into a new table.

Join

Portions of multiple files can be brought together into a single file through use of the *Join* operation. In Figure 7.16 the Late Tapes table is created by joining elements from the Movie, Customer, Inventory, and Rental tables. The Date Out field comes from the Rentals table, while customer name and telephone number are supplied by the Customer table. When the Available field in the Inventory table is equal to "N," the tape is still out, and the Movie Title from the Movie table is joined to the Late Tapes table.

Subtract

Relational database programs have a *Subtract* operation that compares two tables and creates a third table containing the uncommon elements. Figure 7.17 illustrates how the tape Inventory table is subtracted from the Rentals table. The resulting table contains a list of rented tapes that do not have a match in the Inventory table. These situations represent a data integrity problem that needs immediate attention since the Rentals table contains tape numbers that do not exist in the Inventory table.

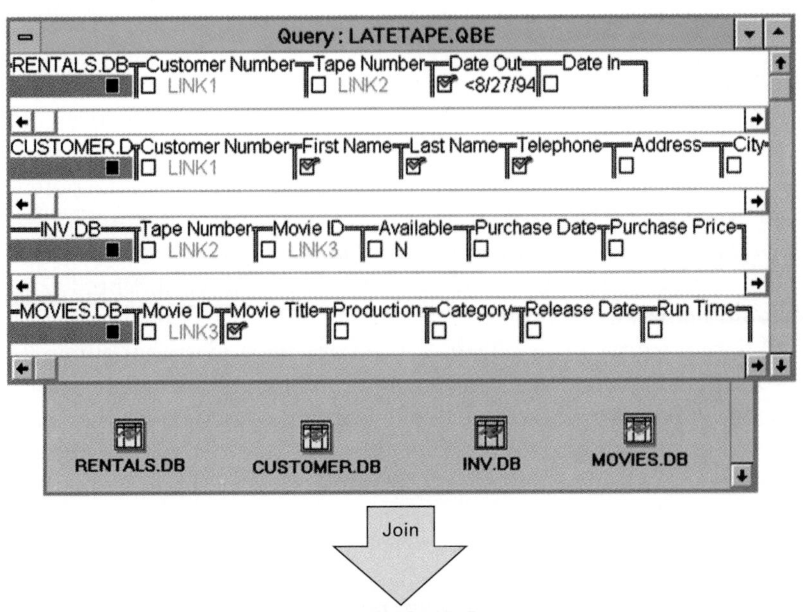

FIGURE 7.16
The *Join* operation links data from different tables to create a new table of common elements.

LATE TAPE TABLE

Date Out	First Name	Last Name	Telephone	Movie Title
8/12/94	Nick	Harris	(616) 555-0034	Casablanca
8/21/94	John	Wilson	(616) 555-7296	Robin Hood
8/25/94	Charles	Billings	(616) 555-0997	Ghostbusters
8/25/94	Martha	Young	(616) 555-5957	Pretty Woman

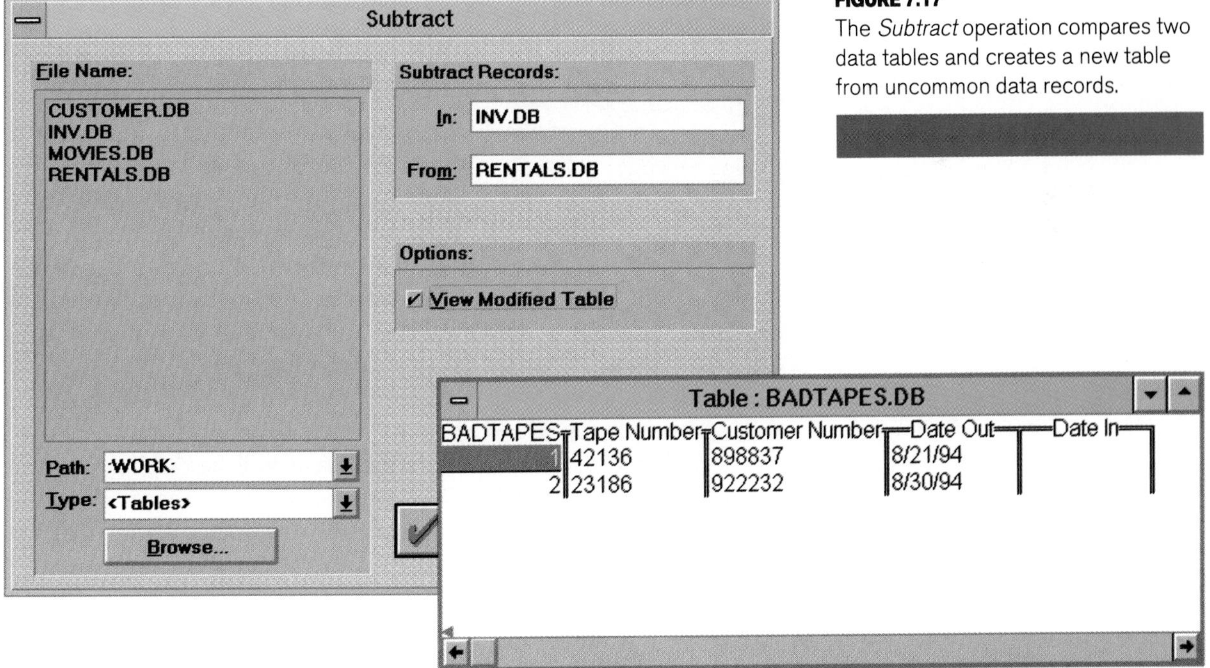

FIGURE 7.17
The *Subtract* operation compares two data tables and creates a new table from uncommon data records.

Pros and Cons of Database Processing

A database can be difficult and expensive to create. The time it takes to customize software, the need for database design expertise, and the cost to set up and maintain a database are its main drawbacks. Before anyone undertakes the job of building a database, the potential advantages should be weighed against the costs (Figure 7.18).

Database systems working on a network with multiple users need special precautions and security. Access to confidential data should be password protected. Special care must be taken to ensure the data integrity of key fields. Procedures must exist that eliminate problems associated with *concurrent updates*. A concurrent update occurs when two different users try to make changes to the same record at the same time. Problems like this result in two customers both being promised the same inventory item. This problem is avoided by having the database management software lock out (prevent access to) other users while the record is being updated.

The main advantage offered by a database is, perhaps, reduction in the cost of developing new applications. Once the database is in place, applications generators make it easy to generate special queries or reports. Procedures for the creation of new computer applications are covered in the chapter on system design and implementation. At this point the important factors are, first, to recognize that application development can be time consuming and costly. The second factor is that most of the cost of application development lies in writing special programs to build, maintain, and access those files. If database management software and a workable application generator are in place, most of the costs of file design and data access programs are eliminated.

Pros and Cons to Database Processing

Pros

1. Allows users easy cross-referencing of related data items.
2. Promotes data integrity by eliminating data redundancy.
3. Once database is in place, application generators help reduce cost of new user interfaces.
4. Application generators also reduce time to develop new user interfaces.

Cons

1. Takes time to develop integrated database files.
2. Users need expertise with application and database design.
3. Multi-user systems need special security procedures and precautions.

FIGURE 7.18
When properly designed, databases expand as users' needs grow while providing them with easy access to a wide range of related information.

Another important advantage of a database lies in elimination of data redundancy. When each application is supported by its own files, it is inevitable that some data content will be duplicated. This means procedures must be established so all occurrences of a data item are updated with each transaction that affects the item. As mentioned earlier, when a video store customer moves, the address must be updated in several files when a file management system is used. This adds cost and complexity to computer operations. Any failure to update a data item reduces the reliability of an organization's computer resources. However, if the video store uses a database, the address needs to be changed only once.

In the days when most databases had to be assembled entirely from scratch, costs could be difficult to justify. Today there are literally scores of user-friendly application generators that work with reliable database management software. Such software reduces costs and efforts, making databases practical for most computer users.

APPLICATIONS FOR DATA MANAGEMENT SOFTWARE

You will find data management systems are the heart and soul of any information system application. Some of these applications can be managed by using personal computer systems. A small business might use a personal computer to maintain inventory and customer records similar to Boomtown Video Rentals' system. In other situations more complex multi-user applications, often related to organizational or public databases, work within computer networks. Airline flight schedules or census statistics fall into this category.

Keep in mind that data management is an important part of modern society. The following sections review some of the most prominent uses for file and database management systems.

Hypermedia

Multimedia applications have merged with data management software to create **hypermedia** applications generators. Hypermedia software creates interfaces with highly flexible access to structured data. Associated data is organized into screen displays called *cards* (records), which incorporate any mix of text, numbers, sound, or graphics. Related cards are grouped together into *stacks* (files).

Hypermedia users navigate through stacks, moving one card at a time. Each card has a unique combination of text, graphs, and/or images that convey information to the user. Hot words or special icons identify links to additional information. At any point in the session, hypermedia users can click on button icons to skip to different cards within the active stack or in other stacks. For example, Figure 7.19 illustrates how hypermedia software can help people plan a vacation to Europe. After selecting a city, in this case Amsterdam, information related to points of interest, lodging, and restaurants is available by activating related buttons.

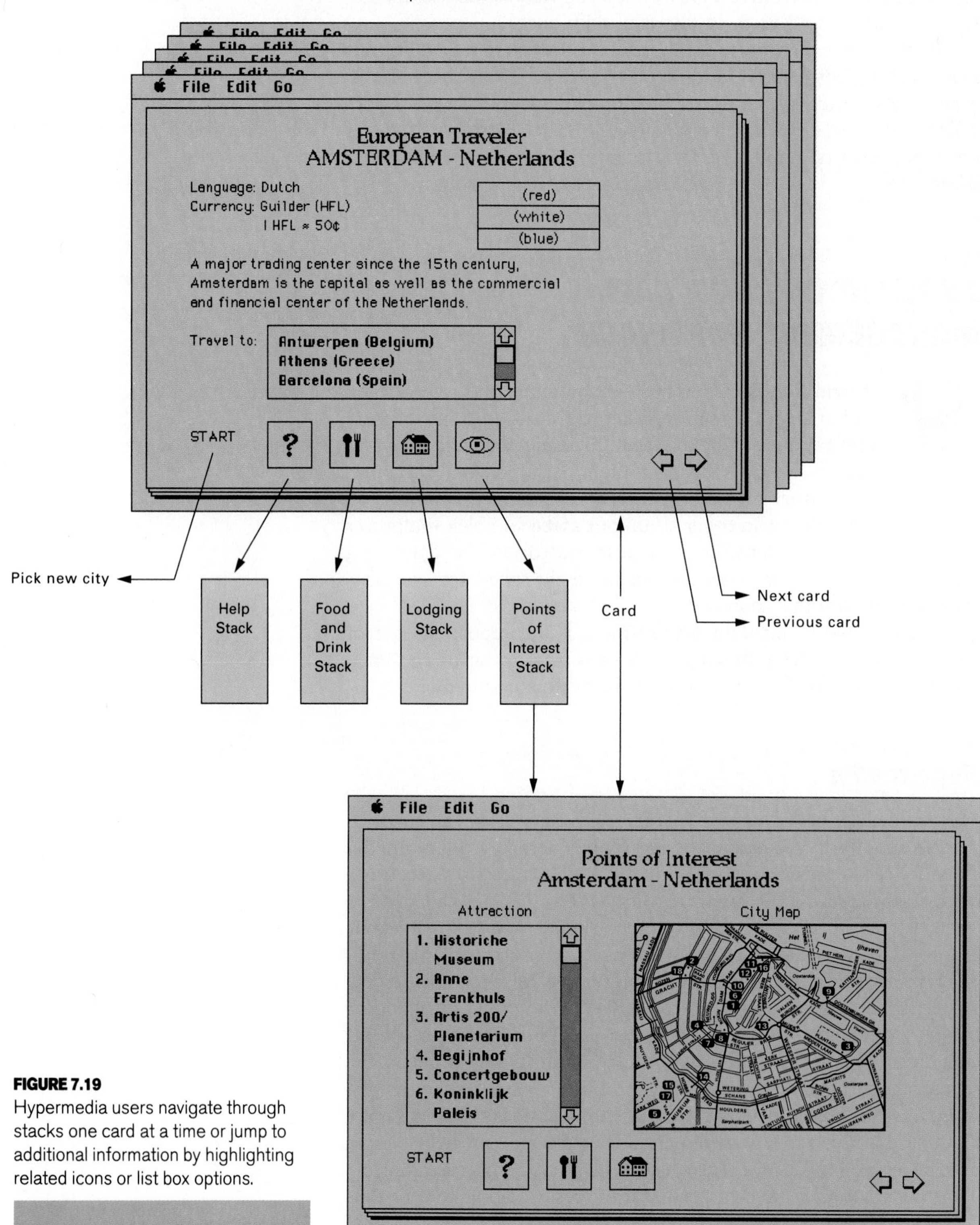

FIGURE 7.19
Hypermedia users navigate through stacks one card at a time or jump to additional information by highlighting related icons or list box options.

Education

Data management systems work behind the scene to help teachers and administrators keep student records up to date. Schools, from elementary to college level, maintain files and databases to keep track of business functions, as well as academic records. Data files for inventory and payroll keep these institutions functioning efficiently.

Teachers can use file management programs on small computers to store student grades and test questions. Test-generating software can select problems and assignments at random from a test bank, or teachers can pick specific questions. Along with the test, the software can develop matching answer keys. Thus, a teacher equipped with a file management system is able to vary test materials with ease. In addition, database software allows teachers to track individual student progress through course materials. By integrating test results with course objectives, database software can create individualized feedback sheets for students. These sheets would identify study materials to review, based on test results.

Counselors use computers to help students determine occupational and academic preferences. Large databases hold volumes of information about educational and experience requirements for a variety of jobs. By tying into these databases, counselors can direct students to careers that match their skills and goals. If a student decides to pursue a further educational degree, another database can help locate scholarship and loan programs.

Public Health

At many hospitals and clinics, computers decrease the time doctors and other professionals often spend in taking patient information and health histories. Patients provide information at computer terminals under prompting from the computer. These entries are incorporated into a patient history file that enables a medical professional to spend more time with patients and less time writing information into history files. When these history files are incorporated into the hospital's database management system, they support medical diagnosis (see Figure 7.20), laboratory analysis, and even patient billing.

Pharmacies use computers to keep track of drug dispensing activities. Prescription records entered into computers can be found quickly for responses to inquiries or for refilling prescriptions. In addition, some databases contain information that helps pharmacists spot potential problems with interactions between newly prescribed drugs and older medications.

Public health officials use databases to store and analyze data concerning new diseases and to monitor potential epidemics. Researchers at the Centers for Disease Control, for example, collect

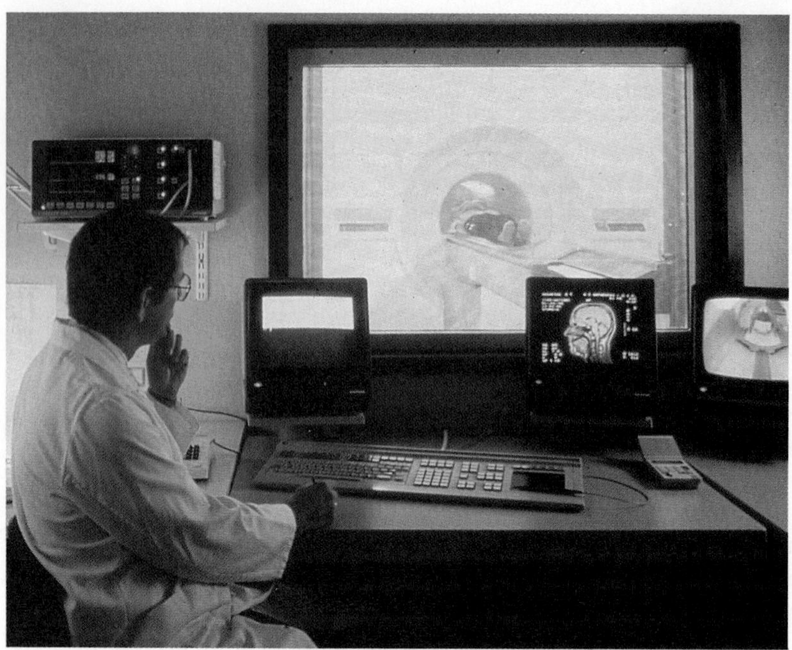

FIGURE 7.20
Medical diagnoses often use database files to help relate patient symptoms to similar cases and medical histories.

data from medical specialists around the country. With the help of database programs, the researchers can keep current on health dangers and suggested treatments.

Another use for databases in public health is the nationwide Poison Control Center. At the center a database is kept, containing information on poisons and their antidotes. Most household products, such as cleaners and medicines, are found in this database. A database program's ability to cross-reference information allows it to access antidotes, based on the brand name or contents of a product. Using data communication software, an emergency center in any state can call the poison center.

Law Enforcement

Police officers, FBI agents, attorneys, and judges all use databases in performing their jobs. Some databases store a vast amount of data about criminal, civil, and contract law. One of the largest law enforcement databases is run by the FBI's National Crime Information Center (NCIC). The NCIC database stores data on crimes, criminals, victims, and stolen properties. State law enforcement agencies can query the NCIC system whenever they need information. They also can add data to the system. This and other information, such as fingerprint images, can be shared by officers and court officials throughout the country.

Some police officers access databases from their patrol cars. A car license can be entered as a key field. The officer enters queries that determine if the car and/or its owner are listed in databases that keep track of stolen cars or "wants and warrants." Responses to the queries let an officer know whether to expect danger in connection with an arrest or when approaching a suspect (see Figure 7.21).

Courts use databases to help judges, legal secretaries, and clerks perform their jobs. The text of a state and/or municipal legal code can be stored in a database and searched for legal precedents or references. Case information and court decisions also are retained in online databases. Other data management systems organize and track information related to court scheduling and inventory evidence.

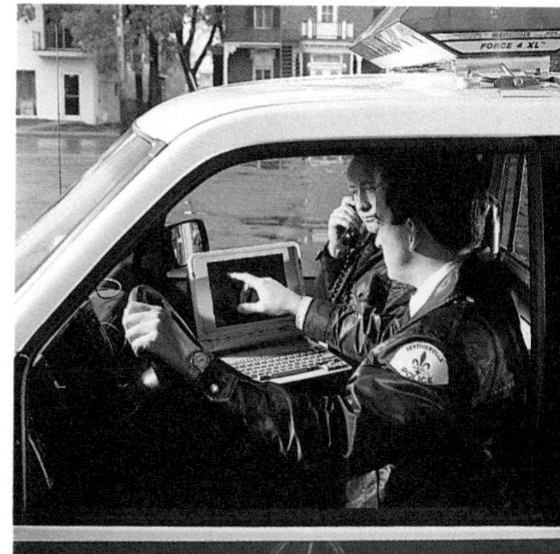

FIGURE 7.21
Access to databases by police officers provides immediate access to "wants and warrants," which helps them prepare and protect themselves.

Automotive Repair

In some cases file and database management systems are replacing small libraries of reference materials. When you take your car for a tune-up, your mechanic could be using a computer-based reference search to check parts numbers and engine specifications (see Figure 7.22). Easy access to information on many models of cars makes these systems ideal for mechanics who service a wide variety of vehicles. In addition, these electronic manuals are easily updated by the

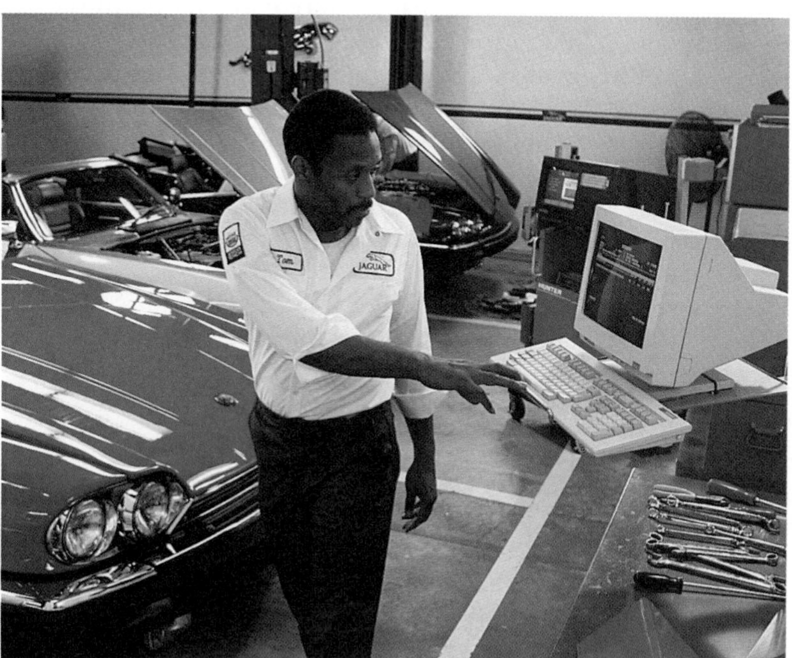

FIGURE 7.22
Access to databases with manufacturer's maintenance specifications and part numbers has replaced paper manuals and parts lists.

manufacturer and require less storage space than printed manuals. The U.S. Navy claims it has made some of its warships over 2,000 pounds lighter by replacing paper copies of manuals with the electronic equivalent.

FIGURE 7.23
Library services are supported by database programs that control patron records and lending activities, and perform reference searches.

Libraries

Databases have found their way into libraries with reference searches (see Figure 7.23). Here computers can search through large databases composed of titles, authors, and subject descriptions by looking for keywords. For example, several library services allow students to search a database for any book or article containing the words "computer-based training" in the title.

Hundreds of hours in research time can be saved by having the computer do the initial search through the literature. Although this service is expensive with specialized databases, it can be cost beneficial if the right keywords are used. On the other hand, someone doing a report on computer literacy who uses just the keyword "computer" will be no better off than before. The books and articles containing that keyword would fill a small library.

Agriculture

Farmers use data management systems to keep livestock records. Original costs, identification, maintenance costs, births, losses due to death, and selling prices are data fields contained in a record assigned to each animal. The data management system maintains individual records of animals and organizes this information for many uses. For example, a farmer might wish to compare original costs with selling prices for all livestock during a specified period. By identifying a few key fields, the farmer can instruct the data management program to locate and display the desired information quickly and easily.

Farmers keep special records on livestock and poultry breeding. The records contain genealogies over multiple generations. This data, in turn, helps scientists and farmers to breed desirable traits into herds or flocks. Examples include milk yield from dairy cows, rapid growth in chickens, large breasts in turkeys, and other characteristics.

Some breeding cooperatives have data management programs to track selected breeds of livestock. Data files on thoroughbred horses, beef and dairy cattle, and other livestock make up different databases.

A Closer Look...

Hypermedia

Many of the topics discussed in this chapter are incorporated into new applications being developed for hypermedia software: integrated data, application generators, and the ability to share software solutions among users. To illustrate these features, let's take a closer look at the hypermedia application for planning the vacation shown in Figure 7.19.

Q Who uses hypermedia?

A Anyone with a need to explore options or learn more about a subject is a potential user of hypermedia. This would include business people, students, travel agents, and workers learning about new equipment.

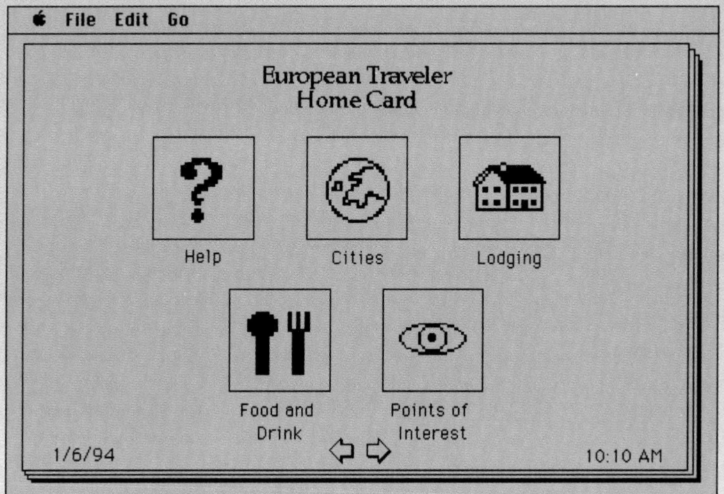

Q What kind of information can you get?

A Information found in a hypermedia stack is limited only by the imagination of the designer. Our European Traveler application contains stacks on each major city, points of interest, lodging, and restaurants. The hypermedia software indexes each stack on a starting, or home, card the user initially sees.

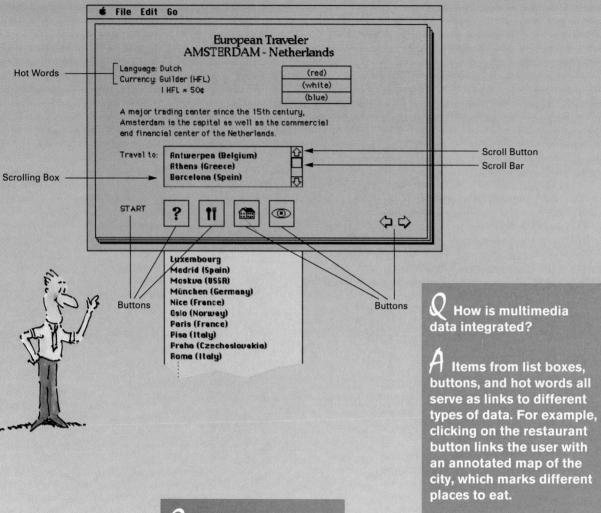

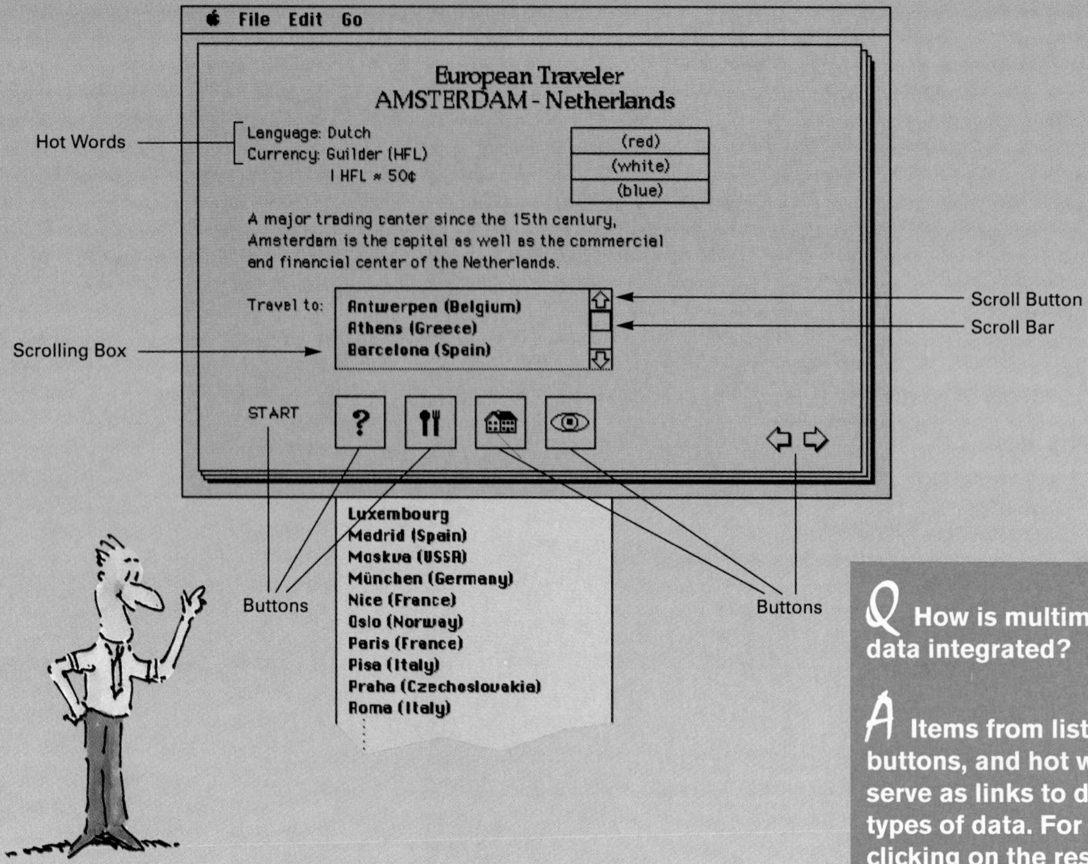

File Edit Go

European Traveler
AMSTERDAM - Netherlands

Hot Words

Language: Dutch
Currency: Guilder (HFL)
1 HFL ≈ 50¢

(red)
(white)
(blue)

A major trading center since the 15th century, Amsterdam is the capital as well as the commercial and financial center of the Netherlands.

Travel to:

Scrolling Box

Antwerpen (Belgium)
Athens (Greece)
Barcelona (Spain)
Luxembourg
Madrid (Spain)
Moskva (USSR)
München (Germany)
Nice (France)
Oslo (Norway)
Paris (France)
Pisa (Italy)
Praha (Czechoslovakia)
Roma (Italy)

Scroll Button

Scroll Bar

START

Buttons

Buttons

Q How is multimedia data integrated?

A Items from list boxes, buttons, and hot words all serve as links to different types of data. For example, clicking on the restaurant button links the user with an annotated map of the city, which marks different places to eat.

Q How do you navigate through all the stacks of information?

A Users navigate through the hypermedia cards by highlighting buttons, using the keyboard or a mouse. Arrow buttons usually take the user sequentially through the active stack, one card at a time. Hot words directly access related information found on different cards in other stacks.

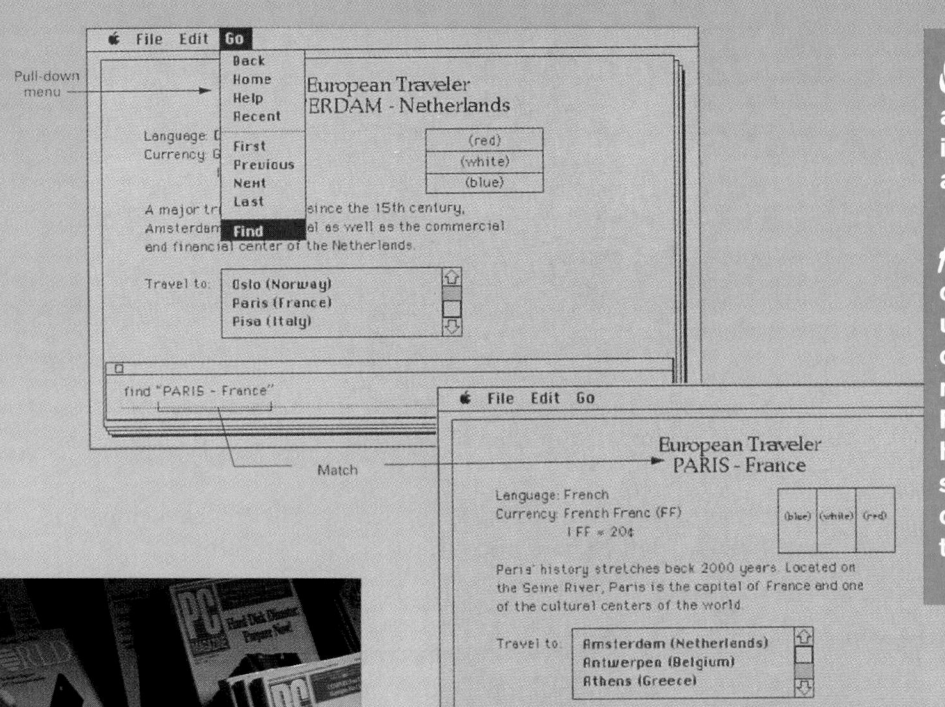

Q How can you directly access different data if no identifying icon (button) is available?

A To go directly to the card for Paris, France, a user would select the Find option from a pull-down menu. Entering "PARIS – France" would send the hypermedia software on a search for the first card it could find with a match to these characters.

Q How do you acquire hypermedia stacks?

A As hypermedia software and applications become more popular, businesses have begun to design and sell stacks to users willing to pay for this service. Magazines and retail stores are the best sources for prepackaged hypermedia stacks.

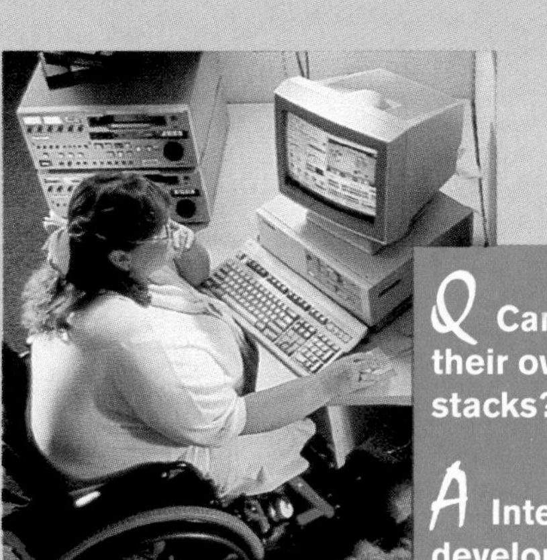

Q Can people develop their own cards and stacks?

A Interested user/developers can change text, create new line art, and link new cards to a stack. Application generators are used to create new stacks. Users start by scripting the relationship one card has to other cards in its own stack and to cards in other stacks.

Chapter Facts

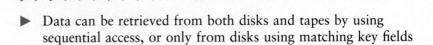

- Data can be retrieved from both disks and tapes by using sequential access, or only from disks using matching key fields to support direct access.
- Batch processing supports sequential access, while real-time processing relies on direct access techniques.
- File management systems access one file at a time, which makes requests for information residing in multiple files more difficult to obtain. Duplicate data across files can also create problems.
- In databases, files are linked by common key fields. This eliminates duplication of data and allows access by multiple application programs.
- Data management software organizes data through a data definition language and allows queries to be made through different user interfaces with the data manipulation language.
- A data manipulation language allows the user to control files and make queries through select, append, update, sort, and index operations.
- Application and report generators help users create data entry prompts, queries, and printed documents.
- A data model reflects the plan a computer system uses when storing and accessing data items.
- Databases can be organized into one of three models: hierarchical, network, or relational.
- Relational database programs can create new tables by using project, join, and subtract operations.
- Databases reduce time and costs for developing new applications while eliminating data redundancy. They can be expensive and difficult to set up.
- Data integrity is critical when data management systems are accessed by multiple users.
- Multimedia applications combined with data management techniques are incorporated into hypermedia application generators.
- Database programs are useful in many areas including education, medicine and public health, law, agriculture, and reference systems.

Terms to Remember

a. application generator
b. batch processing
c. data administrator
d. data integrity
e. data model
f. database management software
g. direct access
h. file management software
i. hypermedia
j. index
k. key
l. query
m. real-time processing
n. report generator
o. sequential access
p. table
q. update

Mix and Match

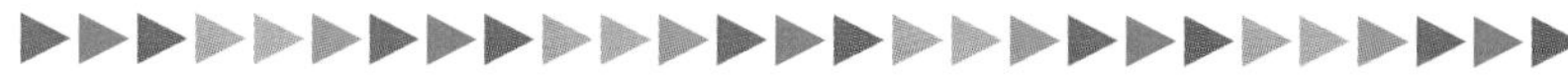

Match the following definitions to the Terms to Remember

1. _____ finding one record without processing other records.
2. _____ user request for information.
3. _____ individual responsible for an organization's data.
4. _____ add to, change, or delete from data in a file.
5. _____ processing data in groups.
6. _____ field used to identify record in a file.
7. _____ multimedia application for data management software.
8. _____ processing a user request as soon as it is input.
9. _____ attribute of a data file whereby every data field is accurate and properly identified.
10. _____ separate file based on a key field, which identifies location of a record within a data file.
11. _____ interface for designing and modifying printed documents.
12. _____ computer program that maximizes access to a flat file.
13. _____ independent file within a relational database.
14. _____ finding an individual record by looking at every record in a file one at a time.
15. _____ computer program that creates, stores, and accesses integrated data files.

16. ____ computer program users work with to design data entry screens, user prompts, and printed reports.
17. ____ plan computer uses for storing and accessing data.

Review Questions

1. What types of storage media are used with sequential and direct access methods?
2. How is the key field used when sequentially accessing a record and when directly accessing a record?
3. What types of access methods are used with batch processing and real-time processing?
4. Why are flat files associated with file management software?
5. What features do file management and database management systems have in common?
6. What are four responsibilities of a data administrator?
7. Explain the function of the Create, Select, Append, Update, Sort, Index, Project, Join, and Subtract operations.
8. What types of user interfaces are represented by the Structured Query Language and Query By Example?
9. Identify five document design features a report generator handles.
10. How can a database lose its data integrity?
11. What are two disadvantages to file processing?
12. Describe the important features of hierarchical, network, and relational database models.
13. What are four advantages to using a database and three potential disadvantages?
14. How do school administrators, teachers, and counselors use file and database management?
15. In what ways can access to a database help doctors, pharmacists, and public health officials?
16. Explain how police officers, FBI agents, and judges utilize file and database management programs to perform their jobs.
17. How can a data management system help an automotive repair technician?
18. How could the use of a reference search help you in school?
19. How does a hypermedia user navigate through the cards in a stack?

Applying What You've Learned

1. Describe two applications (not in the text) for each type of access method: sequential and direct. Include the fields in a typical record and identify an appropriate key field.
2. Use one of the database models described in the text to organize the data that would be needed in one of these applications. Make a general diagram of the data relationships as shown in the text.
   a. recording flights in and out of your local airport
   b. accessing a student database by student number, name, or major
   c. sending advertising to credit card customers based on the types of purchases they make
   d. setting up a reference search system in a library
3. Several database programs exist for use on microcomputers. Information about them can be obtained from computer magazines and retail stores. Investigate one of these programs. Report on the commands it includes, type of model (if known) it uses, its memory requirements, how much data it can hold, and its cost. Find out if classes or tutorials are available to train users.
4. Write a natural language command that would produce the following data:
   a. list of drivers with expired licenses
   b. list of voters who voted in the last local election
   c. list of library patrons with overdue books
   d. names of salespeople who earned more than $1000 in commissions last month
   e. list of employees within a year of retirement
5. Multimedia applications using hypermedia have incredible potential. Describe an application for hypermedia. What type of graphics, images, and sounds would be integrated with text and numbers? How would the stacks be organized? Draw a sample card and identify the different types of data used in the card.

Answers to Mix and Match

1. g 2. l 3. c 4. q 5. b 6. k 7. i 8. m 9. d 10. j
11. n 12. h 13. p 14. o 15. f 16. a 17. e

UNIT THREE

Hardware and Communications

Unit Three explores how computer technology works internally. Chapter 8 explains the different types of processing hardware. Ranging in power from a single-purpose microcomputer to a high-capacity mainframe or supercomputer, the processing hardware is the controlling element. Characteristics of each type of processing hardware are examined along with the problems they best solve.

Computer-generated information is only as useful as the input data and output information. Chapter 9 looks at the different types of input and output hardware involved in a variety of applications. Different techniques exist for entering data of varying types. Peripherals also come in diverse forms to support temporary, permanent, and action output.

People use a variety of equipment to store data in a computer-readable format. Chapter 10 examines magnetic tape and disk media as well as new innovations in optical storage. Special procedures for maximizing disk utilization and minimizing errors are looked at as well.

Chapter 11 concludes this unit with a study of networking applications and associated hardware and software. A mobile society requires that information travel with its members. For this reason, Chapter 11 focuses on how processing power and information are distributed to users, no matter where they are.

QUARTER SALES
Los Angeles
22
HEWLETT PACKARD
LaserJet IIISi

8

Processing Hardware

- From the User's Point of View
- Processing in the Past
  - First generation
  - Second generation
  - Third generation
  - Fourth generation
  - Fifth generation
- Binary Codes for Data and Instructions
  - Machine code
  - Standard codes for data
- The Central Processing Unit
  - The processor
  - Memory
  - CPU operations
  - The anatomy of a microcomputer
- Hardware to Solve Different Problems
  - Mainframes and organizational systems
  - Minicomputers and work group systems
  - Microcomputers and personal systems
  - Specialized processing hardware
- A Closer Look . . . The Making of a Microprocessor

FROM THE USER'S POINT OF VIEW

As with any other technology, present-day computers have built on the hardware designs of the past. Even if you never build a computer system, it is important that you know how the computer itself works. As an automobile driver, it is not necessary that you understand the internal workings of an engine, but this knowledge helps you know the limits of the vehicle and explain performance problems to technicians. Likewise, understanding the processing components of a computer system helps you troubleshoot problems or, at least, adequately explain difficulties to a computer professional. Also, knowing the options available to speed up processing helps you become a knowledgeable consumer when purchasing new computer equipment.

PROCESSING IN THE PAST

Although the visible components of a computer system—such as a scanner or color printer—may be impressive, the real power lies unseen within the processing hardware. The power and speed of processing hardware has increased astronomically since the first computers were built. Over the past fifty years, several unique forms of processing hardware have led people who study computing history to break it into five generations.

First Generation

Before the 1940s there were several attempts to build mechanical computing machinery. Jacquard (Who's Who, Chapter 9), Babbage (Who's Who, Chapter 13), and Pascal (Who's Who, Chapter 1) all attempted and succeeded to varying degrees.

Even as late as 1944, an electromechanical calculator, the MARK1, incorporated mechanical and electrical components to perform simple arithmetic on data. Colossus, developed in England in 1943, was used to decode German military codes during World War II. It is considered the first working electronic computer.

Back in the United States, J. Presper Eckert and John W. Mauchley were building the ENIAC (see Who's Who, Chapter 2). Its processing hardware consisted of 17,000 vacuum tubes, 70,000 resistors, and 5 million soldered joints. *Vacuum tubes,* with their ability to turn off and on, were the components that stored the data and results as they were processed. Each vacuum tube was made of glass and contained electronic circuitry. Other computers, like UNIVAC I (shown in Figure 8.1), and radios and televisions of the day, depended on vacuum tubes. How-

FIGURE 8.1
The first commercially successful computer was the UNIVAC I. The first system was delivered to the U.S. Bureau of Census in 1951, the second to General Electric in 1952.

ever, these tubes were unreliable because the tremendous heat they generated shortened the working lives of the tubes and associated electrical equipment. Replacing tubes slowed processing.

Second Generation

The late 1940s brought an invention that would revolutionize not only the computer industry but the entire world of electronics—the **transistor.** It was a small component that could transfer an electronic signal across a resistor. When transistors were used as the basis for a computer's processing hardware, the problems of heat production and unreliability were significantly reduced. Use of the transistor, developed by Shockley, Bardeen, and Brattain (see Who's Who in this chapter), quickly spread to radios and other electronic devices.

Third Generation

Although people found new uses for the transistor, it still produced too much heat for use in small or enclosed equipment. In 1959, Kilby tested the first **integrated circuit** or **IC** (see Who's Who, in this chapter). The IC is a solid-state circuit made from a semiconducting

(a)

(b)

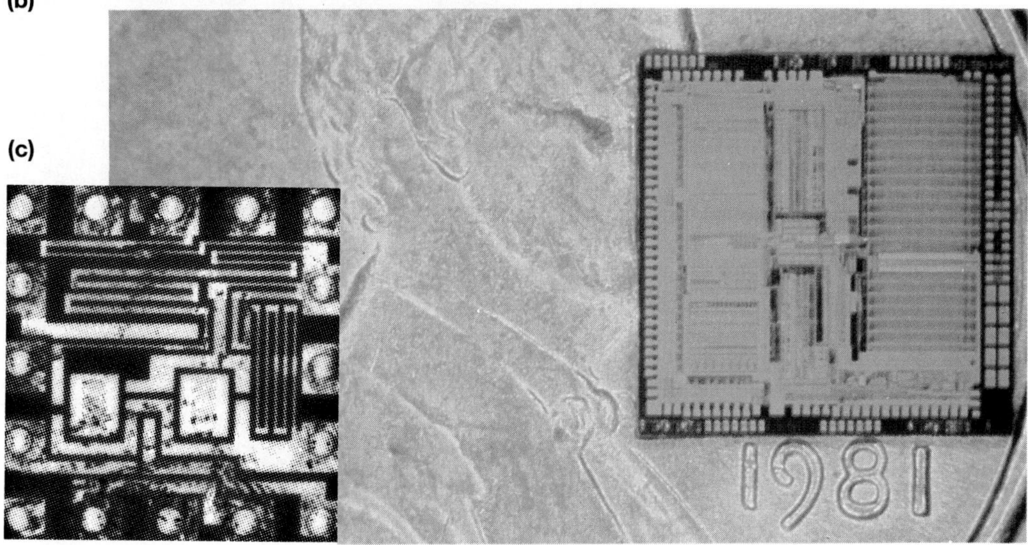

(c)

(d)

FIGURE 8.2
The first four computer generations are represented here by their processing hardware: (a) vacuum tube, (b) transistor, (c) integrated circuit, and (d) microprocessor.

material. The wafer-sized ICs could hold the equivalent of hundreds of transistors. The wafers, called *chips*, made computers smaller, faster, and lighter than their predecessors. The Closer Look at the end of this chapter explains how chips are manufactured.

Fourth Generation

The miniaturization of computer processing hardware continued with the invention of the **microprocessor** by Hyatt and Hoff (see Who's Who in this chapter). Initially designed for use in video controllers, microprocessors found instant success in the computer market. Previously, computer processing capabilities were distributed among several integrated circuits. Microprocessors combined circuits for processing, limited memory, and input/output control on a

FIGURE 8.3
The small, powerful, and user-friendly microcomputer became popular among businesses, homes, and schools.

single chip. The first commercially developed microprocessor—the Intel 4004—was developed in 1971. A few years later, the Intel 8008 expanded the capacity of the original version by providing multiuse arithmetic and control circuitry. The computing power that occupied an entire room during the 1950s can today reside on a slice of silicon smaller than a penny.

Fifth Generation

The microprocessor is still the processing hardware of choice for many computers. However, research into faster ways of processing volumes of data has led to alternatives to this fourth-generation hardware. By combining rows of microprocessors, computer scientists are leading the way into the fifth generation through **parallel processing.** When using this technology, a single computer program is broken down into several modules and processed simultaneously by the parallel processors. Efficiency and speed are considerably increased.

BINARY CODES FOR DATA AND INSTRUCTIONS

Even from the earliest days of computing, the processing hardware of every computer generation used bits and bit patterns to internally represent data and programs. George Boole held that all logical conditions could be described as either true or false (see Who's Who, Chapter 11). Computer circuitry is an application of this theory. When electricity is present, circuits or paths through the computer's processing components may be either open or closed to the electrical pulses. Bit patterns, or combinations of these on/off bits, are how data and programs are processed and stored.

Machine Code

Computer programming languages using English words or abbreviations must be translated into binary codes. When processing hardware is manufactured by different companies, each may have its own binary machine language, or **machine code.** Machine code represents the processor's internal switches with a 0, usually designating an open switch, and a 1, designating a closed switch. Different switch settings perform different operations.

Figure 8.4 shows how one line from a program written in the BASIC programming language might be translated into several lines

FIGURE 8.4
One instruction in the high-level programming language BASIC actually translates into several lines of machine code.

Machine Code

One High-Level Program Instruction		Several Machine Language Instructions
TOTAL = TICKETS * COST	=	1011 0011 1001 0100 (Moves TICKETS from memory to processor) 1111 0101 1101 1100 (Moves COST from memory to processor) 0001 1000 0010 1001 (Initiates multiplication) 1110 1010 0110 0100 (Moves answer (TOTAL) from processor to memory)

of machine code. This line of BASIC code is one of many that make up a complete program. It is used to figure a TOTAL price when purchasing a designated number of TICKETS at a specified COST. The first two binary codes in Figure 8.4 identify the location in memory of the number of TICKETS sold and the COST of each ticket. The next line of machine code tells the processor to multiply TICKETS by COST. The last binary instruction indicates where the results, called TOTAL, are stored in memory.

Standard Codes for Data

As with program instructions, data is also expressed as binary code. All input, whether a keystroke from a keyboard or a scan from a scanner, is converted to zeros and ones. Keystrokes can represent an alphanumeric symbol or a *control character,* which represent special instructions for cursor movement, tabulation, carriage return, and so on. As mentioned in Chapter 6, a scanner converts a photograph into pixels, whose location and color are represented in a binary code. A MIDI uses bit combinations to indicate the pitch and duration of musical notes. Different combinations of bits represent textual, graphical, and audio data. Computers that process data converted to binary digits are called *digital computers.*

A group of bits forms a bit pattern, known as a **byte,** which represents a single alphanumeric or control character. Several standard binary codes exist to represent textual data. As a result, no single standard has been established for all computers. Typically, computers use codes that assign either seven or eight bits per byte. Codes vary according to the type of computer system used.

Most smaller computers use a seven-bit code called the American Standard Code of Information Interchange, or *ASCII* (pronounced as′-kee). ASCII was used originally by the communication industry for transmission over telegraph lines. This code has been adopted as the standard for many computers, particularly personal computers. With ASCII, users can transmit data from one computer to another, even if the machines have different internal coding systems. Noncompatible data from one computer is converted to the widely compatible ASCII code for transmission. The second computer receives the ASCII data and converts the data to its own internal code. Software also exists to convert data to an ASCII file for storage on disk.

As a result, the use of ASCII increases opportunities to share data. A more recent version of ASCII uses eight-bit bytes. This expansion increases the number of bit combinations possible from 128 to 256 and therefore the number of characters that can be rep-

CHARACTER	ASCII BINARY	ASCII DECIMAL	CHARACTER	ASCII BINARY	ASCII DECIMAL	CHARACTER	ASCII BINARY	ASCII DECIMAL
a	01100001	97	A	01000001	65	0	00110000	48
b	01100010	98	B	01000010	66	1	00110001	49
c	01100011	99	C	01000011	67	2	00110010	50
d	01100100	100	D	01000100	68	3	00110011	51
e	01100101	101	E	01000101	69	4	00110100	52
f	01100110	102	F	01000110	70	5	00110101	53
g	01100111	103	G	01000111	71	6	00110110	54
h	01101000	104	H	01001000	72	7	00110111	55
i	01101001	105	I	01001001	73	8	00111000	56
j	01101010	106	J	01001010	74	9	00111001	57
k	01101011	107	K	01001011	75	space	00100000	32
l	01101100	108	L	01001100	76	.	00100001	33
m	01101101	109	M	01001101	77	"	00100010	34
n	01101110	110	N	01001110	78	#	00100011	35
o	01101111	111	O	01001111	79	$	00100100	36
p	01110000	112	P	01010000	80	%	00100101	37
q	01110001	113	Q	01010001	81	&	00100110	38
r	01110010	114	R	01010010	82	(	00101000	40
s	01110011	115	S	01010011	83	)	00101001	41
t	01110100	116	T	01010100	84	*	00101010	42
u	01110101	117	U	01010101	85	+	00101011	43
v	01110110	118	V	01010110	86	.	00101110	46
w	01110111	119	W	01010111	87	/	00101111	47
x	01111000	120	X	01011000	88	<	00111100	60
y	01111001	121	Y	01011001	89	>	00111110	62
z	01111010	122	Z	01011010	90	?	00111111	63

FIGURE 8.5
Eight-bit ASCII is a binary code used in most personal computer systems to represent alphanumeric and control characters. This is only a portion of the 256 bit combinations available.

resented. For example, the bit pattern for the upper-case letter A in 8-bit ASCII is 01000001, a dollar sign is represented by 00100100, and the control character TAB is 00001001 (see Figure 8.5).

Larger computers typically use an eight-bit code called Extended Binary Coded Decimal Interchange Code, or *EBCDIC* (pronounced eb′-sih-dik). The letter A in EBCDIC is 1100 0001 and a comma is encoded as 0111 1101. While ASCII is used most commonly with personal computers and data communication, EBCDIC is used primarily for internal data handling by larger computers.

Once data has been converted into binary form, it is ready to be processed. Processing data to obtain information occurs within the **central processing unit,** or **CPU.** Central processing units condense all the computational functions of a computer into two major components:

- Processor
- Memory

The processor combines arithmetic, logic, and control/communications operations on one or more chips, depending on the size of the computer. Memory requires several chips to store data and programs during a specific IPOS cycle. Operations executed (performed) within the processor and memory are synchronized by an electronic clock built into the CPU. The clock emits electrical pulses or cycles at a fixed rate. For example, the clock speed determines if a microprocessor in a personal computer runs at 33 *MHz (megahertz)* versus 16 MHz. Each megahertz is equal to a million clock cycles per second. These pulses are used to coordinate program execution.

The Processor

Data transformation, although seemingly sophisticated, is actually based on a simple premise. Computers can add and compare values. These operations take place at tremendous speeds within the processor. The speeds are measured in fractions of a second as *milliseconds* (thousandths), *microseconds* (millionths), *nanoseconds* (billionths), and *picoseconds* (trillionths). Instead of executing highly complex operations, a computer conducts many simple operations very quickly. This is the essence of computer processing power.

To make use of this power, the processor relies on three operations:

- Arithmetic
- Logic
- Control/Communication

Arithmetic Operations

All the mathematics a computer performs is, essentially, addition. The computer can add two numbers to obtain a sum. Subtraction is actually negative addition, multiplication is repeated addition,

Who's Who

William Shockley (1910–1989)

John Bardeen (b. 1908)

Walter Brattain (1902–1987)

In the 1940s computers and other electronic equipment had reached a physical impasse. They processed data by means of vacuum tubes, which were bulky, hot, undependable, and consumed a lot of power. Scientists William Shockley, John Bardeen, and Walter Brattain worked together at Bell Laboratories looking for a more reliable replacement for the vacuum tube. After many tests, Shockley theorized that applying an external electrical field to a block of quartz with semiconducting film on one side and a metallic conductor on the other would provide the needed medium. They produced a "junction transistor" and revealed it to the scientific world in 1948. Acceptance was not immediate for the solid-state transistor. Although easier to mass produce than the vacuum tube, the transistor could not be put into existing machines. However, use of the transistor in telephones, hearing aids, and radios brought the three men recognition. In 1956 Shockley, Bardeen, and Brattain were awarded the Nobel Prize in Physics. Just ten years after its invention, the transistor technology was supplanted by a new idea—putting an entire circuit on a single piece of silicon: the integrated circuit.

and division is repeated negative addition. That is, a computer will use addition to find solutions to the following problems:

$6 - 3 = n$	$6 * 3 = n$	$6 / 3 = n$
$6 + (-3) = 3$	$6 + 6 + 6 = 18$	$6 + (-3) + (-3) = 0$

[Here the computer determines the answer (2) by counting the number of −3s that must be added before 0 is reached.]

Simple addition, then, enables the computer to solve complex mathematical problems. Repetitions of arithmetic functions take very little time, since millions of instructions can be processed every second.

Logical Operations

Computer logic is, simply, comparing two values by determining whether a value is equal to, greater than, or less than another value. While this idea is simple, it holds the potential for great processing power. For example, computer logic can determine whether the number of tickets sold is equal to the number of seats in a theater. If so, the show is sold out. Computerized inventory systems depend on this type of logic.

Payroll processing also makes use of computer logic. If the number of hours an employee has worked in a week is greater than 40, the computer can adjust the pay scale to reflect overtime. The program in Figure 8.6 shows how this logic is coded in the BASIC programming language to compute overtime. The resulting values would be the employee's gross earnings.

Computer logic also can be used to sort data into alphabetical or numeric order. As with arithmetic, the computer executes logical functions at ultra-high speeds, performing millions of comparisons per second.

Control/Communication Operations

The processor, under control of the operating system, uses its control/communication operations to direct the flow of data into and out of memory. It also coordinates arithmetic and logic operations. To perform these operations, instructions and related data are sent along wires or buses. The **bus** is the path (circuitry) that connects the CPU with internal components. To send machine code along a bus line, bits or bytes may be collected into **words.** Each word is the number of bits that the CPU can use at a time. A 32-bit computer (a CPU that uses 32 bits per word) can access more data faster than, for example, an 8-bit or a 16-bit computer.

BASIC PAYROLL PROGRAM

```
100 REM *** PROCESSING SECTION OF PAYROLL PROGRAM ***
110 REM PROGRAM CODE TO COMPUTE REGULAR AND OVERTIME PAY
120 OVERTIME = 0
130 IF HOURS > 40
      THEN REGPAY = RATE * 40
           OVERTIME = (HOURS – 40) * (RATE * 1.5)
      ELSE REGPAY = RATE * HOURS
140 GROSSPAY = REGPAY + OVERTIME
```

Example A

Rate = $5.00 and Hours = 40

```
OVERTIME = 0
SINCE 40 IS NOT > 40
  REGPAY = 200 (5.00 * 40)
GROSSPAY = 200 (200 + 0)
```

Example B

Rate = $5.00 and Hours = 45

```
OVERTIME = 0
SINCE 45 IS > 40
  REGPAY = 200 (5.00 * 40)
  OVERTIME = 37.50 ((45-40) * (5.00 * 1.5))
                       5    *    7.50
GROSSPAY = 237.50 (200 + 37.50)
```

FIGURE 8.6
This BASIC program uses a computer's ability to make logical comparisons to compute weekly overtime pay when an employee works over 40 hours.

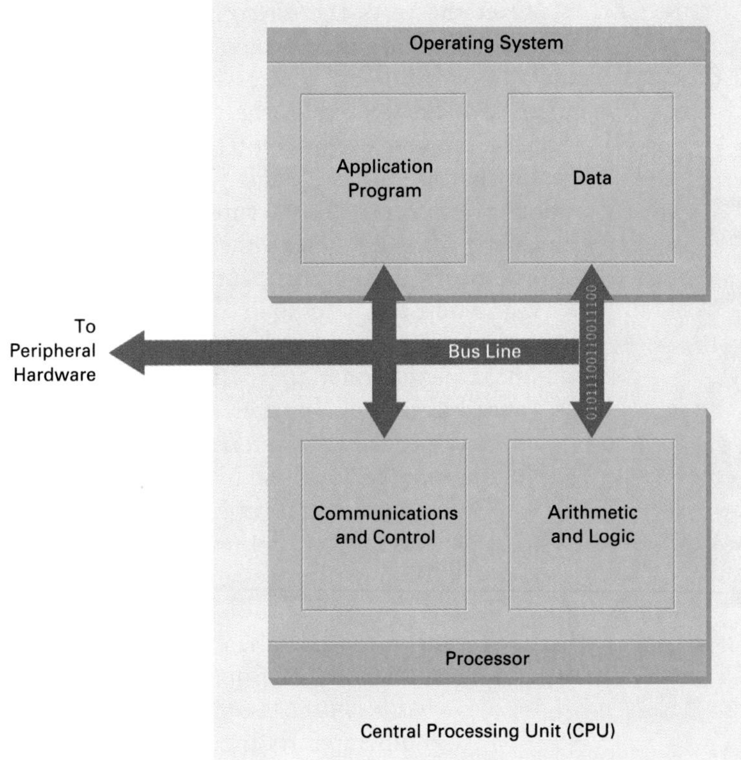

FIGURE 8.7
Data and programs move from memory to the processor through different buses or bus lines.

For example, Figure 8.7 illustrates how data is processed and returned to memory through control/communication operations performed by a processor using buses to move the machine code and related data. Control/communication operations also initiate the arithmetic and logic operations of the processor when needed. Results are then sent back to memory by the processor. As will be explained later the processor communicates with other hardware by sending out electrical pulses along a bus line. The processor uses its control/communication operations to coordinate all aspects of processing.

In the News...

BEFORE CALLING TECHNICAL SUPPORT

1. Reboot the computer and try again.
2. Repeat all steps, following instructions in the manual.
3. Make sure all cables are firmly attached.
4. Remove RAM resident utilities from memory.
5. Check the index in the manual, and see if your problem is listed in the *Trouble Shooting* section.
6. Try doing the task on another system.
7. Compare system requirements to your setup.
8. Ask your in-house expert.

Microprocessor Speeds

IBM and compatible computers with Intel microprocessors

	Processor ID#	Processor Speed
PC	8088	4.77 MHz
PC/AT	80286	8+ MHz
PS/2 Model 80	80386	25+ MHz
PS/2 Model 90	80486	33+ MHz
PS/2 Model 95	Pentium (80586)	66+ MHz

Apple Macintosh and compatible computers with Motorola microprocessors

	Processor ID#	Processing Speed
Mac Classic	68000	8+ MHz
Mac L/T	68020	16+ MHz
Mac SE/30	68030	16+ MHz
Mac II	68030	20+ MHz
Apple Quadra, NeXT	68040	33+ MHz
	68060	66+ MHz

FIGURE 8.8
A microprocessor's processing speed is measured in megahertz (MHz) with 1 MHz equal to a million clock cycles per second.

Over the years the microprocessors controlling personal computers have become increasingly powerful as processing speeds have increased. For example, the original IBM personal computer used an Intel 8088 microprocessor that ran at 4.77 MHz. The latest generation of microprocessors runs at 66 MHz or faster. Figure 8.8 shows the family of microprocessors used by popular microcomputer manufacturers and their related processing speeds. We should point out that when you hear people refer to an IBM or IBM-compatible microcomputer as a 386 or 486 machine, they are referring to the type of microprocessor used by the computer. A 386 computer has an Intel 80386 microprocessor, while a 486 computer uses an 80486 microprocessor.

For applications requiring high-speed mathematical computations, a specialized microprocessor, called a *math coprocessor,* is available. This chip supports the CPU by performing the calculations more rapidly than the processor and is controlled by the primary microprocessor in the CPU.

Some chip manufacturers take a keep-it-simple approach when designing processors to boost processing speeds. The resulting **Reduced Instruction Set Computing (RISC)** processor uses fewer machine codes, which enables it to achieve faster processing speeds by eliminating intermediary steps. Applications calling for real-time graphic displays, like the flight simulator shown in Figure 8.9, are currently taking advantage of RISC technology.

Memory

In memory, data and programs are held only temporarily, just before and after processing is completed. Application programs instruct the computer to execute specific tasks. The machine code for these instructions, and the necessary data, are loaded into memory, where they stay until the processor needs them. After the processor conducts any required arithmetic and logic operations, it returns the results to memory for temporary storage. Memory also is referred to as **primary storage.**

FIGURE 8.9
The processing speed of RISC technology is necessary for the complexity of large-scale simulations.

The relationship between memory and the processor is analogous to you sitting at your desk next to a filing cabinet. You (the processor) are processing information found on your desk (temporary storage). Your in and out baskets are the means by which you receive (input) and send (output) data. Once you have processed information, it is either thrown away (erased) or filed in the cabinet (permanent storage).

The contents of a computer's memory, in most cases, are temporary and constantly undergoing change. This type of memory is known as *volatile memory*. The contents of volatile memory are subject to loss when the power is turned off. Thus, a constant electrical power supply is needed to retain data and instructions in volatile memory. Of course, data, program instructions, and the results of processing can be retained on storage media such as tapes and disks, discussed in Chapter 10. These media are known as **secondary storage.**

In general, memory chips fall under one of two categories: **read-only memory (ROM)** or **random access memory (RAM).** Special-purpose programs are built into ROM chips during manufacturing. Since programs stored in ROM are etched into memory circuits, these programs do not have to be loaded into memory. This permanent software in ROM is called *firmware*. ROM is a form of nonvolatile memory, so it is typically used to hold systems programs and language translators.

In the News...

THE HISTORY OF ELECTRONIC COMPUTING

1946 J. Presper Eckert, John Mauchley and a team of 50 complete the Electronic Numerical Integrator and Computer (ENIAC). The first large-scale electronic digital computer weighs 30 tons, stands two stories, and covers 15,000 square feet.

1947 Grace Hopper documents the first computer bug, a dead moth in a cabinet of the Mark II.

1949 Maurice Wilkes of England's Cambridge University builds the first stored-program computer, the Electronic Delay Storage Automatic Computer (EDSAC).

1950 John von Neumann completes the Electronic Discrete Variable Automatic Computer (EDVAC), the first computer to use binary or digital mathematics.

1951 The Universal Automatic Computer (UNIVAC I), operating at a rate of 2,000 computations per second, is delivered to the U.S. Bureau of the Census as the first American commercially produced computer.

1953 IBM introduces the first magnetic tape device, the Model 726. It can pack 100 characters per inch and move at 75 inches per second.

1954 FORTRAN, or Formula Translation programming language, is developed by John Bakus of IBM.

1956 The term "artificial intelligence" is coined by John McCarthy, Assistant Professor at Dartmouth College.

1959 Jack Kirby of Texas Instruments and Robert Noyce of Fairchild Semiconductor create the integrated circuit.

Commercial and Business-Oriented Language (COBOL) is created.

1960 The first modern computer generation ends as vacuum tubes, punched cards and machine codes give way to second generation transistors, magnetic tape and procedural languages in computer design and operation.

1965 Beginner's All-Purpose Symbolic Instruction Code (BASIC) language is developed by Tom Kurtz and John Kemeny of Dartmouth College.

1967 The third generation is under way, with integrated circuits, floppy disks and nonprocedural languages becoming prominent in computer instruction and usage.

1968 Gordon Moore and Robert Noyce found Integrated Electronics (Intel) Corp. First computer mouse demonstrated.

1969 The Intel 4004 becomes the first microprocessor and paves the way for the microcomputer revolution.

Pascal, named after the famous mathematician, is developed by Niklaus Wirth of Switzerland as a programming language for systems development.

1975 The Cray-1 supercomputer is introduced as the fastest computer on Earth, preforming a million more calculations per second than ENIAC in a space a thousand times smaller.

Microsoft Corp., founded by Bill Gates and Paul Allen, adapt BASIC to the Altair microcomputer.

1977 Apple Computer, founded by Steve Wozniak and Steve Jobs, introduces the Apple II personal computer.

CP/M is marketed by Digital Research as a standard control program for personal computers.

1978 VisiCalc, electronic spreadsheet software, is created by Dan Bricklin and Bob Frankston.

1979 Micropro International releases WordStar, a word processing program.

1981 The IBM Personal Computer debuts; Microsoft's MS-DOS becomes its standard operating software.

Osborne Computer introduces the Osborne I, the first portable computer.

1983 Lotus 1-2-3 takes VisiCalc's place as the leading spreadsheet program marketed by company founder, Mitch Kapor. Windows is presented by Microsoft.

1985 The C++ programming language is developed.

1990 The advent of parallel processing and greatly increased processing power make this the year of artificial intelligence.

1992 Apples announces "Personal Digital Assistant."

1993 Intel P5 chip, Pentium, developed.

2000 Experts predict that computers containing a billion processors will be technologically feasible, exceeding the power of the human brain.

In contrast, RAM is a form of volatile memory used for temporary general-purpose storage. When we think of computer memory, we usually have RAM in mind. Programs and data must be loaded into RAM from outside sources, like disks. If the power to the computer fails, RAM is completely erased. Programs and data must then be loaded again.

To locate needed data or instructions for processing, the computer assigns a number, or **address,** to each byte position in memory (see Figure 8.10). Programmers working with high-level programming languages use words or symbols to assign labels (variable names) to data needed from memory. The computer then associates these labels with its own internal addresses. Once the assigned address is located, the computer retrieves the specified data.

The storage capacity of memory is measured by the number of characters, or bytes, it can hold. Typically, memory is measured in thousands or millions of bytes. A *kilobyte (K)* represents 1024 bytes, which is often rounded to a thousand bytes. A computer with 512K memory, then, provides storage for exactly 524,288 bytes, rather than 512,000. The confusion is a result of rounding 1024 down to 1000 before calculating memory capacity. Memory capacities in newer personal computers often are measured in *megabytes (MB),* or millions of bytes, and larger computers have several *gigabytes* (billions of bytes) of primary memory. Future computers will have *terabyte* (trillion-byte) capacities.

Although internal processing speeds are fast, it is comparatively slow for the processor to acquire the necessary data from storage like a disk. Due to this, the CPU may sit idle during some of the time a program runs.

To minimize waiting time for the CPU and speed up processing, users can now purchase computers, or enhance their existing computers, with a special feature, **cache memory.** Cache (pronounced

FIGURE 8.10
RAM chips temporarily store data and programs. Each byte (character) is assigned a unique location in memory, identified by its address.

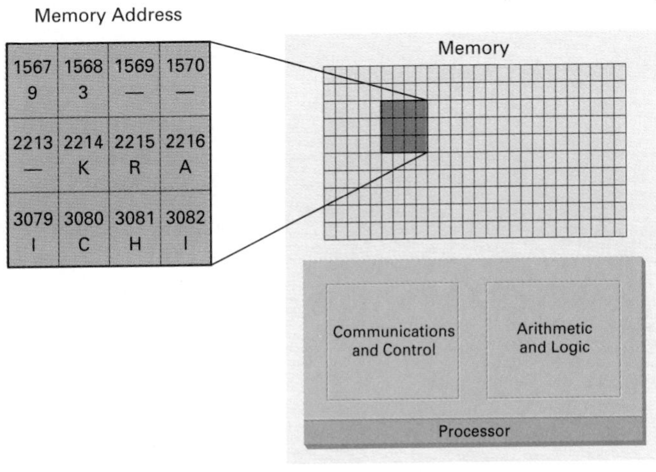

"cash") memory is a part of RAM that holds the data most likely to be needed next by the CPU. When data is retrieved from disk, it is loaded with the other data in that disk area into cache memory. In some cases, cache memory can exceed 512K of storage. As a result, there is a good chance the next data the computer needs for processing is already in cache. Using cache memory supports faster processing because retrieving data from the cache is thousands of times faster than retrieving it from disk.

The data contained in cache memory is not always the data needed, but cache is judged by its hit ratio, similar to a batting average. Hit ratio is the percent of times the correct data is in the cache (a hit) divided by the number of times the CPU goes to the cache looking for data. Effective cache memory has over a 90% hit ratio.

CPU Operations

The question now arises, how does the processor orchestrate all of the actions involved in running a program? All processing, regardless of the operation, is broken into two phases:

- Fetch phase
- Execution phase

During the *fetch phase* the processor's control/communication operation identifies the next program instruction and its address in memory. The instruction is then loaded (fetched) into the processor. For example, in Figure 8.11, four instructions compute ticket sales for a concert. The first instruction, locating the number of tickets sold, is recalled. This completes the first fetch phase in the figure.

The *execution phase* starts at this point, with the processor interpreting the instruction, transferring related data from memory, and performing the appropriate arithmetic or logic operation on the data. In Figure 8.11 the first instruction locates the value 4 (tickets sold) in memory. During the execution phase, 4 is transferred along a bus from memory into the processor. With the completion of this execution phase, the next fetch phase begins.

The fetch/execution cycle is repeated for the single-ticket cost of nine dollars. Once the cost and number of tickets are in the processor, the next fetch/execution cycle results in multiplying these values. When the result, called TOTAL, is returned to memory, the last execution phase in this example is finished.

The processor uses the internal clock cycles to regulate the transfer of data or instructions so the phases do not overlap. The repetition of the fetch/execution cycle continues until all program instructions have been processed. The speed of processing depends on the clock speed of the processing hardware.

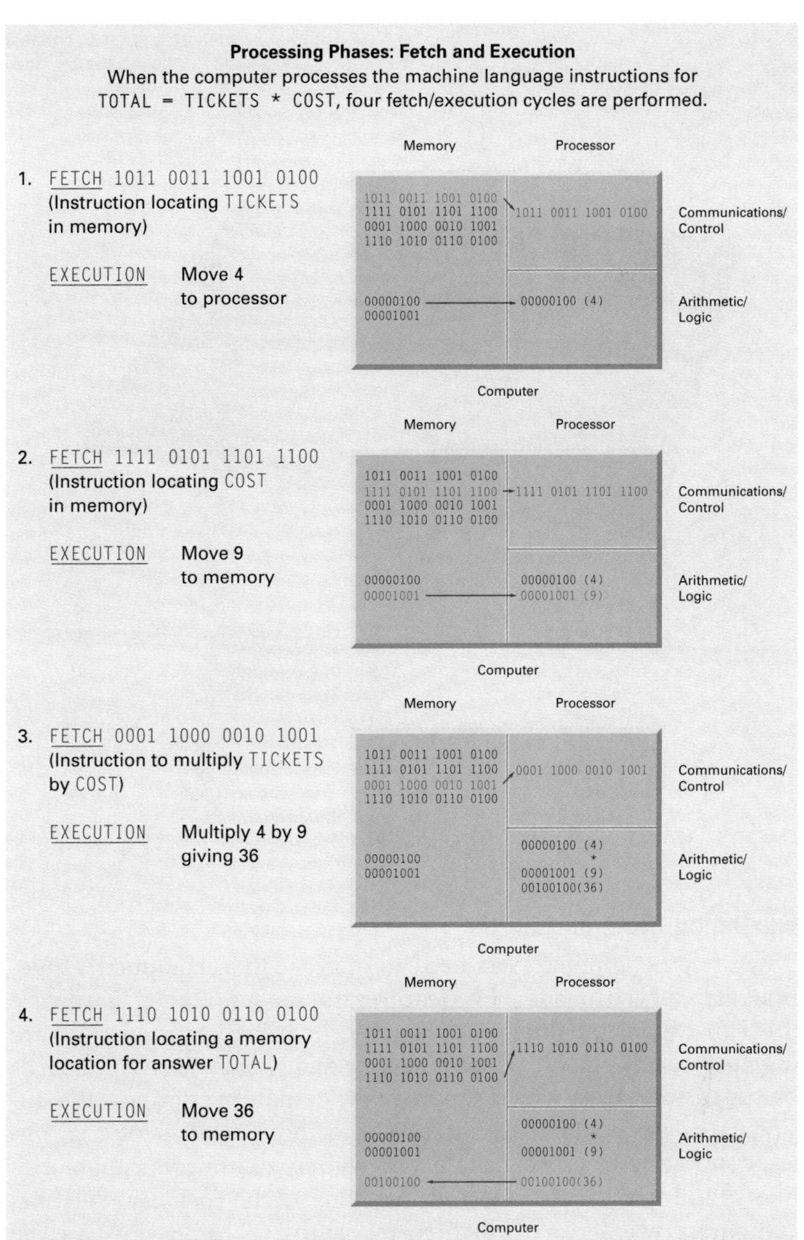

FIGURE 8.11
Four fetch/execution cycles go into computing the purchase price for concert tickets.

The Anatomy of a Microcomputer

The CPU circuitry that once required a room full of vacuum tubes connected by miles of wire now resides on several small silicon chips. A microcomputer's microprocessor, RAM and ROM chips, clock, and other supporting circuitry are interconnected on a single circuit board called the **motherboard.** An example of a motherboard can be found in Figure 8.12.

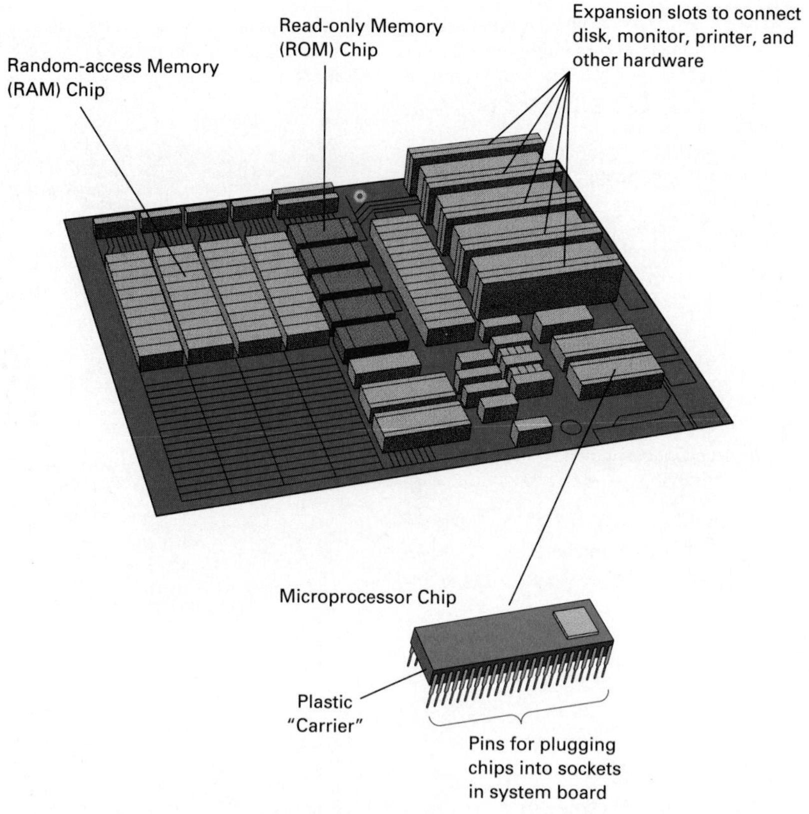

FIGURE 8.12
A microcomputer's microprocessor, memory chips, and expansion slots are found on the motherboard.

Expansion Slots and Cards

When microcomputer users need to increase their computer's functionality, they can add new features to the processing hardware through **expansion slots** on the motherboard. Expansion slots are designed to link the processor and existing memory to circuit boards or **expansion cards,** which support new computing options. Expansion cards are available for increasing memory, adding color graphics, connecting to a fax machine, providing multimedia capabilities like sound and video I/O, and installing cache memory. Personal computers will have from three to eight expansion slots on the motherboard.

Installation of new expansion cards is quite easy. For example, users wishing to add enhanced graphics need only purchase a video graphics adapter (VGA) board and slip it into an expansion slot. New expansion boards are often accompanied by a disk containing a related device driver. The driver must be installed on the system disk. The new graphics capabilities become immediately available after rebooting the computer, although related software packages sometimes need to be installed again.

Who's Who

Jack Kilby (b. 1923)

Robert Noyce (1927–1990)

Marcian Hoff (b. 1937)

Gilbert Hyatt (b. 1938)

Just a few years after the invention of the transistor, two groups of scientists were competing to produce its successor. Jack Kilby worked at Texas Instruments in research. He succeeded in 1959 in building the first working circuit on a chip—an integrated circuit (or IC). Robert Noyce and fellow scientists at Fairchild Semiconductors layered these chips and isolated them with insulating material. Despite their independent work, Kilby and Noyce are recognized as the coinventors of the integrated circuit, precursor to the microprocessor. Noyce and two colleagues left to form their own company to manufacture integrated circuits, Intel.

In 1971, Marcian Hoff, a researcher at Intel, and his coworkers used the idea of the integrated circuit to develop the first working microprocessor, the 4004. The following year they produced the 8008. Although Hoff and his team were credited with the invention, an engineer named Gilbert Hyatt actually had a patent on the single-chip microprocessor in 1970, before Hoff's model. A recent court decision awarded Hyatt with recognition as inventor of the microprocessor.

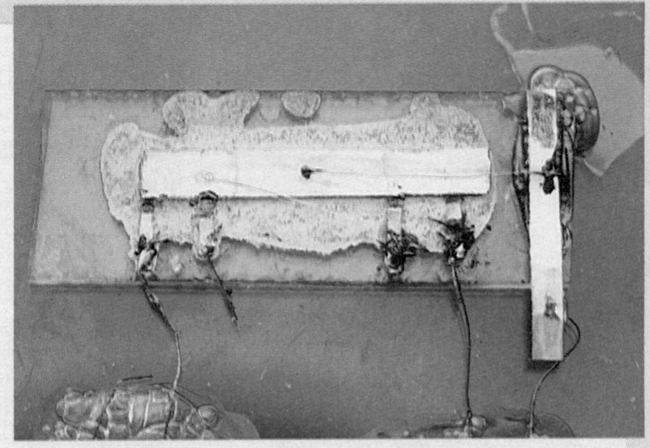

Jack Kilby (top) built the first working integrated circuit (middle). Marcian Hoff (bottom) and others based the design of the microprocessor on IC technology.

I/O Ports

Regardless of the application, the data is input to the computer from hardware external to the CPU. Output is also sent outside of the processing hardware. To accommodate different types of input and output hardware, a computer has several places where the input/output—as well as storage—hardware is connected to the processing unit. These places, connected to the motherboard, are called I/O (Input/Output) ports. Two types of I/O ports are available: serial and parallel. Data is sent between the computer and the attached hardware one bit at a time with a **serial port,** as shown in Figure 8.13. When a **parallel port** is used, the entire bit pattern for a single character is sent at the same time (see Figure 8.13). The I/O port is the point of connection between peripheral hardware and the bus line (see Figure 8.14). The bus line is the internal communication link to the processing hardware.

Different peripheral devices will have different I/O port requirements. The advantage to using a parallel port is that it is faster, since it sends several bits simultaneously. However, the I/O and storage hardware must be physically close to the computer. While serial ports do not provide as high a transmission speed, the peripherals

FIGURE 8.13
Serial and parallel ports allow input and output hardware to be connected to the processing hardware of a computer.

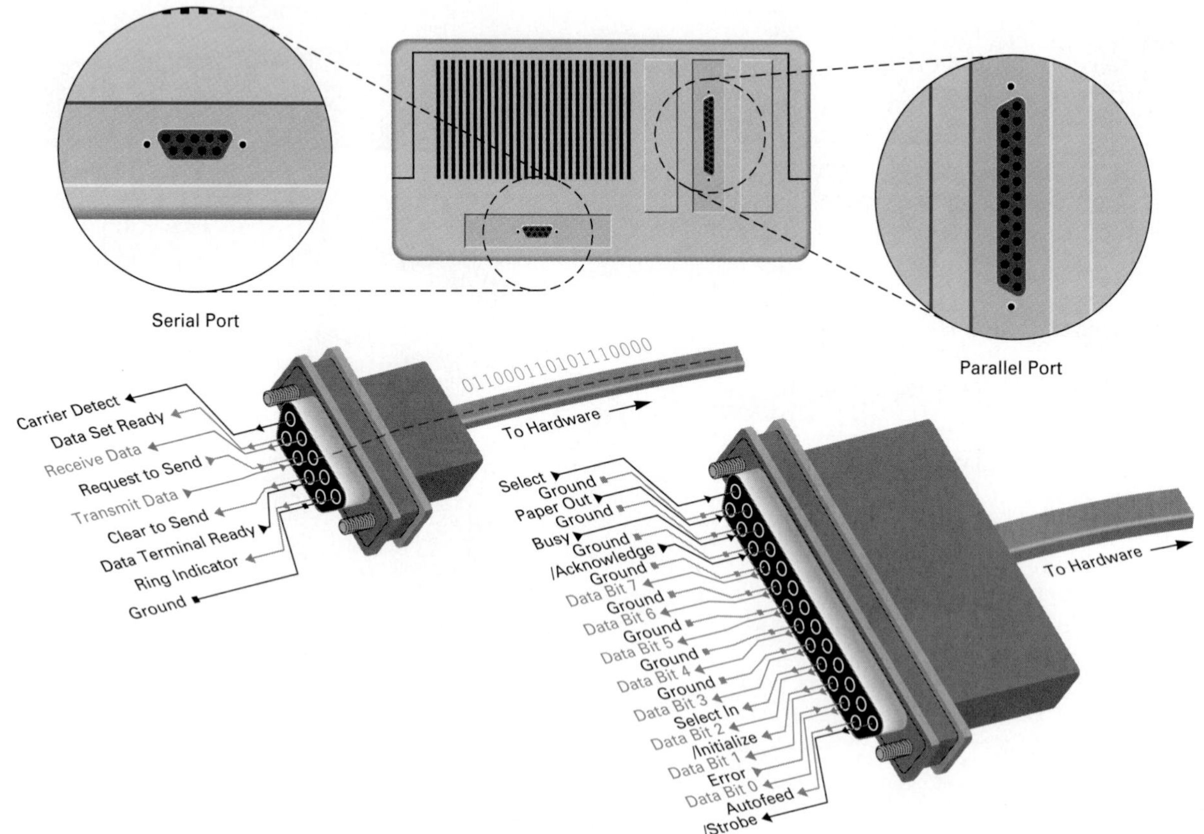

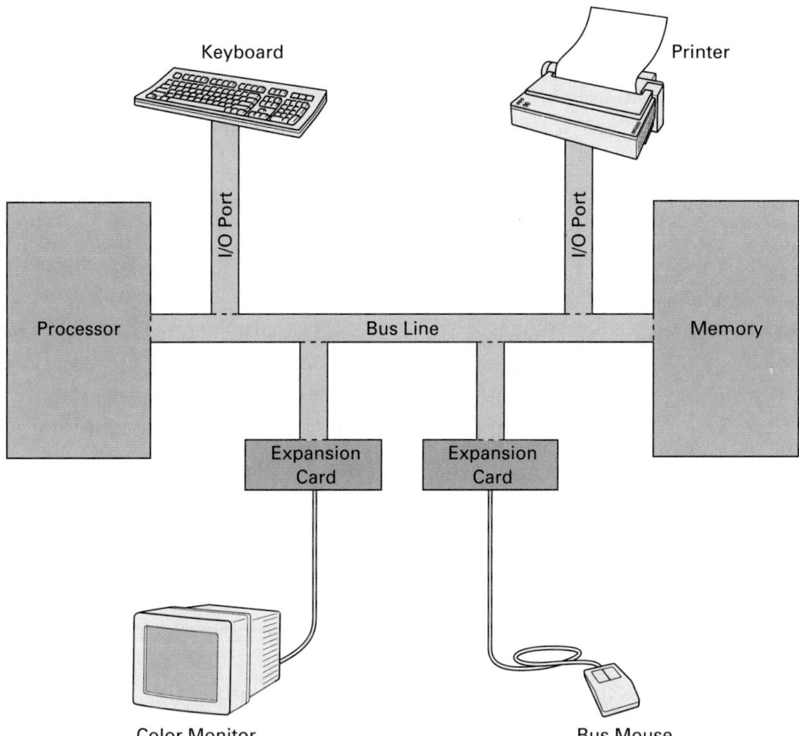

FIGURE 8.14
Bus lines, expansion slots, and I/O ports allow the CPU to be connected to a variety of hardware, expanding the capabilities of a computer system.

can be farther away. Serial ports are used to help send data over telephone and other communication lines. Part of the decision in buying a computer is to be sure sufficient I/O ports and expansion slots are available to handle current and future hardware and processing needs.

HARDWARE TO SOLVE DIFFERENT PROBLEMS

Computers come in various sizes to solve all kinds of problems. Just as operating systems have capabilities that meet different problems, processing hardware also is diversified. In general, processing hardware is characterized by cost, size, storage capacity, number of users, and processing speed. In many cases there is a considerable amount of overlap among groups. Three of the most commonly used sizes for describing computer hardware are:

- Mainframes
- Minicomputers
- Microcomputers

Mainframes and Organizational Systems

Mainframes are large, relatively expensive machines that offer extensive problem-solving capabilities. Mainframes can have memory capacities measured in gigabytes and more. The largest mainframes can process well over 100 million instructions per second, or *MIPS*. They often incorporate several processors. Their operating systems usually handle multiple applications within a time-sharing environment. This provides many users with the ability to perform different processing tasks. Data storage is primarily on hard disks, with tapes used as backup. Mainframes can serve as the heart of an entire network of computers. Other computers of all sizes can be linked to mainframe computers as part of a network, or the mainframe may act as a centralized information resource. When a microcomputer is connected to a mainframe or a computer network, the personal computer is often referred to as a **workstation.** This distinction is made to differentiate between remote processing hardware—that is, a microcomputer connected to a mainframe—and the mainframe itself.

Few individuals or departments within a business require the massive processing capabilities offered by mainframes (see Figure 8.15). These machines are used primarily by government, universities, and large businesses. Such organizations have extensive processing needs as well as the financial means to purchase or lease costly mainframes. People use mainframes for complex problems or

FIGURE 8.15
Mainframe systems are like information-processing factories that can handle the needs of thousands of users.

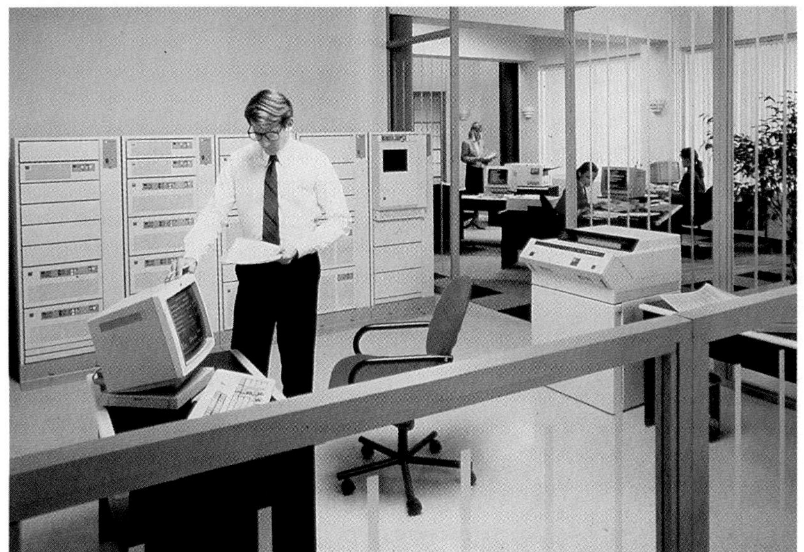

FIGURE 8.16
Minicomputers will fill a large closet and serve dozens of users at the same time.

large-volume jobs. Major banks can process bills for credit cardholders all over the world with the aid of a mainframe. Insurance companies use mainframes to process millions of policies. Large research projects, like the Human Genome Project, use the vast mainframe memory, storage capacities, and fast processing speeds to conduct tests and coordinate operations. Thus, mainframes have met the hefty processing demands of larger organizations.

Minicomputers and Work Group Systems

The minicomputer is a scaled-down version of the mainframe. Both the processing power and cost of minicomputers are less than that of the mainframe. Yet minicomputers have larger memory sizes and faster processing speeds than most microcomputers. They are well suited to the specific needs of smaller work groups of specialists within large organizations, a smaller business subsidiary, or a medium-sized independent business or laboratory. Since minicomputer prices range from about $25,000 to several hundred thousand dollars, many companies prefer to lease rather than buy them.

Memory capacities in current minicomputers are measured in megabytes and can easily range into gigabytes of primary storage. Minicomputers have fast processing speeds and operating systems with multitasking capabilities enabling them to serve more than one user (see Figure 8.16). They can be equipped with drives for diskettes and tape, as well as for hard disks. Tapes and floppy disks are inexpensive media for backing up important data files and programs.

Minicomputers make computer problem-solving power available to more than just large organizations. Data and information held in minicomputers are invaluable to people working together on common problems. For example, researchers who need to locate and share pertinent facts efficiently, or architects working on different subsystems within the same building, would benefit from using a minicomputer. A business' manufacturing plant uses a minicomputer for inventory tracking and process control.

The real-time monitoring of scientific equipment often is assigned to a minicomputer. Many organizations will use several minicomputers as a part of a network instead of one mainframe. The advantage to this design is that not all processing power is dependent on a single machine.

Microcomputers and Personal Systems

Advancing computer technology has brought computers into the home, the schoolroom, and the workplace. Called home computers, laptops, personal digital assistants, personal computers, microcomputers, or micros, these machines are powerful, yet easy to operate.

Every microcomputer is capable of performing jobs once handled by only the largest computers. Purchase prices for micros range from $500 for home units to $10,000 or more for professional models. A typical microcomputer memory unit stores up to 32 megabytes of data. Processing speeds of microcomputers are measured in megahertz instead of MIPS. A microcomputer running at 33 MHz is faster than one running at 10 MHz and works at approximately 4 MIPS.

Microcomputers are designed to be operated by one user at a time, using the keyboard or mouse for data entry and a monitor or printer to display output. Disk drives are used to store data. Some microcomputers, such as cash registers, are dedicated to one job. Others perform a variety of work directed by application programs.

Millions of people have used microcomputers to solve a wide range of problems and to increase their personal productivity. For example, desktop TSR (terminate stay resident) packages for micros work as personal assistants to users. Typically, they provide clocks, calendars, calculators, daily schedule reminders, and scratch pads, all brought to the screen by pressing a few keys. In recent years, design changes have reduced the size of some microcomputers, making computer technology portable and affordable.

Laptop computers (see Figure 8.17) are roughly the size of a large notebook. Their power source, a battery, is completely self contained, yet can be recharged from an electrical outlet. Laptops,

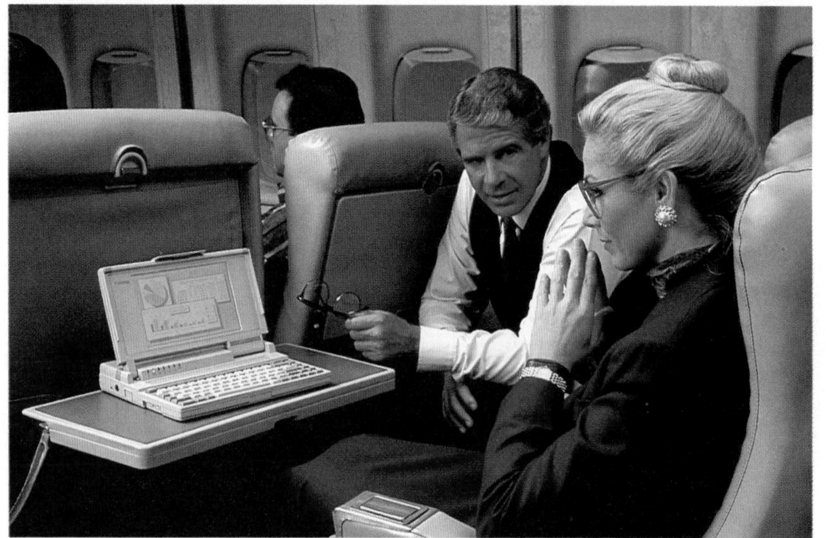

FIGURE 8.17
This laptop computer allows a person to use a computer system under almost any conditions.

sometimes called notebook computers, can contain over 200 megabytes of hard disk memory, 8 megabytes of RAM, floppy disk drives, keyboard, mouse, and a color monitor. Special I/O ports are available to allow a full-size keyboard and monitor to be attached. Power adapters can be used to plug into any electrical outlet throughout the world. Other snap-in modules facilitate connection with an additional battery or serial port, networking or fax equipment. You can even plug a laptop into a car cigarette lighter and power it with a car battery! Obviously, not all laptop computers have all these features, and many of the modules are expensive, but a user need not suffer loss of processing power when downsizing to a laptop.

Even smaller than the laptop computer is the *notepad*, a computer using a pen, or electronic stylus, rather than a keyboard for input. As seen in Figure 8.18, the monitor is rather small and the only apparent form of output. However, tremendous capabilities are hidden in the notepad computer, also called a personal digital assistant (PDA). It can recognize hand-printed text, storing it as a business letter, note, or other document. Rough sketches can be converted to more precise graphic output, such as charts and diagrams. Basic mathematics problems, like addition and multiplication, are calculated when the problem is written on the screen. TSR software, such as a calendar, is available. A notepad computer can also be connected to a printer, fax machine, pager, or disk drive to output or store data. The processing hardware is based on RISC technology. Many people see notepads as changing the way we do personal computing.

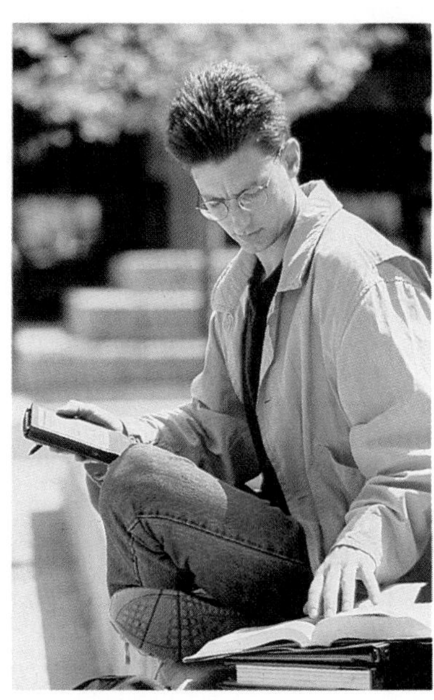

FIGURE 8.18
Notepad computers are designed to use pen input. Information is output on the screen when the notepad is attached to a phone line, printer, or fax machine.

	Cost	Size	Storage Capacity	Number of Users	Processing Speeds
Microcomputer	$500 to $10,000	Fit on desktop	64,000 to 32 million characters	1	Up to 20 million instructions per second
Minicomputer	$25,000 to $250,000	Fill a closet	4 million to 16 billion characters	100s	10 million to 100 million instructions per second
Mainframe Computer	$250,000 and more	Fill a room	32 million characters or more	1000s	100 million or more instructions per second

FIGURE 8.19
Comparison of processing hardware features from small microcomputers to large mainframe computers.

Specialized Processing Hardware

Although microcomputers, minicomputers, and mainframes cover a wide range of sizes, power, and applications (Figure 8.19), they may not be sufficient to handle special processing requirements for some users. As a result, newer and more specialized processing hardware has been developed. This includes

- Embedded computers
- Supercomputers
- Fault-tolerant computers

Embedded Microprocessors

Your new refrigerator, microwave oven, or stereo system probably is equipped with its own microprocessor. These appliances, like many other products, are now being manufactured with embedded computers. An embedded computer is a microprocessor designed to operate within another tool. Embedded computers are, of course, not as flexible as general-purpose computers. They use microprocessors but are not microcomputers. The microprocessors used by embedded computers contain only one preset program (firmware). In addition, these microprocessors do not use standard input, output, and storage hardware. The microprocessor in your refrigerator will not help you write a letter, but it will regulate the refrigerator's temperature to keep your food fresh. The purpose of embedded computers is to expand the capacities of the tools you use (Figure 8.20).

FIGURE 8.20
An appliance with an embedded microprocessor has expanded capabilities, but is not as flexible as a general-purpose personal computer.

Supercomputers

The most advanced and expensive type of computer is the **supercomputer**. Processing speeds in supercomputers range from 200 MIPS and faster. The Cray Y-MP supercomputer shown in Figure 8.21 can process about 500 million mathematical calculations every second. With a price tag that is equally tremendous, from $5 million to $20 million, supercomputer use is usually limited to such organizations as large oil companies, the U.S. Department of Defense, and the National Aeronautics and Space Administration (NASA).

FIGURE 8.21
This Cray supercomputer can process over a half a billion mathematical calculations every second.

Supercomputers are designed using parallel processing to achieve much faster processing speeds than mainframes, but they use this processing power to work on just one complex problem at a time instead of sharing processing time with many users. For example, the U.S. Weather Bureau uses the fast processing speeds of a Cray supercomputer for a single purpose—forecasting the weather. To analyze data from satellites and from hundreds of weather stations, forecasters need a supercomputer's speed.

Oil companies use supercomputers for petroleum exploration by analyzing rock formation and samples. Military strategists use them to simulate defense scenarios. Cinematic specialists use them to produce sophisticated movie animations. Supercomputers are powerful, but they are special-purpose tools.

Fault-Tolerant Computers

Many organizations cannot afford to be without their computer, even for a few minutes. As a result, a few computer manufacturers specialize in building **fault-tolerant computers.** These machines are designed so that they never crash. To achieve this, the manufacturer duplicates all important components of the processing hardware. Fault-tolerant computers have at least two memories, processors, and disk drives, with duplicate wiring to all these parts. Sources of emergency electrical power, like batteries and generators, are also part of the fault-tolerant computer system.

The operating system is designed so that the processing and storage hardware is never used at more than half its capacity. Therefore, when hardware problems occur, the operating system automatically switches processing to the remaining hardware without interruption. Fault-tolerant computers are especially useful in hazardous environments or in situations where an organization cannot afford to be without processing power. Although fault-tolerant computers are more expensive than standard computers, hospitals, scientific laboratories, and nuclear power plants need the hardware duplication and backup they provide.

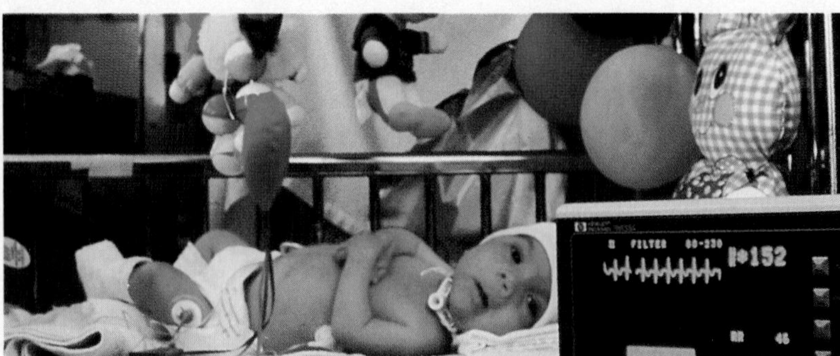

FIGURE 8.22
Fault-tolerant computers are designed with duplicate hardware so an organization is never without processing power.

A Closer Look...

The Making of a Microprocessor

How is a microprocessor made? Even a look under a microscope at a microprocessor does not reveal the numerous steps required to take a hunk of quartz rock and transform it into the wafer of silicon holding the brain of a computer.

Q The circuitry on a microprocessor is so small. Does it start out that way?

A Large detailed drawings of the circuitry are made, sometimes drawn using a computer. Each circuit is hand-checked. Then the drawing is made into a photographic image and reduced to microscopic size.

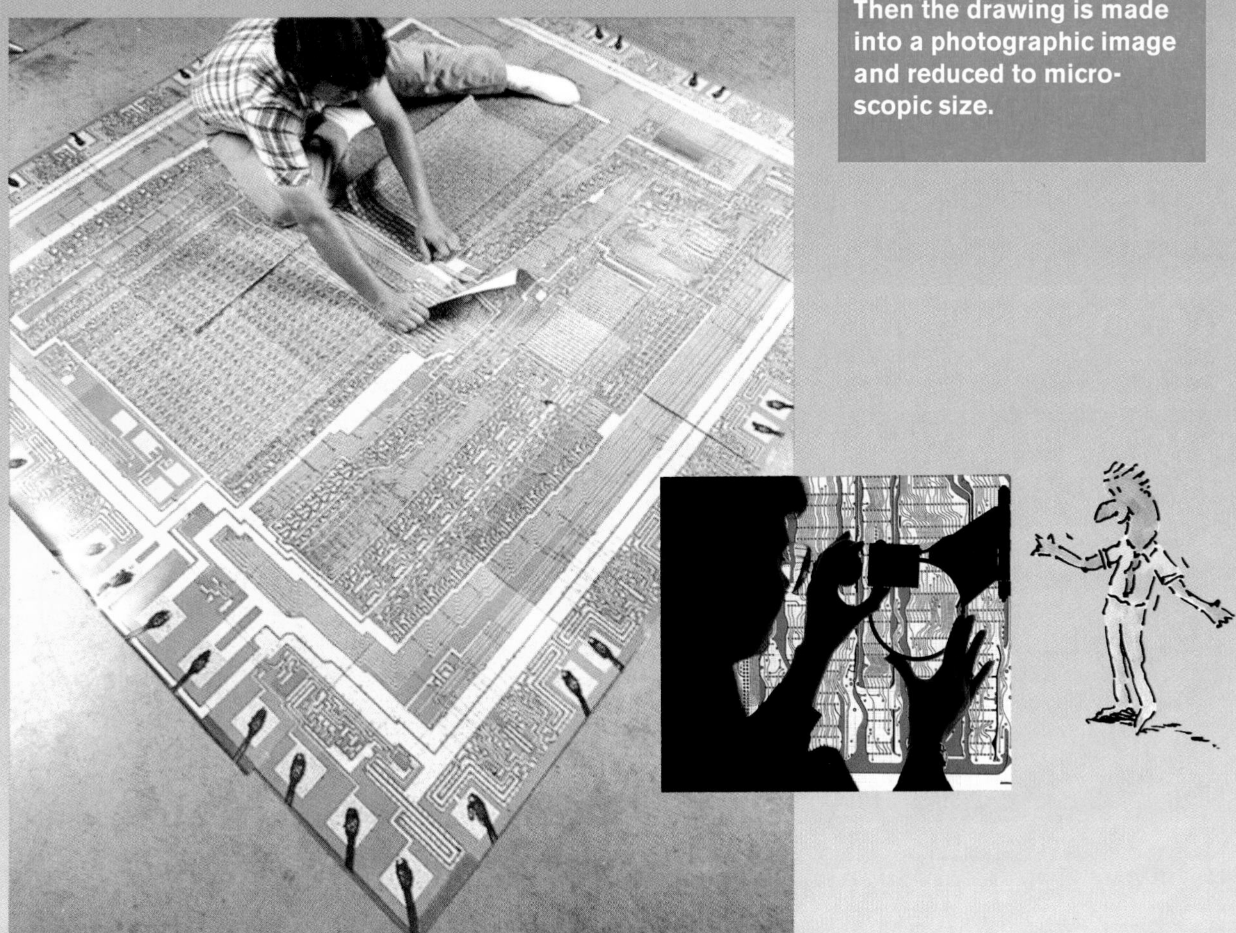

Q Where do you get the silicon for the silicon wafer? And how is it made into a wafer?

A The basic material for an integrated circuit like a microprocessor is a silicate (quartz) rock. It is crushed and melted into nearly pure silicon. This material is formed into rods or ingots two to six inches in diameter and sliced 9–20 thousandths of an inch thick.

Q How does the circuitry get on the wafer?

A A light-sensitive plastic, a photoresist, is applied to the wafer. The circuit design is etched into the photoresist with ultraviolet light shone through a masking plate containing the design. The wafer is dipped into acid to etch the circuit path into the wafer. This process is repeated for each circuit needed.

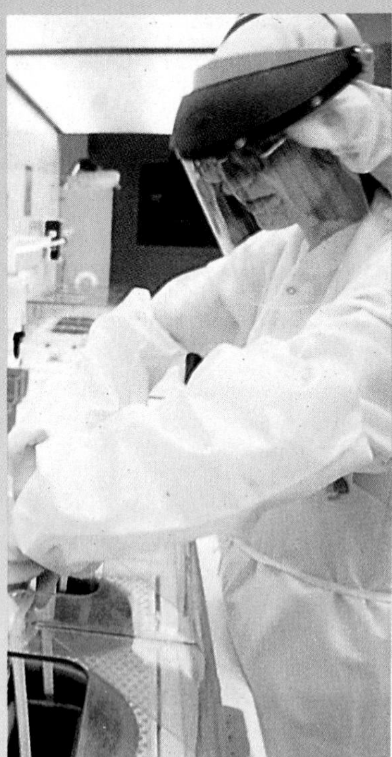

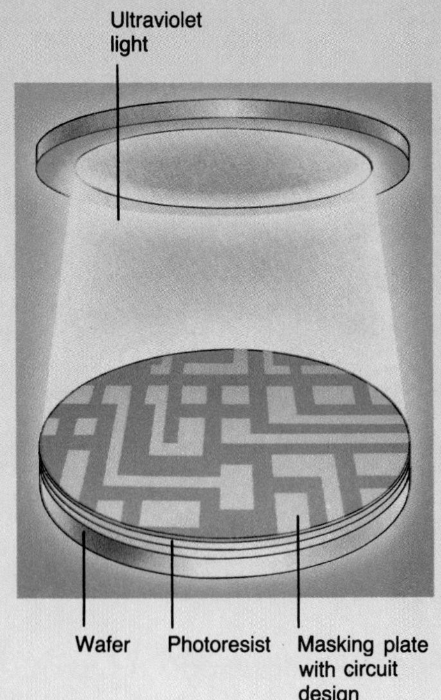

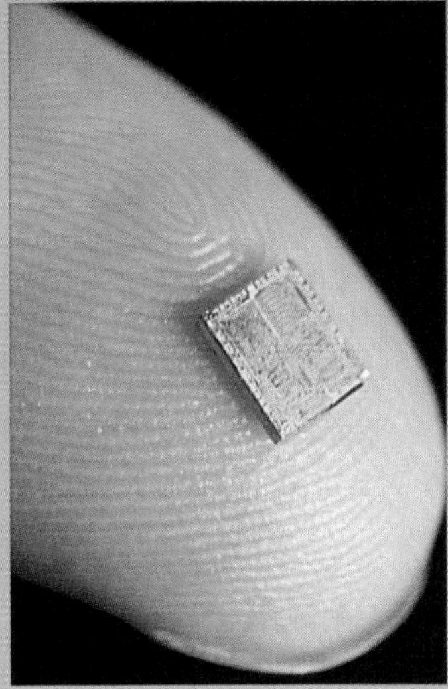

Q **Does each wafer then become one microprocessor?**

A **A wafer contains several hundred microprocessors. When etching is completed, the wafers are cut into individual microprocessors with a diamond saw, each less than one-eighth of an inch square.**

Q **Why are microprocessors manufactured in clean rooms?**

A **A particle of dust can ruin an entire processor. To avoid this, work is done in a "clean room" where much of the handling of the wafers is done by machines. People in the clean room wear protective clothing. It guards them from caustic chemicals and guards the wafers from dirt and moisture.**

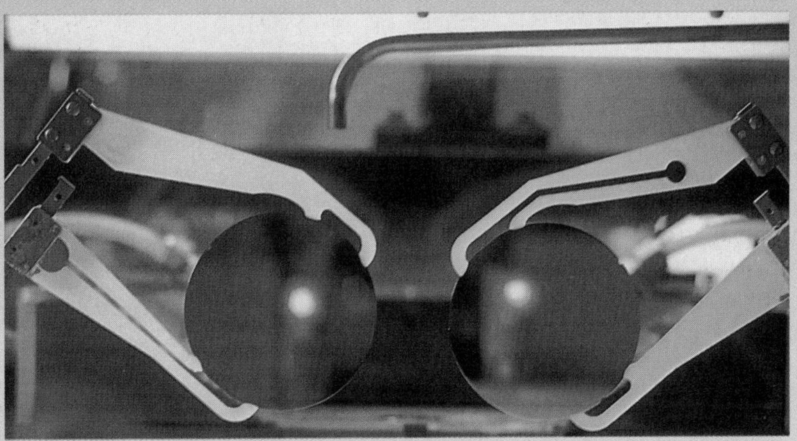

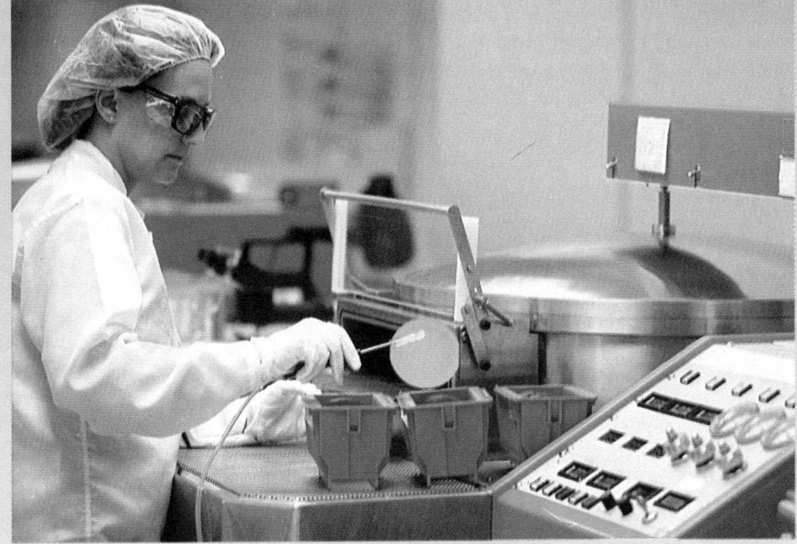

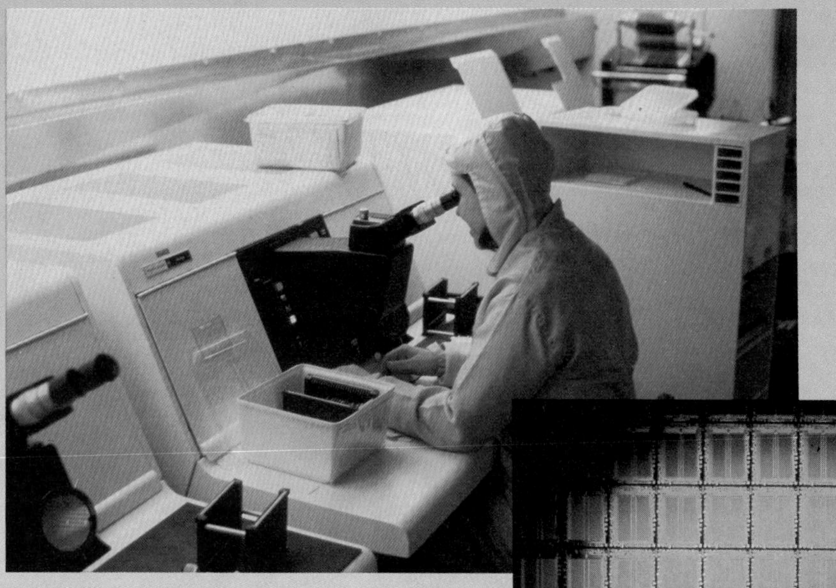

Q How are the microprocessors checked for quality?

A After each series of etchings, the wafer is examined under a microscope. Defective wafers are removed from production. Microprocessors are also tested electronically several times during production.

Q How do the microprocessors fit into the computer?

A Individual microprocessors are attached and wired onto frames. They are then installed on boards that are assembled with other integrated circuits to become the finished microcomputer motherboard.

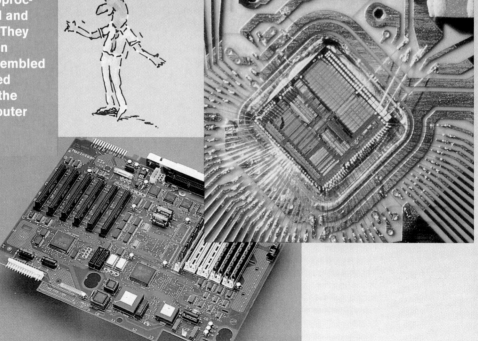

Chapter Facts

- First-generation computers used vacuum tubes for processing hardware.
- Transistors were invented by Shockley, Bardeen, and Brattain in the mid-1950s and became the processing hardware for second-generation computers.
- Third-generation computers used integrated circuits (ICs), which were first tested in 1959 by Jack Kilby.
- Computers from the fourth generation combined many integrated circuits into a microprocessor. This technological breakthrough in the late 1960s is credited to Hyatt and Hoff.
- In the fifth generation, computers become more powerful through the development of parallel processing hardware.
- All processing hardware works on Boole's two-state logic. In digital computers, instructions are put into a binary code called machine code, represented by 1 (presence) and 0 (absence) of electricity.
- Standard binary codes, ASCII and EBCDIC, enable computers to encode data and transfer it over bus lines.
- The central processing unit (CPU), or processing hardware, is made up of the processor and memory.
- The processor performs three types of operations: arithmetic, logic, and control/communication.
- Processing speeds are measured in fractions of a second: millisecond (one-thousandth), microsecond (one-millionth), nanosecond (one-billionth), picosecond (one-trillionth).
- Within the processor, control/communications operations direct the flow of data and instructions along bus lines.
- The speed of the processor is also measured in megahertz, a million clock cycles per second.
- Memory, called primary storage, holds data and programs. It can be volatile or nonvolatile.
- Random access memory (RAM) is temporary storage. Read-only memory (ROM) is preset during manufacturing.
- Data is retrieved in the processing hardware according to its memory location, or address.
- Memory capacity is measured by number of bytes. A kilobyte (K) is approximately 1000 characters. A megabyte (MB) is 1 million characters. Large computer systems have memory capabilities in billions (gigabytes) and, in the future, trillions (terabytes) of characters.

- Processing consists of two phases: the fetch phase and the execution phase. These are coordinated by an internal clock.
- Expansion slots on the motherboard allow additional hardware capacity to be added to the computer's circuitry.
- Serial and parallel input/output ports provide a place where peripheral hardware can be connected to the motherboard.
- Mainframes are large, high-speed computers with billions of characters of memory.
- Minicomputers are smaller than mainframes, but have many megabytes of primary storage and processing speeds measured in MIPS (millions of instructions per second).
- Microcomputers are small but powerful machines. They usually serve only one user at a time but in varying applications. Their processing speeds are measured in megahertz (MHz).
- Laptop computers allow true portability of processing power. Notepad computers involve pen input and can process written text.
- Embedded computers are microprocessors built into appliances and tools. They are permanently programmed to expand the device's capabilities.
- Supercomputers are powerful machines with large storage capacities. They are expensive and used only in applications requiring fast processing of large amounts of data.
- Fault-tolerant computers contain duplicates of all important hardware components. Each component is used only to half capacity. When a component fails, the duplicate takes over.

Terms to Remember

a. address
b. bus
c. byte
d. cache memory
e. central processing unit (CPU)
f. expansion card
g. expansion slot
h. fault-tolerant computer
i. integrated circuit (IC)
j. machine code
k. microprocessor
l. motherboard
m. parallel port
n. parallel processing
o. primary storage
p. random access memory (RAM)
q. read-only memory (ROM)
r. reduced instruction set computing (RISC)
s. secondary storage
t. serial port
u. supercomputer
v. transistor
w. word
x. workstation

Mix and Match

Match the definitions to the Terms to Remember.

1. ____ I/O port that can send or receive data one bit at a time.
2. ____ circuit board designed to fit into an expansion slot of a microcomputer's motherboard to add memory or connect external hardware.
3. ____ circuitry path that connects the CPU with internal and external hardware.
4. ____ simultaneous processing of the same program through the use of several processors.
5. ____ the processing hardware of a computer, containing the processor(s) and memory.
6. ____ a single chip containing input/output control, processing, and some memory circuitry.
7. ____ I/O port that sends or receives one byte at a time.
8. ____ operating language unique to each computer that is made up of bits (0 or 1) representing electronic circuits (off or on).
9. ____ another name for a computer's internal memory.
10. ____ a small, solid state circuit placed with other electronic components on a silicon wafer.
11. ____ small electronic component that is the basis of the second-generation computer.
12. ____ permanent memory, which holds systems programs and language translators.
13. ____ the name given to a personal computer networked to a mainframe.
14. ____ a part of primary storage that holds data for access by the processor. It is faster than disk access.
15. ____ a computer with duplicate processing components that is designed to switch to one set of components when the other set has problems.
16. ____ permanent long term storage of data which usually involves disks or tapes.
17. ____ place where expansion cards can be plugged into the motherboard, expanding a microcomputer's processing power.
18. ____ unique number assigned to each memory location within a computer's processing hardware.

19. ____ powerful, high-speed parallel processing computer capable of handling enormous amounts of data.
20. ____ a group of bits representing a single character.
21. ____ temporary storage for data and programs.
22. ____ a collection of bits representing the instruction or data the CPU can process at one time.
23. ____ the primary circuit board in a microcomputer, containing the RAM and ROM chips and microprocessor.
24. ____ processor designed to achieve faster processing speeds by minimizing intermediary processing steps through limiting the number of complex operations.

Review Questions

1. What is the characteristic technology for the first, second, third, fourth, and fifth computer generations?
2. Describe how Boole's two-state logic is applied to computer-based instructions and data.
3. How are ASCII and EBCDIC used?
4. What are the two main parts of the central processing unit?
5. How is the speed of processing hardware measured?
6. What are the differences between a millisecond, microsecond, nanosecond, and picosecond?
7. Under what simple premise does the processor work?
8. Describe the operations performed by the processor.
9. What are the uses of these types of specialty processing hardware: cache memory, math coprocessor, and RISC?
10. What is stored in memory?
11. Differentiate between volatile and nonvolatile memory.
12. How are read-only memory and random access memory used?
13. Explain how the processor uses memory addresses to locate data and instructions.
14. How do the fetch and execution phases relate to IPOS?
15. What role does the computer's clock play?
16. How are expansion cards and I/O ports used to add to a microcomputer's capabilities?
17. What are five ways to group processing hardware?
18. Identify two types of portable microcomputers and explain how they differ from each other.

19. What are three applications for embedded computers and supercomputers?
20. How does a supercomputer differ from a mainframe?
21. Describe how fault-tolerant computers are different from other computers.

Applying What You've Learned

1. Look at the instructions that come with the school or home computer you use. How fast is the processor? How much main memory does it have? How much memory is contained in RAM? In ROM? What type of secondary storage is available?
2. Classify each processing job by the type of operation it would require: arithmetic, logic, or control/communication. Some problems may require more than one processing operation.
   a. finding a square root of a number in memory
   b. checking the breathing rate of a patient
   c. loading visual data read by a scanner into memory
   d. calculating how many males and how many females are in an employee file
   e. sending to a distant terminal the names of only those customers with unpaid bills
3. Use the ASCII table in Figure 8.5 to encode your full name, including spaces. How many bits does it take? How many bytes? How many characters?
4. Besides those mentioned in the text, what five other organizations could use the continuous availability of a fault-tolerant computer?
5. Bubble memory was once announced as the memory of the future. Research on it has slowed. Read an article on it. Why is it not more popular? What are its advantages? Is another type of nonvolatile memory being developed instead?
6. Besides those mentioned in the text, what are five machines or tools that would benefit from having embedded computers?

Answers to Mix and Match

1. t 2. f 3. b 4. n 5. e 6. k 7. m 8. j 9. o 10. i
11. v 12. q 13. x 14. d 15. h 16. s 17. g 18. a
19. u 20. c 21. p 22. w 23. l 24. r

9

Input/Output Hardware

- From the User's Point of View
- Input Hardware Options
  - Keyboards
  - Pointing devices
  - Terminals
  - Scanners
  - Other input devices
- Output Hardware Solutions
  - Permanent output
  - Temporary output
  - Action output
- Peripheral Design and Safety
  - Repetitive strain injuries
  - Low-frequency emissions
  - Ergonomics
- *A Closer Look . . . Peripherals for Special Applications*

FROM THE USER'S POINT OF VIEW

You may push buttons or use a mouse or look at screens for information every day. A staggering array of other hardware is available to customize a computer system for special input and output needs. We will take a look at the common, as well as uncommon input/output hardware available and discuss the applications where they are used. Each input and output peripheral has one thing in common: when used properly, it helps you become more productive.

INPUT HARDWARE OPTIONS

Despite the variety of processing and storage hardware available, it is the input of data and the output of information that concerns most users. For many, the most easily recognized peripherals are the keyboard, monitor, and printer—hardware related to **input/output (I/O)** operations. I/O operations are where computers and people meet. People enter data into the computer through input hardware. They then receive results of processing from output hardware. Where user/computer interaction is most frequent, user-friendliness is most important.

Interactive processing requires there to be a dialogue between the user and the computer. The user requests service from the computer. The computer responds, often by producing a dialog box, menu, or other screen display. The user enters data in response to the prompts displayed by the computer. The computer continues processing, prompting the user for more data or instructions as necessary. This series of exchanges is characteristic of interactive input and processing. With batch processing, little user involvement is required, so input procedures are often less user friendly. Different types of input peripherals are available to support both types of processing. The following are the most widely used devices.

Keyboards

Most computer systems contain a **keyboard,** still the most widely used input peripheral. Different keyboards usually have some features in common. They have typewriter-like keys for inputting letters, numbers, and other symbols. Cursor control keys manipulate the cursor up, down, left, and right. In addition, **function keys** can activate special software features,

FIGURE 9.1
A special stylus is used to indicate on the keyboard which Chinese character to input.

such as centering in a word processing program, or locating the first worksheet cell. Many software packages allow users to define the activities associated with function keys. These keys let users control several operations by pressing just one or two keys instead of selecting menu options or entering commands.

Many keyboards have numeric keypads for easy input of numeric data. On other keyboards, the keys contain icons rather than alphanumeric symbols. These are useful in fast-food restaurants where the icons represent food items (see Figure 1.5). Also, special keyboards are available for foreign languages, as seen in Figure 9.1, or include keys with scientific characters.

When a key on a keyboard is pressed, the binary code for that character is sent through an I/O port, down a bus line, and into the central processing unit. Some keyboards have small temporary storage areas to allow users to type ahead of the computer system. Characters saved in this buffer will be processed as the CPU becomes available, usually within a matter of seconds.

Pointing Devices

The keyboard is an efficient way to input text, but can be a deterrent for nontypists trying to use a command-driven operating system. The mouse is growing in popularity with the advent of graphical user interfaces. As mentioned in Chapter 3, the user controls a screen pointer by moving a mouse across a desktop or other flat surface. The motion is converted to similar movement on a monitor. When a button on the mouse is clicked, the location of the mouse in relation to icons or menus on a monitor is sent to the CPU.

Despite the mouse's ease of use, it has a disadvantage. In a small work area, room to move the mouse may be limited. People with restricted arm movement may find using a mouse difficult. An alternative to the mouse is a **trackball,** which looks like an upside-down mouse. Rather than move a mouse across a surface, a trackball user rolls a ball mounted in a stationary housing (see Figure 9.2). Like a mouse, a trackball also has buttons for fixing the cursor position on the screen. A trackball can be installed in any port that handles a mouse.

FIGURE 9.2
This trackball, attached to the side of a portable computer, provides an alternative to the keyboard.

Since trackballs require minimal workspace, manufacturers have been including them with laptop computer systems. Some trackballs are temporarily mounted at the side of the computer and removed when necessary. Others are permanently placed in the middle or at the side of the keyboard itself, or even at the side of the monitor. Still others can be held in a user's fingers and the ball moved with the thumb. For less portable personal computers, larger trackballs are available.

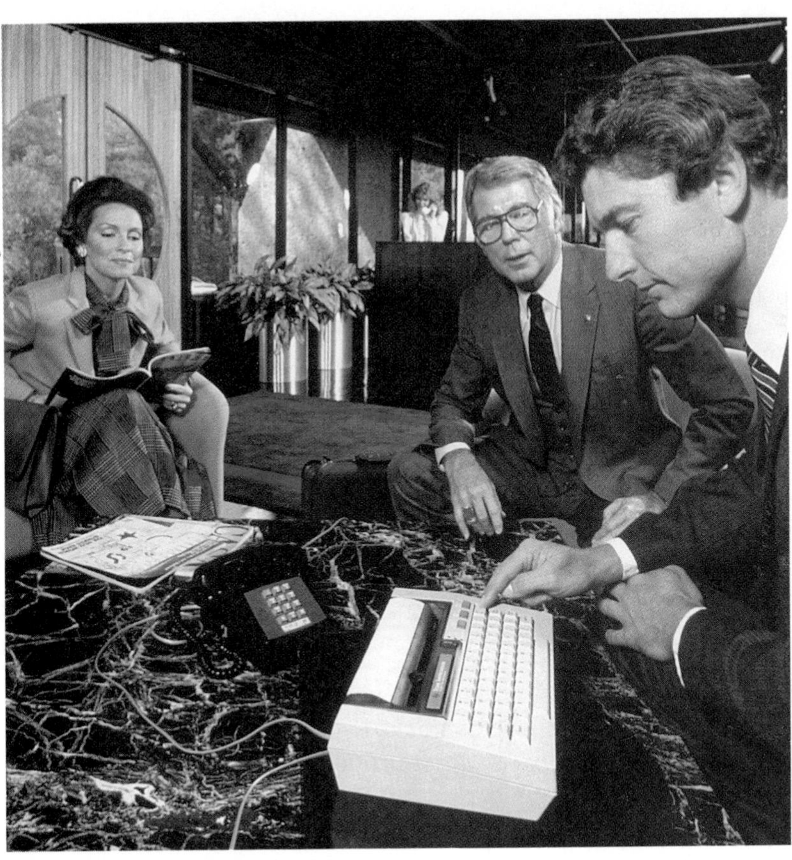

FIGURE 9.3
A hard-copy terminal provides a permanent record of all interactions with the computer.

Terminals

The traditional input hardware for interactive computing is the terminal. The **terminal** is a single piece of equipment with a keyboard and built-in monitor or printing mechanism. If the terminal has a monitor, input data is reproduced, or echoed, on the screen as the user types. Since the data displayed on a screen is not permanent, this display is referred to as *soft copy.*

Some terminals contain a printing mechanism, like a typewriter, instead of a screen. Since these machines produce a paper or *hard copy* of the output, they also are known as *hard-copy terminals* (see Figure 9.3). A popular version of this type of terminal was first produced by the Teletype Corporation in the 1960s. As a result, people sometimes refer to them as teletypes, although these hard-copy terminals are not now in wide use.

Many terminals have little or no built-in processing power. This is what distinguishes them from personal computers or workstations. These terminals rely on communication with a computer (see Figure 9.4). The user inputs data through the terminal while the

FIGURE 9.4
A terminal without processing capabilities of its own can be used to transmit production line information to and from a central factory computer.

computer provides the mathematical, logical, and memory capacity to support processing. The computer returns output to the terminal as needed. Since the performance capabilities of terminals are limited, their cost is quite low. However, terminals place a sizable processing burden on the host computer. Terminals can be seen at tellers' stations in banks, in travel agencies, and in libraries for on-line reference searches.

Some terminals are equipped with built-in processing and memory capabilities to supplement the main computer's processing power. When used within a network, these *intelligent terminals* relieve some of the processing load placed on central computers. Many processing and memory operations, such as editing input and formatting output, are executed entirely within the intelligent terminal. This reduces the need for constant communication between the terminal and the computer. However, even intelligent terminals cannot stand alone as a computer system. They merely act as I/O hardware.

Scanners

While a keyboard, mouse or trackball requires a user to input data by hand, scanners allow input of printed data. A **scanner** reads text, photographs, and graphics that are then converted into bit patterns for processing, storage, or output.

Bar Codes

Scanners and other devices that collect data from products and sales tags as they are purchased are part of **point-of-sale (POS)** systems. Perhaps the most familiar POS system uses the universal product code (UPC) to help update inventory, track daily sales, and print sales receipts at grocery stores. UPC markings on items represent a product number and consist of a series of bars of varying widths. For this reason, the UPC often is referred to as a **bar code.**

When a bar code is scanned, as in Figure 9.5, the light source is reflected off the spaces between the marked bars. This returned light is converted into bit patterns. A decoder in the scanning system translates the bit patterns into meaningful letters and numbers. As shown in Figure 9.6, scanners can resemble guns or wands, which send out a beam of light to reflect back bar patterns as input. Other scanners, like those commonly seen in a grocery store, are built into sales checkout counters and use low-level lasers as the light source.

In the UPC system the pattern on the bar code label represents the manufacturer's product code. Bar codes have been put to many other uses. For example, library books and library cards are marked with bar codes to expedite checkout. Bulk mailings sent by businesses print bar codes related to the address and zipcode at the bottom of an envelope to speed up processing by the post office.

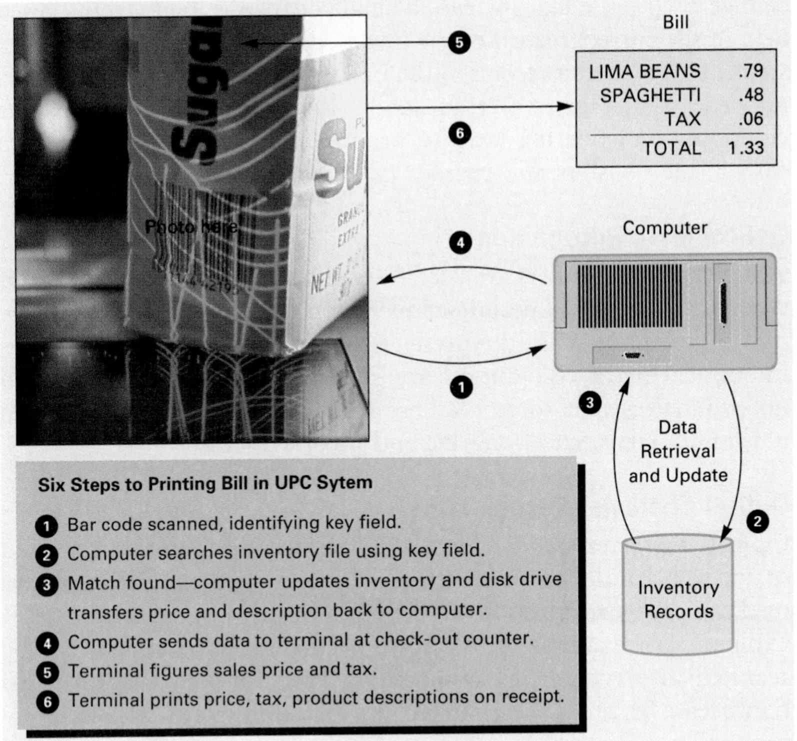

Bill
LIMA BEANS .79
SPAGHETTI .48
TAX .06
TOTAL 1.33
Computer
Data Retrieval and Update
Inventory Records
Photo here
Six Steps to Printing Bill in UPC Sytem
1 Bar code scanned, identifying key field.
2 Computer searches inventory file using key field.
3 Match found—computer updates inventory and disk drive transfers price and description back to computer.
4 Computer sends data to terminal at check-out counter.
5 Terminal figures sales price and tax.
6 Terminal prints price, tax, product descriptions on receipt.

FIGURE 9.5
Bar code scanners initiate a six-step IPOS cycle that updates inventory records and prints grocery bills.

As an inventory control application, the UPC markings identify a stock number. This number is the key field for records in the inventory file. By using the bar code, the computer locates the record associated with that item number. The record contains information about the product, like name, current stock levels, and price fields. These fields are used to generate a customer receipt. This method allows stores to offer special sale prices without having to

FIGURE 9.6
A handheld scanner can input bar codes from a price tag.

change each price tag. Instead, a single change is made to the price field in the correct record of the inventory file. Figure 9.5 shows the steps used to print a receipt in the UPC system. As sales transactions are processed, a log of all transactions is stored on disk or tape. The computer uses this log later to produce reports that help balance cash in the registers and reorder merchandise for the store.

Optical Mark Recognition

Other types of scanners are used to read handwritten characters and typewritten marks. Special scanners for *optical mark recognition (OMR)* methods sense the presence of a pencil mark. Popular uses for optical mark recognition are standardized tests, surveys, and questionnaires. On some of these forms, scanners can distinguish plus/minus signs, check marks, and other symbols.

Optical Character Recognition

Optical character recognition (OCR) permits users to input printed or typewritten documents with a scanner. Entire pages of text are read rapidly by scanners for direct input. Many publishers use OCR scanners. For example, news stories written on typewriters may be scanned into typesetting computers. Type for newer editions of books can be set by scanning pages from previous editions. Law firms scan old contracts to make on-line revisions. Reference services scan current books and magazines to update their holdings. OCR scanners are also used to track packages sent by international delivery services.

OCR scanners are now available for personal computers. They can range in size from a handheld scanner that scans a small area at a time to full-page scanners. When a user scans text, it can be input directly into standard word processing formats for later editing. This eliminates the need to retype a document already in a printed form from some other medium, like a newspaper, or from an incompatible word processing program.

Magnetic Ink Character Recognition

Magnetic ink character recognition (MICR) is similar to OCR methods in that MICR employs computer-readable symbols. However, MICR requires special magnetic ink to record the symbols, as seen in Figure 9.7. MICR coding is used primarily in banking operations to enter data from checks and deposit slips. These banking documents are imprinted along the bottom with MICR symbols that indicate customer account numbers, bank identification, and dollar amounts. A special MICR scanner, also shown in Figure 9.7, reads the MICR character data for routing between banks as storage on tape or disk for subsequent processing.

DAVID M. KROENKE
MERCER ISLAND, WASHINGTON 98040
284
1/15 19 94
19-2/1250
Pay to the order of Postmaster $ 15.00
Fifteen and 00/100 Dollars
FIRSTLINE
SEATTLE-FIRST NATIONAL BANK
MERCER ISLAND BRANCH/MERCER ISLAND 98040
For
⑆125000024⑆ 93178 000⑈ 0284 ⑈0000001500⑈

MICR Characters

FIGURE 9.7
MICR scanners input from a check the bank's and customer's account numbers along with the amount of the check.

Image Scanners

Specialized scanners, called image scanners, are available for inputting graphical data such as drawings, photographs, and maps. As each image is scanned, it is converted into light and dark pixels, similar to a newspaper photo. The pixels are then stored as bit patterns. Such peripherals are available for scanning both black/white and color images. This technique makes the images usable by desktop publishing and graphics packages (Figure 9.8). Law enforcement services can scan fingerprints and store them on file. Analysis programs compare sets of prints to find matches among millions of fingerprint records.

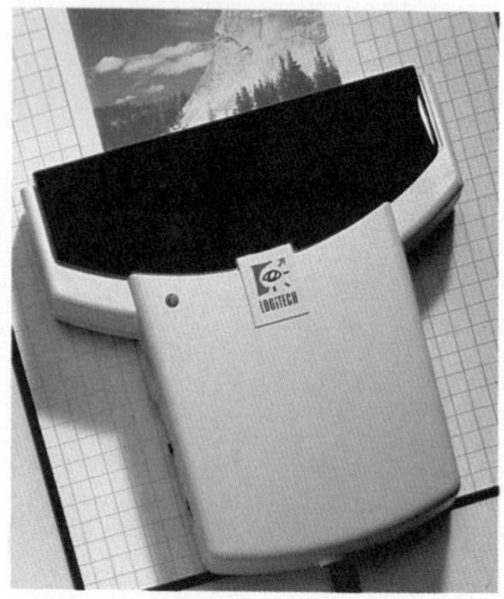

FIGURE 9.8
The page scanner and handheld scanner facilitate direct input of both textual and graphical data.

Other Input Devices

While the keyboard, mouse, and scanners are the most familiar devices for input, other input peripherals are used for special applications. For example, keys and a mouse are not always needed for cursor control. People also use joysticks when playing computer games. The **joystick** looks like a stick shift found in a car with manual transmission. By moving the joystick's arm, players can control the movement and action of characters on the screen. Some drawing software allows use of a joystick for input instead of a mouse.

A handheld, light-sensitive stylus attached to terminals can accept the stylus' position on the monitor as input. People move this **light pen** across a screen to make menu selections or draw shapes (see Figure 9.9). This technology allows input of handwriting as data on a notepad computer, called a *pen-based computer*. Besides note taking, a person could use a light pen or stylus to edit word-processed documents directly on a screen, using common proofreading symbols. Figure 9.10 displays some of the proofreading symbols used in pen-based computer editing. Pen-based computing has increased sharply in the last few years as people use it for everything from personal note taking to text editing and on-site inventory recording (see Figure 9.10).

FIGURE 9.9
By using a light pen, an engineer can alter designs directly on the screen.

An input device similar in use to the light pen is the **touch-sensitive screen**, which enables users to input instructions by merely touching prompts displayed on a screen (see Figure 9.11). These screens can be sensitized so the application of pressure by a finger, pencil, or stylus initiates input. Another type of touch-sensitive

[ ]	selects a word
X	deletes a word
L	inserts a space
∧	inserts a word
✓	displays menu options
9	deletes a character
(tap screen)	selects a menu option or a character
—	flick right (next page)
—	flick left (previous page)

FIGURE 9.10
Software within a pen-based computer can accept handwriting as input, which is useful for editing text appearing on a screen.

screen waits for a finger, etc., to interrupt infrared light beams criss-crossing in front of the screen. The combination of lights that are interrupted determine the screen area used for input. Such screens are especially helpful when people are unfamiliar with computers. Information systems in shopping malls, airports, and amusement parks are now being developed using touch-sensitive screens as the only input hardware.

Drafting or drawing **tablets** work on a similar principle. A stylus or *puck* with crosshairs and buttons is run across the surface of a flat, pressure-sensitive or magnetically sensitive tablet (see Figure 9.12). The pattern of pressure or position of the puck when a button is pushed is sensed by wires under the surface of the tablet, then **digitized.** That is, the location of the stylus/puck is expressed in mathematical terms and transmitted to the computer. The image "drawn" or "traced" on the drafting tablet is echoed on a screen.

By using tablets or light pens, people can input structural drawings into the computer. The drawings then can be viewed and

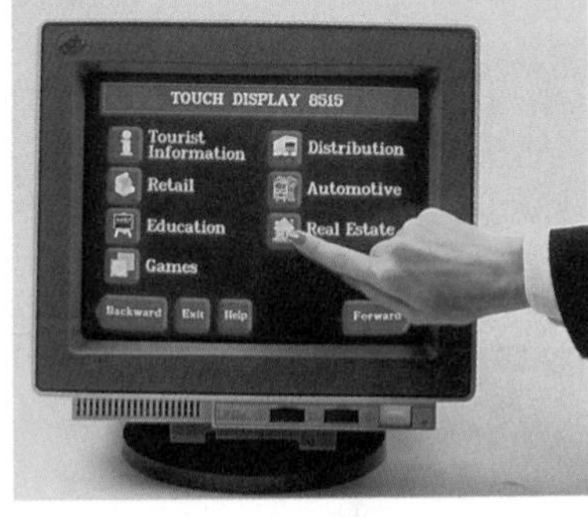

FIGURE 9.11
Touching the screen breaks a matrix of infrared beams, which are used to locate the screen position for input.

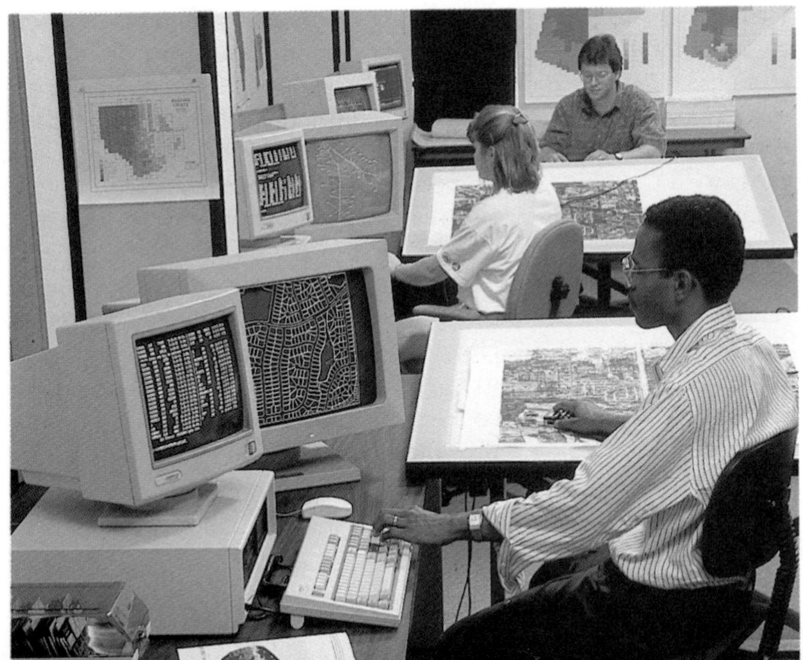

FIGURE 9.12
As the puck is moved across a photograph, the graphical data is digitized and input into the computer.

manipulated as if the objects they represent actually existed. An aircraft engineer can design a plane and input the specifications into the computer. The three-dimensional computer drawing can be tested as a model of the aircraft. Test flights can be simulated and design features evaluated, all under control of the computer. This enables users to detect problems in product designs and to draft new designs before the product is made.

A recent development, the *still camera,* looks on the outside like a regular camera. The user focuses, aims, and shoots a scene. However, instead of being stored on photographic film, the image is digitized and stored on a small disk within the camera. This disk can then be removed and read by a computer. The images on the disk can be transferred for use within graphics software or displayed on a monitor or projector. The same disk can be used many times over.

A telephone with tone dialing is used widely as an interactive input device. While at home, a user can pay utility bills by dialing a number that establishes a connection to a bank computer. Then the user's account number, utility account number, and amount are entered through the phone keys. The computer generates a vocal response that verifies the bill has been paid. A similar system is also used to inquire about airport arrivals and departures by keying in the flight number, day, and destination of a flight. This results in a vocal listing of flight information.

Another type of input peripheral is the credit card reader used by merchants, restaurants, hotels, and gas stations. The credit card is passed through a slot containing a magnetic tape reader. The strip of magnetic tape on the back of the credit card is read to obtain the credit card number. The amount of the sale is entered through a keypad. The computer responds with an approval or disapproval of the sale based on the customer's current credit level.

FIGURE 9.13
A voice-recognition device translates the human voice into digital signals. Clear and careful speaking is a necessity when using this input hardware.

Card readers of various types date back to Hollerith's (Who's Who, Chapter 10) original punched card. Instead of magnetic strips, these cards have holes punched by *keypunch* machines. Different combinations of holes represent text and numbers. Data entry operators use a keyboard on a keypunch machine to punch data on the cards. Computers output data on punched cards by using a *cardpunch.* For instance, utility companies sometimes include punched cards with their bills. Customers return the punched card with payments, and the billing data is read into the computer from the cards by a card reader.

Voice-recognition devices accept spoken commands as input (Figure 9.13). In one typical application a computer using voice-recognition devices accepts spoken commands from people confined to wheelchairs. The individual need only announce the direction and speed. The computer recognizes the spoken words and converts them to output, guiding the wheelchair.

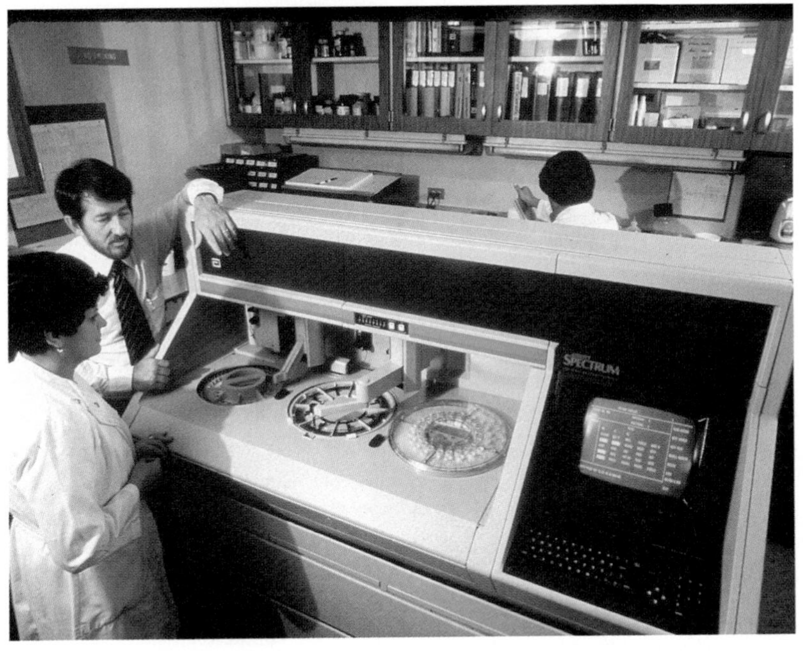

FIGURE 9.14
A sensor is used to detect and input the chemical makeup of a blood sample.

Today's voice-recognition devices still have many drawbacks. Only a limited number of commands are understandable by the devices, and users often need to talk slowly. In addition, computers must be programmed to recognize the speech patterns of those people who will be using the equipment. Currently, many such systems require users to read a list of key terms into the computer to establish a working vocabulary. Still, as hardware specialists continue to refine voice technologies, voice input has the potential to come into wider use. Eventually, computers are expected to accept all voice input. People talking to the computer on their wrist will be a common sight.

In many scientific applications, data input is done through a *sensor,* as in Figure 9.14. When coupled with specialized applications programs, these input devices allow data—such as the chemical makeup of a material, blood components, the movement of land along an earthquake

In the News...

ERGONOMICS OF INPUT

Apple's new ergonomically designed keyboard combats incorrect wrist positioning.

fault, or changes in radioactivity—to be sent to a computer for analysis. No matter what the application, the input peripherals in Figure 9.15 are being developed to make data acquisition timely and accurate.

Hardware	Characteristics
Keyboard	Most popular data entry device. Some come with optional numeric keypads, function keys, and cursor control keys
Mouse, Trackball, Joystick	Used with graphic displays to control cursor
Hardcopy Terminal	Produces permanent results
Scanner	Accepts a wide variety of machine-readable characters, which include optical marks, optical characters, magnetic ink characters, and bar codes
Image Scanners	Accepts graphical data and converts it to pixels
Light Pen	Handheld hardware used to control cursor for graphic input
Touch-sensitive Screen	User touches prompts on screen to control input; no additional hardware needed
Tablet	Supports graphic input through freehand drawing or tracing
Still Camera	Places "photographs" on disk for computer input
Telephone	Used to input numeric data from long distances; some voice recognition hardware is used with telephone input
Credit Card Reader	Used for credit checks during retail purchases
Cardpunch, Keypunch	Puts holes into punched cards representing data
Cardreader	One of the oldest types of input devices, reads data from punched cards
Voice Recognition System	Activated by user's voice after voice has been programmed into the computer; currently accepts limited number of vocal commands
Sensor	Allows direct input of physical data

FIGURE 9.15
Input peripherals are designed to work with a variety of data and user involvement.

OUTPUT HARDWARE SOLUTIONS

The role of computers as problem-solving tools is most visible when users receive and apply the actual results of computer processing. Output peripherals support a great diversity of applications. Generally output hardware falls into three categories:

- Permanent output
- Temporary output
- Action output

Permanent Output

Computer-processed information in the form of printed documents, drawings, and microfilm are examples of permanent output. A vast selection of hardware is available for its production. Different types of permanent output used together give broad support for professional or personal applications. An architect's office, for example,

In the News...

TIPS FOR REDUCING COMPUTER VISION SYNDROME

"viewing distance should be 18 to 30 inches"

- Position the center of the screen about 20 degrees below eye level; viewing distance should be 18 to 30 inches.
- Use a high-resolution monitor.
- Position the VDT so that the office window is at a right angle to the screen. If that is not possible, close the window blinds.
- Reduce overhead lighting to cut glare. If glare persists, use a high-quality antiglare filter.
- Clean the screen and/or filter to remove dust and fingerprints.
- Use an adjustable document holder that puts reference material at the same height and plane as the computer screen.
- Rest your eyes occasionally. Get regular eye checkups; mention VDT work.

Sources: Center for Office Technology; Library of Congress; Optical Coating Laboratory.

might make use of reports, graphics, and microfilm for daily support of operations. The following sections introduce the most common types of permanent output hardware.

Printers

Many organizations produce permanent output for routine business correspondence, payroll processing, billing, and accounting. For example, architects deliver cost estimates and formal bids to clients as professional documents. Many of these applications require the use of a printer. A variety of printers is available, based on the intended application and who is to use the document. The speed of printing may be an important consideration, along with the cost of producing the document.

A popular type of printer for personal computer systems uses *dot-matrix characters*. These characters are formed as a pattern of dots within a matrix. The printer transfers the dots to paper using a print head that contains several pins, as shown in Figure 9.16. Different combinations of pins strike an inked ribbon. As the print head moves across the paper, the pattern of dots required for each character is printed on paper.

The quality of printed characters depends on the number of dots used per character and how the character is printed (see Figure

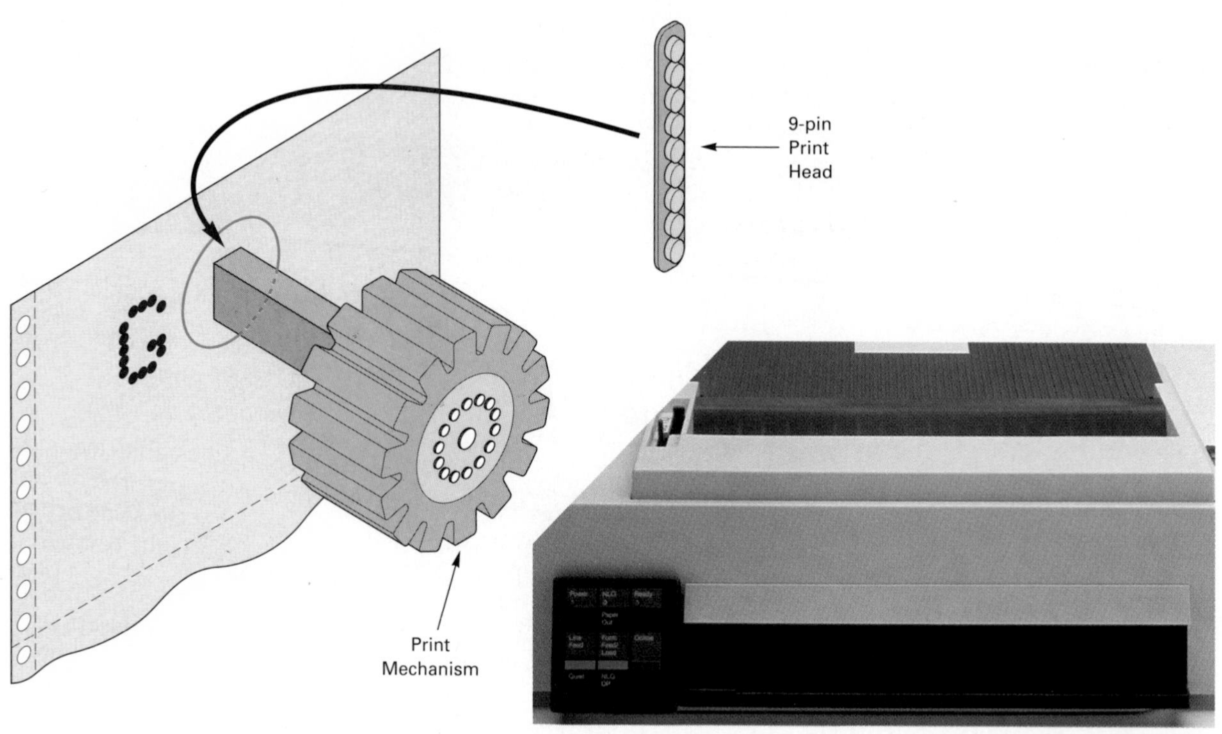

FIGURE 9.16
Draft-quality printers use either 9- or 24-pin print heads.

9.17). The output of an inexpensive printer producing dot-matrix characters generally is not considered to be of professional quality. That is, it does not look as if it has been typed by hand on a high-quality typewriter. A dot-matrix printer using dot-matrix characters is also called a **draft-quality printer** since it may be suitable for a draft, but not a final copy. However, many draft-quality printers can create *correspondence-quality characters* by typing each line twice. The dots are printed a little higher in the second pass, which fills in the character. As you might expect, printing is slower when producing correspondence-quality characters.

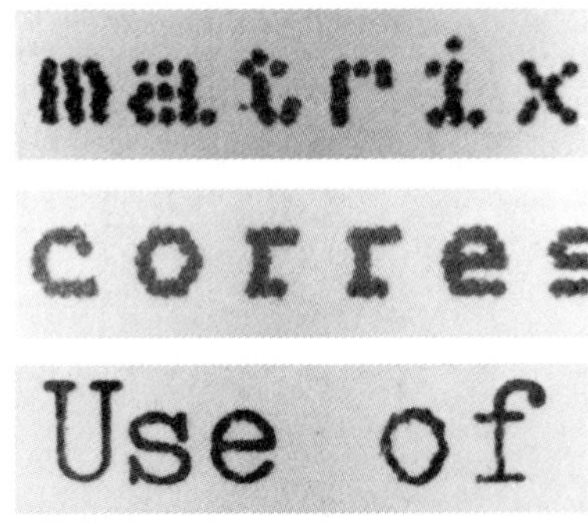

FIGURE 9.17
Printers produce either dot-matrix, correspondence-quality, or full characters.

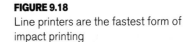

Printers that use *full characters* produce a top-quality output suitable for any business application. Such printers are called **letter-quality printers.** Each number, letter, and symbol available in a full-character printer is solid, like typewritten characters.

Print speeds are determined in part by the amount of text a printer can output at one time. **Serial printers** print one character at a time, generally from 50 to 400 characters per second. **Line printers** output a complete line of text at a time, at a rate of between 100 and 2,000 lines per minute. Using xerographic techniques, **page printers** output a page at a time, reproducing over 300 pages per minute.

Printers use either impact or nonimpact methods to transfer text to paper. Most draft-quality and letter-quality serial printers are impact printers. Both contain print elements that strike a ribbon for character formation. This physical contact is characteristic of impact printers. Line printers represent the fastest form of impact printing. By using either a rotating drum or chain containing every possible letter, number, and special character, a line of print can be quickly formatted. A printed line is created by striking an inked ribbon and paper against the drum or chain with small hammers, as seen in Figure 9.18. Line printers are frequently used with minicomputers and mainframes needing reliable and continuous operation from a printer.

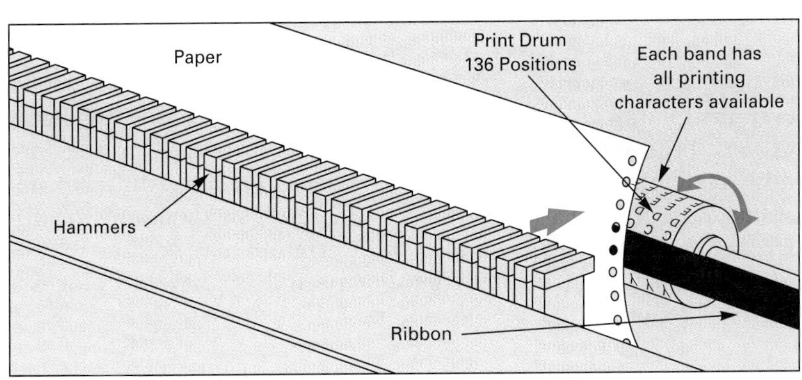

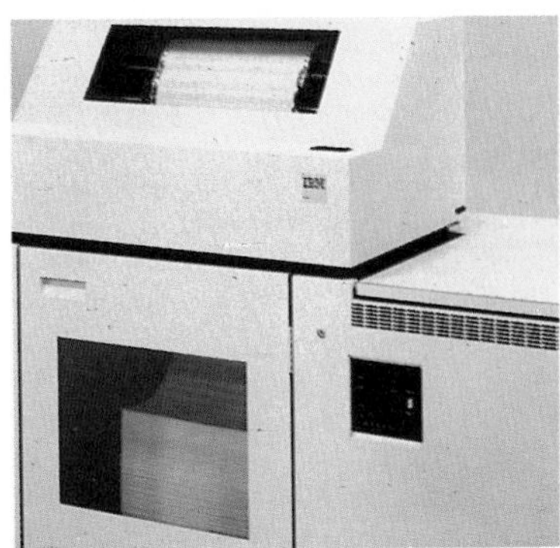

FIGURE 9.18
Line printers are the fastest form of impact printing

Who's Who

Joseph Marie Jacquard (1752–1834)

Joseph Marie Jacquard grew up in pre-Revolutionary France, the son of a weaver and a pattern maker. In his youth he spent many boring hours as a drawboy, lifting the warp strings on a loom for the master weaver to draw the shuttle through them. In 1790 he had an idea to mechanize the loom; however, the French Revolution intervened. In 1801 Jacquard developed a loom that used punched cards to control its operation. Needles fell through holes in the cards and lifted the warp strings; different combinations of punched holes created different designs and patterns in the woven material. Fabric designs and quality improved dramatically. However, the weavers saw the innovation as loss of their jobs. They burned the looms and attacked Jacquard.

The government, recognizing the loom's use, gave Jacquard in 1806 a pension and royalties. This allowed others to manufacture the looms, which quickly spread across Europe. Punched cards were to re-emerge as a data storage media in information processing more than 80 years later in the United States.

Nonimpact printers form characters without using an inked ribbon. *Ink-jet printers,* for example, spray tiny drops of ink to form character shapes on paper. Since characters are formed as a pattern of dots, ink-jet printers are technically dot-matrix printers. However, the quality of ink-jet output generally is much higher than that of most draft-quality dot-matrix printers. Color ink jet printers are now available with jets that can be filled with three different ink colors. The mixing of these colors can result in thousands of different hues. Although a complex color printout may be slow to produce on an ink-jet printer, the clarity and quality of color are extremely high.

Other nonimpact printers form characters with such elements as heat and electricity. A *thermal printer* uses heated dot-matrix wires to print output on specially treated paper. *Electrostatic printers* emit electrical impulses that are reproduced as characters on electrostatic paper. Some fax machines use techniques similar to thermal printers to produce documents on heat-sensitive paper. Output on thermal paper fades quickly when exposed to light but the hardware is often inexpensive.

A nonimpact printer that produces high-quality output at very high speeds is the **laser printer.** Laser printers operate much like copy machines. A controlled beam of intense laser light forms images on an electrically charged drum (see Figure 9.19). These images attract toner particles. The particles, arranged as the images, are transferred to paper. There, heat is used to fuse the particles to the paper. Laser-created documents feature a high-quality print with high resolution a page at a time. This allows users to print their own letterheads, logos, and special forms along with the text, instead of using preprinted forms. Graphic images are output clearly. With new developments in laser print technologies, color laser printers have been developed. Costs for laser printers have steadily declined. As laser printers become more affordable, they are in demand by both individual and commercial users who need high-quality printing at fast speeds.

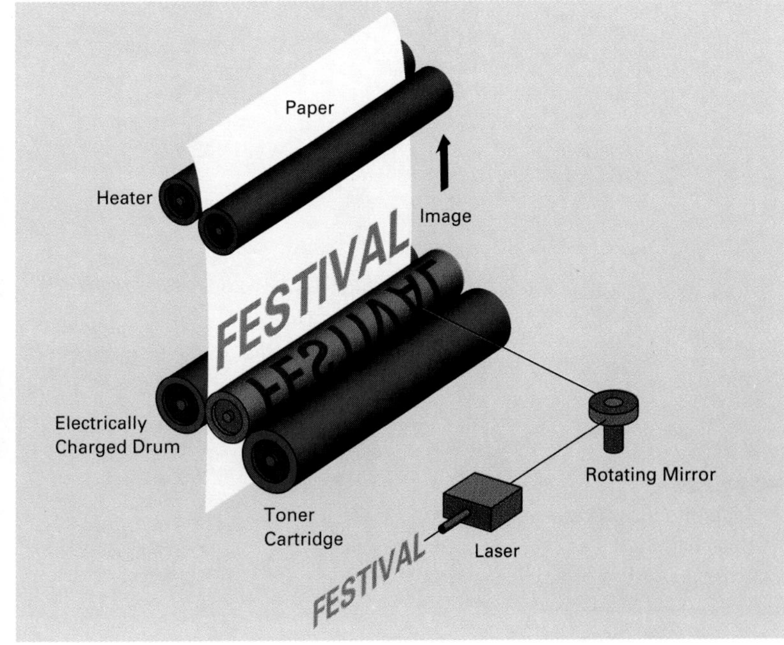

FIGURE 9.19
Laser printers contain a laser that scans across electrically charged drums, creating output rivaling typesetting.

Plotters

Within an architectural firm many computer applications require large graphic output in the form of graphs, maps, charts, and drawings. An architect's designs, for example, require sketches instead of text. One kind of device that produces permanent graphic output in large sheets is the **plotter** (see Figure 9.20). Directed by signals from the computer, the plotter moves a pen across a piece of paper. A plotter equipped with more than one pen can produce multicolor graphic output.

Two types of plotters are available. The flat-bed plotter holds a sheet of paper on a flat surface, then moves a pen across the sheet to form images. With a drum plotter the paper is wound around a drum; then the paper's rotation and pen movement are computer-coordinated to produce an image. Plotters can plot drawings from the size of standard letter paper up to 3 feet by 4 feet. Some drum plotters are capable of producing longer continuous drawings. With both flat-bed and drum plotters, two- or three-dimensional graphics can be created.

The technology used in plotting drawings also makes available output peripherals that will cut templates for signs, or etch plastic surfaces with the same accuracy that a plotter produces in drawings.

FIGURE 9.20
A plotter produces drawn, rather than printed, output.

Plotters and related hardware are high-quality, low-volume devices ideal for output of large drawings, maps, and other detailed graphics. In other words, they produce high-quality output for specialized purposes, but the process is time consuming. As a result, plotters are unable to mass-produce graphic output efficiently.

Microfilm and Microfiche

Large volumes of information can be held in rolls *(microfilm)* or sheets *(microfiche)* of film on which miniature images are recorded. High-capacity microfilm enables users to access a high quantity of full-page images quickly and conveniently. In addition, microfilm is used for permanent preservation of printed information since film is more durable and more compact than paper.

With **computer output microfilm** (COM) techniques, the results of computer processing are transferred—in miniature form—directly onto microfilm or microfiche. On microfilm, pages of data are imaged sequentially on a reel of film. Microfiche is a sheet of film often measuring 4 inches by 6 inches and carrying information equivalent to a 200-page report (see Figure 9.21).

FIGURE 9.21
A COM system produced the microfiche page being examined on this reader.

Microfilm output is used for distribution of airline schedules, automotive parts catalogs, medical x-rays, and lists of books in print. It also is ideal for storing back issues of newspapers and magazines. An architectural firm can use microfilm resources to access information on old blueprints, building codes, and zoning laws.

Temporary Output

In applications that do not require permanent output, video displays and audio responses serve as effective, yet temporary, output. Computer technology brought with it an onslaught of permanent documents. The "paper avalanche" that resulted actually became a hindrance to information retrieval. Locating pertinent pieces of information in the mountain of available documents became a time-consuming chore. Computer technology soon enabled users to locate needed files directly and to receive real-time service. Output used for reference does not have to be printed on paper. Video displays for temporary output have reduced this paper avalanche.

Temporary output also is useful when the information changes rapidly. In airports, screens display up-to-the-minute flight information. At a football field, scoreboards provide temporary output reflecting current scores and statistics. In addition to temporary output displayed on a screen, audio response and interactive devices provide output for immediate, temporary use.

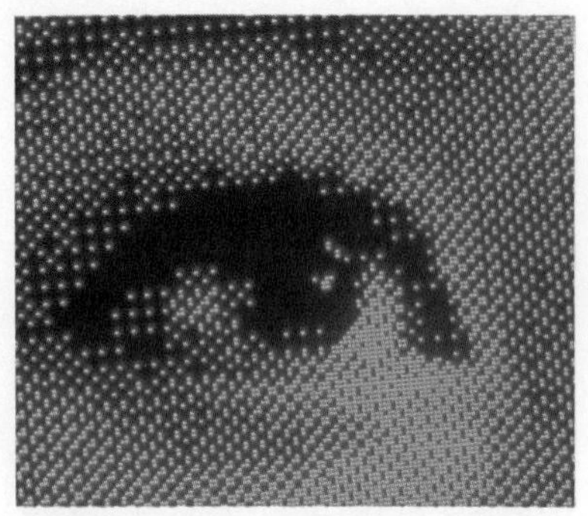

FIGURE 9.22
The display on a VDT is made up of many pixels differing in color and brightness.

FIGURE 9.23
The standards for color monitors differ in the resolution of the screen and in the number of colors displayed.

Video Display Output

Monitors, also called **video display terminals (VDTs),** provide the same information as a plotter or printer, but are more efficient where temporary use of information is desired. Monitors are either *cathode ray tubes (CRTs)* or flat screens. CRTs operate much like television picture tubes. The computer generates signals that move an electron beam across the phosphorus-coated face inside the cathode ray tube. As the beam is turned off and on, it makes the phosphorus glow. These glowing pixels are what we see as images on the screen (see Figure 9.22).

Flat screens are more compact and are used with laptop and pen-based computer systems. CRTs and flat screens usually use the bit mapping of pixels, as described in Chapter 6, for graphic displays. Flat screens for portable computers may employ a *liquid crystal display (LCD)* in which an electric field causes liquid crystals to change intensity and align in a predetermined configuration, creating output characters. Such monitors are very flat, compact, and lightweight.

Images might be displayed on **monochrome,** or single-color, monitors. Typically, monochrome screens display output in green, white, or amber colors on a black background. Multicolored output can be produced by **RGB monitors,** which use red, green, and blue components in each pixel to form full-color images. Many LCD

Monitor Type	Resolution (pixels)	Resolution of Colors
CGA (color graphic adapter)	640 × 200	16
EGA (extended graphics adapter)	750 × 350	16
VGA (video graphics array)	720 × 400	256
Super VGA	1024 × 768	256
XGA (extended graphics array)	1024 × 768	65,536

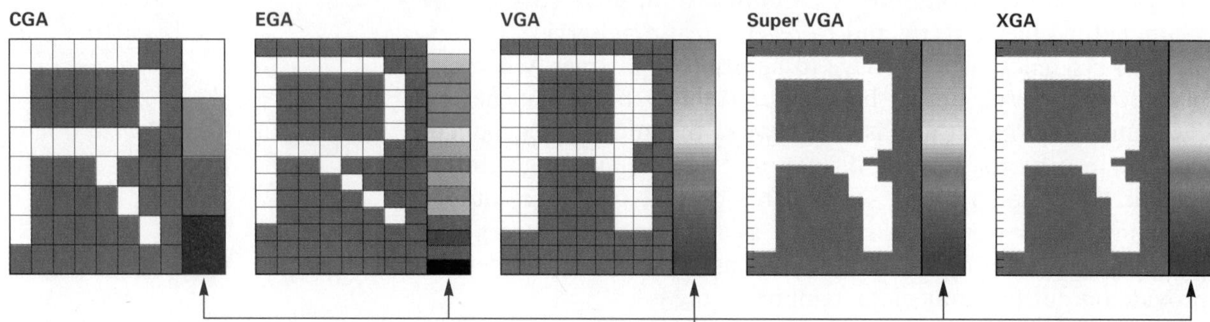

monitors are monochromatic. However, color LCD monitors are available but expensive since each of the color components for a single pixel is controlled by a separate transistor—almost a million transistors per screen.

Over the years standards have been developed for color monitors. These standards are based on the screen resolution and the number of colors available. Monitors with a *CGA (color graphics adapter)* can display up to 640 (height) by 200 (width) pixels per screen in 16 colors. *EGA (extended graphics adapter)* increased the screen display to 640 by 350 pixels with 16 colors available. When *VGA (video graphics array)* was introduced in 1987, it astounded people by its near-photograph-quality display. Monitors with VGA can display from a range of 262,144 colors (up to 256 colors at a time) in any of the 720 by 400 pixels on the screen. *Super VGA,* released two years later, displays 256 colors in 1024 by 768 pixels. *XGA (extended graphics array),* developed in 1990, allows displays in an incredible 65,536 colors on screens 1024 by 768 pixels. Figure 9.23 summarizes the characteristics of color monitor standards. It is easy to see that future developments in this area can only enhance the lifelike quality of graphic displays.

For presentations to audiences, large-screen formats are available. One example is a CRT television screen with a 33-inch-diagonal screen. Another alternative is the *projection plate,* which is a semitransparent plate that fits on top of an overhead projector. The projection plate is directly connected to a computer. The image that normally appears on the computer's monitor is transmitted to the plate and projected on a large screen. Also, output can be sent to an RGB projector that shows the image on a large screen.

Sound and Speech Output

Sound synthesizers create messages—temporary output—that computer users hear. Perhaps the most familiar form of audio output is heard on the telephone in the weather, time, or common operator messages. In this type of temporary output, voice messages may be tape recordings of human voices or artificially created by a *speech synthesizer.*

Uses for sound and speech synthesizers are becoming more wide-ranging. Often delivered through telephones, speech output has been used to provide information about stock market prices and flight departure times. In late-model cars a voice output reminds the driver to turn off headlights or to add fuel to an almost empty tank. Since audio output requires only the ability to hear, it can be of great value to people with visual handicaps and reading disabilities. For example, computers and calculators are available where all output can be heard, if needed.

FIGURE 9.24
Computers help make music by using a sound synthesizer for output.

Action Output

As we have seen, computer processing can result in printed documents and drawings, screen displays, voice recordings, and more. These types of output depend on the sight or hearing of people for interpretation and use. Action output, on the other hand, consists of processing data that initiate some form of movement or process control activity.

One type of action output is produced by **numerical control (NC)** devices. NC machines accept numeric specifications as input. They produce machine parts that meet those specifications precisely as output. Programmable drill presses and lathes are NC machines that output a cutting action. People who once operated manual tools may now program NC machines to produce desired results (see Figure 9.25).

For technicians and engineers, CAD (computer-aided design) technologies support **computer-aided machining (CAM).** Computer-aided machining links numerical control capabilities directly with computer-generated designs by converting CAD designs into specifications used by NC machines. This communication between design and manufacturing equipment is known as **CAD/CAM.** Large metalworking machines are used under CAM systems to prepare tools for the stamping of automotive parts or the fabrication of mobile homes based on CAD designs.

FIGURE 9.25
Precision part production depends on the programmablility and accuracy of a numerical control machine.

FIGURE 9.26
Linking robots on the assembly line creates a flexible manufacturing tool, which performs complex operations.

Many examples of action output are seen in **robotics** systems, where computer-driven machines are programmed to perform work. Robot output can be determined solely by computer programs. In other cases, output is a result of the input of physical data. Some robots are attached to cameras that allow them to "see" their surroundings and adapt their action output according to what they view (Figure 9.26).

The first robots were used to perform dangerous tasks. Robots can do high-risk jobs, such as working among toxic fumes or handling radioactive materials, with no ill effects. The earliest robots thus spared people from health-threatening duties. In recent years people have put robots to many labor-saving uses. For example, a robotic engine manufacturing tool might perform a series of functions: sizing holes in a block, inserting pistons, and putting the engine block head in place. The robots sense the size of each hole, then locate and insert pistons that fit the holes to 0.0001 inch.

The field of medicine has found several uses for action output. In hospital emergency rooms, computers with sensors monitor a patient's vital signs and, as action output, regulate the flow of oxygen or medication to the patient. Embedded microprocessors can send small electrical shocks to muscles to stimulate movement in paralyzed limbs. Computerized pacemakers stimulate heart muscles. In both cases muscle movement is the action output.

PERIPHERAL DESIGN AND SAFETY

The increased use of input and output peripherals in the past two decades has brought about some special health concerns for the human users. When people used only typewriters and pens for business paperwork, there were always breaks in the action. For example, the typewriter carriage had to be returned at the end of each line, paper needed to be changed, and errors had to be manually erased. With the advent of computers, especially word processing programs, it was possible for a person to spend several hours typing at a keyboard and looking at a monitor with little change in hand or body position. It wasn't long before workers were complaining about pain in their wrists and hands, back and neck aches, and headaches due to eyestrain.

Repetitive Strain Injuries

Doctors and researchers have found several causes for many of these symptoms. Continuous typing on a keyboard or use of a mouse results in *repetitive strain injuries* (RSI). In an RSI, the tendons in the arms become inflamed and squeeze the nerves. This causes numbness and pain. Unless the RSI is diagnosed and treated, serious long-term disabilities can develop. Carpal tunnel syndrome, an RSI of the wrist, can cause permanent damage, seriously limiting use of one or both hands. Nearly half of workplace illnesses in private industry can be accounted for by RSI.

Low-Frequency Emissions

Since monitors were introduced in the late 1970s, people have been concerned about the effects of the extremely low-frequency (ELF) emissions from these screens. Rumors of miscarriages and brain tumors caused by VDT emissions have yet to be substantiated by medical researchers. At the very least, many people find the glare from a screen causes eyestrain and headaches. Other workers complain of continuous back or neck pain that seemingly cannot be relieved with routine pain medicine.

Ergonomics

Most of these problems were based on the design of computer equipment and its related workspace. Since most hardware is mass-produced, there was little consideration at first for the need to fit an individual. **Ergonomics** is the study of how the tools and equipment we use can be designed to fit the way the human body moves and works. Health researchers, hardware engineers, office furniture designers, and people who set up the work areas for computer users all are considering ergonomic features when they create a new product (Figure 9.27).

For example, to stem the increase in repetitive strain injuries, designers and medical experts have come up with a variety of solutions. Doctors have designed special splints to put around wrists to prevent injury-causing movement. Surgery has also relieved some sufferers of carpal tunnel syndrome. Hardware designers are attempting to create keyboards that better fit the human hand. These designs include pads on which to rest your palms, letters in different locations on the keyboard, and curved keyboards. There

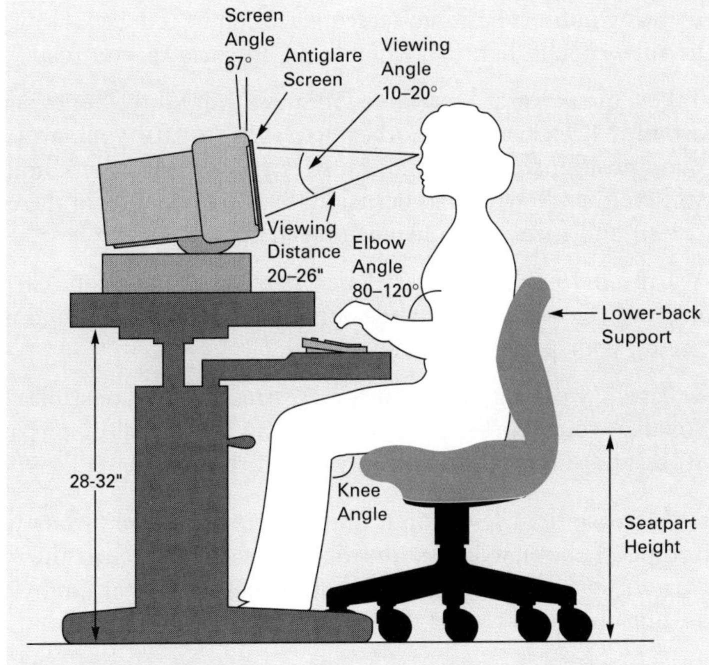

FIGURE 9.27
There are several ergonomic considerations in designing a comfortable work area.

are even keyboards that are shaped like an inverted V, where the hands are placed at the sides, rather than on top. Varying degrees of success have been reported.

To reduce the perceived dangers of monitors, anti-glare screens and changes in screen colors are being used. For those who would like to protect themselves from emissions, there are leaded aprons that can be worn, similar to those used by x-ray technicians. Scientists are constantly trying to reduce the emissions from VDTs. Many European countries have adopted strict standards on monitor emissions. However, manufacturers claim that there has been no definitive proof that continued exposure to these emissions is harmful.

Many of the complaints of back pain and general fatigue are due not to I/O hardware, but to the workspace itself. Bad posture due to sitting on poorly designed chairs, at desks raised to an improper level, or under insufficient lighting can cause many of these complaints. Here are some suggestions to help you achieve safe computing:

- Sit on a chair with rollers built for your height. Your back should be straight but supported, lower arms and thighs parallel to the floor, and feet flat. Chair and desk heights should be adjustable.
- The top of your monitor should be even with your eyelevel. Any documents you are typing from should also be at that level. Adjustable monitor arms and copy holders are available.
- By using indirect lighting, screen glare can be reduced. However, be sure enough light is available on all surfaces you read.
- Take a break for at least fifteen minutes every three hours. Move around, stretch, and do other activities to vary your arm and body positions. At a minimum, stretch your arms every hour or so. Even while working, occasionally look away from the close screen and focus on a distant object.
- Warm up your hand muscles before a long typing job. Clenching and releasing your hands, stretching your fingers, and massaging your palms are all suggested.
- Create a working environment as stress-free as possible. Personalize your workspace and set up an efficient flow of paperwork and information within your work area.

As we increase the use of input and output hardware in our work environments, both workers and designers have reached the same conclusion. We must adjust the equipment to fit our individual needs, not our bodies to fit the equipment.

A Closer Look...

Peripherals for Special Applications

Unique human and technical situations have led to the development of I/O hardware far beyond the traditional keyboard, screen, and printer. Such peripherals are especially important for people with special needs, using physical data, or presentation of output in a unique way. Everyone has different questions to ask when talking about special peripherals:

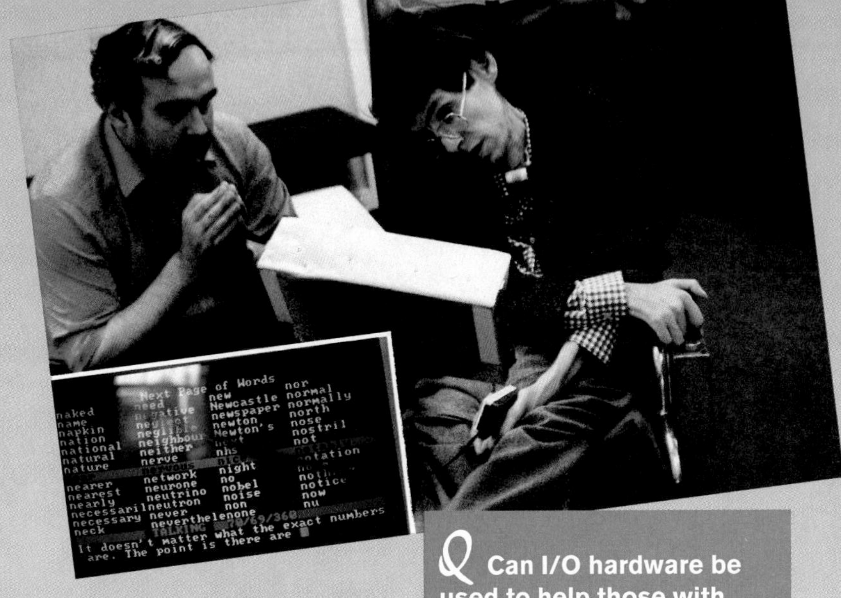

Q Can I/O hardware be used to help those with limited movement communicate?

A A variety of peripherals are available for people who have difficulty using a keyboard. Textual data can be entered through a touch-sensitive screen, voice-recognition devices, or handheld pointer. This physicist uses a button on his armrest to indicate a word and build sentences.

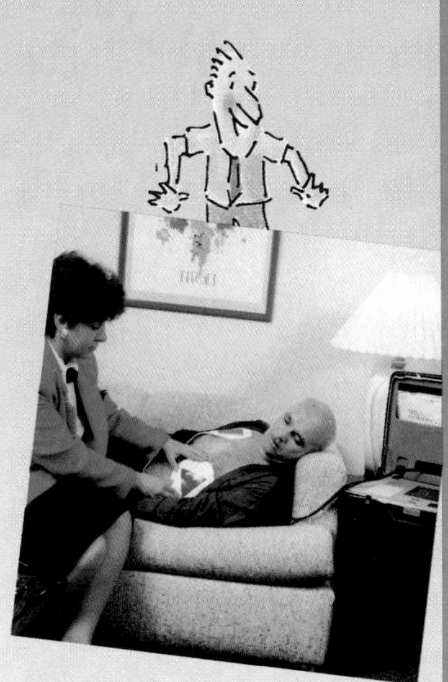

Q What are practical applications for the input of physical data?

A There are a very wide range of sensors available for collecting and inputting many types of physical data. Each sensor detects a specific kind of data, such as radioactivity, seismic movement, presence of certain chemicals in blood, or heart rate. Some sensors will transmit the intensity of the component into a computer, which converts it to numeric data.

Q What kind of output hardware could help the physically handicapped move?

A Special hardware can be used to stimulate a single muscle, allowing movement of body parts previously paralyzed.

Q How are changes in I/O hardware technology affecting entertainment?

A The entertainment industry relies heavily on I/O hardware to improve animation in film, advertisements, and television. This input device contains sensors attached to an actor's face, head, and lips. As he moves, a computer generates similar movements in the on-screen character.

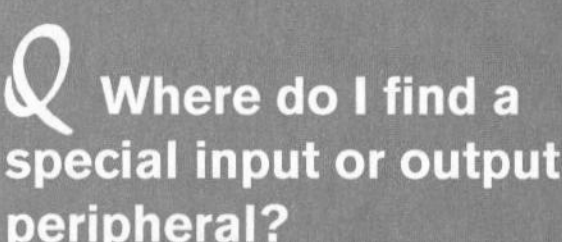

Q Where do I find a special input or output peripheral?

A For many applications, like labs or research stations, the best sources for such hardware are the manufacturers themselves. You can find their names through advertisements in professional journals, or contact a company already using such equipment. Some hardware is still experimental, and information may be available only from the research institution where it is being developed.

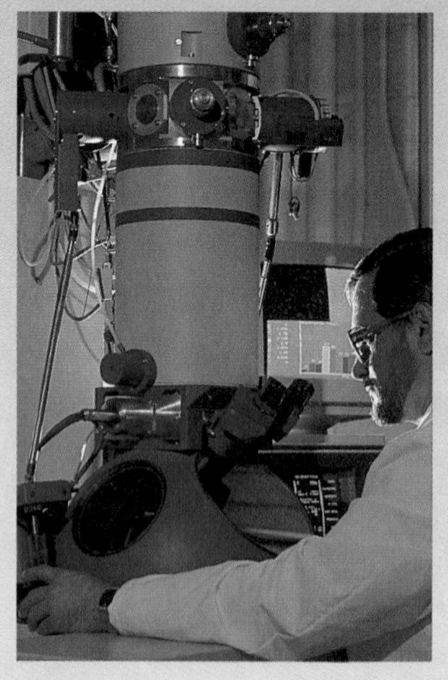

Chapter Facts

- User-friendly computer systems let people take more control of computers. I/O is the link between computers and people.
- Keyboards may contain character keys, special function keys for activating software features, numeric keypads, or icons. Pointing devices, like a mouse or trackball, provide an alternative to the keyboard for data input.
- A terminal is where input is entered or output received. Input is via keyboard, while output is on a screen (soft copy) or typewriter-like printer (hard copy).
- Scanners are used to transfer user-recognizable characters into machine-readable characters. They can scan bar codes, optical marks (OMR), optical characters (OCR), magnetic ink characters (MICR), or graphic images.
- Sensors allow direct input into computers of such physical data as chemical makeup or radioactivity levels.
- Users can input data interactively using a joystick, light pen, or touch-sensitive screen, or drawing on a tablet.
- Voice-recognition systems allow vocal input based on a preprogrammed vocabulary.
- Input also can be sent through telephone tone dialing or a credit card reader.
- Output hardware can be permanent, temporary, or can result in action.
- Permanent output usually is a hard copy from a printer. Print can be in dot-matrix, correspondence, or full characters.
- Printer speeds depend on whether it is a serial, line, or page printer. Print method is either impact or nonimpact.
- Plotters can produce drawings, maps, and pictures as another form of permanent output.
- Photographically reduced images can be stored on microfiche (pages of film) or microfilm (reels of film). COM is high-volume, durable, permanent output.
- Monitors or video display terminals provide temporary output. Graphics are presented through patterns of pixels or by using liquid crystal displays.
- Output can be presented on monochrome or RGB monitors. Standards for color monitors are CGA, EGA, VGA, Super VGA, and XGA.
- Sound synthesizers create sounds as output, while speech synthesizers output spoken words.

- Action output is produced through the programming of robots or by numerical control (NC) machines.
- Action output is used to monitor and stimulate muscles connected to artificial or paralyzed limbs.
- Safety in computing involves protection against repetitive strain injuries and low-grade emissions from monitors. Work areas should be designed with ergonomic considerations.

Terms to Remember

a. bar code
b. CAD/CAM
c. computer-aided machining (CAM)
d. computer output microfilm (COM)
e. digitize
f. draft-quality printer
g. ergonomics
h. function keys
i. I/O (input/output)
j. joystick
k. keyboard
l. laser printer
m. letter-quality printer
n. light pen
o. line printer
p. monochrome
q. numerical control (NC)
r. page printer
s. plotter
t. point-of-sale (POS)
u. RGB (red, green, blue) monitors
v. robotics
w. scanner
x. serial printer
y. tablet
z. terminal
aa. touch-sensitive screen
bb. trackball
cc. VDT (video display terminal)
dd. voice-recognition device

Mix and Match

Match the following definitions to the Terms to Remember.

1. ____ a combination of keyboard with monitor or printer providing input and output to a computer system.
2. ____ the study of how tools, furniture, and equipment can be designed to fit the human body.
3. ____ printer that produces one page of output at a time.
4. ____ machine-readable collection of stripes of varying width used to identify items.
5. ____ input hardware, where each keystroke represents a character.

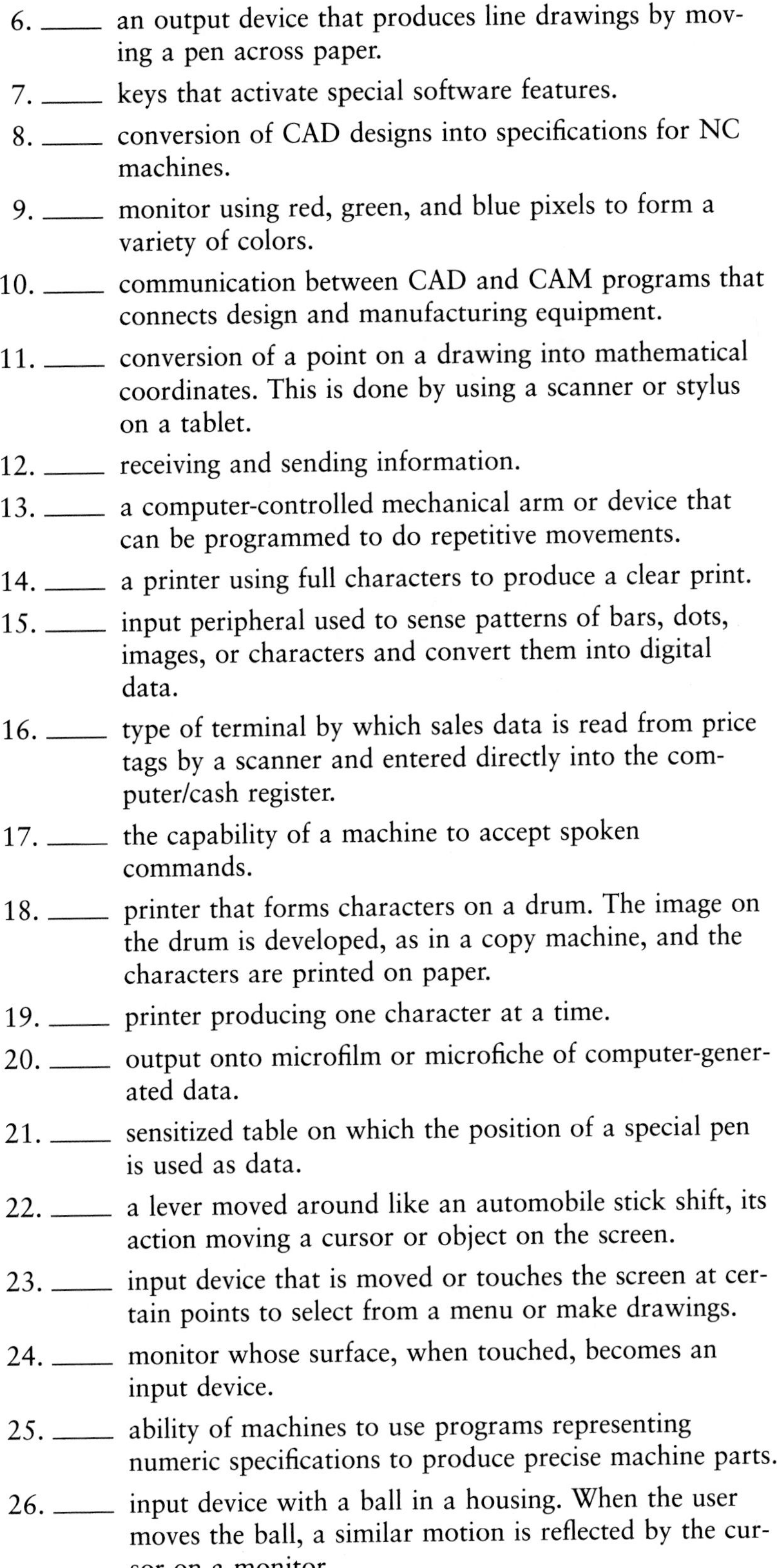

6. ______ an output device that produces line drawings by moving a pen across paper.
7. ______ keys that activate special software features.
8. ______ conversion of CAD designs into specifications for NC machines.
9. ______ monitor using red, green, and blue pixels to form a variety of colors.
10. ______ communication between CAD and CAM programs that connects design and manufacturing equipment.
11. ______ conversion of a point on a drawing into mathematical coordinates. This is done by using a scanner or stylus on a tablet.
12. ______ receiving and sending information.
13. ______ a computer-controlled mechanical arm or device that can be programmed to do repetitive movements.
14. ______ a printer using full characters to produce a clear print.
15. ______ input peripheral used to sense patterns of bars, dots, images, or characters and convert them into digital data.
16. ______ type of terminal by which sales data is read from price tags by a scanner and entered directly into the computer/cash register.
17. ______ the capability of a machine to accept spoken commands.
18. ______ printer that forms characters on a drum. The image on the drum is developed, as in a copy machine, and the characters are printed on paper.
19. ______ printer producing one character at a time.
20. ______ output onto microfilm or microfiche of computer-generated data.
21. ______ sensitized table on which the position of a special pen is used as data.
22. ______ a lever moved around like an automobile stick shift, its action moving a cursor or object on the screen.
23. ______ input device that is moved or touches the screen at certain points to select from a menu or make drawings.
24. ______ monitor whose surface, when touched, becomes an input device.
25. ______ ability of machines to use programs representing numeric specifications to produce precise machine parts.
26. ______ input device with a ball in a housing. When the user moves the ball, a similar motion is reflected by the cursor on a monitor.

27. _____ an impact printer capable of producing dot-matrix characters.
28. _____ a screen that provides temporary output of information.
29. _____ impact printer producing one line at a time with speeds of up to 2,000 lines per minute.
30. _____ a single color, referring to a monitor with one color on a background.

Review Questions

1. What are two pointing devices used for data input, and how do they work?
2. What are the advantages and disadvantages to using a terminal instead of a computer system for input and output?
3. Define four types of machine-readable data read by scanners, and describe an application for each.
4. How does a touch-sensitive screen work, and where could it be used?
5. Describe how a still camera works, and identify an advantage to creating photographs this way.
6. How can a telephone and card reader be used as part of input operations?
7. Describe an application for voice-recognition devices, and identify three limitations to using this equipment.
8. How is a sensor used as an input peripheral?
9. What are the different speeds of serial, line, and page printers?
10. How do ink-jet, thermal, electrostatic, and laser printers work?
11. What are the pros and cons of using a plotter for output?
12. Why would an organization use Computer Output Microfilm?
13. Describe two ways of storing reduced images by using COM.
14. Name and describe the differences in the five standards for color monitors.
15. Describe applications for sound and speech synthesizers.
16. What determines the movement (output) of a robot?
17. What are two health concerns for users of computer systems?
18. How can people help make computing safe and comfortable for themselves?

Applying What You've Learned

1. What input, output, or storage peripherals would be most suitable for these examples of data processing?
   a. updating fast-food restaurant inventories
   b. grading a college entrance exam and reporting the results to the students
   c. spray painting motorcycles on an assembly line
   d. checking driving records for a driver's license renewal
   e. designing and stress-testing an earthquake-proof computer center
2. How could voice-recognition devices and sound/speech synthesizers aid in these situations?
   a. a wheelchair for a paraplegic
   b. a computer used by a child who cannot read
   c. danger and fire alarms for a blind person
   d. ordering from a catalog over a telephone
   e. a computer used by a person learning English
   f. safety features in a building during a power blackout
3. What are five applications for a robot other than those mentioned in the text?
4. Some input/output hardware buyers believe in getting the biggest and fastest hardware they can afford.
   a. What are the disadvantages to this approach?
   b. What are the disadvantages to buying the least expensive hardware?
   c. Would it be better to delay purchasing necessary hardware equipment until the price comes down or to buy the newest equipment now?
5. On the horizon for video equipment is high-definition television. Write a short research report on this upcoming technology. How does it differ from present television? What timeline (and prices) are expected for its release? Are standards established for this technology?

Answers to Mix and Match

1. z 2. g 3. r 4. a 5. k 6. s 7. h 8. c 9. u 10. b
11. e 12. i 13. v 14. m 15. w 16. t 17. dd 18. l
19. x 20. d 21. y 22. j 23. n 24. aa 25. q 26. bb
27. f 28. cc 29. o 30. p

10

Storage Hardware

- From the User's Point of View
- Magnetic Disk Storage
  - Hard and floppy disks
  - Disk storage
  - Disk packs
  - Removable and fixed disks
- Optical Disk Storage
  - CD-ROM
  - WORM disks
  - Erasable optical disks
- Magnetic Tape Storage
  - Tape cartridges
  - Tape labels
- Specialized Storage Hardware
  - Mass storage
  - RAM drives
  - Flash memory
- Maximizing Hardware Performance
  - Parity checking
  - Data compression
- *A Closer Look . . . Building a Personal Computer*

FROM THE USER'S POINT OF VIEW

Hours worth of work can be saved or lost in the blink of an eye when using a computer system. One of the most common mistakes new computer users make is forgetting to copy important data and programs to another tape or disk. Without a duplicate, you could lose valuable information or software if the original is lost or destroyed. You can minimize problems by learning backup procedures and how to properly handle different storage media. Once you appreciate the importance of storage hardware, proper data handling procedures will become second nature.

MAGNETIC DISK STORAGE

The right mix of input and output hardware is essential to a user-friendly computer system. Of equal importance is choosing the correct type of storage media and hardware. Storage media hold data before processing and store the results of processing. The term, **storage media,** refers to the material on which data is recorded. Tapes and disks are the most common media (Figure 10.1).

When data and program files are constantly changing, magnetic storage media are used. A magnetic tape or disk drive records data by magnetizing small areas on the storage media. These magnetized areas store the binary codes representing data or program instructions. When the file is no longer needed, the storage hardware overwrites the binary codes and records new information in its place.

Hard and Floppy Disks

Magnetic disks are the most commonly used storage media because they support both sequential and direct access to data. The primary types of disk drives use either hard disks or floppy disks. Disk drives are

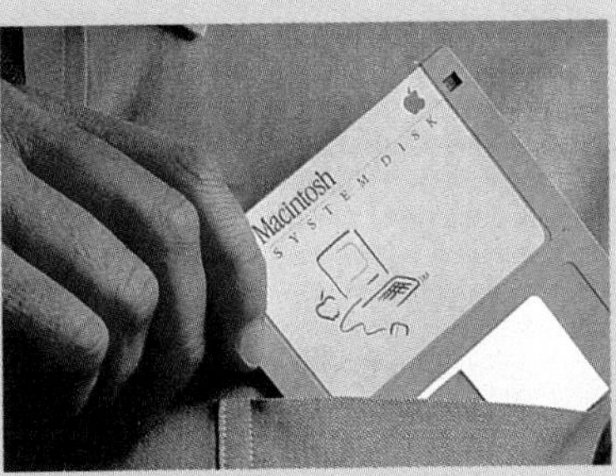

FIGURE 10.1
Storage media like this 3.5-inch diskette keep data and programs when the computer is turned off.

equipped with read/write heads that convert the magnetized spots on disk into a binary code. As the disk spins inside the drive, the read/write head passes over the surface of the disk. The head writes data on the disk by magnetizing spots on the disk's tracks or retrieves data from the disk by reading magnetized spots already there. The disk drive reads the bits as a continuous stream of data. Since each byte of data consists of eight bits, the computer then organizes the bits into bytes.

Moisture and extreme heat or cold are bad for any disk. Magnetic fields associated with electrical equipment like telephone receivers or with paper clips kept in a magnetized holder can erase any magnetic storage media. Dirt and dust damage both the read/write head and the disk surface, if caught between the two (see Figure 10.2). As a result, removable disks must be handled with care and stored in a cool, dry location out of direct sunlight. Disks should never be left in a hot car during the day or a cold car overnight.

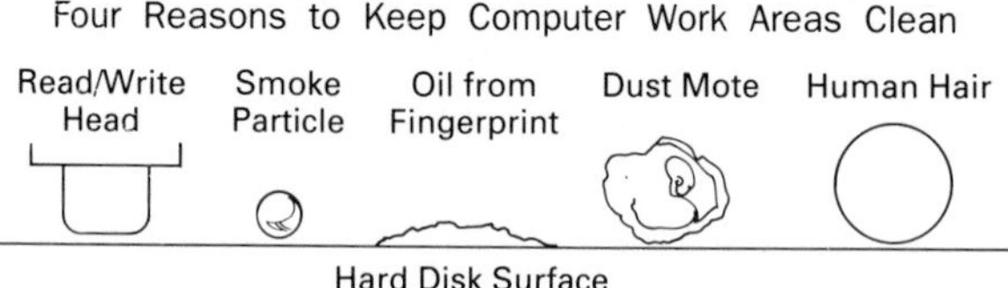

FIGURE 10.2
A disk drive's read/write head is extremely vulnerable to common contaminants that can damage the mechanism and destroy stored data.

When compared to floppy disk drives, hard disks provide users with fast access to stored data. Storage capacities can exceed one billion bytes (gigabytes). Hard disks come in a variety of sizes, from about a 14-inch diameter for minicomputers and mainframes, to a 1.3-inch diameter for portable personal computer systems (see Figure 10.3).

To achieve fast access speeds, the read/write head does not actually touch the hard disk surface, but floats over it. While hard disks are sealed to protect the disk from dirt and dust, a sharp blow dur-

FIGURE 10.3
This hard disk is 1.3 inches in diameter and is designed to work within handheld personal computers.

ing operations can cause a head crash. **Head crashes** occur when the read/write head touches the surface of the disk, resulting in damage to both the disk and disk drive.

Floppy disks, or diskettes, are round, flat, flexible pieces of plastic used primarily for data storage in personal computer systems. Larger systems often use diskettes as media for data entry while relying on hard disks for data storage. Typical diskette sizes are 5.25 inches and 3.5 inches. In the past, 8-inch floppy disks were used. Two-inch diskettes are available, but not widely used. Windows in the diskette cover permit access to the surface for reading or writing of data. Diskettes can wear out, since the read/write heads physically touch the diskette's surface. As a result, it is very important for users to backup data and programs on diskettes.

To safeguard data from accidental erasure, the **write-protect notch** on a 5.25-inch floppy disk can be covered, as shown in Figure 10.4. The smaller 3.5-inch diskettes have a **write-protect window,**

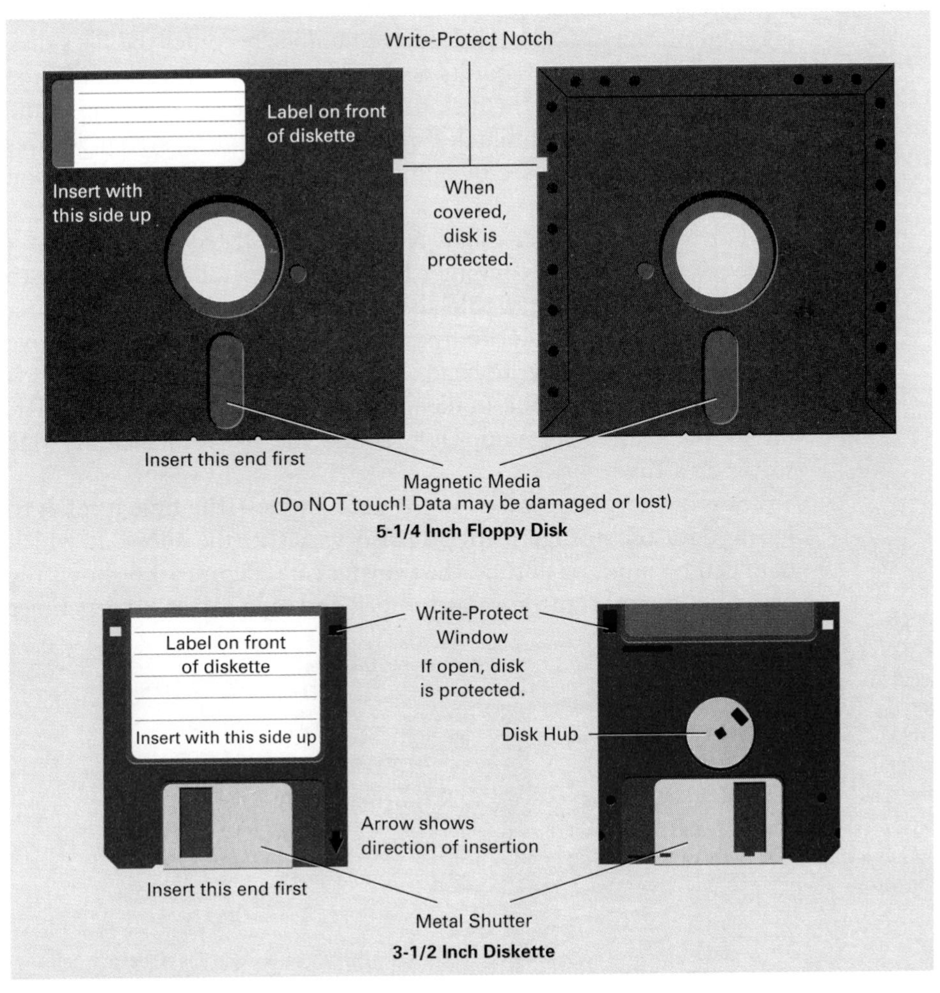

FIGURE 10.4
Data on a 5.25-inch disk is protected from accidental erasure by covering the write-protect notch. Opening a 3.5-inch disk's write-protect window also protects data and programs.

which is opened to protect programs and files from deletion. In both cases data can be read or input from the disk; however, the disk cannot be used to store new output. Data on hard disk can also be write-protected by having the operating system designate selected files as read-only.

Disk Storage

Disk drives store data on disks in concentric circles called **disk tracks.** In Figure 10.5, tracks are subdivided into storage locations called **sectors.** Individual sectors hold one record or one block of records. The computer locates a record by its sector number.

During the **formatting** process, a systems program controls the disk drive as it eliminates any old data and sets up each track and sector. Disk directories also are created during formatting. Directories catalog disk contents by filename and file size along with identifying the date and time each file was stored on the disk. A separate *file allocation table (FAT)* identifies, by sector number, where the file is found on the disk. The disk sector number becomes the file's **disk address.** When a user requests access to a file on a certain disk, the operating system uses the disk drive to look for the filename in the disk directory. When a match is found, the operating system locates a file by accessing the sector number provided by the file allocation table.

For example, a user might request the HOMEWORK file on a diskette. The personal computer DOS would search the directory to find HOMEWORK. It would then use the disk address found in a file allocation table to locate the start of the file. DOS would move the disk drive's read/write heads to the track with the disk address and check that sector for an identifying label for the HOMEWORK file. If the match is found, DOS copies the file into memory one sector at a time.

Storage hardware varies in the **access time**—the time it takes to locate data on storage media. It also varies in the speed at which data can be input or output, the **transfer rate.** Figure 10.6 shows the access times and transfer rates for disk and tape drives. Access times

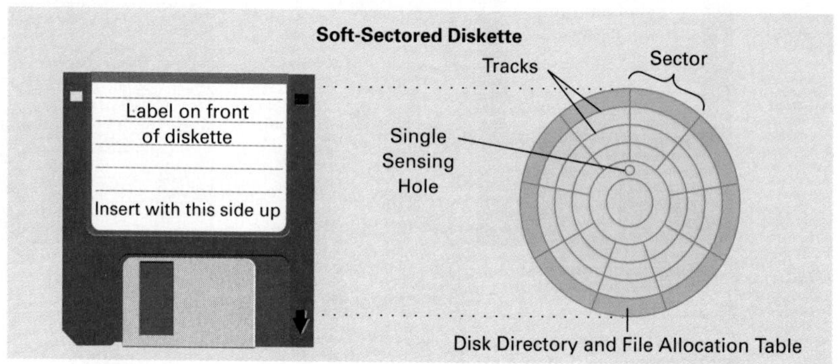

FIGURE 10.5
Computer users format new disks to set up tracks and sectors. A single sensing hole on soft-sectored disks determines where tracks begin (and end). The outside track holds the disk directory and file allocation table.

	Access Time	Transfer Rate	Storage Capacity
Removable Disk Pack	15 to 100 milliseconds*	150,000 to 2 million characters per second	65 million to 32 billion characters
Fixed Disk	5 to 30 milliseconds*	200,000 to 2 million characters per second	10 to 2 billion characters
Floppy Disk	70 to 500 milliseconds*	30,000 to 100,000 characters per second	180,000 to 1.4 million characters
Tape	10 milliseconds* to several seconds	18,000 characters per second	10 million to 60 million characters
CD-ROM Disk	265-400 milliseconds*	Up to 2 million characters per second	Up to 1 billion characters

*millisecond = 1/1000 of a second

FIGURE 10.6
Data storage are available on a wide variety of media. Each storage medium has different access speeds, transfer rates, and storage capacities.

are slower for floppy disk drives, when compared to hard disk drives, because read/write heads must be gently placed on the disk's surface.

The organization of sectors on a disk varies among computer systems. One way computer systems could be compatible with one another is to have disk sectors organized in the same way. This means a disk created by one computer system would be usable on the other system's disk drive.

On hard disks a special magnetized code marks the beginning of each track. Diskette sectors are established according to a sensing hole (see Figure 10.5). **Soft-sectored diskettes** have one sensing hole which physically identifies the beginning of each track. Track sectors on a soft-sectored diskette are identified by the disk drive through formatting.

Diskettes are distinguished not only by size, but also by their storage capacity. Storage capacity is measured by the **density** (bytes per inch) in which data is written on the disk. These disks generally fall into one of three categories: single, double, and quad (high-capacity) density (see Figure 10.7). Diskettes

In the News...

BACKUP TIPS

- Keep multiple copies—redundancy is key to a good backup strategy.
- Test backups frequently.
- Store backups in a secure off-site location.
- Replace disks and tapes regularly with fresh ones.
- Perform incremental backups of critical data throughout the day.

Floppy Disk Maximum Capacities

Size (inches)	Sides (single or double)	Density (double or high)	Capacity (kilobytes or megabytes)
5.25	single	double	180 KB
	double	double	360 KB
	double	high	1.2 MB
3.5	double	double	720 KB
	double	high	1.4 MB

FIGURE 10.7
The most commonly used floppy disks are 3.5 or 5.25 inch. Their storage capacities depend on the data's storage density (double or high).

manufactured with only one usable side are considered single-sided, while double-sided disks use both sides.

Disk Packs

A collection of hard disk platters stacked on top of each other creates a high-capacity storage unit called a *disk pack*. The disk drive that handles a disk pack uses several read/write heads to retrieve data from or output data to a disk surface. Figure 10.8 shows the access mechanism with read/write heads. The disk pack illustrated in the figure provides seven recording surfaces. The bottom surface is not used. When the access arms, which move as a unit, are in a given position, seven tracks can be read—one on each surface. Repositioning of the arm enables seven more tracks to be read.

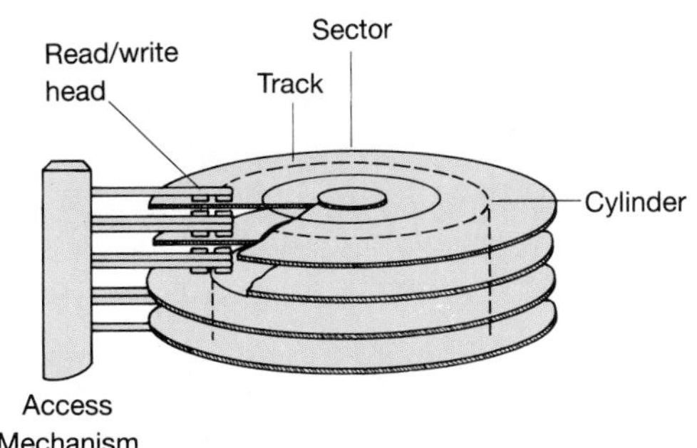

FIGURE 10.8
Direct access to data on a disk is accomplished through movable read/write heads that can access data on one cylinder at a time.

The collection of tracks that can be read at one position of the access mechanism is called a **cylinder.** To locate a specified file on a disk pack, the operating system searches the directory for a matching name and its corresponding disk location. The access mechanism moves to the specified cylinder. Then the read/write head for the correct track is activated, and the beginning of the file is located. The desired data then is copied into memory.

Removable and Fixed Disk Packs

Disk packs can be inserted into a disk drive for temporary use or installed permanently within the drive. Such disks are called *removable disks* or *fixed disks,* respectively. Removable disks lend versatility to disk use. Since disks can be inserted and removed, the number of disks available for use with a drive is countless. Inside a disk drive the removable disk is less vulnerable to dirt and destructive elements in the environment.

Fixed disks are built inside the computer case and sealed from the outside environment to protect the disk. An access light on the front panel is turned on when data is being read or written. A specialized fixed disk design places a read/write head over each track. This design feature supports high-speed access at a more expensive purchase price.

One way of installing a fixed disk into a PC is to insert a *hard card* (Figure 10.9) into an open expansion slot on the computer's

FIGURE 10.9
Hard disks fixed inside a hard card are easily installed into a personal computer's expansion slot on the motherboard.

FIGURE 10.10
Disk cartridges contain a hard disk that can be inserted into or removed from the disk drive.

motherboard. A hard card is an expansion card with a 2-inch fixed disk built inside. These cards provide an easy way to expand a PC's hard disk capacity and are often used with laptop computers. Storage capacities range from 20MB to over 100MB. Another way to increase disk capacity is to install an *external disk drive.* These removable or fixed disk drives usually connect to one of the computer's parallel ports.

Personal computer systems with fixed disks usually have an additional disk drive that handles floppy disks to backup critical data and programs. However, they can also be equipped with *disk cartridges.* Cartridges are hard disks that are mounted and removed from disk drives as shown in Figure 10.10. These storage media are compact, often measuring only 3.5 inches in diameter, but store more than 20MB of data. Cartridges provide portable, interchangeable, high-capacity hard disk storage.

Some cartridge disk drives employ a physics principle observed by Daniel Bernoulli. Aerospace engineers use Bernoulli's law when designing airplane wings, because it deals with the actions of air or liquids when they are flowing at varying speeds over different surfaces. Bernoulli disk drives use this principle to lift the read/write head off the disk surface when the disk is spinning.

Mainframe and minicomputer systems often utilize removable disk packs for data storage and retrieval. Computer operators lock the disk pack into the drive by screwing it into place. As shown in Figure 10.11, some information centers support rooms full of these disk drives.

FIGURE 10.11
Large information centers store huge amounts of data on removable disk packs. Some centers maintain rows of disk drives that directly access data from these disk packs.

OPTICAL DISK STORAGE

Optical storage techniques used by computers are basically the same as those used to record music on compact disks. Each employs lasers and are most often used to store data/music on a permanent basis. **Optical disks** differ from magnetic disk storage by the way data is stored and read from the storage media. A laser beam is used to write and read data on these reflective disks, so they are also known as laser disks. Optical disks support direct access techniques and have more storage capacity than magnetic disks. You will find three different types of optical disks in common use:

- CD-ROM
- WORM
- Erasable

To record data on an optical disk, a high-powered laser burns small pinpoint pits into the disk's surface to represent bit patterns (see Figure 10.12). Therefore, CD-ROM and WORM disks are written on only once. A lower-power laser scans the optical disk's surface to read the bit patterns.

In the form of video disks or compact disks (CDs), optical disks represent a new trend in small, high-capacity storage of images and sound. A single optical disk stores nearly one gigabyte of data on one side. To put this storage capacity into perspective, an optical disk can hold 800 television-quality images or 60 minutes of high fidelity music.

FIGURE 10.12
An optical disk's surface is pitted to represent binary 1s and left smooth for 0s. A clear protective layer is applied to the surface to minimize damage due to rough treatment.

CD-ROM

Optical disks for data storage include the *CD-ROM (Compact Disk with Read Only Memory)*, which is expensive to produce initially but is easily and inexpensively reproduced. CD-ROM is an ideal

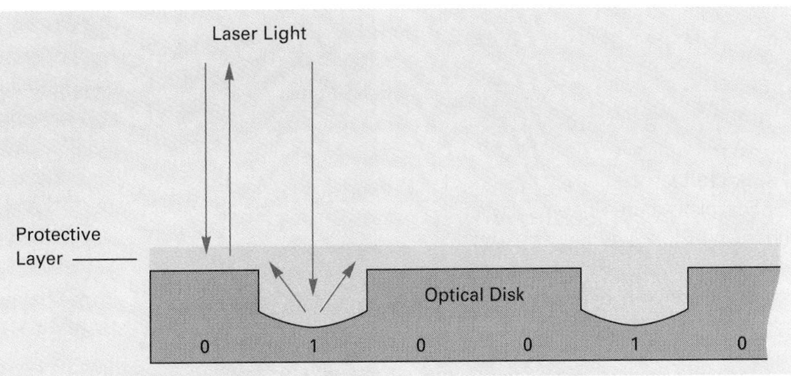

way to distribute large amounts of data, like an online encyclopedia or multimedia presentations.

Since CD-ROMs can hold pictures, this type of storage is well suited for structural drawings used by architects and engineers. Music lovers are drawn to the clear, crisp sound quality available from CDs, which reproduce music free of the tape hiss found with magnetic tape recordings. Video sequences and library references are also recorded for educational applications. Unfortunately, CD-ROM drives (see Figure 10.13) can only read disks; online recording and editing are not possible. The original data recorded on a CD-ROM cannot be changed.

WORM Disks

A *WORM (Write Once Read Many)* optical drive can record data on a blank disk. However, the data on the disk is permanent once it has been recorded. These disks cost over $10 apiece. Personal computer users with a WORM disk drive can create the masters for CD-ROMs.

Practical applications for WORM optical disks usually involve archiving data. Banks and brokerage houses must keep permanent records of every business transaction in which they are involved. WORM disks provide large storage capacities for data that should not be changed for security or legal reasons.

FIGURE 10.13
Optical disks store video-quality images and sounds as well as text. They are used for video games and can store the contents of an entire encyclopedia on a single disk.

Erasable Optical Disks

Erasable optical disk drives can overwrite data like magnetic hard disks and are the most flexible type of optical storage media. However, their cost and slow transfer speeds have kept them from economically competing with magnetic hard disks. The increased storage capacity of optical disk technology gives it great potential as a popular type of storage hardware. While research continues to improve erasable optical disk technology, magnetic storage media are still the storage workhorses for most computer systems.

In the News...

OPTICAL STORAGE DISKS

Best-known for high-fidelity sounds, the compact disk (CD) is synonymous with more than music to a growing number of computer users. This small, optical device can store encyclopedias of information. A single disk can hold as much information as 500 floppy disks.

The optical disk's vast storage capacity and durability make it ideally suited for archiving library materials, storing office files such as insurance claims, or multimedia motion pictures and sounds.

The market for optical storage disks is expected to blossom as advances in technology bring improvements in data retrieval speed, cost, and the ability to change or erase information on a disk.

MAGNETIC TAPE STORAGE

Tape drives, which operate like tape recorder/players, provide a low-cost, high-capacity means of sequentially storing and accessing data. Magnetic tape storage is most often used for batch processing, to record real-time transactions, to archive financial or legal data, or to backup data from disk.

Large computers use tape drives to store and read data on reels of tape. A reel of magnetic tape is a half-inch wide and can store 1,600 to 6,400 characters per inch on its half-mile length. Tape drives attached to early microcomputers used cassette tapes similar to those found in home or car stereo systems. Cassettes and reels are now being replaced by *tape cartridges.*

Tape Cartridges

These cartridges are self-contained in hard plastic shells that are easy to mount in a tape drive and store when not in use. They hold between 40 megabytes and 20 gigabytes of data. Personal computer users utilize tape cartridges to backup important programs and data (see Figure 10.14).

Tape drives record data as magnetized bit patterns. The orientation (polarity) of the magnetized spots on the tape's recording surface represents either a binary 1 or 0. Running down the length of reel tape are eight or nine **tape tracks,** or channels in which bits are held. Combinations of bit positions that cross the tracks represent individual bytes. Figure 10.17 illustrates how nine-track tapes typically store data.

Like magnetic disk drives, tape drives are equipped with read/write heads. To read tape-recorded data, the read/write head senses magnetic spots, then transfers the data to memory. The read/write head also records magnetic spots in track locations to write data on tape. Like disks, tapes are write-protected when data should be used on a read-only basis.

Typically, tapes are driven past the read/write head in a series of start-stop actions. The head reads or writes one record at a time. Then the tape stops momentarily before proceeding to the next record. Consequently, the tape being processed moves forward in quick jerks. To prepare the mechanism for these stops, *interrecord gaps* are inserted between records on tape. Interrecord gaps are similar to the blank sections of tape between songs on a music tape. They identify a record to be read during a single read/write operation. In addition, they provide physical space for the stopping and starting of the tape drives.

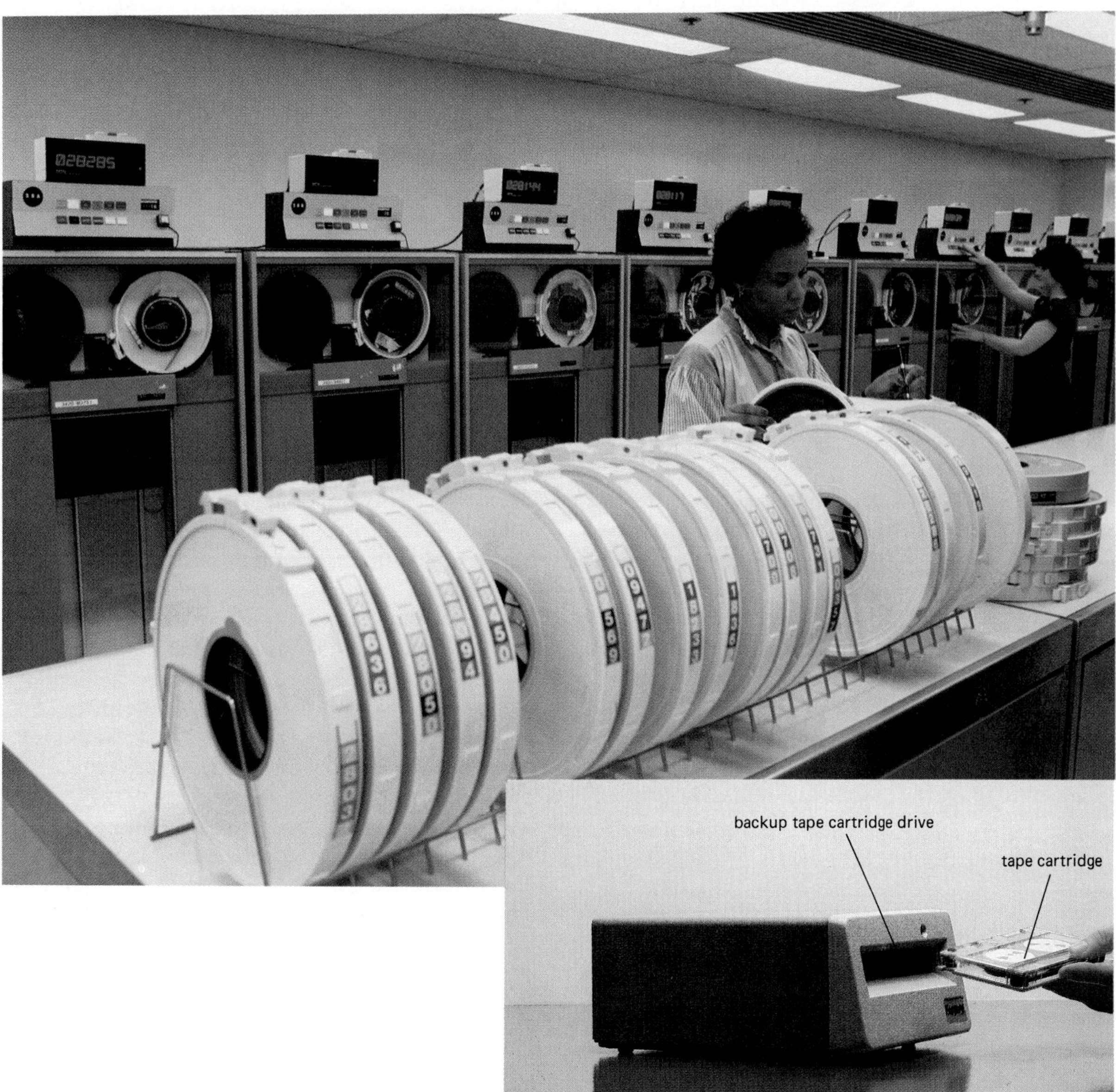

FIGURE 10.14
Tape storage is done with reels or cartridges. In either case, data can be accessed only sequentially.

The tape drive stops at each interrecord gap. Thus, the more gaps on a tape, the less efficient input or output is. To increase computer efficiency, records can be grouped in **blocks.** By using blocking methods, several records can be read into memory or written to the storage media in a single processing operation. Allowances still must be made for starting and stopping the tape. For this purpose *interblock gaps* are inserted between blocks of records as shown in Figure 10.15. Under blocking techniques, the computer pauses less fre-

Who's Who

Herman Hollerith (1860–1929)

In the late 1880s the U.S. Bureau of the Census was headed for trouble. Using methods available, Census Bureau employees took more than 7 years to complete the 1880 count of 50 million. With the population burgeoning to 60 million, it was estimated the 1890 census would require more than 10 years to finish. Dr. Herman Hollerith of the Bureau searched for a better method. As he watched a train conductor punch the tickets of riders with their destination, he was reminded of Jacquard's method of using punched cards to dictate intricate weaving patterns. Inspired, he developed a series of machines that compiled the 1890 census information mechanically. The 1890 census count took only six weeks but results were not announced until December of 1890 in order to double-check the results and assure the public.

Numeric data was punched onto cards, represented by a hole in a specially designated area of the card. Combinations of two holes represented letters of the alphabet. Each card could store 80 digits or letters with 12 places for holes in each column. As the Hollerith machine processed a card, a pin would fall through each card hole into a pan of mercury. This action closed an electrical circuit and registered the count on a meter, so punched holes were translated into meaningful information. Also, using punched cards as a storage medium made it possible to record census data only once and retain the data for future use. This eliminated the need to duplicate work and increased the productivity of the census employees.

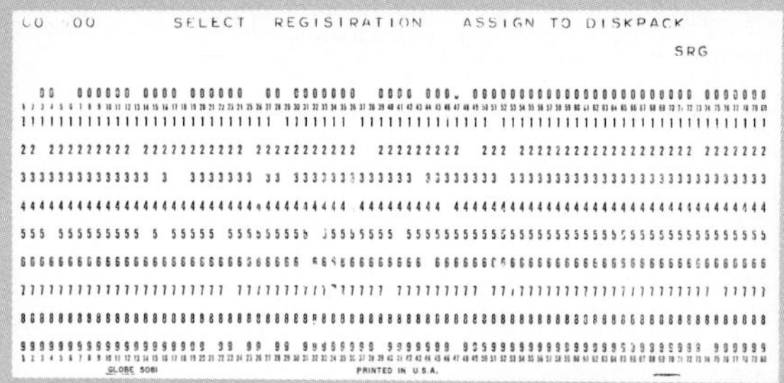

Hollerith received patents for his devices in 1884. He formed his own company, TMC (Tabulator Machine Company), which produced card systems used in accounting and railroad car inventory. After several business ventures, his company merged in 1924 into International Business Machines (IBM), which is the world's largest computer company today.

quently than if records are input one at a time. Also, more records can be stored within the same area. Because blocks of data are more efficiently processed, data is commonly stored in blocks on disk as well.

While it may seem logical that eliminating all gaps on a tape would maximize computer efficiency, this method is not feasible for data processing. Blocks of data to be read or written are held in a

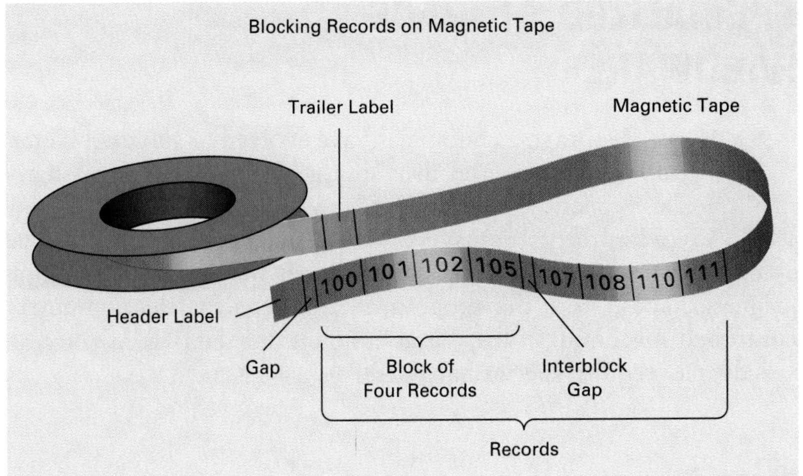

FIGURE 10.15
Records are blocked together on storage media to increase the efficiency of input and output operations.

buffer. A buffer is a portion of the computer's memory that is set aside, like cache memory, for temporary data storage. Unlike cache memory, buffers just store blocks of data and rely on no special input and output routines.

Most buffers are not large enough to accommodate an entire data file. For example, a file with 200,000 records, each with 120 characters, would require a buffer for 24 million bytes. Not even the largest computers have that much buffer capacity. Thus, large files must be broken into smaller, more manageable blocks of data. Typically, files are separated into blocks of records from 1,000 to 2,000 bytes long.

Tape Labels

To locate a requested file on tape for processing, the computer refers to a *header label,* a special-purpose record written at the beginning of a file (see Figure 10.15). A user specifies a file name, then the computer sequentially searches the header labels of files on the tape to find a match. *Trailer labels* mark the end of each tape file and indicate when all data in a file has been processed. They are sometimes referred to as end-of-file marks. Checks for trailer labels are included in programs. When the trailer label is reached during data processing, the program instructs the computer to cease reading the tape.

The only time data is written in a continuous stream on a tape is during disk backup. This procedure is called *tape streaming* because data is dumped (copied) from disk to tape at a high speed. This approach allows personal computer users to backup a hard disk in a short period of time.

SPECIALIZED STORAGE HARDWARE

Special storage technologies have evolved to solve problems traditional tape and disk storage techniques cannot handle. Sometimes extremely dirty or electronically charged environments damage or erase magnetic storage media. Some industrial environments are so harsh that paper tapes, not magnetic tapes, store the program instructions for the computer-controlled machining tools. Large amounts of data or fast access speeds may require special hardware.

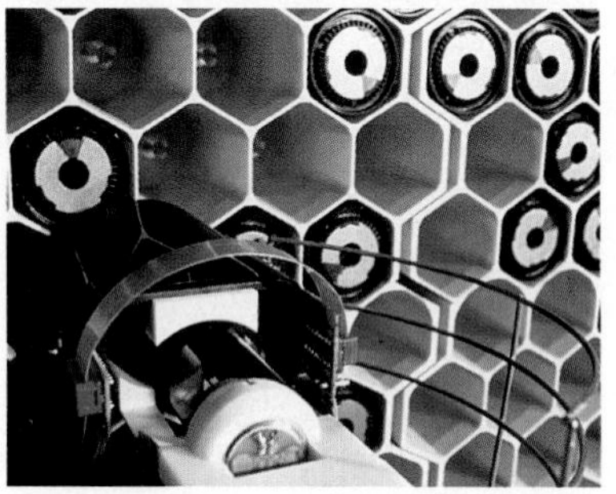

FIGURE 10.16
Each cell of this mass storage system contains a length of magnetic tape, allowing retrieval of huge amounts of data.

Mass Storage

Some organizations require storage and retrieval of extremely large volumes of data. This would include government offices, insurance companies, and historical archives. One type of mass storage contains a honeycomb arrangement of data cartridges that in turn each contain a strip of magnetic tape as seen in Figure 10.16. A mechanical arm goes to the cartridge required and loads the tape within it onto a drum. From there the data on the tape is copied to a magnetic disk for faster access. Retrieval of the cartridge is slower than other storage methods but makes access of vast amounts of data possible. Furthermore, increased storage capacity is relatively easy to add.

RAM Drives

When users need the fastest possible access to data or when additional disk space is not immediately available, RAM memory is set aside to temporarily replace disk storage. A computer's operating system creates a *RAM drive* by setting aside a designated amount of memory, usually when the computer is booted. Memory used by a RAM drive reduces the amount of memory available to application programs.

In other instances, the RAM drive is a separate piece of hardware that connects to the computer through a parallel port or expansion slot. An independent RAM drive is purchased when access speed is critical. This type of storage can be thousands of times faster than a diskette drive. A RAM drive is not a permanent secondary storage solution since RAM memory is volatile. In other words, all the data is lost when the power is turned off. Therefore, backup procedures are even more important when RAM drives are used.

Flash Memory

Recently, a special type of *programmable read only memory (PROM)* has been used as an alternative to RAM drives. These memory chips are nonvolatile and are therefore a true replacement for disk storage. Known as *flash memory,* the contents of these chips can be altered by the computer and the data retained when the power is turned off. Access to data in flash memory is not as fast as a RAM drive, but still many times faster than retrieving data using a disk drive.

Since flash memory does not use any moving parts that draw power, it is used when power consumption must be kept to a minimum. This is particularly important for portable computers relying on battery power. Flash memory is not likely to replace disk drives in other situations because it costs more and physically takes up more space.

MAXIMIZING HARDWARE PERFORMANCE

The primary purpose of any storage hardware is to safely and accurately store data in the minimum amount of space possible. To minimize reading and writing errors, computer systems use different error-checking routines. One of the most common is parity checking.

Parity Checking

Any recording done on storage media requires error checking. A common approach adds an additional bit to every bit pattern to check the data's integrity. This new bit is the *parity bit.*

A coding scheme such as ASCII requires eight bits to make up each byte. On a nine-track magnetic tape, then, eight bits are used to represent a byte of data, leaving one extra track. This track holds the parity bit, used to verify that data is encoded correctly. To do this, the computer instructs the drive to maintain either an even or an odd number of 1 bits in each byte. The bit recorded in the parity track is used to meet that condition. This type of error-checking procedure is known as **parity checking.**

In an example of parity checking, the letter A in ASCII is encoded with an even number of 1 bits: 0100 0001. The computer identifies that two 1 bits are used with the letter A. In an odd-parity-checking scheme, the parity bit is recorded as a 1, bringing the total of 1 bits to three, an odd number. The letter C, coded 0100 0011, would require a 0 parity bit to retain the odd number of 1 bits already in the bit pattern.

By using this odd-parity-checking scheme, the computer would check that each byte contains an odd number of 1 bits before continuing processing. If a byte contained an even number of 1 bits, the computer would attempt to reread the byte. If the error continued to show up after several reads, the record containing the faulty byte would be skipped, and the error reported. Processing of remaining records then continues for most applications; in other cases, all processing stops. Figure 10.17 shows the byte structure of the ASCII code format with odd-parity-bit checking.

Data Compression

Many computer users experience problems when their data storage needs expand beyond the capacity of their storage hardware. Using a **data compression** utility program to compact data on disk is an alternative to upgrading your storage hardware.

Most data compression techniques rely on the simple assumption that bit patterns are often repeated in data files. You see this repetition in the two Ts in the word "letter" or blank spaces in unused areas of a line graph. Graphic data usually has more redundancies than textual data. The data compression software looks for these redundancies and puts a special notation in its place. For instance, instead of repeating a binary code 10 times for 10 spaces, data compression software writes a special notation that essentially says "10 spaces go here." When the notation is read from disk, the data is converted back to 10 independent spaces.

The types of redundancies and what to do with them vary between different data compression schemes. Sometimes expansion cards with a coprocessor and additional RAM chips acting like a disk cache work with the compression software. Data compression techniques supported by a specialized coprocessor are faster than techniques that rely only on terminate stay resident (TSR) software. In either case, you can expect space savings ranging from 40 to 60 percent.

Storing Data on Tape with Odd Parity

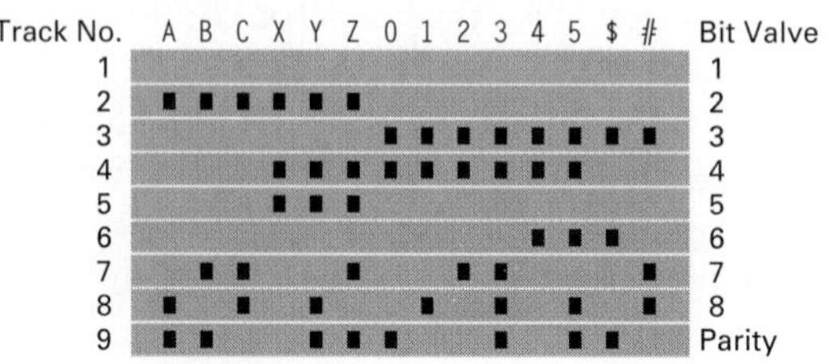

FIGURE 10.17
The parity bit is magnetized only when an odd number of magnetized 1 bits is needed. Computers then use parity checking to look for input errors. An even number of 1 bits indicates an error.

A Closer Look...

Building a Personal Computer

The input, processing, output, and storage hardware discussed in Unit Three are easily assembled into a personal computer system. Assembling a microcomputer from its component parts may sound intimidating. However, even a novice can complete one in a few hours. Although not for everyone, building a microcomputer is no more difficult than adding a few expansion cards to an existing computer system. What follows are a few questions people often ask when interested in building their own personal computer.

Q How do I find the parts I need for building a personal computer?

A Catalogs or stores that specialize in electronic components are a good source for parts. In many cases they offer kits that combine compatible components into one package.

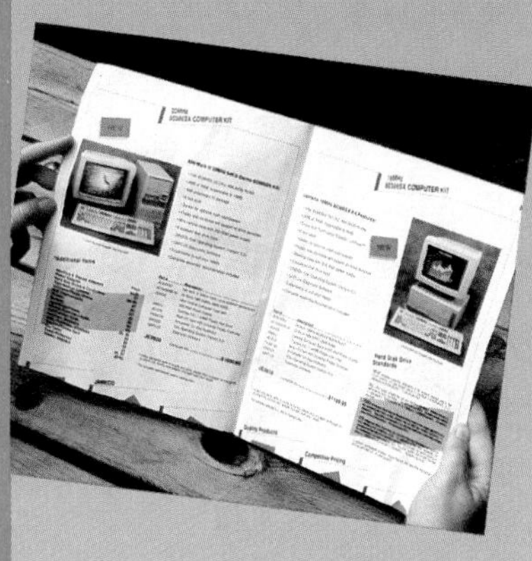

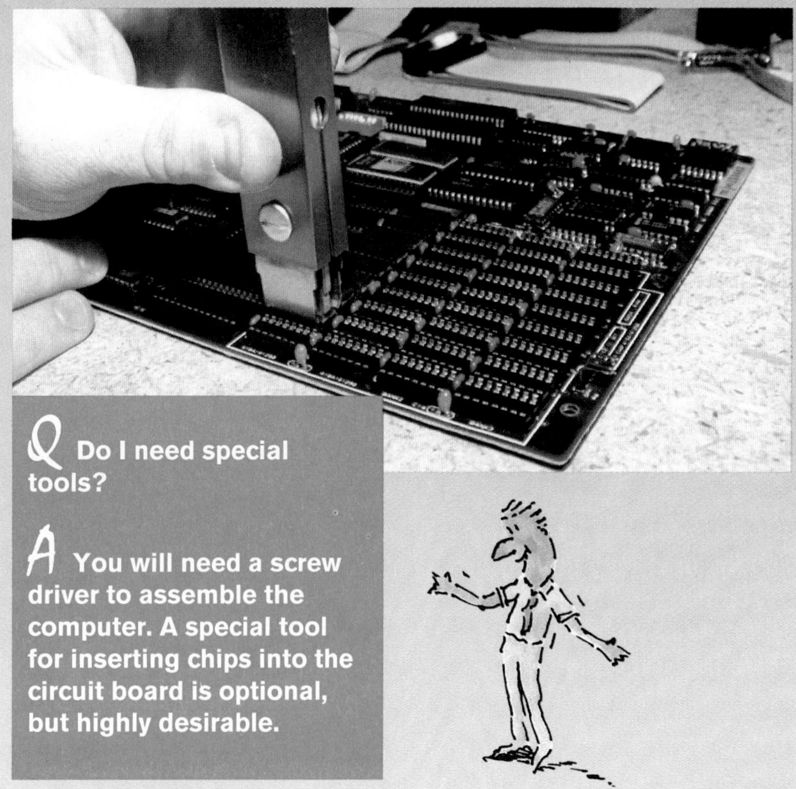

Q Do I need special tools?

A You will need a screw driver to assemble the computer. A special tool for inserting chips into the circuit board is optional, but highly desirable.

Q How do I know which memory chips to use?

A The memory chips and microprocessor must work at the same clock speeds. You can verify this information by reading the codes on the RAM chips. ROM chips are usually installed on the motherboard by the manufacturer before it is sold.

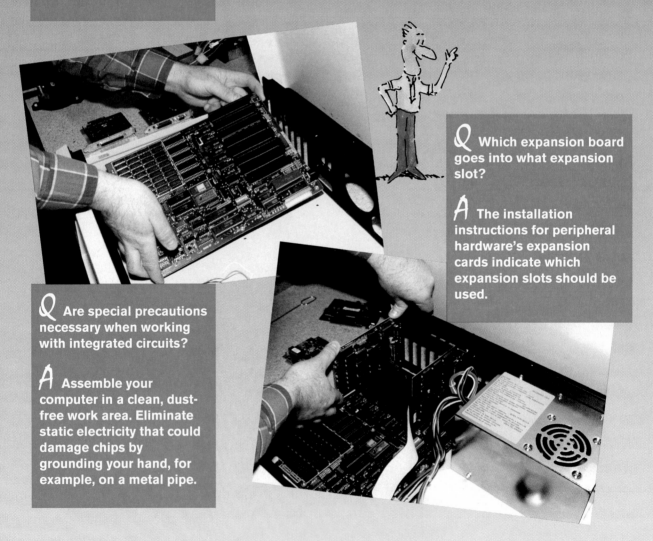

Q Which expansion board goes into what expansion slot?

A The installation instructions for peripheral hardware's expansion cards indicate which expansion slots should be used.

Q Are special precautions necessary when working with integrated circuits?

A Assemble your computer in a clean, dust-free work area. Eliminate static electricity that could damage chips by grounding your hand, for example, on a metal pipe.

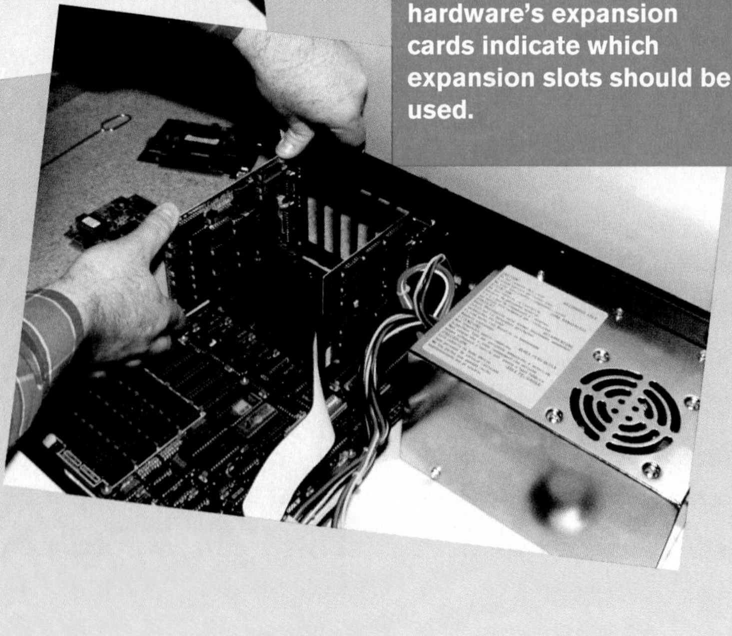

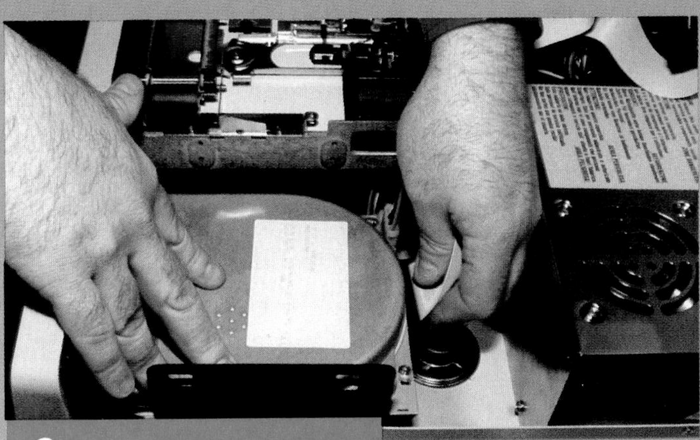

Q What software do I need to start?

A You will need an operating system that is compatible with the computer's microprocessor before booting the machine for the first time. Many times, this software will be part of a PC kit.

Q What disk drives should I use?

A Building your own computer means installing any capacity disk drive you want and cache memory if desired. An additional benefit is that you have the know-how to replace drives when they fail or need to be upgraded.

Q What do I do if it doesn't work when I turn it on?

A If problems occur, unplug the computer and double-check all connections and inserted chips. This error message means the keyboard is not connected. A manual for the operating system and assembly instructions will also provide trouble-shooting tips.

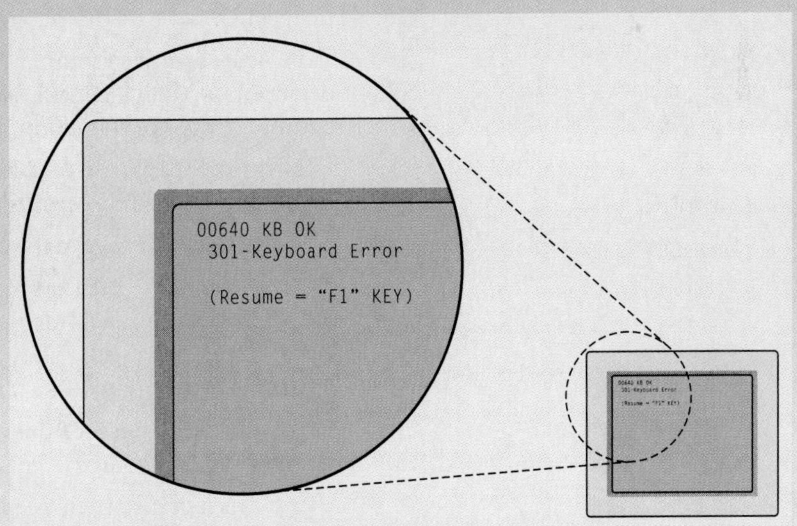
00640 KB OK
301-Keyboard Error
(Resume = "F1" KEY)

Chapter Facts

- Data is captured on storage media for further processing. Tapes and disks are the most common storage media.
- Disk storage is either on hard disks or floppy disks. Data is coded as magnetized spots by the disk drive on the disk's tracks. Tracks are divided into sectors.
- Data must be copied to other media as backup in case the original is lost.
- Disks must be protected from strong magnetic fields, extreme heat or cold, dirt, and dust. Users should never touch a disk's recording surface.
- The disk directory and file allocation table list disk contents and starting locations of files and programs. Sector numbers or cylinders are used to locate the files and programs.
- Disks are either removable or fixed. Disk cartridges are small, removable hard disks used by microcomputers.
- Storage hardware varies by the access time needed to locate data on the hardware and the transfer rate for input or output of that data.
- Data is read from an optical disk using a low-power laser. CD-ROMs and WORM optical disks store data permanently as holes burned into the disk. Erasable optical disks are just becoming available.
- Tape storage media are either reels of tape, cassettes, or cartridges. Data is stored on tracks as magnetized spots.
- Tape records are separated by interrecord gaps to allow the drive to stop/start. Blocks of records are held in buffers in the computer memory as temporary storage.
- Files on tape begin with a header label identifying the file name and end with a trailer label.
- Mass storage through data cartridges is also available for use with large amounts of data.
- RAM drives and flash memory store data in integrated circuits. RAM drives lose data when power is turned off while flash memory retains data through use of PROM chips.
- Parity checking ensures data is correctly written and read by the storage hardware.
- Users can increase their media's storage capacity by using data compression software, which replaces data redundancies with special space-saving notations.

Terms to Remember

a. access time
b. block
c. cylinder
d. data compression
e. density
f. disk address
g. disk track
h. formatting
i. head crash
j. optical disk
k. parity checking
l. sector
m. soft-sectored diskette
n. storage media
o. tape track
p. transfer rate
q. write-protect notch
r. write-protect window

Mix and Match

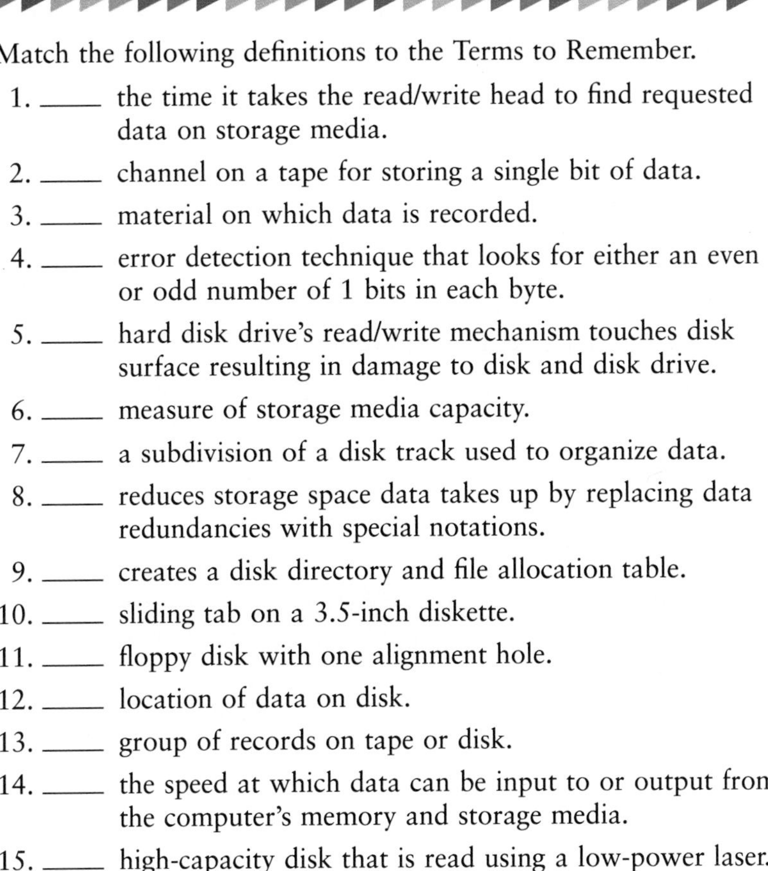

Match the following definitions to the Terms to Remember.

1. ____ the time it takes the read/write head to find requested data on storage media.
2. ____ channel on a tape for storing a single bit of data.
3. ____ material on which data is recorded.
4. ____ error detection technique that looks for either an even or odd number of 1 bits in each byte.
5. ____ hard disk drive's read/write mechanism touches disk surface resulting in damage to disk and disk drive.
6. ____ measure of storage media capacity.
7. ____ a subdivision of a disk track used to organize data.
8. ____ reduces storage space data takes up by replacing data redundancies with special notations.
9. ____ creates a disk directory and file allocation table.
10. ____ sliding tab on a 3.5-inch diskette.
11. ____ floppy disk with one alignment hole.
12. ____ location of data on disk.
13. ____ group of records on tape or disk.
14. ____ the speed at which data can be input to or output from the computer's memory and storage media.
15. ____ high-capacity disk that is read using a low-power laser.

16. ____ one of the concentric circles on a disk surface where data is stored.
17. ____ collection of tracks on a disk pack that can be read at one position of the access mechanism.
18. ____ section cut out of the side of a 5.25-inch floppy disk.

Review Questions

1. Why are magnetic disks the most commonly used storage media?
2. Identify the primary types of magnetic disk storage.
3. What types of environmental hazards can damage a magnetic disk or accidently erase data?
4. What causes a hard disk head crash?
5. How can data on 5.25-inch floppy disks and 3.5-inch floppy disks be protected from accidental erasure by a computer user?
6. What happens when a disk is formatted?
7. How are the disk directory and file allocation table used to locate a file on disk?
8. What are two distinguishing features of a floppy disk? Give an example of each feature.
9. What are the advantages and disadvantages to using disk drives with removable and fixed disks?
10. How are the three types of optical disks different?
11. What is the current limitation to erasable optical disk storage?
12. When is magnetic tape storage used?
13. Why are records often grouped into blocks when recorded on tape or disk?
14. How is a file found on magnetic tape?
15. What types of situations would call for mass storage, RAM disks, and flash memory?
16. What type of problems does parity checking detect?
17. Why would someone want to use data compression?
18. How much time and what tools are needed for building a personal computer?

Applying What You've Learned

1. Some storage hardware buyers believe in getting the fastest and highest-capacity hardware they can afford.
   a. What are the disadvantages to this approach?
   b. What are the disadvantages to buying the least expensive hardware?
   c. Would it be better to delay purchasing equipment until the price comes down or to buy the newest equipment now?
2. Look at the storage hardware available to you in school or at home. What kind is it? Are the storage media fixed or removable? How much data (in bytes) can the media hold? Is access of the data sequential or direct? How fast can the data be accessed? You may need to check manuals for this information.
3. Look up the procedure for formatting a diskette on home or school equipment. Write a user's guide explaining the procedure to new students. Include any necessary pictures and warnings. Exchange this guide with a fellow student to see if it is clearly written.
4. Use the Extended ASCII chart (Figure 8.5) to determine the bit patterns for the letters in your last name. List what the parity bit would be for each character if parity is odd.
5. Explore how optical disks are being presently used in education, training packages, advertising, music, or another field. Write a short report on your findings.

Answers to Mix and Match

1. a 2. o 3. n 4. k 5. i 6. e 7. l 8. d 9. h 10. r
11. m 12. f 13. b 14. p 15. j 16. g 17. c 18. q

11

Networks and Data Communications

- From the User's Point of View
- The Need for Data Communications
  - Telecommunications
  - Teleprocessing
- Networks
  - Network topologies
  - Linking computers within a network
  - Distributed processing
- Data Communications
  - Communication hardware
  - Communication software
- Network Applications
  - Bulletin board systems (BBS)
  - Information utilities
  - Telecommuting and teleconferencing
  - Electronic funds transfer
  - Electronic data interchange
  - Work group computing
- *A Closer Look . . . Information Utilities*

FROM THE USER'S POINT OF VIEW

Informed computer users seem to go through stages as they become comfortable using computer technology. At first new operating procedures and application packages hold your attention as you learn how to use them. Next, you want to share your computer-generated words, graphs, and other information with colleagues and friends. At that point, you will want to learn about data communications hardware, software, and procedures. Linking your personal computer to other computers opens up opportunities to improve personal productivity, to explore new ideas with others, and to communicate with people all over the world. As you might expect, a whole new vocabulary is necessary to explain the communication options available.

THE NEED FOR DATA COMMUNICATIONS

Astronomer Neil Janson pointed to the chart coming out on the printer. "I'm just not sure," he said "It may be a supernova—or just an astronomical aberration!" Neil's assistant, Jamal Manot, nodded without removing his eyes from the output. "Maybe we should send this stuff to Dr. Baranson. It's four A.M. here, but it's noon in England, and she told us to let her know if we find something significant."

With a series of commands, Neil requested the transfer of data from the Rathmore Observatory in the California desert to an office 8,650 kilometers away in Greenwich, England. But the transmission was not direct. First, a message was sent to the observatory's minicomputer with instructions to connect to the research network. Through telephone lines and microwave channels the message traveled from California to another computer in Boston. Using a communication satellite the message then traveled to the Greenwich research computer. When Dr. Baranson was notified via electronic mail that a priority request was waiting in her mailbox, she immediately brought it up on her PC's screen. The data from California was in England for analysis in a matter of seconds (Figure 11.1).

Telecommunications

Regardless of how computers are used, people find an increased need to share information with others. The headquarters of a manufacturing firm must communicate with its regional factories. A university needs to maintain contact with its branch campuses. A computer user at home would like to talk to other users of a new software package. All of these applications involve communication of electronic mes-

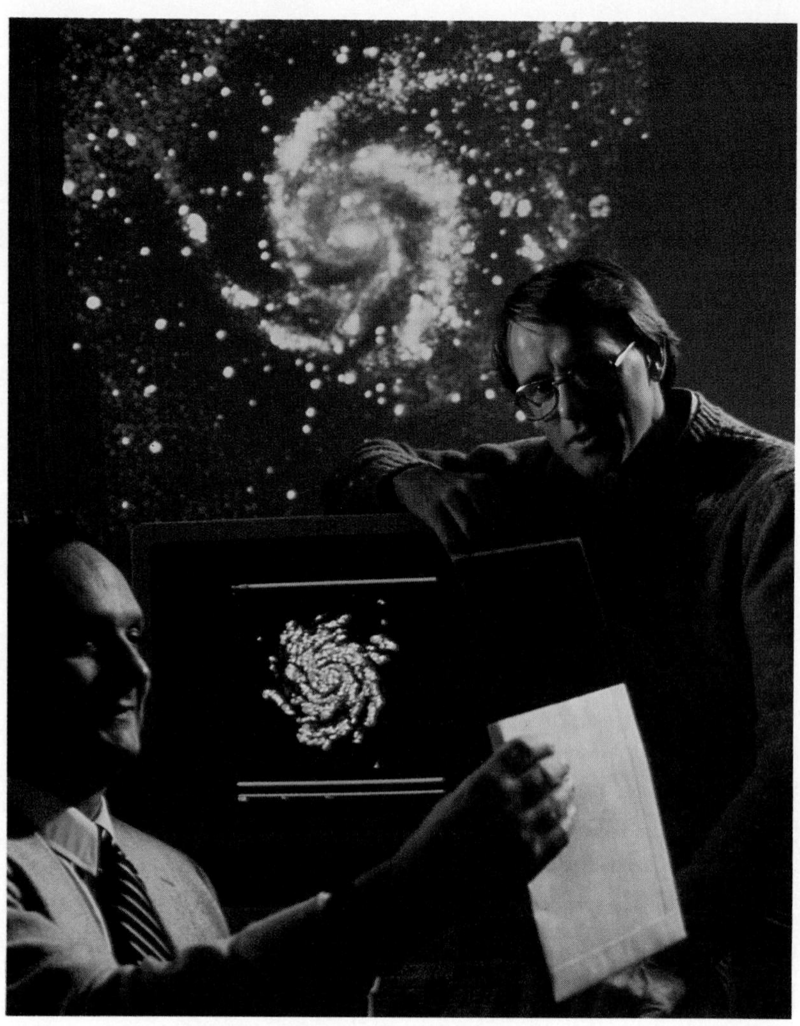

FIGURE 11.1
By using data communication, astronomers can transmit data about celestial phenomena around the world.

sages over a long distance, **telecommunication.** When a computer is involved, the transmission of textual, numeric, audio, or video data is called **data communication.**

Teleprocessing

An important problem for many organizations is where processing power should lie when data is shared over a large geographic area. One popular solution is **teleprocessing.** In a teleprocessing system, communication lines connect remote terminals and printers to a single computer (processor). Consider the problems the airline companies would have without teleprocessing. Millions of people at thousands of locations need to reserve seats, often months in advance.

Coordination of reservations needs to be centralized. Terminals at travel agencies are linked, as part of a teleprocessing system, to a high-speed computer. The central computer keeps track of each ticket request and updates flight information using a database management system. With real-time processing, travel agents can provide up-to-the-minute information on flight schedules. When they book seats on particular flights, that information is sent through communication lines and recorded immediately, in real-time, to prevent overbooking.

NETWORKS

Computer networks support data communication between two or more computer systems. A dozen personal computers in an office linked together to share files and electronic mail is a small-scale network. On a larger scale, multicontinent satellite links enable banks in the world's financial centers and your hometown to exchange data.

Network Topologies

A computer network can be as simple or as complex as user requirements dictate. Three fundamental designs, known as **network topologies,** are used for organizing computer networks:

- Bus topology
- Ring topology
- Star topology

Bus Topology

A *bus topology* connects several computers, or nodes, with a communication channel, often a single cable. A **node** is one computer system within a network. Just as a bus services all the stations along its route, in a bus topology all messages move over a single communication channel to which all nodes are connected. Each node is capable of establishing direct communication through the bus line with every other node in the network. Computers use an internal bus line in a similar manner to connect the processor with its memory and peripheral hardware. Figure 11.2 shows an example of bus topology, sometimes referred to as point-to-point communication.

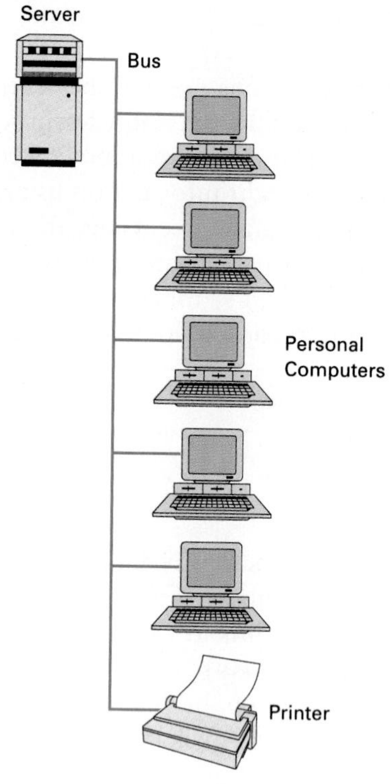

FIGURE 11.2
Bus networks connect computers along a common communication channel.

Hardware, programs, and large amounts of data may also be shared by network users through connections to a special node called a **server.** There are many types of servers—for example, file servers, database servers, and print servers. The computer system assigned as the server shares common hardware resources, such as a high-speed printer, or distributes data and programs to other nodes in the network. The server operates under the control of network system software and usually has a large amount of disk storage capacity.

Consider, for instance, a group of civil engineers and support personnel working within the same office and using a bus network. Design ideas, building schedules, and other data entered into individual PCs would be stored on the database server where others could access it as needed. Everyone also has access to the plotter connected to the server. The bus topology would promote efficient person-to-person communication and the sharing of data.

Ring Topology

Direct communication between nodes is also possible in a *ring topology*. Each node in a ring network is connected to two others, ultimately forming a large circle. An electronic message typically must travel from one node to the next, around the ring, until it reaches the appropriate destination (see Figure 11.3). Electronic messages and other transmissions always travel in the same direc-

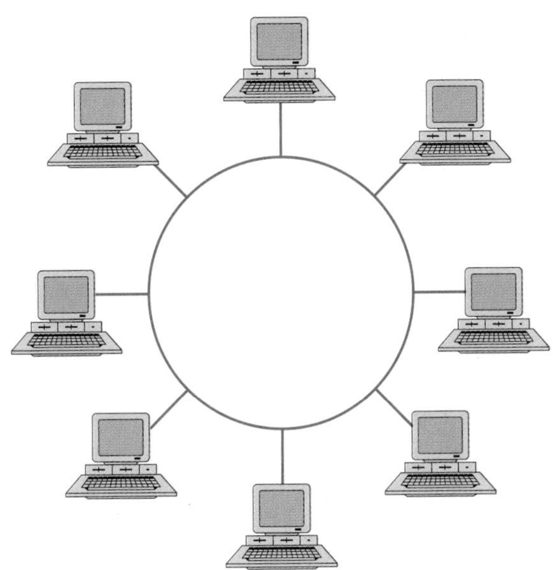

FIGURE 11.3
Ring networks connect one computer to two others as part of peer-to-peer communication.

tion. A ring topology may be used to connect computers at several large universities. Ideas and research can be passed around the network as needed. Institutions do not need to be directly connected to all others for information to be effectively shared.

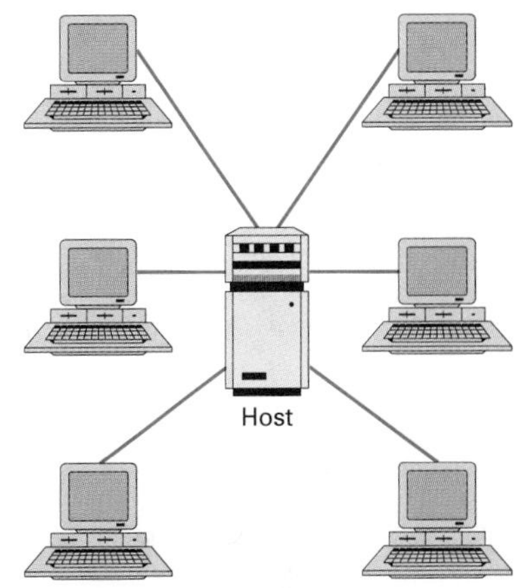

FIGURE 11.4
Star networks form around a central computer system (host), which coordinates communications among the various computers.

Star Topology

At the hub of *star topology* is a central controlling computer that routes all communication requests. As seen in Figure 11.4, each node is linked solely to the central computer, called the *host*. Since no internode connections exist, direct computer-to-computer communication is impossible without going through the host. Instead, the host intervenes to deliver messages to specified destinations. One disadvantage of the star topology is that failure of the host computer shuts down the entire network. A manufacturing plant with computers coordinating different phases of production could use a star network. The host would coordinate activities and maximize production schedules by acting as the intermediary between the other computers.

Hybrid Topologies

Two types of topologies can be linked to form a *hybrid topology*. For example, a central computer might link several bus networks, creating a hybrid of bus and star topologies. The point at which different networks are linked together is called a **gateway.** This hardware contains circuitry and communication software to aid in linking two networks or in connecting a network to a teleprocessing system. Differences in topologies and communication channels between the systems are handled by the gateway. A data communications specialist would be needed to install the gateway.

Linking Computers within a Network

When data is sent between remote computers, several different communication channels may be involved. The **communication channel** is the medium by which data communications take place. The type of channel used dictates the number of users that are simultaneously handled and the transmission speeds.

For the successful marriage of computers and communication devices, data must be coded in a form compatible with both technologies. Computers transmit data as *digital signals* by representing bit patterns as on or off electrical voltages. Telephones and other communication devices use *analog signals,* which express data as patterns of continuous sound frequencies, similar to the human voice (see Figure 11.5). People who want to establish data communication links, therefore, have to make a choice. They can set up communication channels between computer components, which carry digital signals directly from one machine to the next, or they can use standard communication channels to carry data that has been converted into analog signals.

Data Transmission Speeds

The rate of data transmission is often measured by the number of **bits per second (bps)** sent through communication equipment. The speed of data transmission can also be represented by its **baud rate,** or the number of times the transmitted signal changes within a sec-

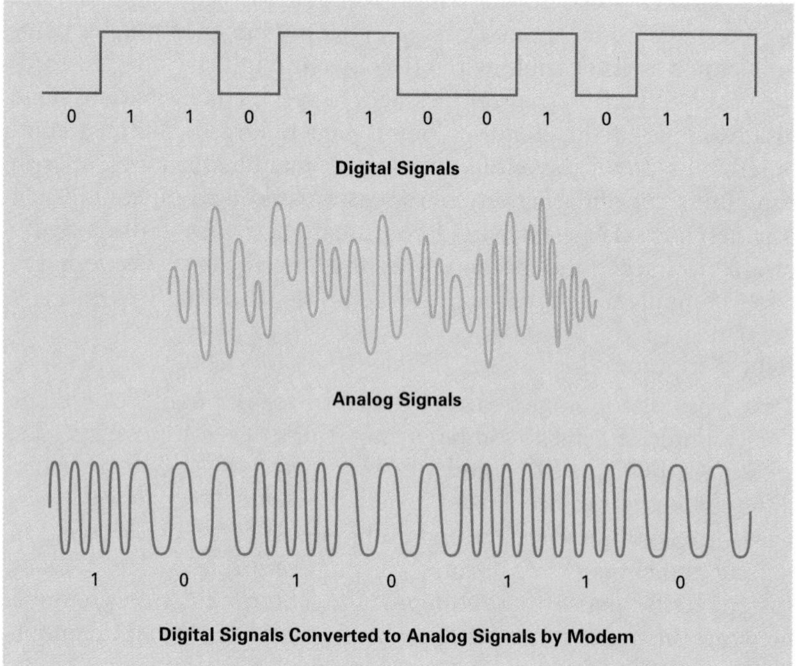

FIGURE 11.5
Computers generate digital signals representing bit patterns, whereas standard telephone lines were designed to handle analog signals in the form of voices and other sound patterns. To use a telephone for data communications, digital signals need to be converted to an analog format.

Data Transmission Speeds

Transfer Rate (bps)	Time to send a 10-page single-spaced document
300	20 minutes
1,200	5 minutes
2,400	150 seconds
4,800	75 seconds
9,600	38 seconds
14,400	25 seconds

FIGURE 11.6
This chart illustrates the impact data transmission speeds have on the time it takes to transmit a 10-page single-spaced document.

ond. The term, baud, is derived from Baudot, the Frenchman who developed a coding scheme for telegraph communications. Often baud rates and bps are incorrectly interchanged. Baud rate varies with the communication hardware used. The speed at which a signal changes is not necessarily equal to the number of bits being sent. At low speeds, such as 300 bps, the baud rate is typically also 300. For higher speeds, data transmission hardware and software make it possible for more than one bit to be transmitted with each signal change. Baud rate is best used to compare transmission characteristics of communication hardware, while bps is a better measurement of data transmission speeds (see Figure 11.6).

Communication Channels

On telephone *(twisted pair)* wires, transmission speed is limited, and opportunities exist for noise on the line and for wiretaps. One pair of twisted wires can handle only one telephone conversation or data transmissions up to 14,400 bps as shown in Figure 11.6. Twisted-pair channels directly connecting two computers in a network can transmit data at speeds exceeding 1 million bps. *Coaxial cables,* similar to those used in cable television networks, accommodate transmission speeds exceeding 10 million bps for short distances. The signal must be amplified to travel more than a mile, but each cable can transmit the equivalent of 80 sets of twisted pairs. Since the cables are insulated, fewer transmission errors are encountered.

Wireless communication channels are available that use infrared or radio frequencies to transmit data. The same radio technology used with cellular telephones can be used to set up wireless computer networks. Fast transmission speeds supporting simultaneous data transmissions are possible using high-frequency radio waves

FIGURE 11.7
Data communications use a wide variety of media (channels) to transmit data around the world.

Communication Channels

Channel	Simultaneous Transmissions
Telephone (twisted pair)	1
Coaxial cable	80
Microwave	672
Optical fiber	2,016

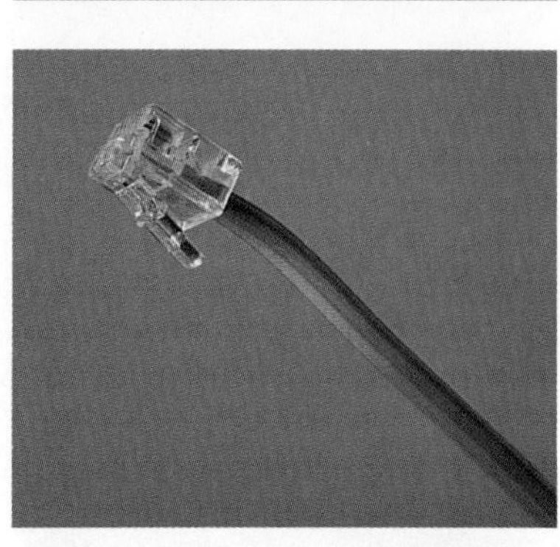

called *microwaves*. This type of communication channel sends data signals at speeds up to 50 million bps through open space. Many long distance telephone calls involve the use of microwave transmissions. As shown in Figure 11.7, a single microwave channel can carry over 670 independent data transmissions. Microwave signals bounced off communications satellites can carry many voice and data signals simultaneously over great distances.

Developments in optical fibers using laser technologies provide ultra high-speed data transmission with speeds reaching one billion bps. An *optical fiber cable,* shown in Figure 11.7, is a collection of spun glass filaments that conduct laser beams. Although expensive, one optical fiber channel can carry over 2,000 simultaneous data transmissions.

Coordinating Data Communication

When computers share a communication channel, arrangements must be made to prevent overlapping data transmissions *(collisions)*. To avoid collisions and other data communication problems, a network uses a set of communication protocols. A communication **protocol** is a set of predefined procedures for establishing, maintaining, or terminating data communication between nodes.

Two common protocols for computers sharing a communication channel involve contention and token passing. These protocols establish procedures that minimize data collisions. These procedures are similar to those used by people when they communicate with one another. For example, people sharing the same telephone line (party line) in rural areas run into problems when two people try to use the telephone at the same time. Collision detection occurs when each caller hears the other dialing. One way to handle this *contention* is for both callers to hang up, wait, and try again.

In the News...

DON'T BE OVERLOADED:

Tips for Fighting E-mail Overload.

For Senders:

■ Cover one topic per message, making it easy for recipients to file, forward, delete, store or answer.

■ Use clear subject headers so the recipient can quickly gauge the message's importance.

■ Do not overdistribute. Prepare distribution lists thoughtfully for different clusters of people.

■ Post general-interest reports in a common file or electronic bulletin board.

For Recipients:

■ Delete it now! Do not clog your in-box with messages you have read.

■ Create electronic folders by topic for easy retreival.

■ Shut off the "beep" notification feature. Look in your in-box several times a day, but do not let the alarm interrupt you every few minutes.

When computers in a network have a similar problem, a contention protocol called CSMA/CD (carrier sense multiple access with collision detection) is used. In other words, when contention occurs as two computers start to transmit along the communication channel at the same time, they both stop and wait a randomly assigned amount of time before retrying. That is, each node waits a slightly different period of time as a means of resolving the contention problem. Networks that use Ethernet standards employ CSMA/CD.

Have you ever been to a meeting where everyone tries to talk at once? One way to handle this problem is to make a rule that only the person with the designated token (gavel, stick, etc.) can talk. When one person has had his or her say, the token is passed to the next person. This procedure is repeated until everyone has a chance to speak. *Token passing* protocols use similar procedures. A special electronic signal (token) is sent continuously from one node to another. Network nodes cannot transmit any data until they receive the token. Once the data is transmitted, the token is sent to the next node in the network. Networks using a ring topology and token passing communication protocols are often referred to as token-ring networks. Other communications protocols are discussed later in this chapter.

The International Standards Organization (ISO) developed a set of protocols to help integrate computer systems produced by different manufacturers. It is known as the *open systems interconnection* model, or *OSI*. The OSI communication standard is subdivided into seven layers as outlined in Figure 11.8. Each layer establishes communications protocols to link dissimilar hardware and software. The OSI model covers everything from the user interface to data transmission and packaging. A company using hardware and software that adhere to the OSI model can link their computer systems to robots on the production line, an engineer's CAD workstation, and the computers used by suppliers.

FIGURE 11.8
The International Standards Organization developed the Open Systems Interconnection (OSI) model as a standard for telecommunicating systems.

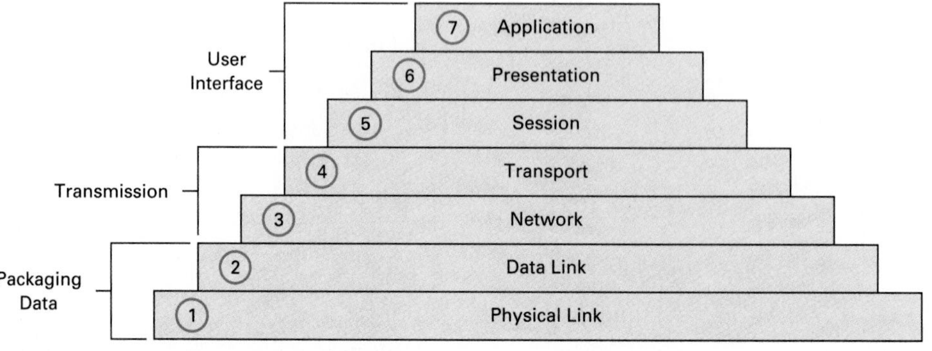

Distributed Processing

There is a great deal of flexibility in the ways data processing is handled on a network. A variety of network configurations support **distributed processing.** By having several computers connected together to share data and processing responsibilities, computer-based processing is distributed back to the workplace where the data originates. The physical placement of each computer is tailored to personal and organizational needs. The following cases demonstrate typical network configurations.

Local Area Network

Although it serves a growing urban area, Harrington and Associates' real estate office has modest data communication requirements. Each real estate agent uses a personal computer in his or her office to write proposals and access records of residential and commercial properties for sale. The PCs are separate from each other, yet they all are located in one building (see Figure 11.9). Harrington chose to link their computers together into a **local area network (LAN).** Any combination of the three network topologies—bus, ring, and star—can be used to create a LAN. This type of network is usually privately owned and connects computers within a confined service area.

The real estate agents share access to a laser printer and to a database of properties currently on the market. Everyone shares the cost of maintaining these resources, making the LAN a cost-effective data communication alternative to one large computer system.

FIGURE 11.9
In this building, personal computers in each office share a laser printer and database maintained by a server at the receptionist's desk.

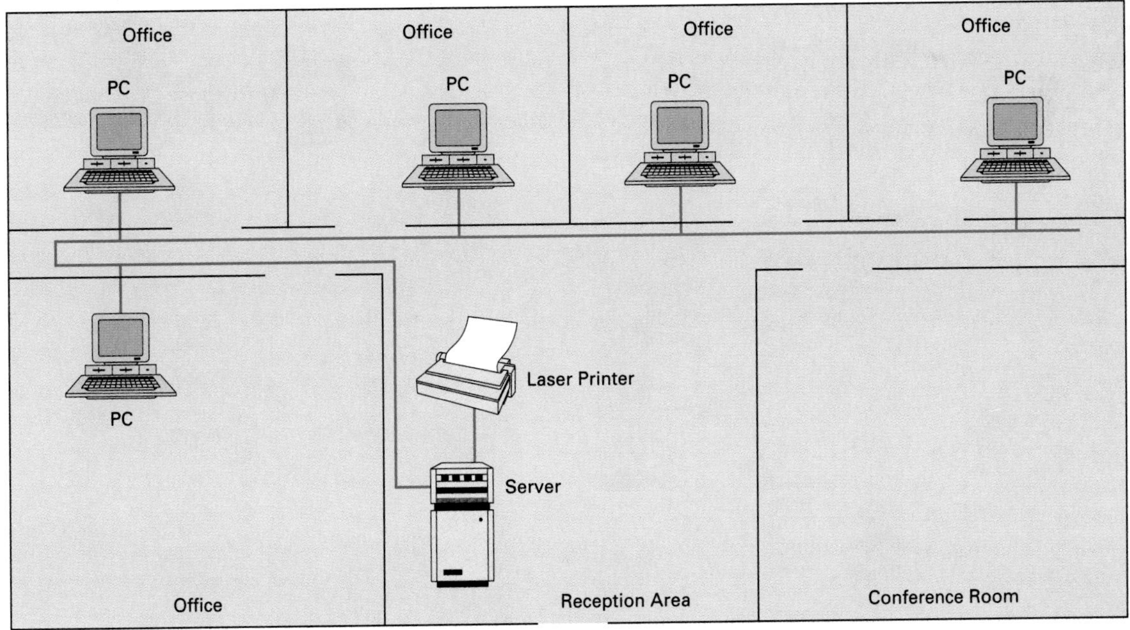

LANs are most efficient when they service a large number of users in a limited area, usually within a few miles. Large office buildings, college campuses, and industrial complexes often use LANs to fulfill their data communication needs.

To connect to the LAN, each computer has a *network card* added to an expansion slot in the motherboard. This special type of expansion card contains the circuitry and I/O ports needed to physically connect to the communication channel.

Wide Area Network

The observatory at which Neil and Jamal work is just one part of a **wide area network (WAN)** illustrated in Figure 11.10. The WAN connecting Neil's California observatory to England is called Internet. It uses fiber optic communications channels along with telephone lines, coaxial cable, and microwave channels to connect hundreds of universities, observatories, and research centers. Nodes include direct input from telescopes, terminals, and PCs in labs, and laptops used by traveling researchers. Each user has his or her own password that must be used to gain access to the network.

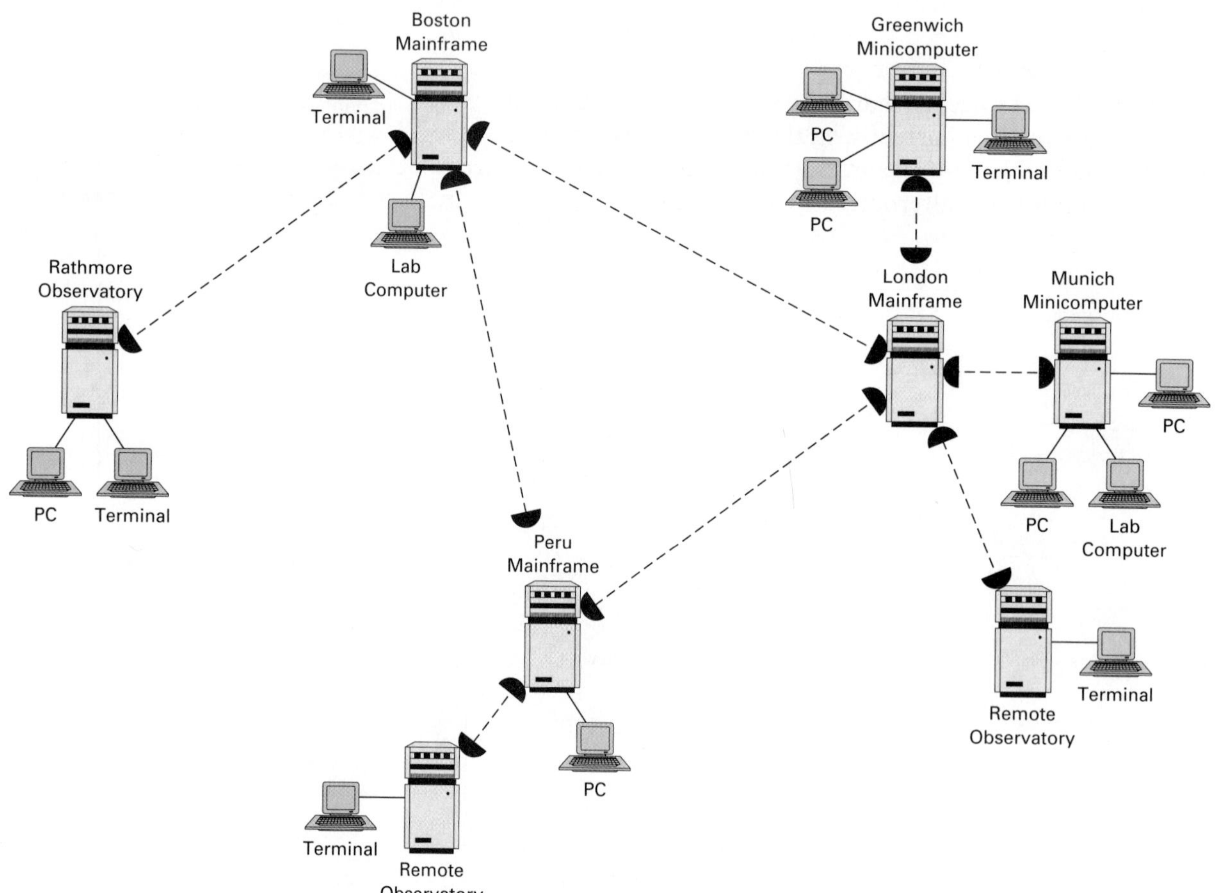

FIGURE 11.10
Rathmore Observatory is connected to a wide area network that connects people and computers over several geographically dispersed areas.

Value-Added Networks (VANs)

WANs provide innovative businesspeople the opportunity to offer additional services to network users for a fee. These services include access to databases, electronic mail, adventure games, and even timesharing with mainframe computers. Businesses that add services to current WAN capabilities create a **value-added network** (VAN). For example, VANs for telephone users are assigned a 900 area code. Several of these pay-by-the-minute VAN services have become very controversial in some areas because of the type of information they deliver to users.

In many countries VANs are under government regulation and are classified as either public or private. Public VANs are available to anyone with communication hardware, and the ability to pay service fees. Later in this chapter the public VANs, sometimes called information utilities, will be discussed in more detail.

Client/Server Computing

Every organization has its own data handling and data processing requirements. A variety of network designs have been developed to meet these needs. For instance, data communication at Northern Bank requires sharing data between three branch offices, located in two adjacent towns, and a credit card authorization center. Automatic teller machines (ATMs) and workstations similar to those shown in Figure 11.11 are hardwired with coaxial cable to a server in each branch. Data processed in the branch office is transmitted by the server using a microwave communication channel to a computer in Northern's main office.

Northern Bank uses a flexible **client/server** network design. In a client/server network, the user's computer, the client, takes on more responsibility than it does in a traditional server-oriented network. The client computer most often handles the user interface software. Northern's ATMs and personal computers acting as intelligent terminals or *diskless workstations* are ideal for displaying menus and accepting data. The teller's personal computer is a disk-

FIGURE 11.11
A client/server design used by this bank supports greater network flexibility because each terminal, the client, is intelligent enough to perform tasks usually taken on by the server in more traditional network setups.

less workstation and does not have disk drives because the data is maintained by the server.

A client/server network is a classic example of distributed data processing. Each client on the network handles its own data entry and error checking. This approach improves network performance by freeing the server to handle other network responsibilities, like accessing the customer database through microwave transmissions to the main office. Furthermore, more ATMs or teller workstations can be added to the network before compromising system performance because each system takes responsibility for its own user interface and data handling.

DATA COMMUNICATIONS

or effective data communication within a computer network, all five components of a computer system are necessary:

- Data: the message itself
- Procedures: a mutually agreed upon method of communication
- Hardware: equipment doing the sending, receiving, and storing
- Software: instructions for data transmission and network operations
- People: users and computer professionals

In a simple personal communication, two people will talk to each other in a language they both understand. The means of connection can be face-to-face talking, the telephone, or a letter. When linking a computer into a network, the communication procedures become a little more involved.

Communication Hardware

Since your telephone operates using analog signals, computer-based digital data must be converted into this format. Modems, multiplexers, and facsimile machines convert digital data into an analog format and back.

Modems

The digital signals of computers and the analog signals used by telephones are made compatible by special devices for encoding and decoding data. These devices are known as **modems,** a term coined from the functions they perform: *mo*dulation and *dem*odulation.

Modems permit two computers linked by analog telephone lines to exchange data. A sending modem modulates digital data into analog form for transmission over standard telephone lines. A modem at the receiving end demodulates the analog signals back into digital form for input to the receiving computer (see Figure 11.12).

Two standard types of modems are available for establishing connections between computers and communication channels: acoustic couplers and direct-connect modems. Users attach *acoustic coupler modems* to their computers using a telephone's handset. Rubber cups on the acoustic coupler fit over the handset earpiece and mouthpiece. The cups are designed to hold the telephone handset securely for sending and receiving sounds, at the same time blocking ambient noises. Once the telephone number of the receiving computer is dialed and the handset is in place, transmission can begin. Signals from the sending computer are modulated, then transmitted through the mouthpiece. At the receiving end a modem receives the signals through the earpiece, demodulates them, and routes them to the receiving computer.

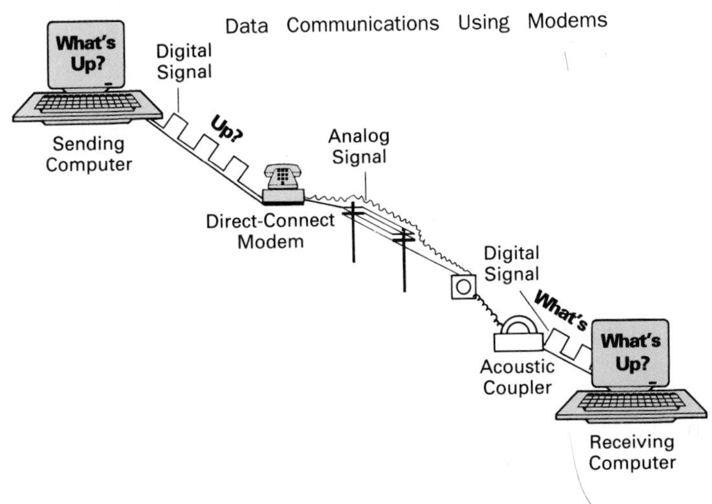

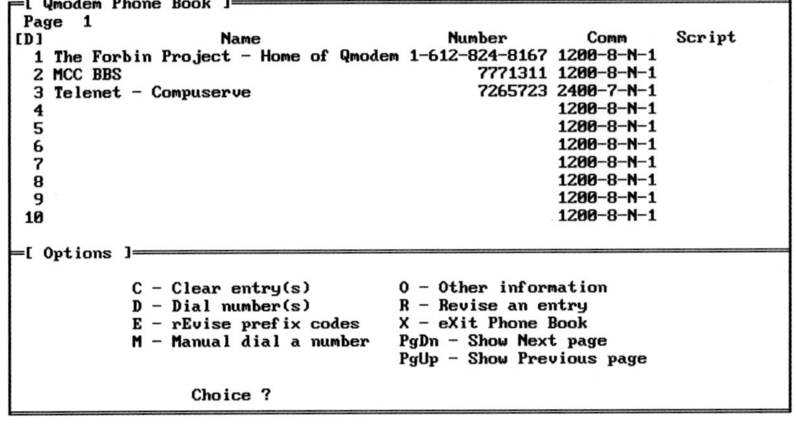

```
=[ Qmodem Phone Book ]=
Page  1
[D]              Name                      Number        Comm       Script
 1 The Forbin Project - Home of Qmodem 1-612-824-8167 1200-8-N-1
 2 MCC BBS                                   7771311 1200-8-N-1
 3 Telenet - Compuserve                      7265723 2400-7-N-1
 4                                                   1200-8-N-1
 5                                                   1200-8-N-1
 6                                                   1200-8-N-1
 7                                                   1200-8-N-1
 8                                                   1200-8-N-1
 9                                                   1200-8-N-1
10                                                   1200-8-N-1

=[ Options ]=

         C - Clear entry(s)          O - Other information
         D - Dial number(s)          R - Revise an entry
         E - rEvise prefix codes     X - eXit Phone Book
         M - Manual dial a number    PgDn - Show Next page
                                     PgUp - Show Previous page

              Choice ?
```

FIGURE 11.12
Modems modulate bit patterns into an analog signal for transmission over standard telephone lines. Another modem then demodulates the signal back into its original digital form.

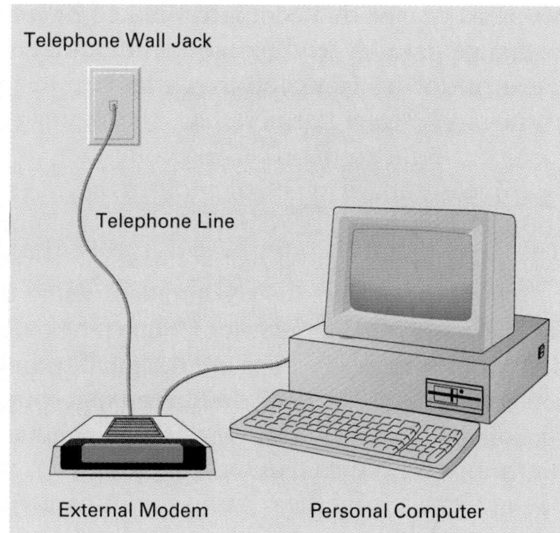

FIGURE 11.13
External modems use two cables to link a personal computer and communication line. One connects to the computer's serial port and the other to a telephone wall jack.

With direct-connect modems, no attachments need to be on the telephone handset because the modem is connected to the telephone jack in the wall. Some direct-connect modems, called *internal modems,* are built into expansion boards and housed inside the body of the computer. A standalone modem called an *external modem* is shown in Figure 11.13. It uses one cable to connect to the computer's serial port and another cable to connect to the telephone wall jack. A person wishing to transmit data need only dial a number to establish the connection. Modulation and demodulation take place within the body of the modem. Direct-connect modems provide data communication that is unhindered by noise interference from the surrounding area.

Multiplexers

Modems are designed to perform only one data transmission job at a time. At large organizations or computer centers, a computer system might need to accept multiple transmissions at once. To handle such large-scale demands, devices known as multiplexers were developed. A **multiplexer** receives signals from several incoming transmissions, combines them, and retransmits them through a single communication channel. In effect, the multiplexer is a switching station. One approach is to have the multiplexer assign a fixed time interval (time slice) to every incoming transmission. As much data as the time slice permits is transmitted. By switching very quickly from one device to the next, all incoming transmissions are sent through the same communication channel (see Figure 11.14).

For example, a large office building with the computer center in the basement and many users on each floor might require a separate cable between each user and the computer. To reduce the number

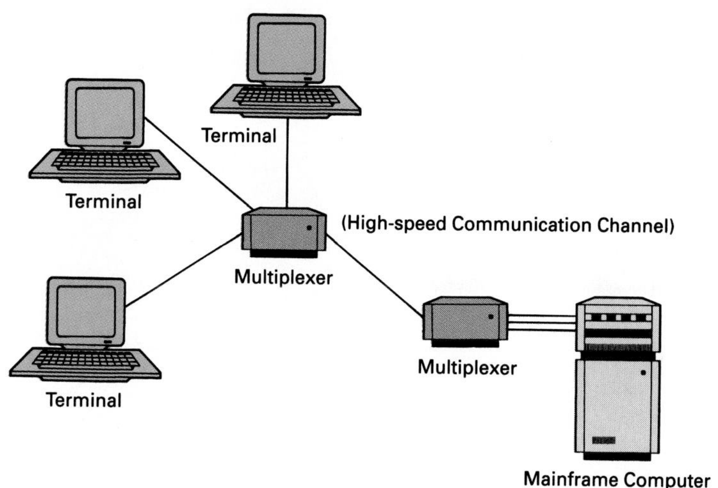

FIGURE 11.14
Multiplexers send data from several workstations through a single communication channel. Another multiplexer at the other end separates the signals back into their original format.

of cables, a multiplexer allows all users on one floor to share a single communication line. The users can operate a variety of input or output hardware simultaneously.

Facsimile Machines

For many organizations the **fax** or **facsimile machine** has become a necessity. Just as a telephone transmits voice messages and a modem digital data, a fax machine transmits images of printed material. The data can be a drawing, a photo, a handwritten document, or even your take-out lunch order (see Figure 11.15).

After dialing up a receiving fax machine, the user inputs the document into the sending fax machine. Just like a modem, the fax machine's scanner converts the document into digital signals that are sent to the receiving fax machine via telephone. The quality of the sending and receiving equipment determines the resolution (clarity) of the output. Early facsimiles were rather grainy and printed on light-sensitive thermal paper that faded with age. More expensive fax machines transmit a page in under a minute and output it on plain paper with a resolution similar to that of an ink-jet printer.

Standalone fax machines are inexpensive and easy to operate. They can even substitute as a copy machine by sending a document to itself. A disadvantage to standalone fax machines is that the hardcopy output cannot be edited or stored on a computer without being re-entered using a keyboard or scanner.

An alternative is the internal *fax board* that slides into the expansion slot of a personal computer. With this device a document can be sent, received, and edited by the computer without ever producing a paper copy. The disadvantage to this approach is that the user must leave the computer on in order to receive incoming faxes.

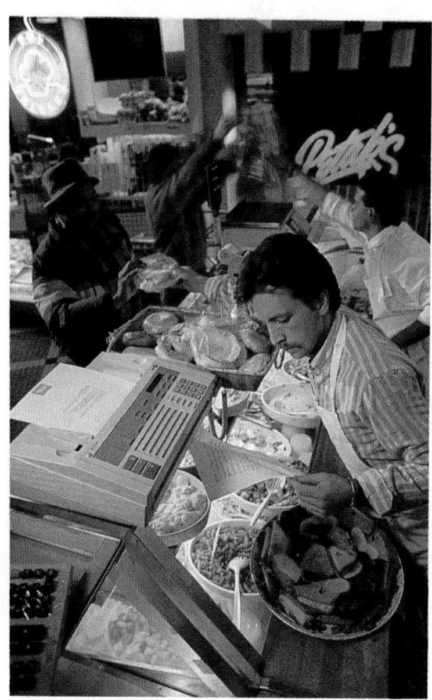

FIGURE 11.15
Many businesses. like this delicatessen, use a fax machine to receive customer orders.

Who's Who

Augusta Ada Byron (Countess of Lovelace) (1815–1852)

The woman considered the world's first programmer came from an elite background. Augusta Ada Byron was the daughter of Lord Byron, the poet. She was educated well and showed an early aptitude for mathematics. Marriage gave her the title Countess of Lovelace. When Charles Babbage brought stories of his invention, the difference engine, to her mother's home, Ada was intrigued by its potential. Babbage and the Countess kept up a correspondence for years. A technical account of Babbage's invention was made public through the writings of General Luigi Menabrea. Countess Lovelace translated the paper and added copious notes. She also included detailed operating instructions—a precursor of computer programs. However, Babbage was never able to get the difference engine to work. She and Babbage attempted to use the difference engine to develop a winning system for the horse races. The invention was no more successful here as she had to pawn her family's jewels twice to pay gambling debts. The Countess died of cancer at age 37, at the same age and of the same cause as her famous father. ADA, a major programming language adopted in the early 1980s by the U.S. Department of Defense, is named in her honor.

In addition, an independent scanner is needed to digitize images and other information that is originally in a printed format.

The speed of data transmission and the diversity of documents that can be sent are advantages to facsimile machines. Signatures that have been faxed are in many cases considered as legally binding as those on original documents. For example, some police cars are equipped with fax machines so that signed search warrants can be immediately sent from the judge to the investigating officers.

Personal Communications Devices

The uses of modems and facsimile machines have become so popular that *fax-modems* are available. These machines combine the data communications capabilities of a modem with the image transmission capacity of a fax machine.

Other combinations of computers and communications technology have also been developed. A laptop or notepad computer with an internal cellular fax-modem is not only a personal digital assistant, but a personal communication device. When linked into a wide area network, informed users literally have a world of information in their purse or briefcase (Figure 11.16).

FIGURE 11.16
Notepad computers combined with cellular modems become personal communication devices you can use anywhere at anytime.

Communication Software

Communication software is the user's interface with the modem. These programs aid the user in dialing up the destination computer, redialing the number when it is busy, providing online help, maintaining file security, and performing other important operations related to data communications. Many communication programs can automatically connect to other computers at a specified time to transfer data. For example, any investor with a personal computer system and modem can dial up and transfer current stock and bond prices into his or her personal database software just after the markets close. The investor does not even have to be present when the transfer occurs.

Depending on the network topology, communication software running on a node has additional network duties. It must be able to handle data from other computers and make the data available to the correct applications program. In addition, the communication software must be able to transfer requests from local applications programs to other computers in the system. These requests could involve data kept on the other nodes.

Communication software is designed to work with a variety of hardware using set communication protocols and transmission speeds. For two people to converse, they must understand each other—that is, speak the same language. For a successful transmission of data, both computers and associated communication software must agree on communication protocols for formatting and transmitting data. Since data sharing involves another computer system and a telephone or other communication channel, there are other compatibility considerations as well.

Synchronous and Asynchronous Transmission

Prior to data transmission, both the sending and the receiving computers must be ready to accept data according to a predetermined spacing of bit patterns. Most commonly, data transmission patterns are *asynchronous*. That is, data is transmitted a single character at a time, byte by byte. A start bit and at least one stop bit are included in every byte transmitted (see Figure 11.17). This enables the receiving computer to recognize when each byte (character) has been transmitted. Asynchronous transmissions generally are used for personal computer communications and VAN connections.

Providing speedier data communication are *synchronous* transmissions, which group data into blocks for transmission. A synchronous data transmission sends several characters at a time as shown in Figure 11.17. Each block is preceded by one or more synchronization bits that serve as a timing mechanism. When the receiving computer encounters the synchronization bits, it is prepared for the arrival of a new block of data. Thus, separate bytes need not be identified by start and stop bits. Synchronous transmissions require special buffers for holding blocks of incoming data. Fast, efficient synchronous communication is used when data transmission speeds exceeding 20,000 bps are required.

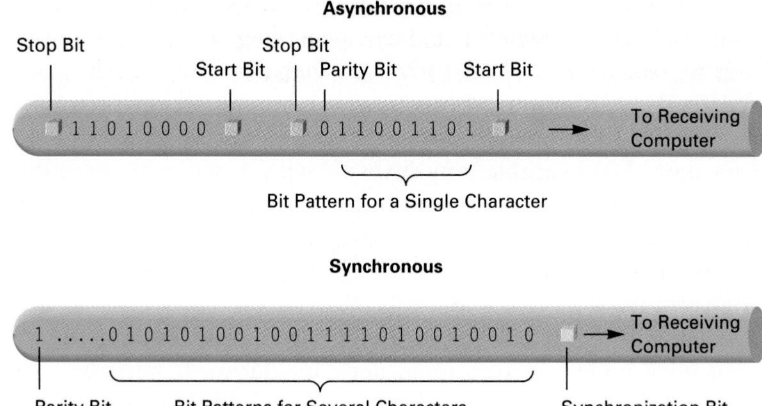

FIGURE 11.17
Asynchronous data transmission sends a single character at a time, while synchronous transmission sends several characters at a time.

Data Transmission Modes

Data transmissions between computers operate in one of two modes, as shown in Figure 11.18. *Half-duplex transmission* permits two-way communication over a channel, but data is transmitted in only one direction at a time. A CB radio, for example, provides half-duplex service. If one party is speaking, the other cannot respond until the message is completed. Half-duplex data communication

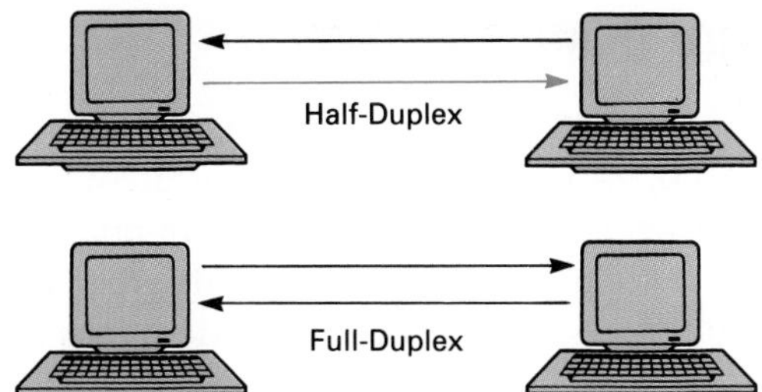

FIGURE 11.18
Data is transferred between computers in a network in one of two ways: half-duplex means only one computer can send data at a time; full-duplex means both computers can communicate simultaneously.

often is used for batch transmission of data. The receiving computer will respond only when it senses that all of the data has been sent.

Simultaneous two-way transmission is accommodated by *full-duplex transmission.* This mode allows each computer to send and receive data concurrently. A telephone conversation is a familiar example of full-duplex transmission. Parties at both ends of the connection can speak or listen at any time during the conversation. Full-duplex communication is primarily used for interactive input and real-time processing.

Error Detection

Data transmission requires communication software to coordinate data communications between computers and to check for transmission errors. One method for detecting transmission errors involves the use of either an odd- or even-parity-checking scheme, just like those utilized by disk and tape storage hardware (see Chapter 10). The receiving computer expects either an odd- or even-parity standard. The sending computer will add a parity bit and turn it on or off for each transmission according to need.

If an odd-parity checking scheme is used, the parity bit is always turned on to make the number of "on," or 1, bits odd. When an even number of 1 bits is detected, an error condition exists. In this situation, the receiving computer requests that the data be transmitted again.

NETWORK APPLICATIONS

Networks—whether wide area or local—expand our ability to use computers as problem-solving tools. Numerous public and private networks now bring a variety of services into corporate offices and private homes. In fact, it is relatively common for organizations to enhance interoffice data communication by linking people together through user-friendly computer networks. Here is a review of some of the most common types of network applications.

Bulletin Board Systems (BBS)

A public access message system, known as an **electronic bulletin board system** (BBS), allows users to communicate with one another, often without charge. By signing onto a bulletin board service, users can share programs, data, and messages with other bulletin board members, as shown in Figure 11.19. Participants in a BBS use modems to gain access to the service. They can scan bulletins left by other users or compose their own messages.

Initially, bulletin boards were used by computer hobbyists, who exchanged information about new technologies and applications for computers. Since then the number of BBSs has grown to accommodate all types of callers. DNA researchers swap information via bulletin boards, as do engineers, physicians, and marine biologists.

Members of a BBS also have access to noncommercial, public-domain software and shareware. The programs are **uploaded** to the bulletin board computer. To upload is to transfer data or programs to another computer. Once the bulletin board receives the public-domain software, it can be copied by any user in the network. This process, the receiving of a program or data from another computer, is called **downloading.**

Despite the low or nonexistent service fee, bulletin boards still require some human intervention. A *system operator* or *sysop* is responsible for maintaining the bulletin board operation, checking that no questionable data or copyrighted software appears on the BBS for downloading, and providing assistance to members.

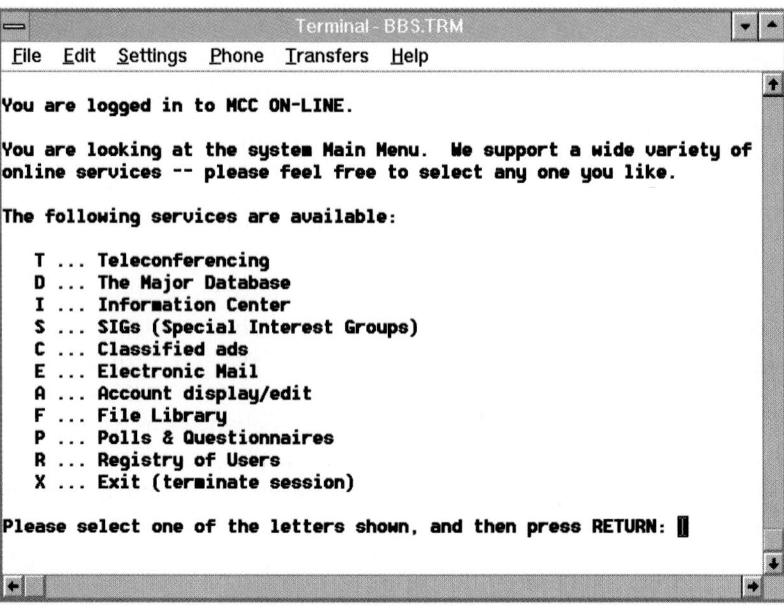

Terminal - BBS.TRM
File Edit Settings Phone Transfers Help
You are logged in to MCC ON-LINE.
You are looking at the system Main Menu. We support a wide variety of online services -- please feel free to select any one you like.
The following services are available:
T ... Teleconferencing
D ... The Major Database
I ... Information Center
S ... SIGs (Special Interest Groups)
C ... Classified ads
E ... Electronic Mail
A ... Account display/edit
F ... File Library
P ... Polls & Questionnaires
R ... Registry of Users
X ... Exit (terminate session)
Please select one of the letters shown, and then press RETURN:

FIGURE 11.19
Electronic bulletin boards provide a variety of services to their users for no or nominal fees.

Who's Who

George Boole (1815–1864)

The logical design on which modern computer circuitry and data communication is based was developed by a self-taught mathematician, George Boole. Boole's theory of logic was that any mathematical expression was in one of two states: true or false. Boole called it zero-one logic; we call it Boolean arithmetic. By combining many elements, each with two states, complex problems could be solved. Boole's life was dedicated to showing that logic had a strong place in mathematics, not just philosophy. His theories also made the design of Babbage's difference engine possible.

Information Utilities

The growth in popularity of personal computers has spawned the development of VANs that provide users with access to expansive databases. These commercial services are known as **information utilities** and are accessible to anyone with a computer, a modem, and a telephone. Information utilities offer convenient access to huge stores of information (see A Closer Look at the end of this chapter).

Information utilities require payment of a minimum monthly fee or a one-time subscription fee, plus charges for time spent online with the network and other possible telephone charges. The time of day and duration of access determine these charges. During business hours, access is most costly. Less expensive access times include late night, early morning, and weekends.

For example, such information utilities as CompuServe, Prodigy, and The Source offer news and business bulletins, banking services, and an online encyclopedia. Also, reviews of films, plays, books, and restaurants can be accessed, along with airline schedules and video games. These utilities provide customer access to software packages, text editors, and programming languages. There is even an online shopping service that lets subscribers purchase sporting goods, appliances, and clothing at a discount. Information utilities target a broad audience of computer users and provide information on many subjects.

The Dow Jones News/Retrieval Service is geared to the needs of businesspeople. The service offers stock market quotations, reports on business and economic news, and profiles of companies. Non-business information provided by the Dow Jones service includes general news stories, weather reports, and online encyclopedias.

In addition to these information utilities, a number of specialized dial-up services have emerged. Career opportunity networks assist people who desire new jobs, and even provide career counseling to network users. Utilities such as dating services target the social interests of users. Other special-interest information utilities provide news in such fields as medicine, law, education, and entertainment.

Telecommuting and Teleconferencing

The ability to access information networks has forced many people to re-evaluate how training and work are done. Already, some people's work takes them outside the office. For example, physically challenged employees can work away from the office when circumstances keep them at home. With the ability to link workers together through computer networks, **telecommuting** is now feasible. A wide range of productivity software, combined with laptop and notepad computers, allows telecommuting people to work at home or at other locations (Figure 11.20).

FIGURE 11.20
Telecommuting allows people to work at home by using a computer to communicate with colleagues at the main office.

Some professionals, such as architects, writers, and computer programmers, can work at home, using a personal computer. Electronic mail systems allow them to keep in touch with their offices. The mail system delivers messages, electronic worksheets, and work assignments to the employee's home computer. If additional data is needed from work, database queries allow employees to access the information and download it to their personal computers. The work is completed at home and transmitted back to the office through use of the same system.

This type of flexibility provides a solution to workers in special situations. Working at home can appeal to people with small children. The ability to work at home allows them to raise a family without sacrificing their careers. Working at home can also appeal to employees with physical handicaps who find it difficult to commute daily to the office.

As you can see, the office environment is no longer bound by walls or limited to a single building. Through computers many of these activities can take place in the home. By using communication networks, individuals at different locations can hold conferences. This **teleconferencing** enables businesspeople to participate in seminars given by experts located around the world without the inconvenience and expense of physically traveling to the seminar.

FIGURE 11.21
Teleconferencing helps people to communicate effectively when separated by great distances.

Electronic Funds Transfer

When you cash a check, another network of computers comes into play. The banking industry has developed a communications network that helps minimize the work involved in transferring money between banks. The **electronic funds transfer (EFT)** system handles financial transactions through a computer network rather than by exchanging cash. This is having a major impact upon society. Through the use of electronic passwords and credit cards, buyers and sellers can advise a bank that a transaction has been completed. The bank completes the transaction by automatically moving the money from the buyer's account to the seller's.

An EFT system provides a solution for problems that continually have plagued buyers, sellers, and banks. Without the use of EFT, buyers have had limited purchasing power outside of their local community. Out-of-town stores would not always accept their checks. Also, many stores do not have credit plans available for major purchases. Sellers, in turn, always had to be on the outlook for stolen or uncashed checks. There was also a delay between the time a buyer wrote a check and the time a seller actually received the money. Banks were caught in the middle, handling millions of checks per day. An EFT system minimizes the need to write checks and for the bank to process the paper involved.

Currently, the French are using a new type of credit card that will help minimize fraudulent electronic transactions. Called a *smart card,* this credit card contains a processor and memory chip that stores and updates the owner's credit information. Every time a transaction is made using this smart credit card, the transaction immediately becomes part of the owner's credit history. If a stolen card is used, the memory chip is wiped clean by a credit card reader. Erasing occurs when the merchant tries to verify the customer's credit through the bank's central computer system.

FIGURE 11.22
Without Electronic Data Interchange (EDI), purchase orders, bills, and other transactions must be manually processed. EDI automates this process by connecting the buyer's and seller's computer systems.

Electronic Data Interchange

For organizations, *electronic data interchange (EDI)* is the electronic exchange of specially formatted business documents for ordering new supplies. The computers of organizations transfer data

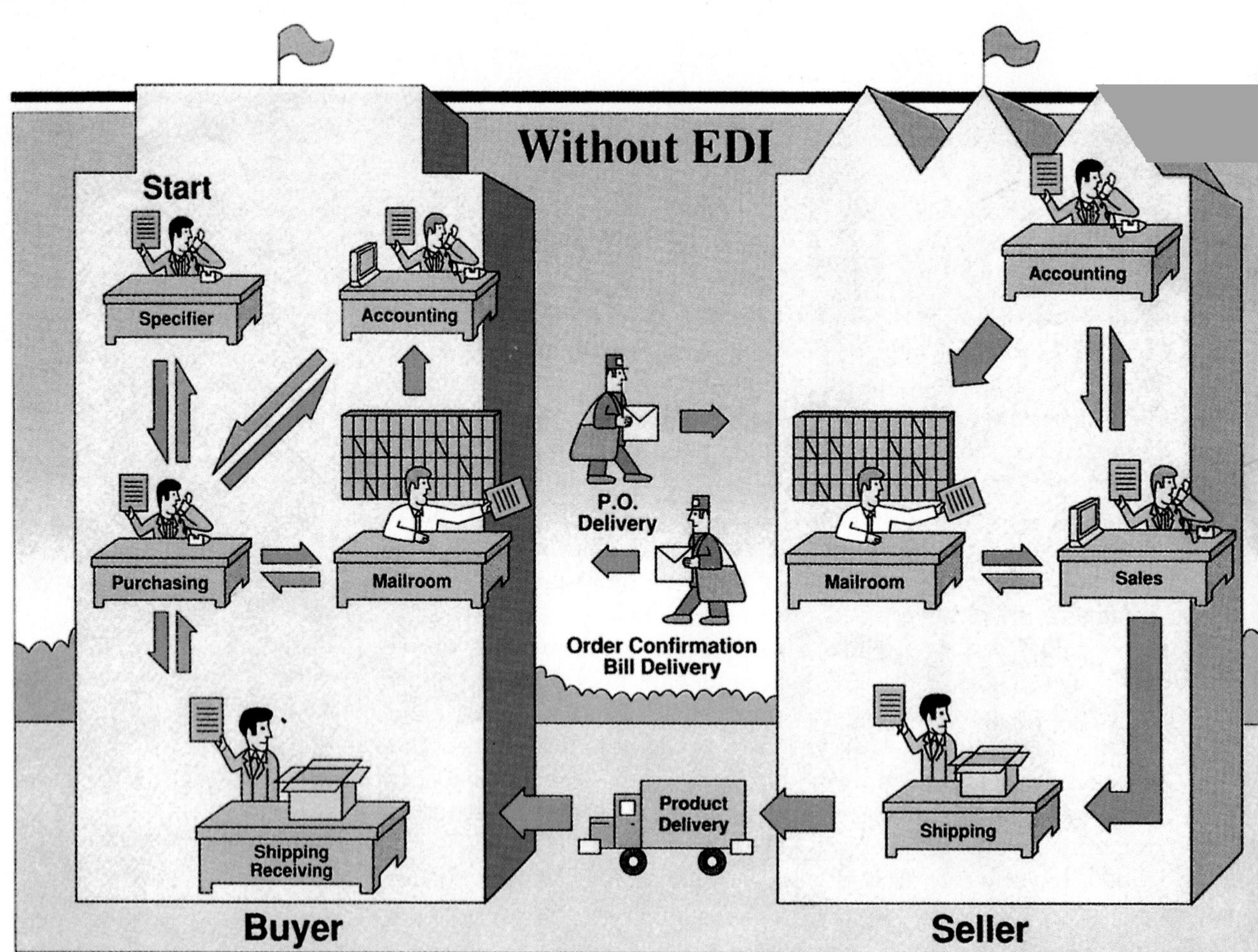

Without EDI, the real power—either at the Buyer Company or the Seller Manufacturing Company—may seem to be vested in the mail room and with

(*SOURCE*: Datamation, *March 15, 1988. Copyright © 1988 Cahners Publishing Company. Reprinted with permission.*)

directly instead of people using paper forms sent through regular mail, as illustrated in Figure 11.22. EDI takes place when a catalog company electronically sends a summary of its customer orders to its suppliers' computers. When EFT is linked to EDI, bank statements are sent to the organization and bills are paid electronically. By using EDI, an organization can cut down on paper work, reduce data entry errors, and increase the efficient management of data.

Work Group Computing

The linking of computers to form networks is changing the way people work. E-mail reduces the time and expense of sending documents or messages through conventional delivery services. Users can send messages to any other user or to everyone in the mail network; thus, they can receive from any other users as well. *Voice mail* is the voice equivalent of E-mail. Messages are recorded and routed to an individual's electronic mailbox, played back as needed, and responses sent to the appropriate person.

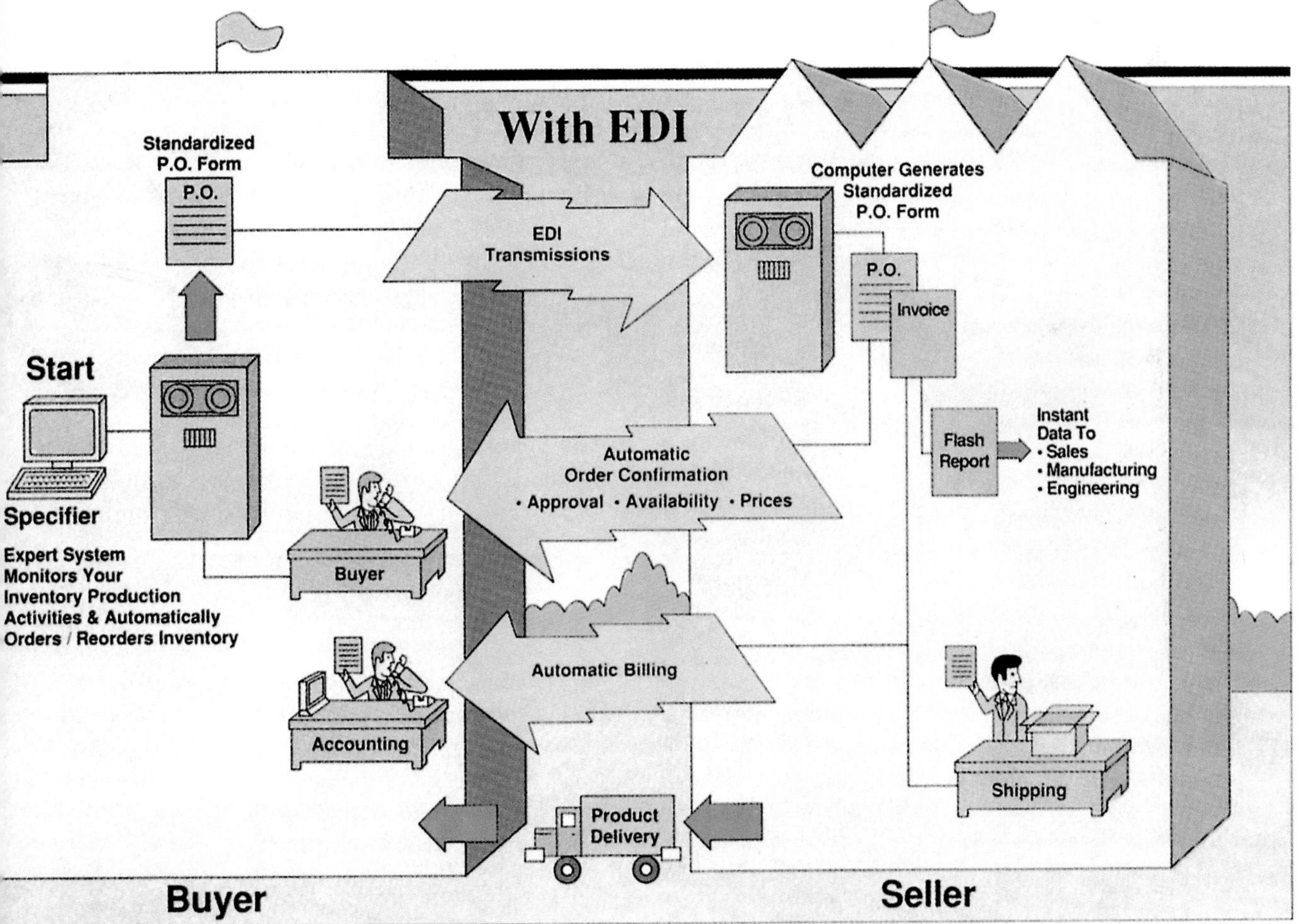

the U.S. Mail. With EDI, orders, confirmations and billing whiz seamlessly between the partners in the transaction.

In the News...

THE TEN DEADLY NETWORK SINS

PC World asked Patrick Corrigan, managing director of the network consulting firm The Corrigan Group, to discuss the most frequent networking mistakes.

1. The "I'll do it myself" installation. Networks are "complicated stuff." Too many companies install their own LAN's without sufficient experience or knowledge, or professional help.

2. The "bargain basement" approach. Shopping for the cheapest hardware and operating system may ease the initial pain of investing in networking technology, but will cost you when you run into the inevitable incompatibilities and inadequate support.

3. Using an untested reseller or system integrater. Too many people are orphaned by a dealer, VAR (value added reseller), or consultant when things don't go right. To save yourself from that fate, get references, particularly from companies that have implemented a LAN in a similar environment.

4. Poor planning and design. Issues such as user account information, directory structures, and deciding who has access to different types of data should be hammered out when the network is installed—with an eye toward future growth.

5. Unrealistic expectations. Most organizations install a network expecting it to be a quick and easy process. Neither is ever true. The payoff might be months—or years—away.

> *"Every company needs a comprehensive disaster recovery plan"*

6. Assuming everything will work when the last wires are connected. Rarely is this the case, even if you've got a professional network installer handling the project. The lesson? Don't move your strategic applications over too quickly. Assume you'll have a shakedown period while all the bugs get worked out.

7. Networks maintain themselves, right? One of the most serious mistakes a company can make is assuming that anyone can manage the LAN. Every network—regardless of size—requires the ongoing attention of a trained network administrator. Backups, application installation and maintenance, management of user accounts, and hardware and software compatibility are just a few of the issues the network manager will have to deal with almost daily.

8. Lack of user training. Many companies don't recognize the need to train users how to work effectively in a networked environment. Instead, users are simply given a password and shown how to log on to the network. Users need to be schooled in issues such as dealing with shared peripherals and shared applications.

9. Improper backup. A major source of trouble for networks of any size is a failure to follow proper backup procedures. Intermediate backups should be done regularly—nightly, ideally—and with proper redundancy. Full backups should be done as often as possible.

10. Disaster recovery? We'll think about that tomorrow. Every company needs a comprehensive disaster recovery plan, but it's particularly critical when your business depends on the smooth operation of the network. Key issues include the impact of the system going down, the amount of time required to get the network back up and running, and designating an individual or individuals who'll be responsible for implementing the recovery plan.

E-mail and voice mail are important features of work group software, **groupware**, which also incorporates public calendars and scheduling, interactive conference calls, and document sharing (see Figure 11.23). Groupware works within a network to help people communicate ideas and resolve problems. It coordinates the flow of information between people to support *work group computing*. People working in different time zones can use groupware features on wide area networks to minimize problems associated with different working hours.

For example, researchers like astronomer Neil Janson use groupware to share information. At the beginning of this chapter Neil used an E-mail system within a wide area network to contact Dr. Baranson in England. After the initial findings were posted on the WAN's electronic bulletin board, other astronomers responded with dozens of E-mail messages asking for more information. To handle this increase in E-mail messages, Neil used the groupware's message filtering feature to redirect all E-mail about the aberration to a special mailbox. *Message filtering* allows a groupware user to automatically sort incoming mail based on personally selected key

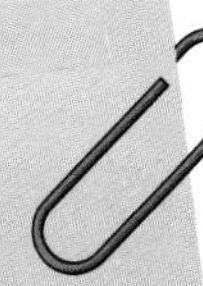

Work Group Computing Using Groupware

Electronic Mail and Voice Mail
- private and public mailing lists
- automatic acknowledgment of mail
- built-in word processing
- fax support
- password security on mailbox
- message filtering

Bulletin Board
- allows response to posted messages
- allows downloading and uploading of data and software
- virus protection

Teleconferencing
- supports video broadcast of participants
- electronic whiteboard
- supports mediation from a designated facilitator

Calendar and Scheduling
- ability to lock out selected times
- automatic checking for common meeting times
- E-mail notification of meeting
- E-mail meeting confirmation

Shared Documents
- private and public files
- password security on files
- supports complex documents
- supports group editing
- maintains readers' log

FIGURE 11.23
Groupware is designed to support work group computing.

words. Any E-mail using a key word is sent to specific mailboxes. Some groupware packages will even signal the user when "priority" mail arrives from a specific person or company.

Many of the E-mail messages requested a teleconference with Neil. During the teleconference the groupware's user interface supported the questions and answers using an *electronic whiteboard.* Participants posed questions by typing on their keyboards or using their notepad's stylus. Neil answered questions in the same way. The electronic whiteboard posted each question and related answer on a designated area of everyone's personal computer screen. Photographic images taken by Neil's telescope and computer-enhanced could be displayed on command by any of the groupware users.

As Neil worked with others in collaborating his findings, he started writing an article about it for an important scientific journal. The groupware document-sharing feature helped Neil distribute rough drafts of the article to colleagues working at the observatory as well as others located at different universities. Furthermore, the groupware's *readers' log* kept track of who had access to, and hopefully read, the paper. Another groupware feature allowed the readers to make editorial comments about the article. These suggestions were independently stored in separate files that Neil could recall when writing the final draft.

FIGURE 11.24
The University of Arizona's Decision Planning Lab uses several groupware features to support interactive problem solving.

A Closer Look...

Information Utilities

Electric and gas utilities have been providing needed services to their customers for years. The explosive growth of personal computers and inexpensive modems has added information utilities to this list. Unlike your local gas and electric companies, which are usually monopolies, there are several information utilities from which to choose. Furthermore, you can subscribe to as many as you want.

Besides a computer and modem, you need to acquire a communication software package before using an information utility. Next you should consider the services that would be of interest to you. Do you want access to current stock market information, electronic catalogs, airline reservations, or E-mail? Do you enjoy playing interactive video games or like to shoot the breeze with others? You should ask these and other questions before going online.

Q With whom would you electronically communicate?

A Besides the data services mentioned in this chapter, an information utility can support many other groupware features. Ask friends and family if they use an information utility. If they do, find out what they like about it and how they use it.

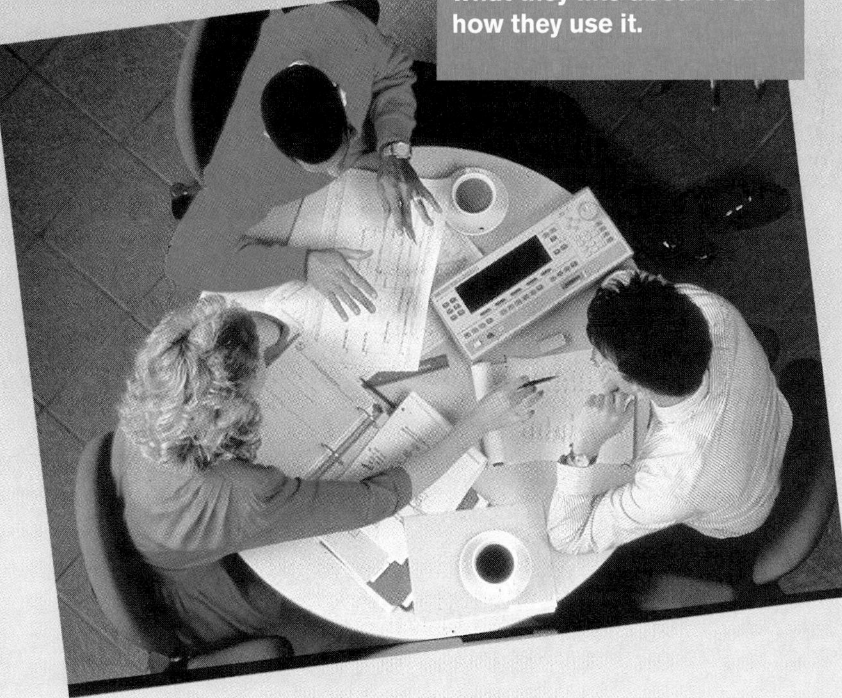

Q Does the information utility provide access through a local or toll-free telephone number?

A Part of the cost of using an information utility is in the charges levied by your local and long distance telephone companies. A local access number or 800 number would save long distance telephone expenses. In addition, make sure that everyone you will work with is also covered by a local access number or toll-free number.

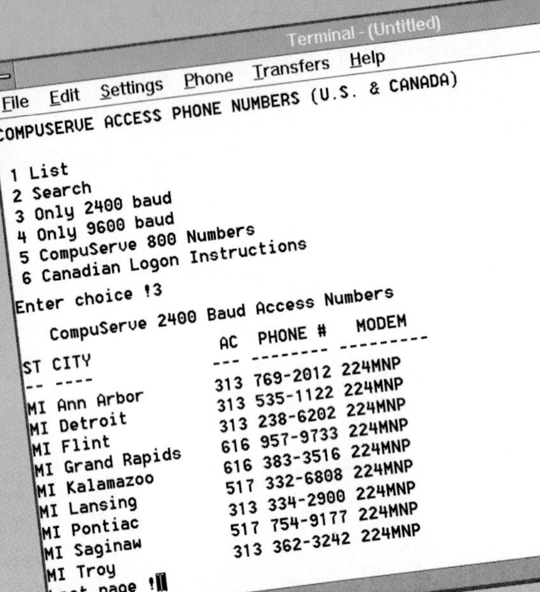

Terminal - (Untitled)
File Edit Settings Phone Transfers Help
COMPUSERVE ACCESS PHONE NUMBERS (U.S. & CANADA)
1 List
2 Search
3 Only 2400 baud
4 Only 9600 baud
5 CompuServe 800 Numbers
6 Canadian Logon Instructions
Enter choice !3
CompuServe 2400 Baud Access Numbers
ST CITY AC PHONE # MODEM
MI Ann Arbor 313 769-2012 224MNP
MI Detroit 313 535-1122 224MNP
MI Flint 313 238-6202 224MNP
MI Grand Rapids 616 957-9733 224MNP
MI Kalamazoo 616 383-3516 224MNP
MI Lansing 517 332-6808 224MNP
MI Pontiac 313 334-2900 224MNP
MI Saginaw 517 754-9177 224MNP
MI Troy 313 362-3242 224MNP
Last page !

Q What is the service fee?

A Expect the utility to charge some combination of a one-time initiation fee, a monthly or an annual basic rate, and/or usage fees based on connect time. Find out if the access fees have a tiered cost structure based on the time of day you use the service.

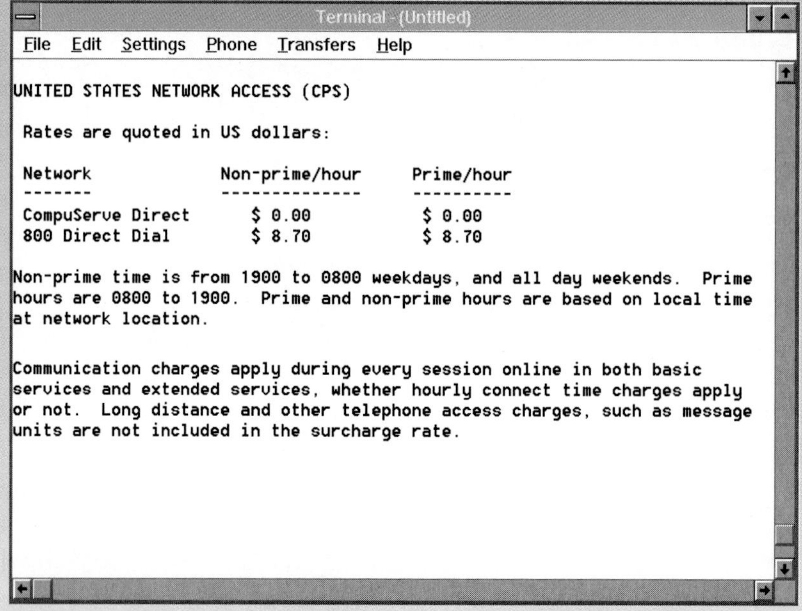

Terminal - (Untitled)
File Edit Settings Phone Transfers Help
UNITED STATES NETWORK ACCESS (CPS)
Rates are quoted in US dollars:
Network Non-prime/hour Prime/hour
CompuServe Direct $ 0.00 $ 0.00
800 Direct Dial $ 8.70 $ 8.70
Non-prime time is from 1900 to 0800 weekdays, and all day weekends. Prime hours are 0800 to 1900. Prime and non-prime hours are based on local time at network location.
Communication charges apply during every session online in both basic services and extended services, whether hourly connect time charges apply or not. Long distance and other telephone access charges, such as message units are not included in the surcharge rate.

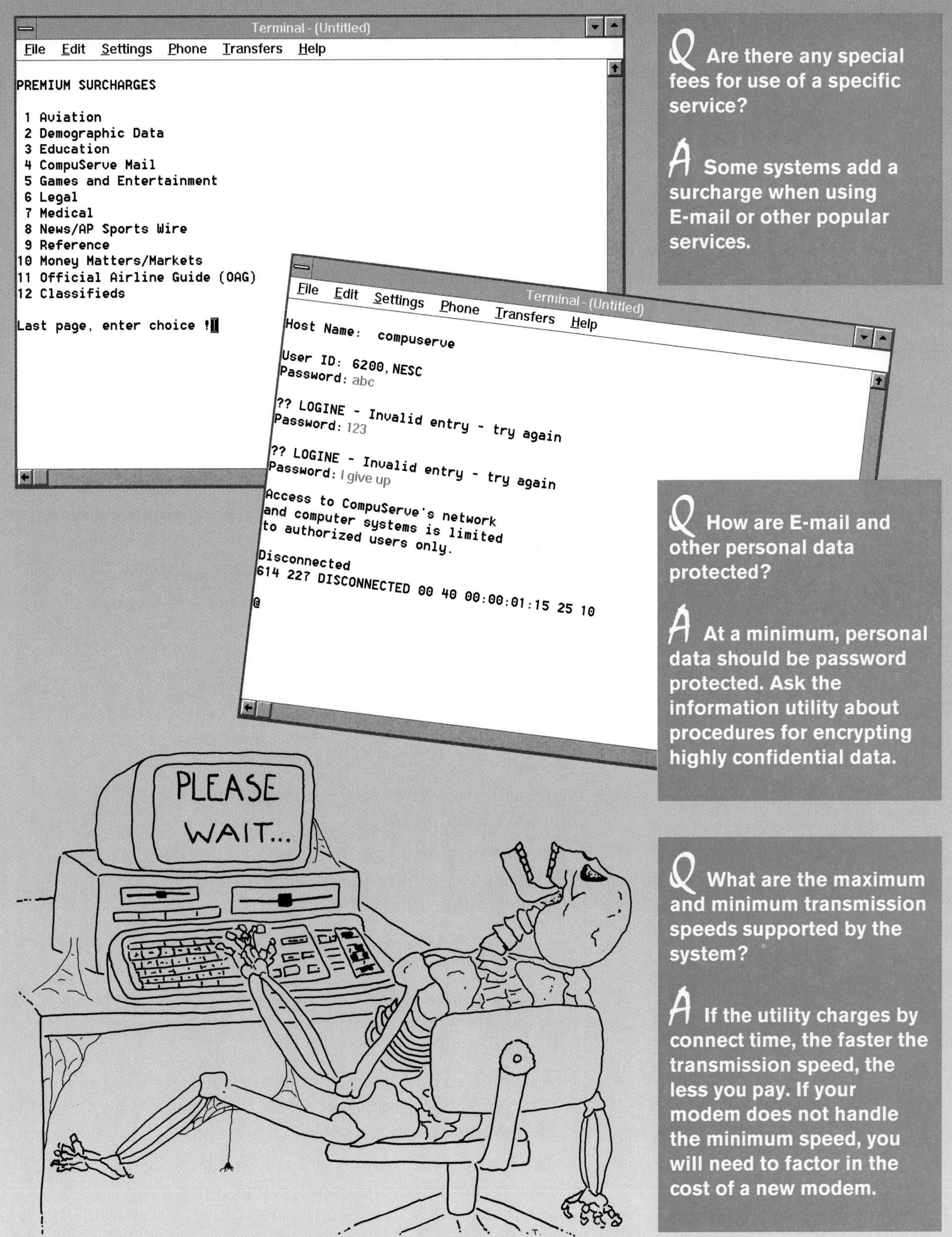
Terminal - (Untitled)
File Edit Settings Phone Transfers Help
PREMIUM SURCHARGES
1 Aviation
2 Demographic Data
3 Education
4 CompuServe Mail
5 Games and Entertainment
6 Legal
7 Medical
8 News/AP Sports Wire
9 Reference
10 Money Matters/Markets
11 Official Airline Guide (OAG)
12 Classifieds
Last page, enter choice !
Terminal - (Untitled)
File Edit Settings Phone Transfers Help
Host Name: compuserve
User ID: 6200, NESC
Password: abc
?? LOGINE - Invalid entry - try again
Password: 123
?? LOGINE - Invalid entry - try again
Password: I give up
Access to CompuServe's network
and computer systems is limited
to authorized users only.
Disconnected
614 227 DISCONNECTED 00 40 00:00:01:15 25 10
@
PLEASE WAIT...

Q Are there any special fees for use of a specific service?

A Some systems add a surcharge when using E-mail or other popular services.

Q How are E-mail and other personal data protected?

A At a minimum, personal data should be password protected. Ask the information utility about procedures for encrypting highly confidential data.

Q What are the maximum and minimum transmission speeds supported by the system?

A If the utility charges by connect time, the faster the transmission speed, the less you pay. If your modem does not handle the minimum speed, you will need to factor in the cost of a new modem.

Chapter Facts

- Telecommunication is electronic communication over long distances. Data communication is the sending and receiving of data electronically.
- The sharing of a single computer's processing power by several terminals over communication lines is teleprocessing.
- Distributed processing involves several computers linked together to share data processed by end-users.
- Network topologies fall into three basic categories: bus, ring, and star.
- Star networks rely on a host computer to coordinate data communications.
- A single communication channel links nodes within a bus network.
- Computers within a ring network are linked to two others forming the ring.
- Gateways link networks with different topologies.
- The transmission speeds through communication channels are measured in bits per second (bps), while baud rates are associated with communication hardware.
- The communication channels available for data communication differ in their transmission speeds. Slowest are telephone lines, out-raced by coaxial cables, microwave systems, and optical fibers.
- Predefined procedures for transmitting data are known as communication protocols.
- Local area networks (LANs) serve a confined area such as an office complex, while wide area networks (WANs) can cover large geographic areas.
- Networks with services beyond data communication are called value-added networks (VANs).
- Powerful personal computers now support client/server network designs where the PCs take over processing once done by the server.
- Data coming to and from computers is in digital form. This must be converted to analog signals to be sent over voice-oriented communication channels.
- Digital/analog conversion is done by modems. Modems can take the form of acoustic couplers and direct-connect modems.

- Multiplexers merge several signals for transmission over a single high-speed communication channel to and from a remote computer.
- Facsimile (fax) machines work like modems but digitize and transmit images from hard copy instead of transmitting computer-generated data.
- Notepad computers with cellular modems become personal communication devices with great flexibility.
- Transmissions of data can be in synchronous or asynchronous patterns.
- Common computer-based transmission modes are half-duplex, used in batch processing; and full-duplex, used with real-time processing.
- Electronic bulletin board systems (BBSs) serve as centers for leaving public messages and sharing public-domain software.
- By accessing an information utility, a user can tap into a variety of online services, such as reservation systems, reviews, market quotes, and encyclopedias.
- Working people can use computer technology to work at home or reduce travel time through telecommuting and teleconferencing.
- Electronic funds transfer (EFT) uses a computer network to handle financial transactions between banks, buyers, and sellers.
- Electronic data interchange (EDI) allows the exchange of business documents between two or more organizations.
- Work group computing is made possible with groupware features that support electronic mail, voice mail, public calendars, meeting schedulers, teleconferencing, and document sharing.

Terms to Remember

a. baud rate
b. bits per second (bps)
c. client/server
d. communication channel
e. data communication
f. distributed processing
g. download
h. electronic bulletin board system (BBS)
i. electronic funds transfer (EFT)
j. facsimile (fax) machine
k. gateway

l. groupware
m. information utility
n. local area network (LAN)
o. modem
p. multiplexer
q. network topology
r. node
s. protocol
t. server
u. telecommunication
v. telecommuting
w. teleconferencing
x. teleprocessing
y. upload
z. value-added network (VAN)
aa. wide area network (WAN)

Mix and Match

Match the following definitions to the Terms to Remember.

1. ____ node within a network that handles special tasks.
2. ____ receiving data or programs directly from another computer.
3. ____ the medium by which data communication takes place.
4. ____ user interface to support professional communications through common calendars, teleconferencing, etc.
5. ____ sending data electronically from one location to another.
6. ____ commercial service wherein users pay for access to a VAN.
7. ____ predefined set of procedures for data communications.
8. ____ putting data processing hardware where data originates.
9. ____ network design where end-user's computer takes on processing tasks traditionally handled by a network server.
10. ____ WAN with additional services available to users.
11. ____ machine that scans, digitizes, and transmits/receives hard copy over communication lines.
12. ____ rate at which data is transmitted though a modem or other communication hardware.
13. ____ hardware that connects different network topologies.
14. ____ meeting of people through a network.
15. ____ long distance communications.
16. ____ description of how computers are interconnected within a network.

17. _____ device that converts a single data transmission between analog and digital signals.
18. _____ computer network that allows financial transactions without the actual exchange of money or checks.
19. _____ one computer system within a network.
20. _____ sending data or programs directly to another computer.
21. _____ public or private network covering a large geographic area.
22. _____ interconnected computers within a confined service area.
23. _____ public access message system that allows users to leave or read messages.
24. _____ working at home using a computer network for communications.
25. _____ device that combines signals from several incoming transmissions to be sent to the same computer.
26. _____ central computer system that exchanges data with physically remote input and output components.
27. _____ measurement of communication channel data transmission speeds.

Review Questions

1. What are the characteristics of the three basic network topologies?
2. In what situations is it best to use bits per second (bps) instead of baud rate?
3. Name four types of communication channels, and identify the transmission capacity associated with each.
4. How are data collision problems avoided when two computers use the same communication channel?
5. How are personal computers connected to a local area network?
6. How is a client/server network configuration different from a more traditional server-oriented network?
7. Why are modems needed for data communication?
8. Describe three ways you can connect a modem to a personal computer.
9. What are the advantages and disadvantages to using a fax board versus a standalone fax machine?

10. When is a computer a personal communication device?
11. What are five services that data communication software provides computer users with modems?
12. What is the difference between synchronous and asynchronous data transmissions?
13. How do half-duplex and full-duplex transmissions work?
14. What are the responsibilities of a bulletin board's sysop?
15. How do information utilities charge for their services?
16. How are electronic funds transfer and electronic data interchange similar?
17. What are six groupware features that could be used for work group computing?
18. What features and options should you look for in an information utility?

Applying What You've Learned

1. Communication software is a critical component of any data communication system. Compare two commercial and/or shareware packages. Identify costs for acquiring the software, maximum transmission speed each can handle, maximum number of entries in its dialing directory, and list any special features you find interesting or useful.
2. If you wanted to join all the computers in your school into a network, which of the topologies would you use? Make a simple drawing of the network, label each node, and identify its location.
3. Educators have been speculating how groupware can change the way classes are taught. Pick a grade and subject. Then describe how students and teachers could use groupware to improve the quality of instruction in their classroom.
4. An electronic mail or voice mail system uses a computer to store correspondence. Potentially, this could make it available to anyone with access to the system.
   a. What could be done to protect the privacy of a person's business or academic correspondence?
   b. What other losses of privacy could occur if electronic mail is used in all departments of a large organization?
5. Telecommuting is slowly becoming accepted in business, but it does have its disadvantages. Name five jobs where telecom-

muting would not be possible. What are five jobs where telecommuting is not only possible but could be an advantage to both workers and employers? What are some additional responsibilities that a telecommuter has?

6. Describe how a consumer-oriented EDI system would work. Do you know of any companies that are allowing personal computer users to use such services?
7. How could an EDI system create marketing opportunities for a business?

Answers to Mix and Match

1. t 2. g 3. d 4. l 5. e 6. m 7. s 8. f 9. c 10. z
11. j 12. a 13. k 14. w 15. u 16. q 17. o 18. i
19. r 20. y 21. aa 22. n 23. h 24. v 25. p 26. x 27. b

UNIT FOUR

Information Systems

When the components of a computer system are thoughtfully combined, they facilitate the sharing of information and they support decision making. Chapter 12 discusses how managers in any organization can sharpen their decision-making skills by using knowledge derived from computer systems. Applications for management information systems and decision-support systems are examined from a user's perspective.

Careful planning must accompany the design of any computer system. In Chapter 13, different approaches to developing and upgrading computer systems are overviewed. This chapter emphasizes that users should be involved when system requirements are identified and evaluated, as well as provided adequate training. In addition, Chapter 13 stresses the responsibilities of the computer professionals who design system components and organize implementation strategies.

An important part of systems design and implementation revolves around the creation of computer programs. Chapter 14 examines the choices computer programmers make between writing new software and modifying existing programs. Design techniques for creating new programs are discussed, as are several of the most common programming languages. Maintenance is presented as an ongoing operation necessary for the long life of any program and associated computer system.

IBM

12

Management and Decision-Support Systems

- From the User's Point of View
- Management Information Systems
  - People using management information
  - Data for management information
  - Organizing data into reports
- Decision-Support Systems
  - Modeling
  - Data analysis using queries
- Tools to Enhance Decision Making
  - Materials requirement planning
  - Self-directed work teams
  - Quality control
  - Total quality management
  - Expert systems
- *A Closer Look . . . Developing an Expert System*

FROM THE USER'S POINT OF VIEW

Management is not restricted to the business world. Any organization, whether it is a large corporation, government agency, school, church, or volunteer society, requires information to control resources and achieve goals. If and when you are in a position to manage others, information technology can help you plan, organize, direct, and control activities. While computers are not magical solutions to every problem, information technology is a powerful tool for effective decision making. You will find that access to complete, correct, and timely data is the unifying factor joining past performance with today's problems and plans for the future.

MANAGEMENT INFORMATION SYSTEMS

Information is a strategic resource for any organization. It is management's role within an organization to use this information to plan events, solve problems, and supervise people. Much of the data from which useful information is derived comes from day-by-day activities—for example, the number of patients served (hospital), sales made (restaurant), or emergency calls (fire station). A **management information system (MIS)** is the collection of systems, both computerized and manual, that provides information about ongoing activities to an organization's decision makers. Every organization has an MIS whether they know it or not. The secretary with last year's employment figures is part of the MIS. So are the contents of a manager's file drawer or a database. A business's annual report, a school's graduation list, or the telephone tree for a volunteer agency are all important parts of an MIS for their respective organizations.

Look again at the definition of MIS. It is a collection of systems but does not necessarily include a computer. An MIS can be composed entirely of data, procedures, and personnel. Computer hardware and programs need not be involved (Figure 12.1).

Early MIS systems centered around hand-kept records. Important data was stored on ledger books, spreadsheets, and file cards. Social security, health care, and other programs have increased demand over the years for information by the government and decision makers. The advent of computers allows people to solve this information problem by organizing data onto tape and disk files.

File processing systems discussed in Chapter 7 were a partial solution to this organization problem, but using separate files made it difficult for managers

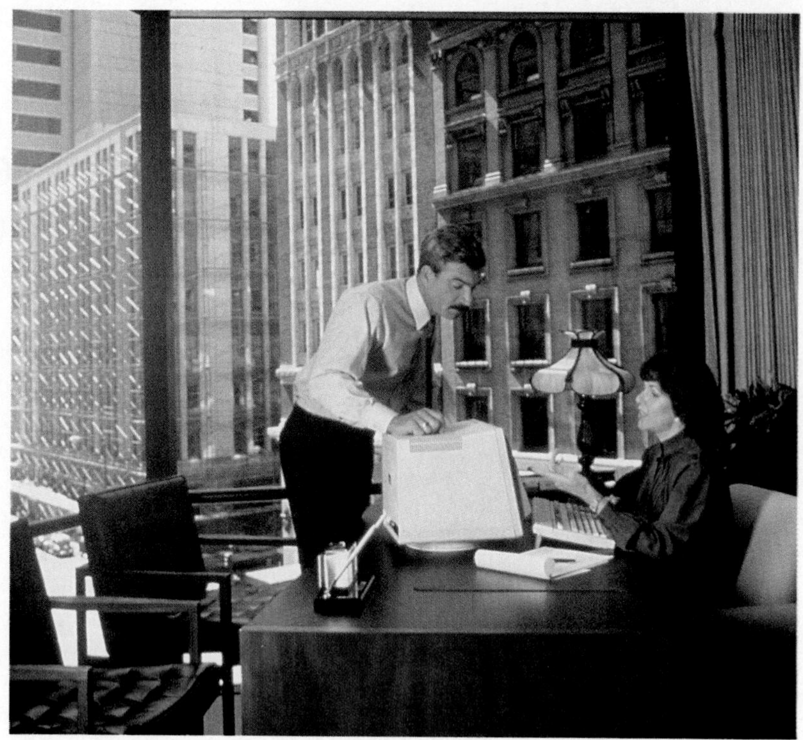

FIGURE 12.1
A management information system is composed of data, procedures, and people. The more organized MIS may include computers.

to obtain related data and keep it updated. Eventually, the volumes of information were more than many file processing systems could handle. Many organizations now use database programs to integrate their data files and plot data relationships, making information more accessible.

Organizations vary with their present use of computers in MIS. Some exclusively use database programs, while others still keep data by hand. This chapter will focus on using computers as part of a management information system.

People Using Management Information

Management in many areas of business needs information to operate. Administration, counseling, engineering, accounting, manufacturing, marketing, education, personnel, public health, and sales are all information-intensive activities. Although the types of information needed are different for each area, the decisions have several features in common.

In general, the amount of detail included in computer-generated information varies with the scope of decision making to be supported. That is, some management decisions demand immediate attention, yet are short-term in nature, and require highly detailed information. Sweeping decisions that will have long-term effects on the organization usually are supported by less-detailed information covering a larger area of interest. For example, a retail store supervisor responsible for the sports department may receive and use detailed computer output showing every sale of equipment sorted by model and size.

A store manager working at the next management level might want to know only the total sales figure for a single department, as compared to sales for the other departments, and total sales for the entire store. At this level the information is used to determine how much space to allocate for an individual department and to decide upon the size of its staff and the value of its stock.

At headquarters for a chain of stores, upper-level management may require only summaries of store-wide figures. The job of top managers is to monitor overall profitability, so an executive may not know what is happening in individual departments. In this sense, information content is far less detailed. But the scope of the information is far greater, involving perhaps hundreds of stores.

This comparison highlights the value of information as a management tool. Problem-solving tools, including computers, must be designed to match information with the responsibilities of the individual and the decisions that he or she makes.

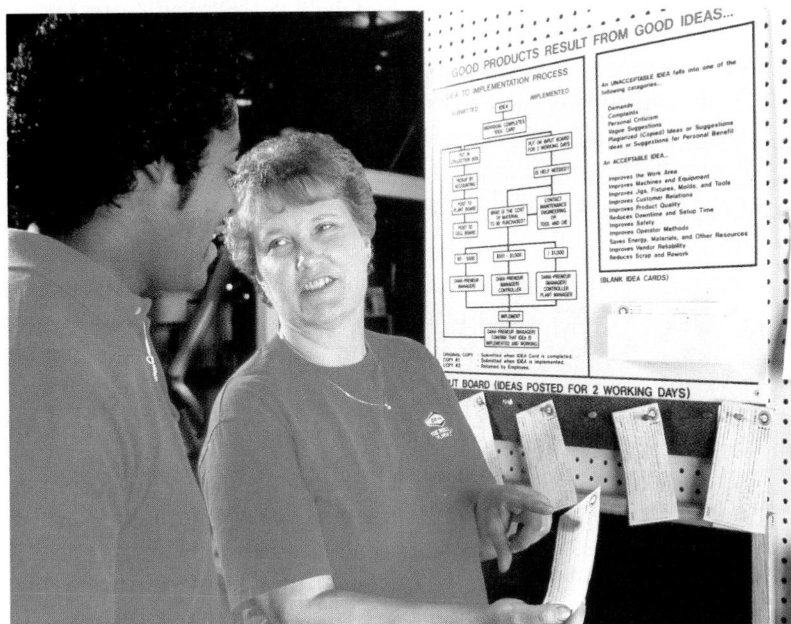

FIGURE 12.2
Front-line management makes operational decisions about daily activities.

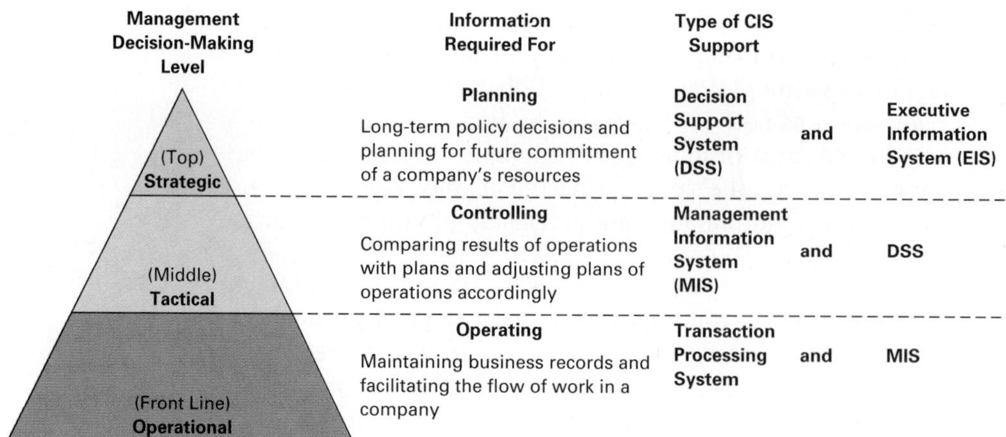

FIGURE 12.3
Management decision-making addresses different goals and concerns as problems are solved at different management levels.

The example of management requirements in the department store situation identifies three levels at which management occurs and decisions are made (see Figure 12.3):

- The department supervisor has responsibilities associated with the day-to-day support of transactions in a single department. The responsibility and accountability of this individual can be described as **front-line management.** Since all of this person's attention is focused on a single organizational unit, he or she has time to digest and react to highly detailed information.
- The manager of the store would be considered part of **middle management.** At this level, a manager is responsible for evaluating the performance of each supervisor and for making whatever changes or adjustments may be necessary to meet sales goals and to keep inventories at reasonable levels. Intermediate levels of detail are required by middle management. In the example, a store manager receives information on sales levels but would not need detailed listings of each sales transaction.
- The president and high-level decision makers of the store chain are part of the organization's **top management,** or *executives.* At this level few short-term decisions on daily operations are made. Instead, decisions by top management have far greater consequences. For example, executive-level people decide where and when to open new stores or to close existing outlets. Top-level executives might decide about what kinds of products and services are to be offered by the chain as a whole. For example, is it profitable for the chain to operate garden shops, automotive service centers, travel agencies, and so forth? The people at this level are charged, broadly, with determining the mission of an organization. They establish the organizational structure and provide the resources needed to fulfill that mission. These responsibilities, collectively, constitute the setting of strategy for the organization.

The specialized problems and degrees of control of the three managerial levels establish different demands for management information. These levels are depicted in Figure 12.3. At the bottom are **operational decisions,** where detailed data is used to complete everyday tasks. As the pyramid shows, the volume of information needed for operational decisions is quite large. Day-to-day operational decisions are made by front-line managers (see Figure 12.2).

Managers at the middle of the pyramid make **tactical decisions.** Here, activities conducted at the bottom level are summarized to provide a broader scope of information. Middle management uses this information to make short-term decisions that impact how, when, and where an organization's resources are used (see Figure 12.4).

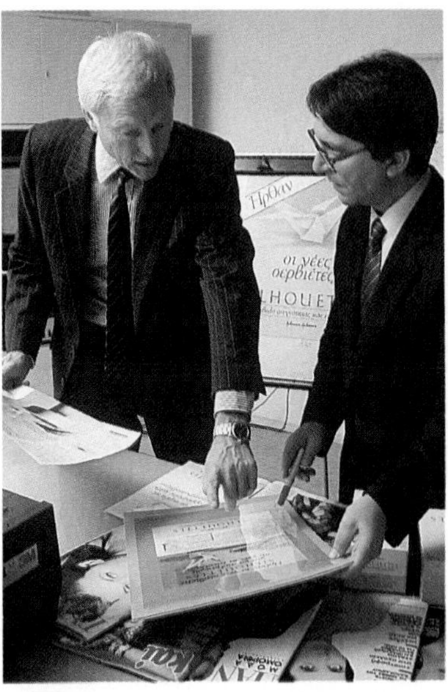

FIGURE 12.4
Middle management makes tactical decisions about short-term problems.

Strategic decisions are made at the top of the pyramid. Information produced at the lower levels is summarized and interpreted before it reaches this strategic level. Thus, strategic decisions require information that is low in volume, yet broad in scope. This type of information is used by top management to make long-term decisions with wide-ranging effects.

The main job of strategic managers is to plan what is to become of the organization. The bottom two levels implement the strategic decisions made by executives. In short, operational managers deal with today's problems, while tactical managers make decisions about this month's stock levels or next season's products. Decisions that make an impact on the whole organization—such as relocating stores, shifting the marketing focus to a new audience, and modifying personnel requirements—are matters left to top management (see Figure 12.5).

While we have examined the management levels of a department store, similar levels exist in other areas. Management of a manufacturing plant would contain a shift supervisor (front-line management), plant manager (middle management), and company president (top management). A university has faculty, department chairpeople, and deans to represent the three management levels. Each level may include a variety of decision makers. In a factory, front-line management would involve foremen as well as shift supervisors. Top management of a university is made up of deans, board of trustees, and a president. Management information systems must be designed to support all levels of decision making.

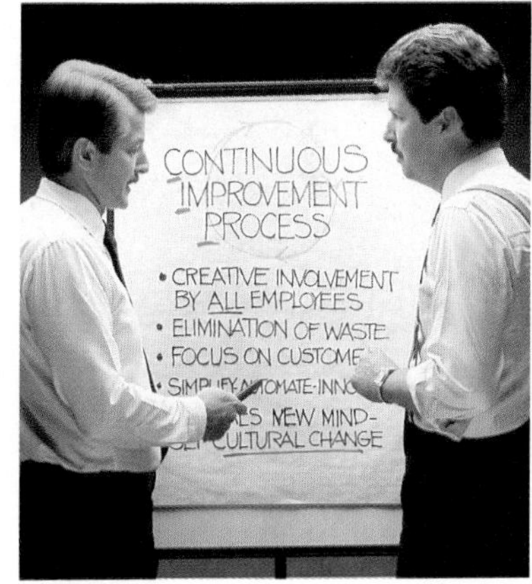

FIGURE 12.5
Top management makes long-term decisions causing wide-ranging effects.

Data for Management Information

Until now, we have been discussing the *management* in management information systems. Of equal importance is the *information.* Information is gathered during different parts of the transaction cycle. The *transaction cycle* is the input, processing, output, and storage of a single transaction. Any system that oversees this process is known as a **transaction processing system.** Whether processing involves completing a single customer order, manufacturing one car, or registering a single student, processing each transaction generates data for the MIS. This represents the day-to-day activities of an organization and is the foundation of any MIS.

As illustrated in Figure 12.6, an organization can divide data into four general areas: financial, personnel, research, and production/sales.

Financial data includes figures about how the organization's resources translate into money. This would encompass data on an organization's profit and loss, assets and liabilities, and other resources of value.

Information about employees and their productivity would be included in **personnel data.** Not only a list of employees, but figures on absenteeism and retirement may be important to management.

Analysis of past performance and plans for future projects is **research data.** For example, stores research potential customers, volunteer agencies investigate sources of future funding, and colleges plan how to recruit certain types of students.

Production/sales data involves numbers about the actual products made, products sold, or services provided. Manufacturing plants would keep inventory levels and raw material orders. Orga-

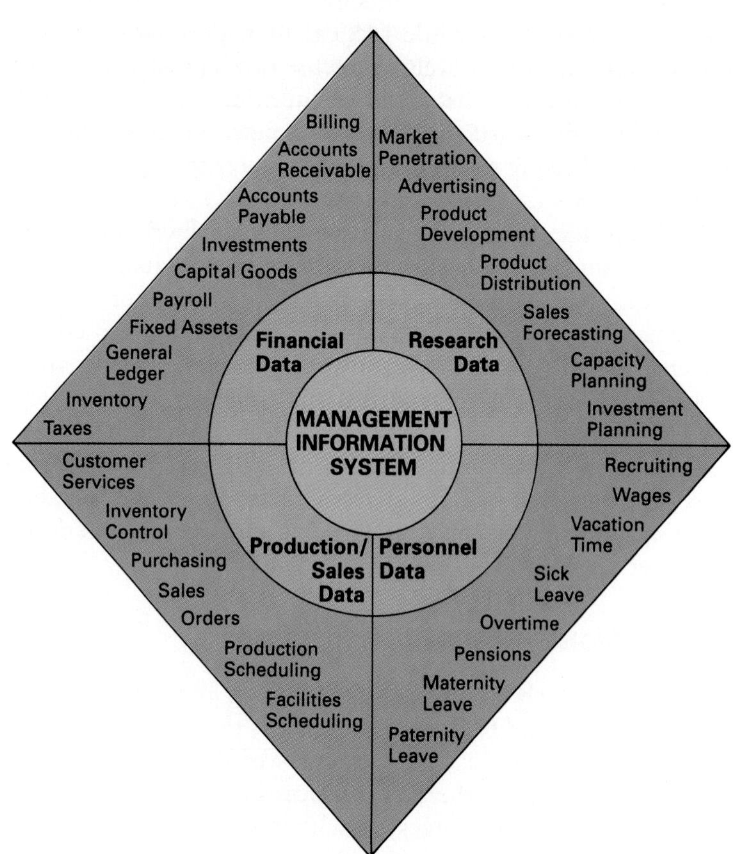

FIGURE 12.6
Data incorporated into an organization's MIS covers finances, personnel, research, and productivity.

nizations that are service oriented—such as schools, churches, volunteer agencies, or travel agencies—would have production/sales data concerning the number of people served and how they were helped.

Organizing Data into Reports

The organization of data and the design of associated reports is critical to the successful use of an MIS. Effective reports are designed to reflect the types of data needed at each management level. Reports are either scheduled for routine use or produced on a demand basis. Since the problems at management levels differ, so does the presentation of information. Report formats generally fall into one of three categories: detailed, summary, and exception reports.

Detailed reports are used by front-line management to examine day-to-day operations. A teacher will use a detailed class report that lists students enrolled in a class. Each student's name and number are displayed on a separate report line.

Detailed reports usually contain one printed line for each item in the database or file. The department store supervisor would use a detailed inventory report to examine the status of each item sold in the department. The report in Figure 12.7 contains the description of items, stock on hand, stock on order, and sales. By using this report, the supervisor can make operational decisions about what stock to reorder or which merchandise to stop selling.

When large amounts of data need to be analyzed, it is not usually practical or necessary to see all of it at one time. In these sit-

Page 2

TIP-TOP STORES

Detailed Inventory Report

Department: Sports — Date: 8/12/9_

Number	Product Description	Stock On Hand	Stock On Order	Stock Below Reorder Point
1101	Leather Basketball	12	0	
1102	Leather Football	3	6	*
1103	8 ft. Jump Rope	24	0	
1104	12 ft. Jump Rope	19	0	
1105	Badminton Birdies	2	15	*
.	.	.	.	.
.	.	.	.	.
.	.	.	.	.

FIGURE 12.7
Detailed reports provide front-line managers with specific data needed for day-to-day decisions.

uations a *summary report* is used. Summary reports condense day-to-day operational data into totals.

Some tactical and strategic decisions can be made by comparing trends in summarized data. Summary reports that show total store sales over several years would help department store executives decide when to close or expand certain stores. A university department chairperson can prepare for top management a request for additional facilities by looking at summaries of classroom and lab use (see Figure 12.8).

Exception reports, like summary reports, result from processing data. Comparisons are used to produce exception reports, which identify departures from normal operations or contain only the data that meets specified conditions.

Early warning signs of an impending problem sometimes can be seen in exception reports. The vice-president of finance for a department store chain may notice increased numbers of unpaid customer

In the News...

THE WINDS OF CHANGE

No change is guaranteed to succeed. Following are some variables that influence change.

■ **Perception.** Make sure people understand the need for change and the reasons behind it.

■ **Involvement.** The more employees involved in decision making, the more committed they will be to the project.

■ **Organizational and departmental culture.** When change is perceived to have a negative impact on a culture, resistance will result.

■ **The stakeholders.** Examine the perceptions, attitudes and behaviors of key stakeholders, for they will set the trend within the organization.

■ **Champions.** Successful change has powerful champions; you may need to find one. Changes without champions often don't succeed.

■ **Time.** Major changes are time consuming and often take longer than people think they should. Estimate on the high side.

■ **Stress.** Stress can have an initial positive impact on productivity. But too much without support to help people cope with it will produce a productivity nosedive.

■ **Training.** Most change requires an extensive investment in training and coaching resources.

Source: QED Information Sciences, Inc.

WHATSAMATTA UNIVERSITY
Summary of Facility Utilization Report
Date: November 5, 199_
Building: Haworth Hall

Hours	Classroom Utilization	Laboratory Utilization
7–8	5%	45%
8–9	60%	95%
9–10	100%	100%
10–11	100%	100%
11–12	100%	100%
12–1	96%	95%
1–2	98%	100%
2–3	83%	100%
3–4	62%	100%

FIGURE 12.8
This summary report encapsulates data related to the utilization of dozens of rooms over several hours.

bills going to collection agencies. The information, available from an exception report that lists overdue accounts, would suggest that executives review the company's charge policy.

Exception reports can highlight both negative and positive trends. A university may produce an exception report listing the names of alumni who have contributed over $1000.00 (see Figure 12.9). The university president would be delighted to see that this exception report contains more large contributions than reports from previous years.

WHATSAMATTA UNIVERSITY
Gold Star Contributors
(contributions over $1000)

Name	Contribution	Alumni
Ms. Elaine Anderson	1,050	71
Mr. and Mrs. Baker	2,100	67/69
Mr. Stanley Borkenstein	1,500	76
Mr. and Mrs. Edward Conelly	5,000	63
.	.	.
.	.	.
.	.	.

FIGURE 12.9
Exception reports focus attention on situations needing immediate action. In this case, each contributor could receive a personalized letter from the university president.

Management information is important for the successful operation of any organization. Decision makers use MISs to oversee what is happening in their organization. However, for strategic planning, it also is necessary to anticipate what is going to happen. As a result, future problems and needs are examined with the help of decision-support systems.

DECISION-SUPPORT SYSTEMS

Important decisions made in organizations may require more information than an MIS can provide. Managers are expected to make intelligent guesses on how today's conditions will affect tomorrow's productivity. They can get help with this problem in two ways. First, managers can use queries to access relevant data from an MIS database. Second, computer professionals help managers create a **model** or mathematical representation of the problem. When these elements are brought together to aid in long-range planning, they become the foundation of a decision-support system. A **decision-support system (DSS)** is a real-time computer system that aids managers in solving problems through queries and modeling (Figure 12.10). Decision-support systems designed specifically for strategic decisions by top-level managers are called **executive information systems.**

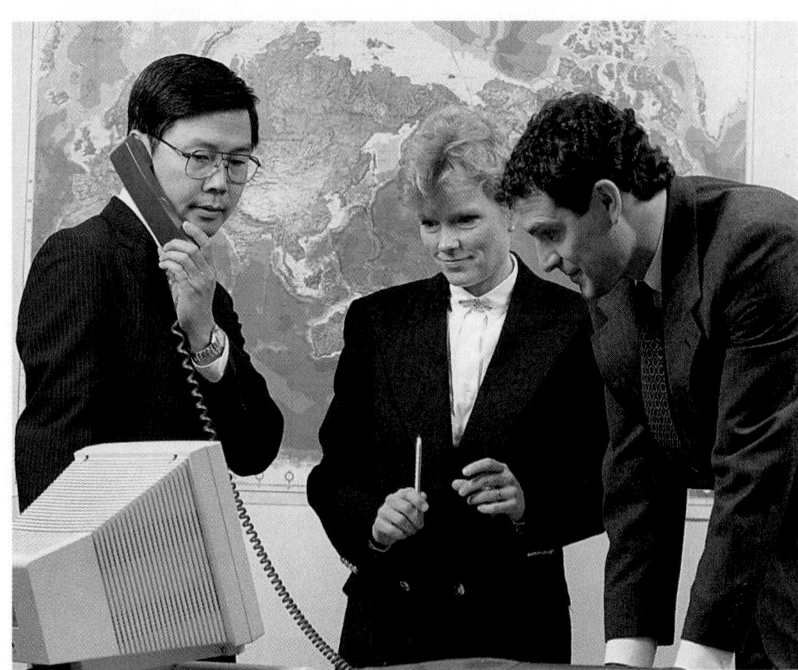

FIGURE 12.10
Decision-support systems do not replace managers but promote problem solving by providing complete and correct information.

DSS users input queries and variables for the model through GUIs and natural language interfaces. Menus, help screens, and other utilities are also included to increase user-friendliness and assist with data entry.

Modeling

Any organizational decision involves forces that work against each other. A department store may wish to maximize profits by expanding services but is faced with increased costs for labor, construction, and maintenance. Another alternative is to raise prices, but managers know that when prices are raised too high, customers will shop elsewhere. How can managers account for all of the interactions, examine all possible alternatives, and still arrive at the best solution? One way is to use a DSS to perform modeling.

For example, the executive who is considering automotive centers for a chain of department stores must look at many factors that will affect the profitability of these centers:

- Does each store already own the land needed to support an automotive center?
- What facilities are needed in the way of buildings, parking, access from busy streets, and so forth?
- How much does the average customer spend on a typical visit to an automotive service center?
- What services should be offered at the centers: Self- or full-service gasoline, brake and muffler service, 24-hour towing?
- How many customers must be served each month for a service center to break even?
- How much money must be invested in equipment and inventory for each center?
- Are there enough trained technicians in the area to staff the centers?

This situation illustrates the fact that there is too much information for one person to process mentally. Detailed records could be accumulated and organized manually, but this could represent a lot of work and take too much time. As a result, computer models are used to assist with this type of complex problem solving.

One type of modeling that evaluates a variety of complex factors is called *linear programming*. Linear programming is a method of finding an optimum solution for a problem by representing each condition or constraint as a mathematical equation (see Figure 12.11). Since many linear models involve a series of complex equations, computers are used for accuracy and to speed up processing.

LINEAR PROGRAMMING MODEL:
Profitability of Auto Service Centers

Goal: To maximize service center profits, given realistic expectations of revenue and cost constraints for capital outlay, labor, inventory, etc.

Question: Which individual services will contribute most to profitability?

Some model variables: x_i = activities associated with service center
x_1 = gas, x_2 = auto parts, x_3 = brakes, x_4 = mufflers, etc.
p_i = profits associated with activity x_i
c_i = capital outlay required for x_i
l_i = first year labor costs for x_i
n_i = start up inventory costs for x_i
r_i = expected revenues for x_i
a_i = advertising budget for x_i
.
.
.

Model:	maximize Σp_i	(profit for all services)
Given:	$\Sigma a_i x_i \leq 23000$	(total advertising budget is \$23,000)
constraints showing	$l_1 x_1 > 12500$	(estimated labor for gas service is over \$12,500)
estimates of costs	$l_3 x_3 = .81 l_4 x_4$	(labor costs for brake dept. 81% of muffler dept. costs)
for each item	$180000 \leq n_2 x_2 \leq 200000$	(auto parts inventory is \$180,000 to \$200,000)
	$c_3 x_3 + c_4 x_4 > 75000$	(break and muffler shops set up costs are over \$75,000)

.
.
.

$$p_2 = r_2 x_2 + .10 c_2 x_2 - l_2 x_2 - a_2 x_2 - .63 n_2 x_2 \ldots$$

show actual make up of profit for each service

↑ depreciation (under $.10c_2x_2$); ↑ auto part inventory turn around (under $.63n_2x_2$)

$$p_3 = r_3 x_3 - .81 l_4 x_4 - a_3 x_3 - \ldots$$

↑ share labor costs with muffler shop (under $.81l_4x_4$)

FIGURE 12.11
This linear program is used to model the costs associated with opening an automotive service center.

Sometimes opposing goals must be met. For example, any automotive service center would like to maximize profit. However, this can be done only under the constraints of meeting payroll obligations, licensing fees, maintenance costs, and so forth. A DSS that uses linear programming would maximize goals while minimizing constraints. Computers help because such calculations often are far too complex to do manually. A disadvantage, however, is that each goal and constraint must be described in precise mathematical terms to realistically model the actual situation.

With a DSS an executive can set up models that reflect different alternatives. In the service center example one decision might involve whether to sell gasoline at service centers. A model can help pull together costs of installing the necessary equipment and storage tanks. Provision is also made for the cost of land, buildings, entrances, and other requirements. When all start-up costs are accumulated, they are processed by a DSS to produce forecasts on depreciation of these costs over a number of years. Then operating costs could be estimated. These include the purchase of gasoline and payroll costs for employees.

In the News...

EXPENSIVE EXECUTIVE TOYS OR PRODUCTIVITY TOOLS

By the year 2000 the so-called executive workstation—more accurately known as the IVDT (integrated voice/data terminal)—will be on everyone's desk, replacing the telephone, the personal computer, the terminal, the modem, electronic mail software, and convenience devices like the calculator, desk and appointment calendars, the Rolodex, even telephone message and memo pads. Extra-fancy models may allow simultaneous communications in voice, text, graphics, image, and video. They might even take dictation.

A survey by Venture Development Corp. (Natick, MA) asked executives to indicate their interest in various IVDT features. The following is a list of the features in order of interest.

1. internal database access
2. ability to run personal computer programs
3. telephone directory
4. single-key access to functions
5. ability to use phone and send data simultaneously
6. screen dialing
7. speed dialing
8. private database
9. electronic mail
10. external database access
11. voice annotation
12. memo writing
13. telephone call log
14. graphics generation
15. calculator
16. voice mail
17. calendar

Who's Who

Thomas John Watson, Sr.

(1874–1956)

As a young man, Thomas Watson sold pianos, organs, and caskets. He joined National Cash Register (NCR) as a salesman. By age 33 he was the third most powerful man at NCR, leaving it to become president of Computing Tabulating Recording Company in 1913 and president of IBM in 1924. From his earliest days as a manager, Watson favored the sales force over technical workers. Although he established research and development groups, he felt that the salespeople, being closest to customers, should generate the ideas for new products and services. He funded the MARK I, an early computer, and then used IBM to beat it out with the IBM SECC in 1947. The SECC could do 21,000 calculations a second. Watson believed that through consistent quality service and respect for customers, one could build a thriving company.

As IBM grew, it produced one of the first general-purpose computers using integrated circuit technology, the System/360, in 1964. It was really a family of computers that allowed customers to choose among nine different processors and seventy types of input/output hardware to customize their system. Watson was much admired by President Roosevelt and was offered the Secretary of Commerce position and an ambassadorship, both of which he declined. He ruled IBM with an iron hand. When his son, Thomas Watson, Jr., took over in 1956, the senior Watson lived only another two months.

Given this picture of costs, the DSS could be used to project different levels of expected income for the gasoline retailing operation. The result of this modeling process is a reliable figure on how much gasoline each center would have to sell every month to cover expenses and produce a profit. Developing this caliber of information might take many weeks if the work is done manually. With a computer, the effort can be completed in hours once the raw data has been gathered and the model created.

Using a DSS in this way helps take both detailed drudgery and guesswork out of major decisions. In the example a decision on whether to sell gasoline comes down to an estimate on how many gallons customers would buy. A DSS could be used to model each element of an automotive center's operation. For example, models could be built and applied to the brake shop, the lubrication facility, the engine diagnosis and repair operation, and any other segments of automotive center business. Once a model of this type is created, executives can "exercise" it to test results under varying conditions. The result would be a projection of the business volume required to reach a break-even point for each area and for the service center as a whole.

Data Analysis Using Queries

While modeling presents an overall view of a problem and tests various solutions, a query involving a data manipulation language can be used to formulate specific "What if?" questions. One advantage to a query is that a manager can use this part of a DSS without the help of a computer professional.

As discussed in Chapter 7, a query uses commands and/or examples to retrieve information from a file or database (Figure 12.12). While sitting at a terminal, a university administrator immediately can raise such questions as, "What if we raise tuition by 5%? How much additional revenue will be generated, assuming enrollments at current levels?" or, "How will hiring two new security guards affect costs for building security?" These answers are solicited merely by typing in the questions, using a few key words.

A query language is easier to use than modeling software for nonprofessionals, but it is limited to a series of single, relatively straightforward questions. Both modeling and data analysis with queries have predictive value that easily surpasses manual forecasting.

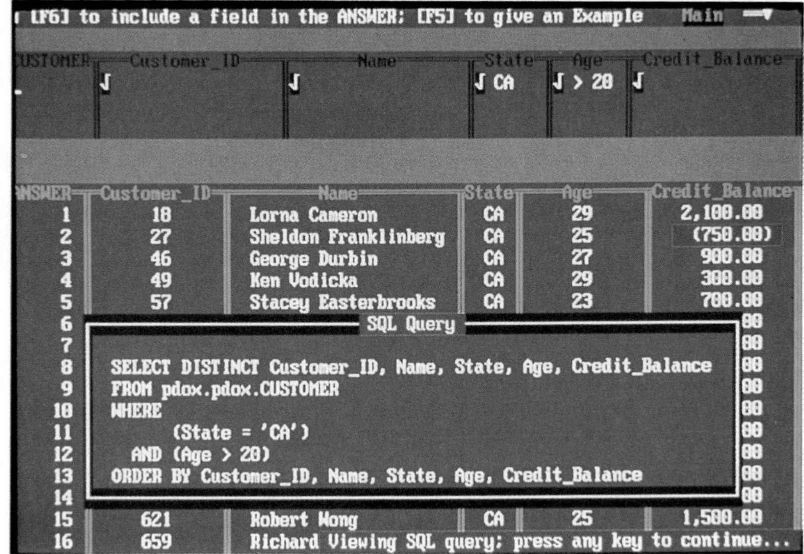

FIGURE 12.12
This display was generated by a query requesting information about customers from California who are over 20 years old.

TOOLS TO ENHANCE DECISION MAKING

Computer-based management and decision-support tools enable people to respond effectively to increased competition and unexpected opportunities or emergencies. By examining important data and modeling different alternatives, managers can make intelligent choices that improve service and profitability.

All of these good things do not automatically happen just because an organization purchases a few computers. Management from the top down must make a commitment to use the technology to increase personal, departmental, and corporate productivity. Organizations of every size need informed users as managers. These people are in the position to determine which collection of decision-making tools work best in their organization. Some of the greatest savings may not come from reduced inventories or personnel, but from better scheduling or the ability to react quickly to changing consumer needs.

An organization's mix of MIS and DSS is dependent on the transaction processing systems currently being used, the organizational structure (centralized vs. distributed decision making), current resources, corporate culture, and the computer literacy of important decision makers. How these systems are used is dependent on organizational goals. Automotive companies and other manufacturers build products and need to track inventories, operating expenses, mean time between equipment failures, etc. Travel agencies, hospitals, law firms, and other service-oriented industries track the number of clients served, billable hours, etc. While these organizations have much in common—for example, payroll—specialized decision-making tools have evolved to meet a variety of organizational needs. Furthermore, personal productivity tools like electronic spreadsheets and presentation graphics software serve unique MIS and DSS applications within every organization.

Materials Requirement Planning

Computer systems have been successfully used for some time in **materials requirement planning (MRP).** In this application, production schedules and current inventory for associated parts and materials provide the data a computer uses to schedule the purchase and delivery of additional supplies. MRP systems help management minimize money invested in inventory, which frees an organization's finances for such other purposes as advertising or research and development (Figure 12.13).

FIGURE 12.13
Materials requirement planning software helps managers track inventory levels and production schedules in order to deliver materials just-in-time.

Some advanced MRP systems support recent manufacturing trends toward just-in-time inventory. *Just-in-time inventory* means that materials or parts arrive shortly before they are needed. Managers use information supplied by an MRP system to schedule just-in-time deliveries of parts and materials. As a result, the manufacturer minimizes finances tied up with inventory and saves money by not having to store materials and parts before they are needed. Japanese industry first used MRP systems for just-in-time inventory in the late 1950s. Both the American and Japanese automotive industries have now gone to this type of inventory system while other manufacturers are starting to follow their lead.

The critical component for the successful implementation of any MIS or DSS system is communication. When DSS provides the information that manufacturing managers need, key decision makers can examine and modify designs and production plans during early phases of the product development cycle. Changes at this stage are comparatively easy and less expensive to make than those made at later stages.

Self-Directed Work Teams

With fast and reliable communications between people being critical to any organization, it should come as little surprise that networks and groupware are becoming popular. The move towards **self-directed work teams** has motivated many organizations to design

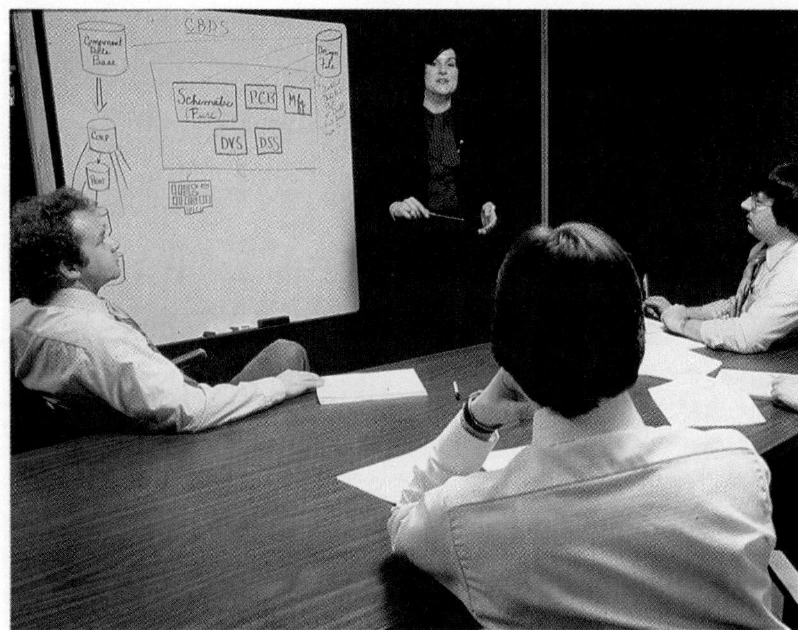

FIGURE 12.14
Self-directed work teams are empowered to make management decisions concerning a specific problem.

computer systems that support group decision making. This type of employee work team is empowered to make management decisions that solve specific problems. For instance, an office furniture company might form a team to design, at a reasonable cost, an ergonomic desk chair. Team members would include a designer, cost accountant, structural engineer, manufacturing engineer, office manager, and representatives from suppliers.

As illustrated in Chapter 11, groupware supports team communication through electronic mail and teleconferencing when members are geographically distributed. Electronic mail also helps people easily collect data from a wide variety of sources. Often information is obtained or decisions are disseminated without the necessity of time-consuming meetings, personal telephone calls, or mass mailings. The chair designer could E-mail rough sketches of new chair designs to other team members. The same groupware system can schedule and coordinate a team teleconference to discuss the designs.

Even when team members physically work in the same building, they can use groupware to support decision making. This groupware application is known as a *group decision support system (GDSS)*. A GDSS uses groupware operating on a network as the means by which team members can define a problem, discuss possible solutions, and delegate responsibilities. Many GDSS users feel more comfortable using the system instead of attending a group meeting because it allows the anonymous submission of ideas and suggestions. As a result, everyone's ideas are given equal weight when considered by the group.

Quality Control

Quality control is the routine checking of a product or process to make sure it meets a predefined standard. Inferior training or raw materials, worn tools, improper equipment setup, or human errors create quality control problems. Quality control often determines the long-term success of a product, service, and organization. Good designs and ideas can fall victim to poor production or service quality as consumers become disgusted with product failures or bad service. Increased competition in the global marketplace has forced many organizations to re-examine their quality control procedures.

Front-line management now uses **statistical process control (SPC)** procedures to eliminate quality control problems before they start. The idea behind SPC is to continually improve a process until every defect is found and eliminated. Manufacturers use SPC procedures because they realize it is cheaper to find a defective part before it is installed and fails. Furthermore, undetected defects adversely affect customer satisfaction. If a defective 50-cent part is found before it is installed, the organization loses 50 cents. If it is installed in a $100,000 machine that is returned or needs service, the expense to the organization is considerably more.

In SPC, workers and/or computers monitor production by statistically selecting certain pieces for detailed inspection. Control charts, like the one shown in Figure 12.15, document whether each

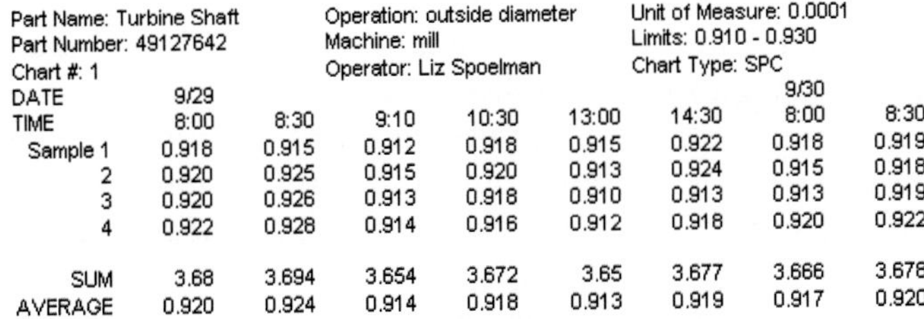

Part Name: Turbine Shaft
Part Number: 49127642
Chart #: 1

Operation: outside diameter
Machine: mill
Operator: Liz Spoelman

Unit of Measure: 0.0001
Limits: 0.910 - 0.930
Chart Type: SPC

DATE	9/29						9/30	
TIME	8:00	8:30	9:10	10:30	13:00	14:30	8:00	8:30
Sample 1	0.918	0.915	0.912	0.918	0.915	0.922	0.918	0.919
2	0.920	0.925	0.915	0.920	0.913	0.924	0.915	0.918
3	0.920	0.926	0.913	0.918	0.910	0.913	0.913	0.919
4	0.922	0.928	0.914	0.916	0.912	0.918	0.920	0.922
SUM	3.68	3.694	3.654	3.672	3.65	3.677	3.666	3.678
AVERAGE	0.920	0.924	0.914	0.918	0.913	0.919	0.917	0.920

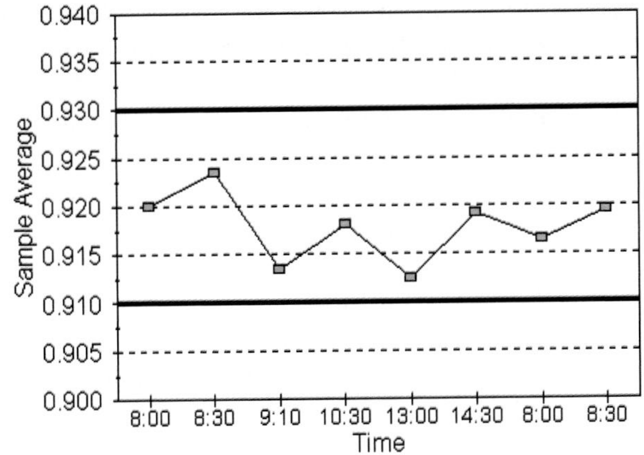

FIGURE 12.15
Statistical process control procedures chart the results of a specific process, looking for trends that indicate potential quality control problems.

piece is within acceptable limits. Statistical packages then analyze this production data to identify current production trends. When the trends indicate that production quality is on the decline, changes are made. For example, in machining new auto parts, a worn cutting tool or drill bit is replaced. Unexpected quality problems are immediately flagged and prompt managers to re-examine the quality of the materials being used or equipment operation and set-up.

SPC procedures are also applied to sales and customer service data. By collecting data directly or indirectly from customers an organization can identify problems. If the statistical trends indicate a decline in service quality, changes need to be made. This may require retraining people or re-evaluating how the services are delivered. For example, an increase in patient complaints about long waits may require a hospital to re-evaluate admission procedures.

Total Quality Management

As a result, **total quality management** is not limited to manufacturing. It is an organization-wide management philosophy that focuses on customer satisfaction through quality control of every service and product. Total quality management can be a goal of service-oriented agencies like hospitals, volunteer organizations like a blood bank, or any government agency. Furthermore, computer-based MIS and DSS can rely on popular personal productivity software to achieve the goals of total quality management.

As mentioned in Chapter 5, the rows and columns in an electronic spreadsheet contain numbers and formulas that can help people project results and choose among alternatives. A spreadsheet allows the manipulation of numbers and organized presentation of the results. Applications that require the summarization of data, or the clear presentation of important data, can be done best on a spreadsheet. Summaries of financial, personnel, research, and production/sales data can be arranged on a spreadsheet in an easy-to-use and familiar format. Other advantages to using an electronic spreadsheet for decision support are listed in Figure 12.16.

After critical data is analyzed, it is necessary to communicate clearly the ideas behind plans or decisions. Information is often communicated most easily through use of graphics, images, and sound. As a result, many spreadsheet and database packages automatically link data with multimedia and presentation graphics packages. When such integration is available, graphic output is easily created by

FIGURE 12.16
Electronic spreadsheets can help managers achieve total quality management goals by presenting data in a clear, easy-to-read format that can be standardized across an organization.

Decision Support Using Electronic Spreadsheets

1. Clear presentation of important data
2. Provides a standard format for exchanging data
3. Inexpensive alternative to some expensive DSS capabilities
4. Allows users to manipulate data to answer "What if . . .?" questions

using existing data from worksheet or database files. No matter which software tools are used, the value of computer graphics within the decision-making process lies in facilitating communication and understanding.

Furthermore, spreadsheets can be one of the building blocks of an organization's MIS. For example, all departments in a hospital could use the same budget template when planning yearly budgets. Each department head would enter data unique to that department. By having a standard format, top management could analyze the budgets for all departments with a global view. Executives would then make strategic decisions based on the entire hospital's financial situation. These decisions could include increasing outpatient services like a sports medicine clinic or extending pharmacy hours for walk-in orders. By using spreadsheets, each department head can adjust his or her budget to reflect strategic plans quickly and easily.

In addition, not every organization can afford the power of a customized MIS or DSS. The blood bank in a resort community needs the data analysis and "What if?" capabilities available on a DSS. An electronic spreadsheet can provide an inexpensive alternative. The agency's director can use the spreadsheet program to get answers to questions like these:

- If tourism increases 10% next summer and traffic accidents increase proportionately, how much blood will be needed?
- How many new donors must be acquired to fill this need?
- How effective have public service announcements been in increasing walk-in blood donors?
- How much more advertising will be needed next summer?

As you can see, electronic spreadsheets and graphics support total quality management at several levels. They organize data in familiar ways and also allow the manipulation of data to obtain answers for some of the "What if?" questions asked of the larger, more expensive DSS. Electronic spreadsheets can play a role in both enhancing existing decision-making functions and serving as a focal point for a small organization's MIS.

Expert Systems

Powerful problem-solving software for decision makers, called expert systems, are some of the first practical applications of work in artificial intelligence. *Artificial intelligence* is the application of computer technology to simulate human thought and judgment. **Expert systems** contain patterns for decision making and probabil-

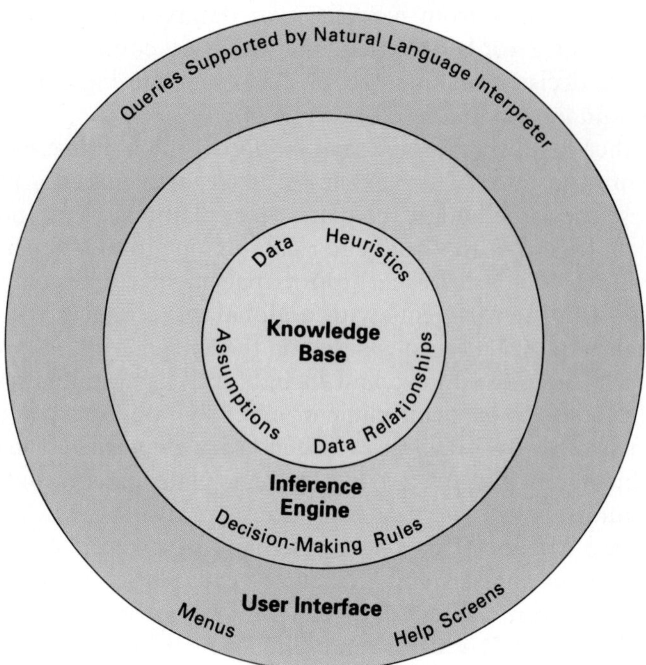

FIGURE 12.17
An expert system's interface provides user access to the inference engine, which works with a knowledge base to draw conclusions and make recommendations.

ities for expected outcomes based on information available from experts. To create an expert system requires more than retrieval of data from large databases. Experts in a specific field *(domain)* are interviewed to obtain their knowledge and the rules by which they make decisions. Such systems have three components: knowledge base, inference engine, and user interface (see Figure 12.17).

The **knowledge base** used by an expert system takes the capabilities of databases one step further. It contains facts, data relationships, and assumptions that the computer professional, working with domain experts, combines together to form the rules used for decision making. The knowledge base for a specific domain, combined with the powerful retrieval and decision-making **inference engine,** drives an expert system. When presented with a problem, the inference engine software can draw new conclusions and add this information to its knowledge base. The vast knowledge base and numerous decision-making rules are made easily accessible to users through the user interface.

One expert system, called Caduceus, contains information about human diseases, related symptoms, and diagnostic tests in its knowledge base. Doctors then enter queries based on symptoms of their patients (see Figure 12.18). The expert system responds with a list of possible diagnoses and the probability of their occurrence.

```
------------------------------------PATIENT 1------------------------------------
(1) Patient's name:(first-last)
**FRED SMITH

(2) Sex:
**MALE

(3) Age:
**55

(4) Have you been able to obtain positive cultures from a site at which Fred Smith
has an infection?
**YES

      --------------------------------INFECTION-1--------------------------------
      (5) What is the infection?
      **PRIMARY-BACTEREMIA

      (6) Please give the date and approximate time when signs or symptoms of
      the primary-bacteremia (INFECTION-1) first appeared (mo/da/yr)
      **MAY 5, 1975

      The most recent positive culture associated with the primary-bacteremia
      (INFECTION-1) will be referred to as:

      ---------------------------------CULTURE-1---------------------------------
      (7) From what site was the specimen for CULTURE-1 taken?
      **BLOOD


My therapy recommendation will be based on the following probable infection(s)
and potential causative organism(s):

INFECTION-1 is PRIMARY-BACTEREMIA
                                                            {Possible identities}
<Item 1> The identity of ORGANISM-1 may be PSEUDOMONAS-AERUGINOSA
<Item 2> The identity of ORGANISM-1 may be KLEBSIELLA-PNEUMONIAE
<Item 3> The identity of ORGANISM-1 may be E. COLI
<Item 4> The identity of ORGANISM-1 may be BACTEROIDES-FRAGILIS
<Item 5> The identity of ORGANISM-1 may be ENTEROBACTER
<Item 6> The identity of ORGANISM-1 may be PROTEUS-NON-MIRABILIS

(46) On a scale of 0 to 4, where higher numbers indicate increasing severity, how
would you rate Fred Smith's degree of sickness?
**3

(47) Does Fred Smith have a clinically significant allergic reaction to any
antimicrobal agent?
**NO

(48) Fred Smith's weight in kilograms (or <number> POUNDS):
**70
                              {note that 2 drugs cover for 6 potential organisms}
[Rec 1] My preferred therapy recommendation is as follows:
In order to cover for Items <1 2 3 5 6>:
     Give: GENTAMICIN
     Dose: 119 mg (1.7 mg/kg) q8h IV [or IM] for 10 days
     Comments: Modify dose in renal failure
In order to cover for Item <4>:
     Give: CLINDAMYCIN
     Dose: 595 mg (8.5 mg/kg) q6h IV [or IM] for 14 days
     Comments: If diarrhea or other GI symptoms develop, patient should be
     evaluated for possible pseudomembranous colitis.

Do you wish to see the next choice therapy?
                                                  {alternative choices are available}
**Y
```

FIGURE 12.18
This is a sample session between an expert system and a medical professional.

It also suggests the least expensive and least painful tests to be administered first. Like a human expert, the expert system will defer on a diagnosis, if not enough information is available.

Expert systems, like people, approach a given problem in different ways. When a **forward chaining** approach is taken, symptoms or situations are provided, and the expert system attempts to identify the problem. With **backward chaining** the problem is described, and the system looks for solutions by identifying possible causes.

People say backward chaining is goal-driven because the expert system starts with an explanation of the results, and its goal is to find evidence that supports these results. Expert systems in market research could use a backward chaining approach to identify target markets. For example, the system could examine demographic data and recommend to a beverage company that it target young adults for cola ads because of their high consumption of the product.

Forward chaining is considered data-driven because the system starts with all the available data and tries to draw a conclusion from it. Medical diagnosis systems, like Caduceus, can use a forward chaining approach. A patient's symptoms are input, and the expert system uses its knowledge base and inference engine to match the symptoms with a successful treatment strategy.

Expert systems are built to *assist* decision makers, not to *replace* them. They can support solutions suggested by experienced personnel and present alternative courses of action. In addition, an expert system can increase the knowledge normally acquired by people through experience. For example, a new intern working in a free clinic would not have the resources or experts found in a hospital. An expert system would expand the intern's own knowledge base by identifying rare illnesses and suggesting possible treatments.

Decision-support systems, like an expert system, do not make final decisions; they only display logical alternatives. The actual decision making is left to people. The idea is to design a system that can draw from a wide variety of specialized data. Users simply would need to ask the right questions.

A Closer Look...

Developing an Expert System

Expert system developers, known as *knowledge engineers,* are finding it difficult to quantify the knowledge of human experts. When asked to describe how decisions are made, people often find it impossible to identify all of the factors involved. Human experts base their decisions on years of experience as well as formal education. As a result, expert systems are costly and difficult to create because identifying all of the facts and recognizing the relationships between those facts is very time consuming. What follows are common questions people have about how expert systems are developed and tested.

Q When is it practical to develop an expert system?

A Expert systems are developed when there is a high demand for limited human resources, that is, experts. At other times, organizations develop expert systems when critical decision makers near retirement age.

Q Who decides what is in a knowledge base?

A The expert works with a knowledge engineer, reviewing problems to decide what is needed in the knowledge base. The knowledge engineer adds the data to the knowledge base, and the expert checks to see if it works properly. If not, changes are suggested and they try again.

Q What type of problems are best handled by expert systems?

A Expert systems work best in clearly defined domain areas. Repairing and maintaining a specific robot would be a practical expert system application. However, developing an expert system to make repair and maintenance decisions for all the equipment in the factory would be impractical with today's tecnology.

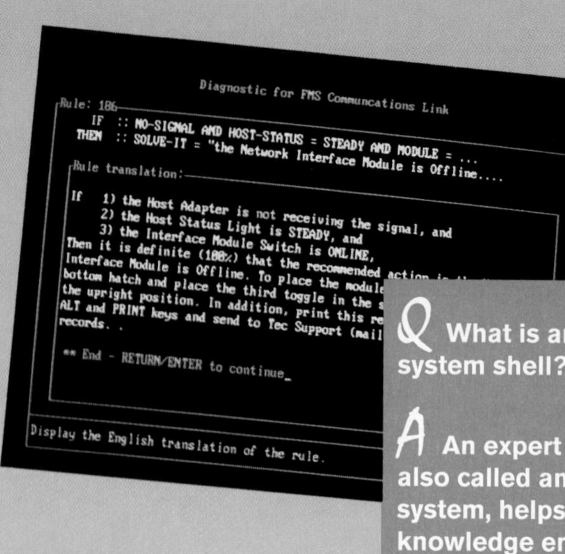

Diagnostic for FMS Communcations Link
Rule: 186
IF :: NO-SIGNAL AND HOST-STATUS = STEADY AND MODULE = ...
THEN :: SOLVE-IT = "the Network Interface Module is Offline....
Rule translation:
If 1) the Host Adapter is not receiving the signal, and
2) the Host Status Light is STEADY, and
3) the Interface Module Switch is ONLINE,
Then it is definite (100%) that the recommended
Interface Module is Offline. To place the
bottom hatch and place the third toggle in the
the upright position. In addition, print this
ALT and PRINT keys and send to Tec Support
records. .
** End - RETURN/ENTER to continue
Display the English translation of the rule.

Q What is an expert system shell?

A An expert system shell, also called an authoring system, helps the knowledge engineer create a customized user interface for a new expert system along with loading data and data relationships into the knowledge base.

Q How do you test an expert system?

A There are two levels of testing. First-level tests are performed on problems the expert has encountered and solved in the past. Second-level tests are performed on new, real-life problems with the expert present to second-guess the system and confirm solutions before they are implemented.

Q Is special computer equipment needed?

A Expert systems can be developed and run on personal computer systems. Ideally, these systems have fast processing speeds and large amounts of disk storage space.

Chapter Facts

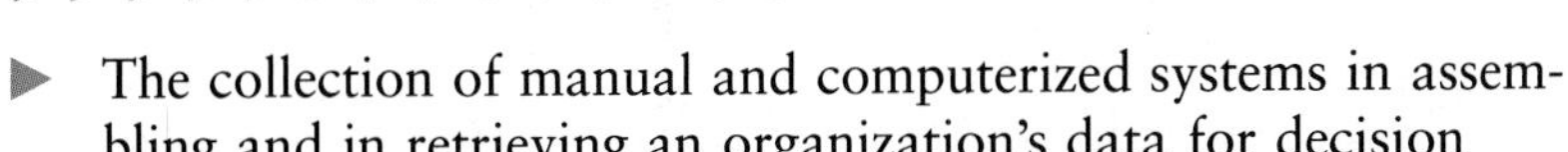

- The collection of manual and computerized systems in assembling and in retrieving an organization's data for decision making is called its management information system (MIS).
- In any organization, management's role is to solve problems, plan events, and supervise people. Management has three levels: front-line management, middle management, and top management or executives.
- Front-line managers make operational decisions about daily transactions. They use detailed reports to show information about each transaction.
- Middle management makes tactical decisions about short-range problems, using summary and exception reports about the organization.
- Top management makes strategic long-range decisions that have far-reaching effects. They use summary and exception reports to show organizational trends.
- Managerial data can be organized into financial, personnel, research, and production/sales groups.
- A decision-support system (DSS) is a real-time computer system that includes modeling software and queries for data retrieval. It is used for long-term decision making.
- Modeling is the mathematical representation of a problem. One way of finding an optimum solution is through linear programming, which uses precise definitions of problem goals and constraints.
- Queries retrieve data to answer "What if?" questions posed by decision makers.
- Materials requirement planning (MRP) applications allow management to schedule the purchase and delivery of supplies in a way that minimizes the money invested in inventory. MRP supports just-in-time inventory systems.
- Management-level decisions are made by self-directed work teams that use group decision-support systems to coordinate the flow of ideas and information between team members.
- Statistical process control (SPC) procedures help organizations maintain high levels of quality control by using statistical analysis of production/sales data to identify potential problems.

- An organization-wide commitment to customer satisfaction through quality control of services and products is known as total quality management.
- Expert systems combine a knowledge base with retrieval and decision-making software. They concentrate in one specific area of knowledge and "learn" by storing the conclusions they draw.

Terms to Remember

a. backward chaining
b. decision-support system (DSS)
c. executive information system
d. expert system
e. financial data
f. forward chaining
g. front-line management
h. inference engine
i. knowledge base
j. management information system (MIS)
k. materials requirement planning (MRP)
l. middle management
m. model
n. operational decision
o. personnel data
p. production/sales data
q. quality control
r. research data
s. self-directed work team
t. statistical process control (SPC)
u. strategic decision
v. tactical decision
w. top management
x. total quality management
y. transaction processing system

Mix and Match

Match the following definitions to the Terms to Remember.

1. ____ group of people who have been empowered to make management decisions to solve a specific problem.
2. ____ contains the facts, data relationships, and probabilities of occurrences used by expert system.
3. ____ short-term decisions made by middle managers.
4. ____ real-time computer system that aids managers in solving problems through data retrieval and modeling.

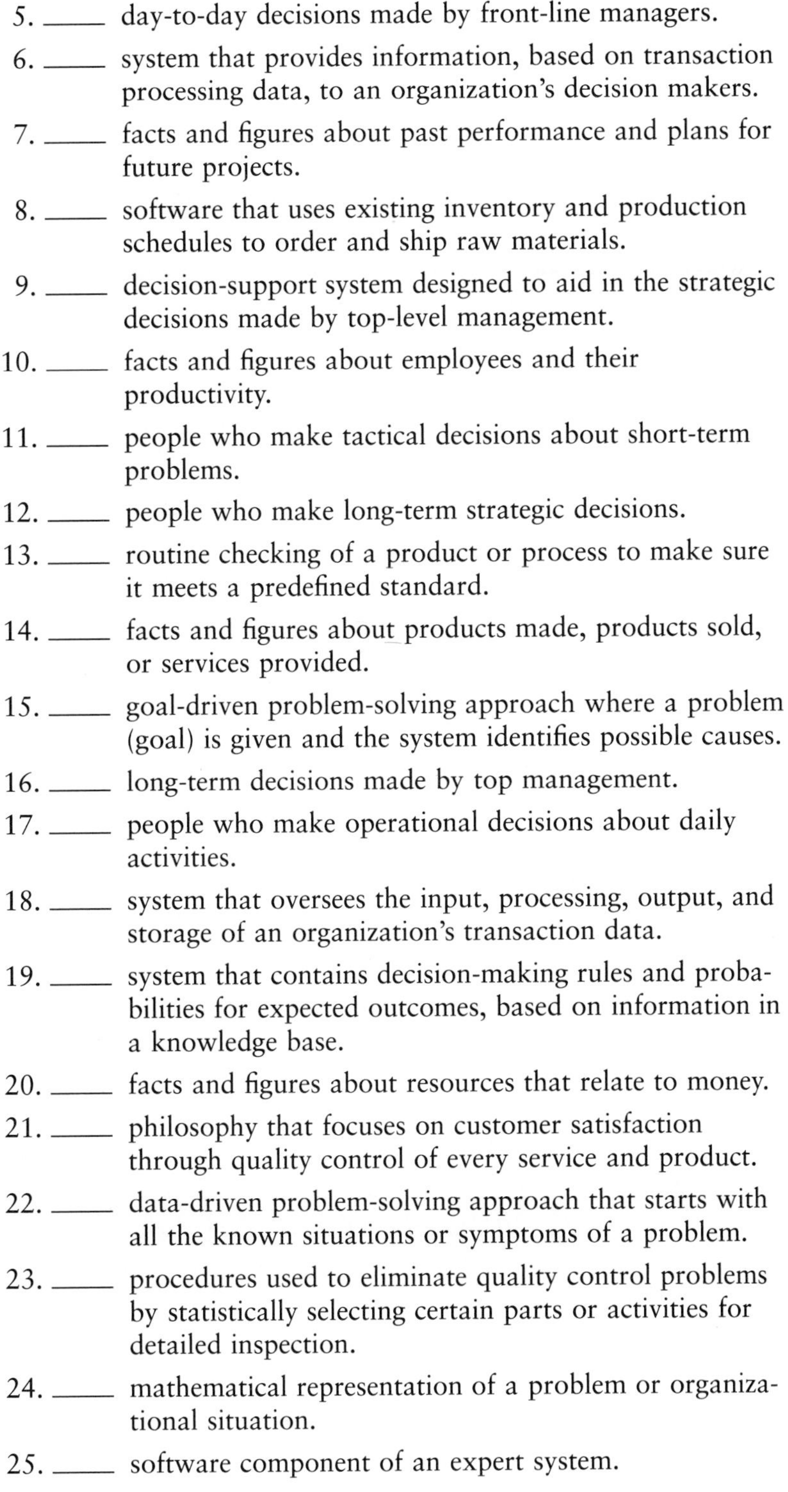

5. ____ day-to-day decisions made by front-line managers.
6. ____ system that provides information, based on transaction processing data, to an organization's decision makers.
7. ____ facts and figures about past performance and plans for future projects.
8. ____ software that uses existing inventory and production schedules to order and ship raw materials.
9. ____ decision-support system designed to aid in the strategic decisions made by top-level management.
10. ____ facts and figures about employees and their productivity.
11. ____ people who make tactical decisions about short-term problems.
12. ____ people who make long-term strategic decisions.
13. ____ routine checking of a product or process to make sure it meets a predefined standard.
14. ____ facts and figures about products made, products sold, or services provided.
15. ____ goal-driven problem-solving approach where a problem (goal) is given and the system identifies possible causes.
16. ____ long-term decisions made by top management.
17. ____ people who make operational decisions about daily activities.
18. ____ system that oversees the input, processing, output, and storage of an organization's transaction data.
19. ____ system that contains decision-making rules and probabilities for expected outcomes, based on information in a knowledge base.
20. ____ facts and figures about resources that relate to money.
21. ____ philosophy that focuses on customer satisfaction through quality control of every service and product.
22. ____ data-driven problem-solving approach that starts with all the known situations or symptoms of a problem.
23. ____ procedures used to eliminate quality control problems by statistically selecting certain parts or activities for detailed inspection.
24. ____ mathematical representation of a problem or organizational situation.
25. ____ software component of an expert system.

Review Questions

1. What are the roles of management in an organization?
2. What types of decisions and problems do the three levels of management handle?
3. What types of reports do the different levels of management need to perform their jobs?
4. What is an advantage and a disadvantage to using linear programming models?
5. How are models and queries used as part of decision-support systems?
6. What determines an organization's mix of management and decision-support software?
7. How does materials requirement planning support just-in-time inventory?
8. How can self-directed work teams use a group decision-support system?
9. Why would some people prefer to use a group decision-support system than to physically attend a group meeting?
10. Why is quality control important?
11. Identify the three components of an expert system and explain how each works.
12. How can expert systems assist experienced and inexperienced people?
13. Why are expert systems difficult to develop?
14. What types of problems are expert systems designed to handle?
15. When is it practical to develop an expert system?

Applying What You've Learned

1. Computers are involved in almost every aspect of an organization's decision making. What type of organization may not need a computer at the present time? If this organization continues to grow, will it be possible for it to exist without a computer in the future? Explain.
2. Pick an organization with which you are familiar. It can be a business, school, or volunteer agency. Name three examples

for each type of data available from an MIS. Describe what might be contained on typical detailed, exception, and summary reports for that organization.

3. MIS and DSS are currently under much discussion in many organizations. Each is difficult to describe precisely, and few people agree on exactly what each should contain. Find an article on either MIS or DSS. Summarize the article and list any new terminology used. How do the concepts presented in the article apply to school, your workplace, or other familiar organizations?
4. With each level of management come different responsibilities and rewards. Interview or read about a person at one of the three management levels. What are the benefits? What kinds of stress and deadlines exist? How far-reaching are the decisions he or she makes and how much responsibility must the manager take if the decision is wrong? What tools does this manager use to help him or her make decisions?
5. A decision support system or expert system provides assistance to decision makers, but actually it does not make the decision. In your chosen career field what types of decisions may be aided by the large base of data available on a DSS or expert system? Are there any decisions that should rely solely on human efforts?
6. Imagine you are an "expert" being interviewed to provide information for a knowledge base. After picking an area of interest to you, list ten different types of data that would have to be included in the knowledge base. For each type of data, name a possible source of that information. Also, list five different types of decisions an expert system in that field should be able to analyze.
7. Statistical process control is being used with a variety of processes. Make a list of five places where SPC could be employed. What production/sales data is used by the system? How would the data be collected?
8. Compare and contrast forward and backward chaining approaches to finding connecting flights from New York to Chicago and then Chicago to Los Angeles.

Answers to Mix and Match

1. s 2. i 3. v 4. b 5. n 6. j 7. r 8. k 9. c 10. o
11. l 12. w 13. q 14. p 15. a 16. u 17. g 18. y
19. d 20. e 21. x 22. f 23. t 24. m 25. h

13

System Design and Implementation

- **From the User's Point of View**
- **Handling Information Problems**
  - Designing new systems
  - System life cycle
- **Life-Cycle Step One: Requirements**
  - Initial review
  - Feasibility study
  - Requirements for a personal computer system
- **Life-Cycle Step Two: Alternative Evaluation**
  - Identifying alternatives
  - Selecting the best alternative
  - Alternatives for a personal computer system
- **Life-Cycle Step Three: Design**
  - Design techniques
  - Hardware
  - Programs
  - Data and procedures
  - People
  - Designing a personal computer system
- **Life-Cycle Step Four: Implementation**
  - Construction and testing
  - Installation
  - Evaluation
  - Maintenance
  - Set-up and maintenance of a personal computer system
- *A Closer Look . . . Project Management Software*

FROM THE USER'S POINT OF VIEW

The chances are good that one day you will need to purchase a small computer system. Historically, systems development was a process that centered on the acquisition or replacement of a mainframe computer system. Many of the lessons computer professionals apply when designing computer systems for businesses can also be applied to purchasing personal computer systems. In fact, the steps in system development are basically the same for the design of any system: a new house, baseball team, formal garden, or personal computer system.

HANDLING INFORMATION PROBLEMS

Computers can introduce a valuable but expensive technology to organizations. Managers may have to learn to think differently before their organizations can realize the potential value of computers. When we look at earlier developments in designing new systems, we can appreciate the extent of change required to harness the power of computers.

Designing New Systems

When the first production computers were introduced in the 1950s, they represented a substantial investment in an unproven, although promising, technology. Computer hardware at this time cost millions of dollars. Developing the software needed to operate the computers required a large investment of time, money, and personnel. However, there was really no choice. Large organizations were finding it impossible to keep up with the information-processing and paperwork requirements of the post-World War II economic expansion.

The computer obviously held the potential solution, but computer technology was too formidable for most managers. As a result, the technology could be utilized only through a new breed of technicians who spoke the language of computers. These computer professionals, for their part, had virtually no understanding of organizational problems or needs. A communication gap formed, which hindered the matching of computer applications and their prospective users.

Developing information systems for computer processing was a major undertaking. The amounts of data involved and the complexity of programs proved formidable. Experienced project managers found some similarities between the activities required to develop a computer system and those associated with the creation and implementation of new products and services. However, comparatively few organizations had experience with systems of this scope.

Because of communication and technological obstacles, many early attempts to develop large computer systems resulted in disaster. One common problem centered around the development of advanced systems that failed to solve the initial data processing problems. This was a major result of the lack of communication between managers and technicians.

Another type of unpleasant surprise came in the form of costs for these **systems development projects.** The steps taken to define and create new system solutions to existing problems demanded time and money. A major airline reservation system developed during the 1950s, for example, was reported to have overrun its original budget by some $40 million. Initial systems for processing checks and deposit slips in banks experienced even greater cost overruns.

System Life Cycle

Once the obstacles in system development were identified, methods for bridging the communication gap were not far behind. A number of organizations devised project development techniques similar to those successful in the defense and aerospace industries. Also, at about this time, the same methods were being used to manage a project aimed at putting an American astronaut on the moon (Figure 13.1).

The method is simple and proven. Any major systems project will involve solving problems that cannot be known or understood completely in advance. There are just too many details associated with a major project. To make projects of this type manageable, the

FIGURE 13.1
The life-cycle approach to systems development was applied to coordinate complex tasks like landing people on the moon.

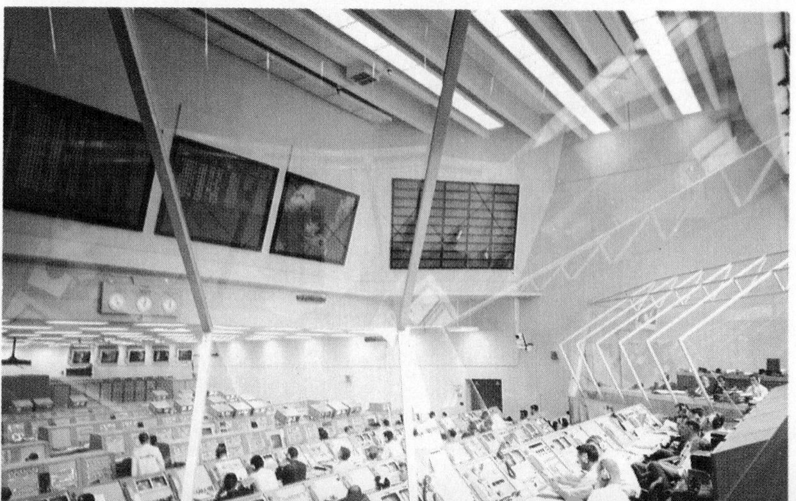

overall job is broken into a series of small activities. These subsets of the problem are small enough to be understood and planned. In the case of space exploration, a different scientific team was assigned to each major area of research: space vehicle structures, life support systems, radiation shielding, navigation, propulsion systems, and so forth.

Similar thinking led computer specialists to devise a project design structure, also known as a *life cycle,* that partitions the job of developing a system into a series of parts, or steps. Management then can understand and monitor projects on a step-by-step basis, taking care to avoid situations in which designs fail to solve problems or major cost overruns occur. As a special precaution, the life-cycle methodology requires users and organizational managers to be involved in the development process.

Users contribute to the process by specifying their needs and reviewing proposed solutions stated in terms they can understand. Top managers review progress at each step in the project. Reports to top managers make it possible to approve the project for further development, to cancel the commitment, or to amend the mission of the project at several junctures along the way. The establishment of control, in turn, provides a framework that promotes effective communication and understanding.

Project control methods are standard within most organizations that develop computer information systems. However, the standards tend to be individualized. That is, each organization generally establishes project structures and reporting requirements to solve the problems defined by its management. The life-cycle or project structure in each organization differs from that of every other organization. This is dictated by the size of the organization, the scope of the problem, and the type of equipment used. Small organizations and individuals that use personal computers have needs different from larger organizations, with minicomputers or mainframes. Nonetheless, there are common requirements for systems development projects (see Figure 13.2). The description of the life cycle presented in the remainder of this chapter is based on those common factors.

A typical life-cycle structure used to guide the development of a computer information system can be organized into the following four steps:

- Requirements
- Alternative evaluation
- Design
- Implementation

Each major step can be broken into a series of phases that are more specific in nature.

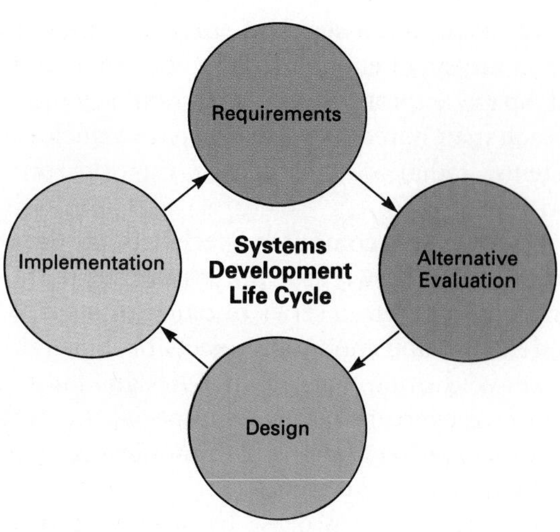

FIGURE 13.2
Systems development conforms to a four-step life cycle that involves defining requirements, evaluating alternatives, design, and implementation.

LIFE-CYCLE STEP ONE: REQUIREMENTS

To avoid developing systems that fail to solve the identified problems, virtually all life cycles begin by defining system requirements. This initial phase tends to be relatively informal and also short in duration. It includes both an initial review of the project goals and a study of the feasibility of reaching those goals (see Figure 13.3).

Initial Review

Systems development should begin with a user request, or at least with close user involvement. Ideally, users who have gained some sophistication with computer capabilities are the first to identify a problem. One or more users develop a formal request (in writing), which is reviewed by the organization's systems development group. Sometimes the systems development process is initiated when employees bring to the computer center manager an idea for improving the existing system or information about new computer software. In an organization that does not have systems development professionals, a user/developer or an outside consultant may investigate a problem and its possible solutions.

The problem or idea is discussed, and a systems analyst—a specialist in computer systems development—is assigned to perform an *initial review.* During this review the analyst interviews users to identify the source of a problem, trying to determine if the problem has a computer-based solution. Sometimes the problem involves lack of procedures or poor management and can be corrected without a new computer solution. If the issue is looking at new software, the analyst will review what the software does and its role in the existing system.

Regardless of the starting point, the initial review is devoted primarily to the analysis of user operations and responsibilities in the specific area being studied. Users are responsible for helping the systems analyst understand the basic operations involved in how the system presently works. Users must also identify the problems, opportunities, and benefits resulting from application of a computer to the issue under study.

Once the user has done this, the systems analyst can make a preliminary estimate of the time and cost involved in implementing the initial idea. The user-identified benefits then can be compared with the costs estimated by the analyst. The analyst's findings are written into the initial review within a couple of weeks and presented to management. At this time MIS managers or other tactical decision makers decide whether the idea has enough merit to pursue an in-depth feasibility study.

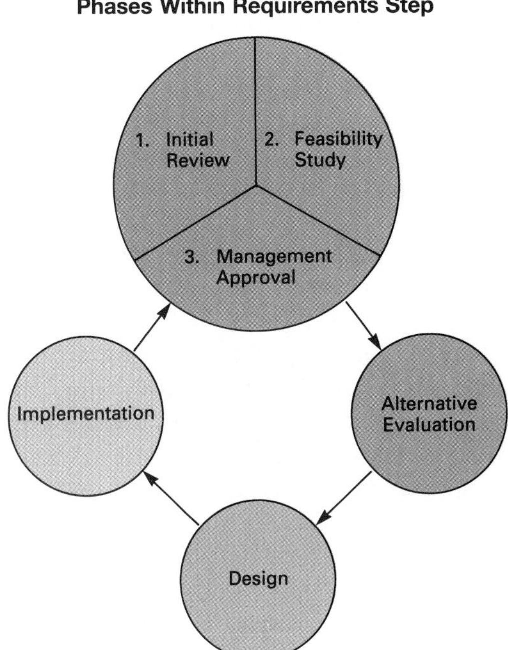

FIGURE 13.3
The requirements step focuses on clearly identifying the problem to be solved.

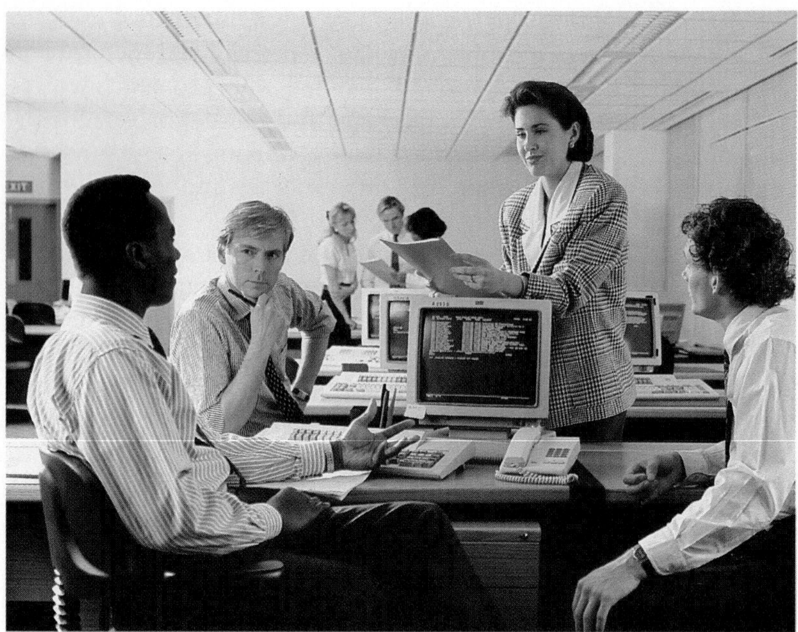

FIGURE 13.4
One way of collecting data for a feasibility study is to have members of the application development team observe and interview users.

Feasibility Study

In the second requirement phase a **feasibility study** is conducted. This study determines whether the project is realistic in terms of time, costs, and resources. Additional users and analysts become involved as part of an **application development team.** This team is responsible for carrying out the systems development project, including the design and implementation of the new system. They gather enough information to define and describe user operations in terms of volumes of transactions, number of people involved, turnaround or deadline requirements, uses for accumulated data, methods of data storage, current problems, and opportunities for improvement.

The main techniques for data gathering are questionnaires, interviews, observations, data flow diagrams, and collecting sample documents. Questionnaires are employed when a large number of users must be involved with a feasibility study. When managers or key people are involved, personal interviews are conducted. Observations and sample documents help team members identify where data originates and where it is used in an organization. The resulting **data flow diagram** (see Figure 13.5) provides a visual representation of how the data and people interact.

At this point the team concentrates on the main applications and work assignments. Experienced analysts follow a well-known guideline: the rule of 80–20. This means that, in any system, 20

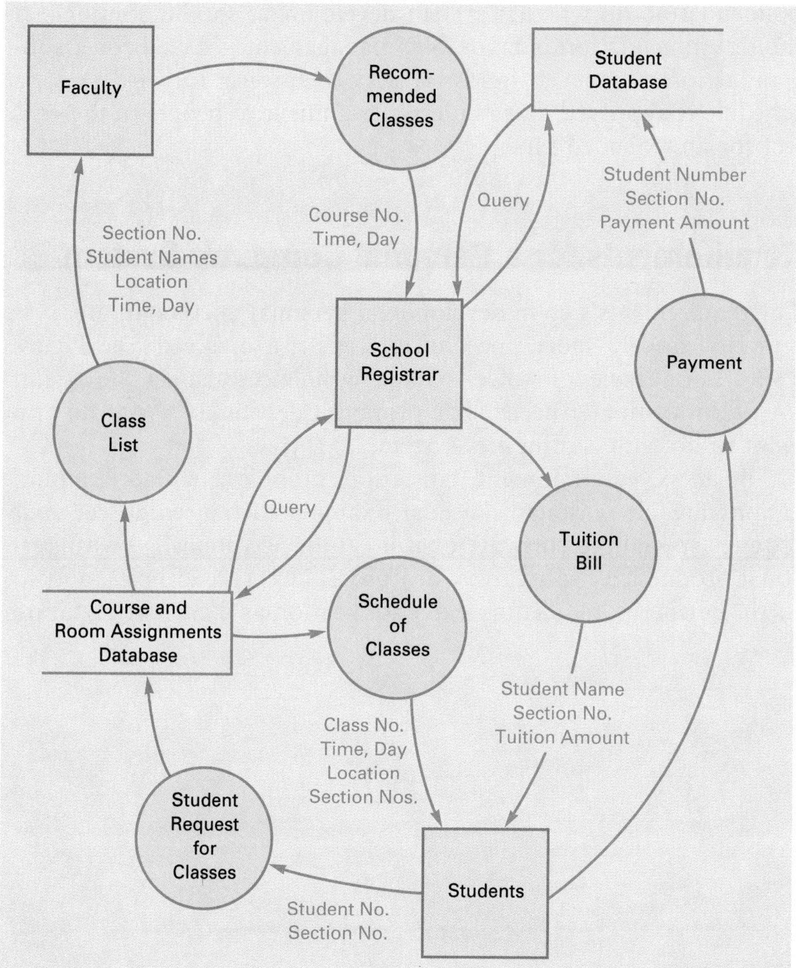

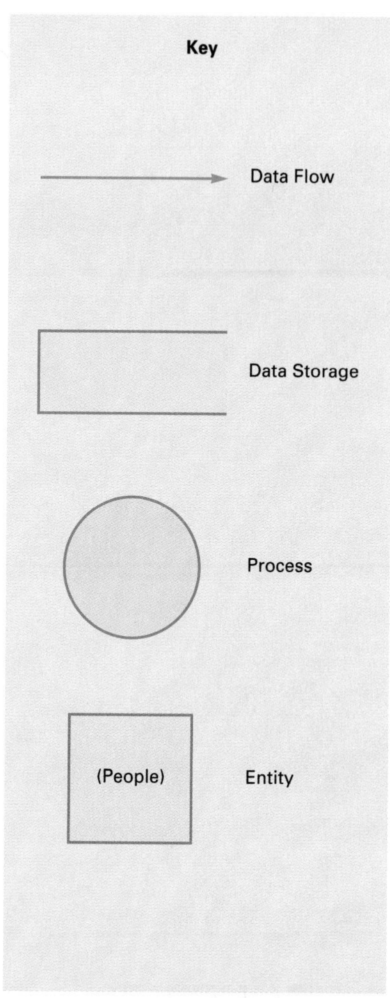

FIGURE 13.5
Data flow diagrams show the movement and processing of data items throughout an application. Circles show a process and boxes show entities, like people, who are involved with the process. Lines and arrows identify how data flows within the application, while open-ended rectangles indicate data storage.

percent of the documents or tasks will represent 80 percent of the work. An important skill for analysts, then, lies in recognizing and concentrating on the 20 percent of the activities and processes that are the key to any system.

The team gains enough knowledge of operations so that it can develop initial plans about the computer equipment to be used, the storage space required, the number of people who will be involved, the overall design or specifications for required programs, and any procedures or training required.

A result of a feasibility study should be a preliminary budget and schedule for the project. These estimates will be refined as part of Step Two: Alternative Evaluation. However, experienced computer professionals should be able to estimate costs and benefits close enough so that managers can make informed decisions. The feasibility report delivered at the end of this phase provides a recommendation on whether system development should continue. If the recommendation is favorable, management is asked for a substantial commitment of funds to carry the project forward. Also, a schedule is approved that requests assignment of people to the project for an extended time.

Requirements for a Personal Computer System

The requirements step in developing a personal microcomputer system is relatively short since fewer users are involved (see Figure 13.6). Initial review involves balancing finances against short- and long-term computer needs. The primary question is "What do you want to do with a computer system?"

Business, entertainment, education, graphics, or telecommunications are all reasonable needs. Examine each need to see if it requires specialized software or if it can be accomplished with personal productivity software: word processing, spreadsheets, and so forth. Furthermore, identify each application as a current or future

In the News...

A PROPERLY PLANNED INTERVIEW CAN BE AN ANALYST'S BEST TOOL

While the methods of obtaining useful information from the user vary greatly, the personal interview will bring the best results and best understanding, if conducted properly.

An important key to excellent interviewing skills is the ability of the analyst to prepare to deal with the different personalities and attitudes of the people being interviewed. If the analyst can modify personal style to complement the personality of the interviewee, then a channel of communication will be established that will allow ideas to be effectively communicated and the needed information to be obtained.

Studies indicate that verbal messages convey 7%, intonations convey 38%, and body language conveys 55% of the total message. Body language is the key factor, and the alert and well-informed analyst and interviewer should take advantage of this fact during the interview.

Listening has specific goals as they relate to the interviewee as an employee:

1. To raise the level of employee motivation.
2. To increase the readiness of subordinates to accept change.
3. To improve the quality of all managerial decisions.
4. To develop teamwork and morale.

Active listening is characterized by a nonjudgemental attempt on one person's part to allow the other person to explore a problem. Use of body language that encourages openness and acceptance should motivate the employee to participate in the interview more fully, and this should be the interviewer's goal in obtaining information. As with other attitudes, openness encourages similar feelings.

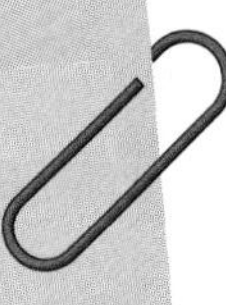

Requirements for a Personal Computer System

1. Identify needs and initial review of finances
2. Personal productivity software vs. specialized software
   a. business
   b. education
   c. graphics
   d. entertainment
   e. telecommunications
3. Location of equipment
   a. electrical outlets
   b. work space
   c. security
4. Who will be using the new system?

FIGURE 13.6
Purchasing a personal computer requires examining finances, needs, and potential locations for using the system once it is set up.

need, since you may be purchasing the system in stages. The general rule at this point is to dream a little. You will quickly become practical as your budget limits the scope of your initial purchase.

Most of the time a personal computer system will not be used by just one individual. List everyone who will have access to the new computer system and see if their needs are included in the initial review. Finally, think about where the computer system will be used. Is there sufficient workspace in this area? Are there enough electrical outlets to power a computer, monitor, printer, etc.? Is the location secure and out of a high-foot-traffic area? By carefully thinking through these concerns, you insure that all of your requirements for the new computer system are included.

LIFE-CYCLE STEP TWO: ALTERNATIVE EVALUATION

The initial step that defines requirements covers the entire scope of the proposed project, including all problems and benefits that can be foreseen. Each succeeding step does the same, but in greater depth. That is, users and computer professionals review the same application repeatedly, in more detail each time. At each step the development team gains a more detailed, clearer view of the problems and methods of solution. The second step involves identifying alternatives and then selecting the best alternative for fulfilling the system requirements (see Figure 13.7).

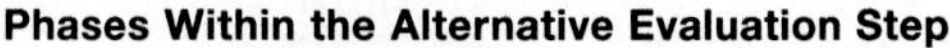

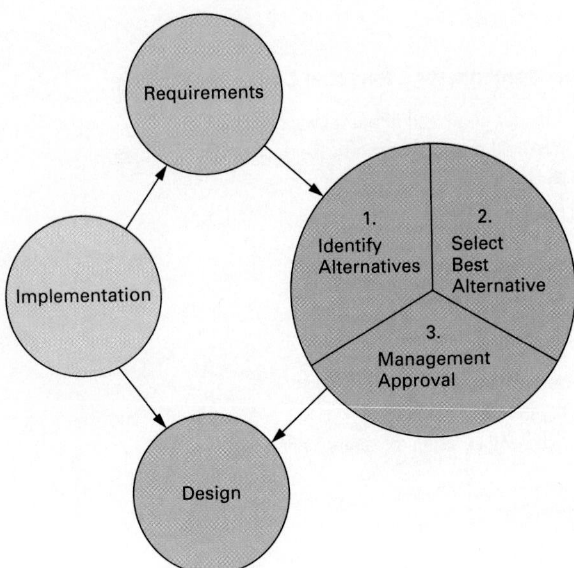

FIGURE 13.7
During the alternative evaluation, every reasonable solution to the problem is examined before a recommendation is made to management.

Identifying Alternatives

A new systems development project affects all five components of a computer system in some way. Even if some components are not directly changed, the systems analyst must examine each to see how it influences the other system components.

When examining available solutions for solving the problem, the applications development team must include a wide range of alternatives. The team tries to describe viable alternatives that meet the requirements defined in the first life-cycle step. Each alternative must specifically address all five components of a computer system. The alternatives will differ by how system components are acquired or modified. This does not necessarily mean that new computer hardware or software will be purchased. Many times, changes in existing procedures or personnel will solve the problem. The systems development process is iterative (repeats). As each component is examined, requirements for the others may change.

For example, a hospital that establishes a new outpatient clinic at a remote location can consider several alternatives. The new clinic can be connected to the hospital's mainframe by adding teleprocessing capabilities, can retain its own client/server network, or can hire an outside agency (**service bureau**) to handle its data processing needs. As shown in Figure 13.8, each of these alternatives, in turn, would require a different mix of personnel, peripherals, software, data organization, and procedures.

Alternatives for a New Outpatient Clinic*

System Component	Alternative 1: Client/Server Network	Alternative 2: Connect to Hospital's Mainframe	Alternative 3: Hire Service Bureau
Hardware	Server, Personal computers, Printers, Network cabling	Terminals, Concentrators Lease telephone line	Service Bureau provides hardware
Programs	Network programs and new applications programs	Use existing programs maintained by hospital	Service Bureau provides programs
Data	Create new files/databases	Use hospital's database	Create new files for every application or create a database
Procedures	Operating, Maintenance, Backup, Data collection, Emergency/Troubleshooting	Data collection Emergency/troubleshooting	Data collection
People	Train existing staff as users Hire and train network/ database administrator	Train existing staff as users	Train existing staff as users

*Note: Cost/benefit analysis and list of intangibles not included

FIGURE 13.8
Identification of alternative solutions to meet the needs of a new system is an important part of the systems development process. Three alternatives are illustrated here.

Not all systems development projects require new hardware. Sometimes it is just a matter of deciding which personal productivity software to use to solve the problem. A large law firm may decide to standardize the word processing packages used by its offices across the country. In this case the computer hardware already exists, and the consulting systems analyst would need to poll the legal secretaries and paraprofessionals to define software requirements. Although the data and hardware would not be affected by the new software, participating personnel must be trained and new procedures written for them. The alternatives would be selected from off-the-shelf word processing software.

Selecting the Best Alternative

Once the alternatives have been selected, the next phase is to pick the one that best solves the problem. In a report to management, alternatives are described in detail along with a **cost/benefit analysis,** which identifies the associated costs and benefits for each alternative. The team also lists its recommendation as to which alternative is the best. This alternative is not always the least expensive

Who's Who

Charles Babbage (1791–1871)

Some time prior to 1822, Charles Babbage and his friend, John Herschel, were checking data calculated manually for the Astronomical Society, when the pair found many errors. In frustration, Babbage remarked to Herschel, "I wish to God these calculations had been executed by steam!" Steam engines were a common source of power in Babbage's day. He began work on a solution. The outcome of the scientist's efforts was a blueprint for the "difference engine." Composed of gears and wheels, the difference engine would compute functions in the form

$$y = a + bx + cx^2 + \cdots + gx^6$$

His work was funded by the British government, but Babbage was never able to complete the difference engine. While he was working on that project, he designed a new device, the "analytical engine." This machine was designed to compute any mathematical function, in any form. While trying to spread word of his inventions, he met the Countess of Lovelace.

Babbage's design for the analytical engine used many ideas now found in modern computers. The "engine" contained a "store" for numeric data that had room for 1000 variables of 50 digits each. Arithmetic operations were done in the "mill." Programs for the mill were to be written on punched cards. The "engine" would perform logical operations by ringing a bell when a variable went below zero or above capacity. The machine also was intended to drive a typesetter for output. All operations were to work mechanically. Unfortunately, Babbage did not finish any of his inventions. He was always flitting between projects and changing specifications—an example of classic errors in the system design process. Just recently, working models of several of his inventions were finally built.

or the easiest to implement. The best alternative must be one that provides the most effective solution to the problem. When this objective is met by several alternatives, cost and time requirements then become deciding factors.

If management is presented with alternatives ranging from the easiest and least expensive to more complex and expensive solutions, they will probably support the team's decision since management knows what alternatives have been rejected. Also, management must consider the hidden or intangible costs and benefits for alternatives. Employee satisfaction or stress, increased availability of management information, and improved customer service are intangible costs and benefits. They may not be classified in dollar terms but are still important to consider. For example, the installation of a new computer system in a department store during the Christmas rush may be most effective in solving a processing problem, but such a solution could be stressful to already harried employees.

The final action in this step is to obtain management approval of the alternative selected by the development team. Projections of costs and benefits will be considered reliable if they are supported by both users and computer professionals. At this time, schedules and budget projections are reaffirmed as management approves the start of the design step. However, it is possible for management to reject the proposal at this point. They may request that another alternative be investigated more thoroughly or dismiss the project altogether if conditions within the organization have changed.

FIGURE 13.9
The alternatives are presented to management for approval along with their comparative costs and benefits.

Alternatives for a Personal Computer System

When examining alternatives for a personal computer system, remember "software drives hardware." In other words, the software you select determines hardware requirements. For instance, minimum internal memory requirements and choice of operating system are dictated by software selection. Some alternatives are just a matter of personal choice—the keyboard layout, for instance. On the other hand, most computer professionals agree that a minimum of two disk drives should be available to simplify copying and backup procedures (see Figure 13.10).

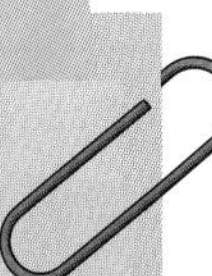

Alternatives for a Personal Computer System

1. Software drives hardware (what do you really need?)
2. Identify necessary system components
   - a. minimum memory
   - b. operating system
   - c. keyboard layout
   - d. two disk drives
   - e. minimum expansion slots
3. Performance vs. price considerations for system components
   - a. hard disk drive
   - b. color vs. monochrome screen
   - c. graphics
   - d. speed of processor
   - e. potential multitasking capabilities
   - f. modem
4. Cost vs. benefits
   - a. intangible costs (learning to operate new software and hardware)
   - b. hidden costs
     - floppy disks
     - printer paper
     - printer ribbons and cartridges
   - c. intangible benefits
     - increased personal productivity
     - competitive edge

FIGURE 13.10
Before purchasing a personal computer system, hardware and software performance must be weighed against price.

At this juncture you must weigh the costs of software and hardware against the benefits. High-speed computers with multitasking capabilities will cost more than slower machines and may not be suitable for your needs. Can you cost-justify a high-capacity hard disk at this time, or will a lower-capacity disk drive suffice? How important are portability, sound, and data communications? Do you need a high-speed laser printer, or can you get by with a draft-quality dot-matrix printer? Internal expansion slots on a personal computer's motherboard provide an opportunity to later add system components you cannot afford at this time. Make sure you have enough expansion slots to accommodate future peripheral purchases.

Personal computer systems do include intangible costs and benefits. While your system may eventually increase your productivity, it will take time to familiarize yourself with new software and hard-

In the News...

HOW SECURE IS "IT"?

Level D—Minimal Protection: no built in security.

Level C1—Discretionary Security Protection: systems provide separation of users and data. Access limitations can be enforced.

Level C2—Controlled Access Protection: makes users individually accountable for their actions through log-in procedures and audit trails. Where most commercial systems fail.

Level B1—Labeled Security Protection: all the protection of the C2 level. In addition, access control beyond password protection, labeling of files with sensitivity levels, and a restriction on the reuse of data by multiple users are required.

Level B2—Structured Protection: B2 level protection is extended to all system resources. B2 systems are classified as "relatively resistant to penetration." Systems must be structured from the outset to be penetration resistant. Stringent configuration management and system administration controls must be present.

Level B3—Security Domains: B3 systems must exclude any code that is not essential to security policy enforcement. Additionally, B3 systems must be designed to be "highly resistant to penetration" and engineered to minimize system complexity.

Level A1—Verified Protection: functionally equivalent to B3 systems. But A1 systems must be formally documented, and the security policy of the system must be proven—mathematically if need be—to be consistent with stated security goals. Also, a formal analysis must be done to identify and analyze any "covert" methods of entry into the system.

ware. New equipment may require new office furniture or perhaps some remodeling work. Hidden ongoing costs include purchasing disks, paper, and printer supplies. You must realize you will spend as much on software and incidentals as you will on hardware. The result of the alternative evaluation step is to complete a list of hardware and software features, without specifying particular brand names.

LIFE-CYCLE STEP THREE: DESIGN

The purpose of the design step is explained best by the end product that marks its completion. Typically, this step concludes with the acceptance of a document called **system specifications.** This is a description that covers, in enough detail to satisfy both management and users, all of the requirements and procedures to be incorporated in the new system.

Included in the system specifications will be designs and samples of all of the transaction forms, input screens, and output documents to be produced. Also included will be descriptions of the procedures to be followed by all involved personnel, as well as related functions and services to be provided by computer professionals. Equipment to be installed is described in general without specific makes and model numbers of devices (see Figure 13.11).

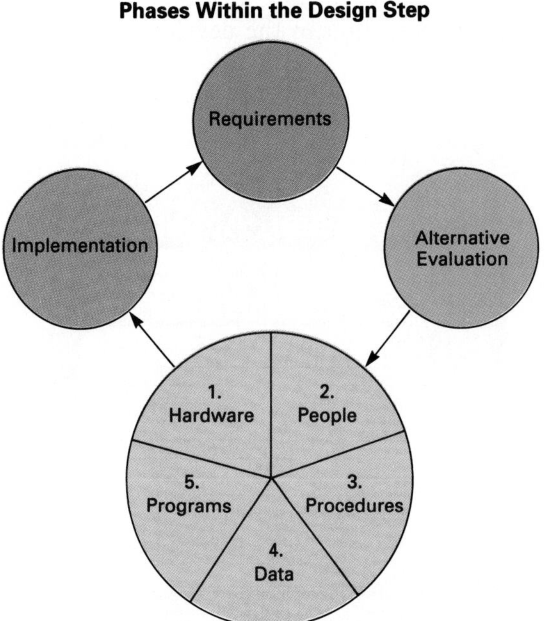

FIGURE 13.11
Each component of a new computer system must be examined as part of the design step.

Design Techniques

To aid in creating and managing the different aspects of an involved system design, two design techniques have been developed: prototyping and CASE. These techniques differ in scope, but their usefulness has made them necessary additions to the repertoire of the systems analyst.

Prototyping

In the design process, models of screens for data input and reports for output need to be mocked up for user and management approval. Since the programs supporting I/O are not necessary at this stage, systems analysts have used pencil sketches or typed samples. Recently, software packages have been developed that specialize in **prototyping,** the modeling or simulation of user interfaces. Prototyping tools give systems analysts the ability to mock up an input screen, complete with menus, windows, help screens, and highlighting. Users input sample data into the prototype, as seen in Figure 13.12. Although the data would not be processed, trying the model gives users a realistic idea of what data input would involve. Any changes users suggest to the screen format can be easily implemented with the prototype software. Sample reports, output screens, and other forms of user interaction with the system can be simulated. With prototyping tools, a systems analyst can model all or just part of a proposed system.

The advantages of prototyping are obvious. It enables users to see exactly what to expect and invites them to become involved with the design of the system. The ease of using prototyping allows fine tuning of user interfaces until they please everyone involved. This eliminates costly changes later in the development process.

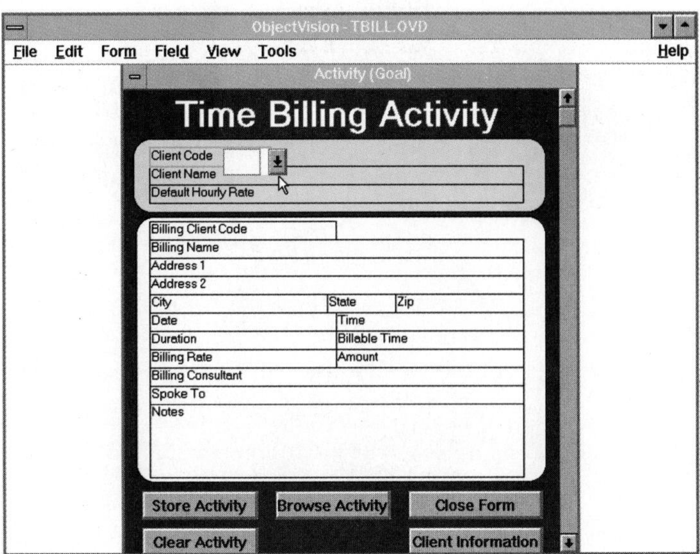

FIGURE 13.12
This prototype allows people to interact with new user interface very early in the design step.

There are some disadvantages to prototyping, especially when users are not well informed. First, the prototype of a report, for example, is just a model and should not be interpreted as a signal that the new report is ready to use. Second, the ease with which changes can be made to a prototype does not reflect the work involved in producing the actual screen or report. Any changes to user interfaces need to be made at the design step, not when the new system is being installed or tested. Third, what users may find desirable in a prototype may be too costly or time consuming to include in the system. Systems analysts and managers must be aware of the pitfalls in using prototyping as well as its benefits to the users.

CASE Tools

While prototyping aids in designing the user interfaces, **CASE (Computer Aided Software Engineering) tools** are software packages that facilitate management of the entire systems development process. Each CASE tool is a program used by computer professionals for a different aspect of the systems development project. For example, CASE tools exist to assist in conducting feasibility studies, developing project descriptions for alternative evaluations, and generating management reports. Many CASE tools use a resident database or *data dictionary* containing information about the system's IPOS cycle and other features of the new system. CASE tools can generate data flow diagrams for the requirements step, diagrams and software code for programmers, and screen designs. By combining these tools, systems analysts have a powerful CASE toolkit that supports each step in a systems development project (see Figure 13.13).

The advantage to using CASE is that many activities can be automated and/or integrated. That means, when the name of a

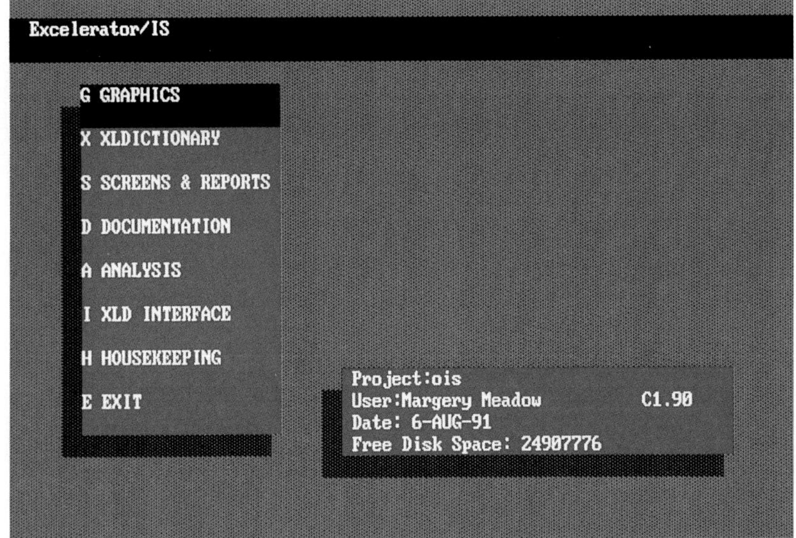

FIGURE 13.13
CASE software provides a variety of management tools for overseeing a systems development project.

report or activity is changed in one part of the system, the changes will be reflected in the data dictionary and other parts of the system. Also, some CASE packages will find inconsistencies in requirements within the system design. This technology improves productivity of the systems analyst and the development team.

Cost is one disadvantage to using CASE tools. Because of the complexity of these tools, only organizations with large systems development projects can maximize their use. Also, there are few standards from package to package. This means that a system developed with one CASE toolkit cannot be easily maintained with another. As this technology evolves, expect to see some standardization in software development tools as well as an effort to make them available to the smaller organization and personal computer user.

Regardless of the design tools used, it is important that all five components of the new system be studied. This is essential whether the system is for a large organization or a personal computer user. Any change to an existing system, no matter how small, will probably have some effect on hardware, programs, data, procedures, and people.

Hardware

If new computer equipment is required, working parameters for selecting it are determined in the design step of the system's life cycle. Secondary storage and memory requirements for computers are chosen. Peripheral equipment, such as printers, must have detailed specifications concerning speed, method of printing, and print style. The keyboard's layout, screen size, screen color options, and screen resolution need to be chosen. Specifications for data communication hardware and software need to be listed. The office facilities to be affected are studied to see where and how any new equipment and/or furniture will be accommodated.

When speed is important, a **benchmark test** compares software and hardware performance against a minimum standard agreed upon by management and the application development team. For instance, a benchmark of three seconds might be set for the response time of a new order entry system. Systems with slower response times during testing are disqualified.

An implementation and installation plan must be developed. If new computer and/or data communication equipment is required, a **request for proposal** (**RFP**) describes hardware specifications, including benchmarks, and requests vendors to propose solutions. The proposals sent by vendors in response to the RFP include descriptions of desired hardware and software, training, and service with associated costs. The RFP is the first step in securing bids and placing orders for new equipment. When a person is acquiring a new personal computer system, comparison shopping at several local computer stores may be substituted for a formal RFP. Large computers and network hardware can require long periods of advanced planning and installation. In many situations the equipment delivery schedule determines when a system can be implemented.

Programs

Existing software can be modified or new programs acquired. If changes need to be made to programs, they can be done by the internal programming staff or hired out to *contract programmers,* who become temporary consultants to the organization. When existing programs do not solve the problem, new programs must be obtained. Sources for new programs include buying them off the shelf from stores or creating them. When programs are purchased from software vendors, they may have to be customized. In any case, detailed program specifications must be written and reviewed by users. The development of program specifications will be covered in more detail in Chapter 14.

Computer professionals use several forms to help users understand what will be involved in the new or changed software. Figure 13.14 includes a **print chart,** which indicates exactly how printed output will look. The **screen layout form** in Figure 13.14 performs a similar function for screen displays. By showing users each form and asking them to approve its design, analysts are increasing the chance that the reports and displays will be effectively used later. When prototyping is available, it can be used to show active models of the print chart and screen layout form.

Data and Procedures

At this time, decisions are made concerning the organization and layout of data. Usually, computer professionals make these decisions since they rarely involve the users directly. The **record layout form** in Figure 13.15 helps the professionals organize the locations of fields within records. Decisions are also made about whether to use a database or file management system (see Chapter 7). CASE tools may help by suggesting data designs for the existing system specifications.

A change in any of the other four computer system components is usually accompanied by a review of present procedures or a change in policy. Operating procedures must be updated or created whenever new hardware or software is purchased. Users and systems analysts will often visit sites that have implemented similar projects to see what procedures they use.

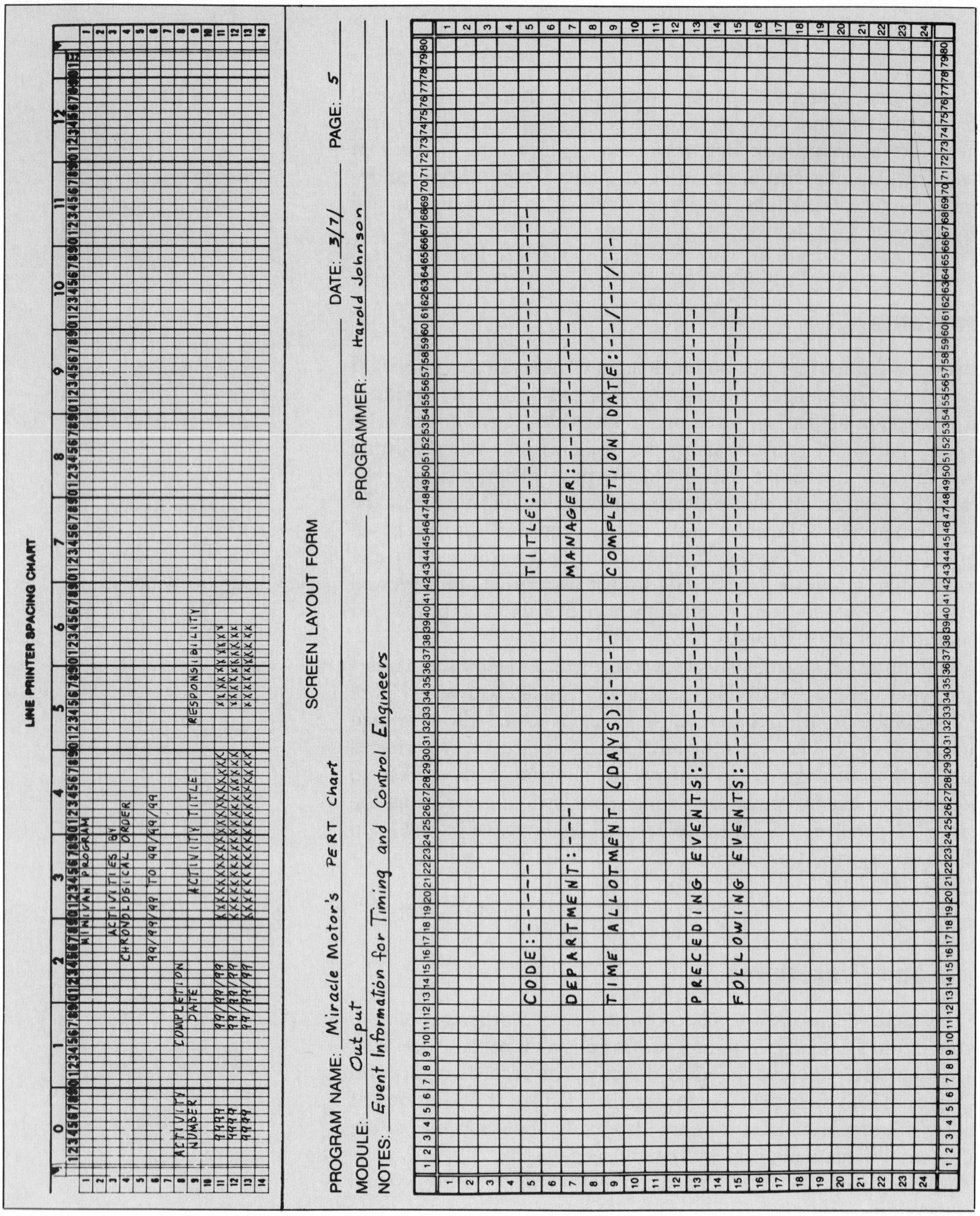

LINE PRINTER SPACING CHART

MINIVAN PROGRAM

ACTIVITIES BY
CHRONOLOGICAL ORDER

99/99/99 TO 99/99/99

ACTIVITY NUMBER	COMPLETION DATE	ACTIVITY TITLE	RESPONSIBILITY
9999	99/99/99	XXXXXXXXXXXXXXXXXXXX	XXXXXXXXXXXX
9999	99/99/99	XXXXXXXXXXXXXXXXXXXX	XXXXXXXXXXXX
9999	99/99/99	XXXXXXXXXXXXXXXXXXXX	XXXXXXXXXXXX

SCREEN LAYOUT FORM

PROGRAM NAME: Miracle Motor's PERT Chart DATE: 3/7/ PAGE: 5

MODULE: Output PROGRAMMER: Harold Johnson

NOTES: Event Information for Timing and Control Engineers

CODE: - - - - TITLE: - - - - - - - - - - - - - - - - - - -

DEPARTMENT: - - - MANAGER: - - - - - - - - - - -

TIME ALLOTMENT (DAYS): - - - COMPLETION DATE: - - / - - / - -

PRECEDING EVENTS: -

FOLLOWING EVENTS: -

FIGURE 13.14
Print charts lay out report formats for users and programmers. Screen layout forms also help these people conceptualize a proposed system design.

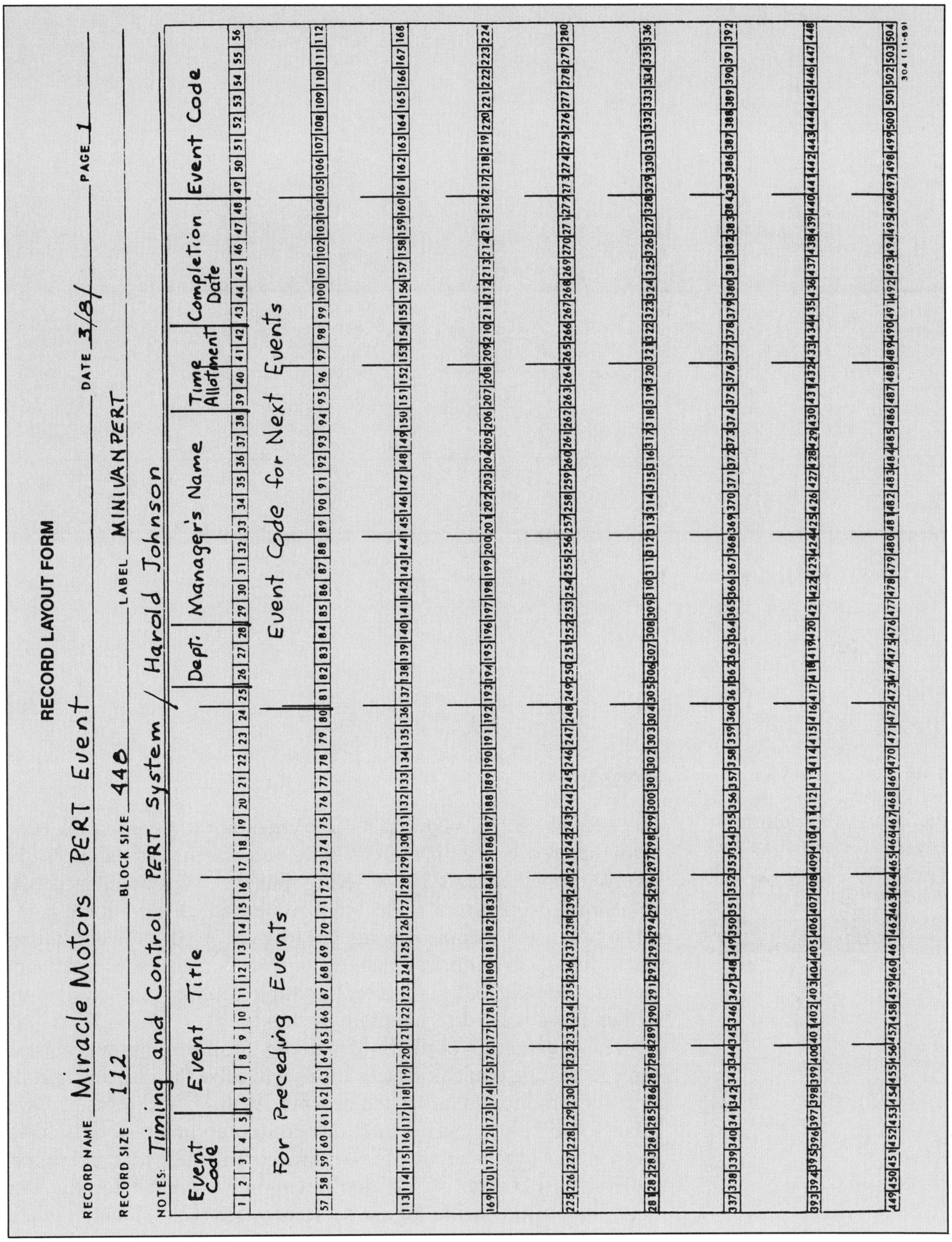

RECORD LAYOUT FORM

RECORD NAME Miracle Motors PERT Event DATE 3/8/ PAGE 1

RECORD SIZE 112 BLOCK SIZE 448 LABEL MINIVANPERT

NOTES: Timing and Control PERT System / Harold Johnson

Event Code	Event Title	Dept.	Manager's Name	Time Allotment	Completion Date	Event Code
1–5	6–25	26–28	29–38	39–42	43–48	49–56

For Preceding Events	Event Code for Next Events
57–80	81–112

304 (11-69)

FIGURE 13.15
Record layout forms allow computer professionals to estimate data storage requirements for a new computer system.

```
Schedule Name:    SurgeryWatch
Project Manager: Pat McNeil
As of date:       7-Oct-94  2:33pm    Schedule File: B:SURGW2A

                                 95                                                     96
                                 Sep      Oct                    Nov              Dec                          Jan
                        Status   17  24   1    9    15   22   29   5    13   19   26   3    10   17   24   31   7    14   21

START PROJECT              D M  .   .    .   ¦    .    .    .    .    .    .    .    .    .    .    .    .    .    .    .
:Market Analysis         + D =========   .   ¦    .    .    .    .    .    .    .    .    .    .    .    .    .    .    .
START PROTOTYPE DEVE       D    .   .M   .   ¦  ¦ .    .    .    .    .    .    .    .    .    .    .    .    .    .    .
:R&D Labels for Inv.     +      .   .++++---¦  ¦ .    .    .    .    .    .    .    .    .    .    .    .    .    .    .
:Manual Development      +      .   .++++++++++++++   .    .    .    .    .    .    .    .    .    .    .    .    .    .
:Modify NightWatch S     + C    .   .    .   ===================   .    .    .    .    .    .    .    .    .    .    .
:Modify Label Gen. S     + r    .   .    .   ------=====--------    .    .    .    .    .    .    .    .    .    .    .
COMPLETE PROTOTYPE         C    .   .    .   ¦ .    .    >>>>>M    .    .    .    .    .    .    .    .    .    .    .

D Done                    === Task          - Slack time (==---), or
C Critical                +++ Started task    Resource delay (---++)
R Resource conflict         M Milestone     > Conflict
r Rescheduled to avoid resource conflict  p Partial dependency
Scale: Each character equals 1 day

TIME LINE Gantt Chart Report
```

FIGURE 13.16
Gantt charts track multiple tasks associated with a systems development project and flag situations where there are resource conflicts in terms of time, equipment, or people.

People

The success of the next phase, implementation, depends on how involved users are with the design of the system. When users are involved, they have a stake in seeing that the new system succeeds. Sometimes people have to be hired to operate new equipment. At other times new people are temporarily involved with consulting and training. It is critical that the application development team identifies the personnel required to implement the new system as well as those needed to maintain it.

The culmination of the third step of a project comes when users agree in writing that the specifications will solve the identified problems and produce the projected benefits. At this point the users have "signed off" the system, and the computer professionals have accepted the specifications they will meet. For their part, computer professionals commit to an implementation schedule for the last step. The **Gantt chart** in Figure 13.16 is often used to identify when different phases begin, to estimate their duration, and to provide an overview of which activities occur concurrently during implementation. Since a major development project may take several years to finish, coordination of personnel and facilities is essential to maintain productivity.

Designing a Personal Computer System

In a smaller systems development project you may agree informally upon a design solution with other users involved. In any case the list of system features evolves into the system specifications, which identify particular brand names and model numbers (see Figure 13.17). Make sure the application packages that you need are easy to use, have readable documentation, and integrate with other software. Your software choices will, to a great degree, dictate hardware manufacturers and models.

Now is the time to get price estimates on hardware and software from local retailers and catalogs. Compare warranties and delivery dates as well as prices. Be aware that retail prices will generally be higher but may include training and service. In either case check that complete systems documentation is available as part of the purchase price. A purchase price may not include necessary cables or paper and extra ribbons for printers. A personalized Gantt chart can help you coordinate the purchase and set-up of equipment. In addition, it can aid you in planning future acquisitions, such as adding a modem, expanding memory, or upgrading to a laser printer.

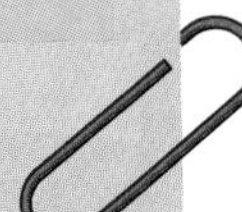

Designing a Personal Computer System

1. Convert a list of features into system specifications
   - a. Software
     - easy-to-use
     - readable documentation
     - integrates with other software
   - b. Hardware
     - compatible with software
     - additional expansion slots
     - ability to add memory
2. Where to get price estimates
   - a. retail stores
   - b. catalogs for complete systems
   - c. catalogs of kits for building your own computer
3. What is included in the price besides hardware/software?
   - a. training
   - b. service
   - c. documentation
   - d. warranty
   - e. ancillaries
4. Create timeline for purchases
5. Purchase system components

FIGURE 13.17
Systems specifications are used to purchase a new personal computer system.

LIFE-CYCLE STEP FOUR: IMPLEMENTATION

Within the context of a system development project, implementation involves the activities that put a new system into operation and those that maintain its successful use. The actual changeover to operational status occurs during the latter part of this step. Gantt charts, like the one in Figure 13.16, identify the initial phases and their expected duration. This last step of the life cycle includes construction and testing, installation, evaluation, and maintenance phases (see Figure 13.18).

Construction and Testing

The activities within this phase are technical in nature. This usually is the point in the project at which users play only minimal roles. Users on the application development team are replaced by technical support specialists, senior programmers, computer operations personnel, data communications specialists, and database administrators. The job is to establish all of the computer-related requirements that will have to be in place before the new system becomes operational.

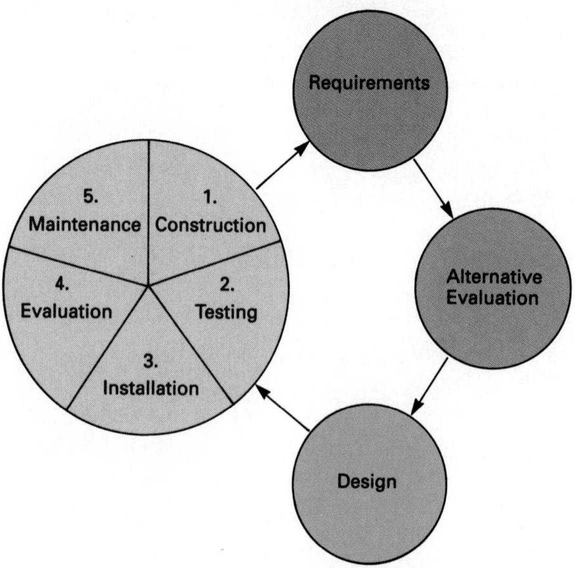

FIGURE 13.18
During the implementation step, all of the components of the new computer system are brought together for installation.

The main activity of the construction phase is the preparation and testing of programs for the new system. If new programs need to be written or purchased programs need to be customized, the coding of program sections or modules is assigned to one or more programmers. Each module is tested as it is written. As connecting modules are completed, testing extends to sets of modules, then to entire programs. In some instances test data may be applied to test multiple programs, or systems of programs (see Chapter 14). When traditional programming techniques are used, this one activity can account for up to 50 percent of the cost of system development. This cost factor has motivated attempts to streamline or shortcut the programming process. Some of these streamlined methods are described briefly in Chapter 14.

Other implementation activities include the installation of new equipment and, after the programs are available, the performance of complete system tests. A **system test** is the actual operation of the new system, carried out by users with real application data. Usually, this data has been processed previously under existing systems. Thus, the expected results are known from previous processing. A system test then serves to exercise a new system to make sure users understand and are satisfied with the results that will be delivered.

Since users perform the system test, it is necessary to complete at least some of the training for the new system. Training efforts must encompass both a core group of users and the computer center personnel who will provide support. To achieve a realistic system test, at least some files that will interact with the new application must be created.

At the conclusion of the testing phase, the new system has been developed in its entirety and is ready for use. Separation of testing from installation serves to reassure users and management. The new system, now fully tested, can be put to work with confidence.

Installation

No matter how extensive preparations might be, stress and some confusion are inevitable when a new system is to be installed. The act of starting up a new computer system is referred to as either **installation** or *conversion*. Emotions can be involved as well as changes in procedures.

At the point of full conversion, use of the old tools and methods ceases. The experience can be like parting with an old friend. Individual employees, for example, may have used the previous methods and equipment for 5, 10, or even 15 years. The old ways worked for them; people were familiar with and comfortable in the routines they followed. If conversion is to be successful, training programs should assure employees that the new ways are for their good and for the good of the organization.

Computer professionals participate in the installation phase primarily as consultants. Analysts and programmers should be available to answer questions and resolve problems. But computer operators should take over the operation of the system. Users should start working with the output they need in their everyday job responsibilities.

Problems will inevitably arise. Any problems that affect the ability of the system to function or the reliability of results should be fixed immediately. Any other problems should be considered part of system maintenance, which is covered later. The goal of installation is an operational system.

One of the major jobs of a system conversion often lies in setting up files or a database to support the new system. Difficulties generally center around the need to tie file conversion to day-to-day operations. For example, major operating crunches were experienced in the days when banks changed from manual bookkeeping methods to online computer systems. Typically, a branch or operating unit of the bank closed out its manual files on a Friday. Immediately a team of temporary employees would enter the offices on Friday evening and work all weekend to transfer thousands of records into a computer file, and also to establish balance controls between computer files and their predecessors.

Because of the extent and importance of the work involved, systems professionals have devised a number of methods that can be used to complete an installation (see Figure 13.19). These include the following four:

- Parallel operation
- Phased transition
- Pilot operation
- Direct cutover

Parallel Operation

Under a **parallel operation** both the existing and the new systems are run, side-by-side, for some time. Results of the two systems are compared to provide both protection and control. The length of time for parallel operation can vary. Usually the old system is retained through one or two processing cycles with the new system. A system that produced month-end accounting reports would be operated in parallel for one or two months.

Parallel operation can provide users a chance to become comfortable with change before old methods disappear. Usually, this method also provides an opportunity to establish the improvements the new system implements. Most important of all, the parallel approach involves the least risk and the most protection for the organization. The disadvantage of parallel operations is that the organization must pay the additional cost in time and labor of running both systems, as well as being able to provide facilities for both the new and old systems.

Phased Transition

A **phased transition** provides the same basic advantages as parallel operation. The difference is that under this method the overlap is piecemeal. In a phased transition, part of the system is put into operation throughout the organization. Once it is working, another part or piece is installed. This phased transition continues until the

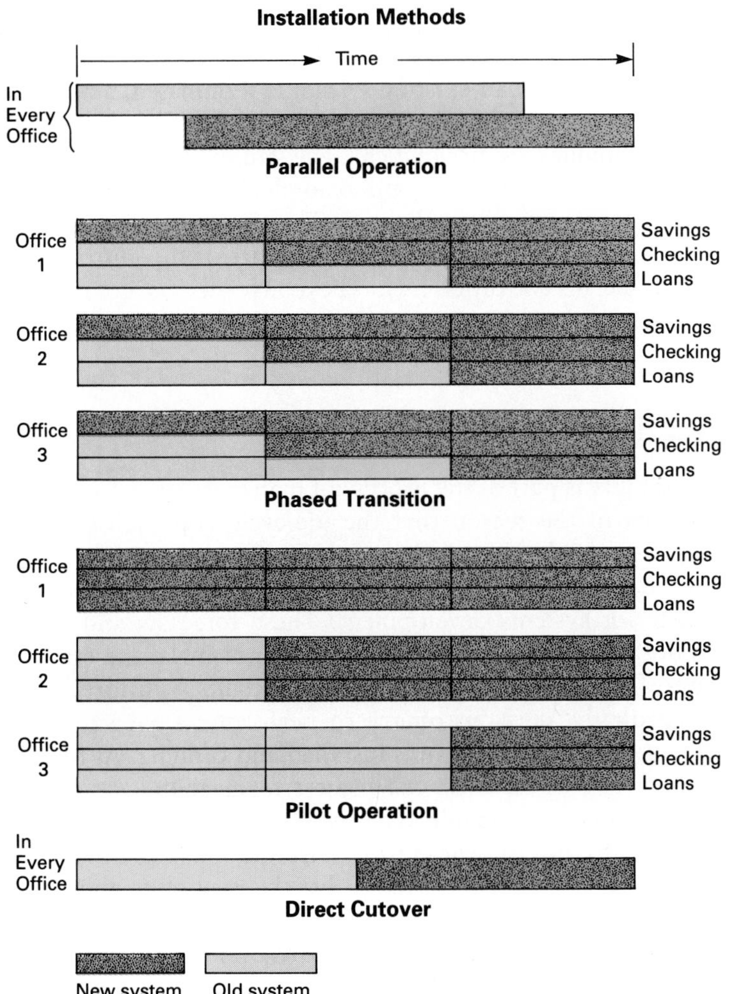

FIGURE 13.19
This chart illustrates different approaches for converting from one system to another.

whole system is in operation everywhere within the organization. Figure 13.19 illustrates how a new bank system might start with computerizing only savings accounts in all its branches, then go to checking accounts, loans, club plans, and others. The idea is that the new system impacts only one portion or function of the organization at a time.

Pilot Operation

A **pilot operation** takes a different approach than is used in a phased transition. Rather than scheduling installation for the entire organization, a small pilot operation is set up. This pilot runs the complete system in only part of the organization until the new system has proven itself. For example, a bank using a pilot operation would install the entire system in one branch office. When it is working properly, the system would be gradually installed in other branch offices one at a time.

Direct Cutover

Under **direct cutover** an existing system is terminated, and the new one takes over immediately. This method generally is used when gradual techniques are impractical. The situation of a bank branch installing online service is a good example. The equipment used by tellers to serve customers is changed. There is no opportunity to use both systems concurrently or to handle part of the customers one way and the others differently. The conversion is complete and immediate.

Evaluation

Accountability is part of the process of management. Accountability also is part of the reason that the life-cycle approach to systems development works. Recall that, at the onset, users and computer professionals are asked to join in identifying both projected benefits and costs for systems development. These forecasts and commitments do little good if management does not make the effort necessary to follow up by comparing actual results with forecasts.

Accordingly, it is customary to perform a review of results shortly after each new system is installed and running. At this point the memories of people on the project team about activities and results are fresh and reliable. They are in an ideal position to pinpoint problems and to benefit from mistakes that can be identified. Also, this usually is a good time to list the new opportunities that already have been uncovered for system enhancement. These potential improvements can be used in the early portions of the maintenance phase, which runs through the entire useful life of a system.

In addition to the review that takes place shortly after installation, many organizations try to hold another review session about

FIGURE 13.20
Evaluation of a new system begins just after it is installed. Another major evaluation of the system often occurs several months later to compare expectations with actual results.

six months after a system becomes operational. This second review is based upon the perspective of experience. The organization has had enough service from the new system so that findings about benefits and savings are well known. This represents an ideal time to compare actual results with projections, and to learn from the successes and difficulties that are identified.

Maintenance

Maintenance begins as soon as a system becomes operational and lasts as long as it is in use. In this sense, **maintenance** encompasses any modification to an operational system. Maintenance meets needs or provides enhanced values for existing systems.

Examples of need for maintenance occur when laws or regulations are changed and computer programs must be modified. For example, if a tax rate changes, a corresponding modification is needed in related programs. The need for modification also occurs on a routine basis, as when the year has to be changed in accounting reports.

Enhancements are recognized opportunities for improvement. These typically are uncovered by users who notice that adding a capability to an existing system may increase its value. As an illustration, a payroll system may be expandable to provide labor cost information for the manufacturing department. The revision to accomplish this may seem minor. However, if this request occurs after the system design has been completed, most computer professionals will avoid changing the design of a system under development. Too much can go wrong. Schedules and budgets can be destroyed. Instead, a list of enhancement opportunities usually is started during the late stages of a development project. These opportunities are carried forward into the ongoing maintenance phase of the life cycle. Figure 13.21 diagrams all phases of a complete life cycle.

Such occurrences as desired early enhancements are commonplace. Even a brand new system can start its useful life with a backlog of maintenance requests. In the course of use, new opportunities

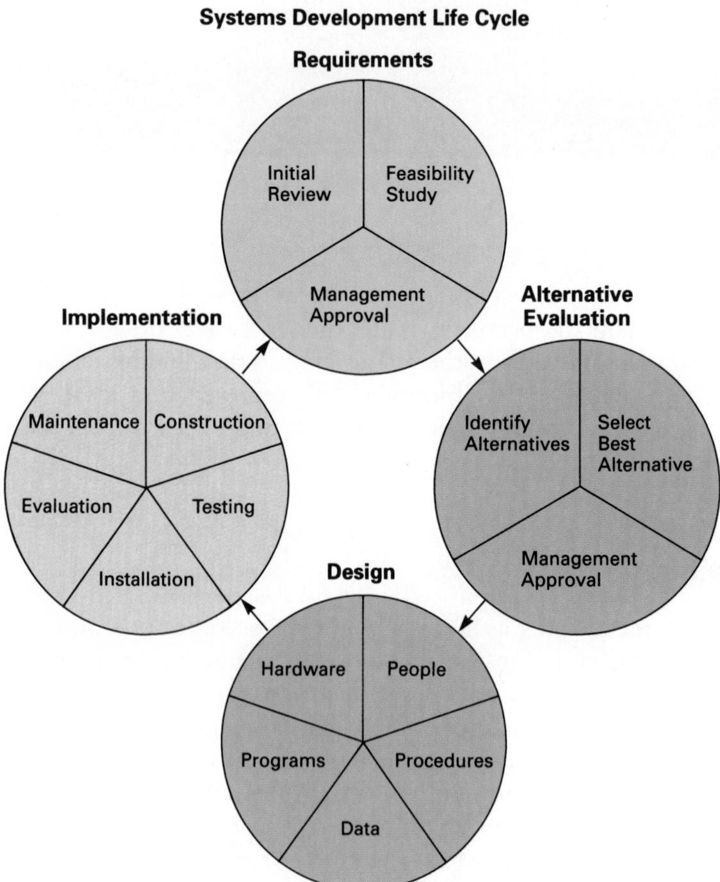

FIGURE 13.21

By following each phase in the systems development life cycle, a new computer system can be created in a cost-effective manner.

will be identified for each application. As these are uncovered, they are reviewed for feasibility, and work is scheduled on maintenance projects, which tend to be miniature versions of systems development projects.

Set-up and Maintenance of a Personal Computer System

The construction and testing of a new personal computer system may be no more involved than removing components from their boxes and making sure the operating system boots properly (see Figure 13.22). Don't forget to keep any warranty or service information that comes with the equipment. Placement of the equipment in a work area may be one of the most critical decisions you make. Look for a clean, dry work environment with plenty of room for materials around the computer. Proper lighting and seating is necessary for user comfort. If improper lighting causes screen glare, special screen shields can be purchased to eliminate it. Computer professionals often recommend using a surge protector and anti-static pads for long equipment life.

Personal computer users can avoid problems by regular maintenance. This includes covering their keyboard when not in use, cleaning disk drive heads and printer, as well as backing up important data and software.

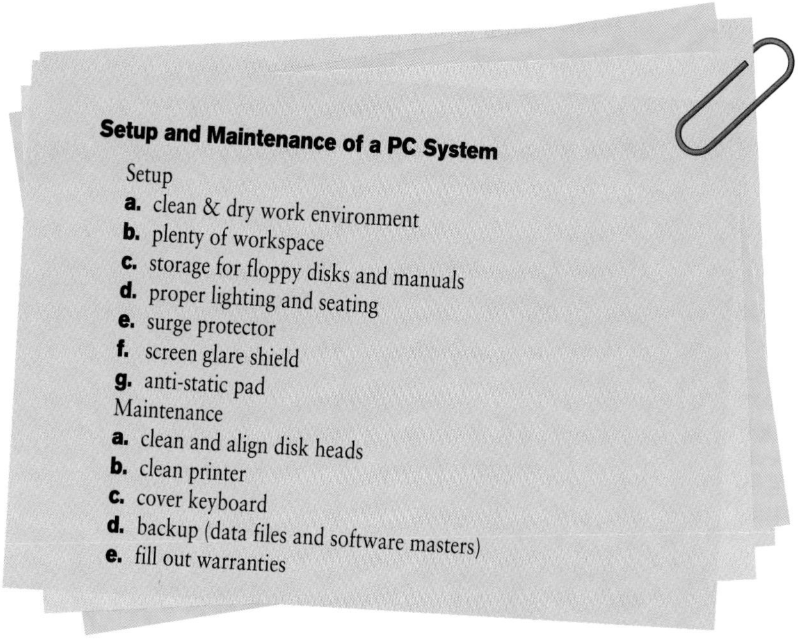

Setup and Maintenance of a PC System

Setup

a. clean & dry work environment
b. plenty of workspace
c. storage for floppy disks and manuals
d. proper lighting and seating
e. surge protector
f. screen glare shield
g. anti-static pad

Maintenance

a. clean and align disk heads
b. clean printer
c. cover keyboard
d. backup (data files and software masters)
e. fill out warranties

FIGURE 13.22
Proper set-up and maintenance of a personal computer ensures that system users can put it to good use.

A Closer Look...

Project Management Software

Specialized software, such as CASE tools, exists to help computer professionals develop new systems. Project management software is a type of personal productivity package that helps people track, plan, and schedule many concurrent projects, whether they involve computers or not. Let's look at a landscaping firm and how its owner uses project management software to assist in organizing the personnel, materials, and equipment needed for several landscaping projects.

Q How can project management software help organize projects?

A The landscaper uses the software to identify critical resources, required deadlines, and the logical order for completing each task. For example, earth is moved and plants are ordered before planting is done. Priorities must be input along with costs, time each worker can spend with the project, and necessary machinery to complete the job.

PROJECT MANAGEMENT

PROJECT: Harrington — START DATE: 4/25; DEADLINE: 6/29

TASK: order plants — PRIORITY: 1
START DATE: 4/26
DEADLINE: 5/12
PERSONNEL:

NAME	WAGE	% TIME
Johnson	14.00	25

EQUIPMENT: none

TASK: level plant bed — PRIORITY: 1
START DATE: 5/1
DEADLINE: 5/7
PERSONNEL: — TOT EST HOURS: 60

NAME	WAGE	% TIME
Wilson, J	12.50	50
Nettle	7.25	75

EQUIPMENT: none

NAME	COST	EST TIME
backhoe	23.00	16 hr
bulldozer	19.00	12.5 hr

TASK: back retaining wall — PRIORITY: 2
START DATE: 5/1
DEADLINE: 5/11
PERSONNEL: — TOT EST HOURS: 75

NAME	WAGE	% TIME
Abrams	9.25	75
Nettle	7.25	25
Quentin	6.25	100

EQUIPMENT: none

NAME	COST	EST TIME
bulldozer	19.00	3.5 hr
dump truck	12.00	5 hr

Project Manager Software Features

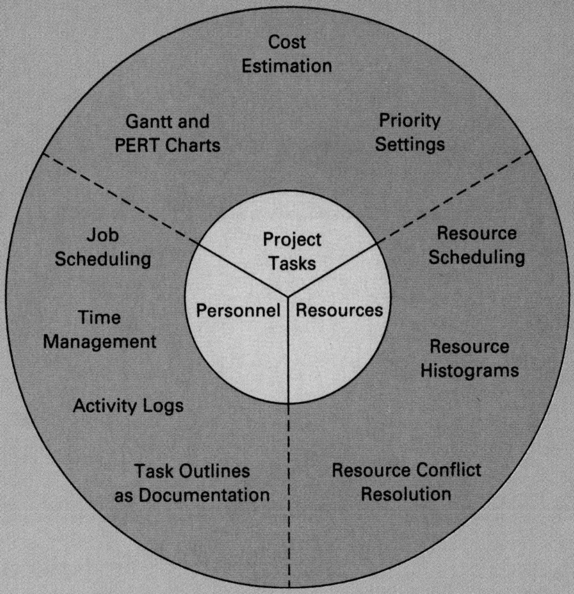

Q What kinds of information are available from the package?

A Project management software provides time management, job scheduling, resource (personnel and material) management, and cost estimation. A Gantt chart, as seen in Figure 13.16, and some of the CASE tools discussed in the text are commonly available with this software.

Q How does the software handle resource conflicts?

A Resource conflicts occur when the personnel, equipment, or materials for a job are not available when needed. This could be due to workers' vacations, a dump truck being used on another job, broken equipment, or late orders. Project management software flags potential conflicts within a single project or between projects and resolves them when possible. For example, worker Nettle is incorrectly scheduled for 45 hours during one week.

PERSONNEL SCHEDULE

PROJECT: Harrington

WEEK: 4/26	WORKER	HOURS	TASK
	Johnson	10	order plants
WEEK: 5/1	WORKER	HOURS	TASK
	Wilson, J	15	level plant beds
	Nettle	40	level plant beds
WEEK: 5/8	WORKER	HOURS	TASK
	*** Nettle	5	level plant beds
	Abrams	10	back retaining wall
	*** Nettle	40	back retaining wall
	Quentin	15	back retaining wall

*** denotes personnel time conflict

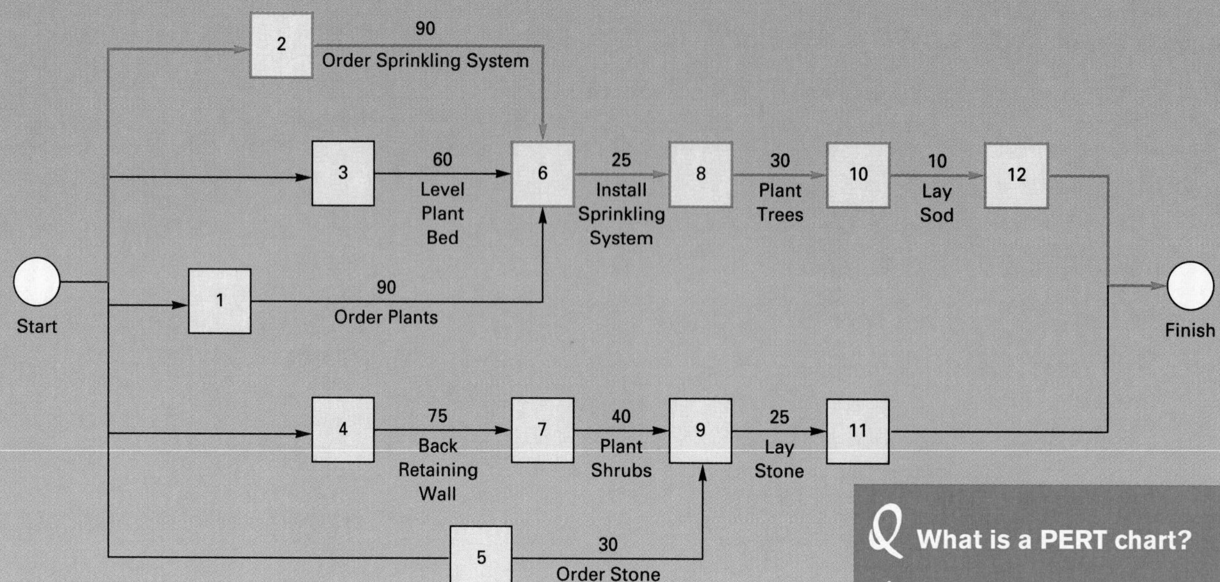

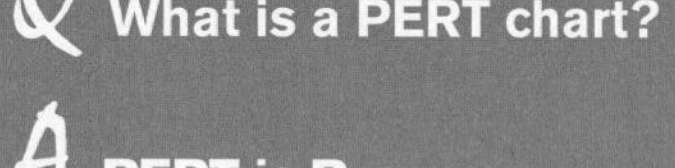

Q What is a PERT chart?

A PERT is Program Evaluation and Review Technique, a key element in project management software. PERT charts show the order and time requirements for each task in a project as boxes connected by lines. The critical path, highlighted in the figure, shows the combination of events requiring the most time. Often several tasks are independent of the others. In landscaping, retaining walls in the backyard can be built while sod is being laid in the front.

Q In what situations is it beneficial to use project management software?

A This software is best used in complex projects that involve many steps, projects taking place in many locations simultaneously, and projects with new managers who need the help of experienced managers not on site.

Chapter Facts

- A systems development project is more easily managed by breaking it down into four life-cycle steps: (1) requirements; (2) alternative evaluation; (3) design; and (4) implementation.
- The requirements step involves three phases: (1) initial review; (2) feasibility study; and (3) management approval.
- In the initial review a systems analyst makes a preliminary estimate of time and costs, deciding whether the project has a computer solution.
- The feasibility study involves other computer professionals and users. They gather relevant data and interview participating users, producing a report of budget and schedule requirements. Management approval is required to proceed.
- During the alternative evaluation step, options are researched by the analysts for comparison through a cost/benefit study. The alternatives, the top choice, and rationale are presented to management for approval.
- The design step involves developing specifications for each of the five system components. Hardware requirements are listed; special forms showing input/output arrangements are approved by users; data file organization is determined; new procedures for operations and training are written; and personnel requirements are listed.
- Prototyping allows the systems analyst to create working models of screens, reports, and other user interfaces.
- A CASE toolkit contains software (CASE tools) and a data dictionary that help systems analysts manage the systems development process using diagrams and charts.
- The implementation step consists of five phases: (1) construction; (2) testing; (3) installation; (4) evaluation; and (5) maintenance.
- During the construction phase, hardware is ordered and software is obtained or written. Programs, hardware, and procedures are then tested—both separately and with a systems test.
- Implementation of hardware can happen as a parallel operation, phased transition, pilot operation, or direct cutover. Evaluation of the entire system occurs immediately after installation and six months later. Maintenance is an ongoing procedure to make necessary changes to software.

- Project management software contains programs to help managers schedule, plan, and track projects. Features include time management, job scheduling, contact tracking, resource (personnel and material) management, and cost estimation programs.

Mix and Match

a. application development team
b. benchmark test
c. CASE (computer-aided software engineering) tools
d. cost/benefit analysis
e. critical path
f. data flow diagram
g. direct cutover
h. feasibility study
i. Gantt chart
j. installation
k. maintenance
l. parallel operation
m. PERT (program evaluation and review technique)
n. phased transition
o. pilot operation
p. print chart
q. project management software
r. prototyping
s. record layout form
t. request for proposal (RFP)
u. screen layout form
v. service bureau
w. system specifications
x. systems development project
y. system test

Terms to Remember

Match the following definitions to the Terms to Remember.

1. ____ method of conversion wherein the old system is removed and the new system is immediately installed.
2. ____ document that shows how output will appear on a screen.
3. ____ changing from an old system to a new system.
4. ____ modeling user interface by users as part of the initial system design.
5. ____ software that uses a data dictionary with charting tools to help computer professionals manage a systems development project.

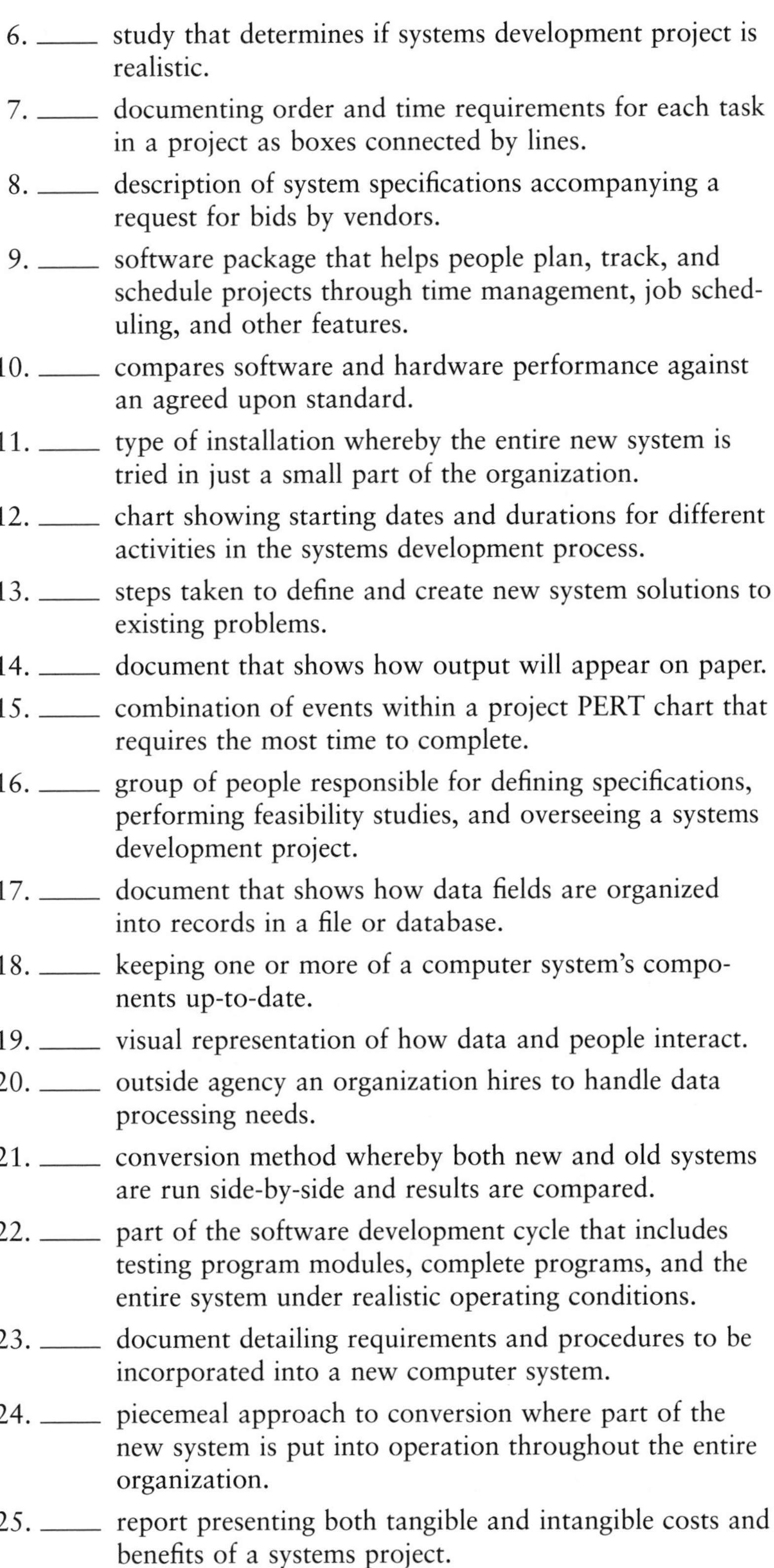

6. ______ study that determines if systems development project is realistic.
7. ______ documenting order and time requirements for each task in a project as boxes connected by lines.
8. ______ description of system specifications accompanying a request for bids by vendors.
9. ______ software package that helps people plan, track, and schedule projects through time management, job scheduling, and other features.
10. ______ compares software and hardware performance against an agreed upon standard.
11. ______ type of installation whereby the entire new system is tried in just a small part of the organization.
12. ______ chart showing starting dates and durations for different activities in the systems development process.
13. ______ steps taken to define and create new system solutions to existing problems.
14. ______ document that shows how output will appear on paper.
15. ______ combination of events within a project PERT chart that requires the most time to complete.
16. ______ group of people responsible for defining specifications, performing feasibility studies, and overseeing a systems development project.
17. ______ document that shows how data fields are organized into records in a file or database.
18. ______ keeping one or more of a computer system's components up-to-date.
19. ______ visual representation of how data and people interact.
20. ______ outside agency an organization hires to handle data processing needs.
21. ______ conversion method whereby both new and old systems are run side-by-side and results are compared.
22. ______ part of the software development cycle that includes testing program modules, complete programs, and the entire system under realistic operating conditions.
23. ______ document detailing requirements and procedures to be incorporated into a new computer system.
24. ______ piecemeal approach to conversion where part of the new system is put into operation throughout the entire organization.
25. ______ report presenting both tangible and intangible costs and benefits of a systems project.

Review Questions

1. How are systems development projects made more manageable?
2. What special precautions should be added to the systems development process to help ensure success?
3. Who performs an initial review, and what are their responsibilities?
4. Who determines if a new computer system has merit and initiates the feasibility study?
5. What data-gathering techniques are part of a feasibility study?
6. Explain the 80–20 rule.
7. Describe how the requirements step applies to the purchase of a personal computer system.
8. Why does the application development team provide management with a list of alternative system solutions?
9. What are three intangible costs and benefits managers must consider when evaluating system alternatives?
10. What decisions are made in the final phase of the alternative evaluation step?
11. What decisions are made when evaluating alternatives for a personal computer system?
12. Name two advantages and two disadvantages of prototyping.
13. Identify an advantage and two disadvantages of CASE tools.
14. What is the purpose of a data dictionary in a CASE toolkit?
15. Use the five components of a computer system to describe the activities and requirements in a set of system specifications.
16. What happens at the end of the design step?
17. What activities are involved in designing a personal computer system?
18. What happens during the construction phase?
19. Who needs to be trained before the system test can occur?
20. What is the purpose of the immediate and six-month follow-up reviews of a completed systems development project?
21. Why are some system modifications in the maintenance phase?
22. Describe the steps in the life cycle of a systems development process. Identify the phases associated with each step.
23. What steps are included in the setup and maintenance of a new personal computer system?
24. Explain features common to project management software.

Applying What You've Learned

1. The systems development life cycle can be applied when any major decisions or purchases are made, even those not involving computer systems. Choose an area where you will have to make a decision in the near future. It could involve school, finding a job or a new place to live, buying a car, or some other decision. Organize your decision making by using the four steps and associated phases in the life cycle. For each step, outline what is involved relating to your decision. Include any ideas on alternatives, feasibility, benchmarks, etc.
2. The type of installation method used depends upon the specific application, the experience of the users, and how involved the change will be. For each installation method (parallel operation, phased transition, pilot operation, and direct cutover), list a situation not mentioned in the text, where this method seems to be the best approach. Briefly explain why you feel the method is appropriate.
3. It is sometimes difficult to list all of the costs and benefits resulting from a systems development project. List two each of tangible costs, tangible benefits, intangible costs, and intangible benefits that may arise from installing a new computer system in a retail store. Use examples different from the text.
4. For each situation described below, list three examples of cyclic, legal, or company policy changes that could result in maintenance for the computer system.
   a. a local branch of a large bank
   b. a college or university
   c. a tax accountant
   d. a public utility such as electric or gas
   e. a local drug store
5. An applications development team involves a variety of people. List the special qualifications and personality traits each of these people should have to be an effective team member: systems analyst, user, network administrator, programmer.

Answers to Mix and Match

1. g 2. u 3. j 4. r 5. c 6. h 7. m 8. t 9. q 10. b
11. o 12. i 13. x 14. p 15. e 16. a 17. s 18. k 19. f
20. v 21. l 22. y 23. w 24. n 25. d

14

Software Development

- From the User's Point of View
- People and Programming
  - Misconceptions about programming
  - The four-step programming process
- Designing the Program
  - Defining the problem
  - Unstructured programs
  - Structured programs
  - Object-oriented programs
  - Tools for program design
  - Testing the program design
- Writing Program Code
  - Language translators
  - Finding program errors
  - Programming languages
- Testing and Debugging
  - Program testing
  - System test
- Documentation and Training
  - User training
  - Program maintenance
- A Closer Look . . . Programming Languages (No Matter How You Say It)

FROM THE USER'S POINT OF VIEW

In this chapter we introduce you to the concepts and languages used to create the instructions for a computer, the program. While you no longer have to learn programming to be an informed user, many people find programming useful for customizing public-domain programs, as a problem-solving tool, and to use advanced features of some software packages.

It is conceivable that you will be involved in a systems design project at some point in your life. Learning about the program development process puts you in a better position to communicate your needs to a computer professional. If we spark your interest, a programming class in one of the languages described may be a logical next step for you.

PEOPLE AND PROGRAMMING

Programs solve problems by controlling data retrieval, processing, and storage within a computer system. Developing efficient, accurate, and user-friendly programs requires organized efforts by trained personnel. Programmers must be made aware of every nuance of the problem and how it affects the organization. They need to have in-depth knowledge of the principles of computer processing, supplemented by total fluency in one or more programming languages. The job postings in Figure 14.1 are typical for people seeking careers in computer programming.

For the end-user, high-level software tools such as CASE and application generators have reduced the need to program. For the user-developer and programmer, however, the importance of programming skills has not diminished. High-level tools make it easier to produce individual modules or entire programs. Some software packages, such as spreadsheets and word processors, provide the opportunity to program macros to automate software operations like printing or file merging. Many database management systems have their own programming languages. However, sound design and effective resource planning remain essential to successful development and implementation of computer systems.

Misconceptions about Programming

If a system requires that new application programs be written from scratch, the programming function can take as much as 50 percent of the overall systems development budget. Even if application packages exist that can be adapted to the needs of a new system, programming is still important. Programming skills still are required to design, develop, and apply computers to solve information problems.

FIGURE 14.1
A variety of opportunities are available for programmers and other professionals.

People inexperienced with computer systems sometimes regard programming simply as the process of writing program instructions, the **code** that causes computers to execute a specific IPOS cycle. This is a long way from the truth. Coding is a relatively minor part of an extensive process that involves problem definition, functional design, technical design, coding, testing, and documentation. Cod-

PROGRAMMER

Duties: Program and maintain Geographic Information System (GIS) and Geographical Exploration Systems using C and Fortran with fuzzy logic programming techniques.

Requirements: 2 years experience in C and Fortran and 3D modeling programs with geophysics applications. Must have knowledge and understanding of fuzzy logic programming techniques.

Salary: 24,000.00 per year.

Send resumes to: Job Service. Job Order No. 1810813 P.O. Box [illegible], Provo, Utah 84603.

Software Development Opportunities

CompuServe, a major communications and information services organization offers systems and applications professionals the kind of environment that will provide long-term professional and personal satisfaction — the latest in proven technology and an appealing lifestyle. We're looking for technical individuals to join our team and provide aggressive development and support.

Be involved in the development of products and services that are used by over 600,000 subscribers of the CompuServe Information Service, work on the micro based interface to the information service, or help us develop our network software so that it can meet the expanding needs of our customers. These and other exciting challenges await you.

Positions available at our Columbus, Ohio corporate headquarters include Programmer through Project Leader levels. Candidates we seek have two or more years of C, Pascal, Assembler or Fortran programming experience in any of the following areas:

- Telecommunications Software and Protocols
- Low Level Systems Development
- Relational and/or Full Text Database Systems
- Implementation of Software Tools
- Macintosh or Windows Applications
- Information Systems Development

lease forward your resume to:
ɔuServe Incorporated
Arlington Centre Blvd.
nbus, OH 43220
tion: Human Resources

"C" Programmer / Analyst

The St. Louis headquarters of an international corporation has an immediate opening for a "C" Programmer/Analyst. This key individual is needed to help develop state-of-the-art Engineering Software for a
·hly regarded as the leader in its industry.

l candidate will have a B.S. degree in
ence or Mathematics along with two
ıce of direct assignments in developing
scientific applications. Experience with
ıdows or other graphical user interface is

offers a comprehensive compensation
ncludes a full range of employee
ıefits, including Profit Sharing.

and salary history to:

"C" Programmer/Analyst
(Dept. W1)
P.O. Box [illegible]
St. Louis, MO 63177

LEE COUNTY, FLORIDA
MANAGEMENT INFORMATION SERVICES DIRECTOR
$42,640 – $63,986

Highly responsible administrative and supervisory work directing Management Information Services, including data processing; systems acquisition and development; operations; networking; and Land Information Systems. Responsibilities include directing the design, installation, and maintenance of a variety of highly complex and specialized systems. Requires four-year degree in computer science, business administration, math, industrial engineering, or related area plus five years responsible data processing experience, including three years of management experience directing a complex computer information center or a computer systems analysis or design unit. Send resume with Social Security number to: **Lee County Personnel, P.O. Box [illegible], Fort Myers, Florida 33908. EOE.**

RESEARCH PROGRAMMER/ANALYST

Duties: Develop Software using "C" and 8088 assembler languages on IBM/PC for use in Data Acquisition, Control and Expert Diagnostic Systems over a digital network connected to remotely mounted microprocessor based equipment. Research and develop techniques for understanding and modeling pneumatic and mechanical systems. Develop an expert system that utilizes the above techniques for determination of operational status, possible problems, and their solutions while device is in active use. Develop network communications protocol for multidrop and point to point devices.

Requirements: B.S. in Electrical Engineering or Computer Science with knowledge of "C" and 8088 assembler langages on IBM/PC, networking protocols, open systems interface modeling and analog to digital conversions. Must have an understanding of physical and mathmatical modeling of pneumatic and mechanical systems. Plus six months experience in real time data systems programming.

Salary: $30,000.00 per year. Send resume to: JOB SERVICE, Job Order No. 1805583, P.O. Box [illegible], Provo, Utah 84603

ing is only the second of four steps in the program development process. The program must be specified and designed in all detail necessary for implementation before the writing of code even begins.

The Four-Step Programming Process

The process of program development falls within the implementation step of the systems development life cycle. Parallel to the purchase, testing, and installation of hardware is the development of software.

The programming process follows a four-step structure of its own, producing application programs that implement the processing portion of a computer system. Like the systems development life cycle described in Chapter 13, program development projects vary with the professionals and organizations involved. However, the overall picture (see Figure 14.2) can be illustrated through four steps in the programming process:

- Designing the program
- Writing program code
- Testing and debugging
- Documentation and training

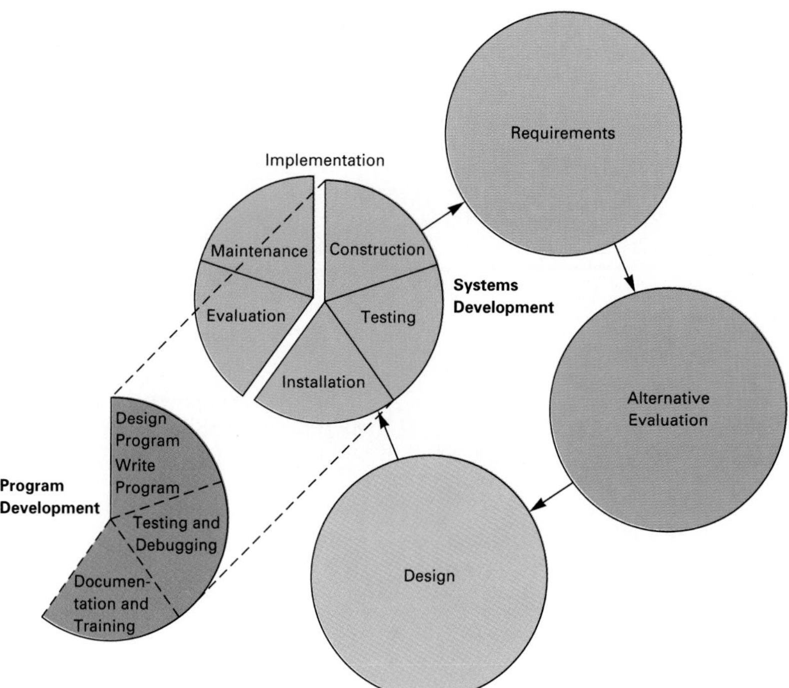

FIGURE 14.2
Program development takes place within the systems development process as part of the implementation step.

DESIGNING THE PROGRAM

Programmers start the process by looking at the **program specifications,** the part of the system specifications that deals directly with program design. Program specifications include what the users expect from the system as well as the technical interpretations of processing requirements prepared by the systems analyst. The print charts, screen layout forms, and record layout forms discussed in Chapter 13 are considered part of the program specifications. In addition, program specifications contain a set of test data to be processed by the program. Complete testing helps to ensure quality, accuracy, and acceptance of programs for use within a system.

Defining the Problem

Remember that, by definition, computer programs solve problems. Initially, the programmer looks at the problem from the user's perspective. Methods of data entry and forms of usable output to be generated must be considered. Here is where a programmer can make use of the prototypes approved by the user. Although trans-

In the News...

USER-DRIVEN COMPUTER TRAINING TIPS

Training is a part of virtually every IS manager's job. New and enhanced systems need someone to explain their operation. Getting your point across will require that your message be presented effectively. Here are a few tips:

■ **Understand Management Objectives** Managers can also identify users who, with extra training, can provide primary support for a department.

■ **Build on the Basics** Without a firm grasp of the fundamentals, a student is sure to lose interest and fall behind as complexities are introduced.

■ **Involve Reluctant Users** Once converted they'll become your advocates. They can also help detect applications and provide constructive feedback.

■ **Vary Presentation Techniques** Consider demonstrations, discussions, visual aids, and hands-on exercises. The more senses involved, the more motivated the student.

■ **Provide Reinforcement** Students build on what they know, so be sure to create situations that reinforce key concepts.

parent to most users, one of the important considerations is the long-term storage requirements for data files. Almost any file created within or maintained by a program will require expansion over time. A programmer who understands both the present and future needs for data storage and retrieval will create a program with a long, useful life.

The same is true for any type of computer program. An expert system for doctors must anticipate the kinds of queries that will be presented and have capacity for expansion. The programmer's understanding of user needs also pays off for programs that support scientific or engineering efforts. Even a macro written for an electronic spreadsheet should be written with long-term, practical use in mind.

Once the problem is understood, the programmer can proceed with designing the program structure in one of three ways:

- Unstructured
- Structured
- Object-oriented

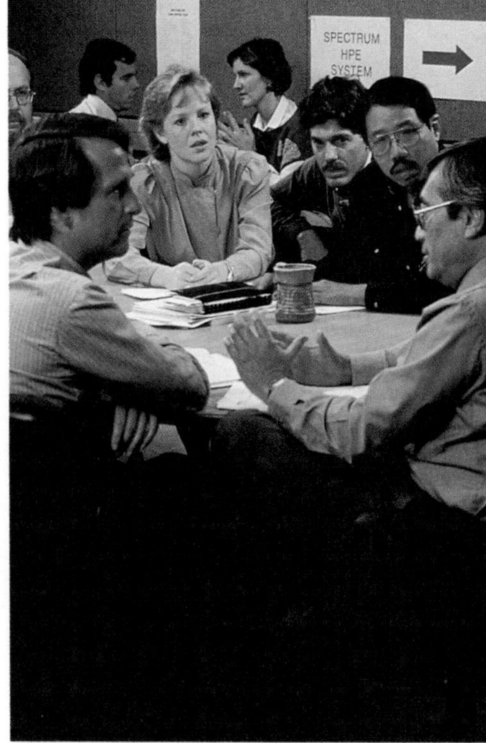

FIGURE 14.3
Problem definition is the starting point for program development.

Unstructured Programs

When computer programming was still in its infancy, programmers had no standard techniques or design methods to follow. Programs were written to solve current problems, but future needs for expanded files or additional program options were not carefully considered. As a result, many programs solved the immediate problem but were difficult to modify or expand later.

Sometimes several major modifications occurred during a program's lifespan. The problems encountered by a maintenance programmer were not unlike those of a family who wanted to winterize a summer cottage. Both were faced with modifying a structure in a way that it was not originally designed to handle. Perhaps the furnace could not keep up with winter temperatures, the windows were not energy efficient and, in general, more room was needed when people were inside most of the day. Sometimes, confronted with these problems, it was easier and more cost efficient to just tear down the cottage and build a new home from scratch.

If a programmer needed to make major changes to a program, similar difficulties could occur. First, the modifications were not always made by the original programmer. Sometimes little or no documentation on the original program was available. Like the summer cottage, the original program was often designed to handle specific applications with little flexibility. These programs would limit the size of files, fail to verify input data, or work with batches of data instead of in real time. Many times programmers found it best to just rewrite the programs from scratch.

Making modifications would have been easier if the original program had not been written in an unstructured manner. **Unstructured programs** were written using a linear approach to problem solving. One instruction followed another until a special condition was reached. When this happened, the program logic branched to another part of the program and continued from there. As programs became more complicated, much branching occurred.

If it was difficult for a maintenance programmer to follow the logic of an unstructured program, it was even harder to modify such a program. The programmer did not always know how new code would affect the rest of the program. Changes to programs were often made in a patchwork fashion, with branches to these patches scattered throughout the program. Someone trying to draw a diagram of the program logic would have lines going in all directions. You can see in Figure 14.4 why unstructured programs were said to contain "spaghetti" code.

During this time, programming was considered more of an art than a science. By the beginning of the 1970s over 85 percent of an organization's programming costs were going for program maintenance. People started looking for ways to reduce these costs and make programs easier to modify.

Structured Programs

As system software was developed, computer scientists recognized that all computer programs, regardless of application, processed data in a series of similar processing steps. This observation altered program development in two important ways.

First, computer manufacturers provided utility software, discussed in Chapter 3, containing processing functions that were standard parts of many programs. These utilities performed such operations as data compression, disk optimization, and hardware emulation. Other utilities made merging and managing large data files easier. Programmers could call up and use these utilities rather than rewrite the code for the frequently used processing functions.

The second change in program development was even more influential. It affected the way programmers approached the programming process itself. This design breakthrough came with the recognition that every program could be written in **structured program** code. In a structured program all aspects of the IPOS cycle can be broken down and coded into three simple structures: sequence, selection, and iteration.

A **sequence** is the normal order for program code. Unless another instruction is inserted, instructions are followed in the same

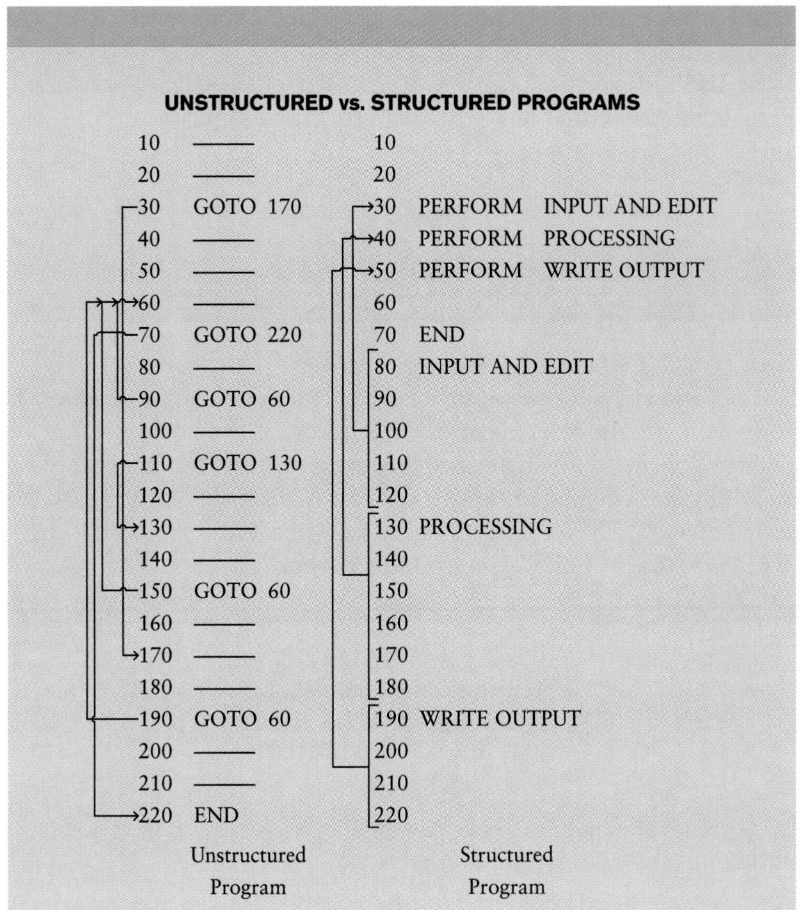

FIGURE 14.4
Unstructured programs are executed in linear fashion, while structured programs execute code modules.

sequence in which they appear within the program. In other words, sequence means that a group of instructions is performed in a preset order. The following segment of a payroll program would be one example. Hours worked and hourly pay rate are entered as data, multiplied to produce the gross pay, and then gross pay is displayed.

```
30 PRINT "ENTER THE HOURS WORKED THIS WEEK"
40 INPUT HOURS
50 PRINT "ENTER HOURLY PAY RATE"
60 INPUT RATE
70 PAY = HOURS * RATE
80 PRINT "GROSS PAY: "; PAY
```

Selection means that one of two alternative sequences of instructions is chosen, based on some condition. For example, the following segment of a payroll program compares hours worked to 40. It uses both the overtime and regular pay calculations when hours are greater than 40. Otherwise, it selects just the regular pay calculations and sets overtime to zero. Regardless of the calculations used, regular and overtime pay are added to get total pay.

```
65 IF HOURS > 40
   THEN OVERTIME = (HOURS - 40) * (RATE * 1.5)
        REGULAR = RATE * 40
   ELSE OVERTIME = 0.00
        REGULAR = HOURS * RATE
70 PAY = REGULAR + OVERTIME
```

Iteration involves a sequence of instructions that is repeated as long as a programmer dictates or until some processing condition changes. In the following example, data is entered, regular and overtime pay are calculated, and total pay is displayed as long as the user enters "YES". This process is repeated until the condition—RESPONSE$ = "YES"—is no longer true.

```
10  RESPONSE$ = "YES"
20  WHILE RESPONSE$ = "YES"
30  PRINT "ENTER THE HOURS WORKED THIS WEEK"
40  INPUT HOURS
50  PRINT "ENTER HOURLY PAY RATE"
60  INPUT RATE
65  IF HOURS > 40
    THEN OVERTIME = (HOURS - 40) * (RATE * 1.5)
         REGULAR = RATE * 40
    ELSE OVERTIME = 0.00
         REGULAR = HOURS * RATE
70  PAY = REGULAR + OVERTIME
80  PRINT "GROSS PAY: "; PAY
90  INPUT "DO YOU WISH TO CONTINUE? (YES/NO)";
           RESPONSE$
100 WEND
110 END
```

The structured approach permits some flexibility. The same program may take many separate forms in the minds of different programmers. In each case, however, the designer establishes segments of code that can be linked to form a workable, quality program.

Another technique in structured programming is to break the code for a program into modules. A **module** is a set of instructions that performs one specific function within a program. For example, most structured applications programs contain separate modules to input data, to check for errors, to perform special processing, and to print reports (see Figure 14.4). A typical module contains no more than a page (about 50 lines) of code and usually can be written in a short period of time by a single programmer. A structured program would consist of several modules, each called upon as needed.

The use of modules and structured programming has several advantages over unstructured programming. Each module is small and considered independent from the other modules in a program. This means that modules for the same program can be written by different programmers and tested separately before being combined into the final program. Modules from one program can be used in another program. Also, if a program needs to be modified, only those modules directly affected need to be changed.

Object-Oriented Programs

Just as structured methodology greatly changed how people program, object-oriented programming is changing the concept of structured programming. **Object-oriented programming** (OOP) is a programming methodology based on objects rather than modules. An *object* is set of programming code that will complete a single task. The object differs from a module in that it contains both descriptions of the data required for the task and the instructions (methods) to perform requested actions. A collection of objects used to solve a problem is considered an object-oriented program.

When a program references an object, it sends a message containing what result is required and lets the object perform the necessary processing. Each object is completely independent of other objects. However, the processing an object performs may be common to several applications. It is common for the same object to be used in several programs, reducing coding time. An object may contain a document, graphic, audio sequence, worksheet, or window as well as any related methods for processing and manipulating these data items.

For example, a payroll system could be written using an object-oriented program. As can be seen in Figure 14.5, several objects would be involved. The COMPUTE PAY object would return an employee's weekly gross pay when given the employee's identification number. This object would access a database to find related information, such as salary schedule or hourly pay, and use this data to return the gross pay amount. Other objects include code for computing TAXES, PAYROLL SAVINGS, MEDICAL deductions, etc. Obviously these few objects would not comprise an entire payroll program. A more complete diagram can be seen in Figure 14.6.

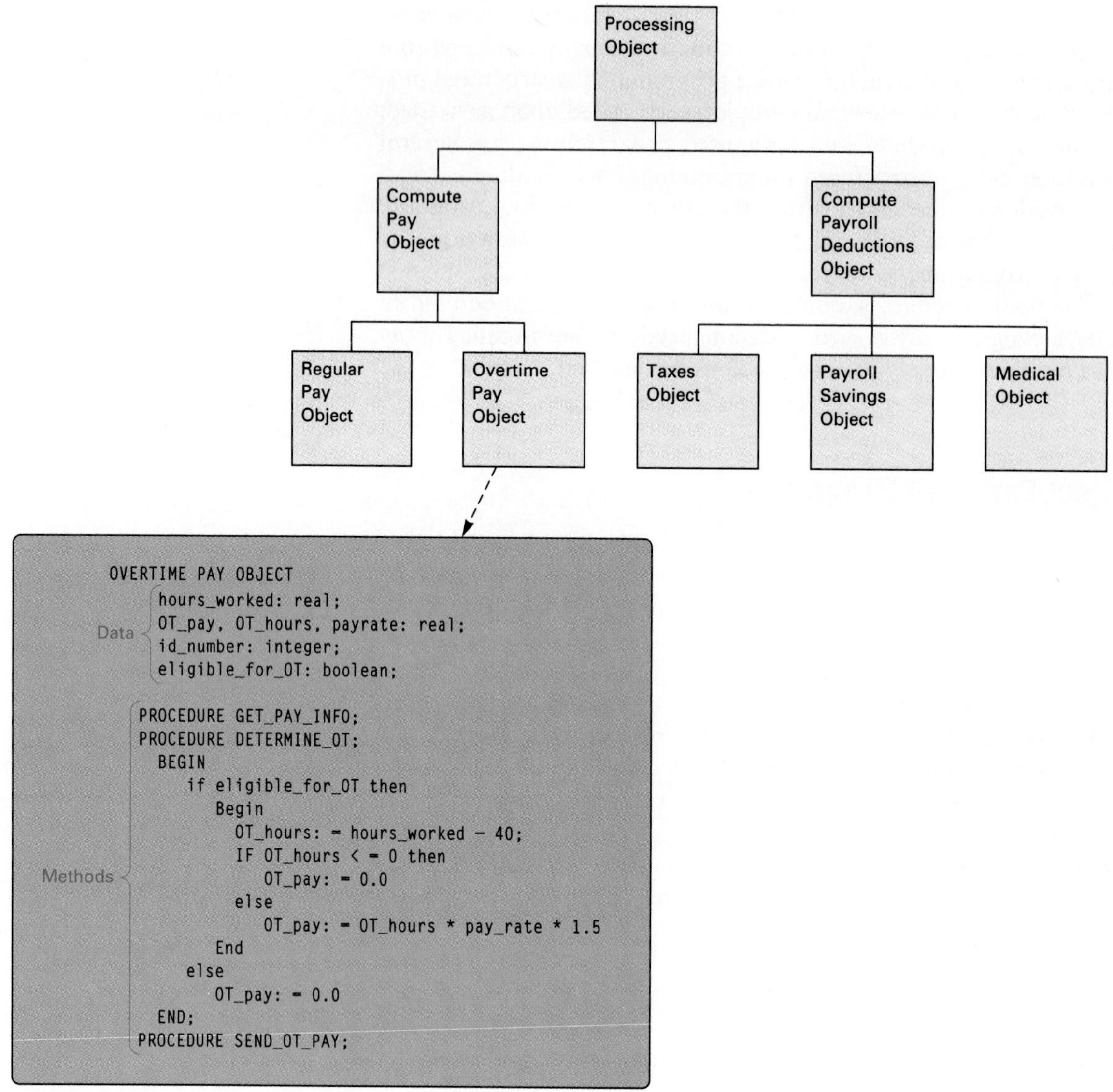
Processing Object
Compute Pay Object
Compute Payroll Deductions Object
Regular Pay Object
Overtime Pay Object
Taxes Object
Payroll Savings Object
Medical Object
OVERTIME PAY OBJECT
Data
hours_worked: real;
OT_pay, OT_hours, payrate: real;
id_number: integer;
eligible_for_OT: boolean;
Methods
PROCEDURE GET_PAY_INFO;
PROCEDURE DETERMINE_OT;
BEGIN
if eligible_for_OT then
Begin
OT_hours: = hours_worked - 40;
IF OT_hours < = 0 then
OT_pay: = 0.0
else
OT_pay: = OT_hours * pay_rate * 1.5
End
else
OT_pay: = 0.0
END;
PROCEDURE SEND_OT_PAY;

FIGURE 14.5
An object contains both the data identifications and necessary instructions for processing.

Figure 14.5 also shows the types of coding found within the single object, OVERTIME PAY. The record retrieved from the database includes the employee's hours worked, hourly pay rate, or salary scale. Methods include computing gross pay and overtime pay if applicable.

OOP is obviously a more complex process than structured programming. This is an initial disadvantage to programmers. However, once an object is written, it can be used in other programs or as a model for other objects. Managing graphic output was one of the first uses for OOP. For example, an object that moves a graphic image to a specified screen location could be used in the free-drawing feature of a graphics package, to define borders in desktop publishing, or for the movement of a missile toward a target in a video game. It is this reliance on previously developed objects that makes object-oriented programming a factor in decreasing the time spent in program development.

Tools for Program Design

Modules and objects become the elements of program design. Figure 14.6 shows a general overview of the structure for a payroll program. This type of graphic representation is called a **structure chart.**

Structure Charts

As seen, a structure chart organizes a program into a series of levels. Modules or objects are identified by rectangles and are executed in order from the top downward and from left to right at each level. This kind of top-down organization is known as a hierarchy. A structure chart is also called a **hierarchy chart.**

Structured programming provides a standard framework within which any program can be designed. The actual processing steps involved in each level of the program are added as additional modules are created or as objects inherit characteristics from higher-level objects. This "top-down" refinement of the program design occurs as the programmer uses design tools to break each module or object into specific program instructions.

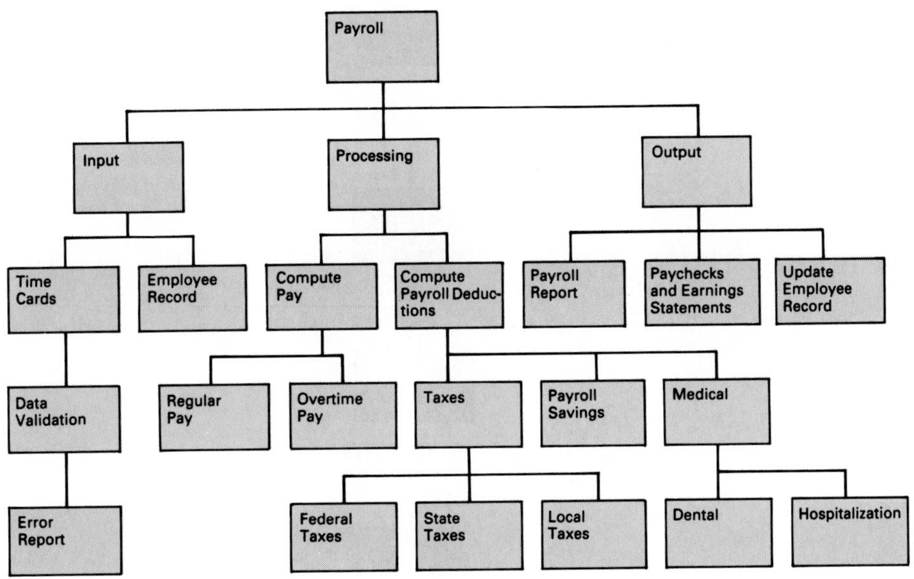

FIGURE 14.6
Structure charts identify the program modules or objects needed to solve a particular problem.

Flowcharts

A common method for defining the steps in a program is through use of a diagram known as a program **flowchart.** A flowchart uses a series of symbols to identify the basic IPOS functions within programs. These symbols, shown in Figure 14.7, are positioned and linked to form a graphic representation of a program's logic. For example, Figure 14.7 shows a program flowchart for the payroll program example. A flowchart is a graphic method for organizing and presenting the specific steps within a program or module.

Pseudocode

While some programmers use flowcharting techniques to represent program steps with symbols, others prefer to use English phrases, or **pseudocode.** Pseudocode became popular because it lends itself

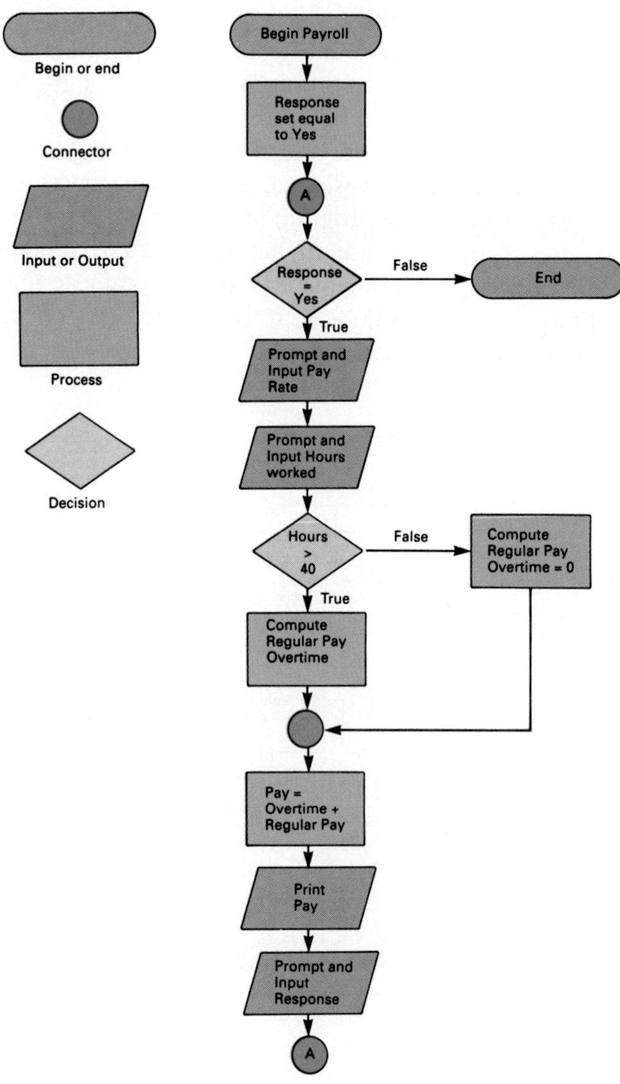

FIGURE 14.7
This flowchart uses symbols and arrows to outline the program logic for payroll processing.

Pseudocode

```
Begin Payroll Program
  Set response = Yes
  Do while response = Yes
    Display "Enter Hours Worked"
    Accept hours
    Display "Enter Hourly Payrate"
    Accept rate
    If hours greater than 40
      Then overtime = (Hours – 40) * (Rate * 1.5)
           Regular = Rate * 40
      Else overtime = 0
           Regular = Rate * Hours
  End-if
  Pay = Regular + Overtime
  Display pay
  Display "Do you wish to continue?"
  Accept response
 End do while
End Payroll Program
```

FIGURE 14.8
Pseudocode outlines in words the logic needed for a payroll program.

to the design of structured programs. Figure 14.8 illustrates the pseudocode version of the payroll program previously flowcharted.

One advantage of designing through use of structure charts, pseudocode, or flowcharting is flexibility. These tools can be translated into program code for any high-level programming language, independent of language rules and syntax. The choice between structure charts, pseudocode, and flowcharting is a matter of personal preference and company standards. Other design tools, not discussed here, are also available. Another benefit is that these design tools provide a basis for reviewing programming operations among all members of an application development team, including users and technicians.

Testing the Program Design

Teamwork in program design and development can help to ensure the quality and reliability of program performance. One important quality control measure is the detailed review of designs before program coding begins. Experienced programmers and/or supervisors review all design documents in a step-by-step procedure known as a **structured walkthrough**. Working together, a small group of computer professionals track the processing of data through the entire

Who's Who

John G. Kemeny (b. 1926)

Thomas E. Kurtz (b. 1928)

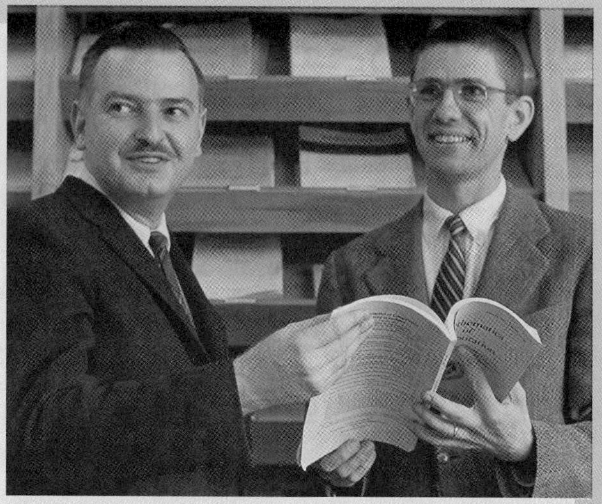

Despite the existence of many computers and such programming languages as FORTRAN and COBOL, programming a computer was complicated in the 1960s. A person needed to have a strong working knowledge of the computer equipment, and the languages lent themselves best to scientific and business applications. John Kemeny (at left in photo) was mathematics department chairman at Dartmouth College in the early 1960s. He had worked on the H-bomb project in Los Alamos and had been an assistant to Albert Einstein. Dartmouth's computer center manager, Thomas Kurtz, convinced Kemeny that the university computer should be time-shared. Together they urged their peers to consider that computer literacy was as important as reading, writing, and arithmetic.

To increase student access, Kemeny and Kurtz developed BASIC in 1964, consisting of 14 different statements. The ease of using BASIC became apparent. Students could program after only two hours of instruction. Many were not science or engineering majors. By placing BASIC in the public domain, the two men allowed its use to spread. Bill Gates wrote a version of BASIC to use on the Altair, an early personal computer. It later became a standard language packaged with all microcomputers. Kemeny and Kurtz tried to set standards for BASIC to unify the many existing versions. In 1985 they released TRUE BASIC, which they saw as a powerful version that could help make programs portable, usable on different types of computers. Although BASIC is no longer the predominant language for college students, many children are taught it in high school and elementary school.

design sequence. The purpose is to identify and adjust any design weaknesses before actual program writing takes place. The more errors that can be uncovered at this stage, the greater the program quality is likely to be.

A vital end product of program design should be a set of test data that will be used to validate programs from the module or object level up through the complete system. **Test data** is an assembled set of data that tries out all of the special processing features and controls of the new program.

For each program function to be tested, test data must include both valid and invalid items. For example, a payroll program might limit the value of checks that can be processed to a minimum of \$20 and a maximum of \$1000. To test this program function, the values $19, $20, $1000, and $1001 might be included in the test data. In this way the data items test the full range of acceptable values and also test to be sure the program can deal with unacceptable data outside both ends of the range.

To test all operational functions of every module, object, and of an entire program, extensive sets of test data may be needed. It is important that preparation of test data be completed during the design stage of program development. The idea of test data is to validate program coding. Quality assurance is greater if development of test data precedes and is separate from the coding operation.

WRITING PROGRAM CODE

If sufficient care is taken with design of programs, coding should be a routine, relatively straightforward process. One instruction in a high-level language usually is written for each line of pseudocode or each flowcharting symbol. To understand the differences in programming languages, we must first see how the computer handles a computer program.

Language Translators

Before the advent of high-level programming languages, computers were complicated to program. Instructions had to be written in the computer's own machine language, which represents internal switch settings as 0s and ls. The complexity of writing machine language

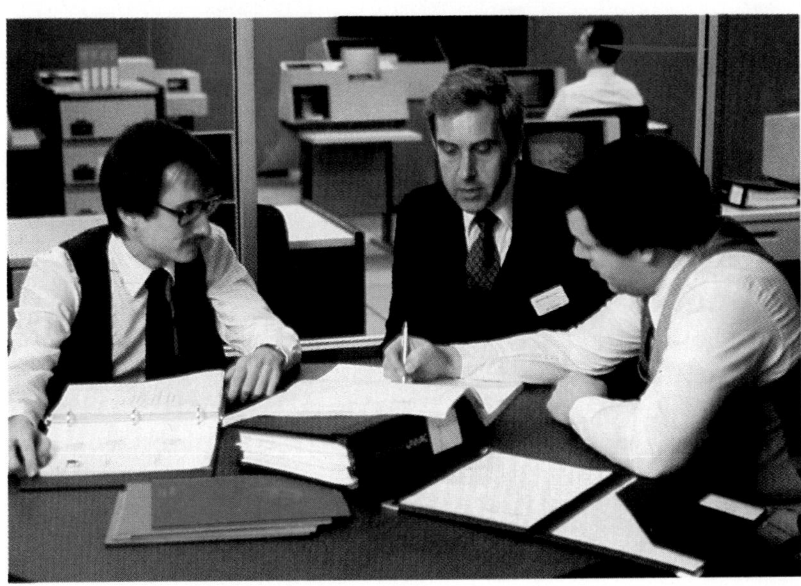

FIGURE 14.9
Structured walkthroughs promote the review and discussion of program design and code with other team members.

programs was addressed in the 1950s when assembly languages made their debut. Programmers using assembly languages relied on translating programs, called *assemblers,* to relieve the burden of coding computer programs in highly detailed machine language. Programs were written in symbolic assembly languages instead of bit patterns. Then assembler software translated the programs into code that the computer could understand. Assemblers generally required one line of assembly code for each machine language instruction to be generated. By today's standards, this method of program translation is simple, but inefficient, since higher-level languages do not maintain this one-to-one relationship. Nonetheless, assemblers were great time-savers in their day.

Although assembler languages are still used for some types of systems programming, they have been replaced by more sophisticated, user-friendly, high-level programming languages and fourth-generation languages (4GLs). These programming languages rely on one of two sophisticated language translators called compilers and interpreters. Like assemblers, they convert program statements written by people into machine instructions. However, for each program statement translated, a compiler or interpreter generates several machine language statements. Compared with assemblers, these language translators allow programmers to write larger, more complex, error-free programs in less time.

Compilers are available for most high-level languages. Figure 14.10 shows the process of translating a program into machine code using a compiler. First, the application program written in a high-level programming language is loaded into memory along with a

FIGURE 14.10
Compilers translate programs written in a high-level language into a complete machine language program or list each instruction that could not be converted.

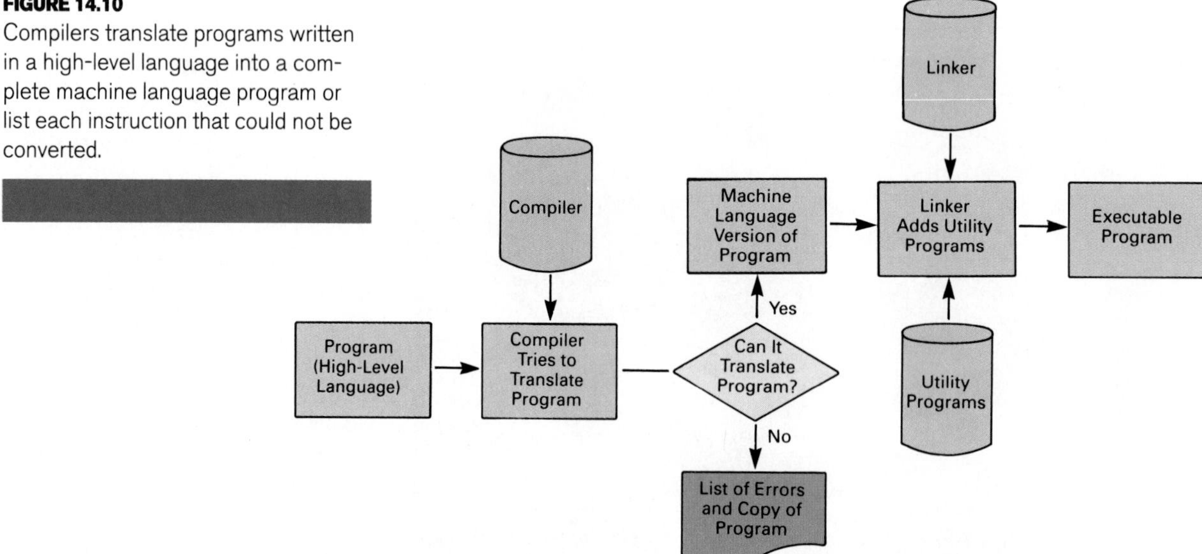

translator program. The compiler checks the program for errors while it is translating the code into machine language.

Syntax errors may prevent the translation from being completed. A **syntax error** is a spelling error or misuse of the high-level language that the computer cannot translate. For example, the COBOL instruction MULTIPLE PAY-RATE BY HOURS GIVING REGULAR-PAY cannot be translated. The COBOL compiler identifies this line as untranslatable because it does not recognize the instruction MULTIPLE. When the programmer corrects the syntax error by replacing MULTIPLE with MULTIPLY, this COBOL instruction can be translated.

In the News...

PROTOTYPING: ADVANTAGES OVER TRADITIONAL METHODS

Most systems developers currently use an approach that was described some 25 years ago to develop today's computer information systems. This development approach, usually termed the Traditional Life-Cycle approach, uses a linear path of analysis, design, development, and implementation phases.

However, the traditional approach to systems development has come under question as information systems grow in complexity and systems development times extend into years. Prototyping has been suggested as an alternative.

An information system's prototype is an early version of a system that contains the most important features of the later production system. The prototype is a model—much like the model used to test a new automobile before it is put into production, or a building before the concrete is poured. With an information system's prototype, the intended users get an early picture of the final production system. This picture allows the users to evaluate the design before the production system is built and implemented.

"Prototyping... incorporates a learning process"

The traditional development approach differs from the prototyping approach in one key aspect: The traditional approach assumes that user requirements can be precisely specified before system construction is attempted. Prototyping, on the other hand, incorporates a learning process into system design. It assumes that precise user requirements are *not* always definable before system construction. While experimenting with a prototype system, users identify, evaluate, and refine production systems requirements. Although prototyping has some problems, it is a vital tool in the development of today's complex information systems.

A word of warning here. The compiler is not going to find **logic errors.** This type of error is translatable but produces the wrong results. In the example above, if the programmer accidentally wrote MULTIPLY PAY-RATE BY EMPLOYEE-NUMBER GIVING REGULAR-PAY, the instruction would be translated. However, the results would be incorrect since employee number is not used in pay calculations. Another example of a logic error would be using a plus sign when a minus sign is needed.

When an error-free translation results, the operating system activates a **linker** program. The linker embeds utility programs needed for input, output, or processing within the translated program. Now the program is complete and ready for use.

At this point the original COBOL program is saved for future updates or modifications. The complete translation, including utilities, is either stored for future use or followed one step at a time, **executed**, by the processing unit. To use a compiler, the computer must have enough memory to store the compiler and the applications program in both its high-level and machine language forms.

Some computers translate programs written in BASIC and other programming languages in a different way, by using an **interpreter**. Interpreters translate and execute one high-level instruction at a time. Each instruction is acted upon after it is translated. Then the translation is discarded. If the program's logic dictates that instructions are repeated, each instruction must be translated again. As seen in Figure 14.11, this process is repeated until the program comes to its logical conclusion or the interpreter finds a syntax error. The advantage to using an interpreter is that it requires a minimum amount of memory. The interpreter needs only enough memory to store the instruction with which it is currently working. This can be

FIGURE 14.11
Interpreters translate high-level language programs into machine code one line at a time, executing each instruction before translating the next. The translation is not saved.

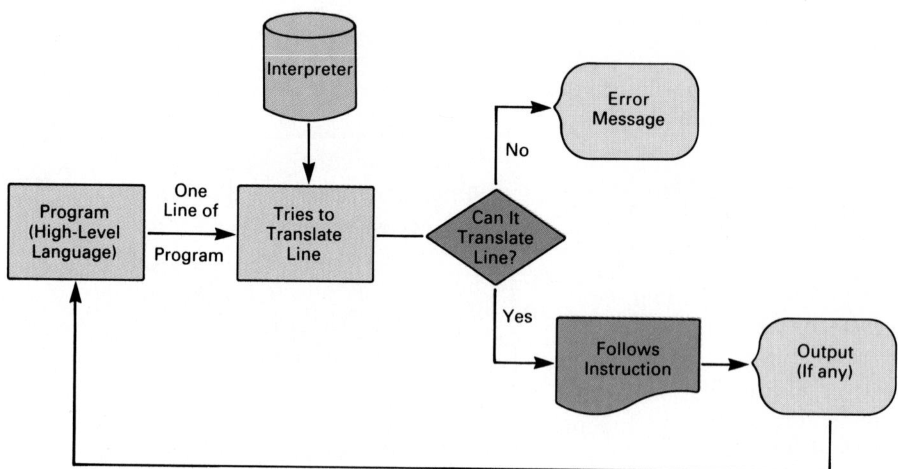

a disadvantage because the translated version of the program is not saved. That means the original program must be translated each time it is used, which slows down processing.

Finding Program Errors

Finding logic errors can be difficult no matter what kind of language translator is used. A finished program, for example, may have 10,000 or more lines of code. Programmers must observe results and apply reasoning to identify the points at which errors occur. Each time a correction is made, it may be necessary to recompile the program involved and to retest the object or module of the program that has been modified. Errors within coded programs are called *bugs*. The process of finding and correcting errors in programs is known as **debugging.** Some high-level-language compilers and interpreters contain debugging features that allow the programmer to follow the program step by step, displaying what is being processed along the way.

Module and object testing of programs should be performed as part of the coding function. That is, a program module or object should not be considered completed until it is tested. Review and structured walkthrough activities typically are integrated with the testing of program routines.

Programming Languages

To code a program design, a programming language is selected with care to meet the specific needs of an application and its users. Through the years, over 200 programming languages have been developed and used for computer processing. The summaries that follow identify and describe only a few of the more popular languages used to implement program designs.

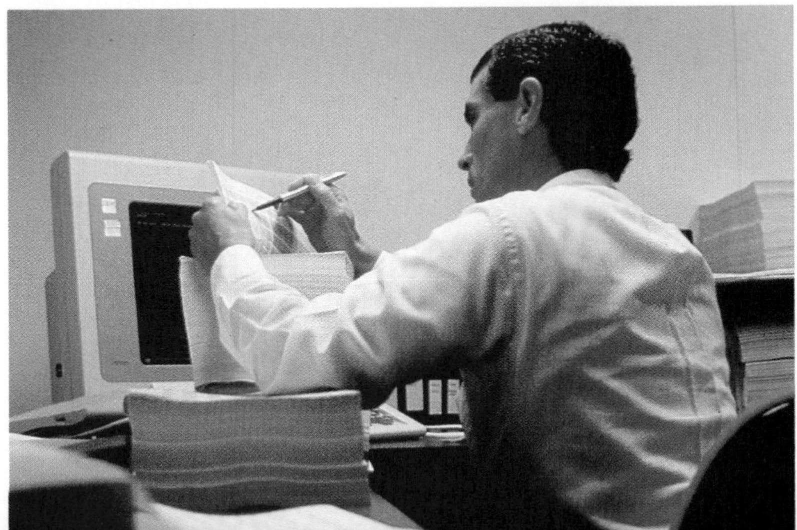

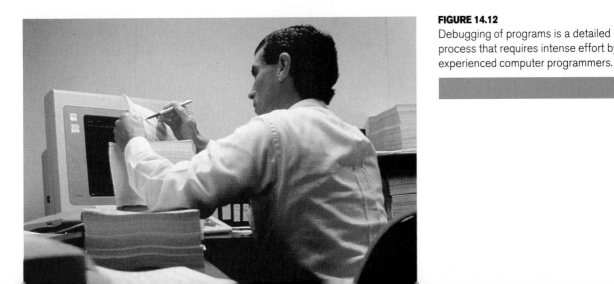

FIGURE 14.12
Debugging of programs is a detailed process that requires intense effort by experienced computer programmers.

FORTRAN

This was the first high-level language. *FORTRAN* (for FORmula TRANslator) was introduced in 1956 to meet the needs of the scientists and engineers who were the predominant users of early computers (see Figure 14.13). This language has limited input/output capacity. Originally, its selection structure was awkward and the iteration structures were very primitive. Programs written in FORTRAN tend to be hard to understand and modify unless they are well documented. With the development of structured programming techniques, new syntax has been added to FORTRAN to make it easier to code properly designed programs.

COBOL

This acronym stands for COmmon Business Oriented Language. *COBOL* development was sponsored by the U.S. Department of Defense in the late 1950s. The language has been in continuous use, with several revisions, since 1960. Billions of dollars have been spent building COBOL programs for mainframe computers. This language, therefore, is still the one most commonly used for business programs (see Figure 14.14).

Because COBOL was designed with business applications in mind, it has been very successful in business environments. An extensive vocabulary exists for defining files, records, and fields. It easily handles disk or tape input/output and has selection and iteration structures that are much better than FORTRAN's. COBOL has also been adapted to the personal computer environment by including syntax to handle screen displays on color monitors, floppy disk I/O, and networks.

FIGURE 14.13
FORTRAN was the first high-level programming language. This FORTRAN program instructs the computer to add two numbers and display the sum on a screen.

```
    Integer Num1, Num2, Sum
    Read (5,10) Num1, Num2
10  Format (I4, I4)
    Sum = Num1 + Num2
    Write (6,20) Num1, Num2, Sum
20  Format (10X, 'The Sum Of', I4, '+', I4, 'IS', I5)
    Stop
    End
```

```
Identification Division.
 Program-ID. Addition.

Environment Division.
 Input-Output Section.
  .
  .
  .
Data Division
 File Section
 FD Data-in
      Label records are standard.
   01 Numbers-to-be-processed.
        05 Number-1-In PIC 999.
        05 Number-2-In PIC 999.

   FD Answer-out
        Label records are omitted.
   01 Sum-to-be-printed PIC X(27).

Working-Storage  Section.
01 Temporary-work area.
        05 Filler            PIC X(10)      Value "The Sum Of"
        05 Number-1-Out      PIC 999.
        05 Filler            PIC XXX        Value "+"
        05 Number-2-Out      PIC 999.
        05 Filler            PIC X(4)       Value "Is".
        04 Sum-Out           PIC 9(4).

Procedure Division.
 Processing-routine.
   Open input Data-in
        Output Answer-out.
   Read Data-in.
   Add Number-1-In, Number-2-In giving Sum-Out.
   Move Number-1-In to Number-1-Out.
   Move Number-2-In to Number-2-Out.
   Write Sum-to-be-printed
        From Temporary-work area.
   Close Data-in
        Answer-out.
   Stop run.
```

FIGURE 14.14
COBOL is the major language used for programming business applications. This COBOL program allows input of two numbers whose sum is computed and then displayed.

BASIC

This programming language was developed during the 1960s at Dartmouth College, specifically for training students to program, regardless of their major. *BASIC* stands for Beginners' All-purpose Symbolic Instruction Code. Implementation of BASIC started on relatively large systems installed on college campuses. When personal computers were introduced, BASIC became a standard programming language both for software developers and for end-users who wanted to program their own applications. This language still is in use for student training and for microcomputer-oriented application software (Figure 14.15).

The examples of the payroll program structures given earlier in the chapter are written in BASIC. They also highlight several problems with this language. Since BASIC was designed before the idea of structured programming, it did not handle iteration as easily as other languages.

In addition, the selection—IF—structure in the original Dartmouth BASIC did not have an ELSE option as shown in Figure 14.16. To get around this limitation, programmers had to have two selection statements. Modifications to BASIC have occurred, taking advantage of the developments in structured programming.

To make up for the lack of easy-to-use selection and iteration structures, there are several variations to the BASIC language. For example, QuickBASIC and True BASIC are two versions of the language that contain statements for structured programming as well as routines for graphics. Visual BASIC allows easy programming of windows, menus, and other GUI elements.

```
10  Input N1
20  Input N2
30  Sum = N1 + N2
40  Print "The Sum Of"; N1;" + "; N2;" IS "; Sum
50  End
```

FIGURE 14.15
BASIC is a relatively easy-to-use language. This BASIC program, which adds two numbers and displays the sum, is shorter than the COBOL program that performs the same task.

```
IF/THEN/ELSE STATEMENT
50 If Hours > 40
      Then overtime = (Hours – 40) * (Rate * 1.5):
            Regular = Rate * 40
      Else overtime = 0.00:
            Regular = Hours * Rate

IF/THEN STATEMENT
50 If Hours > 40
      Then overtime = (Hours – 40) * (Rate * 1.5):
            Regular = Rate * 40

52 If Hours <= 40
      Then overtime = 0.00: Regular = Hours * Rate
```

FIGURE 14.16
Versions of BASIC without the IF/THEN/ELSE selection structure rely on the use of several IF/THEN structures to perform the same task.

LOGO

A more recent programming language designed for educational use is *LOGO,* based on work by Seymour Papert. His interest in psychology and computers led him to new ideas on how to use computers for learning. He helped develop LOGO, which allows even very young students to explore geometric principles. This is done, not as some abstract process, but through the interactive use of computers (see Figure 14.17). The name LOGO is derived from the Greek word *logos,* meaning speech, calculation, or thought. It was used to suggest that the language was meant to be symbolic in nature. These concepts are discussed in more detail in Papert's book *Mindstorms.*

Unlike programming languages used for business or scientific applications, LOGO is an end in itself. This language was not designed to create reports or to track an airplane's flight path. It is to be used only as a learning tool. With LOGO, students can use computers for problem solving. LOGO statements result in the movement of either a turtle on the screen or a real robot turtle. The child programmer is able to explore geometry, applied physics, and art with the results graphically displayed as the path of the turtle.

```
Pendown
Forward 40
Right 90
Forward 40
Right 90
Forward 40
Right 90
Forward 40
Penup
```

FIGURE 14.17
The LOGO program will instruct the computer to draw a square on the screen.

Pascal

This language, developed during the 1970s, is named after Blaise Pascal, inventor of an early mechanical calculator. A strength of *Pascal* is that it was developed specifically to implement structured programming techniques (see Figure 14.18). The Pascal language has been popular in educational curricula for computer scientists and as an alternative to BASIC for the programming of personal computers. Since Pascal was designed for structured methodology, it has been readily adapted to object-oriented programming techniques as well. Newer versions of Pascal contain the code necessary to define objects.

```
Program Add-it (Input, Output);
Var Num1, Num2, Sum: Integer;
Begin
  Readln (Input, Num1, Num2);
  Sum:= Num1 + Num2;
  Writeln (Output, 'The Sum Of', Num1:4, '+',
                   Num2:4, 'Is', Sum:5)
End.
```

FIGURE 14.18
This Pascal program accepts two numbers, then displays the numbers and their sum.

Ada

An even newer language called *Ada* is derived from Pascal. Ada was designed with superior input/output capabilities (see Figure 14.19). Therefore, it was anticipated that Ada would have broader use in industry than Pascal.

Ada is a programming language born in the 1980s. It was named after Lady Ada Augusta Lovelace, an important figure in nineteenth-century computing history. The Department of Defense has sponsored the development of Ada. Their goal is to create a scientific language that would help programmers use good programming techniques and become a national standard like COBOL.

C

C is another example of a computer language that evolved from structured programming concepts (see Figure 14.20). It was developed at Bell Laboratories in 1972. C has many features of high-level languages, yet it is used in bit and byte manipulation for writing systems programs, data communication utilities, and graphics routines. C has many similarities to Pascal in structure and code. It has also been adapted to object-oriented programming.

```
Use Text _10;

Procedure main is
  Type number is integer;
  Package number_10 is new integer _10 (number);
  Num1, Num2, Sum: Number;

Begin
  Get (Num1); Get (Num2);
  Sum: = Num1 + Num2;
  Put ('The Sum Of');
  Put (Num1, Width = 4);
  Put ('+');
  Put (Num2, Width = 4);
  Put ('Is');
  Put (Sum, Width = 5);

  New_Line;

End Main
```

FIGURE 14.19
An Ada program is shown here adding two numbers. As in the Pascal program, processing code is enclosed by BEGIN and END statements.

```
/*Integer version*/

main( )
  {
  int n1 = 0;
  int n2 = 0;
  int sum = 0;

  printf("?"); scanf("%d", &n1);
  printf("?"); scanf ("%d", &n2);

  sum = n1 + n2;

  print ("The Sum Of %d + %d Is %d\n", n1, n2, sum);
  }
```

FIGURE 14.20
The C program adds two numbers and displays their sum.

Like Ada, C is a powerful language with many programming options. As a result, it is not easy for a programmer to become proficient in C. However, C is a *portable language,* which means a C program can be used on many different types of computers with few changes. This is a definite advantage in organizations with many models of personal computers connected by a network.

RPG

RPG stands for Report Program Generator. It was first introduced in 1964 to run on minicomputers with limited memory capacity. As the name implies, RPG was designed to produce business reports. To use RPG, a programmer defines the format in input files by naming fields and specifying their lengths and types—numeric, character, and so forth. Then the programmer defines the operation to be performed on certain fields. The program logic in an RPG program is not developed in a sequence of steps. Instead, specifications for the file description, input, calculations, and output are developed separately. The program in Figure 14.21 shows the four specifications needed to add two numbers.

When RPG was first introduced, it could not handle any type of selections. To meet the ever-changing demands for business reports, RPG has changed. More powerful versions labeled RPGII, RPGIII, and RPG400 have been introduced to handle selections and real-time processing.

```
                FILE DESCRIPTION SPECIFICATIONS
Numbin    IP     F   80              Disk              S
Numbout   0      F   182    OF      Printer
                INPUT FORMAT SPECIFICATIONS
Filein    NS     01
                                           1     30Num1
                                           4     60Num2
                CALCULATION SPECIFICATIONS
01        Num1       Add  Num2       Sum  42

                OUTPUT FORMAT SPECIFICATIONS
Numout    H      207  1P
          OR          OF
                                          34  'The Sum Of 2 Numbers'
          D      1    01
                                          20  'The Sum Of'
                            Num1   3      24
                                          26  '+'
                            Num2   3      30
                                          33  'Is'
                             Sum   3      38
```

FIGURE 14.21
In this RPG program to add two numbers, specifications indicate the input, processing, and output operations.

While the RPG program in Figure 14.21 does not demonstrate all of the RPG capabilities, it does show how each entry for one of the specifications must be written in a designated column. This feature makes RPG unlike the other programming languages previously discussed. RPG implements *nonprocedural programming,* a technique in which it is unnecessary to list and specify processing functions on a step-by-step basis. Instead, the required functions are described in terms of operational parameters that are processed to generate programs, making detailed coding unnecessary.

MODULA-2

Anyone familiar with Pascal and looking at the code of a *Modula-2* program (see Figure 14.22) would notice their similarities. This is because both languages were developed by a Swiss computer scientist, Nicholas Wirth. To increase the use of structured programming techniques in systems program development, Wirth created Modula-2 (called MOD-2). However, the C programming language, with its ability to handle object-oriented programming, has surpassed the use of MOD-2 in systems programming.

```
MODULE Add Numbers;
    FROM InOut IMPORT ReadInt, WriteInt, WriteString, WriteLn;
    VAR number1, number2, sum: INTEGER;

BEGIN
    ReadInt (number1);
    ReadInt (number2);
    Sum: = number1 + number2;
    WriteString ("The sum of");
    WriteInt (number1, 4);
    WriteString ("and");
    WriteInt (number2, 4);
    WriteString ("is");
    WriteInt (sum, 5);
    WriteLn

END Add Numbers.
```

FIGURE 14.22
Two numbers are being added together in this Modula-2 program. Note the similarites to the Pascal program in Figure 14.18.

Fourth-Generation Languages

Fourth-generation languages (4GLs) are starting to gather quite a following. They require the use of a select but powerful vocabulary to access databases. For example, Figure 14.23 shows how a user

```
COUNT customer WHERE city EQUALS New York
201
COUNT customer WHERE city EQUALS New York AND purchase-
description EQUALS guitar and year EQUALS 1990
34
```

FIGURE 14.23
Fourth-generation languages access information from a database through the use of special keywords.

might request customer information from an organization's database. The commands COUNT, WHERE, and EQUALS are part of the fourth-generation language. A similar request in high-level languages could require several lines of code.

A characteristic of fourth-generation languages is that they rely on prior development of a database. Application development is simplified greatly because most of the work in traditional programming goes into development of routines for creating and updating files. Since the database program is responsible for creating and updating files, the 4GL user can concentrate on accessing and formatting needed data.

Natural Languages

Fifth-generation natural language interfaces are currently making their way from research labs into mainstream data processing environments. These nonprocedural languages make it possible for users to address computers in normal human languages without a special vocabulary or syntax. Users present English statements to programs that perform comparisons and develop relationships among described items. Figure 14.24 provides a simple example of a natural language request for customer information.

Compared to the 4GL request, natural language interfaces make assumptions about user requests. For example, the second request in Figure 14.24 just asks how many guitars have been purchased. The computer assumes that the user still is asking for information about customers in New York City. To date, the major applications

How many customers do we have in the Big Apple?

I don't know what you mean by the Big Apple.

New York City

The XYZ Company has 201 customers with addresses in

New York City

How many purchased guitars this year?

34

FIGURE 14.24
Natural languages, which represent the latest way of communicating instructions to a computer, are much more flexible than earlier programming languages.

of natural languages have been for decision support and expert systems. To implement these interfaces, programmers use an **authoring system** to create the customized screens, data retrieval functions, and database setups necessary for the complexity required by these applications.

Figure 14.25 summarizes major strengths and weaknesses of the most popular high-level languages.

FIGURE 14.25
Since computer languages were designed to handle problems in different fields, each has its own strengths and weaknesses.

Summary of Application Program Languages

Language	Applications	Strengths	Weaknesses
Ada	Scientific	Easy to structure programs	Complex, takes time to master
BASIC	Educational, Simple Scientific, and Business	Easy to learn, widely used with microcomputers	Difficult to structure, weak Input/Output capabilities
C	Systems and Graphics	Portable, easy to structure programs	Complex, takes time to master
COBOL	Business	Self-documenting, easy to structure programs, widely used	Verbose, complex computations, awkward
FORTRAN	Scientific and Graphics	Handles complex computations and graphics	Difficult to structure, weak Input/Output capabilities
Fourth Generation	Access to Databases	Simplifies program development	Limited to database applications
LOGO	Educational	Easy to learn, allows simple graphics	Few applications outside of education
Modula-2	Systems	Self-structuring	Not object-oriented
Natural	Decision Support Systems Expert Systems	Uses English and other human languages	Limited to database applications
Pascal	Educational and Scientific	Easy to structure programs	Weak Input/Output capabilities
RPG	Business	Easy to generate business reports	Difficult to structure, complex computations, awkward

TESTING AND DEBUGGING

Attention to testing requirements takes place throughout the design and coding steps of a project. Then, as a final quality check, a system test is performed prior to release of the new system to users. A system test involves two major sets of activities:

- Testing sections of programs and complete programs
- Testing the system under realistic operating conditions

Program Testing

When programs are written in modules or objects, they are put through a series of top-down test procedures. The bottom level of a program is an individual module or object. As previously mentioned, every programmer is responsible for testing program sections as they are written.

A problem can arise in testing modules because part of the test involves checking the interconnections among modules. To check program modules, stub testing techniques often are employed. **Stub testing** is the execution of selected program modules to see if they interact correctly. Quite often the stub is an incomplete module designed to stand in for other, more complex modules. It may do no more than display that the stub has (or has not) been executed in the proper sequence. In some instances standard stub modules are used that input data to or receive output from the module being tested. Although, in OOP, objects are not interconnected, stub testing is still done to check logical flow through the object. In every new program each section must be tested and debugged before it is included in the overall system.

The testing situation is similar even if only program maintenance is being done. If the program was designed by using structured techniques, just one or two sections can be modified without having to recode the other modules. Each changed module or object is tested separately and then joined with the rest of the program.

At the next level of testing, groups of modules or hierarchies of objects are tested. This process builds until complete portions of structured programs are tested as integrated units. Ultimately, the entire set of programs that forms an application is processed with a complete set of test data. When all debugging and recompilation of programs is complete, a full test can be performed.

This procedure is repeated many times until a program is tested completely and is ready for integration into the overall system. At that point the program becomes part of the system test.

System Test

A system test, as described in the previous chapter, involves operation of the complete system, including new equipment and documented procedures by users or by an independent team of employees. System tests usually are performed with realistic data input. The use of previously processed data serves to provide known results against which tests can be compared.

A requirement for a realistic test situation is that all of the documentation needed to operate and maintain programs and application procedures be available. System documentation should be part of the test, which determines whether the system is ready to be turned over to users.

During a system test, program bugs or shortcomings often are discovered. It may be necessary to modify programs before final acceptance of the system. For these reasons it is important to keep a log of all findings during a system test and to use this log to be sure that programming and system documentation is modified to reflect all changes.

After an in-house system test is complete, many commercial software developers run two more types of tests on the software. Pre-release copies of the software, with documentation, are sent to a selected group of users outside the company. These people field-test the software in real-life situations. This step of system testing, called *beta testing,* may help to find additional bugs in the software.

Some commercial developers even have on-site usability testing labs. People using the new software in the lab are monitored as to how they use the software. Recording actual keystrokes or mistakes made by the users can help developers make improvements in future software versions.

DOCUMENTATION AND TRAINING

Recall that enhancement of programs is a requirement built into the very nature of computer systems. As soon as a new system becomes operational, it usually is subject to modification. Either to meet regulations or to capitalize on newly discovered opportunities, computer applications are modified throughout their useful lives.

From a programming standpoint, this means that the documentation prepared by any programmer must be readable and usable by any other programmer. In this way, any programmer can be assigned to modify both programs and supporting documentation as enhancement is required.

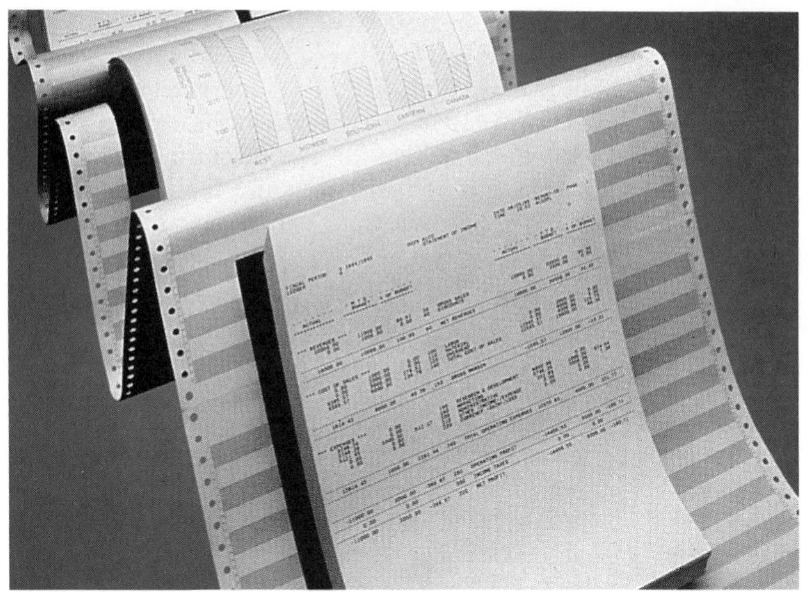

FIGURE 14.26
Complete documentation includes user guides, sample reports, and screen displays. It is necessary for correct use of the program.

Careful documentation also is important because, in most instances today, programming is a team effort. Many computer systems require programs large enough to warrant assignment of at least two and possibly over 50 programmers to the same project. To promote better communication among programmers, it is imperative that professionals within any organization follow the same standards for design and documentation. This helps to ensure that the modules and objects will interact smoothly during program execution. This is especially true when developing software for public use—perhaps a new application package. Uniform methods must be followed in preparation of structure charts, flowcharts, pseudocode, and other documentation.

User Training

Programming is a major part of the implementation step of a systems development project. Toward the end of the implementation step, extensive user training must take place. In addition, computer operators and other personnel require training. At these levels everyone needs extensive documentation. Manuals must be prepared both for training sessions and for reference during ongoing operation of the system. Complete documentation of program design and coding must be included in the data library, along with copies of the storage media that hold the programs.

In short, a lot of loose ends and technical details must be tied together before a system is operational. This final step of a programming project is set up, in large part, to ensure that all the necessary details are accounted for. This step should end with a meeting at which the project manager, the director of computer operations, and the data librarian review all documentation in detail, request any additions, and ultimately accept the documents and the storage media. This review evaluates the efficiency and the quality of the programming effort, providing a learning experience and a basis for improvement of future projects.

Program Maintenance

As will be discussed in Chapter 15, operational programs can become a basis for use of the computer in security breaches and theft. Therefore, once programs are turned over to operations personnel, procedures must be put into place that guard against both misuse and obsolescence of programs and their supporting documents.

For every disk or tape kept within a data library, records of its use should be established and maintained. The original code is checked out only to authorized people. These people must account for everything they do to the programs. Any changes must lead to amendment of the master and distributed copies of code documentation and manuals. Different edition, or **version**, numbers should be assigned to each modified edition of documents and media. Responsible people must not lose sight of the fact that program documentation and media are major assets of their organization. These assets must be guarded and handled with the same level of care accorded to money and securities.

FIGURE 14.27
User training must be completed before programs are put into regular use.

A Closer Look...

Programming Languages (No Matter How You Say It)

As with human languages, programming languages differ in vocabulary and the structure of sentences. The following examples represent a simple IPOS cycle with an iteration. To emphasize language differences, the same functions are shown in COBOL, BASIC, and Pascal code. Also included is programming code from dBASE III PLUS, a popular database management system. Each program allows input of two numbers from a disk file, computes their sum, finds the larger number, and stores the numbers, larger value, and sum on a different disk file. The same idea can be expressed several ways within the same language, so a programmer can develop a style—not unlike a novelist.

COBOL

```
FILE-CONTROL.
    SELECT DATA-IN
      ASSIGN TO DISK.
    SELECT DATA-OUT
      ASSIGN TO DISK.

FD  DATA-IN
    VALUE OF DATA-IN IS "A:DATAFILE.IN'.
    01  NUMBERS-TO-BE-PROCESSED.
        05  NUMBER-1-IN     PIC 999.
        05  NUMBER-2-IN     PIC 999.

FD  DATA-OUT
    VALUE OF DATA-OUT IS "B:RESULTS.OUT".
    01  OUTPUT-LINE-1.
        05  FILLER          PIC X(11)  VALUE "THE SUM OF ".
        05  NUMBER-1-OUT    PIC ZZ9.
        05  FILLER          PIC X(5)   VALUE " AND ".
        05  NUMBER-2-OUT    PIC ZZ9.
        05  FILLER          PIC X(4)   VALUE " IS ".
        05  SUM-OUT         PIC ZZZ9.
    01  OUTPUT-LINE-2.
        05  FILLER          PIC X(17)  VALUE "LARGER NUMBER IS
        05  MAXIMUM-OUT     PIC ZZ9.

WORKING-STORAGE SECTION.
01  END-OF-FILE             PIC X.
```

BASIC

```
10  OPEN "A:DATAFILE.IN" FOR INPUT AS
      FILE#1

20  OPEN "A:DATAFILE.IN" FOR OUTPUT AS
      FILE#2
```

Pascal

```
VAR number_1, number_2, sum, maximum :
  INTEGER;

ASSIGN (infile, "A:DATAFILE.IN);
RESET (infile);
ASSIGN (outfile, "B:RESULTS.OUT");
REWRITE (outfile);
```

dBASE III PLUS

```
select 1
use DATAFILE     (data already stored in
                   database)

select 2
use RESULTS      (report file already
                   formatted in database)
report form RESULTS to file
  B:RESULTS.DBF
```

Q How are fields, records, and files set up for the data?

A In all four examples the input file "A:DATAFILE.IN" is located on the disk in drive "A" and made ready for access. An output file called "B:RESULTS.OUT" is also set up on the disk in drive "B" for later use.

Q What code is required to read the two numbers from the file on disk?

A Each data value is read from the disk and assigned a variable name (NUMBER1 and NUMBER2), storage areas whose names remain constant but whose contents change with the data. The number of variable names and the order in which they are read must be specified in the program.

COBOL

```
OPEN INPUT DATA-IN.
READ DATA-IN AT END MOVE 'Y' TO
  END-OF-FILE.
```

BASIC

```
30  INPUT#1, NUMBER1, NUMBER2
```

Pascal

```
READLN (infile, number_1, number_2);
```

dBASE III PLUS

```
get NUMBER1, NUMBER2

skip (goes to next record)
```

Q Can we just use a plus sign and an equal sign to get the sum?

A No, each programming language uses a slightly different method to do an arithmetic operation like addition. Most languages still require the mathematical signs we are accustomed to, but the form the computation takes may look different. The answer is assigned its own variable name. In this example the variable name SUM is used.

COBOL

```
ADD NUMBER-1-IN, NUMBER-2-IN GIVING SUM.
```

BASIC

```
40  SUM = NUMBER1 + NUMBER2
```

Pascal

```
sum := number_1 + number_2;
```

dBASE III PLUS

```
store NUMBER1 + NUMBER2 to SUM
```

Q How do you code a logical operation, such as finding out which number is larger?

A Most languages include a decision statement of the following form:

IF a comparison is true
  THEN perform an action
ELSE if it is not true
  THEN perform a
    different action.

COBOL

```
IF NUMBER-1-IN > NUMBER-2-IN
  MOVE NUMBER-1-IN TO MAXIMUM
ELSE
  MOVE NUMBER-2-IN TO MAXIMUM.
```

BASIC

```
50  IF (NUMBER1>NUMBER2)
    THEN MAXIMUM = NUMBER1
    ELSE MAXIMUM = NUMBER2
```

Pascal

```
IF number_1 > number_2 THEN
   maximum := number_1
ELSE
   maximum := number_2;
```

dBASE III PLUS

```
if NUMBER1 > NUMBER2
  store NUMBER1 to MAXIMUM
else
  store NUMBER2 to MAXIMUM
```

Q Is output to a disk similar to input?

A Usually there are different program statements for input and output. However, both must show which drive contains the referenced disk, the name of the file on the disk, how many variables there are, and the order in which they are stored.

COBOL

```
MOVE NUMBER-1-IN TO NUMBER-1-OUT.
MOVE NUMBER-2-IN TO NUMBER-2-OUT.

WRITE OUTPUT-LINE-1.
WRITE OUTPUT-LINE-2.
```

BASIC

```
60  PRINT#2 "THE SUM OF "; NUMBER1;
      " AND "; NUMBER2; " IS "; SUM

70  PRINT#2 "LARGER NUMBER IS "; MAXIMUM
```

Pascal

```
WRITELN (outfile, 'THE SUM OF ',
  number_1:3,' AND ',number_2:2,
  ' IS ', sum:4);
WRITELN (outfile, 'LARGER NUMBER IS ',
  maximum:3);
```

dBASE III PLUS

```
@MLINE,    1 say "THE SUM OF"
@MLINE,   12 say NUMBER1 picture "999"
@MLINE,   16 say "AND"
@MLINE,   20 say NUMBER2 picture "999"
@MLINE,   23 say "IS"
@MLINE,   26 say SUM picture "9999"

@MLINE+1, 1 say "LARGER NUMBER IS"
@MLINE+1,18 say MAXIMUM picture "999"
```

Q How can I make the program repeat the same IPOS cycle?

A For any iteration the program must contain what code is to be repeated and how many times to cycle through the code. In this example the IPOS cycle will be looped through over and over until all the data in the input file has been processed. EOF stands for end of file.

COBOL

```
PERFORM PROCESSING-LOOP UNTIL
  END-OF-FILE = 'Y'.
PROCESSING-LOOP.
 WRITE OUTPUT-LINE-1.
 etc.
```

BASIC

```
30   INPUT#1, NUMBER1, NUMBER2

60   PRINT#2 "THE SUM OF "; NUMBER1;
       " AND "; NUMBER; " IS "; SUM
       etc.

80   IF EOF(1) THEN GOTO 90
     ELSE GOTO 30

90   END
```

Pascal

```
WHILE NOT EOF(infile) DO
  BEGIN

WRITELN (outfile, 'THE SUM OF',
  number_1:3,' AND ',number_2:3
  ' IS ', SUM:4);
  etc.

  END;
```

dBASE III PLUS

```
do while .not. eof()

@MLINE, 1 say "THE SUM OF"
 etc.

enddo
```

Chapter Facts

- Programming is more than just writing code. Properly designed programs require a four-step process: (1) designing the program; (2) writing the program code; (3) testing and debugging; and (4) documentation and training.
- Good design methods for programs include structured programming. In a structured program, all code is organized into one of three structures: (1) sequence, (2) selection, and (3) iteration.
- Programs can be organized by modules, each handling a specific function. Single modules can be modified without affecting the logic of the entire program.
- Object-oriented programming is another program organization method wherein an object contains both descriptions of the data and the processing code to generate a specified result.
- Program design is done through a structure chart in a top-down manner. Flowcharts and pseudocode show step-by-step programming logic. Before code is written, logic is reviewed in a structured walkthrough. Test data to examine all conditions of the program is also collected.
- Language translators convert high-level languages into machine language.
- Assemblers convert assembly language programs into machine language, each instruction representing one machine instruction.
- Compilers translate entire programs line by line. If errors are found, they are listed. If the translation is error-free, a linker program embeds needed utilities. The translation is then executed.
- Interpreters translate, then execute, the program one line at a time. This continues until the program is completed or an error is found. The translation is not saved.
- A programming language is chosen that best fits the particular application. A variety of languages are available, including FORTRAN, COBOL, BASIC, Pascal, Ada, C, RPG, and Modula-2. Special languages also exist to aid in accessing databases (fourth-generation languages) and for decision-support and expert systems (natural languages).
- Bugs in the program code and logic are detected through another structured walkthrough. Each module is tested independently through stub testing. Finally, the entire program is tried out on the test data.

- Documentation is important when maintaining programs and in team programming. The latest versions of programs and documentation should be carefully stored.
- Program maintenance is an ongoing procedure involving modifications for cyclic operations, new laws, and changes in company policy.

Terms to Remember

a. authoring system
b. code
c. compiler
d. debugging
e. execute
f. flowchart
g. hierarchy chart
h. iteration
i. interpreter
j. linker
k. logic error
l. module
m. object-oriented programming (OOP)
n. program specifications
o. pseudocode
p. selection
q. sequence
r. structure chart
s. structured program
t. structured walk-through
u. stub testing
v. syntax error
w. test data
x. unstructured program
y. version

Mix and Match

Match the following definitions to the Terms to Remember.

1. ____ the process of finding and correcting program errors.
2. ____ basic structure of a computer program whereby one or two alternate sequences of instructions is used, based upon a tested condition.
3. ____ software package that helps computer professionals create a customized user interface and associated data management system.
4. ____ program that translates and executes one high-level language instruction at a time. Translations are not saved.
5. ____ basic structure of a computer program whereby instructions are executed in the order in which they appear.

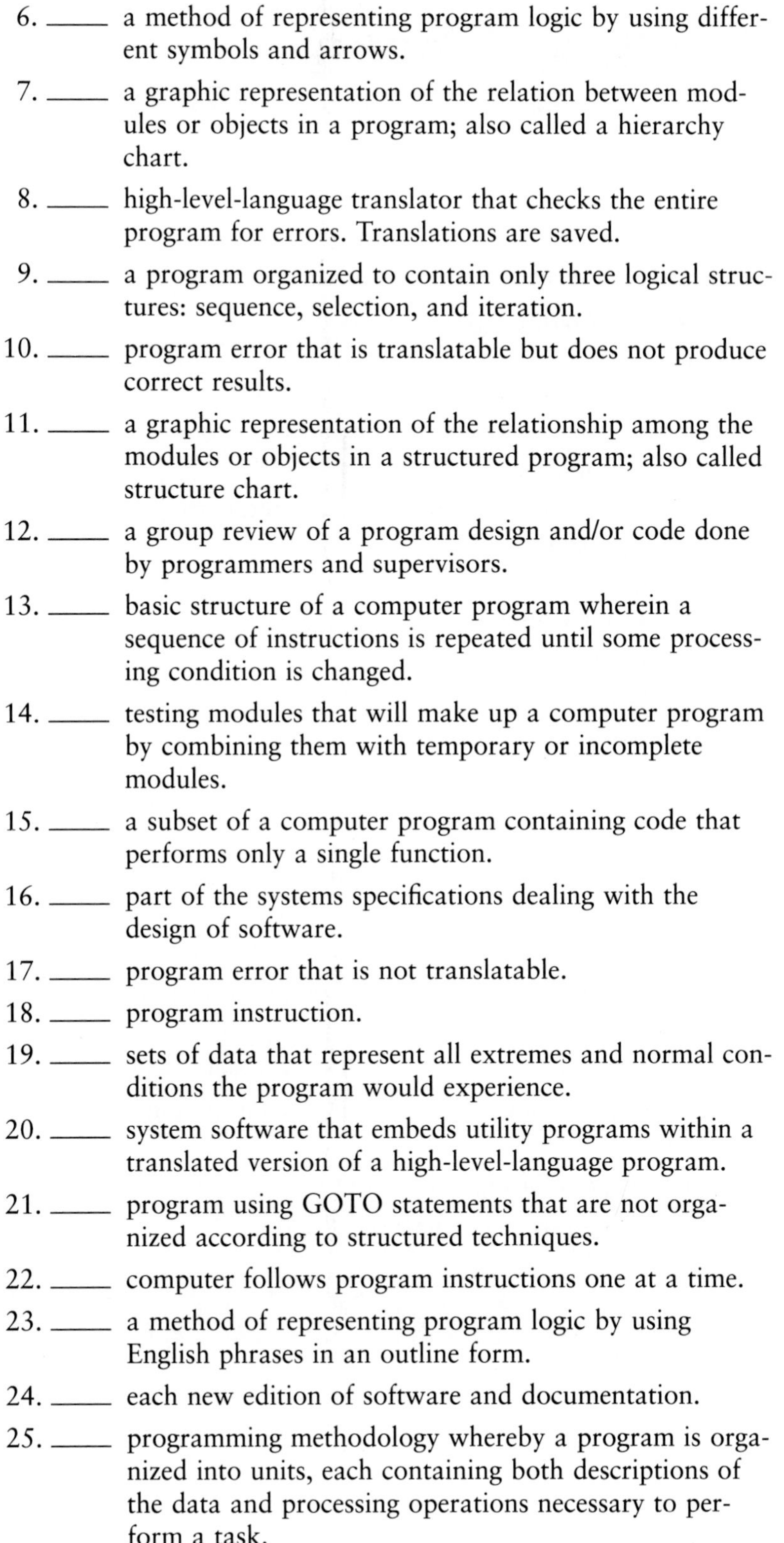

6. ____ a method of representing program logic by using different symbols and arrows.
7. ____ a graphic representation of the relation between modules or objects in a program; also called a hierarchy chart.
8. ____ high-level-language translator that checks the entire program for errors. Translations are saved.
9. ____ a program organized to contain only three logical structures: sequence, selection, and iteration.
10. ____ program error that is translatable but does not produce correct results.
11. ____ a graphic representation of the relationship among the modules or objects in a structured program; also called structure chart.
12. ____ a group review of a program design and/or code done by programmers and supervisors.
13. ____ basic structure of a computer program wherein a sequence of instructions is repeated until some processing condition is changed.
14. ____ testing modules that will make up a computer program by combining them with temporary or incomplete modules.
15. ____ a subset of a computer program containing code that performs only a single function.
16. ____ part of the systems specifications dealing with the design of software.
17. ____ program error that is not translatable.
18. ____ program instruction.
19. ____ sets of data that represent all extremes and normal conditions the program would experience.
20. ____ system software that embeds utility programs within a translated version of a high-level-language program.
21. ____ program using GOTO statements that are not organized according to structured techniques.
22. ____ computer follows program instructions one at a time.
23. ____ a method of representing program logic by using English phrases in an outline form.
24. ____ each new edition of software and documentation.
25. ____ programming methodology whereby a program is organized into units, each containing both descriptions of the data and processing operations necessary to perform a task.

Review Questions

1. In what ways is computer programming different from the misconceptions people have about the programming process?
2. Identify the four steps in the programming process.
3. Identify the three structures found in a structured program.
4. How is a program module different from an object?
5. What are two advantages of using structure charts, flowcharts, or pseudocode to design a program?
6. How do structured walkthroughs help reduce costs and enhance program quality?
7. How does a line of pseudocode or a flowcharting symbol relate to program code?
8. Describe two activities that help programmers check the reliability of their programs.
9. How are assemblers different from high-level-language translators?
10. Explain the differences between an interpreter and a compiler. Give an advantage and a disadvantage to using each.
11. Identify the types of applications associated with these programming languages: FORTRAN, COBOL, BASIC, LOGO, Pascal, Ada, C, RPG, Modula-2, fourth-generation languages, and natural languages.
12. What activities are associated with a system test?
13. How can the design of structured programs help in program maintenance?
14. What is one requirement for a realistic system test?
15. Identify two reasons why program documentation is important.
16. What happens during a documentation review?
17. What is program maintenance?

Applying What You've Learned

1. Designing tools, such as pseudocode and flowcharts, are used for more than just programming projects. They are similar to term paper outlines, assembly instructions, recipes, and wiring diagrams. Use both flowcharting and pseudocode to give a

step-by-step analysis of how to solve one of the following:
a. change a flat tire
b. drive to some remote or hard-to-get-to place
c. start up a computer and load in a program
d. solve a long division problem in math

2. Several hundred computer programming languages have been developed over the years. Some are now obsolete, while others are used only in specialized applications. Report on a programming language not mentioned in the text. Find out about its main use, when and where it was developed, and some advantages or disadvantages of the language. SNOBOL, FORTH, APL, PL/1, LISP, and ALGOL are some languages. Other language names can be found in ads for programmers, computer dictionaries, or guides to published books.

3. It takes a special person to be a programmer. What professional skills do you think would be most beneficial? What personality traits could make a programmer effective? What traits might hamper a programmer on the job?

4. It is important that test data be developed that tries out all options and extreme conditions in a program. It should also include invalid or incorrect data to make sure that it is picked up by the program. For each application, describe a set of test data.
   a. checking to see that a valid date is input into a program in the form mm/dd/yy, like 06/24/94
   b. keeping reservations for a hotel
   c. scheduling classes and rooms for a small college
   d. computing telephone bills

5. User training is an important, but sometimes neglected, aspect of program development. For one of the applications programs or languages available in school or at home, examine the users' guides and existing documentation. List what types of help are available for beginning users (tutorials, workbooks, and so forth). What special features (appendices, error lists, and so forth) are available for advanced users? Does the quality and amount of training material seem sufficient for people to learn the program on their own? What would improve the materials?

Answers to Mix and Match

1. d 2. p 3. a 4. i 5. q 6. f 7. r 8. c 9. s 10. k
11. g 12. t 13. h 14. u 15. l 16. n 17. v 18. b
19. w 20. j 21. x 22. e 23. o 24. y 25. m

UNIT FIVE

Technological Trends

Chapter 15 discusses the potential abuses to personal privacy by organizations using computer systems. Ethical issues related to using technology are examined. The chapter also enumerates warning signs for computer crimes and helps people identify ways to protect their computer systems from viruses and other destructive programs. As a result, protecting systems from electronic invasions, natural disasters, and fraudulent schemes becomes an important concern for every computer user.

Finally, Chapter 16 takes a close look at future trends in technology. As career options related to these trends are explored in detail, the need for continuing education is emphasized. New career paths related to technological developments will open up for people with the prerequisite skills or the willingness to acquire them. Many of these skills will center on the ability to operate and maintain a computer system.

15

Privacy, Ethics, Crime, and Security

- **From the User's Point of View**
- **Privacy**
  - Invasions of privacy
  - The right to privacy
- **Ethics**
  - Ethical issues
  - Ethical guidelines
  - Our responsibilities and opportunities
- **Crime**
  - Examples of computer crime
  - Types of computer crime
  - Signals of potential computer crime
  - Crimes against computers
- **Security**
  - Controls for small computer systems
  - Maintaining security of large computer systems
- *A Closer Look . . . Privacy—Is It Still Possible?*

FROM THE USER'S POINT OF VIEW

Information has become a valuable asset for both individuals and organizations. As you become comfortable working with technology, you will naturally explore new methods for gathering, storing, and exchanging data. With this power, there is also potential for abuse. Used with malice or neglect, computer technology can become a tool for committing crimes or infringing upon your individual rights to privacy. In this chapter we will explore these rights, discuss related ethical issues, identify some of the warning signs of computer abuses, and describe how to maintain the security of computer systems.

PRIVACY

Computers can store personal information about every aspect of your life. The personal information held about you in a computer file can be used for beneficial purposes. A nation understands the make-up of its citizens by maintaining census data on individuals. Your financial records can be exchanged electronically between banks and credit offices, perhaps to expedite processing of a loan application. The positive uses for personal data files abound. However, computer-based data files also are prime targets of abuse. Consider the following hypothetical case.

The first of the month has arrived and your rent payment is due. However, you feel your landlord has neglected his maintenance duties. You notify the landlord that you have decided to hold your rent payment in escrow as allowed by city ordinance until the dispute is settled. Eventually, you reach an agreement and pay your rent. Life seems to have returned to normal—until you discover that your landlord has adversely affected your credit and credibility.

When you apply for a car loan, your application is denied because you are listed as a poor credit risk. You ask why, but the car agency doesn't know. After looking into the matter, you find that your landlord reported you to a credit agency for nonpayment when you legally held back your rent. In addition, when looking for another place to rent, you are constantly turned down. Later, you find your name on a list of "troublemakers" shared among local landlords in the area.

- Have you been treated unfairly for asserting your legal rights as a tenant?
- Has your privacy been violated when information about you was reported to the other landlords?

- Is your landlord guilty of violating your constitutional rights by reporting false or incomplete information to the credit agency?
- Were the credit agency and car dealer too willing to accept unverified information about your creditworthiness?

In this case you may be the victim of misused computer technology. Your privacy may have been invaded; a crime may have been committed. Certainly your landlord has behaved in an unethical manner by not providing completely accurate information. The credit agency may be guilty of negligence for not verifying the information. Computer technology was used to your disadvantage.

Invasions of Privacy

Computers don't invade anybody's privacy. People do. Since computer systems are designed to be user friendly, it may not be difficult for unauthorized people to get access to personal data. People must be able to protect their computer files and limit file access only to authorized users.

The protection procedures used depend on individual situations. For example, consider what happens when you ask for credit. The prospective creditor asks you to provide information about yourself, your financial situation, and any loans you have made in the past. You should carefully read anything you sign, especially papers related to borrowing money. Almost every loan application has a provision under which you give the prospective lender permission to check on your credit status. Lenders need to know an individual's financial history to protect their investments. This means that lenders can contact computer credit services, banks, retailers, or others with whom you have done business.

Once you give permission to have your credit checked, you have given up some of your rights to privacy (Figure 15.1). Before you sign, be sure you understand what rights you are surrendering. You also should come to an understanding with the party that asks for permission to investigate you. For example, you can ask what happens if negative information is reported. Make it clear that you feel you have a right to see and explain any negative reports that might be issued. On the other hand, if you know of past problems with credit or other personal information, it is better to explain the problem in advance. If the information will disqualify you, save the embarrassment of authorizing an information search. Don't apply for credit until you are fairly sure you will qualify. Be aware that computer files may contain information on almost any business transaction in which you have been involved.

If you learn of any negative information reported about you, be aware you have the right to correct any errors. There have been instances in which bad credit information has been entered into the wrong records. Also, businesspeople can make unjustified or incomplete reports about your actions, as in the example of the rent dispute.

FIGURE 15.1
When authorizing a personal credit check, you surrender some of your rights to privacy.

The Right to Privacy

The right to privacy—to various extents—is guaranteed by law. The best known legal basis for claims to privacy are contained in the Fourth Amendment of the U.S. Constitution. The Fourth Amendment protects U.S. citizens from "unreasonable searches and seizures . . . of person, house, papers and effects." This language is general and has been subject to considerable debate and many lawsuits. To clarify the meaning of the Fourth Amendment, Congress has passed a number of laws, including the following eight.

Freedom of Information Act (1970)

Personal data maintained by the federal government became accessible to any citizen who wanted it through the Freedom of Information Act of 1970. Unless release of the data threatens national security or infringes upon someone else's privacy, information must be furnished in response to requests.

Fair Credit Reporting Act (1970)

Also in 1970, Congress passed the Fair Credit Reporting Act. This law gave individuals the right to examine and, if desired, challenge information held in their credit files. It also prohibits the exchange of credit information with unauthorized users.

Privacy Act (1974)

The Privacy Act of 1974 was aimed at reducing the amount of irrelevant information collected by federal agencies and maintained in government computer files. These agencies are required to reveal how they intend to use the information they keep. In addition, permission must be obtained from affected individuals before the information is used for other than the stated purposes. The effectiveness of this act is dampened by the difficulty in establishing the relevance of an item of data. As another shortcoming, the law applies only to government agencies.

Education Privacy Act (1974)

The Education Privacy Act restricts access to grades, evaluations, and other computer-based data maintained by private and public schools. It also establishes a student's right to examine and challenge personal data maintained by these systems.

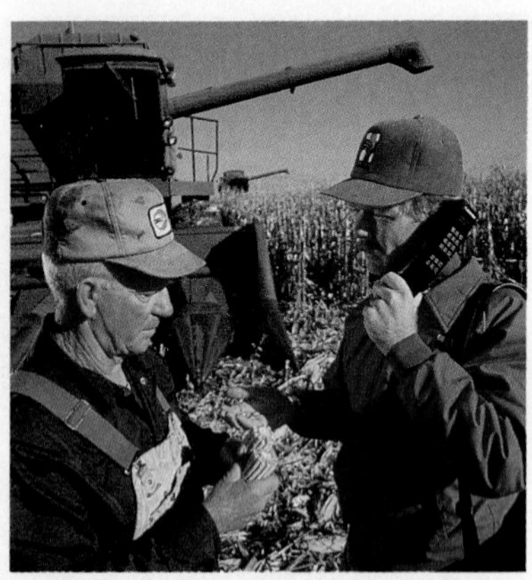

FIGURE 15.2
Personal privacy can be invaded in many ways—for example, eavesdropping on cellular telephone conversations.

Right to Financial Privacy Act (1978)

This government legislation sets strict guidelines for federal agencies wishing to review bank accounts. However, this law does not regulate state agencies or bank employees.

Electronic Communications Privacy Act (1986)

The Electronic Communications Act provides privacy protection to communications involving new forms of technology (Figure 15.2). In particular, this legislation clearly identifies electronic mail and makes it a federal crime to intercept these computer-based transmissions.

Video Privacy Protection Act (1988)

The Video Privacy Act specifically bars retailers from selling or disclosing video-rental data without a court order or the consumer's consent. This legislation was enacted after a list of video tapes rented by U.S. Supreme Court nominee Robert Bork was printed by a Washington newspaper at the time of his confirmation hearings.

Computer Matching and Privacy Act (1988)

Through this legislation, federal agencies are regulated in the types of government computer files they can match to verify personal information. Matches are made to determine if a person may be ineligible for federal benefits or defaulting on government loans. A person can challenge the information if incorrect.

ETHICS

Privacy and the use of computer-based data are at the heart of a broader issue—ethical standards. Ethical standards usually are not established by government legislation, although ignoring ethical issues could mean engaging in illegal activities. Instead, **ethical standards** are a set of principles a person uses when considering the rights, privileges, and anticipated responses of all persons and groups likely to be affected by an individual's or organization's actions.

Ethical Issues

Many ethical issues are outside specific legal precedents or fall into gray areas within the law. Therefore, a personal ethical standard must supply the principles for specific courses of action. These standards come into play when selling a used car. Is it unethical to sell the car "as is" without mentioning the bad brakes and the crack in the engine block? Consider these technology-based ethical issues.

- Not registering or paying the registration fee for a shareware package you commonly use.
- Reading someone's E-mail without permission.
- Using your company's computer system for personal business activities.
- Purchasing a software package with a limited license agreement for your personal computer and installing a copy of the package on the computer at work.
- Publishing a research paper, which uses a database collected by others, without their permission.
- Misrepresenting environmental or performance statistics by rounding off data values before the final analysis is performed.
- Using, without permission, a colleague's worksheet template or expert system to help you put together a bid for a competing project.
- Monitoring, without their knowledge, employees' data entry rates and number of breaks, using their own computer systems.
- Firing an employee, based on data that was obtained by unapproved work monitoring or from unverified sources.

Quite often ethical blunders arise from miscommunications and the mishandling of people. These errors take place when one person does not take the rights of others into consideration before engaging in an activity or two sides have conflicting viewpoints.

Ethical Guidelines

Many organizations are establishing ethical guidelines for members and employees (see Figure 15.3). These organizations feel that high ethical standards equate to good employee performance, healthy customer relations, and fewer legal problems. Consultant Darlene Orlov (cited by Cole, 1991*) has clients ask 12 questions when considering potentially unethical actions.

- Is the situation legal?
- How do you feel about the situation? Are you feeling unusually anxious? Are you feeling fearful?
- Does your conscience bother you?
- Will any rules, policies, or regulations be violated?
- Is the proposed action consistent with past practice?

*Cole, Diane. "Companies Crack Down on Dishonesty," *Managing Your Career,* published by the *Wall Street Journal,* Spring 1991, pp. 8–11.

The ACM Code of Ethics and Professional Conduct*

PREAMBLE

Commitment to professional conduct is expected of every member (voting members, associate members, and student members) of the Association for Computing Machinery (ACM). This code identifies several issues professionals are likely to face, and provides guidelines for dealing with them. Section 1 presents fundamental ethical considerations, while Section 2 addresses additional considerations of professional conduct. Statements in Section 3 pertain more specifically to individuals who have a leadership role, whether in the workplace or in a professional organization such as ACM. Guidelines for encouraging compliance with this Code are given in Section 4.

1. General Moral Imperatives

As an ACM member, I will...

1.1 Contribute to society and human well-being,
1.2 Avoid harm to others,
1.3 Be honest and trustworthy,
1.4 Be fair and take action not to discriminate,
1.5 Honor property rights including copyrights and patents,
1.6 Give proper credit for intellectual property,
1.7 Access computing and communication resources only when authorized to do so,
1.8 Respect the privacy of others,
1.9 Honor confidentiality.

2. More Specific Professional Responsibilities

As an ACM computing professional, I will...

2.1 Strive to achieve the highest quality in both the process and products of professional work,
2.2 Acquire and maintain professional competence,
2.3 Know and respect existing laws pertaining to professional work,
2.4 Accept and provide appropriate professional review,
2.5 Give comprehensive and thorough evaluations of computer systems and their impacts, with special emphasis on possible risks,
2.6 Honor contracts, agreements, and assigned responsibilities,
2.7 Improve public understanding of computing and its consequences.

3. Organizational Leadership Imperatives

As an ACM member and organizational leader, I will...

3.1 Articulate social responsibilities of members of an organizational unit and encourage full acceptance of those responsibilities,
3.2 Manage personnel and resources to design and build information systems that enhance the quality of working life,
3.3 Acknowledge and support proper and authorized uses of an organization's computing and communication resources,
3.4 Ensure that users and those who will be affected by a system have their needs clearly articulated during the assessment and design of requirements, and that later the system must be validated to meet requirements,
3.5 Articulate and support policies that protect the dignity of users and others affected by a computing system,
3.6 Create opportunities for members of the organization to learn the principles and limitations of computer systems.

4. Compliance with the Code

As an ACM member, I will...

4.1 Uphold and promote the principles of this Code,
4.2 Agree to take appropriate action leading to a remedy if the Code is violated,
4.3 Treat violations of this code as inconsistent with membership in the ACM.

*Draft revision, February 12, 1992, *Communications of the ACM*, May 1992, pp. 94–95.

FIGURE 15.3

Many organizations ask their members or employees to subscribe to a code of conduct and ethics.

- How would you feel if the details of this situation appeared on the front page of the local newspaper?
- Does this situation require that you lie about the process or the results?
- Do you consider this to be an "extraordinary" situation that demands an unusual response?
- Are you acting fairly? Would you want to be treated this way?
- Would you be able to discuss the proposed situation with your immediate supervisor? The president of the organization? Your family? The organization's clients?
- If a close friend of yours took this action, how would you feel?
- Will you have to hide or keep your actions secret? Has someone warned you not to disclose your actions to anyone?

When in doubt, ask for advice. Another person's point of view is often missing when unethical actions occur. By getting another perspective before acting, you can shed new light on the situation.

Our Responsibilities and Opportunities

Privacy and ethical issues often arise from a volatile mixture of our personal point of view and the use of information. Some type of computer-recorded information is maintained for nearly every person in the United States. It starts when we are born—most birth certificates now are computer-generated. Computer-maintained records about us continue to be created and accessed throughout

FIGURE 15.4
Managers monitoring the work of employees without their knowledge is one of many ethical issues facing people working with information technology.

our lives. If misuse of this information is to be avoided, preventive measures have to come from us.

Knowledge and legislation are the tools we have to control the impact technology has on society. As citizens, we have the responsibility to make our voices heard when abuses occur. We can do this through consumer power and by knowing and insisting on our rights. If you become involved with the design or operation of computer systems, you will have the opportunity to ensure that the system is responsibly designed and made secure to reduce the potential of misuse.

CRIME

Information is power. Constructive use of information opens great potential for improvements and benefits. The fact that millions of computers exist establishes that they are wanted and that they are serving the needs of people and organizations. Used properly, computers are powerful and valuable tools.

However, computers can be and have been misused. In the hands of a dishonest person with special knowledge about sensitive systems, the computer can become a powerful, hard-to-detect tool for the criminal.

Examples of Computer Crime

The news media have detailed hundreds of crimes that involved computers. To make matters worse, experts fear that reported cases make up only a small portion of overall computer crime since many such crimes go undetected, and many that are detected are not reported. The five situations described below provide examples of the dangers involved.

Michigan State University

Michigan State University has a large time-sharing computer system that supports research and is used by teachers and several thousand students. A few years ago, two students developed and implemented a plan to steal passwords and computer time from other users.

The plan was simple. Many students went to the computer lab to complete assignments on personal computers linked to the larger system. Knowing this, the thieves wrote a program that mimicked the larger computer's security program. Unsuspecting students would enter their passwords into a personal computer running with the thieves' fake program. The program would store the passwords, then display an error message. Thinking the computer was out of order, students would move to another machine. They never knew their passwords had been stolen. The thieves would collect the passwords and use the accounts later.

An alert university programmer eventually tracked down the thieves. The programmer was unaware that his password had been stolen until he noticed activity reported on his account at 2 a.m. His suspicions that someone was tampering with his account were confirmed when subsequent reports of activity at odd hours led to the capture of the culprits. Computer-based recordkeeping contributed to their downfall.

Pacific Telephone Company

Jerry Schneider was a whiz kid who built his own computer system when he was 10. By the time he was in high school, he had started his own electronics company. Schneider started out as a *hacker,* a self-taught computer hobbyist who may use his knowledge to gain unauthorized access to computers. While he was a part-time college student, Schneider discovered a way to steal electronic equipment from Pacific Telephone Company. He retrieved old computer printouts and other documentation from a Pacific Telephone trash container to acquire correct account numbers, passwords, and procedures. Then, using a computer in his home, he ordered parts without being billed for them.

Schneider had expensive telephone components delivered to his home and to other locations. Once, he used his computer to order delivery of a $25,000 switchboard to a manhole cover at the intersection of two streets. He picked up the switchboard in a Pacific Telephone truck he bought at a company surplus auction.

Much of the equipment Schneider stole in this way was resold to Pacific Telephone. In fact, he used the company's own computer system to determine which stock levels were low, so he would know what items to steal. Schneider's crime spree ended when one of his own employees turned him in after a dispute over pay.

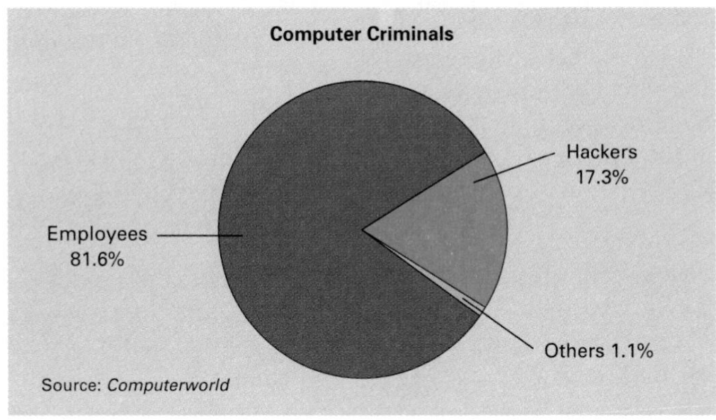

FIGURE 15.5
Although most computer crimes are committed by employees of an organization, hackers are responsible for many crimes as well.

Penn Central Railroad

The case of Penn Central Railroad revolved around missing boxcars. The computer criminals in this case tampered with a computerized freight flow system, and boxcars were routed to a small railroad company outside of Chicago. There the boxcars seemed to have disappeared. The computer system was modified so that the missing boxcars would not be reported.

Investigation indicated that the boxcars had been repainted and used by other railroad companies. According to some estimates, about 400 boxcars were stolen in this manner. But Penn Central wished to minimize attention to the crime and chose not to prosecute.

Equity Funding Corporation

Equity Funding Corporation was a group of companies that handled investments and insurance. Top-level managers from some of these companies lied about company profits to attract investors. In addition, they created volumes of fake insurance policies, then sold

In the News...

TAKING A BYTE OUT OF COMPUTER CRIME

According to the Better Business Bureau, the vast majority of computer crimes are preventable. Consider the following security measures:

Employee hiring. Conduct thorough background checks on all potential EDP employees. Check with former employers, verify technical skills, and check credit histories.

Controlling access to facilities. Maintain a log book with times and names of all who have access to the computer facilities. Allow only employees who work with the computer to sign in.

Physical security. Separate computer facilities from other departments in a secure, isolated area. Provide the appropriate personnel with proper identification that can be verified at the entrance.

Protective devices. Take advantage of all the security devices built into the computer system. Have the company that sold or leased you the equipment explain how password rotation, security codes, and code scrambling devices can control access.

Storage procedures. It is essential to have a duplicate set of all vital tapes, software, and company data stored in a secure, isolated storage space accessible to only top EDP executives.

Audits. Conduct periodic security checks both internally and independently.

"Keeping in mind that some computer crimes are so sophisticated that they may take months, even years, to detect and unravel, management should be constantly on the alert for possible indications of wrongdoing," warns the Better Business Bureau.

them, packaged with valid policies, to other insurance companies. The system was programmed to report only valid policies for auditing purposes. Once the scam was uncovered, more than 20 people were convicted of federal charges. Estimates of losses were as high as $2 billion.

Your Hometown

Computers are used for the same types of criminal activity every day in schools, homes, and businesses. A computer user shares a new program with a friend or associate by making an illegal copy of the software (see Figure 15.6). This type of criminal activity seems quite small by comparison to the Equity Funding or Pacific Telephone cases. When many small crimes are added together, however, the sum represents the theft of millions of dollars in software each year.

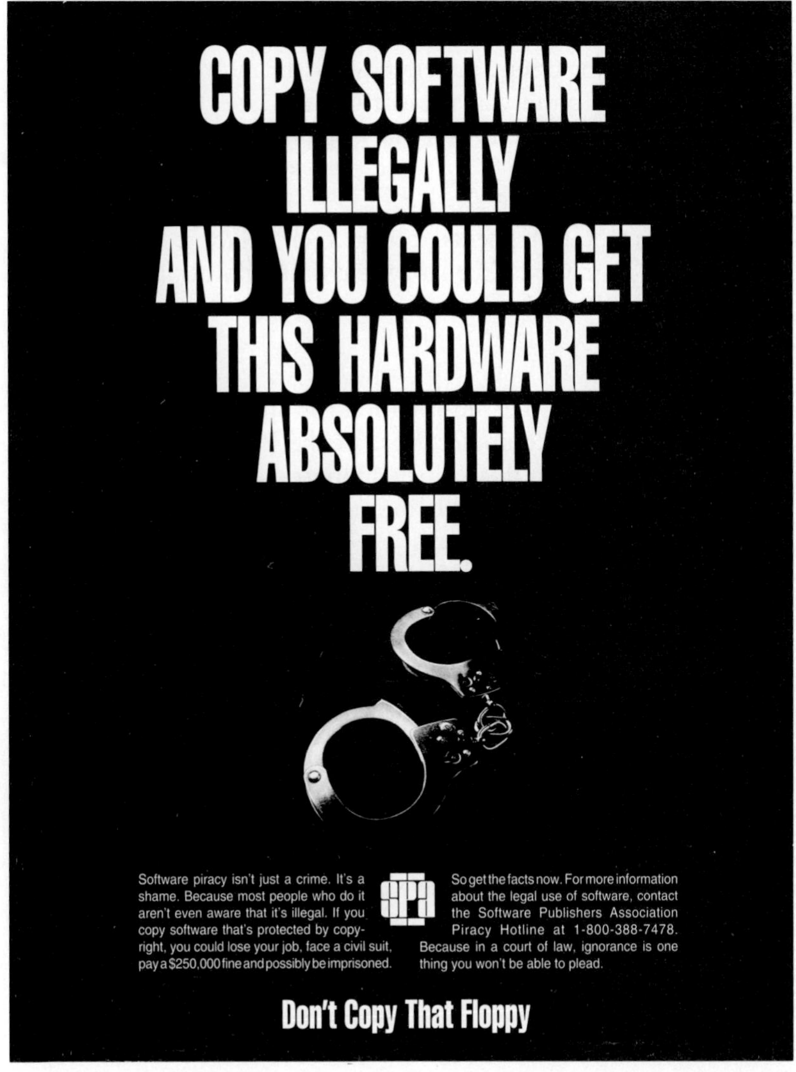

FIGURE 15.6
Copying software for a friend is a computer crime if you do so with copyrighted programs.

Software houses have started to take legal measures to fight back. The Lotus Development Corporation collected a sizable out-of-court settlement from the Heath Group, whose employees allegedly made illegal copies of the Lotus 1-2-3 spreadsheet software. Recently, colleges have been convicted of breaking a copyright law and putting too many copies of a software package on a network, resulting in a large fine. Such actions illustrate the software houses' view that transferring programs without permission is stealing. Copying software is no different from walking out of a store without paying for merchandise.

Types of Computer Crime

Each of the five cases presented above involves a fraud in which the perpetrator uses deceit or misrepresentation for unlawful gain. When the value of the item is greater than $500, the act becomes a felony, or a major crime, under the laws of most states. Although the potential for fraud was present in each case, different types of crimes were committed. In summary, the five categories are these:

Stealing Computer Time

The Michigan State students robbed their fellow computer users first of their passwords, then of their time allocations. Computer time is money.

Stealing Data

Financial data, customer information, or special designs or plans can be stolen from computer files. In the Pacific Telephone case, data was stolen from a trash bin to support the computer-aided theft of expensive equipment. With the use of paper shredders, illegal access could have been reduced.

Manipulating Data

The Penn Central case showed that data could be manipulated to direct events and people's actions—in this case the rerouting of boxcars.

Changing Programs

This method was used to cover up the crimes committed by Equity Funding executives. Usually, this type of computer crime is committed by computer professionals.

Stealing Computer Programs

Software buyers often do not realize they have purchased merely the right to use software, not the software itself. In most cases, users are restricted to making a single copy of original diskettes which may be used only for backup. This means that the software is not legally theirs to give to others. As a result, one of the most widespread crimes involves the illegal copying of software. Since theft of computer data and software often involves making copies, the original remains intact. As a result, these types of computer crime often are difficult to detect.

Signals of Potential Computer Crime

In places where computer crimes have occurred, a number of warning signs have been noted. Most of the signs indicate poor control of the computer system or a lack of education on the part of users. The most common signs include some that you may have observed:

- The computer system seems to run people instead of people running the system.
- People expect computers to solve major problems that already exist, when these problems really indicate other underlying difficulties.
- Users cannot communicate with the computer professionals.
- Users are not asked to contribute ideas during the planning stages of systems development; instead, they are told how the system will be designed.
- No clear-cut procedures are established for who may use equipment and when it may be used.
- Documentation of system design and use is incomplete.
- Decision makers participate in programming and troubleshooting activities.
- Computer professionals are given no guidelines within which to work.
- Access to data and software facilities is easy and uncontrolled.
- Errors in processing occur frequently, but without adequate investigation.
- People are not held specifically accountable for the system operations.

As you can see, all five components of a computer system must be protected from computer crime. Access to hardware and software must be limited to qualified people. Data must be complete, accurate, and monitored for illegal changes. Procedures must be developed to help people operate and control the system properly.

Crimes against Computers

In the cases described earlier, computer systems are used as tools to support fraudulent activities. In the mid-1980s a new problem arose wherein computer hardware, software, and data were the target of malicious damage. The cause of the damage is a computer program called a **virus.** The virus invades a computer system by attaching itself to other commonly used programs (host). After the host program is loaded into the computer memory, the virus permanently installs itself on the new computer system. Once installed, the virus can display unwanted messages, erase data, or even promote activities that damage hardware (see Figure 15.7).

Viruses and other destructive programs have several modes of operation. What follows are brief descriptions of some of the most troublesome.

Worms

While a virus attaches itself to other programs, another type of parasitic program, called a *worm,* is self-contained. Worms cause prob-

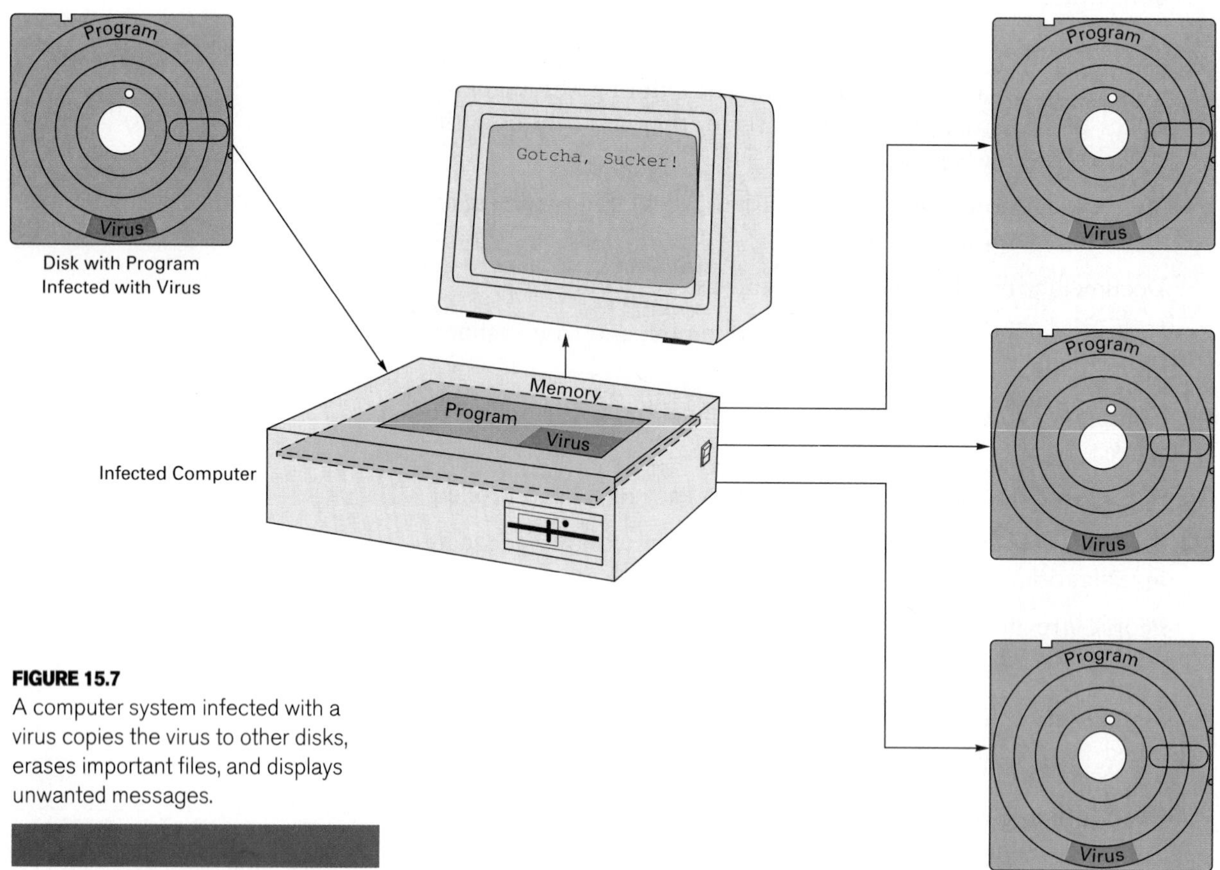

FIGURE 15.7
A computer system infected with a virus copies the virus to other disks, erases important files, and displays unwanted messages.

lems by continuously duplicating themselves in every available memory address. As a result, they fill a computer's memory and bring all other processing activities to a halt.

Trojan Horses

The Trojan horse from Greek mythology was used to conquer the city of Troy by soldiers hidden inside this "victory" gift. The same devious plan is used with *trojan-horse* software. In this case the trojan-horse program hides inside another program and erases data while the user examines the other software. Game demonstrations can potentially hide trojan-horse programs and, as the unsuspecting user shoots down alien invaders, the trojan-horse program erases their hard disk. Trojan-horse software is technically different from a virus because it is not self-replicating.

Time Bombs

Time bombs are similar to trojan-horse programs. Both hide within innocent-looking software packages and do not duplicate themselves like a virus or worm. The difference is that time bombs are time dependent. They often are introduced to a computer system as an "inside" job. Disgruntled, fired employees leave their employers a time bomb as a going away present. The time bomb is hidden within software commonly used by the organization and activates at a preset time to delete critical files.

Virus, Worm, Trojan-Horse, and Time Bomb Protection

Common sense goes a long way in protecting your computer system from destructive programs. Your first line of protection is to limit software acquisition to packages purchased from reliable vendors or shareware distributors. Software copied from a "friend" could prove to be a mistake. Commercial **antivirus software,** also called a *vaccine,* is available that can detect common viruses, worms, etc. Some operating systems have built-in antivirus features. This software should be used to scan every disk before you use it.

If you suspect that your system has been invaded, look for telltale warning signs. What follows are several of the most common signs of an infected system:

- Changes in the size of data files or operating system utility programs
- Unexplained loss of data
- Changes to icons, menus, or windows
- Increase in disk activity during booting
- Strange messages appearing on the screen or printer
- Decrease in available memory

If you suspect that your system has been infected, turn off the computer immediately. This means turning the power off, not resetting the machine. Some viruses can survive a reset. Next use antivirus software to scan your disks, starting with the operating system disk that boots your computer or your system's hard disk. Many of the antivirus programs not only spot unwanted programs, but can delete them and repair the damage done to files.

In some cases, files must be deleted to save the rest of the computer system. If clean backup copies exist, this option presents few problems. If your backup is infected, drastic actions are still needed to protect uninfected programs and files.

SECURITY

Preventing computer crime and the invasion of individual privacy or viruses is a matter of security. In this sense the term *security* applies to all measures designed to protect computers and information resources against unauthorized activities. Even with an extensive security system in place there is no such thing as complete protection for a computer system and its information assets.

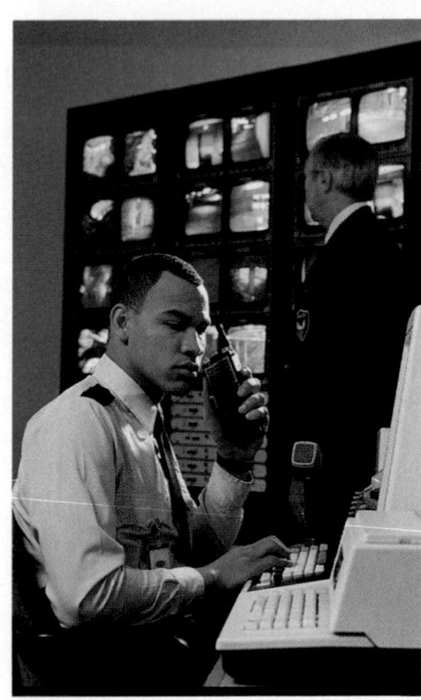

FIGURE 15.8
Building a secure computer system takes time and additional resources.

With many computer systems, demands for immediate processing overshadow security concerns. People are so involved with getting their work done that the monitoring of operations is slack. Input is not as controlled as it should be, and output is not always checked for accuracy and completeness. Often, security components are left out of the programs as programmers concern themselves only with the processing tasks to be completed.

The cost of security is another consideration. Building a secure system takes time and resources. Once security measures are in place, the system may be more expensive to operate. If operations personnel spend half of each workday verifying output, half of their salaries is spent on security or, figuring it another way, the cost of completing work assignments is doubled. Built-in security features in programs require the processing of more instructions. The result is a slow-down in processing as well as a demand for more computer power.

People must strike a balance between no security and nearly complete security. The cost of security should be weighed against the price of potential losses. Security needs should be defined according to the data and the equipment they protect. In a school setting, for example, a system that keeps student grades merits stricter security than a system producing class rosters.

Controls for Small Computer Systems

Small computers are a personal resource. To protect data and equipment, the user must decide who has access, then enforce this decision. Effective enforcement depends on two factors: physical controls and data security measures.

Physical Controls

The physical protection of equipment can be a difficult task. Often computer equipment is located in locked, windowless rooms to deter unauthorized individuals from entering. The pieces of equipment themselves are chained down. In addition, each piece might have a unique serial number. This expedites inventory and allows for easy identification of misplaced or stolen items. Special care needs to be taken with portable computing equipment. Locks are available for some laptop computers when not in use.

Physical security requires more than control over unauthorized access to computer equipment and programs (Figure 15.9). Disas-

Physical Controls to Secure Computer Systems

1. Place computer equipment in areas of limited access from the outside
2. Physically secure equipment to floors and tables
3. Place identification numbers on all equipment, manuals, and software
4. Restrict physical access to authorized people
5. Build computer centers to withstand natural disasters
6. Provide smoke detectors and fire suppression systems that do not harm electronic equipment
7. Place unused storage media in secure library
8. Copy-protect software
9. Use data encryption when storing data and software on storage media

FIGURE 15.9
Computer systems of all sizes can be protected by these common-sense controls.

Who's Who

Seymour Papert (b. 1928)

Seymour Papert, in his youth, traveled all around Africa since his father was involved in studying the tsetse fly. He noticed the discrepancy between his excellent schooling and the lack of education for South African blacks. He and his friends tried to organize classes for the native children but were turned down by both administrators and white parents. Later, in college, he still believed in political activism but studied what he considered a neutral subject, mathematics, to avoid trouble.

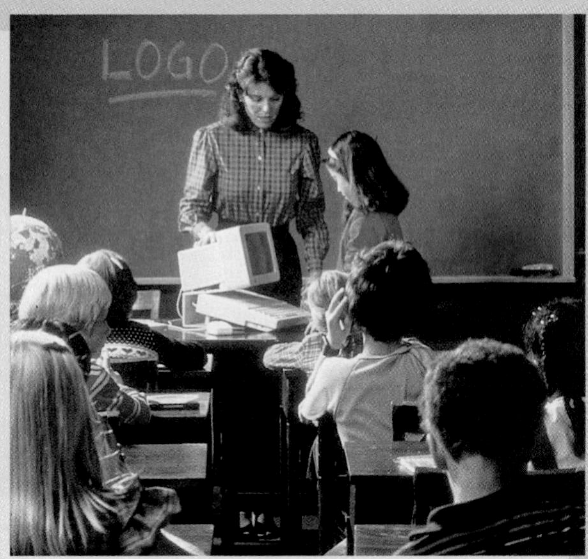

In 1959, Jean Piaget, the developmental psychologist, invited Papert to work with him. Together they studied how children learn. Papert saw a way to influence how all children could be exposed to solid methods of learning, regardless of background. He developed a programming language called LOGO that allows children to control the actions of an animal on a computer screen. LOGO builds upon some basic theorems of geometry, which the children seem to discover themselves. LOGO is now used worldwide and in over one-third of American elementary schools. Papert succeeded in making children problem solvers; in fact, as he puts it, they solve problems that Papert, himself, has not thought of. Recently he has been involved in a project to get computers into third world schools, especially Costa Rica.

ters such as fires, floods, and earthquakes are major threats that occur unpredictably but require preparation and readiness. Protective and recovery measures must be in place, ready for instant activation. For small computer users this means storing master copies of software and hardware serial numbers in a local bank's safety deposit box or a small, personal, fireproof safe. In addition, smoke detectors and waterless fire extinguishers are a must for every office or home with a personal computer system.

Locked away in a drawer or safety deposit box, disks are relatively safe from unauthorized access. Also, many software houses add **copy protection** to their programs. This prevents utility software from reading a program on one disk and transferring it to another. While copy-protection schemes secure software, data-encryption programs help users protect important data. **Data encryption** is the act of scrambling data and programs stored on disk so that a copy of the data is unintelligible without a decoding program. Encryption programs, once the domain of large computer systems, are now available to small computer users. They are especially useful to encode data sent over public transmission lines.

Data Security Controls

After physical security measures have been established, logical measures take over to ensure that sensitive data is kept confidential. Physical security is external; access to the computer itself is controlled. Data security, on the other hand, is internal, and takes place after access to the system has been established.

When small computers are linked to other systems, another type of data security, system passwords, comes into play. **Passwords** are a special combination of letters, numbers, or symbols known only by the user and may be required to access special software, bulletin boards, information utilities, and electronic mail systems. Varying degrees of security clearance can be indicated by an individual's password. Some software, when purchased, contains a **site license**—that is, permission to use the program only by a certain number of users at a designated location. Passwords would ensure the specifications of the site license are followed.

Bulletin board users might be issued a personal password permitting them to read and leave messages. A bulletin board operator (sysop) has a special password enabling him or her to assign passwords to new users, deny access to system abusers, remove messages, and even modify the bulletin board program.

Passwords and special accounts can separate and secure the work of individual users on networks. An added control is restricting the hours that users can access the service. But passwords are effective only if they are kept secret. The possibility that confidential information will be leaked is ever present.

Maintaining Security of Large Computer Systems

Computer crime within an organization usually is discovered by accident—when it is discovered at all. In some cases the failure of a computer system is the first clue that a crime is being committed. As the failure is being inspected and corrected, the crime is exposed. Few systems in existence today provide complete protection against computer crime. Computer professionals thus are faced with the challenge of designing systems that will detect unauthorized use of computers.

To meet this challenge, auditors working with computer professionals have developed special security procedures for computer systems. The procedures, known as **electronic data processing (EDP) controls,** work with all five components of the computer system. The basic categories of EDP controls are:

- Management controls
- Computer center controls
- Input, processing, and output controls

Management Controls

Over the years, professionals have learned that management must be closely involved with data processing decisions. When decision makers do not take an active part in the control of data processing, they invite trouble. The idea behind **management controls** is that the mere awareness by top managers of the processing activities taking place can increase the security of a computer system considerably. While managers need not participate in the physical tasks required to process data, they should set the direction of processing activities (Figure 15.10).

Computer Center Controls

With **computer center controls,** a close watch is kept on computer center resources. Of course, the use of equipment must be restricted to authorized personnel. Users may be required to use a magnetically encoded plastic card or a combination applied to an electronic lock to enter a computer room. Closed-circuit television cameras may monitor and record the entrance of all persons admitted to the computer center. *Biometric security devices* use biological information, like fingerprints, voice patterns, retina patterns, and signatures, to identify authorized users (Figure 15.11).

Summary of Management Controls

1. Management demonstrates knowledge and supports security measures for organization's computer center.
2. Management sets direction for computer center activities.

FIGURE 15.10
By taking an active role in overseeing computer operations, management plays an important part in the system's security.

FIGURE 15.11
Physical characteristics are used to determine accessibility to secure computer environments. Here a person's fingerprint is scanned, providing unique identifying information.

Responsibilities in the computer center should be separated. To prevent any one employee from gaining unlimited access to the system, at least two categories of data processing employees should be created: operations personnel and development personnel. The operations group controls the equipment and application programs in use, while the development group creates new systems. These divisions complement each other and provide security checks and balances.

Another computer center control lies in scrupulous recordkeeping. All processing needs should be accommodated within a precise

In the News...

HACK-ATTACK RESPONSE

What to do if victimized by a hacker:

- Promptly notify your network security officer and law-enforcement authorities.
- Select one authoritative person, such as the IS manager, who will be the main point of contact and the person called to testify.
- Start keeping records, collecting and securing evidence and compiling cost information.
- Plan what you will say and do if the intruder contacts you.
- Provide technical assistance to investigators.
- Do NOT "clean up the system" (which destroys evidence) or discuss the case over unsecured electronic mail.

Source: Federal Bureau of Investigation. *Computerworld* January 25, 1993

Summary of Computer Center Controls

1. Access to computer center is controlled.
2. Responsibilities in computer center are separated into operations and development.
3. Activities are scheduled and kept.
4. Operations personnel are supervised and not allowed to change schedules.
5. Operating procedures are documented.

FIGURE 15.12
Computer center controls help to ensure the security of information processed and stored by computers.

schedule. Procedures and job schedules need to be documented and verified. Supervisors must examine operations to verify that the procedures are followed, and records of computer activity need to be reviewed regularly. In addition, schedules and procedures must be stable—that is, operators should not be able to change them easily and frequently (Figure 15.12).

Equipment use also needs to be recorded to ensure that only authorized personnel gain access to computer tools. This measure protects the equipment from damage and helps ensure delivery of output to the right people. Limiting access to the computer room reduces traffic and helps eliminate errors.

In addition to protecting computing resources during normal operations, equipment in a computer center should be arranged to withstand the earth's rumblings and other natural disasters. Every computer center needs a **disaster recovery plan** containing procedures that specify measures to be applied if computer or data resources are damaged or destroyed (Figure 15.13). The recovery plan can include use of a *hot site,* which is a complete backup computer center available for immediate use, or a *cold site,* an empty facility ready to accept an organization's computing equipment at a moment's notice. Use of backup files, staff training in recovery procedures, and plans to notify clients and customers must also be in place.

Input, Processing, and Output Controls

Management has the responsibility of organizing **input, processing, and output controls** (Figure 15.14). Input controls affect data before it is entered into the computer. Managers need to establish a standard form for input data. Operations personnel must be instructed to reject input presented in improper form.

When appropriate, output should be compared against *control totals* made independently of the computer system. People use control totals to double-check the accuracy of figures produced by the computer system. Typically used as part of batch input, the transactions to be processed are counted manually, and the total recorded. A control total is determined by making manual calculations independent of the computer system to check input operations.

In financial applications, the control total does not necessarily deal with money. Before processing a batch of payroll time sheets, the hour amounts on all time sheets would be added and recorded as the control total. Once processing is completed, computer-generated totals are compared with the control total. Any discrepancies indicate a possible error in data entry.

Input into network applications is harder to control. System programs can use passwords and account numbers to accept only certain input from designated users or locations. A bank customer who has been issued an ATM (automatic teller machine) personal identification number can access a personal bank account from anywhere around town. If someone is foolish enough to leave the password in a wallet, and the wallet is stolen, an unauthorized person can gain access to the account. The system has no control over this security break. Users would be wise to protect their passwords and change them periodically.

Controls over the processing of data rely mainly on documentation. Procedures and schedules must be stated clearly and strictly

FIGURE 15.13
Organizations dependent on their computer systems must have disaster recovery plans in place in case of natural disaster.

followed for effective security of a computer system. Supervisors have the responsibility to monitor operations to make sure these conditions are being met.

Online systems pose special security challenges because transactions can often be difficult to trace. For example, a special sales price might be changed several times online, without producing a written record of the transaction. The absence of these records presents a major security risk. As a result, online programs often instruct the computer to record each change on an **activity log.** An activity log, or summary of online activity, is used to correct errors or to assist auditors in reviewing records.

The operations department should keep records of all processing errors and system failures. Each correction requires documentation. Data processing supervisors can review these records to trace unauthorized activity or other problems. The records also help supervisors evaluate employee performance.

Finally, people need to control the output from all data processing activities. Procedures for distributing output must be documented and followed. Only authorized users should have access to output. These users need to examine returned outputs for completeness and accuracy. Checking control totals, as previously noted, raises the level of security in output.

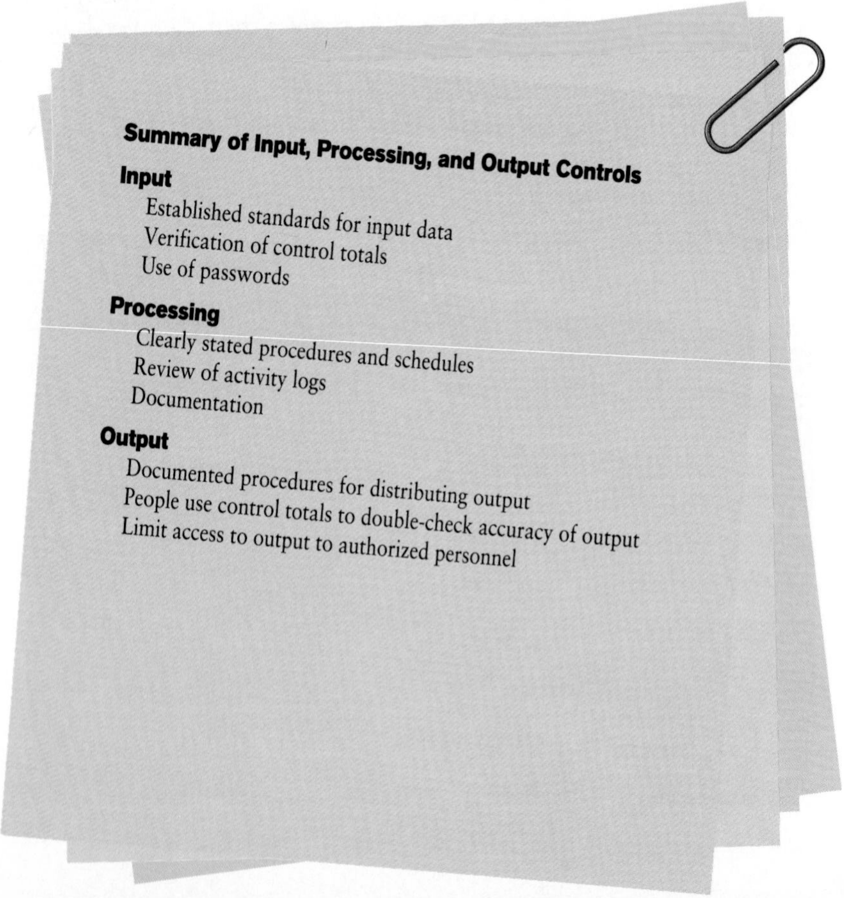

Summary of Input, Processing, and Output Controls

Input

Established standards for input data
Verification of control totals
Use of passwords

Processing

Clearly stated procedures and schedules
Review of activity logs
Documentation

Output

Documented procedures for distributing output
People use control totals to double-check accuracy of output
Limit access to output to authorized personnel

FIGURE 15.14
Input, processing, and output controls that contribute to the security of computer-maintained information are summarized in this checklist.

A Closer Look...

Privacy—Is It Still Possible?

At one time or another everyone receives junk mail, answers an unsolicited telephone call during dinner, or has a salesperson invade their personal space without permission. As these frustrating situations occur, several questions immediately come to mind. What follows are answers to some of these questions.

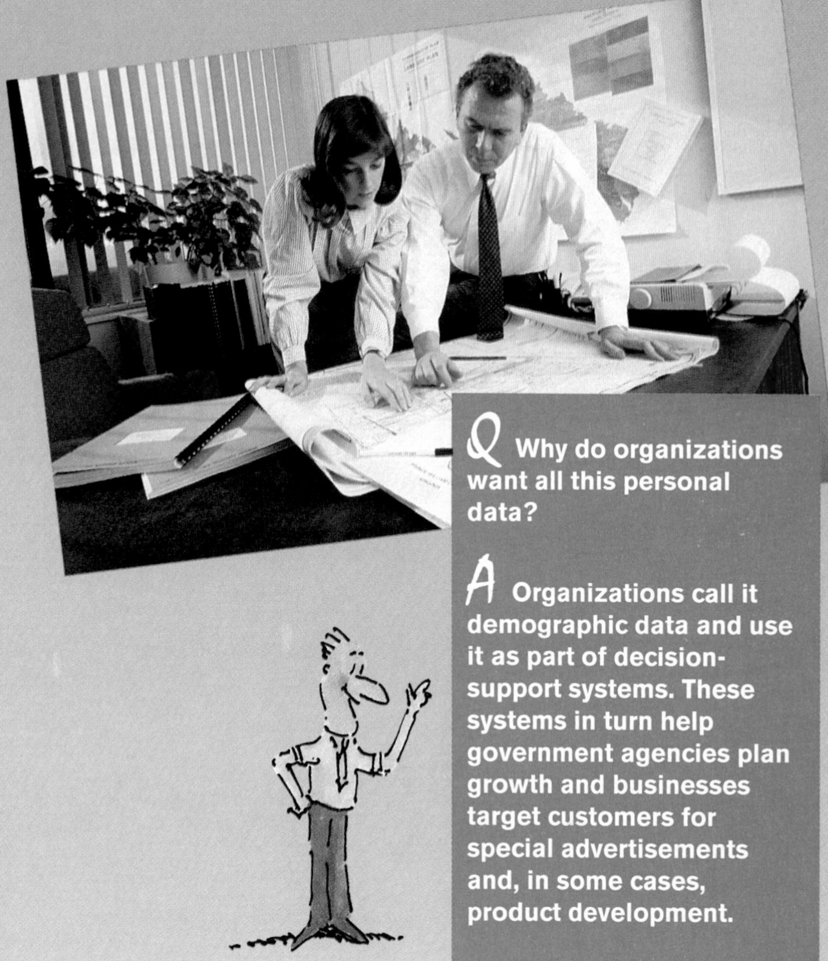

Q Why do organizations want all this personal data?

A Organizations call it demographic data and use it as part of decision-support systems. These systems in turn help government agencies plan growth and businesses target customers for special advertisements and, in some cases, product development.

Q How do organizations get my name, and how do I stop them?

A Answering surveys, filling out warranty cards, and public documents like birth certificates and deeds all generate personal data that organizations buy and sell. You cannot stop all of it, but when given the option of including personal information, JUST SAY NO!

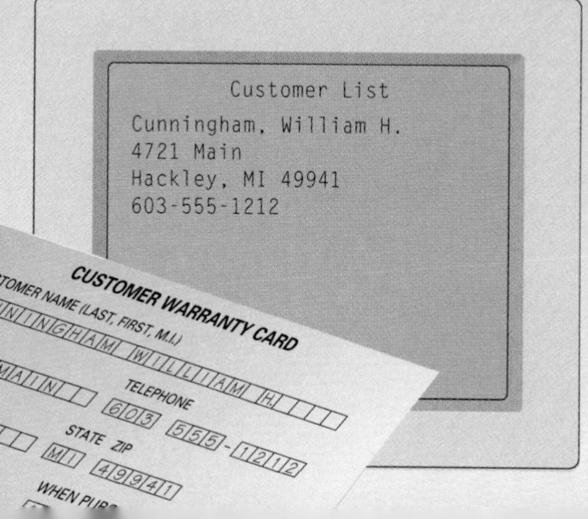

Customer List
Cunningham, William H.
4721 Main
Hackley, MI 49941
603-555-1212
CUSTOMER WARRANTY CARD
CUSTOMER NAME (LAST, FIRST, M.I.)
CUNNINGHAM WILLIAM H
ADDRESS
4721 MAIN
CITY
HACKLEY
TELEPHONE
603 555-1212
STATE ZIP
MI 49941
WHERE PURCHASED
DISCOUNT STORE
APPLIANCE STORE
GIFT

Q Can I remove my name and information from a database?

A Usually not, but you do have the right to verify the accuracy of credit information or records maintained by the government. In some cases, like catalog mailings, you can write the organization and ask them not to send information. The federal government has special forms for requesting a copy of your records. Credit information is available, but you may have to pay to see it.

SOCIAL SECURITY ADMINISTRATION

Request for Earnings and Benefit Estimate Statement

To receive a free statement of your earnings covered by Social Security and your estimated future benefits, all you need to do is fill out this form. Please print or type your answers. When you have completed the form, fold it and mail it to us.

1. Name shown on your Social Security card:

First Middle Initial Last

2. Your Social Security number as shown on your card:

☐☐☐-☐☐-☐☐☐☐

3. Your date of birth: Month Day Year

4. Other Social Security numbers you have used:

☐☐☐-☐☐-☐☐☐☐

☐☐☐-☐☐-☐☐☐☐

5. Your Sex: ☐ Male ☐ Female

6. Other names you have used (including a maiden name):

7. Show your actual earnings for last year and your estimated earnings for this year. Include only wages and/or net self-employment income covered by Social Security.

A. Last year's actual earnings:

$☐☐☐,☐☐☐.00
Dollars only

B. This year's estimated earnings:

$☐☐☐,☐☐☐.00
Dollars only

8. Show the age at which you plan to retire: ☐☐ (Show only one age)

9. Below, show the average yea…
between now and when you…
earnings will be added to th…
give you the best possible e…

Enter a yearly average, not …
show earnings covered by Soci…
performance or scheduled pay increases or bonuses. … but
this is that we estimate retirement benefits in today's dollars, but
adjust them to account for average wage growth in the national economy.

However, if you expect to earn significantly more or less in the future due to promotions, job changes, part-time work, or an absence from the work force, enter the amount in today's dollars that most closely reflects your future average yearly earnings.

Most people should enter the same amount that they are earning now (the amount shown in 7B).

Your future average yearly earnings:

$☐☐☐,☐☐☐.00
Dollars only

10. Address where you want us to send the statement:

Name

Street Address (Include Apt. No., P.O. Box, or Rural Route)

City State Zip Code

I am asking for information about my own Social Security record or the record of a person I am authorized to represent. I understand that if I deliberately request information under false pretenses I may be guilty of a federal crime and could be fined and/or imprisoned. I authorize you to send the statement of earnings and benefit estimates to the person named in item 10 through a contractor.

Please sign your name (Do not print)

Date (Area Code) Daytime Telephone No.

ABOUT THE PRIVACY ACT
Social Security is allowed to collect the facts on this form under Section 205 of the Social Security Act. We need them to quickly identify your record and prepare the earnings statement you asked us for. Giving us these facts is voluntary. However, without them we may not be able to give you an earnings and benefit estimate statement. Neither the Social Security Administration nor its contractor will use the information for any other purpose.

Form SSA-7004-PC-OP1 (9-89) Destroy Prior Edition

Q Are there any situations where it is desirable to provide personal information?

A Decisions are based on data in an information society. Therefore, personal data often helps you sell yourself when it comes to job, credit card, loan, insurance, and other applications. Situations like census tabulations and income taxes require you to provide complete and correct data by law.

Q How can I protect my name and other personal data and keep it from people who misuse it?

A First and foremost, do not provide personal data unless it is required. If the data is being misused, ask to have it removed. Your next step is to seek a restraining order or court injunction. Since many of the federal laws involve only public databases, you could also become involved in advocacy work on new privacy legislation for privately maintained databases.

Chapter Facts

- Computer abuse and its prevention involve four issues: individual privacy, ethical standards, computer crime, and computer system security.
- Consumers' rights to privacy are covered legally by the Fourth Amendment to the United States Constitution and several privacy acts.
- Ethical standards take the rights of others into consideration.
- The impact of computers can best be controlled through the education of consumers and legislation.
- To steal computer time, programs, and data, and to change data or programs are the major types of computer crime.
- Eleven warning signals often identify organizations that are vulnerable to computer crime.
- Viruses, worms, trojans, and time bombs can infect unprotected computer systems by erasing programs and data along with damaging equipment.
- All computer systems can benefit from physical controls and data security. Special protection should be taken against natural disasters and fires. Data encryption and other protections against illegal copying also are useful.
- Organizations with large computer systems need EDP (electronic data processing) controls. These include controls for management, the computer center, data input, processing, and output.
- The best way to protect personal privacy is to not give other people or organizations personal data unless it is absolutely necessary.

Terms to Remember

a. activity log
b. antivirus software
c. computer center controls
d. copy protection
e. data encryption
f. disaster recovery plan
g. electronic data processing (EDP) controls
h. ethical standards
i. input, processing, and output controls
j. management controls
k. password
l. site license
m. virus

Mix and Match

Match the following definitions to the Terms to Remember.

1. _____ procedures to be followed if an organization's computer center is disabled or destroyed.
2. _____ destructive computer program that invades a computer system by attaching itself to other commonly used programs.
3. _____ computer program that identifies disk files that have been infected with a virus, worm, or other destructive programs.
4. _____ set of rules a person or organization uses when considering the rights of others.
5. _____ security procedures by which managers take control of data processing and set the computer center's direction, but not through direct participation in processing activities.
6. _____ computer professionals are divided into operations and development groups.
7. _____ legal copyright that restricts the number of users or locations at which a program can be accessed.
8. _____ scrambling characters on a disk.
9. _____ procedures for accepting data and keeping control totals.
10. _____ a summary of online activities kept for security purposes.
11. _____ special combination of letters, numbers, or symbols known only to the user.
12. _____ a way of storing software on disk that prevents illegal copying by system utilities.
13. _____ security procedures for all computer system components.

Review Questions

1. When can a creditor legally invade a person's privacy?
2. Describe the rights defined by the following:
   a. Fourth Amendment of the Constitution
   b. Freedom of Information Act of 1970
   c. Fair Credit Reporting Act of 1970

d. Privacy Act of 1974
e. Education Privacy Act of 1974
f. Right to Financial Privacy Act of 1978
g. Electronic Communications Privacy Act of 1986
h. Video Privacy Protection Act of 1988
i. Computer Matching and Privacy Act of 1988

3. Why would an organization establish ethical guidelines?
4. Identify 12 questions you should consider before taking potentially unethical actions.
5. What are two means of controlling computer impact?
6. Identify five types of computer crime.
7. What are 11 warning signals of computer crime?
8. How are computer-oriented worms, trojan horses, and time bombs different from a virus?
9. Identify two procedures you can use to protect a computer system from destructive programs.
10. What are six warning signs of an infected computer system?
11. What type of physical security is provided by copy protection and data encryption?
12. What are nine types of physical controls that can be used to secure a computer system?
13. How can data be protected after access to a computer system has been established?
14. Describe three EDP controls that are oriented toward protecting an organization's computer system(s).
15. What is the best way to protect your personal privacy?

Applying What You've Learned

1. Some people say, "The best way to catch a criminal is to think like a criminal." Using the warning signs and physical controls mentioned in the text, make a list of five ways security could be improved in your school computer lab or room containing a home computer. Describe any new procedures or people that would have to be involved.
2. It is part of our legal system to make the punishment fit the crime. Some computer criminals are teenagers or younger. Do you think it is fair to try them as adults? Are prison and/or fines reasonable punishments for them? What would be other ways they could make restitution for their computer crimes? Write a short paper explaining your views.

3. Design an activity log or software sign-out sheet for the people using equipment at school or at home. Include space for names, times, equipment used, and other information needed to monitor security.
4. Research one of the biometric security devices mentioned in the text or one you have seen elsewhere. What biological characteristic does it detect and how? What is the cost? Where do you think such a device could be best used? Where would the device be inappropriate?
5. Most programs on diskette can be easily copied despite any regulations or copyrights. If you produced a program to be sold and wished to protect it from being copied, what would you do? Write what you think is a reasonable software copyright agreement.
6. Computer technology allows managers electronically to monitor the work of employees. Computers can track errors, count keystrokes, and even monitor breaks. Do you think employees have a right to know when their work is being monitored? Should this data be used to determine raises and promotions? What limits, if any, should be placed on the use of electronic work monitoring? Would you have any problems working for an organization that electronically monitored employees?

Answers to Mix and Match

1. f 2. m 3. b 4. h 5. j 6. c 7. l 8. e 9. i 10. a 11. k 12. d 13. g

16

Keeping Up With Change

From the User's Point of View

An Information Society
- Consumer electronics
- Computer-integrated workplaces
- Global economy and the cashless society
- Emerging technologies

Skills Updating
- On-the-job training
- Workshops and conferences
- Recreational and professional publications

Career Paths
- End-user computing
- Information systems
- Computer science
- Computer engineering
- Professional organizations

A Closer Look . . . Emerging Technologies

FROM THE USER'S POINT OF VIEW

Technological innovations are altering the very fabric of our society. Computers are helping to interconnect schools, decentralize businesses, and link consumers to an endless variety of news, information, and entertainment. The speed at which innovations take place foreshadow how fast career skills and requirements change. It is likely that you will change jobs several times in your life. If you view your work as part of a career path, instead of just performing a specific job, education becomes a continuing process. You will find that keeping up with changes requires both an understanding of how technology impacts you and the willingness to learn how to take advantage of it.

AN INFORMATION SOCIETY

For most of its history the computer has been a tool with great problem-solving potential. The challenge has been to identify problems and develop appropriate computer solutions. Today, computers have brought us to the threshold of what has been called an **information society.** An information society consists of a large group of people within a country or region where most workers generate or depend upon information for performance of their jobs. Today, information is one of the United States's largest exports. News services, banks, insurance companies, and television stations are just a few of the organizations that collect data, process it into information, and store it as a major part of their business (Figure 16.1). As consumers, we buy some of this information as newspapers and cable television.

The use of technological tools requires an understanding of how the tools work and what they can be expected to do. The day of simply pressing a button or turning a crank in performance of a job is nearly over. People preparing themselves for tomorrow's workforce must realize that good-paying manual labor jobs will be harder to find. Fewer jobs will require people to move or assemble parts. Those currently performing such jobs must seriously consider retraining in skills compatible with developments in technology.

Consumer Electronics

As a result of technological research, microprocessors and memory chips are being embedded into many products we use each day. In every aspect of our society, increasing numbers of intelligent consumer goods have made our life easier and more interesting. In

FIGURE 16.1
In an information society workers generate and depend upon information to perform their jobs.

turn, users are finding it important to understand basic computer concepts so they can maximize the usefulness of these products.

Smart Homes

As Andrea is leaving for work she has a last-minute conversation with her house. The conversation goes something like this:

> "Computer, close all windows and lock the doors after I leave."
>
> *"Do you want any windows left open for ventilation?"*
>
> "What would you recommend?"
>
> *"Best cross-ventilation today will be achieved by opening the kitchen and southwest master bedroom windows."*
>
> "Make it happen and record the local and national news, stock market closing, and weather for me after 6:00 p.m."
>
> *"Do you still want a search of the news media for downhill ski sales?"*
>
> "Yes. Also, scan for any news on the expected buyout of Technocorp. Let me know immediately of any large sales of its stock on the Exchange."
>
> *"Your curling iron is on."*
>
> "Turn it off and also run an in-depth diagnostic on the high-definition television in the den. What is the probability of failure in the next two weeks and what preventive maintenance measures should be put in place?"
>
> *"Acknowledged."*

The basics for smart houses became a reality in the 1990s. Built around a local area network, the smart house is a good example of a distributed processing system. Each appliance, smoke detector, and sensor has its own processor and memory (Figure 16.2). These devices are self-sufficient and communicate with a personal computer. Homeowners then use voice recognition or a central console to activate the desired combination of equipment anywhere in the house. Furthermore, the voice recognition system replaces the need for security keys because the system unlocks doors on command using unique biometric data, the human voice.

Smart homes provide increased safety and energy efficiency. Lights automatically turn off when people leave a room. Heating and cooling depends on whether people are at home or not. Sensors in the lawn determine when the lawn is watered, but only if the water utility doesn't override the system during periods of water conservation.

In older homes gas leaks or accidental electric shocks are always a possibility. These problems are eliminated in smart homes. Electric and gas systems are kept inactive until the appropriate appliance is connected to the system. Once connected, the built-in processor

FIGURE 16.2
Security, utility, and maintenance systems are networked in a smart house to provide its owners with optimum control.

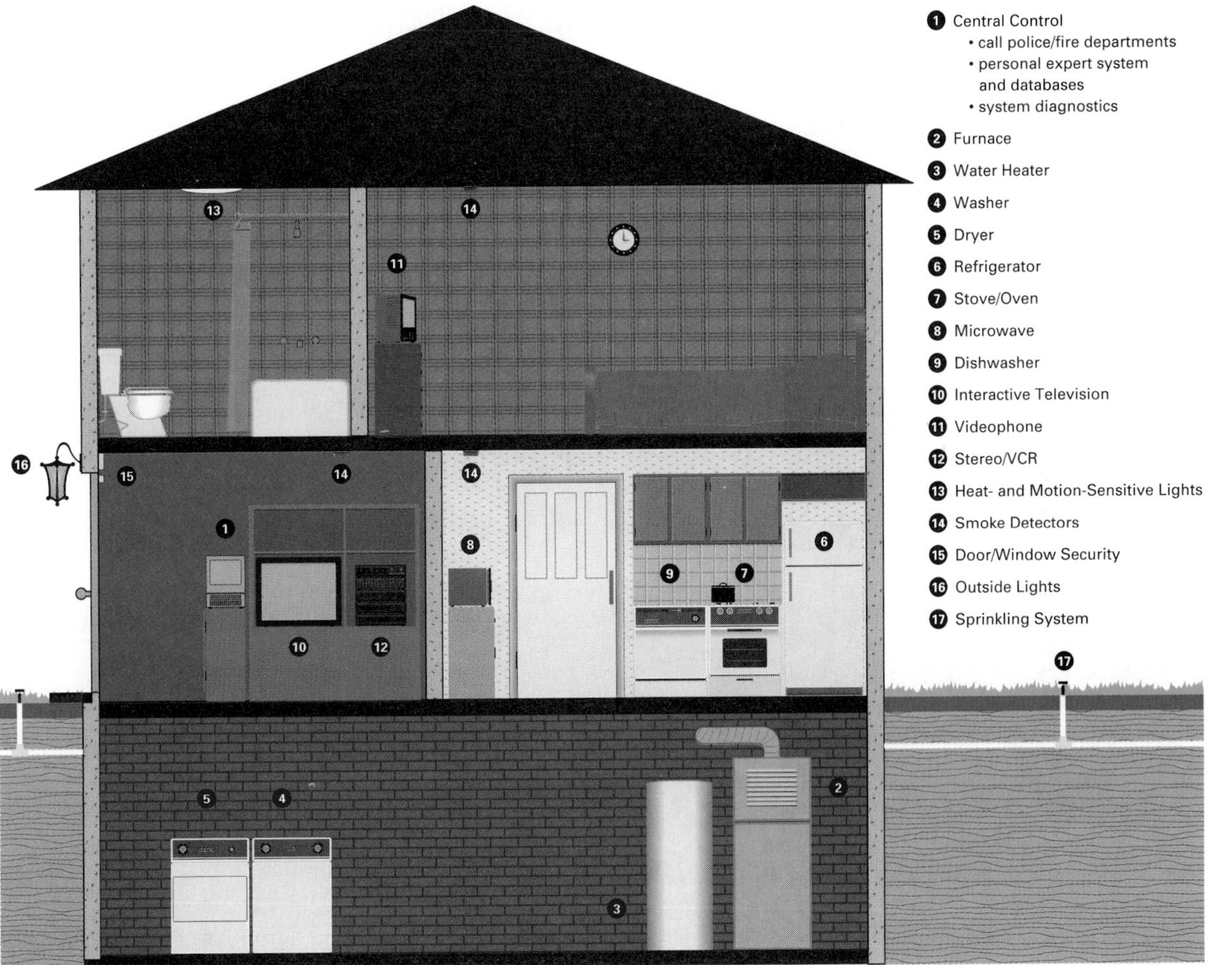

identifies itself and gas or electricity is supplied. This prevents children from getting shocked when poking fingers into open electrical sockets since the power is kept off until an intelligent appliance is plugged in.

Although a completely smart house would require special wiring and outlets, homeowners can now purchase software packages that control security systems, lights, and appliances and work on certain personal computers. Ranging in cost from under $100 to several thousand dollars, these home systems are a glimpse of the future.

Smart Transportation

While smart homes are coming, smart cars are already here. As shown in Figure 16.3, automobiles presently use embedded microprocessors in anti-lock breaks, air bags, climate controls, transmissions, carburetors, instrument panel controls, power steering, suspension control, security, and sound systems. New cars are being manufactured with I/O ports into which diagnostic equipment is plugged. Mechanics use computers to analyze automotive functions

FIGURE 16.3
Automobiles are large users of embedded computers.

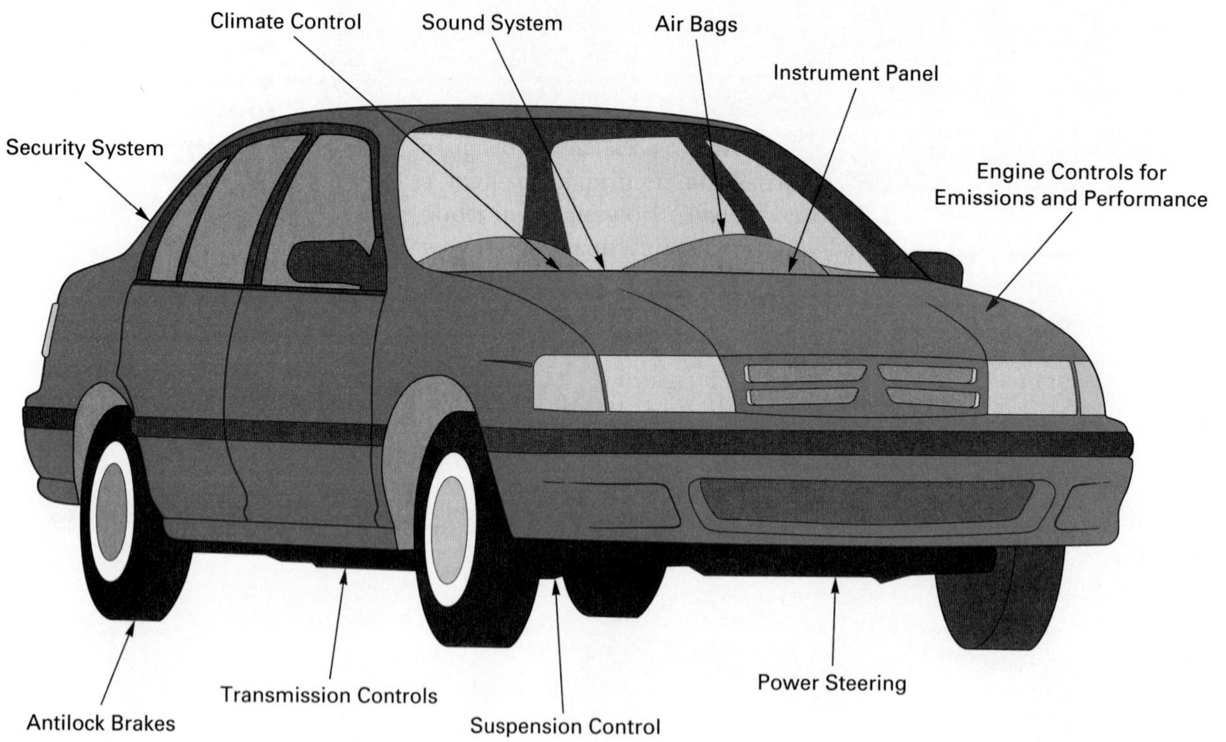

and identify the parts that need servicing or changing. Increased reliability and serviceability for cars has resulted from the harnessing of computers.

Future computers will help drivers arrive at their destinations. Already, some cars have the ability to display road maps, stored on a CD-ROM, on a screen near the driver for guidance. An antenna links the car with global positioning satellites to pinpoint the car's location. The driver can change the display to the traffic or weather report by using a touch screen or voice input. A similar device, without user input, already exists on international airplane flights. Overhead screens display the plane's location, along with information like miles/kilometers and time to destination.

Car radios take on a new look through a nationwide Radio Broadcast Data System. Over 500 stations will transmit not only music but the title and artist of the music. This information will appear on a small display on the radio itself. A listener can also program the radio to find only stations of a certain format, like Rock and Roll or Country. Listeners will also automatically be informed of important weather and traffic information.

On the horizon is automated driving on the proposed IVHS (Intelligent Vehicle/Highway System). Cameras and sensors along the highway would monitor and control traffic flow. When a problem, like a stalled car, is detected, IVHS will lower surrounding cars' speed through receivers in the cars themselves. Turning our car over to autopilot will increase fuel efficiency and reduce driver frustration, but will require us to change how we view driving. Cars of the future may literally drive themselves.

FIGURE 16.4
A new generation of consumer electronics makes voice, image, and data communication easier.

Home Entertainment and Communications

Recreational applications for consumer electronics have increased dramatically. Many homeowners are plugging a variety of equipment into telephone and cable television services (see Figure 16.4). Combined with information utilities, high-definition televisions, and other video services, home entertainment is taking on a new look and broader capabilities.

One of the benefits of living in an information society is the increased availability of leisure time activities. Information utilities help by letting people play or preview games at home through their personal computers and the utility's computer network. People from around the world can play together through these communications networks. Their options range from a chess challenge to participating in complex adventure games that involve several players.

In the near future these same networks will allow users to preview first-run movies, see an off-Broadway play, watch a concert in Europe, or even look at a TV show you missed. When a selection looks interesting, you can rent it by having the utility download it to your television. Anticipating this trend toward customized entertainment, some video rental stores have expanded into the music CD market. You will soon be able go to a store and record exactly the pieces of music you wish on a CD, picking from thousands of selections.

Another way people can spend their leisure time is talking to their television sets. Some cable television users now have control boxes that are linked to the cable company's computer. The control box becomes input hardware that lets the viewer respond to the televised program. The result is **interactive television.** National or regional polls can be taken as viewers punch the appropriate button on their control boxes to respond to posed questions (Figure 16.4). Interactive television lets people tell the station which shows they like or which politician they support. They can order a product shown on television or request a pay-per-view program. Students can even return answers to questions a teacher poses as they watch educational television.

Catalog wholesalers are working with information utilities to showcase their products. Once connected to the system, users identify what they want, and the computer searches through the product line to find the requested information and prices. With interactive television, customers can request a demonstration of a product or see clothing modeled before making a purchase. Billing and payment will be done electronically, and users can request their bank balance to see if they are within their budget. By connecting a television, VCR, CD-ROM drive, and a personal computer, people will be able to access a vast range of information utilities and television stations, receiving and responding to individualized data retrieval.

Virtual Reality

Through the use of complex programs, audio and visual data, and specialized hardware, we can now take computerized entertainment one dimension further. Imagine walking on the moon or swimming into an underwater volcano two miles under the ocean. A virtual reality can put you there. In a **virtual reality,** the user is immersed in a computer-generated environment.

At a minimum, users wear earphones, eyegoggles, and gloves containing sensors to help interact with the virtual reality. Some virtual realities require bodysuits. The eyegoggles, as seen in Figure 16.5, show the wearer three-dimensional views of a computer simulation. As the user moves his or her head, the view changes. Movements of the hands or body act as input that takes the user through the virtual reality scenario. Sensors in the gloves allow the user to move and pick up virtual objects. The actions of the user are responded to by the virtual reality program.

At the present time, a limited number of virtual realities are available. Due to the expense of equipment and software, the best simulations are still in research labs. However, some firms offer a

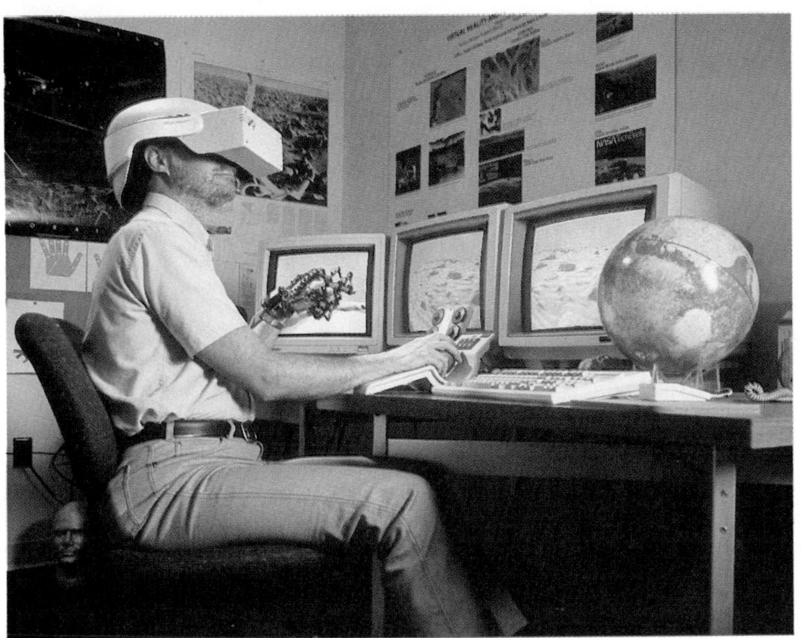

FIGURE 16.5
Virtual realities can allow a person to experience, through sight and touch, unusual situations, like walking on another planet.

pay-to-play opportunity, where a virtual reality game can be rented by the minute. Software exists for less evasive and expensive virtual realities. For example, a person can design a new home and then use a mouse to travel through the 3D images of the rooms displayed on a computer screen.

It is the potential of virtual reality that most excites computer scientists and users. Education would drastically change as a student could learn anatomy from the inside of the human body or a fireman could train on equipment in a virtual reality of a burning house. Manipulating objects in a virtual reality is already being used to help victims of spinal cord injuries to relearn complex motor skills. A person can explore a volcano on Venus in a virtual reality used for scientific research. With virtual reality you are *in* a movie or video game, not just watching it.

Computer-Integrated Workplaces

Many of our jobs have been directly or indirectly affected by changes in technology. From designing consumer goods, and manufacturing, distributing, and marketing those goods, to researching the materials for the products of tomorrow, innovations in computers and technology alter both where and how we work. If the changes take place at our desktop or worksite, we notice them immediately. However, many new technological ideas are showing up behind the scenes as well.

We have come a long way since Henry Ford offered people a car in any color they wanted, as long as it was black. Today, any automotive salesperson can deliver a car to you that has the exact options and colors you want. By entering customer specifications into an integrated manufacturing system, a matching car can be found or built. The trend toward "customized" mass-produced goods continues to increase. Rather than produce an item and hope the customer will like it as is, products like trucks, cars, modular housing, furniture, and clothing are made to order at mass-production prices.

To facilitate the speed of designing and producing new and customized products, engineers can quickly create prototypes with their personal computers. The computer controls an ultraviolet light source aimed at the surface of a vat filled with photocurable polymers, plastic that hardens when exposed to light. Wherever the light hits, the liquid turns solid, forming a thin layer of hard plastic. The floor of the vat is lowered and the liquid surface is again exposed to light. This creates a second layer of plastic on top of the first. By repeating this process, called *stereolithography,* customized parts, both hollow and solid, can be quickly built up (see Figure 16.6). These include not only machine parts but identical copies for museums of priceless, fragile sculptures that would not survive handling.

Stereolithography is one of several computer applications that speed up the manufacturing process. Combined together these pro-

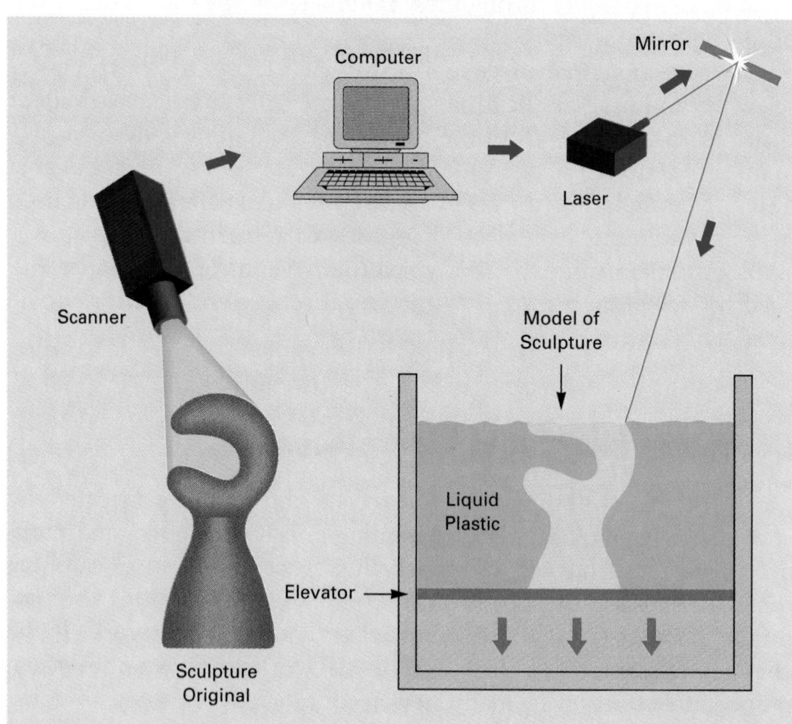

FIGURE 16.6
By exposing liquid plastic to ultraviolet light, a 3D model can be built with more precision and in less time than by traditional milling methods.

cesses are known as **computer-integrated manufacturing. CIM,** as it is called, is a combination of computer-aided design (CAD), computer-aided machining (CAM), numerical control (NC), robotics, and materials resource planning, which are unified by common data communications protocols.

When an order comes in for a custom product, like a car, the specifications are input into a database. CAD systems manipulate this data into useful designs and identify materials. These materials specifications become part of just-in-time inventory. Resource planning software schedules when the actual production begins. As the car is being built, the specification data will affect both humans and machines. People will know what color upholstery to install, and the path a welding robot takes will be unique to the model and options ordered.

In the News...

THE RISE OF THE VISUAL COMMUNICATOR

Picture, for a moment, the stereotypical programmer. Now, think of an artist. Do the two images you conjure up look much alike?

For most people, the answer is no. But in today's world of graphical computing, there's a growing need for a new type of developer: an individual who combines the traditional skills of a programmer with the visual talent of a graphic artist.

Graphic arts skills have never been part of the programmer's curriculum, but the usability of today's applications has quickly become dependent on the visual syntax. In order to create maintainable applications, it's essential that the visual representation of the functions make sense.

Standards have been scarce to nonexistent in this area, leaving programmers and software developers to their own devices. In many cases, their programs include elegant and sexy pictures —but do they communicate? Just as we can recognize a stop sign by its shape, a common set of iconographic standards would help us recognize the myriad images popping up in our software programs.

Global Economy and the Cashless Society

The impact of the information society is far reaching. Data is electronically exchanged between financial markets around the world, affecting the price of wheat in the Ukraine, the value of the yen in Japan, and the unemployment rate in Mexico. Our ability to immediately exchange ideas, transactions, and funds through international networks allows businesspeople to compete in a global economy. For example, bids and construction crews to build a new oil rig in the North Atlantic can as easily come from Japan or southern Europe as from Canada or Iceland.

To support this global economy, the banking industry has developed an interconnected electronic funds transfer (EFT) system, which minimizes the work involved in transferring money between banks. As a result, most bank employees must be able to handle financial transactions through a computer network as easily as they handle cash. Through the use of electronic passwords and credit cards, computer literate end-users can advise their banks to pay their rent and other bills electronically. The bank completes the transaction by automatically moving the money from their account to the landlord's and other designated accounts (Figure 16.7).

The success of EFT, EDI, and other computer-based networks has some people even talking about a **cashless society.** Instead of using coins, paper money, or checks we would make all of our purchases as electronic transactions. In such a society, checks and money would be eliminated. All purchasing and payments would be handled electronically. Individuals and businesses would have universal account numbers. When workers are paid, their employers make electronic deposits to employee accounts. At the same time the employer's account would be reduced. A cashless society may

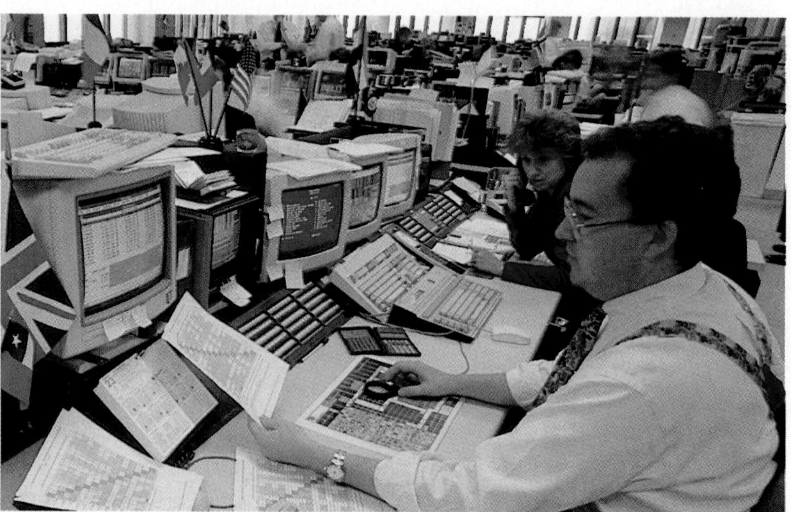

FIGURE 16.7
In a cashless society, all transactions would be completed electronically. Coins and currency would be obsolete.

be far in the future, but we have certainly become less likely to carry large amounts of cash for a transaction than use a credit card or check.

Emerging Technologies

Although no one can accurately predict the future, we can do a good job of guessing by looking at recent technological trends. What could be found only in a research laboratory a few years ago, like a personal digital assistant, now is commercially available. Another trend is that products originally developed for commercial purposes are redesigned for individual consumers. Bar code readers, originally for inventory control, gave way to image scanners for personal computers. Other technologies, like the use of 3D graphics in CAD, went far beyond the design industry for use in advertising, video games, and sophisticated simulations of medical procedures. Several trends on the technological horizon let us glimpse into the future.

Superconductor Materials

From research labs, animation studios, and users of large databases come requests for faster, more powerful, and more efficient computers. This continual drive for increases in performance has led to the development of two major innovations in processing hardware, superconductivity and optical computers. These discoveries, along with parallel processing, are leading us into the fifth computer generation.

To speed up the transfer of data and programs within computer hardware, researchers have sought to reduce the resistance of the materials conducting the electricity. The late 1980s brought a materials science breakthrough, **superconductors.** Superconductors lose all resistance to the flow of electricity at a given temperature. These materials provide the fastest possible means of electronically transmitting data within and between computer components (see Who's Who in this chapter). Superconductors are helping computers break processing speed barriers.

Optical Computers

While some scientists are looking for performance improvements with superconductors, others are developing computers that do not even use electricity to operate. Research is being done on the use of fiber optics for both data transmittal and its processing. Fiber optic cables are currently used as a communication channel to transmit data as light pulses. Current research is on the development of a processing unit containing very fast light-activated switches (see Figure 16.8). An **optical computer** would use these switches and fiber

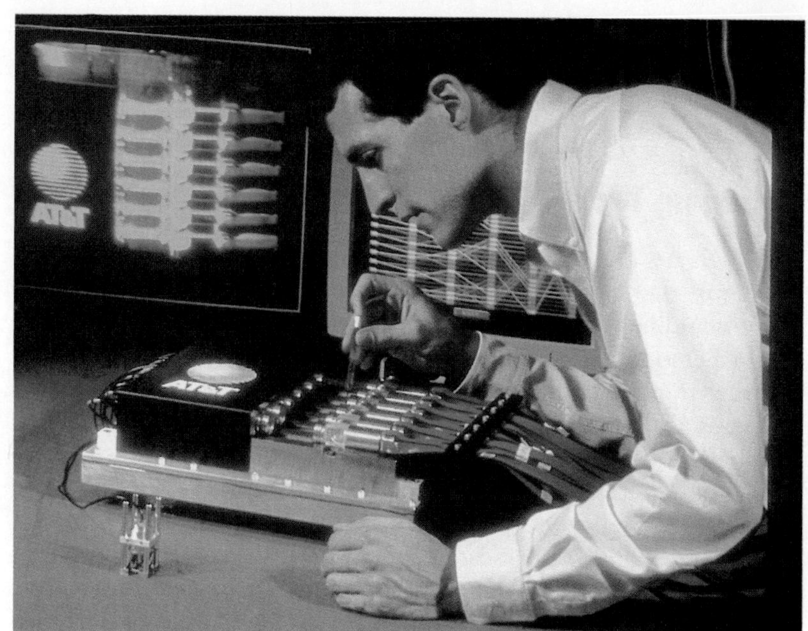

FIGURE 16.8
Light, rather than electricity, is the power behind the circuitry of optical computers.

optics to increase processing and data transmission speeds. Additional advantages are that optical computers generate less component-degrading heat and have less electrical interference than those completely dependent on electricity.

Electronic Superhighways

Fiber optics is also the key to increased quantity and quality of data communications. As telephone and cable-television companies replace copper wires with fiber optic cables, the potential of connecting personal computers—sharing voice, video, as well as textual data—into a worldwide network becomes a reality. Recently, telephone companies have been buying cable operators, home shopping services, and entertainment industries. Hardware and software manufacturers are collaborating on user-friendly interfaces for handheld personal computers that control access to a 500-channel interactive television network. All these ventures are based on the assumption that within the next few years most homes, businesses, and institutions will be linked by a high-speed wide area network consisting of fiber optics, the electronic superhighway. Informed users will travel on this highway to explore new ideas, discuss world events, and negotiate peaceful solutions.

Artificial Intelligence

Technological research is becoming introspective as well. In the growing area of **artificial intelligence (AI)**, computers are simulating human thought and judgment. AI synthesizes computer science, psychology, linguistics, and other specialized fields to perform tasks with humanlike logic. Expert systems, discussed in Chapter 12, are one application of artificial intelligence.

Among the AI developments expected are heuristic problem-solving techniques. The term *heuristic* describes a method by which problems are solved through application of general rules and information based on experience. Instead of following sequences of instructions to devise solutions, heuristic software applies rules proven to be effective in the past. As an example, heuristic techniques are being used to develop programs that can sort and grade produce, efficiently pack a truck or boxcar with different sizes of containers, control complex air and ground traffic, and even play chess. People in these situations evaluate a constantly changing environment but act according to preset rules, acquiring experience as they go. AI systems use the rules given to them as well, learning from experience so as to apply this information to new experiences.

When Andrea gave instructions to her home computer, she was actually using a very sophisticated expert system. The ability to make decisions based on probabilities, like predicting television failure, is an attribute of an expert system. In the future, it will be common to find such systems in homes and the workplace. When Andrea arrived at her desk, a computer-animated image on her monitor reviewed her schedule: a teleconference with a coworker in South America, a request for the latest budget figures from the boss, and a reminder to research potential customers for the new company product.

On her videophone, Andrea meets with her South American colleague. Although she doesn't speak Spanish, and he doesn't speak English, a language translator allows them to communicate. Information he requests is immediately sent to him via Andrea's fax machine. She uses her notepad computer and stylus to send a copy of the proposed budget to her boss and reads his handwritten comments on the monitor. To assist in her product research, the expert system looks for the phone number of the market research firm she used last year and automatically dials it, allowing Andrea to leave a voice mail message. She also instructs the computer to let her know when her call is returned.

Management of Andrea's schedule, calls, use of peripherals, and databases access are under control of her personal expert system. Besides acting as a secretary, the software can scan information services for user's requests, screen phone calls and voice mail, and provide other personal services requiring decision making and priority setting. Owning a personal expert system, available on a personal computer at work or as part of a smart home, may come sooner than you think.

With the aid of personal expert systems, education can be individualized and on a need-to-know basis. For example, as you get ready to build a new deck in the backyard, the list of building materials is put together with the help of an expert deck construction

PERSONAL EXPERT SYSTEM

? This fish has white bubbles growing around its fins and gills. What's wrong?
☛ You have identified a swordfish. This fish is susceptible to a fish virus known as Ich.

? Can I cure it?
☛ All the fish in your tank need to be treated.

? What should I do?
☛ α Ich Treatment for fresh water fish:

1. add I tsp. Malashite Green for each 10 gallons of water
2. raise water temperature to 83 degrees.

FIGURE 16.9
Personal expert systems use artificial intelligence techniques to help you solve common problems in your home or workplace.

system you have downloaded from an information utility. The materials are ordered from the local lumberyard through the same network. As you start cutting lumber and pounding nails, the expert system helps you figure out how to construct the deck in the easiest, safest, and most efficient way. Similar home tutors will be available for interior design, landscaping, electrical wiring, plumbing, and a variety of do-it-yourself projects. A personal expert system could even help you diagnose problems with your tropical fish as illustrated in Figure 16.9.

SKILLS UPDATING

Computers bring about changes in society rather quickly, taking only months rather than years. When changes occur that rapidly, obsolescence of hardware, as well as of knowledge and skills, is bound to be a major problem. *Obsolescence,* present in any technology-driven field, describes the rate at which equipment and its associated skills and knowledge become outdated and, eventually, useless.

In the past, new generations of hardware and software have been introduced about every 10 years. However, it is not uncommon to presently see a new version of software released within a year of its predecessor. The maximum storage capacity of a memory chip has doubled every year in the past ten, with corresponding decreases in cost. Computer equipment purchased today will probably have to be replaced, along with its accompanying software, within a decade.

Technological obsolescence has both good and bad effects for computer professionals and users. On the positive side, the rapid rate of change means that new jobs and entirely new career opportunities are being made available. For qualified people, change represents opportunity. However, with each change comes the necessity of knowing how to use the new technology. To remain current and competitive, users must constantly keep their knowledge and skills updated. Education does not stop with a diploma, certificate, or degree.

FIGURE 16.10
Computer literacy skills are an integral part of many workplaces.

On-the-Job Training

Many people in the work force find that computers have become essential tools in their industries or occupations. These people recognize that knowledge and skills about computers and their uses can improve their chances of career growth. An important characteristic of computers from a job-performance standpoint is that they are general-purpose tools. Computers can be configured with different combinations of devices and adapted in infinite ways to the needs of specific users and applications. This means that each computer-using organization is faced with the need to train its employees on the unique features of its own computer systems (Figure 16.10).

On-the-job training sessions tend to be brief, specific, and practical. Typically, an organization prepares special manuals to be used for training. These are companion pieces to reference manuals that can be used to look up solutions to problems after a computer system is operational.

Most on-the-job training programs, then, deal with specific applications. Sessions usually run from a half-day to as long as one week. Employees are expected to leave these sessions and move right into regular use of equipment and procedures as part of job performance.

Training programs within organizations also deal with general or administrative skills as well as with specific computer topics. For example, many organizations run in-house seminars on management topics such as supervisory skills, stress management, financial operations, and decision making.

In addition, organizations often sponsor attendance by employees at colleges or technical institutes. For qualified courses of study, the company often will reimburse an employee for all or part of the tuition associated with job-related study. If enough employees need the same training, a class may be offered at the job site taught by either in-house trainers or professional educators.

Workshops and Conferences

Many opportunities for improving skills exist beyond on-the-job training programs. Organizations send selected employees to workshops and conferences. These opportunities occur away from the working environment and may involve expertise not found locally. A **workshop** or *seminar* concentrates on a single topic and can last from a few hours to several days. In many ways, workshops are like formal schooling. There are lectures, demonstrations, and materials to read. However, the participants are usually not tested or graded.

Conferences concentrate on broader subjects. A conference might focus on robotics, CAD, or multimedia. Many speakers discuss different aspects of a subject over several days. Presentations at conferences are usually one to two hours long, with several presentations occurring at the same time. There is often a display area, as seen in Figure 16.11, where vendors and publishers can demonstrate related products.

Workshops and conferences both provide a means for people to share ideas, new techniques, and information with others who have common interests. These activities, along with on-the-job training, often are called *continuing education.* To avoid technological obsolescence of their knowledge and skills, people who work with computers typically are required to spend a quarter to a third of their time (personal and working) in continuing education. Therefore, other sources for continuing the learning process, distinct from schools and job-related training, also are important.

Recreational and Professional Publications

People who perform similar jobs or who work in a specific industry develop interests in common. Computer professionals, for example, are interested in new hardware and software developments, in new application packages, or in new ways to install and use their systems. In the medical field, interests center around new medications or treatments. Manufacturing engineers share interests in information about new types of production techniques or tools. Businesspeople need to know what products and services their competition provides.

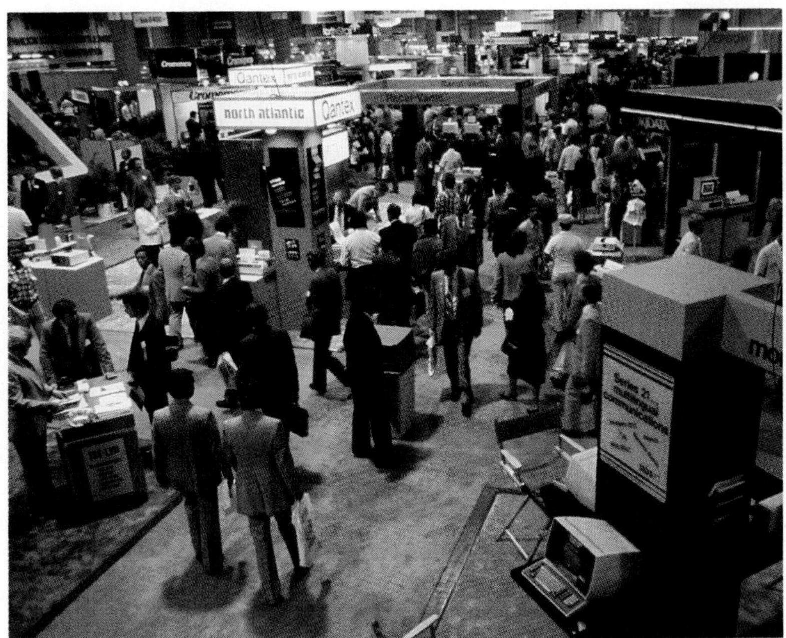

FIGURE 16.11
Conferences provide opportunities for users with common interests to meet each other and view new technology.

A major branch of the publishing industry has evolved to meet these continuing education needs. Special-interest newspapers, journals, newsletters, and magazines are published to supply information to specific groups of readers (see Figure 16.12). In all, tens of thousands of professional publications are produced regularly. More than 700 of these deal directly with computer-related topics, and many more cover applications of computers in particular industries or professions.

Part of the continuing education effort for every computer professional and serious end-user should include reading of one or more special-interest publications. You will almost certainly encounter a number of these publications at school and in the workplace. You should make it a practice to review the contents of such publications carefully and regularly. Subscribe to or arrange to read some of these publications, perhaps in the public or company libraries.

A good way to evaluate a professional publication is to review its table of contents. Then read the articles that match your interests. At the very least, be aware that professional publications will establish an information lifeline that you will need to keep your knowledge base from becoming obsolete.

CAREER PATHS

One job does not make a career. Those of us with an eye toward the future can make the most of our working lives by realizing that our careers will probably be a series of related jobs or a **career path.**

If we identify long-term career goals, we can make intelligent decisions regarding a career path that will lead us to those goals. Otherwise, we could aimlessly jump from one job to another, dissatisfied with our accomplishments at each step. Or worse yet, we could stay in the same job because we have nothing better to do.

FIGURE 16.12
Reading recreational and professional publications provides an easy way to keep your knowledge up-to-date.

Career goals are never easy to choose and are certainly subject to change. But having a career goal in mind does help when writing a resume, applying for a new job, or selecting new fields to study. The computer field offers opportunities to persons with wide ranges of knowledge and skills. A few jobs are open to persons with high school education. However, far greater opportunities, with higher growth potential, are open to those who go on to college.

Almost every college curriculum has been affected by recent developments in computers, microelectronics, and data communications. As a result, many students are trained as end-users as part of their degree requirements. Students interested in working with

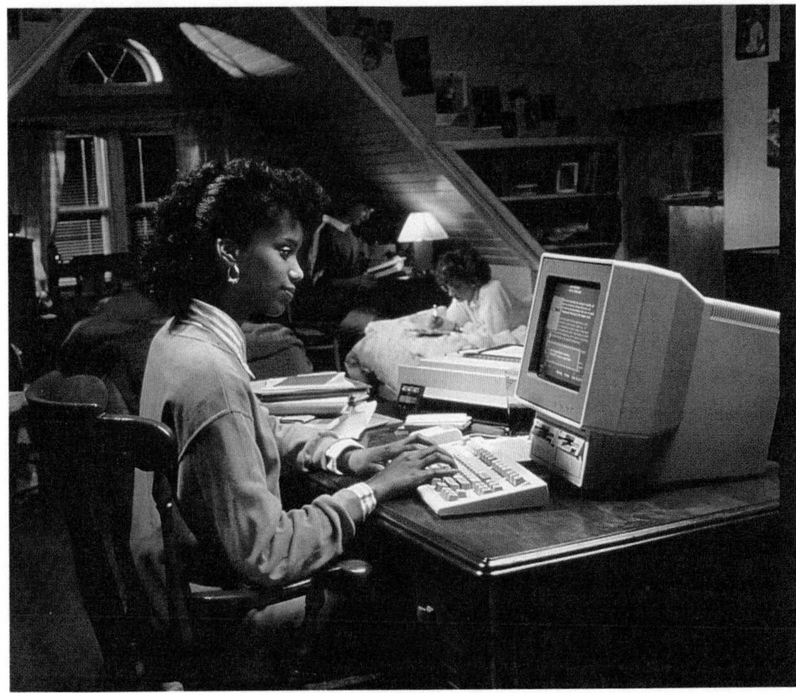

FIGURE 16.13
Computer technology has had an impact on almost every college curriculum.

computers and related technology all of the time have the option of training to be computer professionals. College-level courses can qualify people for a number of job specialties. These specialty areas include:

- End-user computing
- Information systems
- Computer science
- Computer engineering

End-User Computing

Just as computers have affected every facet of human social and working experience, so also have computers become an integral part of virtually every academic department at the college level. This development has been logical and necessary. When computers were new, colleges and universities tended to have a single, comparatively large computer center that served all academic departments. Students from a variety of departments acquired their computer knowledge from this central facility.

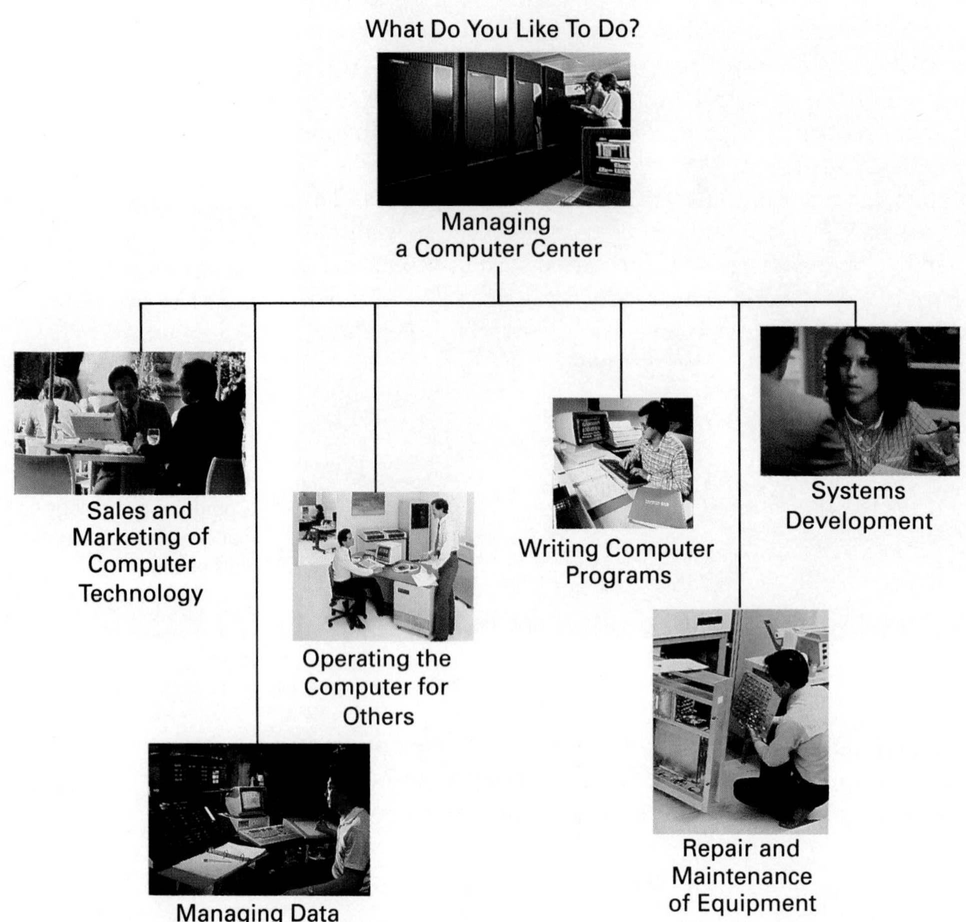

FIGURE 16.14
Many career goals and interests can be met in jobs related to computer information systems.

Now, personal computers can be found in many academic departments. After a general introductory class, specific field-related applications are taught within the appropriate departments. To illustrate, medical and nursing schools use computers to train students in patient monitoring, medical diagnosis, support for patient care, and even administration of hospitals and medical offices. Similarly, departments in science, engineering, business, education, liberal arts, fine arts, social science, and other specialties also tend to have equipment, software, and courses designed to meet special needs of their present students and future computer users.

Information Systems

The work associated with keeping computer systems and networks running and delivering services required by users provides a number of career opportunities. Some of the specific job descriptions were covered in earlier chapters. Specialties within this career area include computer operations, data entry and control, database management, network specialist, systems analyst, computer programming, and software engineering (Figure 16.15).

As computer systems became more sophisticated, great shortages of qualified people developed. There has been a continuous demand since the 1950s for people with the skills to design and successfully implement new computer-based knowledge systems. The recent need that has emerged is for a new category of specialist—people trained to create and install information systems in business, scientific, manufacturing, and educational organizations. Accordingly, the specialty of **computer information systems (CIS)** evolved and is now a popular major on many college campuses.

FIGURE 16.15
Computer professionals working with information systems have many career paths they can follow.

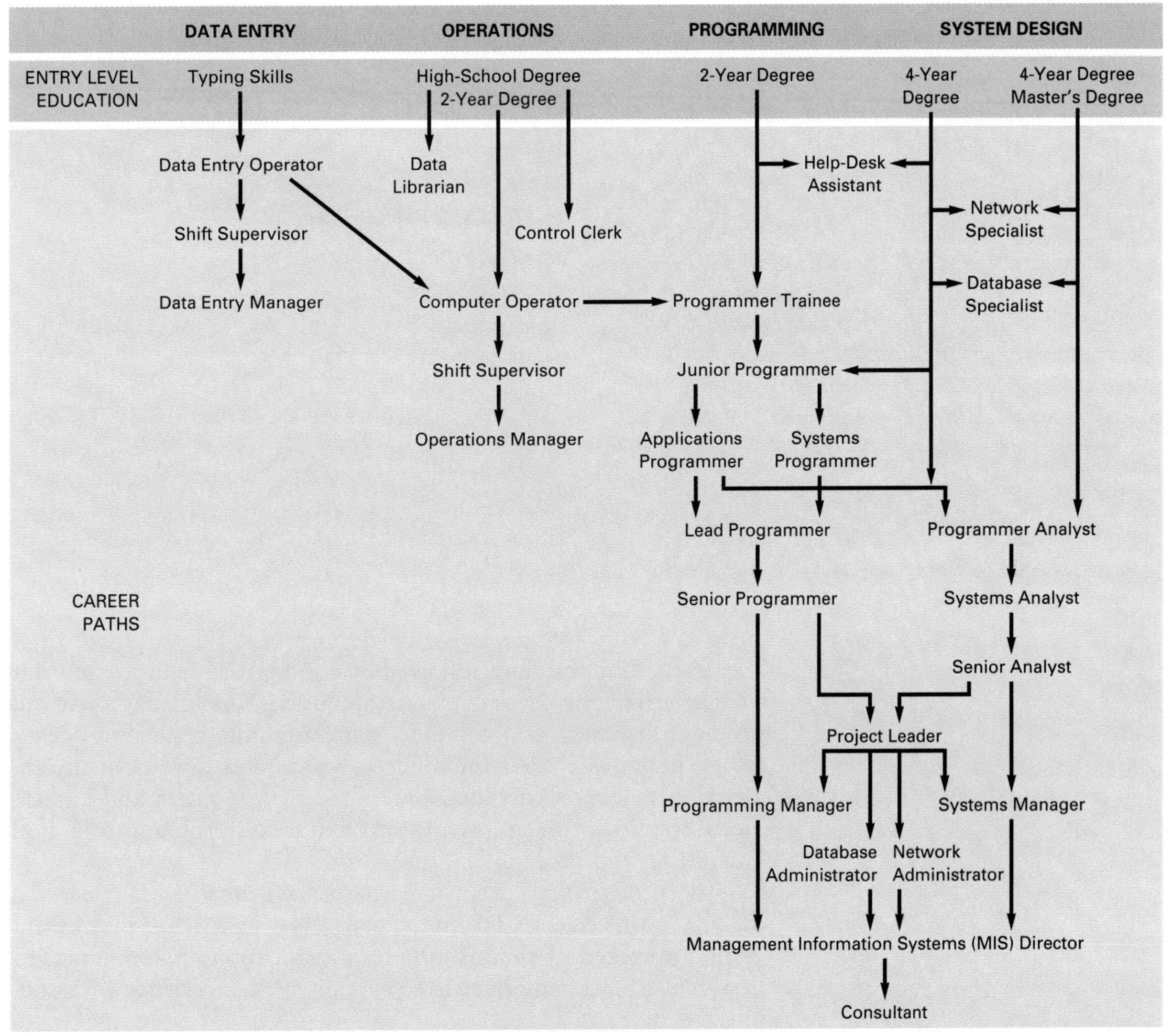

Who's Who

J. Georg Bednorz (b. 1950)

Karl Müller (b. 1927)

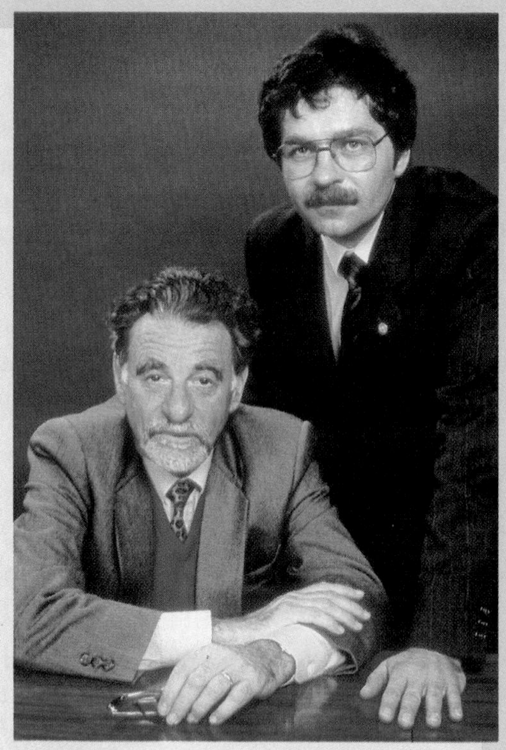

Since its discovery in 1911, superconductivity has intrigued engineers and physicists. A superconductor is a material that loses all resistance to the flow of electricity when cooled to a low temperature. Despite many years of research it was impossible to predict which materials could be used as superconductors. Scientists saw great potential for superconductors as a means to transport electricity efficiently and inexpensively. But expensive equipment was needed to bring the materials down to very low temperatures.

In the early 1980s two researchers, J. Georg Bednorz and Karl Müller, at IBM's research laboratories in Zurich, tried a variety of compounds that they could easily make. For a while they had to share lab equipment with others and almost lost their funding. After reading an article about French research in an unrelated area, Bednorz decided to add copper to a mixture of lanthanum, barium, nickel, and oxygen. In early 1986 Bednorz and Müller were able to show that superconductivity started in their material at a temperature of 35 Kelvins (−397°F or −238°C). This was 12 Kelvins higher than any previous studies and was a big step on the road to superconductor practicality. Their research was painstakingly done but greeted with skepticism. As scientists were able to replicate their results, other research in the area proliferated. Bednorz and Müller were awarded the 1987 Nobel Prize in Physics.

The CIS curriculum followed at hundreds of colleges and universities stresses a series of courses in business and management and includes a sequence in computer programming, application generators, networks, telecommunications, systems development, and decision making. Individuals interested in computers and applications-oriented problem solving will find a CIS program to be both interesting and profitable.

CIS professionals can also earn a *Certificate in Data Processing (CDP)*. To receive a CDP, individuals must pass a five-part examination prepared by the Institute for Certification of Computer Professionals (ICCP) and have five years of work experience with computerized information systems. Two years of college course work can substitute for two years of work experience.

A CDP candidate must pass all five sections within three years. Once a section has been passed, it does not have to be taken again. If a section is failed, it can be retaken. The five sections of the exam are:

- Data processing hardware
- Computer programming and software
- Principles of management
- Quantitative methods and accounting
- Systems analysis and design

Individuals who have received a CDP place these initials following their name to show others their professional certification. The CDP is only one of several certifications available to computer professionals. A *Certificate in Computer Programming (CCP)* is also available through the ICCP by specialized tests covering business, scientific, or systems programming. Proper certification can help professionals advance along their chosen career path (see Figure 16.15).

Computer Science

Early computers were specialized computation devices. Computation, in turn, is part of the province of mathematicians. Therefore, mathematics departments of educational institutions have been involved with computers since the earliest days. Through the years, the mathematically oriented study of computers has evolved into a specialty that deals with the control of the data manipulation capabilities of computers. Today, people who specialize in techniques for designing systems software and apply these techniques to the handling of data and programs are known as **computer scientists.**

Demands for qualified computer scientists have grown with the introduction of more advanced software. System software, remember, controls operation of computers and serves to make application of computers easier for users. It is not unusual for a large computer installation to have more money tied up in system software than in computer equipment. Computer scientists are people whose prime responsibility is to develop and maintain system software. They take classes in computer programming, in data structures, and in the design of such system software as operating systems and compilers. People with this experience work for hardware manufacturers, for software developers, and as technical specialists responsible for software maintenance within organizations.

Who's Who

Alan Turing

(1912–1954)

Alan Turing, who became famous in computing, started out young and gifted in mathematics. In trying to prove an important theorem (Gödel's theorem of incompleteness in arithmetic) in 1935, he designed a computer precursor, the Turing machine. Actually, the Turing machine was an abstract rather than physical machine. It was designed to have three components: a control unit, two-way infinite tape, and a read-write head. The read-write head would process commands found on the tape. These instructions would then be acted on by the control unit. The Turing machine would also test a command before executing it to see if it could adversely affect results. This was an attempt by Turing to see if machines could be taught to "think." Later Turing designed a "thinking machine" that simulated a human contemplating chess moves based on a previous play. In 1950 one of Turing's scientific papers defined the Turing Test for artificial intelligence: an intelligent machine could respond to a user with such a human-like manner that the user could not distinguish machine from person. Turing's inventions supported the need for practical computing machines and provided much of the basis for computer science theory.

Computer Engineering

Persons who complete coursework in **computer engineering** specialize in the development, manufacture, and assembly of computer hardware. At most universities, studies in computer engineering are associated with the discipline of electrical or electronic engineering; however, computers play an integral part in the job of mechanical, chemical, and bioengineers. Persons entering this highly diversified field usually specialize, since the body of knowledge is so great. Computer engineers have become like doctors, who have found it impossible to keep up with all the knowledge associated with their field.

Specialties within computer engineering include the design and building of integrated circuits, the development of storage hardware, the design of output hardware, and the interaction of hardware and software. Computer engineers also work with other researchers to design the parallel processors, optical computers, and

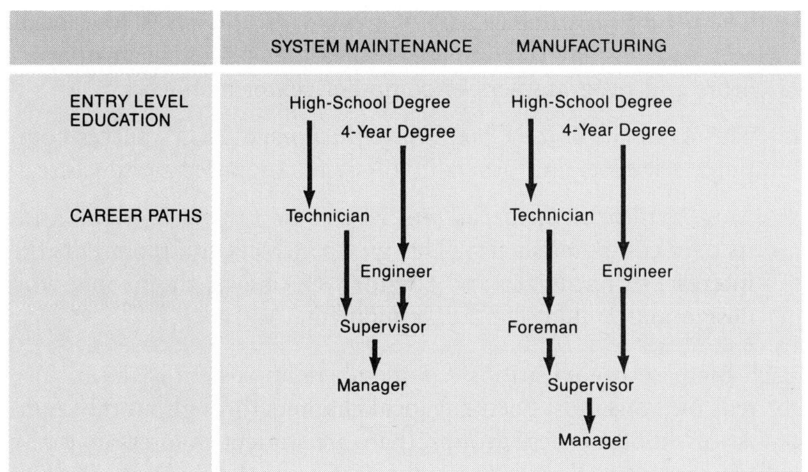

FIGURE 16.16
Electrical and electronics engineers can follow career paths in computer manufacturing and systems maintenance.

superconductor circuitry on the cutting edge of technology. Persons who pursue specialties involving processing equipment and associated software are called **computer architects.** Computer architecture encompasses the work of configuring computer systems to achieve specific performance.

Success in computer engineering calls for completion of courses in mathematics, physics, electronics, system software, circuit design, project management, and manufacturing methods (see Figure 16.16). Through the years, processing functions have shifted back and forth between hardware and system software. One result has been a parallel development of many hardware and software features. In response, many colleges and universities are coordinating and/or combining their programs in computer engineering and computer science. The term *computer architecture* often is used to describe this combined specialty.

Professional Organizations

A variety of professional organizations have evolved to support different computer-oriented career paths. Members of these professional organizations enjoy meeting with each other to exchange ideas and information along with establishing peer contacts. Thousands of professional, trade, and business associations serve millions of members in specialized industries or jobs. Members are attracted by common, shared interests (Figure 16.17). As examples, each of the four major computer disciplines has at least one association serving its specialized needs:

- The *Association for System Management (ASM)* has a membership that consists largely of systems analysts for various organizations.

- The *Data Processing Management Association (DPMA)* appeals to a wide variety of computer professionals ranging from operators and programmers to computer center managers.
- The *Association for Computing Machinery (ACM)* serves computer scientists and others involved in computer architecture.
- The *Institute of Electrical and Electronic Engineers (IEEE)* has its own computer society. This group attracts and represents the interests of hardware and circuitry specialists, the people who design and build computer equipment.

Each of these organizations has membership rosters that run into the tens of thousands. Each has local chapters throughout the country. As offshoots of these groups, there are student chapters on many college campuses. Future computer professionals can begin to align themselves with the disciplines they wish to follow and can begin to build working relationships that can support life-long careers.

In addition to these computer-industry organizations, many other associations and societies have subgroups that specialize in computer applications. Examples include associations serving the health, education, banking, insurance, and petroleum fields. In each case, managers, professionals, scientists, and other serious computer users have a chance to exchange ideas and views with computer professionals who have chosen to specialize in the needs of specific fields.

FIGURE 16.17
Membership in a professional organization promotes new ideas and personal growth.

Ways in Which Professional Organizations Support Personal Development

1. Provide personal and professional contacts
2. Support student members
3. Provide local meetings and presentations
4. Publish newsletters and magazines
5. Sponsor seminars, training sessions, conferences, conventions, and trade shows
6. Provide certification of professional skills

Typical participation in a professional organization begins with membership in a local chapter or group. These local entities have regular meetings, usually at least once a month. Officers of the chapters are responsible for planning meetings, discussions, and presentations on new developments of special interest to members. Often the national organization has a staff that helps to provide speakers or materials for local meetings.

Most associations or societies publish newsletters or magazines for their members. In addition, organizations sponsor and conduct workshops, training sessions, conferences, conventions, or trade shows. These activities can play important roles in the continuing education of end-users and professionals.

A Closer Look...

Emerging Technologies

We have discussed in this chapter the potential impact of optical computers, superconductive materials, and artificial intelligence. Other technological trends will have a tremendous impact on narrow groups of users—for example, computer-aided prosthetics for the physically challenged, or computer-based trading by financial arbitrageurs.

A few new technologies just emerging from research and development laboratories have the potential to change everyone's life. What follows are some questions you may never have thought to ask about emerging technologies.

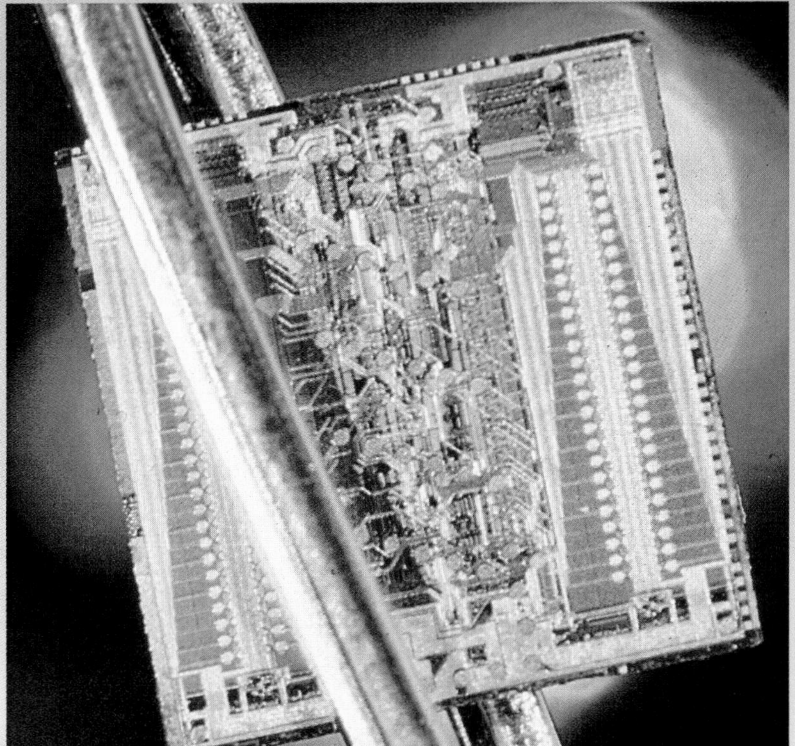

Q What is a neural network?

A Computer scientists want to simulate a person's ability to recognize patterns. To do so, they are integrating thousands of specialized processors, a kind of silicon neuron, onto chips. Neurological connections in the human brain are modeled by the movement of electrons through the circuitry. These **neural networks** are taught basic discriminations through a set of learning trials. For instance, the difference between your voice and a friend's is taught by providing different examples. The system tries to guess after each example and learns to discriminate the difference through trial and error.

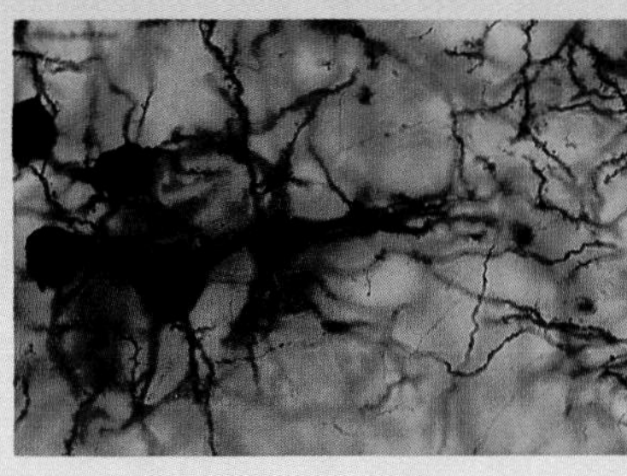

Q What types of work do nanomachines perform?

A **Nanomachines** incorporate gears, levers, lenses, ball bearings, and sensors that are smaller than the period at the end of this sentence. These microscopic machines could clear a person's clogged arteries, clean up pollutants, continuously sense air pressure in your tires, or intravenously manufacture and administer life-supporting drugs. Like a tiny bulldozer, a nanomachine can move atoms across a surface, creating man-made molecules.

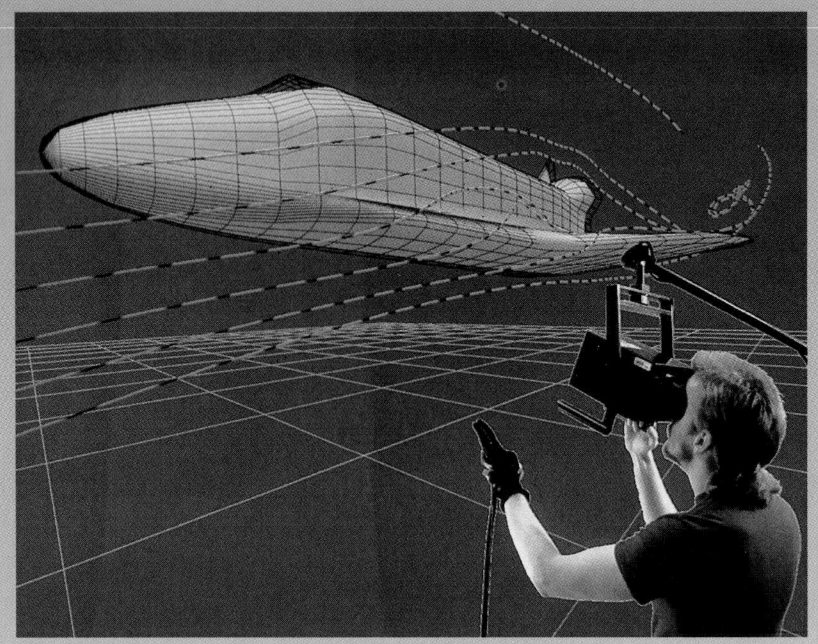

Q Will image processing require new hardware?

A Yes, it will if multimedia, computer-aided design, desktop publishing, virtual reality, and other visually oriented applications are to reach their full potential. Image-processing capabilities mean users work with line art, photographs, video images, and animation as easily as words and numbers. New video-quality screen displays, high-resolution scanners, and affordable color printers will support professional and personal applications of image processing.

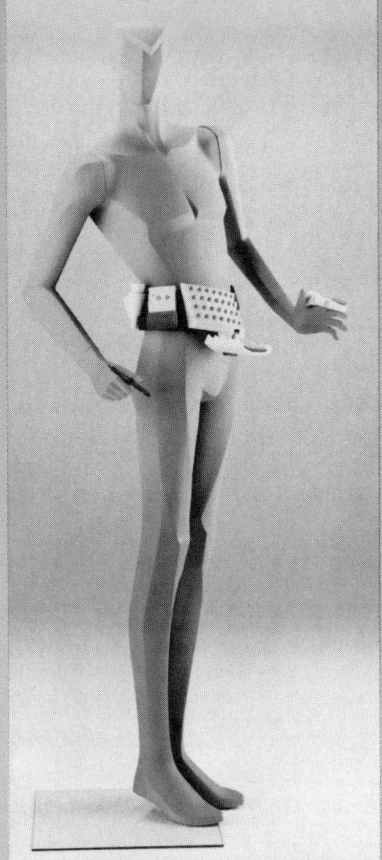

Q What comes next after portable computers?

A Engineers and fashion designers are collaborating on wearable computers. Their goal is to create hardware that is comfortable and enhances job performance. For example, a computer used to take inventory would include an optical scanner on the hand or arm, with a voice-activated database system worn around the neck. An emergency medical technician uses a sensor on his hand to read vital signs, which are displayed on goggles and sent ahead to the hospital.

Q What's in the future for holograms?

A A hologram is a 3D image that seems to float in space and changes as you move around it. Holographic images can now be seen on credit cards, magazine covers, and posters. However, they require hours of precisely filming an object from many angles. Researchers are using supercomputers to take a computer-generated object, rotate it, and store the images for later projection. Although only simple shapes can now be created, graphic workstations of the future will allow a user to create a hologram interactively, as he or she draws it on a screen.

Q What is in the future for robots?

A By combining artificial intelligence and robotics, researchers are creating robots that learn from their movements. One scientist is using the behavior of insects to build multilegged robots that detect and avoid obstacles for exploring the planet Mars. A robotic arm that learns a precise, complex movement like buttering bread, holds promise for the advancement of user-controlled artificial limbs.

Chapter Facts

- We now live in an information society where many people's work generates or depends on information.
- Computer literate workers are critical to an organization's success within the global economy.
- New homes can be wired for intelligent appliances, which make them safer and more energy efficient.
- Automobiles employ embedded computers to control operations, passenger comfort, and security.
- Information utilities could offer a wide range of entertainment options, including the ability to preview and rent the latest video games and first-run movies.
- Interactive television enables customers to give direct feedback to the television station. It also allows students to quickly send back answers to questions seen on educational television.
- Virtual reality allows people to experience a 3D computer simulation by using special gloves, goggles, and body suits.
- CAD, CAM, robotics, materials requirements planning, and a communication standard work together as part of computer-integrated manufacturing (CIM).
- International Electronic Fund Transfer (EFT) systems use computer networks to handle financial transactions that support a global economy.
- A possible extension of EFT would involve a cashless society wherein checks and money would not be accepted.
- By using superconducting materials in computers, processing speed and efficiency can be greatly improved.
- Optical computers use light waves and fiber optics to operate the processing hardware.
- By linking homes and businesses with fiber optic cable, an electronic superhighway will be created that can transmit text, voice, video, and audio information.
- Artificial intelligence uses heuristic rules to make decisions like a person would.
- Personal expert systems will manage database access, voice mail, scheduling, and other services for us. In the near future, expert systems will help homeowners improve and repair their houses.
- Technological obsolescence has created new opportunities for qualified people but necessitates continual updating of skills.

- Workers can keep their skills up-to-date by participating in on-the-job training, workshops, and conferences.
- Professional publications provide a way for specialists to keep up with the newest research in their area.
- Career opportunities as computer professionals exist in many areas, each requiring different skills and formal education. Some groom people for promotion into higher-level positions.
- Professional organizations foster communication among peers, offer chances for continuing education, hold local meetings, publish journals, and sponsor student chapters.

Terms to Remember

a. artificial intelligence (AI)
b. career path
c. cashless society
d. computer architect
e. computer engineering
f. computer information systems (CIS)
g. computer-integrated manufacturing (CIM)
h. computer scientist
i. conference
j. information society
k. interactive television
l. nanomachine
m. neural network
n. optical computer
o. superconductor
p. virtual reality
q. workshop

Mix and Match

Match the following definitions to the Terms to Remember.

1. ____ an area of specialization concerning the creation of systems in business, science, education, and manufacturing.
2. ____ array of processors integrated into a communication network that mimics connections in the human brain.
3. ____ a professional meeting covering a broad subject area. It includes concurrent presentations and product displays.
4. ____ series of related jobs.
5. ____ computer-generated images displayed as three-dimensional output in a set of goggles and controlled by the physical movements of the user.

6. _____ manufacturing system that utilizes the features of CAD/CAM, robotics, and numerical control, linked together by a communications standard.
7. _____ software application that simulates human thought and judgment by use of heuristic problem-solving techniques.
8. _____ extremely small machine.
9. _____ person who specializes in developing techniques for designing system software and their applications in managing data and programs.
10. _____ a society where all financial transactions are done electronically, based upon an individual's universal account number.
11. _____ material that loses all electrical resistance at a set temperature.
12. _____ person who specializes in developing processing equipment and associated systems software.
13. _____ a television containing a cable control box that lets users communicate through the control box to the television station.
14. _____ educational meeting concentrating on a single topic.
15. _____ experimental processing hardware using optical switches for processing and optical fibers to transmit data.
16. _____ computer field specializing in the development, manufacturing, and assembly of hardware.
17. _____ an area containing a large group of people whose work generates or depends upon information.

Review Questions

1. What implications does an information society have for good-paying manual labor jobs?
2. How do smart homes increase the homeowner's safety and the home's energy efficiency?
3. What are ten applications for embedded computers in cars?
4. Identify three trends for cars of the future.
5. How could information utilities compete with cable television and video rental stores?
6. Describe four applications for interactive television.

7. How does stereolithography work? Name two applications for it.
8. What will travel along the electronic superhighway?
9. What are six uses for personal expert systems at home? What are four uses for personal expert systems in the workplace?
10. Identify a good and a bad effect of obsolescence for computer professionals and users.
11. Describe the focus of on-the-job training, workshops, and conferences.
12. What is a good way to review professional publications?
13. Describe the skills associated with people graduating from college programs in computer information systems, computer science, and computer engineering. Identify classes associated with each area of study.
14. How can a computer professional earn a CDP or CCP?
15. How do professional organizations support personal development?
16. Relate the orientation of the Data Processing Management Association (DPMA), Association for System Managers (ASM), Association for Computing Machinery (ACM), and Institute of Electrical and Electronic Engineers (IEEE) with college programs discussed earlier.

Applying What You've Learned

1. Some people look forward to a cashless society, while others would find it undesirable. What are some positive aspects of living in a cashless society? Some negative aspects? How could a cashless society be abused? Would you foresee a decrease in money-related crime? Would a cashless society improve social conditions?
2. As computer equipment becomes obsolete, we are faced with the problem of disposing of the hardware in an environmentally sound way. This problem also includes old stereo and VCR players, outdated copiers, etc. Suggest three ways to handle the growing mound of unwanted technological hardware.
3. Smart cars promote improved security, comfort, fuel efficiency, and environmental safety. What is a disadvantage to using many embedded computers in cars?

4. Find five job ads for computer professionals in the newspaper. What additional qualifications and educational requirements are listed besides those mentioned in the text? What salaries and other benefits are stated? How much experience is required? Do any sound like jobs you would like to have some day? Why or why not?
5. Check your local and/or school library for professional publications related in some way to computers. Make a list of them, including what type of professionals they are written for, how often they are published, and whether they are sponsored by a professional organization. Be sure to include noncomputer industry publications, such as those in medicine, business, and manufacturing.
6. It is becoming more common for people to make "mid-life career changes." That means a middle-aged person will completely change the type and area of work he/she is doing. This often involves going back to school or starting out at a low paying job in a new field.
   a. What are the advantages and disadvantages of this?
   b. Why do you think a person would want to make such a change?
   c. Do you think employers would want to hire a person like this?
   d. Could you see yourself making a change like this? Why or why not?
7. Although computers are constantly increasing in power and speed, there are still some things they cannot do. Describe three problems that are too big for computers to solve.

Answers to Mix and Match

1. f   2. m   3. i   4. b   5. p   6. g   7. a   8. l   9. h   10. c
11. o   12. d   13. k   14. q   15. n   16. e   17. j

A

Introduction to MS-DOS/PC-DOS

- **From the User's Point of View**
- **Personal Computer Start-Up Procedures**
  - System orientation
  - How to boot a PC
  - Setting the printer's top of page
  - Hard copy of screen displays
- **DOS Commands and Utility Programs**
  - Formatting a new (or old) disk
  - Changing the default drive
  - Creating copies of files
  - Displaying the disk directory
  - Renaming files
  - Deleting files
  - Undeleting files
  - Making subdirectories
  - Changing from one subdirectory to another
  - Customizing the DOS prompt
  - Copying files to a subdirectory
  - Removing subdirectories from disk
- **System Shut-Down**

FROM THE USER'S POINT OF VIEW

Before starting to use personal productivity software or learning to program, you need to review operating procedures for IBM and compatible personal computers. The following DOS tutorial provides a brief overview of some of the more important personal computer operating system instructions. Some of these instructions prepare new disks for processing, help you locate disk files and programs, and provide a convenient means of copying important disk resources. You need access to a personal computer to complete the tutorial. Instructions or data you should enter into the computer using the keyboard are printed in red and preceded by a ■.

PERSONAL COMPUTER START-UP PROCEDURES

IBM and compatible personal computers use a disk operating system (DOS) developed by the Microsoft Corporation. Called **MS-DOS,** it is the most commonly used operating system in the world. Licensed and distributed by IBM Corporation as **PC-DOS,** this operating system has evolved through many revisions up to version 6.0 and beyond.

System Orientation

Booting describes the procedure for starting up a computer system. IBM and compatible microcomputers automatically look for and load a command program, named COMMAND.COM, from the operating system into memory as a part of the booting process.

Since a disk with DOS must be in a designated disk drive when booting a microcomputer, associated procedures will vary. The disk drive reading DOS is referred to as the *system drive*. A disk drive storing data (or programs) is referred to as the *data drive*. Use the information below to identify the system drive used by your microcomputer system.

One-Diskette System

The floppy disk drive is labeled drive A. Therefore, the system drive is drive A, and after booting, the DOS disk is removed and drive A becomes the data drive. This configuration is rare because most systems have access to a hard disk or disk storage through a network server as well as the removable diskette.

Two-Diskette System

The second floppy disk drive is labeled drive B. This drive is usually under or to the right of drive A. In this configuration the system drive is drive A, and the data drive is drive B.

Hard Disk and One-Diskette System

Personal computers with hard disk drives identify these drives as drive C. The system drive is drive C, although when a DOS disk is in drive A during booting, drive A is used instead of C, and there is no drive B, since B is reserved for a second floppy disk drive.

Hard Disk and Two-Diskette System

Any personal computer system with a hard disk (drive C) uses it as the system drive when the computer is turned on with drive A empty. Disk drives A and B are used as data drives and backup.

Computer within a Local Area Network (LAN)

The system drive is usually drive A, and the DOS disk contains special network programs. After the system is booted, disk drives A and B are used as data drives. Depending on the LAN configuration, alternative disk space is available through a server. This disk space is identified by drives D through Z. LAN users may be asked to enter a password to identify themselves as part of the booting.

How to Boot a PC

A personal computer's booting procedure will vary between systems. However, they all have two things in common:

1. Power needs to be turned on.
2. DOS must be available on a disk accessible to the system.

Before You Start

If your system has a hard disk, it will be used as the system drive when the floppy disk drives are empty. Most systems are designed to look first for DOS on a floppy disk before trying the hard disk. If you do not have a hard disk, locate drive A, which is the system drive for floppy disk-based systems. Carefully follow the actions marked by the (■) symbol described below for the system drive used by your personal computer.

5.25-Inch Floppy Disks

- ■ Open the system drive latch (see Figure A.1).
- ■ Position the disk with the label on top and the write-protect notch to the left, also shown in Figure A.1.
- ■ Gently push the DOS disk into the system drive until it stops and will not go further without force.
- ■ Close the drive latch.

3.5-Inch Diskettes

- Position the disk with the label on top and the write-protect window (see Figure A.2) to the left.
- Firmly push the DOS disk into the system drive until it locks into place.

FIGURE A.1
Layout of 5.25-inch disk along with two popular disk drive door mechanisms.

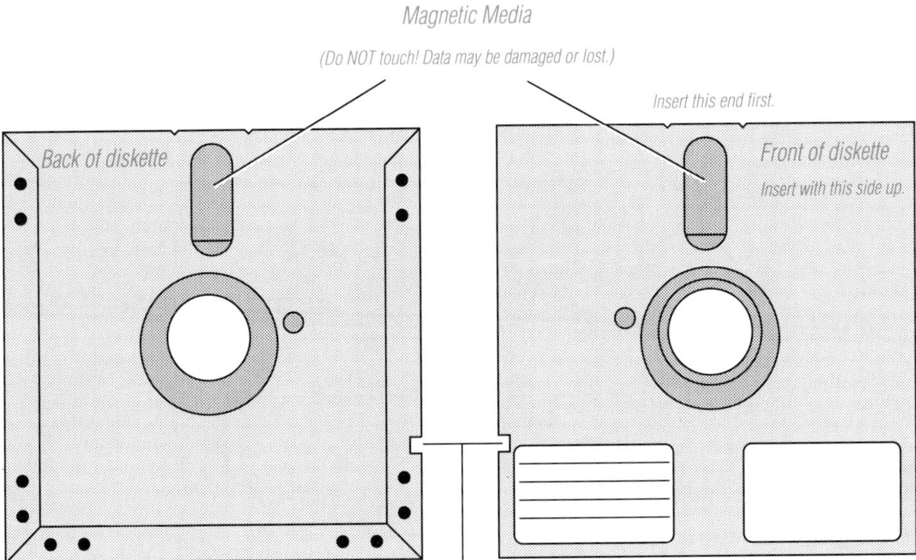

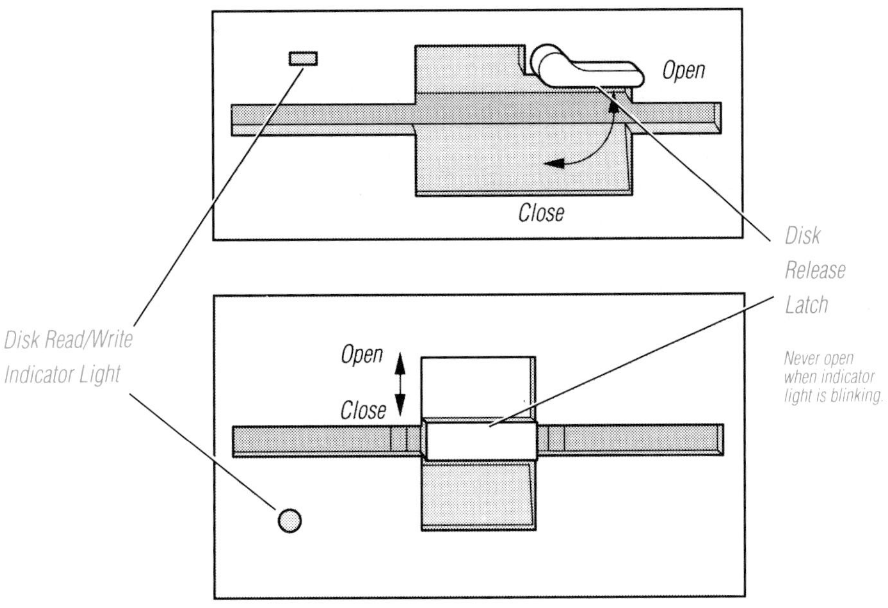

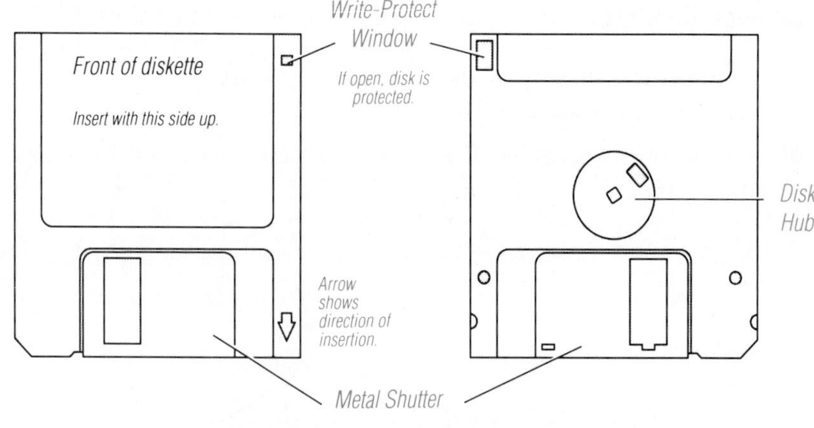

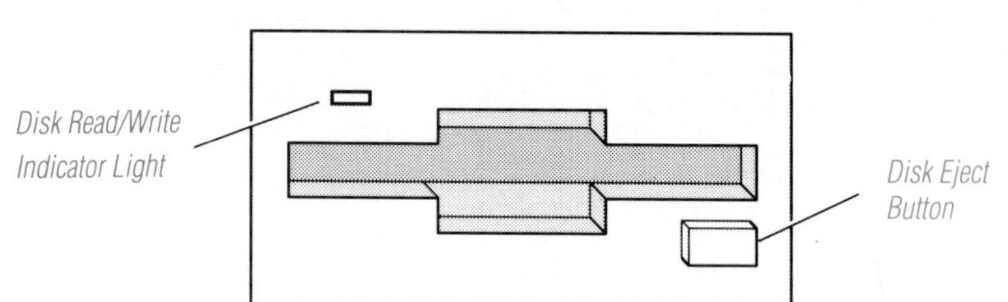

FIGURE A.2
Layout of 3.5-inch disk along with disk drive door mechanism.

Hard Disk

■ Remove any floppy disks currently in the floppy disk drive or drives.

Turning on the Computer

You are now ready to turn on the microcomputer. The ON/OFF switch may be found on the right side of the computer near the back, on the back, or on the front right side.

■ Turn on the computer.

▶ Most computers turn on a light in the front of the drive.

Finally, if the screen does not turn on with the computer, turn on the screen. The ON/OFF switch is usually on the right side of the screen near the bottom or on the top, right side near the back.

■ Turn on screen if it is not already on.

▶ Displays current date.

If your computer system follows the standard booting steps, the current date is displayed on the screen. Many computer systems are customized to display menus, launch a GUI, or describe special procedures or copyright infringement policies. What follows is a description of the standard booting procedures.

The screen will usually display a prompt asking you to verify the system date and time. The `mm-dd-yy` prompt is asking for one- or two-digit entries for the month, day, and year. May 19th of 1994 is entered as `5-19-94`. As you can see in Figure A.3, each entry is separated by a hyphen. The entry for the current time is similar. Enter the hour, minute, and seconds (if desired), separated by colons.

FIGURE A.3
Booting procedures for IBM and compatible personal computers.

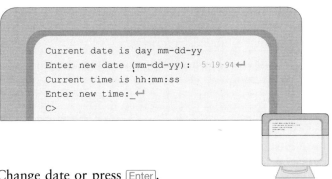

```
Current date is day mm-dd-yy
Enter new date (mm-dd-yy): 5-19-94↵
Current time is hh:mm:ss
Enter new time:_↵
C>
```

Floppy Disk System
1. Insert DOS disk into drive A
2. Turn on computer
3. Turn on screen if necessary
4. Turn on printer when available

Hard Disk System
1. Confirm drive A is empty
2. Turn on computer
3. Turn on screen if necessary
4. Turn on printer when available

- Change date or press [Enter].
  - ▶ Displays current time.
- Change time or press [Enter].
  - ▶ Displays capital letter and > symbol.

After the entering of the date and time, the booting process is complete. The system now displays the letter associated with the system drive, followed by a > symbol. For example, microcomputers using drive A as the system drive display A>. Hard disk systems defaulting to drive C display C>. This display is known as the **DOS prompt.** It tells the user that DOS is ready for instructions. In addition, the DOS prompt identifies the default drive.

Setting the Printer's Top of Page

Since a hard copy of output is often the final result of a session with your computer, you will need to turn on the printer. If there is more than one printer available, make sure you know which printer is attached to your computer and find its ON/OFF switch. It is usually on the side of the printer.

- Turn on printer.
  - ▶ Power/online light turns on.

When the printer is first turned on, it automatically places itself online. In other words, it is in communication with the computer. An online light, next to the online button, should be on.

Top-of-Form

Laser printers print one page at a time and always start at the top of a new page. If you are using a dot-matrix printer, it should be positioned to start printing at the top of a sheet of continuous fan-fold paper. To check this, you will need to explore inside the printer. We must see if the printing mechanism is even with the perforated edge separating the continuous-form paper. If you are using a laser printer and/or a LAN print server, skip to the next section on "Hard Copy of Screen Displays."

- Open the printer's hinged front panel.
- Check to see if the printing mechanism is even with the top of the paper (see Figure A.4).

If the printer is already set for top of page, skip on down to the next section—"Hard Copy of Screen Displays." If not, we will need to make the adjustments with the printer offline. Offline means the printer will not accept output from the computer.

NOTE: Using the paper roller handle is not recommended for adjusting the paper when the printer is on.

- Press online button once.
  - ▶ Online light goes off.

The two buttons shown in Figure A.4 near the online button are the form feed button (often marked as FF) and the line feed button (marked LF). These buttons adjust the paper by activating the tractor feeds and/or paper roller.

Line Feed

Like the Carriage Return key on an electric typewriter, every time you press the LF (**line feed**) button, the printer skips to the beginning of the next line. Use this button to line feed down to the top of the next page.

- Press the line feed button enough times to position the next perforated edge just above the printing mechanism (see Figure A.4).
  - ▶ Paper moves through printer until it is at top of next page.
- Turn printer off.
  - ▶ Online light goes off.

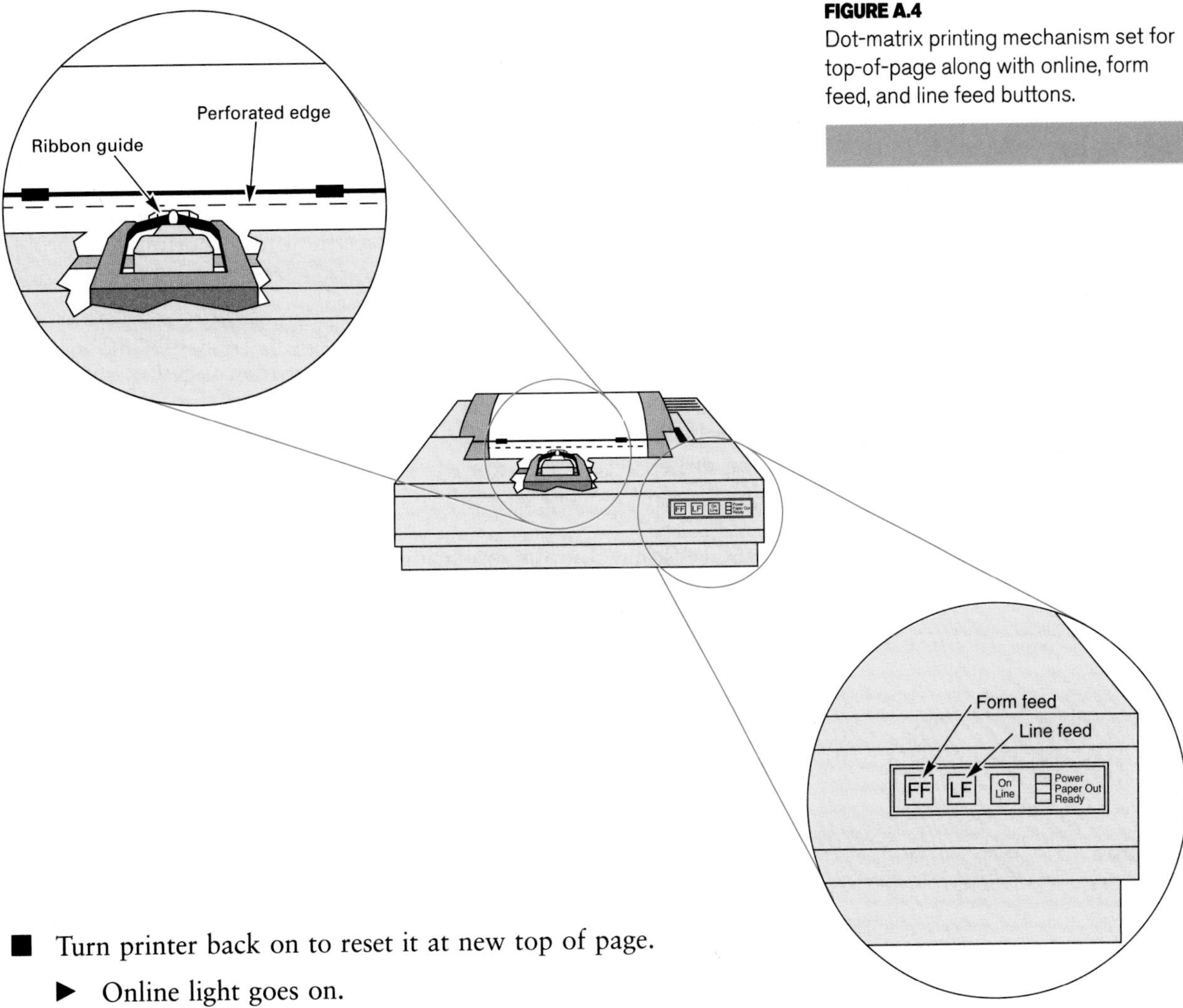

FIGURE A.4
Dot-matrix printing mechanism set for top-of-page along with online, form feed, and line feed buttons.

- Turn printer back on to reset it at new top of page.
  - ▶ Online light goes on.

Form Feed

With the top of page properly set, the **form feed** button should always return the printer to this orientation. Remember, the printer must be offline for either the line feed or form feed button to work.

- Take the printer offline by pressing the online button once.
  - ▶ Online light goes off.
- Press the FF (form feed) button once.
  - ▶ One full sheet of paper feeds through the printer, leaving the print mechanism at the top of the next page.
- Press the online button once.
  - ▶ Online light goes on.

Hard Copy of Screen Displays

With the printer properly set at the top of page, we are ready to make it work. One use for the printer at this stage is to help you document problems. People new to personal computers will soon find themselves working with their computers when no one is around to help. During these times questions pop up or insurmountable problems arise. Sometimes the only solution to a problem is to turn the computer off and start from scratch by booting it again. It happens to the best of us!

Whenever questions or problems appear, remember to print a copy of the screen on the printer. You can then use this output to help explain the situation to a more knowledgeable person when he or she becomes available. A hard copy of the screen is obtained by using either a combination of the Shift and PrtSc keys or just the Print Screen key. The procedure depends on the keyboard in use.

NOTE: Personal computers sharing one printer through a LAN server or switch box may require special procedures for printing screen displays. In some situations, you will be unable to print the screen displays on printers shared by more than one computer. If your system cannot use the Print Screen key, skip to the next section on "DOS Commands and Utility Programs."

■ Turn on printer and adjust it to the top of page if it is not already set.

▶ Online light is on.

Find either the PrtSc or Print Screen key on your keyboard. If you have the PrtSc key, you will need to hold down one of the Shift keys while using it.

FIGURE A.5
Things that can go wrong with a printer.

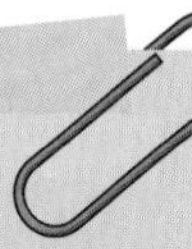

Printer Doesn't Work?

- Unplugged?
- Offline? (online light not on)
- Cable connections are not tight
  —Cable to printer?
  —Cable to computer?
- Do you share a computer with someone else?
  If yes, is there a switch that needs to be changed?

■ Press Print Screen key or the Shift + PrtSc key combination.

▶ Printer outputs current contents of screen display. If not, see Figure A.5.

■ Take the printer offline.

▶ Online light goes off.

■ Press Form Feed button.

▶ Ejects page with screen printout.

■ Put printer back online.

▶ Online light goes on.

DOS COMMANDS AND UTILITY PROGRAMS

What follows is an introduction to some of the most important instructions DOS uses. Each DOS instruction, like Copy or Format, is entered after the DOS prompt, using a similar word order or syntax: first the DOS instruction, a space, and then a list of the file or program names and the disk drive on which they are found. The designated drive and filename become one word, for example, B:\EXAMPLE.TXT. A colon always follows the drive letter, B: in this example. The \ (backslash) indicates the file is located on the primary or root disk directory. A period separates the filename EXAMPLE, from the filename extension TXT.

Lists of filenames are separated by a space. Acceptable file or program names use any combination of letters or numbers up to eight characters. You can use either upper- or lower-case letters. Filenames cannot include spaces. If necessary, use a hyphen instead of a space, as in LAB-1. The DOS User's Manual lists other acceptable characters. A three-character filename extension is permissible if it follows a period, for instance, ANNUAL.RPT would be allowed.

DOS instructions are either internal commands or external utility programs. Internal **commands** are performed by the COMMAND.COM program that is loaded into memory during booting. These operations can be performed at any time. External **utility programs** must be loaded from disk before being executed. These utility programs are found on one or two DOS disks that are purchased with the computer hardware. Floppy disk users must be sure the appropriate DOS disk is in the default disk drive before executing a DOS instruction that relies on an external utility program. When DOS cannot find a utility program, it displays `Bad command or filename`. Hard disk systems and computers within a LAN should be configured to access utility programs at any time.

Formatting a New (or Old) Disk

Formatting a new disk requires the *Format* utility program. Systems booted using a floppy disk must have the system disk in the system drive. Your computer can't load and execute the external Format utility program if it can't find it. If your computer has both a hard disk and dual floppy disks, follow instructions for single floppy disk systems.

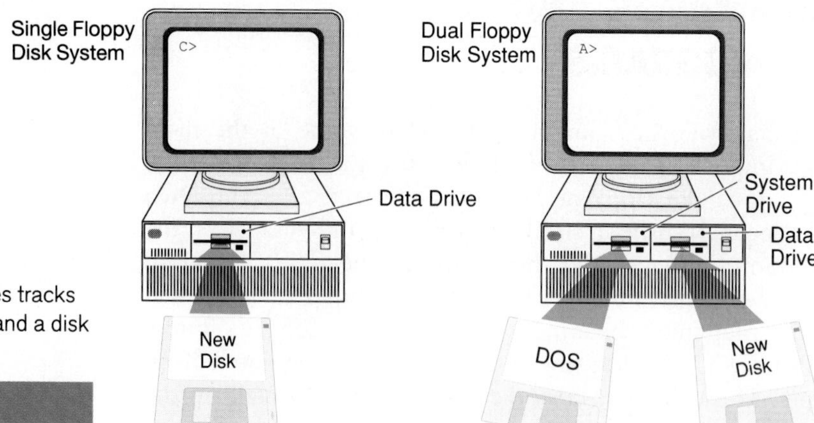

FIGURE A.6
Formatting a new disk creates tracks and sectors for storing data and a disk directory.

- Single floppy disk: place new floppy disk in drive A.

  Dual floppy disk: place the DOS disk in drive A and a new floppy disk in drive B.

- Close the drive door(s) to secure the floppy disk(s).

The floppy disk drive with the new disk is the target drive (Figure A.6). To format a new disk, enter `Format` after the DOS prompt, skip a space, and type the drive designation for the target drive, followed immediately by a colon. Skip another space and enter `/V`. Now press the Enter key (shown below as [Enter]). The computer will walk you through formatting a new disk by displaying a series of prompts. If the following prompts do not appear, check the Error Correction Checklist in Figure A.7 and try again.

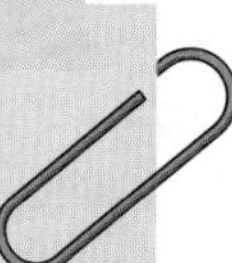

Error Correction Checklist

If a DOS message indicates an instruction has not been executed properly, check the following:

1. Disk(s) is (are) properly positioned in the drive, not upside down or backward. (See Figure A-1 for 5.25-inch disks and Figure A-2 for 3.5-inch disks.)
2. Disk drive door(s) is (are) closed.
3. The DOS instruction and all filenames are followed by a space.
4. There are no spaces between the drive letter, colon, search path and filename in the DOS instruction; for example, A:\PROJECTS\EXAMPLE.TXT is correct.

FIGURE A.7
Things to check when a DOS instruction does not work.

- Single floppy disk: users type `Format A: /V` [Enter]

  Dual floppy disk: users type `Format B: /V` [Enter]

  ▶ `Insert new diskette for drive ?:`
  `and strike ENTER when ready`

NOTE: If the error message `Bad command or filename` appears instead, enter `cd\`, press the Enter key, and try again. If the error message persists, ask your instructor for help.

- Press [Enter]

  ▶ `Head: 0 Cylinder 0`
  (Different displays are possible.)

  ▶ `Formatting ... Format Complete`
  (This message may vary.)

  ▶ `Volume label (11 characters, Enter for none)?`

- Enter YOUR LAST NAME [Enter]

  ▶ `730112 bytes total disk space`
  `730112 bytes available on disk`
  (These numbers will vary, depending on the type of disk used.)

  ▶ `Format another (Y/N)?`

- Type `N` and press [Enter]. If you have another disk to format, type `Y` and press [Enter].

The critical information is displayed by DOS after you have entered your name. The number of bytes (characters) of total disk space should equal the bytes available on disk as shown in Figure A.8. If not, the system displays a third line, which lists the number of bytes in bad sectors.

NOTE: When bad sectors appear, don't panic. Take the disk out of the drive and put it back in. Then try to format the disk again. Most often the disk will format without problems on a second or third try. If the bad sectors persist after three attempts, return the disk to the store from which it was purchased and exchange it for another disk.

DOS provides PC users alternatives within each instruction. The /V that was part of the Format instruction you just entered is an example of an optional parameter (**switch**). Use of these switches is not mandatory. However, they allow the user a greater level of control over DOS activities.

```
A>format b: /v
Insert new diskette for drive B:
and press ENTER when ready...

Checking existing disk format.
Formatting 1.44M
Format complete.

Volume label (11 characters, ENTER for none)? trainor

    1457664 bytes total disk space
    1457664 bytes available on disk

        512 bytes in each allocation unit.
       2847 allocation units available on disk.

Volume Serial Number is 1D68-10DD

Format another (Y/N)?n

A>
```

FIGURE A.8
DOS display when formatting a high-capacity 3.5-inch diskette.

When used with the Format instruction, the /V or "volume" switch prompts DOS to ask for an eleven-character **volume label** (an internal label), which is stored as part of the disk directory. You entered your last name as the volume label. DOS versions 4.0 and higher automatically ask for a volume label, which eliminates the need to use this switch.

Several switches are available and described in detail in the DOS User's Manual. Later we will outline two switches used by the directory (Dir) command. These optional parameters are identified by a slash (/) and follow the DOS instruction after the drive designations. We have found that DOS provides more descriptive error messages when you include a blank space in front of each switch. Do not confuse the slash (/) that designates a switch and the backslash (\) that identifies the root directory.

Changing the Default Drive

The **default disk drive** is the drive DOS uses when no disk drive letter is included in an instruction. To change the default drive, enter the letter of the drive you wish to become the new default drive, and immediately follow it with a colon (:). Then press the Enter key (see Figure A.9). Many computer systems require that a formatted disk be in the new default drive before you change to it.

- Single floppy disk: type *A:* [Enter]

Dual floppy disk: type *B:* [Enter]

▶ DOS prompt changes to `B>` for dual floppy disk users and `A>` for single floppy disk users.

NOTE: If you do not have a disk in the drive, DOS displays the message: `Not ready error reading drive ?.` No harm is done. Insert a disk and press the `R` key for retry. When the disk drive is unavailable, DOS displays: `Invalid drive specification.` This message informs the user that DOS was unable to accomplish a task as instructed. DOS messages usually occur with spelling errors or incomplete instructions. When an error occurs, review the message, identify the mistake, and try again.

- Single floppy disk: ask your instructor which disk drive should be the default drive for the remainder of this lesson. We will assume you will be using drive C as the default unless otherwise instructed.
- Single floppy disk: type `C:` [Enter]

  Dual floppy disk: type `A:` [Enter]

  ▶ Changes DOS prompt.

Creating Copies of Files

The internal *Copy* command is one of the most versatile DOS instructions. It lets you backup an important file by transferring a duplicate to another disk. Files are copied from one location to another by identifying the file's name and disk location, the *source* along with the location of the backup disk or *target* (Figure A.10).

- Single floppy disk: type
  `Copy C:\command.com A:\command.com` [Enter]

  Dual floppy disk: type
  `Copy A:\command.com B:\command.com` [Enter]

  ▶ `1 file(s) copied`

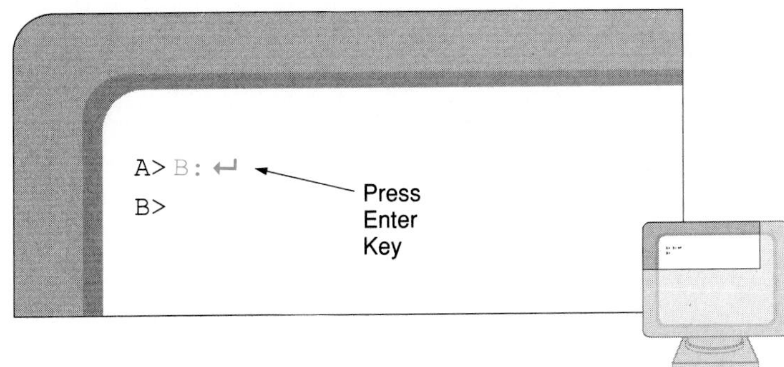

FIGURE A.9
Changing the system's default disk drive.

```
A>copy a:\command.com b:\command.com
        1 file(s) copied

A>
```

FIGURE A.10
Copying a file makes a duplicate of the original.

NOTE: If the system does not report `1 file(s) copied`, run through the error correction checklist in Figure A.7 before trying again.

DOS provides several shortcuts when using the Copy command. For example, if a drive designation is not specified, DOS will use the default drive. When you want to change the filename, all you have to do is change the spelling after the target drive designation. As a result, your next action will copy COMMAND.COM from the source drive to the target drive and change the file name of the copy to NEWCOPY.LAB (see Figure A.11).

▶ Displays DOS prompt.

■ Single floppy disk: type
`Copy command.com` *A:*`\newcopy.lab` [Enter]

Dual floppy disk: type
`Copy command.com` *B:*`\newcopy.lab` [Enter]

▶ `1 file(s) copied`

If the filename is not included after the target drive, DOS will use the original file name for the duplicate. Therefore, `Copy A:\COMMAND.COM B:\` will create a duplicate file called COMMAND.COM on the root directory of the disk in drive B.

```
A>copy command.com b:\newcopy.lab
        1 file(s) copied

A>
```

FIGURE A.11
Copying command.com and changing name of duplicate to newcopy.lab.

Displaying the Disk Directory

A disk's **root directory** is created during formatting. The directory, along with a file allocation table (FAT), is used by DOS to locate data files and programs on a specific disk. The *Dir* instruction, an internal command, lists these files and programs on the screen. If a disk drive is not specified after Dir, DOS will display the directory of the disk in the default drive.

■ Type `Dir` [Enter]

▶ Displays disk directory in default drive.

To look at the directory of another disk, follow Dir with a space, the disk drive letter, and a colon. For example, `Dir B:` displays the disk directory in drive B. Because the list of files in a directory can be rather long, there are two switches that will help you keep the contents of the directory from scrolling off the screen.

`/P` The "page" switch forces DOS to stop when the directory listing fills the screen. The message `Strike a key when ready...` allows you to continue displaying the remaining portions of the directory.

`/W` The "wide" switch forces DOS to eliminate the size, date, and time from the directory display. Five file names and extensions appear on each line to compress the directory listing.

These switches can be used in combination when a directory in the wide mode scrolls off the screen.

■ Single floppy disk: type `Dir A:\ /W` [Enter]

Dual floppy disk: type `Dir B:\ /W` [Enter]

▶ Displays files currently on your newly formatted disk (see Figure A.12).

NOTE: If you forget to close the drive door, DOS will display this message:

```
Not ready error reading drive ?
Abort, Retry, Fail?
```

Older versions of DOS display:

```
Not ready error reading drive ?
Abort, Retry, Ignore?
```

These messages will also appear if the disk is unformatted or when no disk is present in the disk drive. In any case, make sure a formatted disk is in the drive, close the door, and press `R` for retry. If the message persists, press `A` for abort. Remove the disk and try another disk in its place.

```
A>dir b:\ /w

 Volume in drive B is TRAINOR
 Volume Serial Number is 1D68-10DD
 Directory of B:\

COMMAND.COM      NEWCOPY.LAB
        2 file(s)       95690 bytes
                      1361408 bytes free

A>b:

B>ren newcopy.lab nextname.lab

B>dir

 Volume in drive B is TRAINOR
 Volume Serial Number is 1D68-10DD
 Directory of B:\

COMMAND  COM      47845 04-24-92   3:52p
NEXTNAME LAB      47845 04-24-92   3:52p
        2 file(s)       95690 bytes
                      1361408 bytes free

B>
```

FIGURE A.12
DOS display of B drive disk directory using "wide" switch before renaming NEWCOPY.LAB to NEXTNAME.LAB.

To reduce the amount of typing in the following DOS instructions, you need to make the disk drive with your data disk the default disk drive.

- Single floppy disk: type `A:` [Enter]

  Dual floppy disk: type `B:` [Enter]

  ▶ Displays new DOS prompt (either `A>` or `B>`).

Renaming Files

What if a filename needs to be changed? The *Rename* command performs this operation simply by entering the command and old filename, followed by the new filename. You have the option of using the abbreviation *Ren* instead of Rename. The drive designation, if used, precedes only the old filename. In other words, it is incorrect to use a drive designation before the new filename.

- Type `Ren newcopy.lab nextname.lab` [Enter]

  ▶ Displays DOS prompt

- Type `Dir` [Enter]

  ▶ Displays every filename on your data disk.

Take a look at the disk directory displayed on the screen and in Figure A.12. The filename NEXTNAME.LAB should have replaced NEWCOPY.LAB in the display.

Deleting Files

The *Del* and *Erase* instructions perform the same function. Both instructions are used to remove files from the disk directory. When doing so, you must identify a file by its name, extension, and disk location (if it is not in the default disk drive).

■ Type `Del  nextname.lab` [Enter]

  ▶ Displays DOS prompt.

The file NEXTNAME.LAB is deleted from the work disk directory. Unlike the Copy command, DOS does not provide a message that reports the file is deleted. As shown in Figure A.13, DOS just displays another prompt after deleting the designated file. Once it is erased, it cannot be recovered by any DOS version before 5.0. However, commercial software is available that can restore deleted files if the problem is identified before any new files are added to the disk.

Undeleting Files

If you are using DOS version 5 or higher, you can use the *Undelete* command to recover files deleted with Del or Erase. These commands do not actually remove the file from disk. Instead, a ? symbol replaces the first character in the filename stored in the disk direc-

FIGURE A.13
Deleting NEXTNAME.LAB from root directory in drive B. DOS versions 5 or higher also allows users to undelete files erased from disk using the Del or Erase commands.

```
B>del nextname.lab

B>ver

MS-DOS Version 5.00


B>undelete nextname.lab

Directory: B:\
File Specifications: NEXTNAME.LAB

    Deletion-tracking file not found.

    MS-DOS directory contains    1 deleted files.
    Of those,    1 files may be recovered.

Using the MS-DOS directory.

      ?EXTNAME LAB    47845  4-24-92  3:52p  ...A  Undelete (Y/N)?y
      Please type the first character for ?EXTNAME.LAB: n

File successfully undeleted.



B>
```

tory. When DOS sees this symbol in the filename, it is programmed to use the related disk space as needed.

To determine whether you can use the Undelete command, you need to know what version of DOS the computer is using. The *Ver* command displays the DOS version number currently running in the computer.

■ Type `ver` [Enter]

▶ `MS-DOS version 5.00`
(DOS name and version number will vary)

If you are not using version 5 or higher, skip to the next section on "Making Subdirectories."

When using the Undelete command, you restore the file by replacing the ? symbol in the filename with the original character as shown in Figure A.13.

■ Type `undelete nextname.lab` [Enter]

▶
```
Directory: ?:\
File Specifications: NEXTNAME.LAB
    MS-DOS directory contains     1 deleted files.
    Of those,     1 files may be recovered.
Using the MSDOS directory.
    ?EXTNAME  LAB      47845   4-24-94   3:52p   ...A
    Undelete (Y/N)?
```

■ Type `y`

▶ `Please type the first character for ?EXTNAME.LAB:`

■ Type `n`

▶ `File successfully undeleted.`

Making Subdirectories

When a disk is formatted, a root directory is created to catalog the filenames of data and programs stored on the disk. The DOS *Mkdir* command, or its abbreviation *Md,* makes new directories, called **subdirectories.** New subdirectories are attached to the root directory or other subdirectories as shown in Figure A.14. The root directory and subdirectories appear as file folders when graphical user interfaces are used with DOS (see Appendix B: "Introduction to Microsoft Windows").

Subdirectories work like electronic file folders in organizing programs and data according to common attributes. As illustrated in Figure A.14, a well-organized hard disk has a DOS subdirectory for storing DOS utility programs, other subdirectories for application packages, and separate subdirectories for related data.

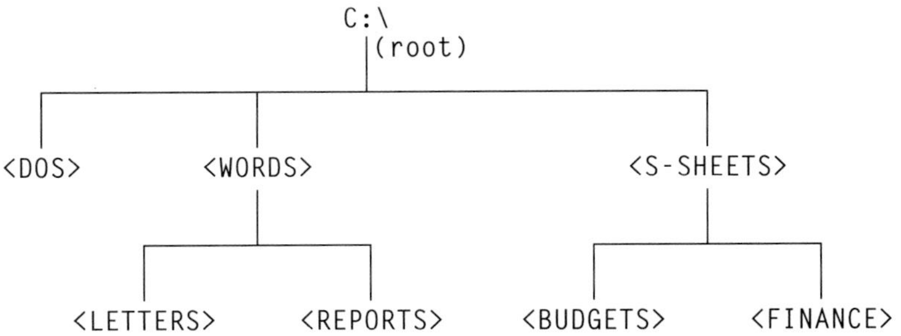

FIGURE A.14
New subdirectories are appended to the root directory. Additional subdirectories can be subordinate to those attached to the root.

Each subdirectory is given its own name when created. Names given to subdirectories must follow the DOS rules for naming files and programs. When making a new subdirectory, the user must identify to DOS how the subdirectory relates to the root directory. This description is called the **search path.** In Figure A.14 the LETTERS subdirectory is subordinate to the WORDS subdirectory. In turn, WORDS is subordinate to the root directory.

Previously, we have used the notation *A:* to identify a search path to drive A's root directory. The notation *A:\PROJECTS* identifies a search path to the PROJECTS subdirectory. Let's start by making a new subdirectory, called PROJECTS, on the default disk, using the Md command.

■ Type `Md \projects` [Enter]

▶ Displays another DOS prompt.

To verify that the PROJECTS subdirectory has been appended to the default directory, display the root directory in the default drive.

■ Type `Dir` [Enter]

▶ Displays disk's root directory.

Somewhere within the directory you should find `PROJECTS <DIR>`. As you can see on your screen and in Figure A.15, subdirectories

```
B>md \projects

B>dir

 Volume in drive B is TRAINOR
 Volume Serial Number is 1D68-10DD
 Directory of B:\

PROJECTS     <DIR>      05-26-93   9:34a
COMMAND  COM     47845 04-24-92   3:52p
NEXTNAME LAB     47845 04-24-92   3:52p
        3 file(s)      95690 bytes
                     1360896 bytes free

B>
```

FIGURE A.15
Making new subdirectory PROJECTS subordinate to root directory in drive B.

are listed in the disk directory to which they are subordinate (appended). A <DIR> appears to the right of the subdirectory name to identify the entry as a subdirectory.

NOTE: If you are using an older version of DOS and were unable to undelete NEXTNAME.LAB, this file will be absent from the list of filenames.

Changing from One Subdirectory to Another

The *Chdir* or *Cd* command activates different directories. This adds a new wrinkle to the status of the default drive. Until now the root directory has always been the **active directory.** When DOS defaulted to a disk drive, the root directory was used. The change directory command now lets users change the active directory. To activate another directory, such as the PROJECTS subdirectory, precede the desired subdirectory name with Cd, a space, and the search path.

- Type `Cd \projects` [Enter]
  - ▶ Displays another DOS prompt.
- Type `Dir` [Enter]
  - ▶ Displays PROJECTS subdirectory.

A new subdirectory contains a least two file references. They are shown in the directory on your screen as . <DIR> and .. <DIR> (see Figure A.16). These entries reference the current subdirectory (.) and

```
B>cd \projects

B>dir

 Volume in drive B is TRAINOR
 Volume Serial Number is 1D68-10DD
 Directory of B:\PROJECTS

.            <DIR>        05-26-93    9:34a
..           <DIR>        05-26-93    9:34a
        2 file(s)               0 bytes
                          1360896 bytes free

B>prompt Today is $d$g

Today is Wed 05-26-1993>prompt

B>prompt $p$g

B:\PROJECTS>
```

FIGURE A.16
Changing directory (Cd) to PROJECTS makes it the active directory when drive B is the default drive. Users can customize the DOS prompt to include the active path and subdirectory name as well as the default disk drive.

the directory to which it is appended (..), in this case the root directory. These references can be used with the Cd command. For example, `Cd ..` is a valid reference to the root directory when PROJECTS is the active directory. `Cd \` always returns the user to the root directory on the default disk.

Customizing the DOS prompt

The DOS prompt displays the active directory when you customize it using the *Prompt* command. Special codes like `$p` (path), `$d` (date), `$t` (time), and `$g` (> symbol) indicate which data is included in the prompt. Entering the Prompt command by itself returns the screen prompt back to its original format as shown in Figure A.16.

- Type `Prompt Today is $d$g` [Enter]
  - ▶ Displays DOS prompt with today's date.
- Type `Prompt` [Enter]
  - ▶ Returns DOS prompt back to its original format.
- Type `Prompt  $p$g` [Enter]
  - ▶ Displays DOS prompt with path to active directory.

Copying Files to a Subdirectory

You do not have to change to a subdirectory to copy or delete files from it. In this case you will copy the file COMMAND.COM from the root directory to the PROJECTS subdirectory and change its name to UPDATE.LAB (see Figure A.17).

```
B:\PROJECTS>copy \command.com \projects\update.lab
        1 file(s) copied

B:\PROJECTS>dir

 Volume in drive B is TRAINOR
 Volume Serial Number is 1D68-10DD
 Directory of B:\PROJECTS

.            <DIR>        05-26-93   9:34a
..           <DIR>        05-26-93   9:34a
UPDATE   LAB        47845 04-24-92   3:52p
        3 file(s)        47845 bytes
                       1312768 bytes free

B:\PROJECTS>
```

FIGURE A.17
The Copy command can duplicate designated files on any disk or subdirectory as long as a path to the target drive and directory precedes the filename.

■ Type `Copy \command.com \projects\update.lab` Enter

▶ `1 file(s) copied`

■ Type `Dir` Enter

▶ Displays PROJECTS subdirectory with UPDATE.LAB.

Removing Subdirectories from Disk

Proper disk management dictates the constant addition and removal of subdirectories as projects and software come into use or become inactive. The *Rmdir* or *Rd* command removes a subdirectory from the disk's hierarchy of directories. Users enter either command and follow it with the search path and subdirectory name. While the root directory cannot be removed, all other directories are fair game.

A subdirectory must be empty except for the "." and ".." entries before removing it. This means all files and subordinate subdirectories must first be deleted or removed. Therefore, UPDATE.LAB must be deleted before the PROJECTS subdirectory is removed.

```
B:\PROJECTS>del update.lab

B:\PROJECTS>cd \

B:\>dir

 Volume in drive B is TRAINOR
 Volume Serial Number is 1D68-10DD
 Directory of B:\

PROJECTS     <DIR>      05-26-93   9:34a
COMMAND  COM     47845 04-24-92   3:52p
NEXTNAME LAB     47845 04-24-92   3:52p
        3 file(s)       95690 bytes
                      1360896 bytes free

B:\>rd \projects

B:\>dir

 Volume in drive B is TRAINOR
 Volume Serial Number is 1D68-10DD
 Directory of B:\

COMMAND  COM     47845 04-24-92   3:52p
NEXTNAME LAB     47845 04-24-92   3:52p
        2 file(s)       95690 bytes
                      1361408 bytes free

B:\>
```

FIGURE A.18
The DOS Rd command removed PROJECTS from the hierarchy of drive B subdirectories.

Furthermore, you cannot remove an active subdirectory. As a result, you must delete UPDATE.LAB from the PROJECTS subdirectory and use the Cd command to change back to the root directory.

- Type `Del update.lab` [Enter]
  - ▶ Displays another DOS prompt.
- Type `Cd \` [Enter]
  - ▶ Displays DOS prompt with root directory backslash.
- Type `Dir` [Enter]
  - ▶ Displays root directory (note reference to PROJECTS subdirectory in Figure A.18).
- Type `Rd \projects` [Enter]
  - ▶ Displays another DOS prompt.
- Type `Dir` [Enter]
  - ▶ Displays root directory (note removal of PROJECTS subdirectory as shown in Figure A.18).

NOTE: If you cannot remove a subdirectory that appears to be empty and devoid of subordinate directories, check to make sure the subdirectory you are removing is not the active directory. When this is not the problem, there is a possibility that hidden files created by some software packages may exist in the subdirectory. **Hidden files** are not displayed with the Dir command. If hidden files exist on a subdirectory, your best alternative is to use commercially available utility programs that are designed to delete this type of file.

SYSTEM SHUT-DOWN

When you are through for the day, the computer system needs to be shutdown. People with their own computers at work usually leave their computers on during the day and turn them off before going home. Those sharing a computer with others usually shut down the computer when they have completed an assignment. As a result, others know the computer is not being used when they find it turned off.

- Remove any floppy disks from their disk drives, return them to their protective covers, and store them in a safe place.
- Turn off computer.
- Turn off printer, if necessary.
- Turn off monitor, if necessary.

Chapter Facts

- IBM and compatible personal computers use MS-DOS or PC-DOS to control internal operations and to manage system resources.
- A DOS disk must be available to the computer system before it is booted.
- A printer's form feed and line feed buttons move paper through the printer one page and one line at a time, respectively.
- Pressing either the Print Screen key or Shift + PrtSc key combination prints a copy of the screen display on the attached printer.
- DOS commands are permanently stored in the computer's memory and can be executed from the DOS prompt at any time.
- DOS utilities are stored on disk and the disk must be in a disk drive before the utility is run. FORMAT is an example of a disk utility.
- Formatting a disk prepares it for use on a computer system by creating tracks, sectors, and a root directory.
- Entering a disk drive letter, colon, and pressing the Enter key makes the designated drive the new default drive.
- The DOS Copy command duplicates the contents of a data file or program on a new disk or subdirectory. A new filename can be assigned to the duplicate.
- A list of data files and programs stored on a disk is displayed using the DOS Dir command.
- Filenames are changed using the Rename command. REN is an acceptable abbreviation.
- The Erase or Del commands remove a data or program file from the disk directory. In some cases the Undelete command can reactivate the filename.
- Users can determine which version of DOS their computer is using by running the Ver command.
- New directories are placed on a disk with the Md or Mkdir command. These subdirectories can be placed in the root directory or other subdirectories.
- The Cd or Chdir command changes the active disk directory used by DOS.
- Users customize the DOS prompt with the Prompt command by adding the date, time, or active directory.

- Before a subdirectory is removed from a disk with the Rd or Rmdir commands, all files and subordinate directories currently stored within it must be removed.

Terms to Remember

a. active directory
b. command
c. default disk drive
d. DOS prompt
e. form feed
f. hidden file
g. line feed
h. MS-DOS
i. PC-DOS
j. root directory
k. search path
l. subdirectory
m. switch
n. utility program
o. volume label

Mix and Match

Match the following definitions to the Terms to Remember.

1. ____ disk operating system developed by the Microsoft Corporation for personal computer systems.
2. ____ button on the printer that moves paper to the top of the next page.
3. ____ screen display of letter associated with default disk drive and greater than sign.
4. ____ description of subdirectory or file location on disk with respect to the disk's root directory.
5. ____ primary disk directory that is created when the disk is formatted.
6. ____ filename that is not displayed as part of the disk directory.
7. ____ DOS instruction that can be executed at any time.
8. ____ 11-character label user adds to disk directory.
9. ____ operating system IBM distributes with its line of personal computers.
10. ____ directory added to root directory.
11. ____ directory DOS uses as a default.
12. ____ optional parameter designated by using a slash and letter.

13. ____ button on the printer that moves paper one line at a time.
14. ____ drive DOS uses when no disk drive designation is included in an instruction.
15. ____ system program stored on DOS disk.

Review Questions

1. How do you boot an IBM or compatible personal computer?
2. How is the top-of-page set on a dot-matrix printer?
3. What key(s) are used to output a screen display to the printer?
4. Identify the rules for acceptable DOS filenames.
5. What situation must exist before a DOS utility program can be used?
6. How do you format a new disk?
7. What procedure is used to change the system's default disk drive?
8. What is the DOS syntax for copying a file from one disk to another, keeping the same name? How do you change the name of the duplicate when copying?
9. Explain how you would display the disk directory of any disk in any disk drive.
10. How do you rename existing disk files?
11. Which DOS instructions delete files from disk? How would you recover a deleted file?
12. How are new subdirectories created on a disk?
13. Explain how you use DOS to change the active disk directory.
14. How would a user customize the DOS prompt to include the search path to the active directory?
15. Explain how to copy a file from one subdirectory to another, keeping the same name. How do you change the name of the duplicate when copying?
16. What is the DOS syntax for removing an existing subdirectory from a disk?
17. Identify the conditions that must exist before a subdirectory can be removed from a disk.
18. What are the common steps for shutting down a microcomputer system?

Applying What You've Learned

1. A volume label can be added to the disk directory when a disk is formatted. Use a DOS reference manual to find out what DOS instruction allows you to change the volume label.
2. DOS recognizes many more DIR switches than were discussed in Appendix A. Use a DOS reference guide for version 5 (or higher) to find the switch that prompts the Dir command to display filenames in order by their creation date. How would you display files in order by their file size?
3. How could you use a single Copy command to duplicate all the files in one disk directory to another disk? (Hint: The answer involves the use of wildcard characters.)
4. Describe a situation where the Undelete command would not work. Assume the command has been entered properly.
5. Customize the DOS prompt to display the time. When does the time in the display change?
6. Use a DOS reference guide to find a DOS instruction that identifies the presence of a hidden file on disk.
7. A general rule for file management on disk is to make separate subdirectories for data files and application packages. For example, users are encouraged to create one subdirectory for their word processing program and other subdirectories for letters, reports, etc. Graphically illustrate how you would organize subdirectories on a hard disk. Assume you are using at least three different application packages. Do not forget to account for DOS utility programs.

Answers to Mix and Match

1. h 2. e 3. d 4. k 5. j 6. f 7. b 8. o 9. i 10. l
11. a 12. m 13. g 14. c 15. n

B

Introduction to Microsoft Windows

- From the User's Point of View
- Personal Computer Start-Up Procedures
  - System orientation
  - How to boot a PC
  - Loading windows
- The Program Manager
  - Using a mouse
  - Selecting operations from drop-down menus
  - Executing program options
- Common Window Features
  - Title bar
  - Sizing a window
  - Scroll bars
  - Maximize and minimize window size
  - Control box
- The File Manager
  - Formatting a new (or old) disk
  - Copying files
  - Displaying two directories
  - Renaming files
  - Creating new folders
  - Copying a file to a file folder
  - Moving a file to another file folder
  - Deleting files
  - Removing a file folder
- System Shut-Down

FROM THE USER'S POINT OF VIEW

Before starting to use personal productivity software or learning to program, you need to review operating procedures for IBM and compatible personal computers. The following Windows tutorial provides a brief overview of some of the more important procedures associated with Microsoft Windows 3.1. These procedures help you prepare new disks for processing, locate disk files and programs, and provide a convenient means of copying important disk resources.

You need access to an IBM or compatible personal computer using Microsoft Windows and a new floppy disk to complete the tutorial. Since Windows requires lots of internal memory and makes extensive use of disk storage, we assume you are using a personal computer with a hard disk or have access to a local area network. Instructions or data you should enter into the computer using the keyboard are printed in red and preceded by a ■.

PERSONAL COMPUTER START-UP PROCEDURES

IBM and compatible personal computers use a disk operating system (DOS) developed by the Microsoft Corporation. Called **MS-DOS,** it is the most commonly used operating system in the world. It is licensed from Microsoft and distributed by IBM Corporation as **PC-DOS.** Recently Microsoft enhanced DOS's user friendliness by creating a compatible graphical user interface (GUI) called **Windows.** A new version of Windows, Windows NT, is in itself an operating system and does not need DOS to operate.

System Orientation

Booting describes the procedure for starting up a computer system. IBM and compatible personal computers automatically look for and load a command program, named COMMAND.COM, from the operating system into memory as a part of the booting process.

Since a disk with DOS must be in a designated disk drive when booting a personal computer, associated procedures will vary, depending on the number and types of disk drives. The disk drive reading DOS is referred to as the *system drive.* A disk drive storing data (or programs) is referred to as the *data drive.* Use the information below to identify the system drive used by your personal computer system.

Hard Disk and One-Diskette System

Personal computers with hard disk drives identify these drives as drive C. The system drive is drive C although when a floppy disk with DOS is in drive A during booting, drive A is used instead of drive C. In this configuration there is no drive B, since B is reserved for a second floppy disk drive.

Hard Disk and Two-Diskette System

Any personal computer system with a hard disk (drive C) uses it as the system drive when the computer is turned on with drive A empty. Floppy disk drives A and B are used as data drives.

Computer within a Local Area Network (LAN)

The system drive is usually drive A, and the DOS disk contains special network programs. After the system is booted, disk drives A and B are used as data drives. Depending on the LAN configuration, alternative disk space is available through a server. This disk space is identified by drives D through Z. As part of the booting procedure, LAN users may be asked to enter a password to identify themselves.

How to Boot a PC

A personal computer's booting procedure will vary between systems. However, they all have two things in common:

1. Power needs to be turned on.
2. DOS must be available on a disk accessible to the system.

Before You Start

If your system has a hard disk, it will be used as the system drive when the floppy disk drives are empty. Most systems are designed to look first for DOS on a floppy disk before trying the hard disk. If you do not have a hard disk, locate drive A, which is the system drive for floppy disk-based systems. Carefully follow the actions following the ■ symbol described below for the system drive used by your personal computer.

LAN with 5.25-Inch Floppy Disks

■ Open the system drive latch (see Figure B.1).

■ Position the disk with the label on top and the write-protect notch to the left, also shown in Figure B.1.

■ Gently push the DOS disk into the system drive until it stops and will not go further without force.

■ Close the drive latch.

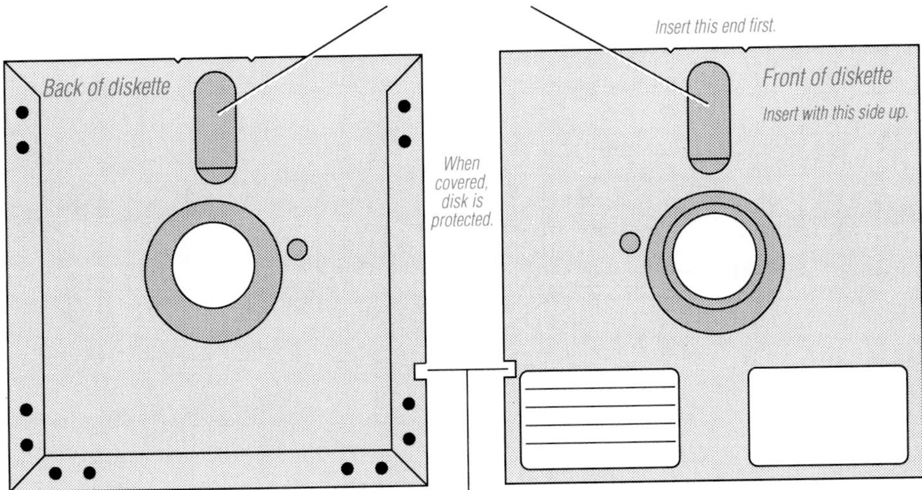

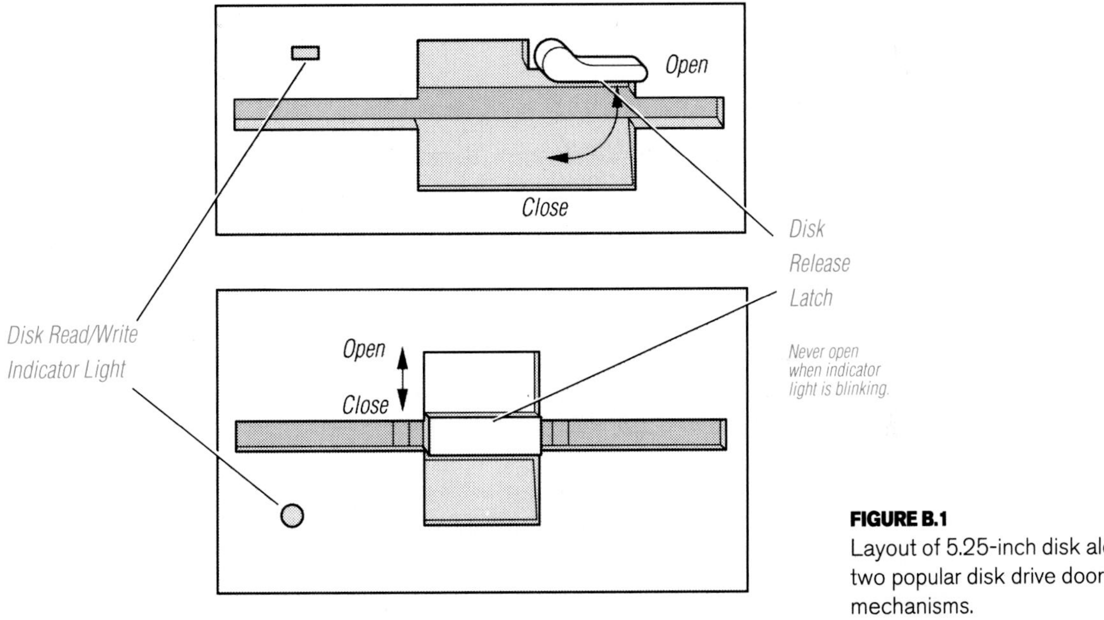

FIGURE B.1
Layout of 5.25-inch disk along with two popular disk drive door mechanisms.

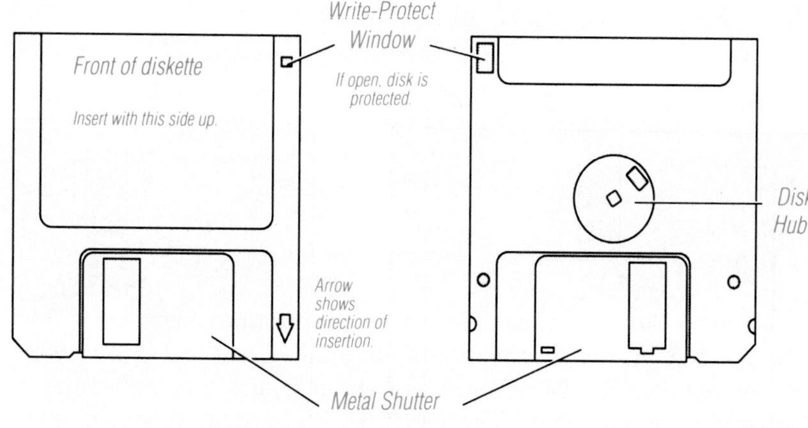

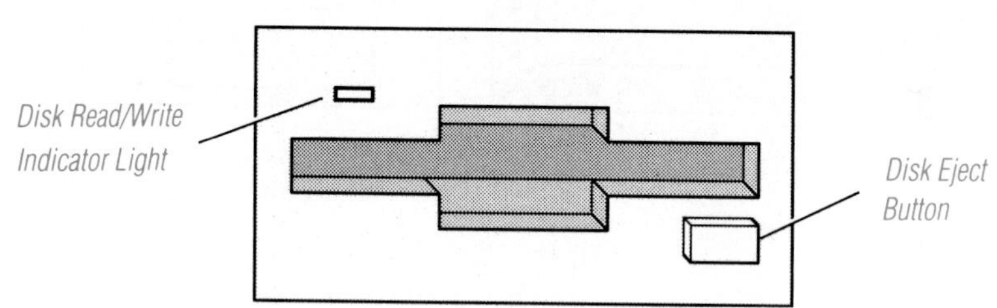

FIGURE B.2
Layout of 3.5-inch disk along with disk drive door mechanism.

LAN with 3.5-Inch Diskettes

- Position the disk with the label on top and the write-protect window (see Figure B.2) to the left.
- Firmly push the DOS disk into the system drive until it locks into place.

Hard Disk

- Remove any floppy disks currently in the floppy disk drive or drives.

Turning on the Computer

You are now ready to turn on the personal computer. The ON/OFF switch may be found on the right side of the computer near the back, on the back, or on the front right side.

- Turn on the computer.
  - ▶ Most computers turn on a light in the front of the system drive.

Finally, if the screen does not turn on with the computer, turn on the screen. The ON/OFF switch is usually on the right side of the screen near the bottom or on the top, right side near the back.

■ Turn on screen if it is not already on.

▶ Displays current date.

If your computer system follows the standard booting steps, the current date is displayed on the screen. Many computer systems are customized to display menus, launch Windows, or describe special procedures or copyright infringement policies. What follows is a description of the standard booting procedures.

The screen will usually display a prompt asking you to verify the system date and time. The `mm-dd-yy` prompt is asking for one- or two-digit entries for the month, day, and year. May 19th of 1994 is entered as `5-19-94`. As you can see in Figure B.3, each entry is separated by a hyphen. The entry for the current time is similar. Enter the hour, minute, and seconds (if desired), separated by colons.

■ Change date or press [Enter].

▶ Displays current time.

■ Change time or press [Enter].

▶ Displays capital letter and > symbol.

After the entering of the date and time, the booting process is complete. The system now displays the letter associated with the system drive, followed by a > symbol. For example, personal computers

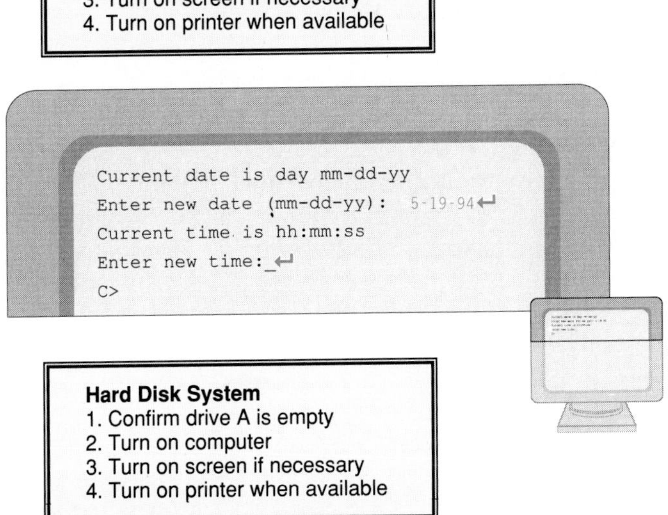
Floppy Disk System
1. Insert DOS disk into drive A
2. Turn on computer
3. Turn on screen if necessary
4. Turn on printer when available
Current date is day mm-dd-yy
Enter new date (mm-dd-yy): 5-19-94↵
Current time is hh:mm:ss
Enter new time:_↵
C>
Hard Disk System
1. Confirm drive A is empty
2. Turn on computer
3. Turn on screen if necessary
4. Turn on printer when available

FIGURE B.3
Booting procedures for IBM and compatible personal computers.

using drive A as the system drive display `A>`. Hard disk systems defaulting to drive C display `C>`. This display is known as the **DOS prompt.** It tells the user that DOS is ready for instructions. In addition, the DOS prompt identifies the default drive, which is used when no other disk drive is specified.

Loading Windows

After entering the date and time, you have completed the booting process. Windows can now be loaded into memory from disk. We use the abbreviation WIN to load Windows. You can skip to "The Program Manager" section if your screen currently looks like Figure B.4.

- Type `win` and press Enter.
  - ▶ Loads Windows and displays `Program Manager` screen shown in Figure B.4.

Windows is a user-friendly interface that reduces the time required for understanding basic computer operations and for learning new applications. Currently on the screen is the desktop, your window into the computer. The **desktop** is aptly named since you work with images on the screen in the same way that you work with papers, folders, and office tools and supplies laid out on an actual desktop. This desktop metaphor is the basis for all screen displays and processing activities under the control of Windows.

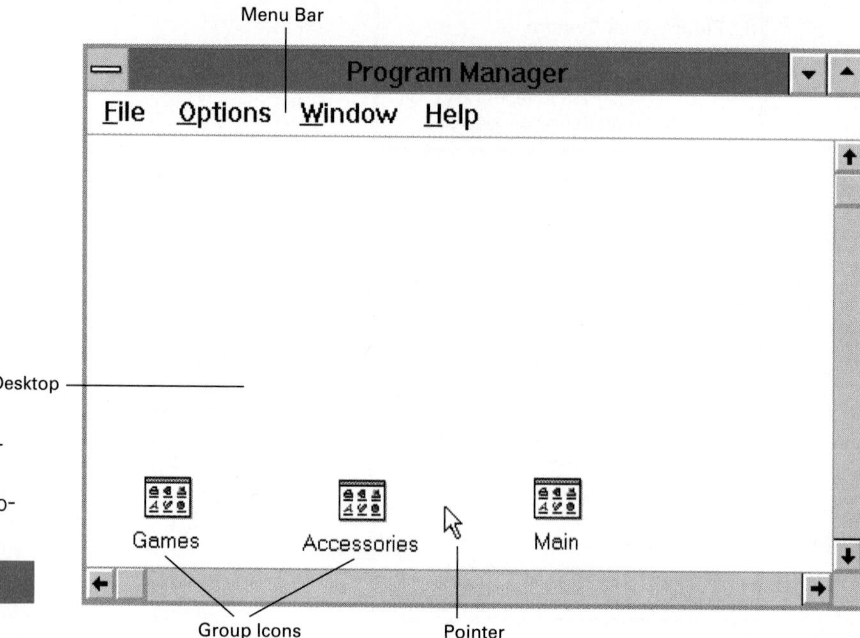

FIGURE B.4
The Program Manager window provides a desktop from which DOS operations and other application programs are executed.

THE PROGRAM MANAGER

The opening window is usually the `Program Manager`. It contains **group icons** that organize each program and data file available to the system. Users open a group icon displayed in the Program Manager window by double-clicking the mouse (pressing the left-mouse button twice in rapid order) with the pointer on the desired icon. The desktop in Figure B.4 contains three group icons, which identify games, main system controls, and accessories such as calendars and calculators. When opened, each group icon displays a collection of program icons associated with application packages and other programs the user has installed.

Across the top of the screen, under `Program Manager`, is the **menu bar.** The menu bar permits access to several drop-down menus, each containing processing commands. The `File`, `Options`, `Window`, and `Help` menus are seen in Figure B.4. These menu titles are standard whenever you view the `Program Manager` but can change with various software packages.

All choices from the menu bar, as well as icon manipulations, are controlled primarily with the mouse. Keyboard alternatives are available, but will not be discussed in detail as a part of this brief introduction. As you grasp and move the mouse across a flat surface, a *screen pointer* moves in a corresponding fashion around the screen. When you work within the desktop, the pointer is shaped like an arrow (see Figure B.4); however, it changes into other shapes, depending on the activity in progress.

Using a Mouse

You can lift the mouse and set it back down again without changing the location of the pointer on the screen. You will need to do this whenever you do not have room to move the pointer across the screen in one continuous movement of the mouse, as in cramped quarters.

At first, using a mouse may seem awkward. However, this device's operation will soon become second nature, and the speed and ease with which you can do things with a mouse will increase your productivity many times over.

A basic technique for working with Windows is to select an icon and either activate it or move it around the screen. You select an icon by pointing to it with the arrow pointer and **clicking** (pressing) the mouse button once. You must select an object before you can use it. In this tutorial, clicking will always refer to pressing the left mouse button.

- Move the arrow pointer so that its tip is within the `Main` icon.

NOTE: If the `Main` window is already open, as shown in Figure B.8, close the window and any other open windows by skipping forward to the section on the "Control Box."

- Press and release the left mouse button once.
  - ▶ The icon name, `Main`, is highlighted and a control menu is displayed as shown in Figure B.5.

The control menu is closed by clicking on any open area of the desktop.

- Move pointer off the `Main` icon and into an open desktop area.
- Click mouse button.
  - ▶ Closes control menu.

You can move and reposition an object on the desktop by holding down the left mouse button while moving, **dragging,** the icon.

- Select the `Accessories` icon and hold down the left mouse button without releasing it.
  - ▶ Highlights `Accessories` icon.
- While holding down the button, move the mouse up and to the left to reposition the icon on the screen.
  - ▶ The icon's label disappears as it is dragged.
- Release the mouse button.
  - ▶ The icon is repositioned in its new location.

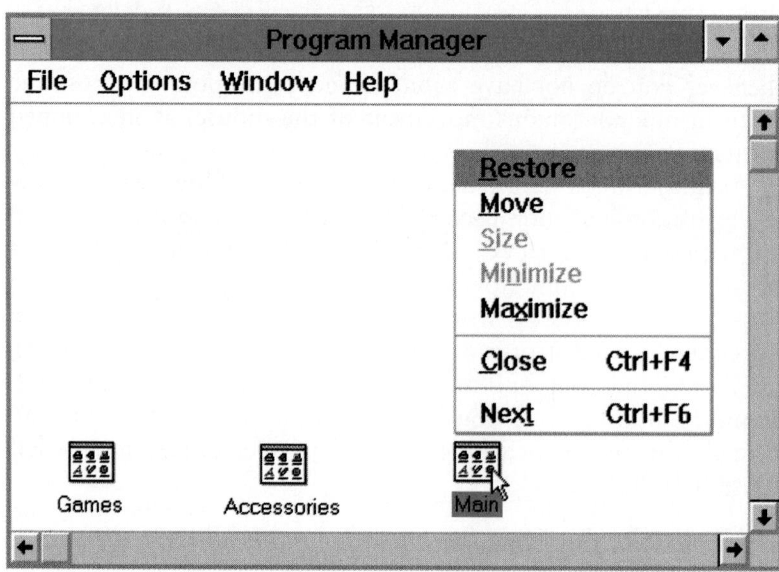

FIGURE B.5
Pointing and clicking on a group icon activates the control menu and highlights the icon name.

These clicking and dragging techniques are used for other mouse operations besides selecting and moving icons. They will become basic techniques for controlling all activities you perform with the computer.

Selecting Operations from Drop-Down Menus

We need to explore how operations are executed by using the mouse to access drop-down menus. The menu bar contains the titles of all available menus (see Figure B.4). You select one of the drop-down menus by clicking on the menu title, for instance, Help. Drop-down menu options stay hidden in the menu bar until the user selects that title. When the menu is selected, it opens to list program options. Once an option is selected, the menu rolls back up into the menu bar.

- Click on the `Help` menu in the menu bar.
    - ▶ The selections in the `Help` menu are displayed as shown in Figure B.6.

This `Help` menu can be of great assistance as you learn how to use Windows and related programs. It is designed to answer questions about specific problems because it is *context-sensitive help*. This means the information displayed when Help is activated concerns the screen display currently being used. In other words, if you are playing a game and ask for help, the Help screen provides information about the game.

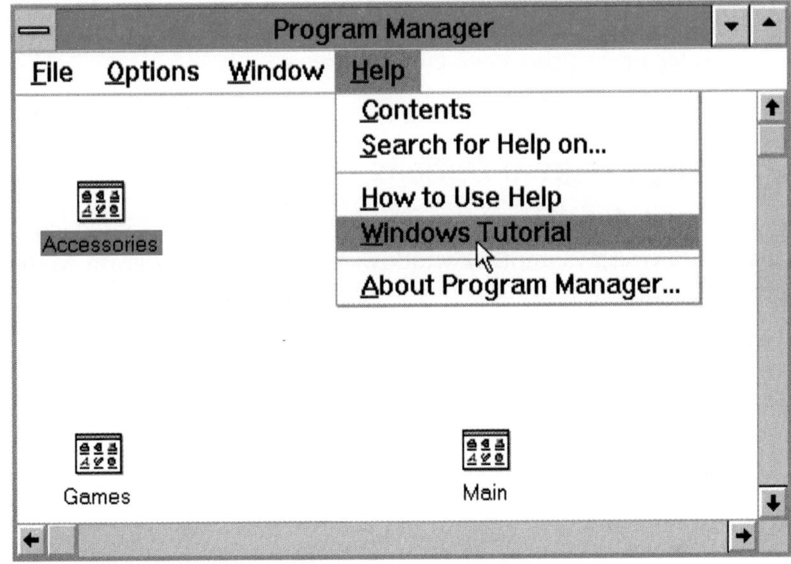

FIGURE B.6
Drop-down menus, like Help, are activated by clicking on the menu name.

■ Click on Windows Tutorial.

▶ Displays opening screen on Windows Tutorial.

This interactive tutorial introduces basic mouse and Windows skills. If you have time, walk through one or both of these tutorials.

■ Press ESC.

▶ Asks you to verify that you want to exit the tutorial.

■ Press the y key.

▶ Returns to Program Manager window.

If you decide not to choose one of the menu items, simply move the pointer outside the menu so that no item is selected. Click the mouse button. The menu disappears and you are back to the desktop.

You can easily scan the menus to see all of the options available on the menu bar.

■ Click on the File menu and hold down the mouse.

▶ The options under File are revealed.

■ Without releasing the mouse, slowly drag the pointer along the menu bar horizontally from left to right.

▶ As each menu title is passed, its drop-down menu is shown.

■ Release the mouse button.

▶ All highlighting of menus is turned off.

NOTE: Some of the names of the menu items may appear dimmed. These are menu options that are not appropriate or that cannot be carried out at that instant. You cannot select a dimmed title. These items will become available at different times and under other processing circumstances.

Executing Program Options

Applications are activated by double-clicking on the associated icon. This action overlays another window on top of the Program Manager and makes additional icons available to users.

■ Select the Main icon and double-click on it without hesitating between clicks.

▶ Displays a window similar to Figure B.7.

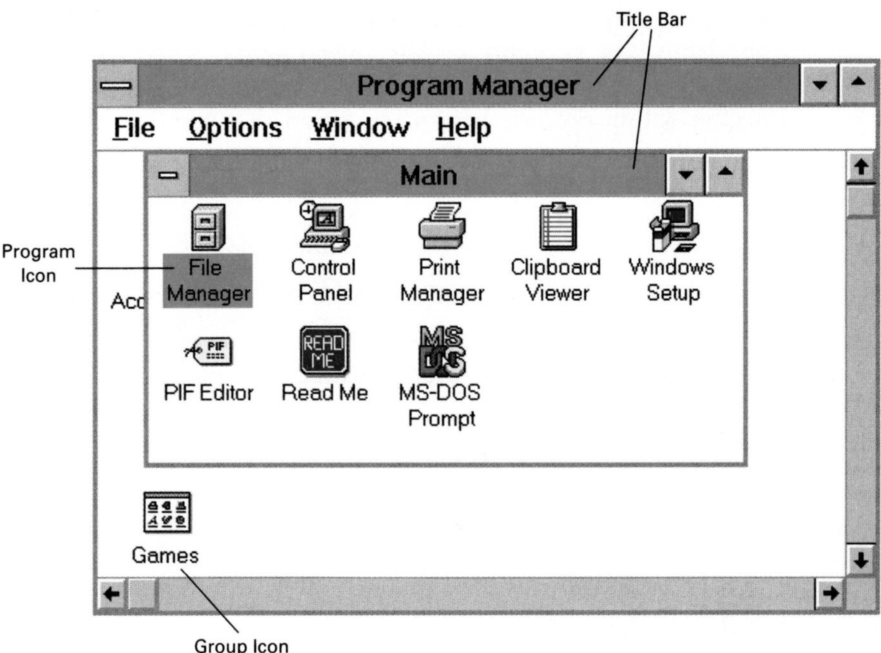

FIGURE B.7
Double-clicking on the Main icon results in overlaying the Program Manager window with the Main window.

NOTE: There are two other ways to open a window aside from double-clicking on the icon. First click on the icon. You can then highlight the `Restore` option of the Control menu shown in Figure B.5 or use the `File` menu to select the `Open` option.

COMMON WINDOW FEATURES

ou now have on your computer screen the `Main` window overlaid on the `Program Manager` window. Each window has common descriptive and functional parts that need exploring.

Title Bar

The window's name, like `Program Manager` or `Main` in Figure B.7, appears in the **title bar** across the top of the window. At both ends of the title bar are small boxes that will be discussed later. Below the title bar of application windows is the menu bar, which lists names of various drop-down menus. Windows associated with group icons, like `Main`, do not have menu bars.

Windows can be moved anywhere on the screen by clicking and dragging within the title bar to reposition the window. You may need to do this if you have several overlapping windows on the screen at the same time.

- Move the pointer within the `Main` title bar.
- Hold down the mouse button and drag the pointer somewhere else on the screen.
  - ▶ The outline of the window is dragged with the pointer.
- Release the mouse button.
  - ▶ The window snaps into its new position.
- Use the mouse to center the `Main` window in the space available.

FIGURE B.8
Users change a window's size by dragging one corner to a new screen location or by clicking on the maximize or minimize buttons found in the top right corner of each window.

Sizing a Window

You have complete control over the location and size of each window. Not only can you drag a window around the screen, you can grab the line around the window, called the *window frame,* and drag it to a new screen location to change the window's dimensions.

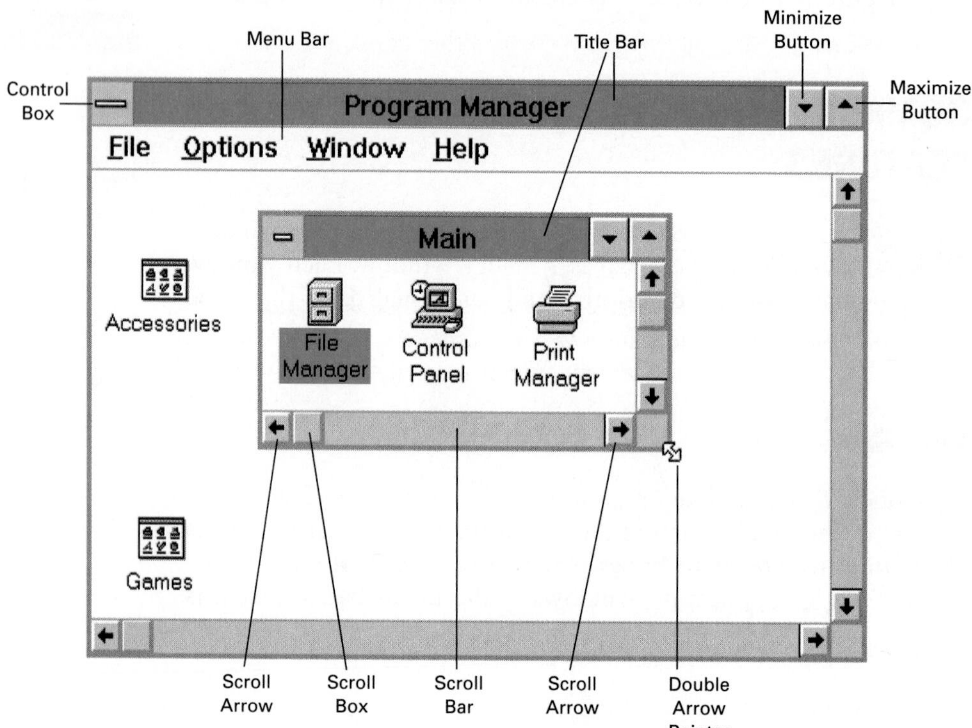

- Position the pointer so the tip touches the bottom right corner of the `Main` window.
  - ▶ Pointer changes to a double arrow as shown in Figure B.8.
- Hold down the mouse button.
  - ▶ Lines in the window dim.
- Drag the window's corner toward the upper left-hand corner of the screen until at least one icon falls outside the dashed lines.
  - ▶ The window outline follows the pointer.
- Release the mouse button.
  - ▶ The window is contracted to reach the pointer location. Any icon outside that area of the desktop will be covered.

Scroll Bars

When a window is reduced in size, **scroll bars** appear along the right and lower edges of a window (see Figure B.8). A **scroll box** within each scroll bar identifies which portion of the window is currently being viewed. Dragging the scroll box or clicking on the **scroll arrows** brings hidden icons into view. You can tell if there are hidden icons in the window because of the presence of a scroll bar.

- Click once on the scroll arrow that points right or down.
  - ▶ Icons in window move off toward the left or up.
- Click within the scroll bar.
  - ▶ Icons in window move in opposite direction.

Maximize and Minimize Window Size

In Figure B.8, the maximize and minimize buttons appear in the upper right corner of the window. The *maximize button* is on the right and appears as an up arrow. When it is clicked, the window expands to fill the screen. At this time the double-arrow *restore button* takes its place. When the restore button is clicked, the window returns to its previous size. Double-clicking on the title bar also maximizes the associated window.

- Click once on the `Main` window maximize button.
  - ▶ `Main` window expands to fill the screen.
- Click on the restore button.
  - ▶ Window returns to its previous size.

FIGURE B.9
Clicking on the minimize button (down arrow) found in the title bar converts the Program Manager window into an icon.

The *minimize button* appears as a down arrow and is located to the left of the maximize button. It is used to convert a window to an icon as shown in Figure B.9. Double-clicking on the icon restores the window.

■ Click the minimize button once in the `Program Manager` title bar.

▶ Window is replaced by an icon in the lower left corner of the screen.

■ Double-click on the `Program Manager` icon.

▶ `Program Manager` window returns to its original size.

Control Box

When you are finished using a window, you put it away by double-clicking on the *control box* in the upper left corner (see Figure B.8). A single click on the control box activates the window's Control menu. We previously saw a Control menu in Figure B.5 when highlighting an icon. Before closing the `Main` window you should resize the window so it includes all the available icons.

■ Drag `Main` window frame to expand window to include the `File Manager`, `Control Panel`, and other icons.

■ Double-click on the `Main` window control box.

▶ The window disappears into the Main icon in Program Manager window.

THE FILE MANAGER

Later in this tutorial you will be learning how to copy and delete files. To do that, you will be using a floppy disk (diskette). Recall from Chapter 10 that before a disk can be used for storing programs and data files, it must be initialized or formatted. When you are using Windows to format a new disk or any type of file manipulation like copying or deleting, the File Manager icon found in the Main group icon needs to be activated.

■ Double-click on the `Main` icon.

▶ Overlays `Main` window on Program Manager.

■ Double-click on the `File Manager` icon.

▶ Displays Directory Tree window on `File Manager` window.

■ Maximize the `File Manager` window if it isn't already.

▶ `File Manager` window fills screen.

The `File Manager` window in Figure B.11 contains a Directory window that is split into two sections: tree and directory. Normally, applications and documents are organized within disk directories in some systematic fashion. When graphically displayed, this hierarchy of disk directories looks like a tree, hence the abbreviation directory tree or tree. A disk directory appears in the tree as a **file folder** icon 🗀. A folder can be found within another folder (directory) and may itself contain other folders. These folders are actually DOS subdirectories (see Appendix A). The manner in which applications and documents are organized within folders (and within folders within those folders) is up to the user. There should be some logic to the grouping scheme, however, to make it easy to locate related applications and documents.

When a folder/directory is highlighted in the tree, the right side of the Directory window displays a list of filenames. These are the data files and programs stored in the highlighted directory.

■ Maximize the Directory window, if it is not already.

■ Click on the `View` menu and select `Tree and Directory`.

▶ Splits the `File Manager` window into two parts, if it wasn't already.

■ Click on the `Tree` menu and select `Expand All`.

▶ Displays the complete directory tree for the default disk.

Formatting a New (or Old) Disk

You need a 5.25-inch or 3.5-inch disk that can be formatted. Remember, formatting a disk erases all files and programs. When a disk is formatted, the user can add a *volume label.* The volume label is added to the disk directory and can be up to 11 characters long. We recommend limiting the volume label to letters and numbers. In this tutorial you will use your last name as the volume label.

- Remove any disks in drive A.
- Click on the `Disk` menu and select `Format Disk` by clicking once.
  - ▶ Displays `Format Disk` dialog box as shown in Figure B.10.
  - ▶ Verify that disk A is selected to be formatted. If not, click on down-arrow box to open menu and drag down arrow until it highlights correct drive letter.
- Click on the text box to the right of `Label:`

FIGURE B.10
Users respond to a series of dialog boxes when formatting a new disk.

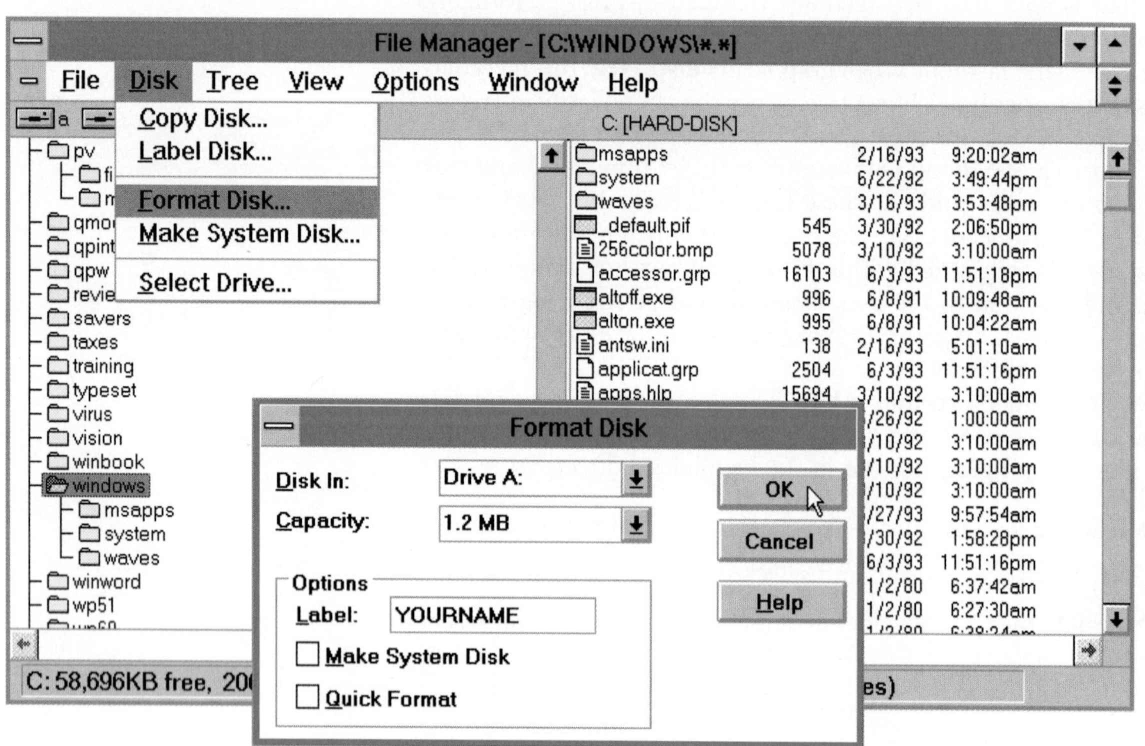

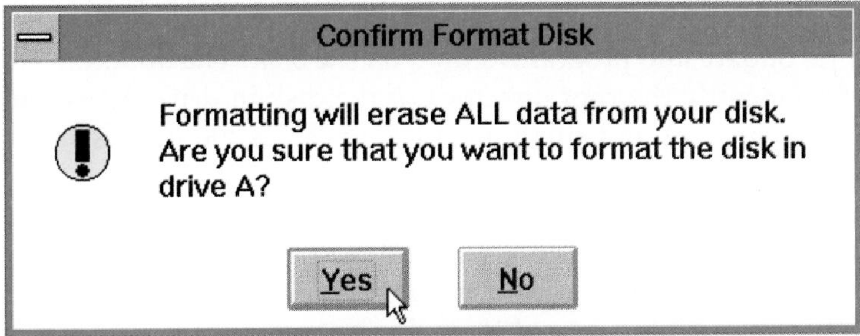

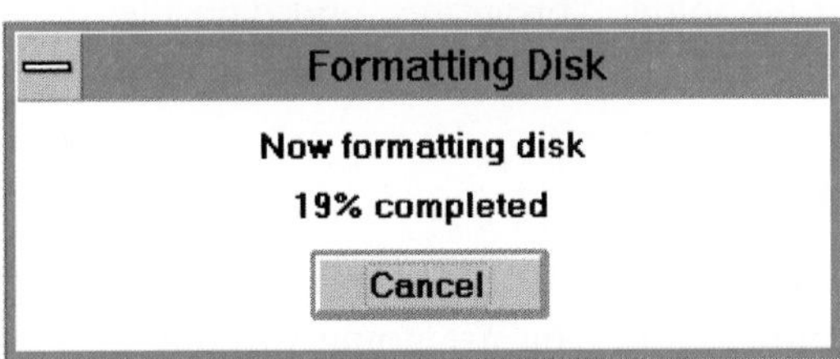

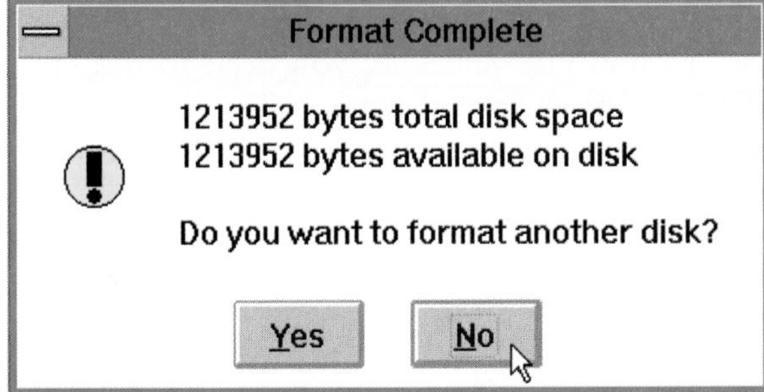

- ▶ Flashing cursor appears in text box.

■ Type your last name and press Enter.

- ▶ Displays Confirm Format Disk dialog box, which reminds users the disk will be erased.

■ Insert disk to be initialized into drive A.

■ Click on the `Yes` button.

- ▶ Displays `Formatting Disk` dialog box, which shows percent completed as disk is formatted.
- ▶ Displays `Format Complete` dialog box and asks `Do you want to format another diskette?`.

■ Click on the `No` button.

- ▶ Returns to `File Manager` window.

When a disk is formatted, a **root directory** is created to catalog the filenames of data and programs stored on the disk. The notation `A:\` is used to identify the root directory of the disk in drive A. As you have seen, the root and subdirectories appear as file folders. They work like electronic file folders in organizing programs and data according to common attributes (see Figure B.11). A well-organized hard disk has DOS and Windows subdirectories for storing utility programs, other subdirectories for application packages, and separate subdirectories for related data. Every computer system has a unique mix of file folders, programs, and data files.

Copying Files

The File Manager helps you copy important files by duplicating them onto another disk. You are going to copy a file called `COMMAND.COM` to drive A. First you must locate `COMMAND.COM` in the disk directory.

To find `COMMAND.COM`, you need to display the contents of the default drive's root directory. This is accomplished by using the scroll arrows to the left of the directory tree to scroll the \ icon into

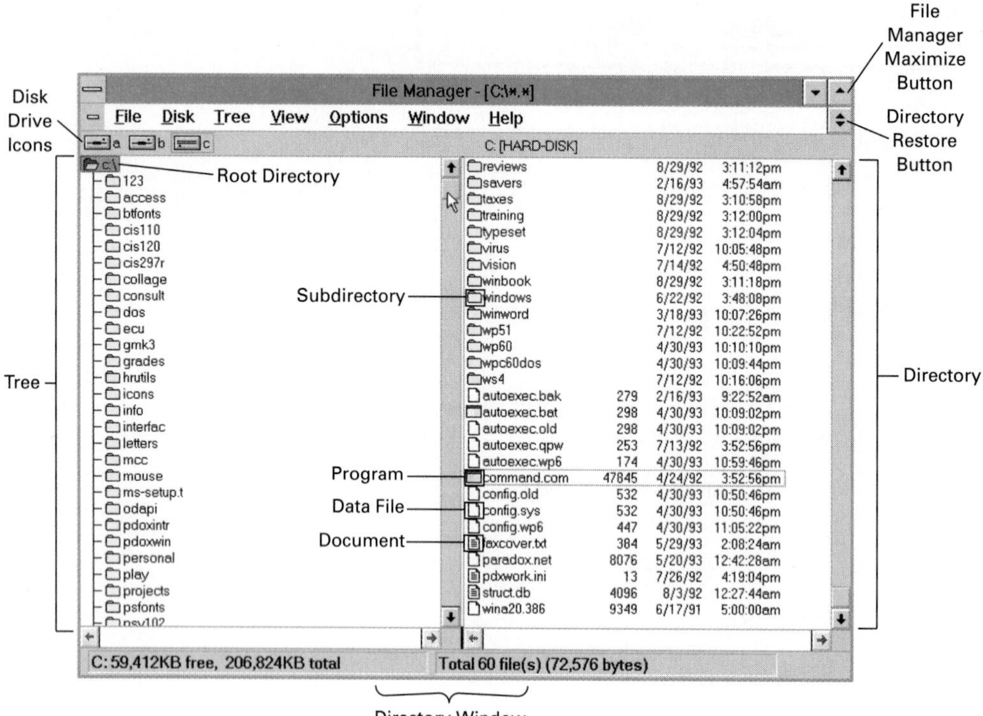

FIGURE B.11
Programs and data files are organized into folders (subdirectories), which are added to the disk's root directory.

view. If drive C is the default drive, you are looking for the `C:\` icon. Clicking on the \ icon displays the directory's contents in the next window. If your computer is already displaying the contents of the root directory, as shown in Figure B.11, you can skip to the section on "Displaying Two Directories."

■ Drag the scroll box to the immediate right of the directory tree up to the top of the scroll bar (see pointer in Figure B.11).

▶ The \ file folder is at the top of the directory tree.

■ Click on the \ file folder.

▶ Highlights icon, if it is not already.

■ Click on the down scroll arrow to the right side of the Directory window until `COMMAND.COM` scrolls into view.

■ Click on `COMMAND.COM` or associated icon.

▶ `COMMAND.COM` appears in the disk directory similar to Figure B.11.

NOTE: All file folders are listed in alphabetic order before programs and data files.

Displaying Two Directories

It is often helpful to display two disk directories at the same time. Checking the dates on backup files or copying files to your backup disk are both situations where displaying the source and target drives is useful. *Source* refers to the disk drive and original filename, while the *target* is the destination drive and name of the copy.

■ Click on the `Window` menu and select `New Window`.

▶ Opens another window with the default disk tree and directory.

■ Click on the `Window` menu again and select `File`.

▶ Horizontally splits screen and shows default disk tree and directory in both views, if it is not already.

■ Click on the drive A icon in the top window.

▶ Highlights drive A icon and displays drive A disk tree and directory.

■ Click on `COMMAND.COM` or the associated icon found in the lower window.

▶ Highlights `COMMAND.COM`.

■ Drag the COMMAND.COM icon to the drive A directory as seen in Figure B.12.

 ▶ Displays Confirm Mouse Operation dialog box shown in Figure B.12.

■ Click on Yes button.

 ▶ Displays Copying dialog box and copies COMMAND.COM to drive A root directory.

This drag and drop approach to copying a file is quick, easy, and assures you that both files have the same name. To change the name of the copy, you use the Copy option in the File menu. Acceptable filenames use any combination of letters or numbers up to eight characters. Filenames cannot include spaces. If necessary, use a hyphen instead of a space. The DOS User's Manual lists acceptable characters. A three-character extension is permissible if it follows a period—for instance, NEWCOPY.LAB.

FIGURE B.12
Dragging a program or data file icon from one directory window to another copies the related disk file to another disk.

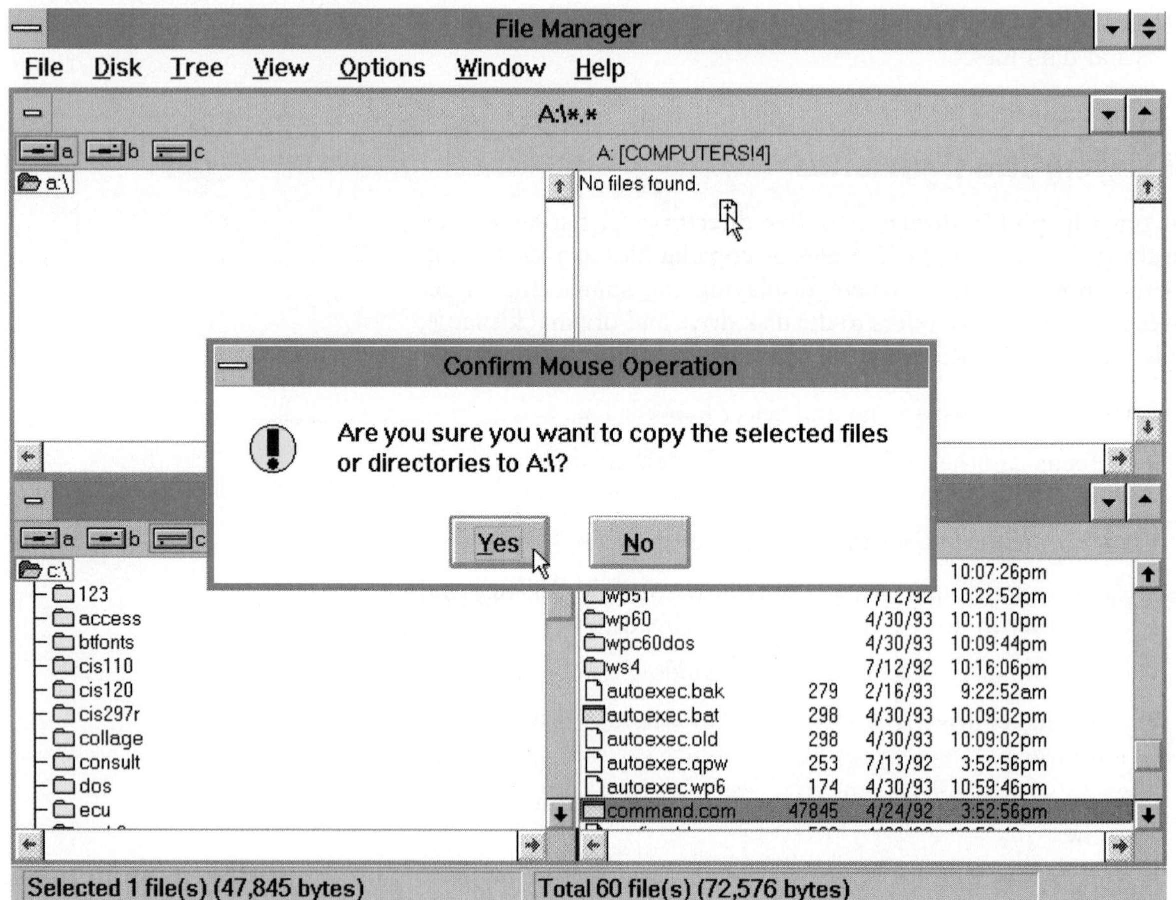

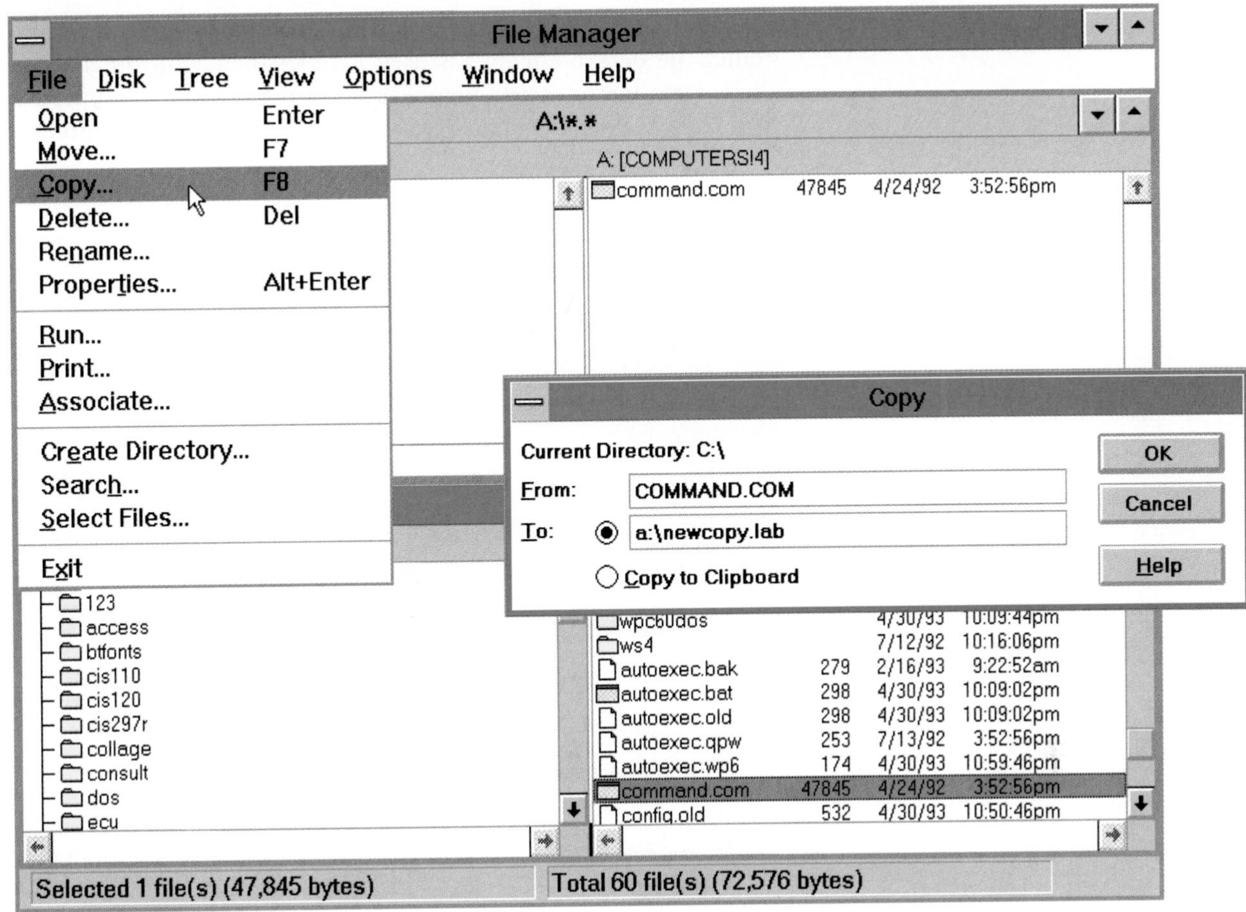

FIGURE B.13
Changing filenames when copying files to another disk requires the Copy option from the File menu, the target drive designation, and a new filename for the duplicate.

- With `COMMAND.COM` highlighted in the lower window, click on the `File` menu and select `Copy` similar to Figure B.13.
  - ▶ Displays `Copy` dialog box.
- From keyboard type `A:\newcopy.lab` and press Enter.
  - ▶ Copies file to drive A and changes name to `NEWCOPY.LAB`.

NOTE: Pressing Enter initiates action just like clicking on the OK button. Anytime a button is highlighted as the OK button is in Figure B.13, pressing Enter is the keyboard alternative.

Take a close look at the filenames and icons in the drive A directory. Even though these files are duplicates of one another, different icons are displayed. Windows used the program icon for `COMMAND.COM` and data file icon for `NEWCOPY.LAB`. The icon assignment illustrated in Figure B.11 is determined by the extension. Executable programs use filenames with the extensions `.COM`, `.EXE`, or `.BAT`. As a result, COMMAND.COM is assigned the ▭ icon for an executable program. The data file icon ▯ is used for filenames with other extensions. Data files created by application programs are recognized by Windows as documents and are assigned a data file icon containing four lines ▤.

Renaming Files

What if a filename needs to be changed? The File Manager performs this operation through the Rename option on the File menu. As illustrated in Figure B.14, you are going to change NEWCOPY.LAB to NEXTNAME.LAB.

- Make the drive A window active by clicking on the title bar.
- Click on the NEWCOPY.LAB icon.
  - ▶ Highlights NEWCOPY.LAB.
- Click on the File menu and select Rename.
  - ▶ Displays Rename dialog box as shown in Figure B.14.
- From keyboard type nextname.lab and press [Enter].
  - ▶ Changes name to NEXTNAME.LAB.

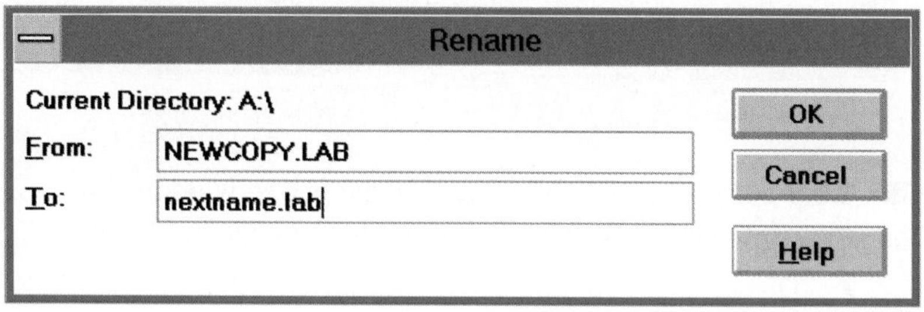

FIGURE B.14
Filenames are changed by using the Rename option from the File menu.

Creating New Folders

As you begin working with the computer, you will create documents using a variety of applications software. Over time, these documents will need to be organized in some fashion—by subject, type of application package used, and so on. You will need to establish a filing system where related documents are placed within folders (*subdirectories*) on your disk.

To create new folders for organizing software and documents, you must make sure that you open the folder within which you want to put the new folder. With the root directory of the disk in drive A active, you are going to create a new directory called PROJ-

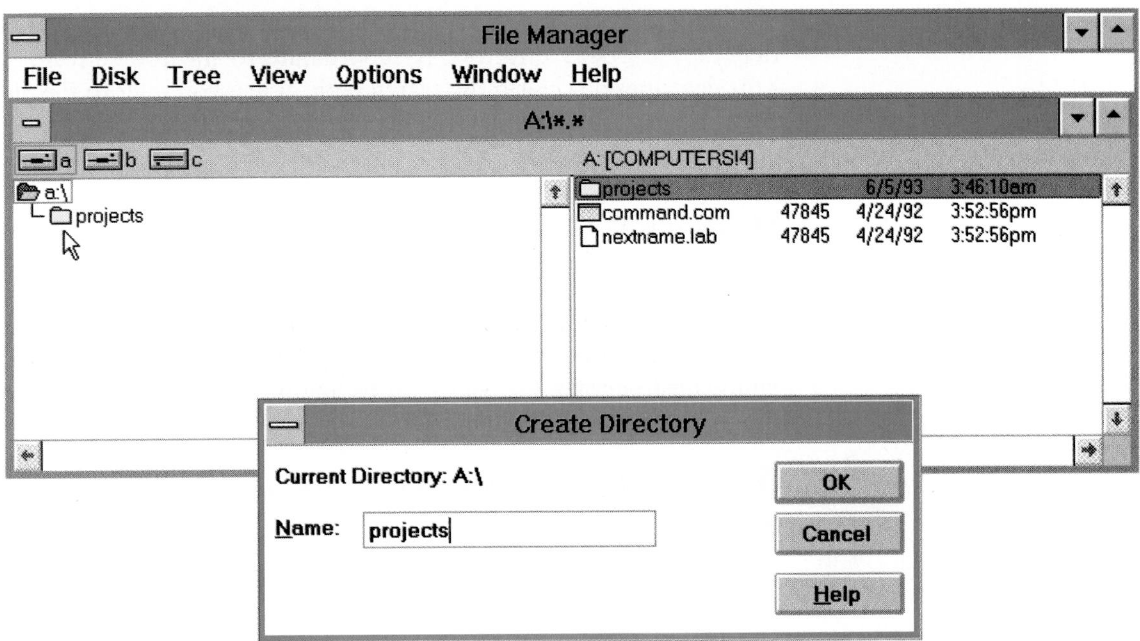

FIGURE B.15
A file folder icon identifies a disk subdirectory, which is used to organize programs and data on the disk.

ECTS. When naming a new subdirectory, you must follow the DOS rules for filenames—that is, up to eight characters in the filename and three characters in the optional extension.

- Make sure the a:\ folder is open.
- Click on the `File` menu and select `Create Directory`.
  - ▶ Displays `Create Directory` dialog box in Figure B.15.
- Type `projects` and press Enter.
  - ▶ Adds a file folder labeled `PROJECTS` to the tree and root directory as shown in Figure B.15.

Copying a File to a File Folder

Copying files to this new file folder is just as simple as copying files from one disk to another. To show you how, let's copy `NEXTNAME.LAB` from the root directory to the `PROJECTS` folder and change the filename to `UPDATE.LAB` as we copy it.

- Make sure `NEXTNAME.LAB` is highlighted.
- Click on the `File` menu and select `Copy`.
  - ▶ Displays `Copy` dialog box.
- Type `a:\projects\update.lab` and press Enter.
  - ▶ Displays drive A root directory.

We used the notation *A:\PROJECTS* to identify to Windows/DOS that the PROJECTS directory is subordinate to the root directory. This description is called the **search path.** When you refer to the file UPDATE.LAB, the search becomes *A:\PROJECTS*\UPDATE.LAB.

Moving a File to Another File Folder

Earlier you copied a file from one disk to another using the drag and drop technique. This approach moves a file instead of copying it when icons are dragged between file folders on the same disk. If you want to copy a file using this technique, hold down Ctrl while dragging and dropping the icon.

- Drag the nextname.lab icon over the projects icon.
- Release mouse button.
  - ▶ Displays Confirm Mouse Operation dialog box.
- Click on Yes.
  - ▶ Displays Moving dialog box.
  - ▶ Nextname.lab disappears from drive A root directory.
- Click on the projects icon under the a:\ icon in the directory tree.
  - ▶ Displays PROJECTS subdirectory with UPDATE.LAB and NEXTNAME.LAB as shown in Figure B.16.

Deleting Files

At some time you will want to delete an unwanted file or files from disk. This task is easily accomplished by highlighting the files and pressing Delete or selecting the Delete option from the File menu. To demonstrate this action, we will delete both files in the PROJECTS directory. Both files can be highlighted at the same time by holding down Ctrl while clicking on the file icon.

- Click on the update.lab icon, if it is not already highlighted.
  - ▶ Highlights filename and icon.
- While holding down Ctrl, click on the nextname.lab icon.
  - ▶ Highlights both nextname.lab and update.lab names and icons (see Figure B.16).
- Press Delete.
  - ▶ Displays Delete dialog box as shown in Figure B.16.

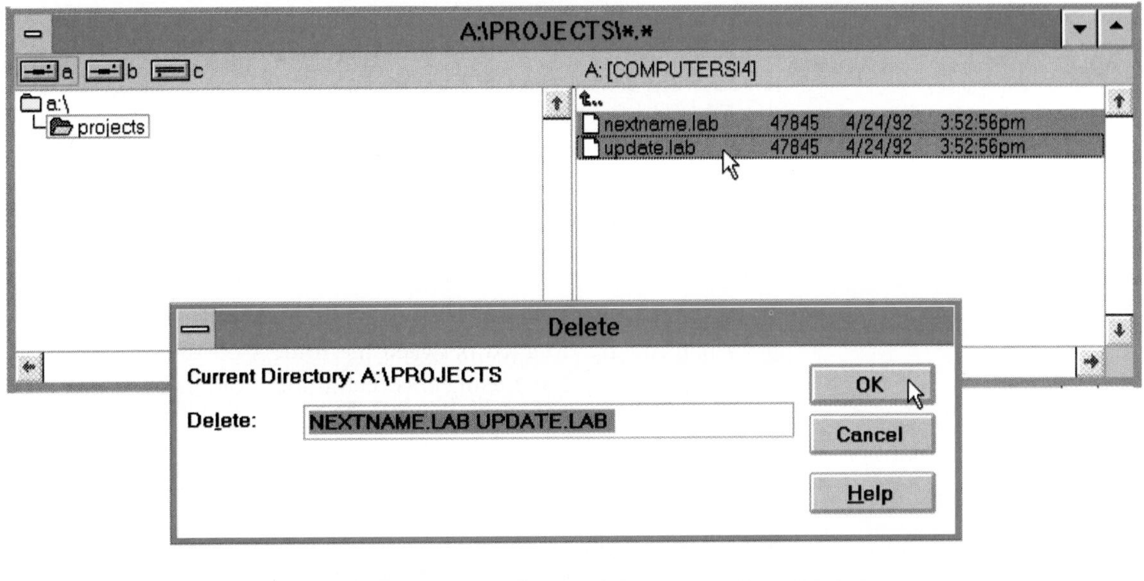

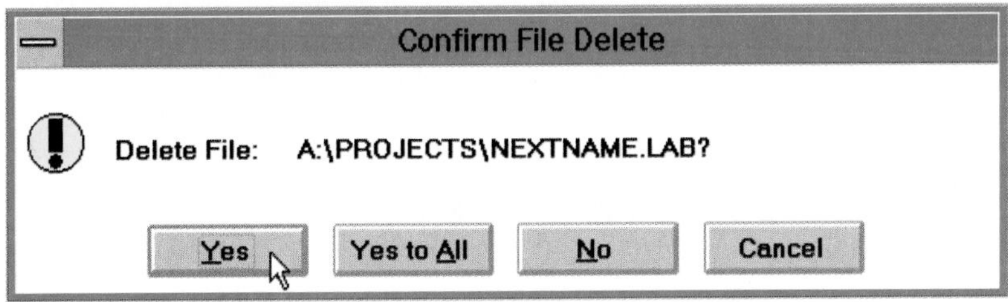

FIGURE B.16
Delete dialog box asks users to confirm a file deletion before removing the file from the disk directory.

- Click on OK.
  - ▶ Displays Confirm File Delete dialog box.
- Click on Yes after visually confirming the correct file is being deleted.
  - ▶ Displays another Confirm File Delete dialog box.
- Click on Yes after visually confirming the correct file is being deleted.
  - ▶ Only ↑.. is left in the disk directory.

Removing a File Folder

Proper disk management dictates the constant addition and removal of file folders as projects and software come into use or become inactive. While the root directory cannot be removed, all other folders (subdirectories) are fair game. A file folder must be empty except for ↑.. before removing it. ↑.. represents an internal index linking the file folder to the root directory or another file folder. If you try to delete a directory with files in it, Windows will systematically ask if you want to delete each file.

File folders, like files, can be deleted by highlighting the associated icon and pressing [Delete]. An alternative is to highlight the icon and select the Delete option from the File menu. As with many Windows features, there are several ways to accomplish the same action.

- Click on the projects icon in the directory tree.
- Click on the File menu and select Delete.
  - ▶ Displays Delete dialog box as shown in Figure B.17.
- Click on OK.
  - ▶ Displays Confirm Directory Delete dialog box.
- Click on Yes.
  - ▶ Removes projects folder from drive A directory tree.

SYSTEM SHUT-DOWN

When you are through for the day, the computer system needs to be shut down. One good rule of thumb is to never turn off a computer while an application program is still running. Always exit the program you are using and return to the Program Manager before turning off the equipment. Some people will go one step further and return to a DOS prompt before shutting their systems down. Ask your instructor which procedure is preferred at your school.

- Double-click on File Manager control box at top left corner of the screen.
  - ▶ Returns to Program Manager window.

NOTE: If you do not double-click fast enough, Windows displays the Control box menu. Click on Close to exit the File Manager.

- Close any open windows.
- Double-click on Program Manager control box at top left corner of screen.

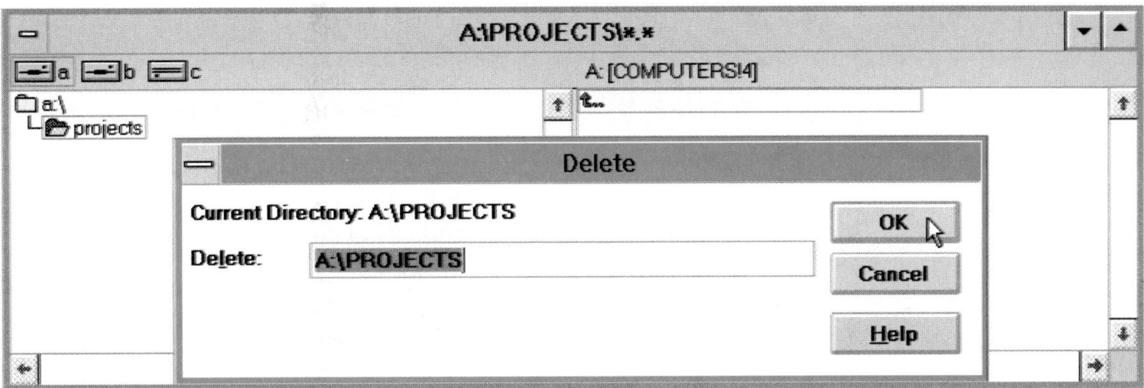

FIGURE B.17
Files, programs, and other folders must be removed from a subdirectory before it is deleted.

- ▶ Displays `Exit Windows` dialog box shown in Figure B.18.

- Click on `OK`.
  - ▶ Displays DOS prompt.
- Remove work disk from drive A, return it to a protective cover, and store it in a safe place.
- Turn off computer.
- Turn off monitor, if necessary.

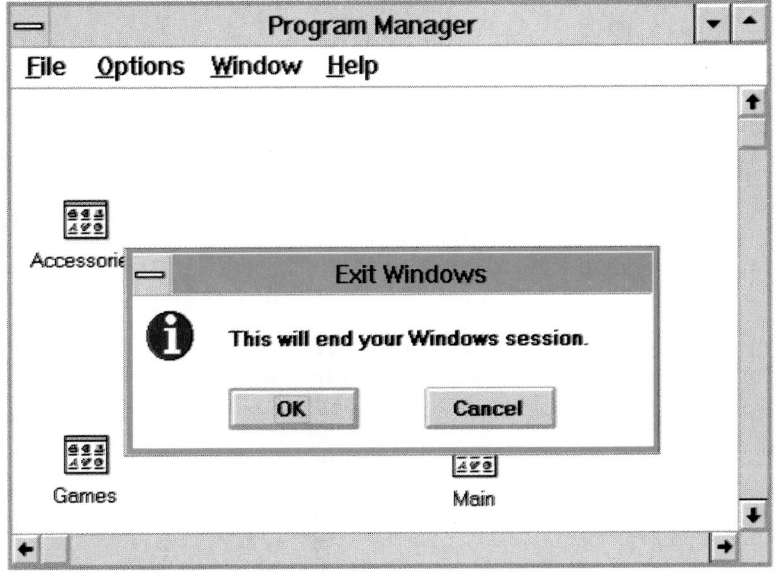

FIGURE B.18
Always exit a program and return to the Program Manager or DOS prompt before turning off your computer system.

Chapter Facts

- Windows is a graphical user interface that uses a desktop metaphor to represent different computer operations as icons. File folders, calendars, and calculators are icons found on the desktop.
- Pull-down menus are found in the menu bar.
- Icons and menus are selected on the desktop by moving the mouse to locate the screen pointer over the item. Clicking the mouse button once the pointer is touching the item activates the menu or associated application program.
- Icons and windows are repositioned on the desktop by using the mouse to drag them to a new screen location.
- A diskette must be formatted using the File Manager. Users do so by responding to a series of dialog boxes to select alternatives and label the disk.
- Windows are identified by the name in the title bar.
- The dimensions of a window are altered by dragging the window frame to a new screen location or by clicking on the maximize and restore buttons.
- Clicking on the scroll arrows and dragging the scroll box to a new location within the scroll bar changes a window's view.
- Double-clicking on the control box closes a window.
- Application programs, data files, and documents are organized into different file folders (subdirectories).
- New file folders can be created, renamed, and deleted at any time.
- Files are moved from one file folder to another by dragging the associated icon over the other folder. Files are copied from one disk to another in the same way. More than one file can be moved or copied at the same time.
- The File Manager provides menus that help the user create new folders, rename files, delete files, remove folders, etc.
- More than one Directory window can be open at the same time.
- Filename extensions determine which icon is assigned to a program or data file.
- A file folder must be empty before it is removed from the disk directory.
- Exiting Windows returns the user back to a DOS prompt.

Terms to Remember

a. clicking
b. desktop
c. DOS prompt
d. dragging
e. file folder
f. group icon
g. menu bar
h. MS-DOS
i. PC-DOS
j. root directory
k. scroll arrow
l. scroll bar
m. scroll box
n. search path
o. title bar
p. Windows

Mix and Match

Match the following definitions to the Terms to Remember.

1. ____ horizontal area across the top of a window, which displays the window's title.
2. ____ icon found in the File Manager that represents a specific disk subdirectory.
3. ____ square within a scroll bar that identifies which portion of the window or list box is currently being viewed.
4. ____ icon found in the Program Manager that organizes related programs and data files.
5. ____ primary disk directory that is created when the disk is formatted.
6. ____ operating system IBM licenses from the Microsoft Corporation and distributes with its line of personal computers.
7. ____ repositioning icon or window on screen by pointing to it and holding down mouse button while moving pointer to a new screen location.
8. ____ graphical user interface developed by the Microsoft Corporation to be used with MS-DOS or PC-DOS.
9. ____ pressing the mouse button once to initiate action or to select a program option.
10. ____ arrow found at either end of a scroll bar.

11. ____ description of how to find a subdirectory or file by identifying a disk drive and the subdirectory's (or file's) location with respect to the disk's root directory.
12. ____ screen layout associated with graphical user interface that uses icons that represent documents, file folders, calculators, and other office tools.
13. ____ horizontal area that runs across the top of a window and displays menu titles.
14. ____ area that appears on the right or lower edges of a window or list box when only a partial view is available.
15. ____ screen display of letter associated with default disk drive and greater than sign, for example, A> or C>.
16. ____ disk operating system developed by the Microsoft Corporation for personal computer systems.

Review Questions

1. How do you load and run Windows?
2. How do you move an icon around the desktop?
3. Describe how an option is selected from a drop-down menu.
4. Why are some menu options dimmer than others?
5. What are three ways to open a window?
6. Describe four ways to alter the size of a window.
7. How do you close a window?
8. How do you format a new disk using Windows?
9. Explain how you would use Windows to display two disk directories at the same time.
10. What are two different procedures for copying a file from one disk to another, keeping the same name? How do you change the name of the duplicate when copying?
11. Identify the rules for acceptable DOS/Windows filenames.
12. What are the three types of file icons?
13. How do you rename an existing disk file using Windows?
14. How are new file folders or subdirectories added to a disk?
15. What are two different ways to use Windows to delete files from disk?
16. How do you highlight more than one icon at the same time?

17. What conditions must exist before a subdirectory can be removed from a disk?
18. How do you use Windows to remove an existing subdirectory folder from a disk?
19. How do you exit Windows and return to the DOS prompt?

Applying What You've Learned

1. A volume label can be added to the disk directory when a disk is formatted. Use a Windows reference manual to find out what File Manager option allows you to change the volume label later.
2. Use a Windows reference guide to find the File Manager feature that allows you to protect a file from accidental erasure. (*Hint:* These files are said to be read-only.)
3. Use the File Manager to display filenames in order by creation date. How would you display files in order by their file size? Which presentation format do you prefer? Explain your answer.
4. A general rule for file management on disk is to make one file folder for related documents and another file folder for each application package. For example, users are encouraged to create one folder for their word processing program and other folders for letters, reports, and so forth. Graphically illustrate how you would organize file folders on a hard disk. Assume you are using at least three different application packages.
5. If your computer system uses a color monitor, how would you change the color of the desktop? How would you change the title bar color? What colors should not be used for the desktop? Explain your answer.

Answers to Mix and Match

1. o 2. e 3. m 4. f 5. j 6. i 7. d 8. p 9. a 10. k
11. n 12. b 13. g 14. l 15. c 16. h

C

Introduction to the Apple Macintosh

- **From the User's Point of View**
- **Personal Computer Start-Up Procedures**
  - System orientation
  - Macintosh desktop
- **Using the Mouse and Initializing a Diskette**
  - Pointing, clicking, and dragging
  - Initializing a diskette
  - Selecting operations from pull-down menus
- **Common Window Features**
  - Title bar
  - Size box
  - Scrolling a window
  - Zoom box
  - Close box
- **Applications, Documents, and Folders**
  - Creating new folders
  - Renaming a folder
  - Deleting an object
  - Copying an object within a window
  - Moving an object to a different window
- **Shutting Down the System**

FROM THE USER'S POINT OF VIEW

The Apple Macintosh is noted for its user-friendly interface, which reduces the time required for understanding the machine and learning new applications. The recent introduction of System 7 provides Macintosh users with a flexible operating system that maintains all the elements of Apple's well-known graphical user interface. Even if you have experience with other computers, you probably need to learn some new skills for working with the Macintosh. Yet, once you have learned these basic techniques, you can apply them to virtually any type of processing task you undertake.

You will need access to a Macintosh personal computer with a hard disk and a new 3.5-inch diskette to complete this tutorial. Since Macintosh operations require lots of internal memory and make use of disk storage, we assume you are using a computer with a hard disk or have access to a local area network. Menu options or data you should enter using the mouse or keyboard are printed in red and preceded by ■.

PERSONAL COMPUTER START-UP PROCEDURES

All models of the Macintosh operate in the same way; they differ basically in their physical sizes, memory capacities, and processing speeds. For all practical purposes, you can move easily from one model to another with few noticeable differences. The operations manuals for the systems explain any minor differences in using various machines.

A typical computer system (Figure C.1) comes equipped with five peripherals: monitor, keyboard, mouse or other pointing device, one or more disk drives for storing and retrieving information, and a

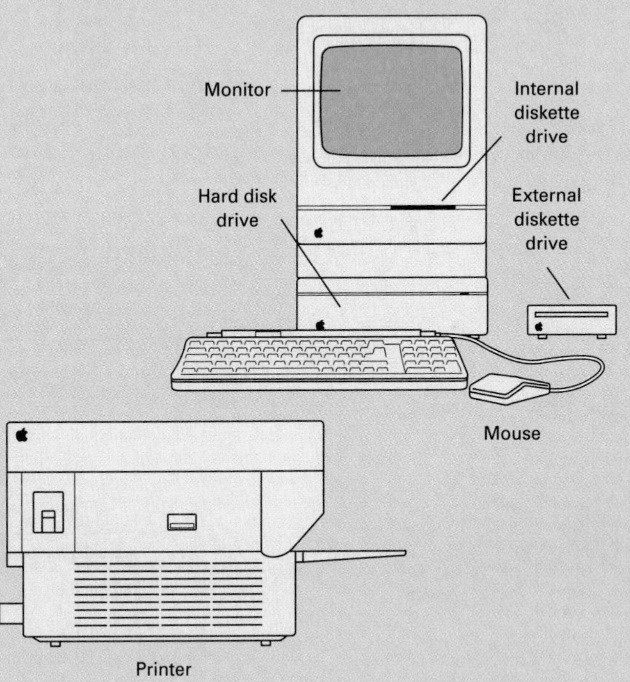

FIGURE C.1
A typical Macintosh system includes several types of peripheral hardware.

printer. Procedures differ slightly when using a hard disk instead of a diskette drive. The hard disk holds all the critical operating system programs.

In this tutorial, we will assume you are using a hard disk and either the System 6 or System 7 operating system. The diskette drive is primarily used to load new software onto the hard disk and as a means of backing up important data.

System Orientation

Besides the hard disk, you will be using either the **internal diskette drive,** which is built inside the computer housing, or an **external diskette drive** attached by cable connected to an I/O port. Macintosh systems use 3.5-inch diskettes (see Figure C.2). The diskette is inserted metal end first, label side up, into the drive until it locks into place.

- Check to see that all the diskette drives are empty.
- Turn on the machine. The ON/OFF switch is at the top right corner of the keyboard, on the back of the computer, or on the left side.

If your computer system follows the standard booting steps, the Macintosh desktop screen appears, similar to Figure C.3, after a welcome message. Many computer systems are customized to display menus, launch application programs, or describe special procedures or copyright infringement policies. What follows is a description of the standard desktop features; your system could be a little different.

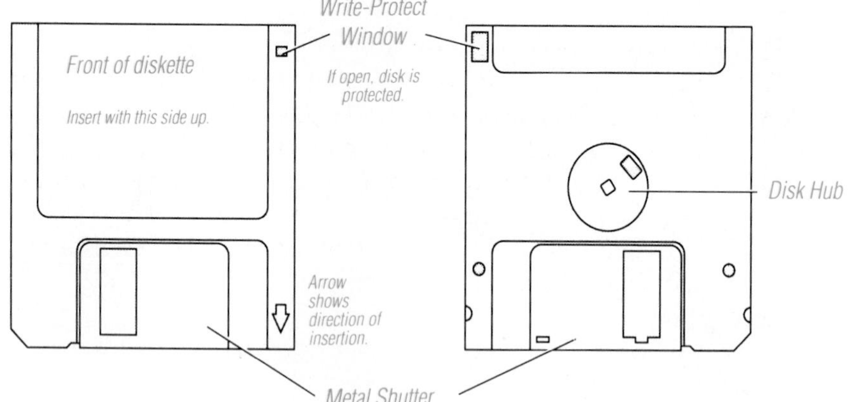

FIGURE C.2
The 3.5-inch diskette is the size commonly used in Macintosh systems.

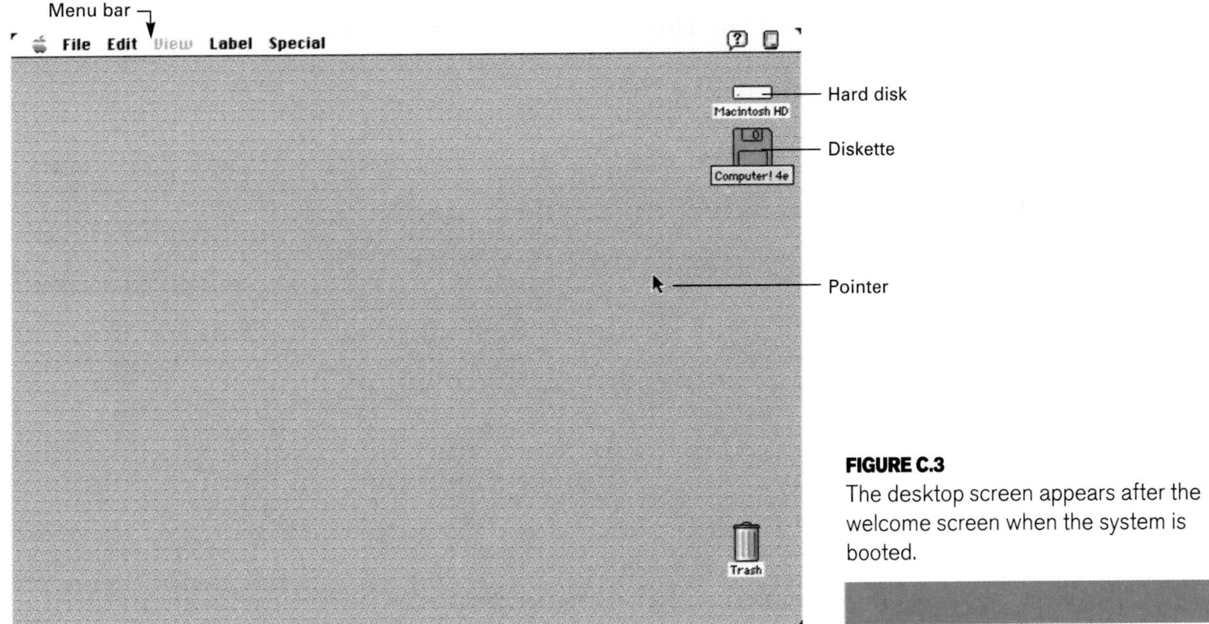

FIGURE C.3
The desktop screen appears after the welcome screen when the system is booted.

Macintosh Desktop

Currently on the screen is the Macintosh **desktop,** your window into the computer. The desktop is aptly named, since you work with images on the screen in the same way that you work with papers, folders, office tools, and supplies laid out on an actual desktop. This desktop metaphor is the basis for all screen display and processing activities of the Macintosh computer system. A special system program called the FINDER manages all of the work on the desktop.

The desktop opening screen contains icons for each piece of storage hardware being used by the system. The desktop in Figure C.3 displays three icons. In the top right corner of the screen is the *disk icon* for the hard disk, labeled Macintosh HD. Your computer might use another label. A diskette icon would be displayed instead if the system had been booted from a diskette. Below the Macintosh HD icon is the icon for the user disk in one of the diskette drives. In Figure C.3 it is labeled `Computer! 4e`. In the lower right corner is the *trash icon* where you discard items no longer needed on the desktop.

Across the top of the screen is the **menu bar.** The menu bar permits access to several menus, each containing processing commands. The *apple icon* 🍎 and the titles `File`, `Edit`, `View`, and `Special` each represent a different menu and are shown in Figure C.3. These titles are standard whenever you view the desktop, while different ones appear with various software packages and versions of the operating system.

USING A MOUSE AND INITIALIZING A DISKETTE

All choices from the menu bar, as well as icon manipulations, are controlled primarily with the mouse. As you grasp and move the mouse across a flat surface, a *screen pointer* or pointer moves in a corresponding fashion around the screen. When you work within the Macintosh desktop, the pointer is shaped like an arrow (see Figure C.3). However, it changes into other shapes, depending on the activity in progress.

You can lift the mouse and set it back down again without changing the location of the pointer on the screen. You will need to do this whenever you do not have room to move the pointer across the screen in one continuous movement of the mouse, as in cramped quarters.

At first, using a mouse may seem awkward. However, this device's operation will soon become second nature, and the speed and ease with which you can do things with a mouse will increase your productivity many times over.

Pointing, Clicking, and Dragging

A basic technique for working with the Macintosh is to select an icon and either activate it or move it around the screen. You select an icon by pointing to it with the arrow pointer and clicking the mouse button once. You must select an object before you can use it.

- Move the arrow pointer so that its tip is within the trash icon.
- Press and release the mouse button once.
  - ▶ The icon is highlighted to indicate that it has been selected.

You can move and reposition an object on the desktop by **clicking** (pressing the mouse button while on the icon) and **dragging** (holding the button down while moving the mouse), as illustrated in Figure C.4.

- Select the Trash icon and hold down the mouse button without releasing it.

▶ `Trash` is highlighted, if not already so.

■ While holding down the button, move the mouse to reposition the icon on screen.

▶ The outline of the trashcan is dragged along with the arrow.

■ Release the mouse button.

▶ The icon snaps into place at its new location.

■ Use the mouse to drag the `Trash` icon back to its original place.

These clicking and dragging techniques are used for other mouse operations besides selecting and moving icons. They will become basic techniques for controlling all activities you perform with the computer.

Initializing a Diskette

Later in this appendix you will be learning how to create, copy, and delete files. To do that, you will be using a diskette. Recall from Chapter 10 that before a disk can be used for storing programs and data files, it must be initialized or formatted.

Obtain a new 3.5-inch diskette that has not been initialized. On the metal shutter or disk label is printed how many sides of the diskette can be initialized (single-sided or double-sided). Some older Macintosh machines will accept only one-sided diskettes. Newer

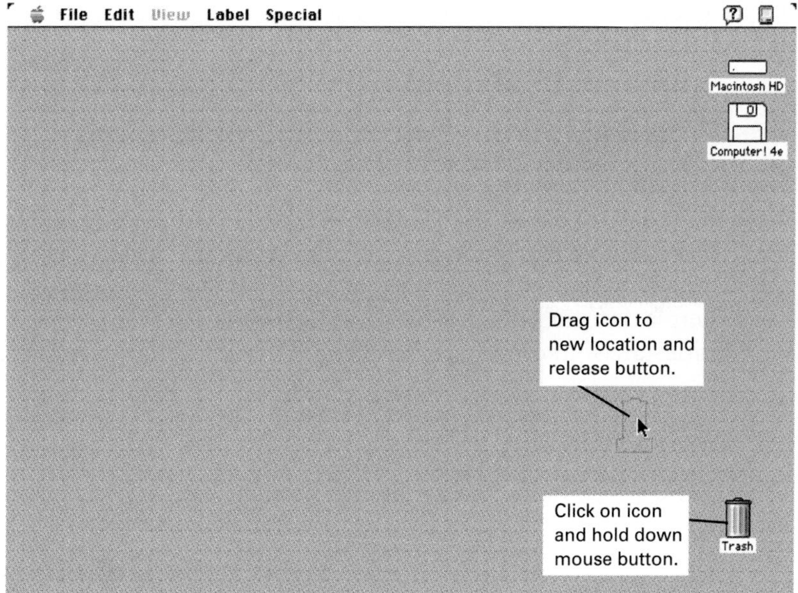

FIGURE C.4
Icons are moved around the desktop by clicking and dragging them.

computers will accept diskettes of both types. Check the user's manual if you have questions as to which diskettes can be used.

A new diskette is automatically initialized by the Macintosh the first time it is inserted into a disk drive. At that time the user is asked to enter a label that can be up to 27 characters long (including spaces). You can use any characters on the keyboard except the colon (:). You will use your last name as a label on your diskette.

■ Insert the new diskette to be initialized into the diskette drive.

▶ Displays the first dialog box shown in Figure C.5. *Note:* When you are using lower-capacity diskettes, the system will ask if you are using a `One-Sided` or `Two-Sided` diskette.

■ Select `Initialize`. If a lower-capacity diskette is used, click on either the `One-Sided` or `Two-Sided` option (as dictated by the diskette).

▶ Displays the next dialog box shown in Figure C.5.

■ Click on `Erase`.

▶ Displays the last dialog box shown in Figure C.5.

■ Type in YOUR LAST NAME and click on `OK`.

Pointer changes to a watch, telling the user to wait. Three boxes will appear in succession on the screen containing these messages:

```
Formatting disk...
Verifying Format...
Creating Directory...
```

A diskette icon labeled with your last name appears on the right side of the screen.

Selecting Operations from Pull-Down Menus

Besides clicking and dragging, computer operations are initiated by using the mouse to access pull-down menus. The menu bar contains the titles of all available menus (see Figure C.6). You select one of the menus by pointing to it and holding down the mouse button. For example, information about your Macintosh and common system utilities are found using the apple icon menu.

■ Click and hold the mouse button on the apple icon at the left side of the menu bar.

▶ The selections in the apple menu are displayed.

NOTE: Having to hold the mouse button to keep the menu in view is how pull-down menus are different from drop-down menus. Drop-down menus stay open when the user clicks on the menu title.

■ Drag the pointer downward to `Control Panels`.

FIGURE C.5
These dialog boxes require the user to approve each step in initializing a diskette.

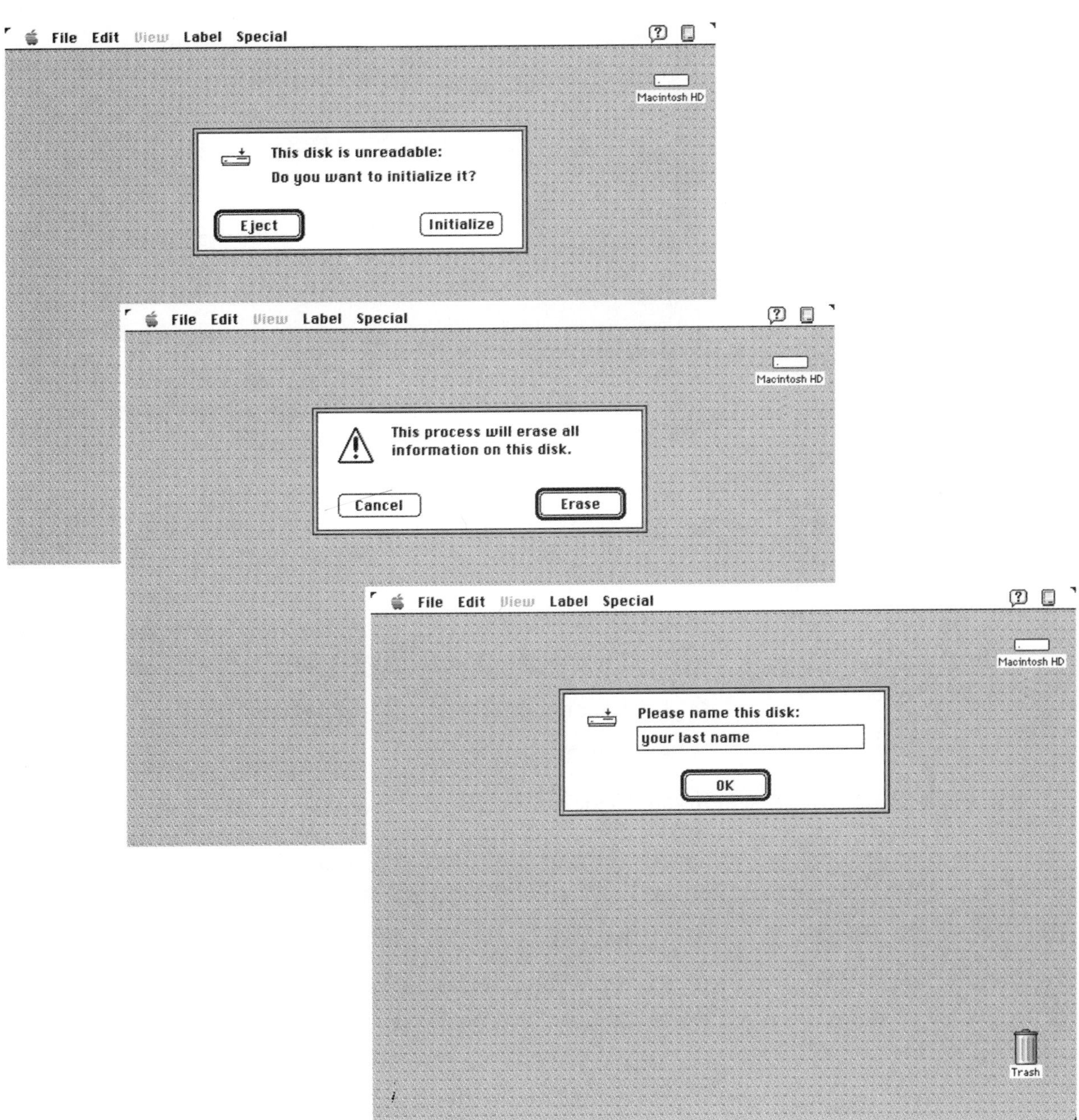

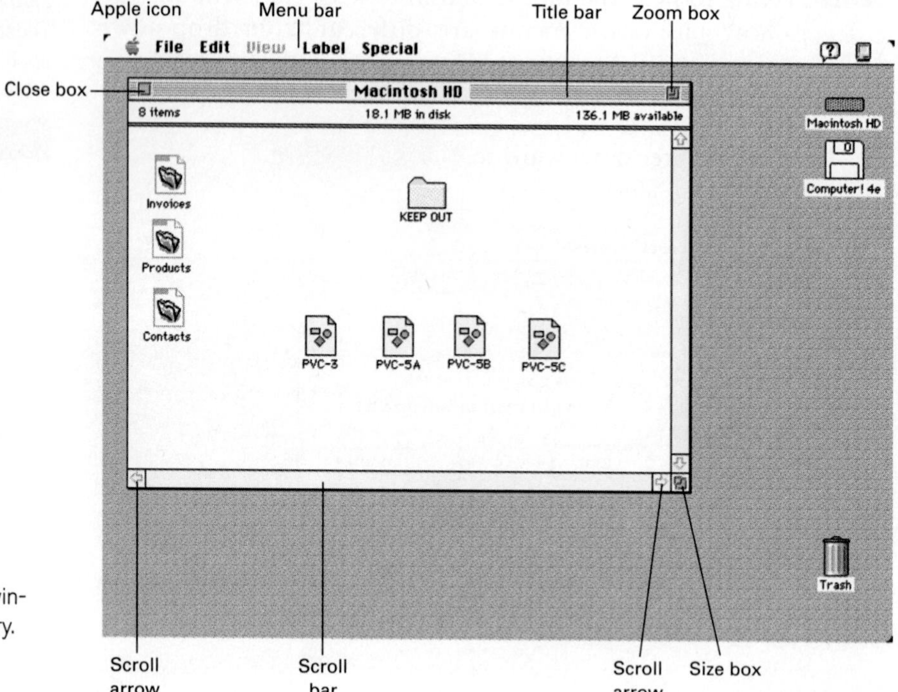

FIGURE C.6
Clicking on a drive icon opens a window that displays the disk directory.

■ Release the mouse.

▶ Opens the `Control Panels` window.

Windows are closed by clicking on the close box (see Figure C.6) found in the window's upper left corner.

■ Click on the `Control Panels` close box.

▶ Closes window.

If you decide not to choose a menu item, simply move the pointer outside the menu. Then release the mouse button. The menu disappears and you are back to the desktop. You can easily scan the menus to see all of the options available on the menu bar.

■ Click on the apple icon and hold down the mouse button.

▶ The options under the apple menu are revealed.

■ Without releasing the mouse button, slowly move the pointer to the right along the menu bar.

▶ As each menu title is passed, its pull-down menu is shown.

■ Release the mouse button.

▶ All highlighting of menus is turned off.

NOTE: Some of the names of the menu items may appear dimmed. These are menu commands that are not appropriate or that cannot be carried out at that instant. You cannot select a dimmed title. These items will become available at different times and under other processing circumstances.

COMMON WINDOW FEATURES

The disk icons that appear on the desktop when you start the system (see Figure C.4) must be opened to make their contents accessible. The easiest way is using the mouse to double-click (click twice rapidly) on the icon.

■ Double-click on the hard disk icon.

▶ Displays a directory window similar to Figure C.6.

The options represented by the icon are available for use. When a disk icon is opened, the desktop is overlaid with a window that displays the disk directory (see Figure C.6). The directory window shows the contents of the disk. The window is made up of several descriptive and functional parts.

NOTE: There are two other ways to open a window aside from double-clicking on the icon. The first is to highlight the icon; then use the `File` menu to select the `Open` option. The second is to highlight the icon; then hold down the ⌘ key and type `O` (the letter, not the number).

Title Bar

The window's title appears in the **title bar** across the top of the window. It contains the name of the disk or other object that has been opened, in this case `Macintosh HD`, and horizontal lines on either side of the title. At both ends of the title bar are small boxes. The left box is the close box you used to put away a window.

Below the title bar is summary information about the directory's contents, including the number of items the directory contains and the size of the directory. Figure C.6 shows 8 items available on the hard disk. These 8 items take up 18.1 MB of disk space, with 136.1 MB still available.

Windows can be moved anywhere on the screen by moving the pointer within the title bar and dragging to reposition the window. You may need to do this if you have several overlapping windows on the screen at the same time.

- Move the pointer within the title bar.
- Hold down the mouse button and drag the window somewhere else on the screen.
  - ▶ The outline of the window is dragged with the pointer.
- Release the mouse button.
  - ▶ The window snaps into its new position.

Use the mouse to center the window in the space available.

Size Box

In the bottom right corner of the window is the *size box*. By dragging the size box, you can resize the window to make it as small or large as you need.

- Select the size box and hold down the mouse button.
  - ▶ Lines in the window become dashed.
- Drag the size box toward the upper right-hand corner of the screen until at least one icon or filename falls outside the dashed lines.
  - ▶ The window outline follows the pointer.
- Release the mouse button.
  - ▶ The window contracts to reach the pointer location. Any icon or filename outside the reduced window disappears.

Scrolling a Window

Along the right and bottom edges of the window are **scroll bars** and **scroll arrows** that permit you to move around in the directory. In some cases, not all of the contents of the directory can be displayed in the window at one time. Some of the items are hidden outside the window frame. The scroll bars and arrows are used to bring these items into view. You can tell if there are hidden objects in the directory because the scroll bars are shaded, and the number of items you see in the window does not match the item count shown under the title bar, as it does it does in Figure C.6.

- Click once on the scroll arrow that points right.
  - ▶ If the scroll bar is shaded, icons in the window move toward the left.
- Click once on the scroll arrow that points down.

▶ If the scroll bar is shaded, icons in the window move up.

As you click, watch the **scroll box** found within each scroll bar. When there are hidden objects outside the window, scroll boxes appear within the scroll bars. By dragging these boxes, you can quickly scroll the window from top to bottom or left to right. The scroll boxes will move up or down, left or right, moving opposite the action of the icons in the window.

■ Drag a scroll box in one of the scroll bars to a new location.

▶ Icons in the window scroll in the opposite direction.

Another way to move quickly through a window is to click in the shaded area of the scroll bar.

■ Click in the shaded area of one of the scroll bars.

▶ The scroll box moves in the direction of the pointer and the icons in the window move in the opposite direction.

Zoom Box

In the upper right corner of the window is the *zoom box* (see Figure C.6). When it is clicked, the window expands to nearly fill the screen; when it is clicked a second time, the window returns to its previous size, as set by the size box.

■ Click once on the zoom box.

▶ Window expands.

■ Click again on the zoom box.

▶ Window returns to its original size.

Use the scroll boxes and size box to adjust the window so that all icons show.

Close Box

When you are finished using a window, you put it away by using the *close box*. As mentioned earlier, every window has a close box on the left side of the title bar.

■ Click once on the close box.

▶ The window shrinks and disappears into the disk icon.

APPLICATIONS, DOCUMENTS, AND FOLDERS

Disk windows contain icons representing programs and the data files that are processed by those programs. Programs are called *applications* within the Macintosh environment and data files are called *documents*. The particular icons used are devised by the authors of the software.

Normally, applications and documents are organized in some systematic fashion (see Figure C.7). They are grouped together and are placed within **folders.** A folder is found within a window and may itself contain other folders. The icon of a folder resembles a conventional filing folder 🗀, in keeping with the desktop metaphor. The manner in which applications and documents are organized within folders (and within folders within those folders) is up to the user. There should be some logic to the grouping scheme. This makes it easy to locate related applications and documents.

Creating New Folders

As you begin working with the computer, you will create documents for the applications you use. Over time, these documents need to be organized in some fashion—by subject, type of application package used, and so on. You will need to establish a filing system where related documents are placed within folders on your disk.

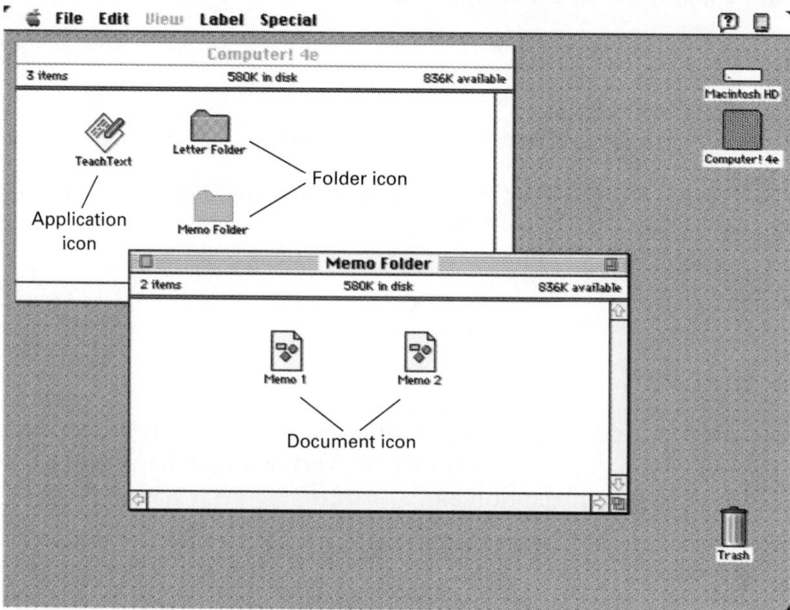

FIGURE C.7
Applications, folders, and documents are represented by different types of icons.

To create new folders for organizing applications and documents, you must make sure that you are in the proper window or folder within which you want to put the new folder. Its window must be active, which means it is on the screen with the title bar darkened. In Figure C.7 the Memo folder is active.

■ Click twice on the diskette icon with your last name.

▶ Displays an empty window.

■ From the `File` menu select the `New Folder` option.

▶ A folder icon appears with the name untitled or empty folder.

Renaming a Folder

The folder is automatically named when you create it, so you can rename it just by clicking on its icon and typing the new name. You need to click explicitly on an icon or on its name to change that name, even if the icon is already selected. You can tell whether an icon has been properly selected for renaming by moving the arrow pointer over its name. The arrow pointer turns into an I-beam pointer, a pointer shaped like the letter I. It indicates that typing is permissible. After typing, click somewhere outside the icon to assign the name.

■ Move the arrow pointer in the folder label until it is behind the last letter.

■ Click on the mouse button once.

▶ The name is no longer highlighted and there is a vertical flashing line (insertion pointer) after the name.

■ Press [Backspace] or [Delete] enough times to delete the old label.

▶ The insertion pointer will back over and delete a character each time it is pressed.

■ Type `Projects Folder`.

▶ The new folder name is centered beneath the icon.

■ Click outside the icon.

▶ The folder icon is no longer highlighted and the new name of the folder is saved.

NOTE: The above method will also allow you to change just part of the folder name by backspacing over only the characters you wish to delete. Another way to change the folder name is to click on the folder name and move the pointer anywhere within the folder name. The arrow is now the I-beam pointer. Without clicking the mouse button, press Backspace once. The entire old filename is deleted, and you may type in a new name.

Deleting an Object

Every user will occasionally need to clean off the desktop by getting rid of some objects. You can erase a folder, application, or document by dragging its icon to the trash. To see how deletion is done, we will create a new folder and then dispose of it.

- From the `File` menu select the `New Folder` option.
    - ▶ Icon appears, labeled untitled or empty folder.
- Drag the new folder icon until it covers the trashcan.
    - ▶ `Trash` icon is highlighted.
- Release the mouse button.
    - ▶ The folder icon disappears into the trash. The trash icon bulges and is no longer highlighted.

At this point, the trash icon contains the folder. The folder can be retrieved by opening the trash window and dragging it to another place on the screen. When you change disks or shut down the system, the trash will be emptied, and the files contained in it will be permanently erased.

Copying an Object within a Window

When you drag icons from one disk window or icon to another disk window or icon, you are also copying them. A duplicate copy of the file on the source disk is created on the target disk with the identical name. If you drag folders from one disk to another, the entire folder, including its enclosed applications and documents, is copied. If you drag an object from one folder to another folder on the same disk, the object is moved, not copied.

Any time the Finder is active, you can make an identical copy of a folder within the same window. Let's start by making a copy of an object on the system disk.

- Click once on the hard disk icon.
    - ▶ The icon representing the disk operating system is highlighted.
- Double click on the disk icon to open the system disk window.

- ▶ Displays the system window.

■ Double click on the System Folder.

NOTE: The System Folder could be located inside another folder. If you cannot find this folder, ask your instructor or lab assistant for help in locating it.

- ▶ Displays the System Folder window similar to Figure C.8.

NOTE: If the System Folder does not use document icons as shown in Figure C.8, click on the View menu and select By Icon.

■ Click on Clipboard icon.

- ▶ Icon is highlighted.

■ From the File menu select the Duplicate option.

- ▶ Displays a highlighted copy of the icon labeled Copy of Clipboard File or Clipboard Copy, possibly overlapping other icons.

■ Drag the new icon to a clear area of the window.

■ Change the icon's name to Newcopy Lab by following the procedure illustrated previously in "Renaming a Folder."

You now have two identical copies of the same information under two different names.

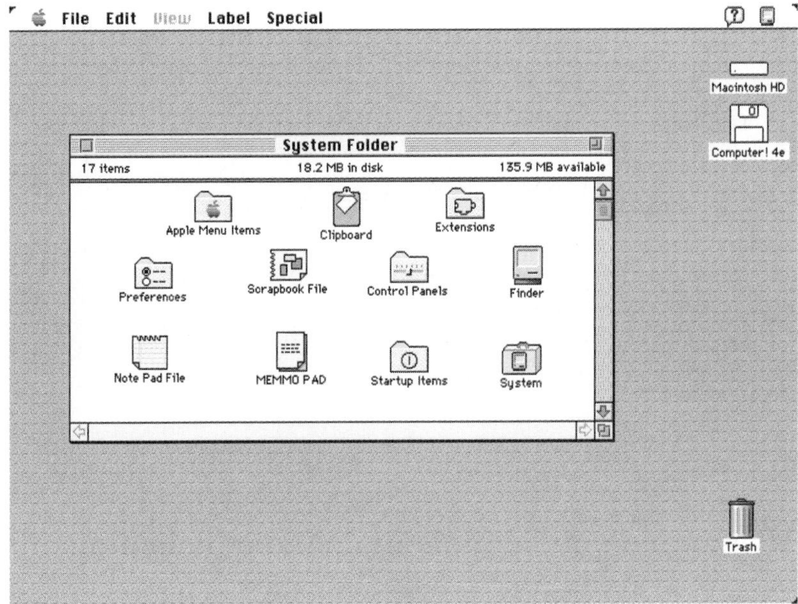

FIGURE C.8
When the system folder is opened, icons representing different desktop tools are available for execution.

Moving an Object to a Different Window

To transfer a folder or other object to another disk involves moving the icon outside of its source window and closing that window. The proper window on the target disk must then be opened and the icon moved into it. If a machine with only a single diskette drive is used, diskettes must be exchanged several times.

We will move `Newcopy Lab` from the systems window on the hard disk into the `Projects Folder` on your floppy disk. Both windows will be open at the same time and overlap (see Figure C.9). When more than one window is open, only one will be active. This is the window whose title bar contains horizontal lines. Inactive windows do not have lines in their title bar.

■ Select `Newcopy Lab` and hold down the mouse button.

 ▶ Icon is highlighted.

■ Drag the icon on top of the disk icon with your last name.

 ▶ Dialog box displays `Items remaining to be copied: 1.`

■ When copying is complete, double-click on the icon with your last name.

 ▶ Disk window opens. Both the `Projects Folder` and `Newcopy Lab` icons appear in the window.

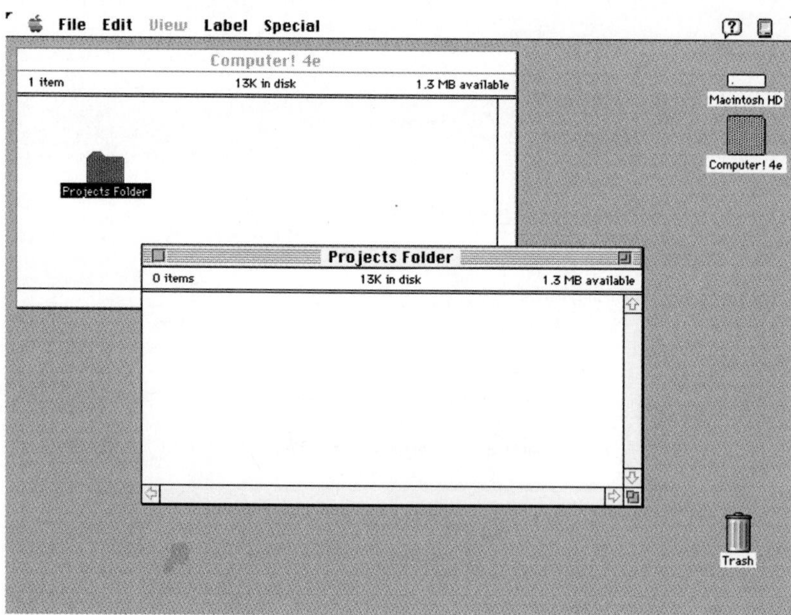

FIGURE C.9
Each time a folder is opened, its window overlays other windows and it becomes the active window.

- Drag the Newcopy Lab icon on top of the Projects Folder window.
  - ▶ Icon is placed within Projects Folder window and disappears from the window.

Although the Newcopy Lab icon does not appear on the screen, it is easy to check that it is in the Projects Folder.

- Open the Projects Folder window by double-clicking on the icon.
  - ▶ Projects Folder contains the Newcopy Lab icon.
- Close the Projects Folder window.
- Close all open windows.
  - ▶ The desktop is cleared.

SHUTTING DOWN THE SYSTEM

After you have completed your work on the computer, you can shut down the system by choosing Shut Down from the Special menu. At this point, Macintosh informs you that you can now turn off the machine, or restart if you wish. On the Macintosh II the Shut Down command turns the machine off, and it is not necessary to press the ON/OFF button on the back of the machine.

- From the Special menu select the Shut Down option.
  - ▶ Some systems display the closing box seen in Figure C.10.
- Turn off printer or other peripherals, if necessary.

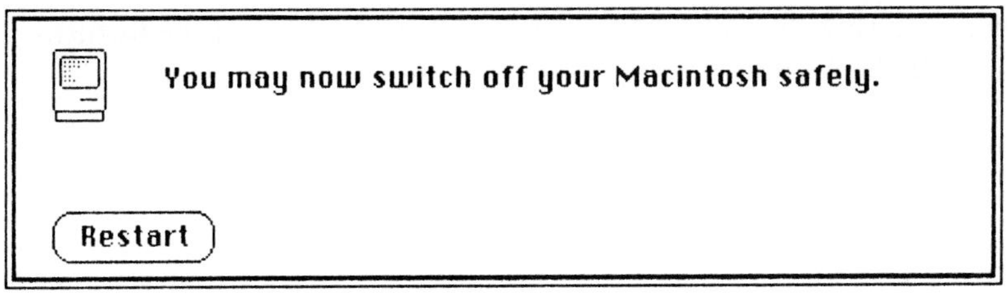

You may now switch off your Macintosh safely.

Restart

FIGURE C.10
Appearance of the closing display ensures safe shut-down of the system.

Chapter Facts

- The Apple Macintosh personal computer is usually attached to a keyboard, mouse, monitor, printer, hard disk drive, and diskette drive.
- System start-up procedures involve booting the operating system from the hard disk when the power is turned on.
- Floppy disk drives can be either internal or external.
- The graphical user interface uses a desktop metaphor to represent different computer operations as icons or menus.
- Items are removed from the desktop by dragging the associated icon over the trash icon.
- Icons and windows are repositioned on the desktop by using the mouse to drag them to a new screen location.
- A new diskette is automatically initialized (formatted) when it is inserted into the disk drive for the first time. Users respond to a series of dialog boxes to select alternatives and label the disk.
- Windows are identified by the name in the title bar.
- The dimensions of a window are altered by dragging the sizing box to a new screen location or by clicking on the zoom box.
- Clicking on the scroll arrows and dragging the scroll box to a new location within the scroll bar changes a window's view.
- Applications and related documents are organized into different file folders (subdirectories).
- New file folders can be created, renamed, and deleted at any time the Finder is active.
- Files are moved from one file folder to another by dragging the associated icon over the other folder. Files are copied from one disk to another in the same way.
- Selecting the Shut Down option from the Special menu turns off the computer.

Terms to Remember

a. clicking
b. desktop
c. dragging
d. external diskette drive
e. folder
f. internal diskette drive
g. menu bar
h. scroll arrow
i. scroll bar
j. scroll box
k. title bar

Mix and Match

Match the following definitions to the Terms to Remember.

1. ____ horizontal area that runs across the top of a window and displays menu titles.
2. ____ icon representing a group of related programs and data files.
3. ____ screen layout associated with graphical user interface that uses icons that represent documents, file folders, calculators, and other office tools.
4. ____ area that appears shaded on the right or lower edges of a window or list box when only a partial view is available.
5. ____ repositioning icon or window on the screen by pointing to it and holding down mouse button while moving pointer to a new screen location.
6. ____ found at either end of a scroll bar.
7. ____ square within a scroll bar that identifies which portion of the window or list box is currently being viewed.
8. ____ pressing the mouse button once to initiate action or to select a program option.
9. ____ disk drive built inside computer housing.
10. ____ horizontal area across the top of a window, which displays the window's name.
11. ____ disk drive connected to computer by attaching cable to I/O port.

Review Questions

1. What are the peripherals commonly used by a Macintosh personal computer system?
2. Describe the start-up procedure for a Macintosh computer system.
3. How do you move an icon around the desktop?
4. How is a new diskette initialized?
5. What is the maximum length of a disk icon label on the Macintosh desktop?
6. How are pull-down menus different from drop-down menus?
7. What are three ways to open a window?
8. What are two ways you can alter the size of a window?
9. How do you close an open window?
10. How are related programs and data files organized on the desktop?
11. Which menu and menu option creates a new file folder?
12. How would you rename a folder or icon?
13. What is the purpose of the Trash icon?
14. Which menu and menu option are used to make a copy of an object within a window?
15. How is an object moved from one window to another?
16. What is the procedure for shutting down the system?

Applying What You've Learned

1. Use the View menu to display applications and document names in a window like a table of contents, instead of as icons. Describe the procedure you would use. Which presentation format do you prefer? Explain your answer.
2. How could you duplicate all the files in one disk and drag them to another disk at the same time? (*Hint:* The answer involves using the keyboard.)
3. Describe how you would undelete a file placed in the trash. When would this undelete procedure not work?

4. A general rule for file management on disk is to make one file folder for related documents and another file folder for each application. For example, users are encouraged to create one folder for their word processing program and other folders for letters, reports, and so forth. Graphically illustrate how you would organize file folders on a hard disk. Assume you are using at least three different application packages.
5. If your computer system uses a color monitor, how would you change the color of the desktop? How would you change the highlight color for icon labels? What colors should not be used for the desktop? Explain your answer.

Answers to Mix and Match

1. g 2. e 3. b 4. i 5. c 6. h 7. j 8. a 9. f 10. k
11. d

Programming Personal Computers in BASIC

- **From the User's Point of View**
- **The Basics about BASIC**
  - Loading the BASIC interpreter
  - BASIC commands
  - Flowcharting simple problems
  - Listing and running BASIC programs
  - Saving and loading BASIC programs
- **Performing Computations**
  - Numeric constants
  - Variables
  - Arithmetic operators
  - Operation hierarchy and the use of parentheses
- **Repeating Program Instructions**
  - Infinite loop structure
  - Batch programs using READ and DATA statements
  - Using BASIC print zones for output headings
  - The TAB function and remark statement
- **Controlling Program Loops**
  - Loops with an exit
  - The IF. . .THEN statement
  - Column totals
  - Output formatting
- **Working with Text**
  - String input and output
  - Designing output
- **More on Loops**
  - Loops and the FOR. . .NEXT statement
  - Nested FOR. . .NEXT loops
- **Tying It All Together**
  - Defining requirements
  - Program design
  - Need for program documentation and clarity

FROM THE USER'S POINT OF VIEW

BASIC is a good first computer language for you to experience. It was developed at Dartmouth College in the mid-1960s for students with no programming background. In fact, the name BASIC is an acronym that stands for Beginners' All-purpose Symbolic Instruction Code. The language was designed with you in mind, and this presentation is for beginners. As you read through Appendix D, you will find out why BASIC is used to introduce beginners to programming.

To complete this appendix, you need access to an IBM or compatible personal computer that uses DOS. If you are not familiar with operating the computer, look at Appendix A. You will also need access to BASICA, Microsoft BASIC, or GWBASIC. This interpreter can be on either a hard disk or separate floppy. Third, you need a formatted disk to store programs. Commands or statements you should enter into the computer are printed in red.

THE BASICS ABOUT BASIC

BASIC is available for every personal computer. In fact, it was built into many of the early PCs. The program that translates your BASIC language instructions into binary values of the computer's machine language is often available in a ROM (Read-Only Memory) chip inside the personal computer. A more advanced BASIC version, called BASICA, is also available on the DOS disk. BASICA, GWBASIC, and other versions contain the additional instructions necessary for advanced programming.

BASIC is a good choice for the beginning programmer because it is extremely forgiving in syntax, compared with other languages. **Syntax** is the collection of rules for a language. The English language has many rules, such as capitalizing the first letter of a sentence and putting a period at the end. BASIC, also a language, has its own rules. But the rules in BASIC are fairly lenient in that you can leave spaces where you wish, you can indent lines if you like, and so forth.

Since BASIC was written for the beginning programming student, it provides error diagnostics to help you to locate and correct some, but not all, of the more common errors or bugs. Error diagnostics appear as **error messages** on the screen, often adjacent to the line containing the error.

Also, you will be able to make good use of some things you learned in algebra when you program in BASIC. You don't have to know quadratic formulas and polynomials; but you will use the concepts of constants and variables, setting up formulas, and working through a problem one step at a time.

Since most programmers start their problem solving by drawing a flowchart, using pseudocode, or making a hierarchy chart, you will also find that it is especially easy to get from these design tools to a working BASIC program.

One more thing about BASIC: It is a powerful language, but it is also easy, and it is fun! You will be coding, running, and understanding some fairly sophisticated BASIC programs very quickly.

Let's take a look at a copy of a correctly written BASIC program and run it.

```
LIST
10 PRINT "Enough talk! Let's code some programs!"
20 END
RUN
Enough talk! Let's code some programs!
Ok
```

What you see is a listing of the program, and the output it produced when it was RUN (executed).

Loading the BASIC Interpreter

Your PC should be booted and the DOS prompt should be displayed. The prompt will probably be A> if you boot from a DOS disk, or C> if you have a hard disk system. It is easy to load the BASIC interpreter. However, before you load BASIC, you will want to be sure you have a formatted data disk available on which you can store some programs. If you do not have a data disk, you should format one before you load BASIC (see Appendix A).

Now simply type: `BASICA` (or `GWBASIC` or the command provided by your instructor to load the BASIC interpreter). Press [Enter]. The BASIC language interpreter will be read into the memory of the computer from the diskette or the hard disk. When the program is loaded, you will see an opening screen with the product name and possibly a copyright message. Then you will notice the BASIC prompt:

```
Ok
```

This prompt is displayed whenever the BASIC interpreter is ready and waiting for instructions from you.

BASIC Commands

Most of the DOS commands mentioned in Appendix A will not work when you are in the BASIC language interpreter. BASIC has a unique set of **commands**, executed by the computer as soon as the command is entered. The following are the main BASIC commands you will need, each with a brief explanation.

CLS

If you type and enter **CLS** (CLear Screen), the screen will clear and the cursor will appear at the top left corner. Any program you have typed or read into the machine will remain in memory; only the screen is erased. (If you are at the keyboard of a PC as you read this, go ahead and try it!)

NEW

NEW command erases any program in memory that you have loaded or written but will *not* erase the BASIC language interpreter itself. This is a handy way to clear the computer's memory if you have finished working with one program and want to start on another, or if you just feel like starting over with the same program. NEW is the opposite of CLS. When NEW is used, the memory, not the screen, is cleared. (*Warning:* The NEW command can also erase a program you do want to keep, so be careful when using it.)

LIST

The **LIST** command causes all lines of the current program to appear on the screen. The latest version of each line is shown, and the program lines are displayed in line number order.

LLIST

The **LLIST** command works just like the LIST command, except that the program is output on an attached printer.

RUN

The **RUN** command causes the program currently in the memory of the computer to execute; that is, each instruction is translated and followed.

Other commands in BASIC related to saving and loading programs to and from a disk will be discussed later.

The line printed at the bottom of the screen of most computers when BASIC is used provides shortcuts for keying some of the commands listed above. To the left or along the top of the keyboard are 10 Function keys, labeled F1 through F10. Some keyboards have 12 Function keys, labeled F1 through F12. The bottom line of the screen refers to the special meanings assigned to those keys. You can LIST your program by keying in the letters L, I, S, and T, or you can just press [F1] instead. [F2] enters the RUN command. Notice the arrow to the right of RUN. This indicates that [F2] not only types the RUN command, but also enters it. [F3] and [F4] start the SAVE and LOAD commands that you will use in conjunction with your floppy disk. If you wish to turn off the display of function keys, enter **KEY OFF. KEY ON** will restore this line to the screen. Programmers usually memorize the meanings of [F1] through [F4] quickly, as they are the function keys most often used.

Flowcharting Simple Problems

Simple sequence problems closely follow the IPOS cycle upon which data processing is based. The programs accept input data that is either keyed into the keyboard or read from a data file on disk. The data is then processed and output as information, which is displayed on the screen, printed on paper, or stored in a disk file. Figure D.1 is a flowchart for a simple sequence program. This figure also illustrates some of the flowcharting symbols you will be using.

The flowchart in Figure D.1 relates to calculating college tuition as a function of the number of credit hours taken. The tuition is $43.75 per credit hour. The input is the number of hours, and the output is the total tuition. The processing involves multiplying the input hours by 43.75 to get the total tuition.

In Figure D.1 the same symbol, a parallelogram, is used to represent both input and output. To obtain the number of hours, the computer will pause and wait for you to enter the value from the keyboard. The parallelogram is also used to show that the tuition is output. When flowcharting, programmers usually note the source of the input (keyboard or disk) and where the output is going (screen or printer).

To start coding the BASIC program, the flowchart is used as a guide. The START symbol is not coded into BASIC; it serves only to show where the flowchart begins. A flowchart can be many pages long, so using START can be helpful. Each of the remaining symbols of the flowchart determines what type of BASIC statement will be used. BASIC **statements** are the instructions that make up a BASIC program. In Figure D.2 note that each BASIC statement has a number that starts each line. A blank space follows the line number and precedes the **keyword,** which specifies the command or action to be performed.

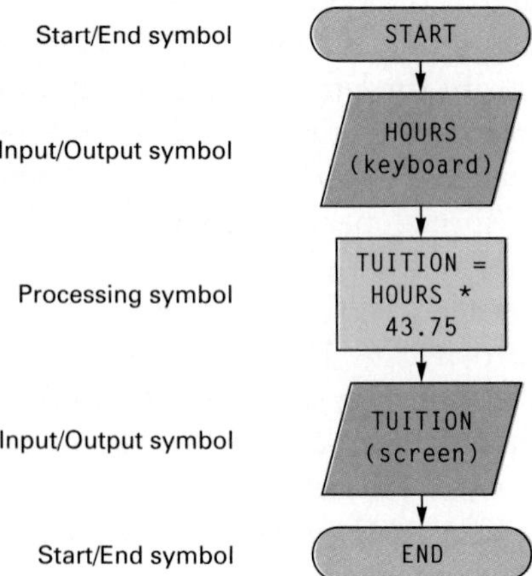

FIGURE D.1
A simple sequence structure illustrates the use of common flowcharting symbols.

```
10 INPUT HOURS
20 LET TUITION = HOURS * 43.75
30 PRINT TUITION
40 END
```

FIGURE D.2
BASIC code for simple program sequence flowcharted in Figure D.1.

BASIC statements are different from BASIC commands in two ways. BASIC statements have line numbers. When a statement is entered into the computer, the line number dictates where it is placed within a program. The statements in the program are not executed until the user types RUN. On the other hand, BASIC commands do not have line numbers and are executed immediately after they are entered.

An Input/Output flowcharting symbol that references the keyboard dictates the use of an **INPUT** statement. The INPUT statement accepts data from a keyboard. The rectangular process block indicates that a **LET** statement is to be used to perform arithmetic operations. The I/O symbol referencing the screen is represented by the **PRINT** statement. By using PRINT, output is displayed on the screen. Finally, the **END** statement speaks for itself, and is used at the very end of every program to stop execution. The combination of user input and rapid output makes this program interactive.

This program is keyed, one statement at a time, and [Enter] is pressed at the end of each line. If you detect an error in a line before the line has been entered, press the [Backspace] until you reach the place where the error occurred. Then type over the error. If an error is not detected until after you have depressed [Enter], the entire line can simply be retyped. When you re-enter a line, be sure to use the same line number, since BASIC retains the latest version of each line. Statements are usually numbered starting with 10, and incremented by 10, to allow room for later insertion of lines you may have forgotten, or to alter your program. This numbering plan is a programming custom but not a requirement of BASIC.

Spacing within a statement is mostly left up to the programmer. You must leave at least one space after the line number and at least one space after the keyword that begins each program statement. Other than that, spacing is entirely up to you. Most programmers like to leave a space on either side of an equal sign and the arithmetic operators (+, -, *, /). The BASIC interpreter is not particular about whether you key in letters in upper or lower case. Except for text that appears between double quotes, BASIC converts everything to capital letters.

Listing and Running BASIC Programs

After keying in the program in Figure D.2, correct any errors by either overstriking or keying in replacement lines. At this point it is usually a good idea to use the LIST command. This command will produce a display of your program on the screen, all sorted by line number, and in capital letters. Take one final look at the program to see if you can spot any errors. Errors can be corrected by simply typing over the incorrect statement.

To start program execution, type RUN, followed by pressing [Enter]. When the interpreter translates your INPUT statement, it will flash a question mark on the screen and wait for you to enter a data value. If you enter `15` and press [Enter], the program will cause `656.25` to be displayed. The `Ok` prompt is then displayed to indicate readiness for another instruction. Figure D.3 shows the whole session to this point.

Saving and Loading BASIC Programs

If you have a two-diskette system, you can save a copy of your program by placing the DOS disk into drive A and your data disk into drive B. The program will not be erased from memory by the save process. If you are using a one-diskette system, place your data disk into drive A.

You first need to think up a unique name for your program. BASIC program names follow the same naming conventions as DOS filenames. Program names begin with a letter and contain only letters, numbers, and hyphens. Program names should be eight or fewer characters long and may have up to a three-character extension. In BASIC always use the extension .BAS so that your BASIC program files stand out when the disk directory is listed. We will save the first program under the name TUITION1.BAS.

FIGURE D.3
List and run program that computes tuition payment.

```
LIST
10 INPUT HOURS
20 LET TUITION = HOURS * 43.75
30 PRINT TUITION
40 END
RUN
? 15
 656.25
Ok
```

The **SAVE** command, which transfers a copy of the program in memory to the program disk, is used as follows:

```
SAVE "A:TUITION1.BAS"
```

Either key in SAVE or use F3. The A: will save the program on the disk in drive A. Users of two-diskette systems can replace the A: with B:. If you leave off the A: or B: drive designation, your program will be saved on the disk in the default drive. The default drive was used to load DOS or the BASIC interpreter.

The **LOAD** command, which transfers a copy of a program from disk into the computer's memory, is as follows:

```
LOAD "A:TUITION1.BAS"
```

To illustrate the process, after saving your program, you could then erase the program from memory by entering a NEW command. If you LIST the program now, there will be nothing to list. Then use the LOAD command to bring a copy of the program in from the disk, and use the LIST command to display the program. Try it!

PERFORMING COMPUTATIONS

To understand how BASIC works, you need to learn a few rules. The INPUT, PRINT, and END statements are self-explanatory. The LET (computation) statement, however, is a little more involved. First, almost every version of BASIC allows you to omit the word LET, and most programmers choose to do so. A LET statement commonly consists of a variable name, an equal sign, and an expression. The expression may be a constant, an arithmetic formula, or a variable. Figure D.4 gives a few examples of valid LET statements.

In simple sequence programs the variables to the right of the equal sign will be those that were entered by the user or involved

```
20 LET PAY = HOURS * RATE
30 NEWQUAN = 354 + OLDQUAN
40 GRADE = ( T1 + T2 + T3 ) / 3
50 K = 2
60 TUITION = HOURS  *  43.75
```

FIGURE D.4
Examples of acceptable BASIC expressions with and without LET as a keyword.

in a formula. The variable on the left will be where the result (or answer) is stored. The value of this variable may eventually appear as output. For each statement in Figure D.4 you tell the computer to do the following:

1. Get the current values of those variables to the right of the equal sign from memory.
2. Perform the indicated mathematical operations on them.
3. Store the result in the variable to the left of the equal sign.

Numeric Constants

Everything to the right of the equal sign in a LET statement is considered part of the **expression.** An expression consists of constants and/or variables, and one or more arithmetic operators, such as addition, subtraction, division, and multiplication signs. Let's take a closer look at each component of a BASIC expression.

A whole number that does not have a decimal point is called an **integer constant.** It can be positive or negative with an optional plus sign if it is positive. Examples of integer constants would include your room number, the number of people in a bus, and the number of this page. Integer constants usually are used for counting. Note that your social security number and your phone number are *not* valid integer constants, since they usually are written with hyphens between the digits. Valid integer constants in most BASIC interpreters are from −32768 to +32767, inclusive.

A **fixed-point constant** has a decimal point. However, digits to the right of the decimal point are optional. Fixed-point constants can have up to seven digits of accuracy, and are either positive or negative. As with integer constants, the plus sign is optional. The computer doesn't understand some people-oriented symbols, so you cannot use commas, percent signs, or dollar signs within a fixed-point or integer constant.

Variables

Most versions of BASIC allow variable names to be up to 40 characters (letters and/or numbers) long. A **variable** is a name that you use to represent a data value so that the same instruction can be used for several different data values. For example, if you ran the program in Figure D.3 again and were to enter 17 instead of 15, the program coding itself wouldn't have to be changed, just the data value. The variable HOURS took on the value 15 the first time the program was run and the value 17 the second time.

```
PAY87          GROSSTODATE     NETPAY
TOTAL4         BOOKPRICE       GRADE
TUITION87                      COST
```

FIGURE D.5
Valid BASIC variable names.

This use of variables illustrates how a program is coded for the general case and then used for many data values. Variables usually are named so that you can easily tell what they represent. In other words, you can go ahead and name the variables in your program X or R2D2, but it would be difficult to understand this sort of program! Figure D.5 delineates a few valid variable names.

Arithmetic Operators

BASIC uses the same common arithmetic operators you use in math class. However, a few changes are necessary to be able to code complex formulas. Figure D.6 shows the most useful BASIC arithmetic operators. A few others are described in the BASIC user's manual for more advanced programming.

Figure D.7 shows how some fairly simple algebra equations would be converted into BASIC LET statements with these five arithmetic operators. Notice that, just as in algebra, parentheses are used to indicate that a particular operation is to be done first. Also note that most symbols, such as pi, have no BASIC equivalent, and a specific value (like 3.141593 for pi) must be used. In algebra, multiplication could be indicated with no operator at all. For example, 3(6) means multiply 3 times 6. In BASIC the asterisk *must* be used to show multiplication: 3 * 6.

Algebra	Meaning	BASIC	Examples	
+	Addition	+	A + B	C + 4
-	Subtract	-	E - 3.2	G - H
x or ·	Multiply	*	HOURS * 43.75	
/ or ÷	Division	/	K / 4.65	
X^2	Exponentiation	∧	X ∧ 2	

FIGURE D.6
Arithmetic operators used within BASIC expressions.

Algebra	BASIC
Grade $= \frac{T1 + T2 + T3}{3}$	10 GRADE = (T1 + T2 + T3) / 3
Area $= \pi r^2$	20 AREA = 3.141593 * R ∧ 2
Celsius $= \frac{5}{9}$ (Fahrenheit − 32)	30 C = 5/9 * (F − 32)

FIGURE D.7
Converting algebraic expressions into BASIC LET statements.

Operation Hierarchy and the Use of Parentheses

The third example in Figure D.7 may raise some questions: What about the parentheses? Are they necessary? Both pairs? The answers are not always easy or obvious. In fact, in this case the first pair of parentheses is not needed. But the second pair is, since if they were left off, the formula would be evaluated as

$$COST = \frac{5 * F}{4} * Q$$

not

$$COST = \frac{5 * F}{4 * Q}$$

These two statements would not produce the same result. It helps, then, to know how the computer will evaluate an expression, so as to determine if parentheses are needed. Figure D.8 shows the hierarchy of arithmetic operations, the order in which the operations are performed. Anything inside parentheses is evaluated first. If the parentheses are *nested* (within each other), the innermost pair is evaluated first. All exponentiations are evaluated next. All multiplication and division are done next, then all addition and subtraction.

In each expression, the BASIC interpreter scans the expression and performs common operations from left to right. Multiplication and division are grouped and performed together; so are addition and subtraction. As a result, in the expression 3 * 6 − 4 / 2 + 5, division and multiplication occur before addition and subtraction, to produce a result of 21.

```
1. Parentheses ... innermost first
2. Exponentiations
3. Multiplications and Divisions
4. Additions and Subtractions
```

FIGURE D.8
Hierarchy of arithmetic operations used by BASIC translator.

REPEATING PROGRAM INSTRUCTIONS

Glance at Figure D.3 again. If you were a college registrar, what suggestions would you have for improving the program? It would certainly be more useful to have a paper copy of the output. This is easily corrected by using an **LPRINT** statement. By using `30 LPRINT TUITION` you would get the output on paper, instead of on the screen.

Used in its present form, the program also has to be RUN for each student. Someone will have to sit at the computer, key and enter RUN (or press [F2]), wait for the question mark, and then enter one piece of data each time. Also, the output is not user friendly at all. It is just a long list of question marks, numbers, and the word RUN. So, you have no control over how the computer prints the answers. The output is delivered where the designers of BASIC decided the output should go, and not necessarily where you want it. In other words, BASIC contains defaults, or standard procedures the interpreter follows when a programmer does not provide other instructions.

Infinite Loop Structure

Figure D.9 compares the flowchart for the hours and tuition problem with a simple variation called an **infinite loop** structure. Obviously, the infinite loop structure gets its name from the fact that there is no easy way out of the loop. The loop is formed by inserting a **GOTO** statement just before the END statement. The GOTO statement (all one word in BASIC) transfers execution to another

FIGURE D.9
Comparison of flowcharts and program code between simple sequence and infinite loop structures.

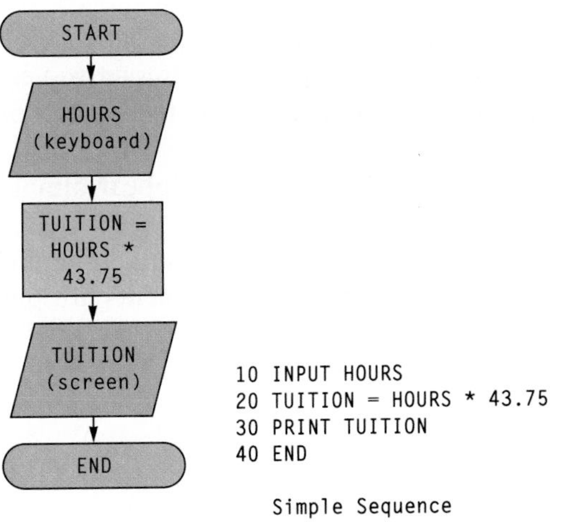

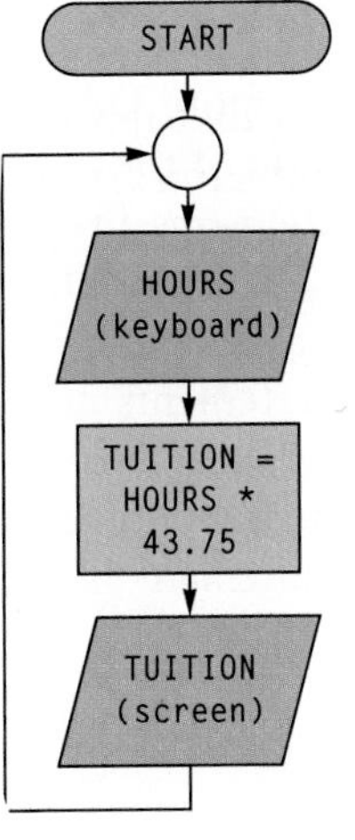


```
10 INPUT HOURS
20 TUITION = HOURS * 43.75
30 PRINT TUITION
40 GOTO 10
50 END
```

Infinite Loop

FIGURE D.10
Sample run of tuition program with infinite loop structure.

```
RUN
? 10
 437.5
? 15
 656.25
? 17
 743.75
?
```

line in the program. As the program is executed, the same group of code is repeated over and over, requesting a value for HOURS each time the INPUT statement is reached. This eliminates having to key RUN for each input value, but it doesn't eliminate having to sit in front of the PC, waiting for each of the question marks to show up. A run of this program would look something like Figure D.10.

What will stop the program iteration, short of pulling the computer's plug? You can stop the loop by breaking the circuit momentarily. Do this by holding down [Ctrl] and pressing [Break]. This will return the familiar `Ok` prompt.

Batch Programs Using READ and DATA Statements

This modification of the program doesn't address the need of the user to constantly input data through the keyboard. One solution is to supply all of the data needed within the program itself. In this way, when input is required, the data within the program is used and there is no waiting for a user's response. When data is input in a group or batch, the program is said to use batch processing.

To convert this program for batch processing, you replace the INPUT statement with a **READ** statement, and add the data in one or more **DATA** statements. Figure D.11 shows the interactive version of the infinite loop structure program, and the batch version of the same program.

The DATA statement in the batch program can appear almost anywhere in a BASIC program. Most programmers keep DATA statements near the READ statement if there is just a small amount of data. For larger amounts of data, the DATA statements are put at the end of the program, before the END statement. The DATA statement is a **nonexecutable statement,** which means that it per-

```
10 INPUT HOURS                  10 READ HOURS
20 TUITION = HOURS * 43.75      20 DATA 10, 15, 17
30 PRINT TUITION                30 TUITION = HOURS * 43.75
40 GOTO 10                      40 PRINT TUITION
50 END                          50 GOTO 10
                                60 END

    Interactive                       Batch
```

FIGURE D.11
Comparison of interactive and batch versions of an iteration (loop) structure using BASIC code.

forms no operations by itself. As a result, it is never the destination of a GOTO statement. A DATA statement doesn't do any calculating, or printing, or actual data input. It is a statement that holds data until needed by a READ statement. There can be several DATA statements in a program. You will see examples of this later.

When the batch version of the program in Figure D.11 is executed, no ? symbols appear. The program pulls the values for HOURS from the DATA statement as needed. Figure D.12 shows a run of this program. The user did not have to hit [Ctrl] + [Break]. The program quit when it ran out of data and displayed the error message `Out of DATA in 10`. A problem has crept into the picture: No longer can the user see what the data values are without LISTing the program. In the interactive mode the data values appear on the screen, right after the question marks. Now there is just a column of answers.

This problem can be corrected by **echo-printing** the data values. Echo-printing means that all input values are also displayed as output. Figure D.13 shows the program modified for echo-printing, together with the output produced. Note that, although the shaded column numbers are not printed on the paper or the screen, they are printed in the book so you can see where the output appears. The computer is placing things where BASIC wants to place them, according to the defaults written into BASIC by its designers.

```
RUN
 437.5
 656.25
 743.75
Out of DATA in 10
Ok
```

FIGURE D.12
The batch program using READ and DATA statements in Figure D.11 produces this output. The error message occurs when the READ statement in line 10 runs out of data stored in line 20.

```
10 READ HOURS
20 DATA 10, 15, 17
30 TUITION = HOURS * 43.75
40 PRINT HOURS, TUITION
50 GOTO 10
60 END

          1         2         3
12345678901234567890123456789012 etc.

 10            437.5
 15            656.25
 17            743.75
Out of DATA in 10
Ok
```

FIGURE D.13
Program is written to echo the input (hours) on same line as the output (tuition costs).

Using BASIC Print Zones for Output

If output is printed according to BASIC defaults, the computer is very predictable: numerical values are printed in **print zones** which run every 14 columns across the screen or page. Since there are 80 columns on the screen and printer using 8.5- by 11-inch paper, this means that five full print zones appear on a line. Partial print zones cannot be used, so there will be 10 columns left over on the right side. Figure D.14 shows the print zones on a screen.

Look carefully at Figure D.13 again. Notice that each number was left-justified within a 14-column print zone. The computer

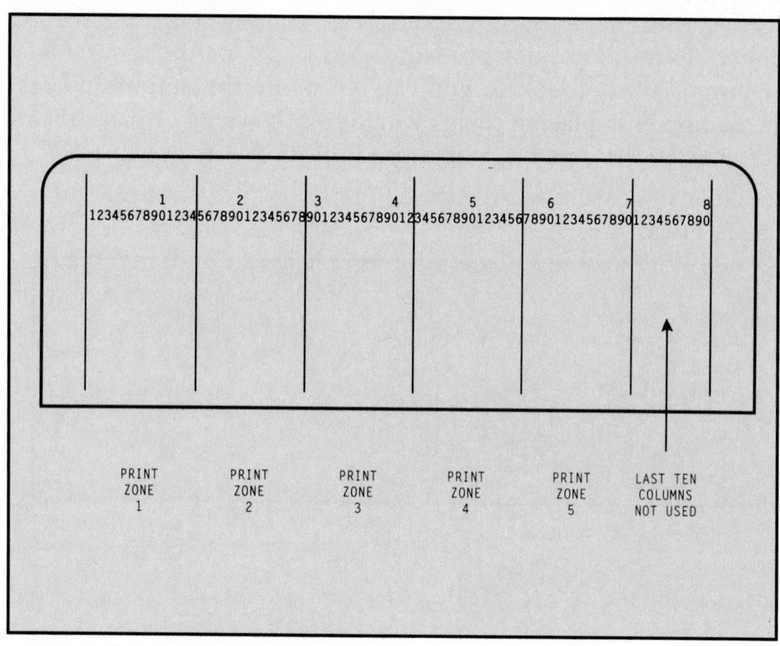

FIGURE D.14
Output from a BASIC program defaults to print zones spaced 14 columns apart.

```
10 READ HOURS
20 DATA 10, 15, 17
30 TUITION = HOURS * 43.75
40 PRINT HOURS; TUITION
50 GOTO 10
60 END

         1         2
1234567890123456789012 etc.

 10  437.50
 15  656.25
 17  743.75
Out of DATA in 10
Ok
```

FIGURE D.15
This program code is the same as that found in Figure D.13 except a semicolon separates HOURS and TUITION in line 40, not a comma. As a result, output data items are placed next to each other.

always allows a space for the sign of a number, whether it is printed or not. In the example, columns 1 and 15 are blank because all the numbers are positive.

Another possibility exists for spacing the output. If the comma between the output variables in line 40 of the program is replaced with a semicolon, the 14-column print zone rule is ignored, and the computer simply leaves one space (plus an extra space for the sign, if the value is positive) and then prints the next value. Figure D.15 shows the output with this modification of line 40. Compare this to the output in Figure D.13.

Headings

The output shown in Figure D.15 suggests that some of the problems associated with a simple sequence program used for the tuition computation are solved. Many data values can be put into DATA statements. The program will execute unattended. The output forms a table, composed of rows and columns, when echo-printing of the data is done. Tables are useful in presenting large quantities of output since the row-and-column format facilitates understanding.

One of the remaining problems is that the output is not really user friendly. This can be remedied by adding some headings to the table. Headings are easy to code in BASIC. All that needs to be done is to place the desired heading between a pair of double quotation marks in a PRINT statement. To illustrate, consider the examples in Figure D.16. Of course, the same examples could be output to the line printer if the PRINT in each line were changed to LPRINT.

Almost anything can be placed between the double quotes—letters (both upper and lower case), numbers, spaces, and symbols. The only symbol that cannot be used is, of course, a double quote. In each case the character immediately following the opening

FIGURE D.16
Headings add clarity to columns of numbers and make printed output easier to read.

```
10 PRINT "The number of hours is:"; HOURS
10 PRINT "The tuition equals"; TUITION
10 PRINT "For"; HOURS; " hours, pay $"; TUITION
10 PRINT "***    ABC Company    ***"
10 PRINT "I B M    Personal    Computer"
```

double quote is printed in the first column, the next character in the second column, and so on. Figure D.17 shows the example program with multiple headings added. A report title has been added, as well as some column headings. Note that a plain PRINT statement causes a blank line to be "printed." This output is certainly better than the original, but it can still be improved. The letterhead and report title could be centered, TUITION could have both decimal places printed and the `Out of DATA in 10` error message could be eliminated.

FIGURE D.17
The PRINT statements in lines 10–70 add a letterhead, title, and column headings to the tuition program.

```
10 PRINT "Whatsa-Matta-U"
20 PRINT "Anywhere USA"
30 PRINT
40 PRINT "Tuition Report"
50 PRINT
60 PRINT "HOURS", "TUITION"
70 PRINT
80 READ HOURS
90 DATA 10, 15, 17
100 TUITION = HOURS * 43.75
110 PRINT HOURS, TUITION
120 GOTO 80
130 END
RUN

         1         2
123456789012345678901234567 etc.

Whatsa-Matta-U
Anywhere USA

Tuition Report

HOURS         TUITION

 10            437.5
 15            656.25
 17            743.75
Out of DATA in 10
Ok
```

The TAB Function and Remark Statement

Headings are easily centered by using the TAB function in a PRINT statement. The **TAB function** doesn't automatically center the heading, it just positions the cursor or printhead at the column indicated. This action is similar to using tab keys on a typewriter. Figure D.18 illustrates the previous program with the TAB function added. Notice that the number following TAB is enclosed in parentheses. These numbers (4, 5, 4, and 15) were chosen so as to print the headings centered over the report.

The program in Figure D.19 shows two additional features. By using the hyphen within quotations in line 160, the column totals will look underlined. Any symbol could have been used; you are not limited to just the hyphen.

Figure D.19 also introduces the **REM** (for REMark) statement. REM is another nonexecutable statement, like the DATA statement. The computer skips REM statements, but they serve an important function. REM statements document the program and provide a place for the programmer to put in notes and blank lines for easier understanding of the code. For example, a REM statement could contain the name of the programmer, the date the code was written,

```
10 PRINT TAB(4); "Whatsa-Matta-U"
20 PRINT TAB(5); "Anywhere USA"
30 PRINT
40 PRINT TAB(4); "Tuition Report"
50 PRINT
60 PRINT "HOURS"; TAB(15); "TUITION"
70 PRINT
80 READ HOURS
90 DATA 10, 15, 17
100 TUITION = HOURS * 43.75
110 PRINT HOURS, TUITION
120 GOTO 80
130 END
RUN

         1         2
123456789012345678901234567 etc.

   Whatsa-Matta-U
    Anywhere USA

   Tuition Report

HOURS         TUITION

 10            437.5
 15            656.25
 17            743.75
Out of DATA in 10
Ok
```

FIGURE D.18
The TAB function found in lines 10, 20, 40, and 60 allows a programmer to override default print zones and place output in any column of the screen or paper.

```
10 REM  My Name          9/30/9x
20 REM
30 REM  Program to calculate tuition
40 REM   cost, as a function of no
50 REM   of hours.  Enter DATA in
60 REM   line 190.  Program is Inf.
70 REM   loop, so an 'Out of DATA'
80 REM   error will occur.
90 REM
100 PRINT TAB(4); "Whatsa-Matta-U"
110 PRINT TAB(5); "Anywhere USA"
120 PRINT
130 PRINT TAB(4); "Tuition Report"
140 PRINT
150 PRINT "HOURS"; TB(15); "TUITION"
160 PRINT "-----"; TAB(15); "-------"
170 PRINT
180 READ HOURS
190 DATA 10, 15, 17
200 TUITION = HOURS * 43.75
210 PRINT HOURS, TUITION
220 GOTO 180
230 END
```

FIGURE D.19
Column headings have been added to the program flowchart. The PRINT statement in line 160 outputs a series of hyphens to underline words printed in line 150. REM statements document the program.

what the program does, etc. Many schools require students to place certain information in REM statements, such as assignment number and section or class number.

Note that some of the REM statements, like lines 70 and 90, have no code to the right of REM. These lines just serve as a way to put blank lines within the code. They do not result in blank lines on the output. Any program can contain as many REM statements as the programmer thinks necessary. You may want to add several more within Figure D.19.

CONTROLLING PROGRAM LOOPS

So far our program has used the sequence and iteration program structures. Another type of BASIC command will help eliminate the Out of DATA message at the end of the output. This error is caused by lack of a logical exit for the loop.

Loops with an Exit

Loops with an exit contain the third program structure, selection. To exit a loop without an error statement, you will need to use the IF...THEN statement. This statement is different from other statements we have seen in that it uses two key words instead of one.

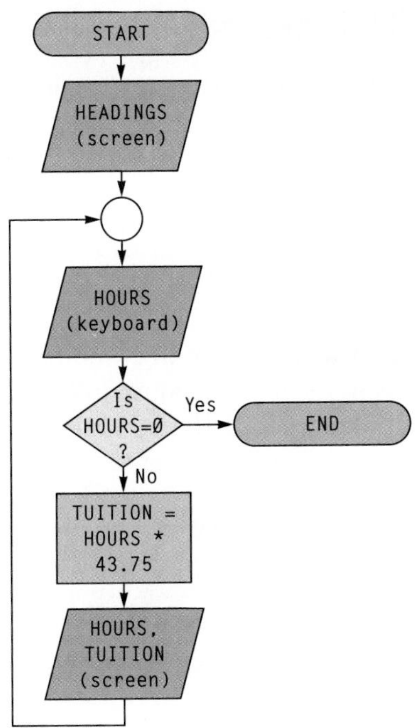

FIGURE D.20
Program flowchart of iteration (loop) structure with a logical exit and termination.

In a flowchart, the diamond-shaped symbol indicates use of an IF...THEN statement in the program. The flowchart in Figure D.20 is identical to the one in Figure D.9, except that the diamond-shaped decision symbol, together with the END block, has been added. Inside the decision symbol, a question is asked that can be answered only "Yes" or "No." Program control is transferred to different lines within the program, depending on the answer to the question.

In line 195 of Figure D.21 the question is whether *HOURS is equal to 0.* Note that if HOURS *is* equal to zero, then control passes to the END block in line 230. But if HOURS is *not* equal to zero, the program continues through the sequence to line 200.

```
180 READ HOURS
190 DATA 10, 15, 17, 0
195 IF HOURS = 0 THEN 230
200 TUITION = HOURS * 43.75
210 PRINT HOURS, TUITION
220 GOTO 180
230 END
```

FIGURE D.21
The IF ... THEN statement in line 195 provides a logical exit from the program loop when 0 hours is read from the DATA statement in line 190.

Why is HOURS being compared to a zero? This zero value in the decision block is called a **sentinel value,** or sometimes *trailer value.* It is a value chosen by the programmer that would never realistically appear in the DATA statements of the program. In the present case zero is chosen as the sentinel value since a student would not register for zero credit hours. Other possibilities for sentinel values in this program include any negative number, and possibly any positive number greater than 25 or so, depending upon the maximum credit hours a student is allowed to take. This sentinel value is placed at the end of the regular values in the DATA statement. Compare line 190, the old DATA statement in Figure D.19, with this new DATA statement used in Figure D.21:

```
190 DATA 10, 15, 17, 0
```

The IF . . . THEN Statement

This IF . . . THEN statement checks each value of HOURS that is READ to see if it is the sentinel value. The general form of the **IF . . . THEN** statement is:

```
line number  IF  logical expression  THEN  statement
```

The statement after THEN may use any executable BASIC statement. In special cases where a GOTO statement is needed, the GOTO can be left off and just the line number referenced. Otherwise a complete BASIC statement must follow the THEN. Figure D.22 shows several examples of IF . . . THEN statements.

FIGURE D.22

Programmers find a lot of versatility in the selection statement IF . . . THEN.

```
100 IF X = 0 THEN GOTO 940
100 IF HOURS > 40 THEN 800
100 IF EMPLNO < 99999 THEN 150
100 IF TIME >= 10 THEN PRINT "It's about time."
100 IF HOURS <= 40 THEN OVERTIME = 0
```

Notice that values can be tested for conditions other than equality. In the second example of Figure D.22, HOURS is being tested to see if it is greater than 40, and in the third example the *less than* symbol is being used. There are six **logical operators** used in BASIC programs. They are listed in Figure D.23.

With the sentinel value of zero having been added to line 190 of Figure D.21, the decision block for the program will have to be coded as follows:

```
195 IF HOURS = 0 THEN 230
```

If line 190 contained, say, a −1 instead of a 0 as the sentinel, then the affected two lines would be

```
190 DATA 10, 15, 17, -1
195 IF HOURS = -1 THEN 230
```

FIGURE D.23

Six logical operators are available for use within the IF . . . THEN statement.

```
= equal to
< less than
> greater than
<> not equal to
<= less than or equal to
>= greater than or equal to
```

Line 195 could also be coded as

```
195 IF HOURS < 0 THEN 230
```

The same output would be produced in either case. The choice of a sentinel value, and the way it is tested in the IF . . . THEN statement, are up to the programmer. Figure D.21 leaves off all of the REM statements and PRINT statements for the headings, showing just the processing loop and exit for the flowchart in Figure D.20.

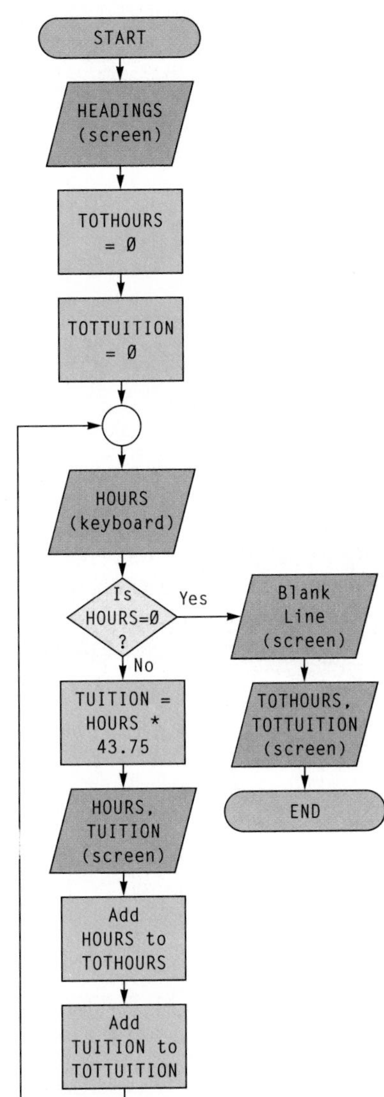

FIGURE D.24
Program logic to compute total hours and tuition costs has been added to the flowchart.

Column Totals

This program is an ideal situation to introduce another important concept in programming, maintaining totals. Since the output has two columns, HOURS and TUITION, it is desirable to keep a total for each column. Totals are accumulated on a computer just as on a calculator. First, the machine is cleared, or set to zero. Then each number is added to a running total when it is entered.

Since two totals are needed, one for HOURS and one for TUITION, the representative variables can be called TOTHOURS and TOTTUITION. Any valid BASIC names would do, but these suggest what the variable names represent.

Figure D.24 shows the flowchart for the program including keeping totals. As HOURS is read and TUITION is computed, each is added to its respective total within the loop. After the sentinel value has been detected, the totals are displayed on the screen. The two statements after the heading is displayed serve to initialize each of the totals to zero. Some versions of BASIC allow you to leave these statements out because all variables are set to zero automatically at the start of the program. However, good programming practice suggests that you always initialize your variables, as shown in this example.

Figure D.25 shows the program that results when the flowchart is coded. For the sake of brevity, the REMarks and the PRINT statements that print the report heading and title are not shown. The program segment in Figure D.25 picks up the program at line 150, where the column headings are printed.

Note how a few extra spaces indenting each of the statements in the loop (lines 270–320) make the loop easier to detect. Since spacing before the keyword is not dictated by BASIC, indentation can help to organize a complex program. REM statements have also been placed throughout the program to aid in documentation clarity.

Figure D.26 shows the output for the program in Figure D.25. Again, the report heading and title are not shown. The column headings are underlined and there is no error message. Also, some quick addition proves the totals to be correct. But the way in which

```
150 PRINT "HOURS"; TAB(15); "TUITION"
160 PRINT "-----"; TAB(15); "-------"
170 PRINT
180 REM
190 REM   ***   Initialize running totals   ***
200 REM
210 TOTHOURS = 0
220 TOTTUITION = 0
230 REM
240 REM   ***  IPO loop  ***
250 REM
260 READ HOURS
270   DATA 10, 15, 17, 0
280   IF HOURS = 0 THEN 370
290   TUITION = HOURS * 43.75
300   PRINT HOURS, TUITION
310   TOTHOURS = TOTHOURS + HOURS
320   TOTTUITION = TOTTUITION + TUITION
330 GOTO 260
340 REM
350 REM   ***   Print totals and END   ***
360 REM
370 PRINT
380 PRINT TOTHOURS, TOTTUITION
390 END
```

FIGURE D.25
This BASIC program follows the program logic outlined in Figure D.24 and illustrates column totals, REMark statements, and an indented loop.

the numbers are printed, which is left justified within the print zone, makes the output look incomplete. Figure D.27 shows what can happen when numbers of various lengths are printed in a left-justified format. This formatting can be corrected by altering the PRINT statements within the program.

Output Formatting

Left justification within a print zone is a BASIC default. This sort of output is not acceptable to most people. One way to override the default is to use the TAB function. Another technique involves a

```
           1         2
123456789012345678901234567 etc.

HOURS          TUITION
-----          -------

 10             437.5
 15             656.25
 17             743.75

 42             1837.5
Ok
```

FIGURE D.26
The BASIC program in Figure D.25 produces this screen output.

```
10 READ NUMBER
20 DATA .004, .0678, .12, 3.45, 67.89, 456.726
30 PRINT NUMBER
40 GOTO 10
50 END

         1         2
12345678901234567890123 etc.

 .004
 .0678
 .12
 3.45
 67.89
 456.726
Out of DATA in 10
Ok
```

FIGURE D.27
Sample program and associated output showing how output is left justified in a print zone.

modification of the PRINT statement called PRINT USING. To use PRINT USING, you must decide how you want the output to look and determine which value to be printed takes up the most columns. In the program of Figure D.27, the number 456.726 is the widest. Assume that the programmer intends to print all the data as dollars and cents, rounding off that value to the closest penny. That would output 456.726 as 456.73. The original PRINT statement in Figure D.27 is

```
30 PRINT NUMBER
```

If it is changed to

```
30 PRINT USING ''###.##''; NUMBER
```

The output then looks as follows:

```
         1         2
1234567890123456789012 etc.
   0.00
   0.07
   0.12
   3.45
  67.89
 456.73
```

Compare this output to that in Figure D.27 to see how the rounding was done and what columns were used for the output. Note that the computer put a leading zero in front of numbers with values of less than 1.00. Also, all the decimal points are lined up, and values have been rounded to two decimal places.

Referring back to the program in Figure D.25 and the output produced in Figure D.26, several lines will be changed to format the output. Given these changes:

```
300 PRINT USING "##            ###.##"; HOURS, TUITION
370 PRINT " --            -------"
380 PRINT USING " ##           ####.##"; TOTHOURS, TOTTUITION
```

Figure D.28 shows the new output.

```
         1         2
123456789012345678901234 etc.

HOURS            TUITION
-----            -------

 10               437.50
 15               656.25
 17               743.75
 --              -------
 42              1837.50
```

FIGURE D.28
Numeric output from PRINT USING "##   ###.##"; HOURS, TUITION.

APPLYING WHAT YOU'VE LEARNED

Each of the first three problems can be done in a variety of ways. The list below represents optional approaches. The problem assignments follow.

a. Simple interactive sequence program.

b. Simple sequence program using batch processing.

c. Infinite loop within an interactive program.

d. Infinite loop program using batch processing.

e. Same as *d* above, but add headings and echo-print all inputs. Don't use the TAB function for headings.

f. Same as *e* above, except use the TAB function to center all headings.

g. Same as *f* above, except use a sentinel to exit the loop.

Your instructor will suggest which of the above organizations to use for your particular assignment. If you are using these exercises for other than class assignments, it is suggested you work each of the problems, beginning with *a*. Then modify the program gradually through the *b* to *g* options. This will give you experience in the complete range of techniques delineated in the chapter thus far.

1. Code a BASIC program that will calculate the miles (or km) per gallon you get with your car or motorcycle. Input data would be the starting and ending odometer readings, and the number of gallons of gasoline necessary to fill the tank on the second visit to the gas station.

2. Code a BASIC program that will calculate the ending balance for your checking account. Input data would be your starting balance, the total deposits you make during the period, the totals of the checks that have cleared during the period, and the service charges (if any).

3. An instructor tells you that your grade in his/her course is a function of how well you do on the four semester exams. The first exam counts 10 percent of your grade, the second counts 20 percent, the third counts 30 percent, and the final exam counts 40 percent. All exam grades and the course grade you print out are on a scale of 0 through 100. Input will be a five-digit student number, plus the four exam grades for each student. Output will be all the exam scores and a final score. (*Hint:* The final grade will be 10 percent of the first grade, plus 20 percent of the second grade, plus 30 percent of the third grade, plus 40 percent of the final exam.)

4. Your class takes an exam. Each student received a numerical grade of 0 through 100. Code a BASIC program that will accept these grades, and calculate and print the class average. Your program should work for any number of students in a class and make use of a sentinel to exit the processing loop. You do not need a student number or name as data.

Now modify your program so that it not only calculates the class average, but also finds both the lowest and the highest grades, thereby allowing you to calculate and print the range. (*Hint:* Set the first grade equal to some variable, such as LET HIGHSCORE = GRADE. Then compare each grade to HIGHSCORE. If the new grade is > HIGHSCORE, let HIGHSCORE equal the new grade.)

5. You have a dilemma. You are studying in your room and are really hungry for a pizza. You look in the campus newspaper and notice a number of pizza shops with delivery service. You want to get the most pizza for your money and decide to code a BASIC program that will accept input data for a number of different shops. For each shop you collect data on the diameter of the pizza, the price, and the delivery charge. You decide to go with the one offering the lowest cost per square inch of pizza. Code a BASIC program that will produce a nice-looking table of your results. (*Hint:* The area of a circle in square inches is equal to pi times the square of the radius in inches. Give each pizza shop a number, not a name.)

WORKING WITH TEXT

The examples so far have used only numeric input and output values. While this might be sufficient for a limited number of applications, users want output tables to include non-numeric variables, such as names, streets, and states. Businesspeople require descriptions of products sold on invoices. Names of employees on checks, and even form letters full of text are written on the computer. It is relatively easy to work with such nonnumeric data, since BASIC is well suited for the task.

String Input and Output

String variables are variables that may contain any combination of text and numeric data. They are formed just like numeric variables, except that the variable name has a dollar sign ($) at the end. Here are some examples of valid string variables:

```
PERSON$          ITEM$          STATE$
STREET$          STUFF$         PRODUCT$
PRINTERTYPE$     FOODITEM$      BOOKTITLE$
```

To learn how to work with string variables, study Figure D.29 carefully. This shows the program listing and the output produced by a simple program that prints a list of some friends' telephone numbers. Lines 10 through 40 print simple headings and, of course, lines 50 through 80 form a loop-with-an-exit structure. When WHO$ takes on the value "last," the exit is made to the END. Note that the phone numbers also are treated as string data. This is because, although they contain digits, the hyphen in the middle would prevent them from being numeric values.

Of course, problems seldom are as simple as this. Figure D.30 shows the output produced by a program that processes information about the books owned by a student. Assume these are the texts for courses taken during a semester, and that the price the student can get for the book when it is sold back to the bookstore is 50 percent of the new book price. The PRINT USING statement will

```
10 PRINT TAB(3); "Telephone Numbers"
20 PRINT
30 PRINT TAB(2); "NAME"; TAB(16); "NUMBER"
40 PRINT
50 READ WHO$, NUMBER$
60   IF WHO$ = "last" THEN 99
70   PRINT WHO$, NUMBER$
80 GOTO 50
90 REM ***  Data values   ***
91 DATA "Erika", "123-4567"
92 DATA "Brian", "234-5678"
93 DATA "Suzie", "345-6789"
94 DATA "Frank", "456-7890"
95 DATA "last", "0"
99 END

         1         2
123456789012345678901234567 etc.

  Telephone Numbers

 NAME          NUMBER

Erika          123-4567
Brian          234-5678
Suzie          345-6789
Frank          456-7890
```

FIGURE D.29
This BASIC program is designed to process string variables in the form of names and telephone numbers.

be used for all numeric output, including the totals. Fairly simple headings and a report title will be included. However, REMarks won't be shown in an effort to keep the program listing a little shorter.

```
         1         2         3         4         5         6
1234567890123456789012345678901234567890123456789012345678901234567
                                 Ima Student

                          Textbooks for Fall '93

                                         New         Used
Author          Title          Course     Price       Price    Condition
------          -----          ------     -----       -----    ---------

Jones     Cemetery Design    CD-402      24.95       12.48      Good
Smith     Druid History      HS-512      19.50        9.75      Worn
Davis     Bookbinding        JR-315      14.68        7.34      Bad
Ames      Winemaking         CM-220      34.95       17.48      Terrible
Hening    Spectroscopy       PH-642      25.00       12.50      Shot!
                                         ------      -----
                                         119.08      59.54
                                         ======      =====
```

FIGURE D.30
Program output represents different types of string data. Associated program listing is shown in Figure D.31.

Designing Output

Frankly, the table in Figure D.30 was not produced by sitting at the keyboard and trying different spacing and TAB settings. It is much easier to plan the table on a sheet of graph paper or a print chart first. That way, the programmer can see what spacing looks best for the headings and the output lines. Also it saves a lot of time in coding and debugging the program.

Figure D.31 is a listing of the program that produced the table. When looking over the program, several things will become obvious. First, there are a lot of PRINT statements. This is typical. Normally, a very large portion of almost any program consists of PRINT statements. In the typical program you also would find that there are about as many REM statements as there are PRINT statements. Notice that the statements in the loop are indented to make the loop stand out from the remainder of the program. All in all,

```
10 PRINT TAB(26); "Ima Student"
20 PRINT
30 PRINT TAB(22); "Textbooks for Fall '93"
40 PRINT
50 PRINT
60 PRINT TAB(41); "New"; TAB(51) "Used"
70 PRINT "Author"; TAB(15); "Title"; TAB(28); "Course"; TAB(40);
   "Price"; TAB(50); "Price"; TAB(58); "Condition"
80 PRINT "------"; TAB(15); "-----"; TAB(28); "------"; TAB(40);
   "-----"; TAB(50); "-----"; TAB(58); "---------"
90 PRINT
100 READ AUTHOR$, TITLE$, COURSE$, NEWPRICE, CONDITION$
110    IF AUTHOR$ = "Done" THEN 200
120    USEDPRICE = NEWPRICE / 2
130    PRINT AUTHOR$; TAB(10); TITLE$; TAB(28); COURSE$;
140    PRINT TAB(40); USING "###.##"; NEWPRICE;
150    PRINT TAB(50); USING "###.##"; USEDPRICE;
160    PRINT TAB(60); CONDITION$
170    TOTNEWPRICE = TOTNEWPRICE + NEWPRICE
180    TOTUSEDPRICE = TOTUSEDPRICE + USEDPRICE
190 GOTO 100
200 PRINT TAB(39); "------"; TAB(49); "------";
210 PRINT TAB(39); USING "###.##"; TOTNEWPRICE;
220 PRINT TAB(49); USING "###.##"; TOTUSEDPRICE;
230 PRINT TAB(39); "======"; TAB(49); "======"
240 REM
701 DATA "Jones", "Cemetery Design", "CD-402", 24.95, "Good"
702 DATA "Smith", "Druid History", "HS-512", 19.50, "Worn"
703 DATA "Davis", "Bookbinding", "JR-315", 14.68, "Bad"
704 DATA "Ames", "Winemaking", "CM-220", 34.95, "Terrible"
705 DATA "Hening", "Spectroscopy", "PH-642", 25.00, "Shot!"
706 DATA "Done", "0", "0", 0, "0"
999 END
```

FIGURE D.31
String and numeric data in lines 701–706 are read and processed by this BASIC program to create output shown in Figure D.30.

the structure of the program is very similar to that of the tuition program developed earlier.

Several features, however, of Figure D.31 require further comment. Lines 10 through 50 print report titles. The TAB functions were determined by laying out the table output on sheets of graph paper. Lines 60 through 90 print the column titles. The titles are two-line titles, underlined as indicated by line 80. Notice that statements 70 and 80 each take up two lines of the listing of the program. Actually, BASIC statements can be up to 255 characters long, and since a line of the screen is only 80 characters, word wrap is used to create additional lines. In other words, when entering a long line, just keep typing without pressing [Enter] until the whole line is entered. Then press [Enter].

Lines 100 through 190 form the main processing loop of the program. Note that four of the five variables are string variables, but NEWPRICE does not need the "$" since it will contain numerical values. The sentinel value is the string "Done," checked for in line 110.

Lines 130 through 160 print a single line of output. Four lines of code are used for a couple of reasons. First, the PRINT statement would have been very long if it had been put on one line. This long statement would have been difficult to edit and correct if errors had been found in it. To connect all four lines of the PRINT statement, a semicolon (;) is put at the end of each line included in the statement except the last. This semicolon keeps the cursor on the same output line instead of returning it to column 1 of the next line.

Lines 170 and 180 increment the totals TOTNEWPRICE and TOTUSEDPRICE with the current values of NEWPRICE and USEDPRICE. Line 200 underlines the columns of data values, and lines 210 and 220 print the totals. Note the semicolon at the end of line 210 to keep the cursor on the same output line so that the other total can be printed. Line 230 prints a double underline below the totals, and, of course, the END follows.

The DATA statements in lines 701 through 705 are similar to previous examples, but note carefully that there are no double quotes around the NEWPRICE. This variable contains numeric values and not strings. In line 706 dummy values must be included for the four variables in the READ statement other than the AUTHOR$ variable, although AUTHOR$ is used for the sentinel. These dummy values in the DATA statement supply a value to each variable READ in line 100. This is done because if any of the dummy values were missing, an `Out of DATA` message would stop program execution.

MORE ON LOOPS

ssume you would like to print the years 1994 through 2000 in a column down the screen. Of course, one way that this could be done is to code the following:

```
10 READ YEAR
20 DATA 1994, 1995, 1996, 1997, 1998, 1999, 2000
30 PRINT YEAR
40 IF YEAR = 2000 THEN 60
50 GOTO 10
60 END
```

This program would accomplish the task, but if the program was modified so that you need a listing of 100 years, keying all of those numbers in DATA statements would be time consuming and error prone.

Loops and the FOR . . . NEXT Statement

Consider, instead, the following way of accomplishing the task:

```
10 YEAR = 1994
20 PRINT YEAR
30 IF YEAR = 2000 THEN 60
40    YEAR = YEAR + 1
50 GOTO 20
60 END
```

With this coding, it doesn't matter how many values you want printed. The number of statements in the program remains the same. All you need to do is change the final year in line 30.

BASIC has an even easier way to accomplish the same task. Compare the following coding with the previous program listing.

```
10 FOR YEAR = 1994 TO 2000
20    PRINT YEAR
30 NEXT YEAR
40 END
```

The output produced by the two programs is identical. Lines 10 through 30 of the second program comprise a **FOR . . . NEXT** loop. FOR . . . NEXT loops are merely shortcuts for more cumbersome coding. In this FOR . . . NEXT loop the interpreter sets YEAR equal to the first value, 1994. YEAR is incremented by 1 every time it reaches the NEXT YEAR statement. At this point execution is returned to the FOR statement, and the value of YEAR is compared to the last acceptable value, which is 2000 in this example. If YEAR is not greater than 2000, program execution proceeds to the next line. However, if YEAR is larger than 2000, program execution skips over the loop and continues to the line after the NEXT statement.

FOR . . . NEXT loops make it easy to do one or more operations a specified number of times. The program even can be interactive, with the user providing INPUT for the starting and stopping year numbers. Note that when you enter more than one value after the ? printed by the INPUT statement, the data values must be separated by a comma, or a comma and a space.

```
10 PRINT "Key starting and stopping years,"
20 PRINT " separated by a comma, and then"
30 PRINT " press the (ENTER) key."
40 INPUT STARTYEAR, ENDYEAR
50 FOR YEAR = STARTYEAR TO ENDYEAR
60   PRINT YEAR
70 NEXT YEAR
80 END
```

The use of the FOR . . . NEXT loop is illustrated further with the following problem. Assume you are a teacher facing a big stack of examinations to grade. Each is a 50-question multiple-choice exam, with each question worth two points. You would like to make up a table with the number of questions missed in the first column and the grade, on a 0–100 scale, in the second. Figure D.32 shows "no-frills" coding and partial output. Of course, the program could have been expanded with PRINT USING statements, headings, and so forth, but the intention here is to discuss the logic of loops and the FOR . . . NEXT statement.

Some of these same ideas can be used to build a table showing the gross income a student would make in a part-time job. Assume the job pays $4.37 per hour and the student works a different number of hours each week, from 1 to 40 hours. Figure D.33 leaves out the headings to show a bare bones listing and part of the output.

```
10 FOR MISSED = 0 TO 50
20   SCORE = 100 - (MISSED * 2 )
30   PRINT MISSED, SCORE
40 NEXT MISSED
50 END
RUN
 0                        100
 1                        98
 2                        96
===========================
 49                       2
 50                       0
Ok
```

FIGURE D.32
A grading table for a 50-question quiz is computed and printed within the FOR . . . NEXT loop in lines 10–40.

```
10 FOR HOURS = 1 TO 40
20   PAY = HOURS * 4.37
30   PRINT HOURS, PAY
40 NEXT HOURS
50 END
RUN
 1           4.37
 2           8.74
 3           13.11
=====================
 39          170.43
 40          174.80
Ok
```

FIGURE D.33
The FOR . . . NEXT loop in lines 10–40 contains code that figures hourly pay rates for people working 1 to 40 hours at $4.37 an hour.

Here again, the output could be improved considerably by adding headings and changing line 30 to include a PRINT USING clause. The following statement would work well:

```
30 PRINT USING "##       ###.##"; HOURS, PAY
```

Most business problems that utilize tables and lists such as pay, interest, and deposits can make good use of the BASIC language FOR . . . NEXT statement. In these applications the computer is simply being asked to do error-free counting.

Nested FOR . . . NEXT Loops

As you may have guessed, it is possible to have loops inside of loops, just as it is possible to have sets of parentheses inside other parentheses in BASIC LET statements. Some problems lend themselves nicely to this sort of application of the nested FOR . . . NEXT loop.

For example, suppose you decide to open a savings account at the bank with a $10.00 deposit. Each month you will add $10.00 to your account. The bank pays an interest rate of 6 percent annually and that compounding is done on the last day of each month. Therefore, you will be making 0.5 percent per month (0.005). For simplicity, assume you opened the account on January 1, 1990, and you would like to know how much money you will have in the account on December 31, 1997. You realize that you will have seven years, each with 12 months, or a total of 84 months of deposits and interest, so you could code the program as shown in Figure D.34. This method requires you to figure out how many months are in the period in which you will be earning interest and making deposits.

```
10 DEPOSIT = 10
20 FOR MONTH = 1 TO 84
30   DEPOSIT = DEPOSIT * 1.005
40   DEPOSIT = DEPOSIT + 10.00
50 NEXT MONTH
60 PRINT "Value on Dec. 31st, 1997 = $"; DEPOSIT
70 END
```

FIGURE D.34
A FOR ... NEXT loop is used to compute savings over 84 months at 6% per year.

Consider the coding in Figure D.35, where nested FOR ... NEXT loops are used. The programs in both Figure D.34 and Figure D.35 produce the same output, $1055.94. Indenting of some of the statements is entirely up to the programmer. However, when using two loops, the indenting makes it easy to see what statements are associated with which loops.

```
10 DEPOSIT = 10.00
20 FOR YEAR = 1990 TO 1997
30   FOR MONTH = 1 TO 12
40     DEPOSIT = DEPOSIT * 1.005
50     DEPOSIT = DEPOSIT + 10.00
60   NEXT MONTH
70 NEXT YEAR
80 PRINT "Value on Dec. 31st, 1997 = $"; DEPOSIT
90 END
```

FIGURE D.35
This program compounds interest by using a nested FOR ... NEXT loop.

To illustrate the use of nested FOR ... NEXT loops further, consider another problem. Assume your young sister is at an age where she will soon be learning multiplication tables. You want to print up such a table to assist her. You decide that a 10 by 10 table will do nicely, so you code the program in Figure D.36. Again, the REM statements are omitted. But this time you have to use PRINT USING, or the table would not have straight columns. Also, the loops are indented for clarity in reading the program.

```
10 PRINT TAB(5);
20 FOR HEADING = 1 TO 10
30    PRINT USING "###      "; HEADING;
40 NEXT HEADING
50 PRINT
60 FOR SYMBOL = 1 TO 61
70    PRINT "-";
80 NEXT SYMBOL
90 PRINT
100 FOR ROW = 1 TO 10
110    PRINT USING "## "; ROW;
120    FOR COL = 1 TO 10
130       NUMBER = ROW * COL
140       PRINT USING "###      "; NUMBER;
150    NEXT COL
160    PRINT
170 NEXT ROW
180 END
RUN
```

```
          1         2         3         4         5         6
1234567890123456789012345678901234567890123456789012345678901234567890 etc.
```

```
       1      2      3      4      5      6      7      8      9     10
-------------------------------------------------------------
  1 |  1      2      3      4      5      6      7      8      9     10
  2 |  2      4      6      8     10     12     14     16     18     20
  3 |  3      6      9     12     15     18     21     24     27     30
  4 |  4      8     12
  5 |  5     10
=============================================================
 10 | 10     20     30     40     50     60     70     80     90    100
Ok
```

FIGURE D.36
BASIC program to print multiplication tables from 1 * 1 to 10 * 10.

A few elements of Figure D.36 require some clarification. Lines 20 through 40 display the top heading line, using a FOR . . . NEXT loop to generate the numbers 1 through 10. Lines 60 through 80 use another loop to repeat the "-" symbol across the screen. While ROW = 1 in line 100, the column takes on all 10 of the values from 1 to 10 in the loop between lines 120 and 150. Since you want those 10 numbers all printed on one line, a semicolon is put at the end of the PRINT USING statement in line 140. That semicolon keeps the cursor on the same output line, ready to print the next number. After all 10 numbers have been printed on a line, you want to print the next 10 values on a different line. The plain PRINT statement in line 160 returns the cursor to the beginning of the next line, to get ready to print a new line of the table. Line 110 generates the column of numbers (1–10) on the far left of the table.

Notice it is possible to get 10 numbers on each line, instead of the five that would have been the maximum if the standard 14-column print zones had been used. Since the largest number in the table is 100, the PRINT USING statement in line 140 includes three ###

symbols. Furthermore, there are three blank spaces inside the double quotes. These three blanks produce the spacing between the numbers in the body of the resulting table.

Experiment with this program by keying it into your personal computer. Change the row and column limits in lines 100 and 120 and alter the USING clause in line 140. You will also be able to see first-hand what would happen if the final semicolon were to be eliminated from the PRINT USING statement.

TYING IT ALL TOGETHER

This section closes with an example that not only uses a FOR . . . NEXT loop, but also most of the other BASIC programming concepts discussed, such as totals, string I/O, PRINT USING, the TAB function, headings, and underlining. Assume you are a college freshperson, sitting with your parents and planning what you can reasonably expect your expenses will be for your next three years in college. Assume that you have kept track of your major expenses for your first year, and they totaled \$10,000.00, broken down as follows:

Tuition	\$5,500.00
Room	1,500.00
Board	2,000.00
Books	800.00
Fees	200.00

Defining Requirements

You estimate that inflation will cause all five categories of expense to go up 7 percent per year. In other words, your tuition for your sophomore year will be 107 percent of your freshman year tuition, your junior year tuition will be 107 percent of your sophomore year amount, etc. The other categories of expenses will increase in a similar manner. You want to know not only what the expenses will be for each of the next three years, taking into account the 7 percent per year inflation, but also what the total expenses will be for each year. You also want to know the totals for each of the five categories for all four years, and the grand total for all five categories of expense over the full four-year period. This is a tall order, but it turns out to be a reasonably easy program to code. The most time-

```
Expenses     Fresh.    Soph.     Junior    Senior    Total
--------     -------   -------   -------   -------   -------

Tuition      5500.00   5885.00   6296.95   6737.74  24419.69
Room         1500.00   1605.00   1717.35   1837.56   6695.91
Board        2000.00   2140.00   2289.80   2450.09   8879.89
Books         800.00    856.00    915.92    980.03   3551.95
Fees          200.00    214.00    228.98    245.01    887.99
             --------  --------  -------   -------   --------
            10000.00  10700.00  11449.00  12250.43  44399.43
            ========  ========  ========  ========  ========
```

FIGURE D.37
College expenses output produced by programs listed in Figure D.38 and Figure D.39.

consuming job turns out to be designing what the output should look like. Look first at Figure D.37, which shows the desired output of the program. As usual, the report title, date, and such are omitted for simplicity.

Program Design

Figure D.38 is a listing of the program that produced the output of Figure D.37. The comments that follow are intended to help you study this program. Keep in mind that some of the coding, indentation, and placement of REM statements are based on programmer preference. Also, it is important to note that many of the techniques used in this program make the program easier to modify should future changes be needed.

Fifteen of the 48 statements in the program are REM statements. This documentation is useful in segmenting the program into shorter modules. Lines 40 and 50 print simple headings. The TAB function has been used here, but some programmers might prefer to use one long string for each line, handling the spacing with spaces between the words, like this:

```
40 PRINT "Expense   Fresh.   Soph.   Junior   Senior"
```

Lines 100 through 140 initialize the five totals that are used. Most versions of BASIC automatically set all variables equal to zero when program execution begins, so these statements are not absolutely required. However, many programmers choose to include them, since they seem to enhance understanding of the program by others. Note that spacing has been adjusted in the statements to make all columns align properly for ease in reading. Many versions of BASIC allow multiple statements on a line, and the five statements could all have been put on one line by separating each statement with a colon. To do this, you would remove lines 110 through 140 and rekey line 100 as

```
10 REM
20 REM   ***   Print Headings   ***
30 REM
40 PRINT "Expenses"; TAB(15); "Fresh."; TAB(25); "Soph."; TAB(35);
         "Junior"; TAB(45); "Senior"; TAB(55); "Total"
50 PRINT "--------"; TAB(13); "------"; TAB(24); "-----"; TAB(35);
         "------"; TAB(45); "------"; TAB(55); "-----"
60 PRINT
70 REM
80 REM   ***   Initialize Totals   ***
90 REM
100 TFRESH  = 0
110 TSOPH   = 0
120 TJUNIOR = 0
130 TSENIOR = 0
140 GRAND   = 0
150 REM
160 REM   ***   Main Processing Loop   ***
170 REM
180 FOR ROW = 1 TO 5
190   READ EXPENSE$, FRESH
200   PRINT EXPENSE$; TAB(11);
210   SOPH   = FRESH  * 1.1
220   JUNIOR = SOPH   * 1.1
230   SENIOR = JUNIOR * 1.1
240   TOTAL = FRESH + SOPH + JUNIOR + SENIOR
250   PRINT USING "#####.##  "; FRESH, SOPH, JUNIOR, SENIOR, TOTAL
260   TFRESH  = TFRESH  + FRESH
270   TSOPH   = TSOPH   + SOPH
280   TJUNIOR = TJUNIOR + JUNIOR
290   TSENIOR = TSENIOR + SENIOR
300   GRAND   = GRAND   + TOTAL
310 NEXT ROW
320 REM
330 REM   ***   Print Totals   ***
340 REM
350 PRINT TAB(13) "--------  --------  --------  --------  --------"
360 PRINT TAB(13);
370 PRINT USING "#####.##  "; TFRESH, TSOPH, TJUNIOR, TSENIOR;
380 PRINT USING "#####.##"; GRAND
390 PRINT TAB(13) "========  ========  ========  ========  ========"
400 REM
410 REM   ***   Data Values   ***
420 REM
430   DATA "Tuition", 5500
440   DATA "Room   ", 1500
450   DATA "Board  ", 2000
460   DATA "Books  ",  800
470   DATA "Fees   ",  200
480 END
```

FIGURE D.38
BASIC program to compute college expenses over four years. Note the use of REM statements for documentation.

```
100 TFRESH = 0: TSOPH = 0: TJUNIOR = 0: TSENIOR = 0:
GRAND = 0
```

The main processing loop does not include anything new. The DATA statements have been put at the end of the program to make the main loop easier to read. Since the length of EXPENSE$ can vary, line 200 uses the TAB function to get each line over to column 11 after EXPENSE$ is printed. Lines 210 through 230 calculate the last three years of expense, and line 240 calculates the total of the four years. The PRINT USING in line 250 utilizes the same format for each of the five numbers to be printed: three blank spaces followed by a six-digit number, rounded to two decimal places. Lines 260 through 300 increment the appropriate totals. The main processing loop consists of five iterations, after which the totals are printed in lines 350 through 390. These statements produce some underlining, and you will want to pay particular attention to how the spacing is accomplished.

Of course, the program is not complete until a PRINT statement has been added to print a report title. You may also want to add PRINT statements for the date and a note to inform the report user that 7 percent inflation rate per year is assumed. Also, the program might be modified so that more (or fewer) expense categories can be used. This could be done easily by altering the terminal value in the FOR statement in line 180. A better way might be to insert an INPUT statement somewhere above the main processing loop and ask the user to key the number of expense items into a variable. The variable would then take the place of the 5 in line 180. You could also make data entry interactive by changing the READ in line 190 to INPUT and eliminating the DATA statements. You are urged to try some or all of these suggested modifications at the keyboard of your personal computer. Feel free, too, to try different PRINT USING spacings, headings, and data.

Need for Program Documentation and Clarity

Now that you have studied the output in Figure D.37 and the program that produced it in Figure D.38, look carefully at Figure D.39. You needn't key this program into a computer unless you would like to do so. Both programs will produce *exactly* the same output. The program in Figure D.39 uses single-letter variables that are not meaningful to anyone but the programmer. No REM statements have been included, and whenever possible, multiple statements have been put on a single line. Although Figure D.39 may involve less typing, it would be a very difficult program to modify and debug, especially if you were not the original programmer. Clarity of code is as important as correct output for a useful program.

This introduction to BASIC covers a fairly large portion of the language. You can write some powerful programs with this material and produce some nice-looking tables and reports. Try your own programs and/or modifications of those you have reviewed.

Virtually any bookstore or library will have many books on the BASIC language, should you have the desire and the opportunity to further your study. Don't fail to check into the BASIC manual that came with your DOS or BASIC disk. While most of these manuals

```
1 PRINT "Expenses      Fresh.    Soph.     Junior    Senior    Total"
2 PRINT "--------     --------  --------  --------  --------  -----"
:PRINT
3 DATA Tuition,5500,Room,1500,Board,2000,Books,800,Fees,200
4 FOR R=1 TO 5:READ E$,A:PRINT
E$;TAB(11);:B=A*1.07:C=B*1.07:D=C*1.07:T=A+B+C+D
5 PRINT USING"#####.##  ";A,B,C,D,T:TA=TA+A:TB=TB+B:TC=TC+
C:TD=TD+D:G=G+T
6 NEXT R
7 PRINT TAB(13);"--------  --------  --------  --------  --------"
:PRINT TAB(13);
8 PRINT USING"#####.##  ";TA,TB,TC,TD,G
9 PRINT TAB(13);"========  ========  ========  ========  ========"
:END
```

FIGURE D.39
This abbreviated program accomplishes the same task as the program in Figure D.37, but it is harder to read and therefore harder to modify.

are mainly for reference, you now know enough about the language to enable you to read them and to understand BASIC statements and commands not covered here.

One of the things you will find in a more extensive treatment of BASIC is that many more functions are available. You can find the sine, the square root, the tangent, the logarithm, and more, and can program your own functions. BASIC even has a function for generating random numbers. You will also want to see how to use subroutines in your programs. Subroutines are handy when it is necessary to have the program use an identical sequence of instructions at more than one place in the program. Instead of coding the sequence of instructions over and over, control can be transferred to a single subroutine each time.

BASIC also includes a large number of functions for the manipulation of strings. These functions join strings, select one or more characters or symbols from either end or the middle of a string, and count the number of characters in a string.

Also you can read about how to write BASIC programs that will sort long lists of data items. Be on the lookout for instructions that will allow you to build and work with data files stored on disks.

Finally, you are bound to find references to some of the newer versions of BASIC that support structured programming. You will see such functions as WHILE . . . WEND loops, IF . . . THEN . . . ELSE statements, DO . . . UNTIL and DO . . . WHILE loops, and other techniques that give the BASIC programmer many of the advantages of structured programming concepts. The possibilities are endless.

Chapter Facts

- BASIC was designed for beginning programmers from all backgrounds and fields of interest.
- Many PCs come with ROM BASIC. More advanced BASIC, like BASICA or GWBASIC, is diskette-based.
- BASIC statements have line numbers and are not executed until the program is RUN. BASIC commands have no line numbers and are executed immediately.
- To correct an error on a line you have not entered, backspace to get to the error and type over it. If the instruction has been entered, the entire statement must be retyped.
- Spacing in a BASIC statement is optional except between a line number and a keyword. Line numbers usually start at 10 in increments of 10 for ease in modifying.
- When the INPUT statement is executed, a question mark is displayed to indicate the computer is waiting for instructions or data.
- BASIC programs are named using the same conventions as DOS files. Filenames should include a .BAS extension.
- Numeric constants contain only plus/minus signs, numbers, and decimal points.
- Hierarchy and use of parentheses is similar to mathematics. Order of hierarchy: 1) parentheses, innermost set first; 2) exponentiation; 3) multiplication and division, left to right; and 4) addition and subtraction, left to right.
- Infinite loops can be formed using GOTO statements. The user must stop the program run to break the loop.
- Batch programs can use READ/DATA statements to embed the data within the program itself. Interactive programs include INPUT statements.
- Unless combined with a USING clause, the PRINT and LPRINT statements will display a data value within a single print zone, with a 14-column default.
- Within a PRINT or LPRINT statement, semicolons display data values next to each other, while a comma prints each data value within a separate print zone.
- Each IF . . . THEN statement compares values and variables using one of the logical operators =, <>, <, <=, >, or >=.
- Using an IF . . . THEN statement with a sentinel value in a DATA statement provides a logical exit for a loop.

- Textual data is stored in string variables. Every string variable name ends in a question mark.
- A semicolon at the end of a PRINT statement causes the cursor to remain on the same line for the next output.
- Multiple INPUT values can be entered on the same line if data values are separated by a comma or a comma and a space.
- FOR . . . NEXT statements create a program loop. Nested FOR . . . NEXT statements allow loops to be executed within other loops. The inner loop is completed before the outer loop.
- More than one BASIC statement can be placed on a line if each statement is separated from the next by a colon.
- Proper program documentation consists of using meaningful variable names, having single statements per line, and including sufficient REM statements to allow easy reading, documentation, and debugging of a program.

Terms to Remember

a. command
b. echo-printing
c. error message
d. expression
e. fixed-point constant
f. infinite loop
g. integer constant
h. keyword
i. logical operator
j. nonexecutable statement
k. print zone
l. sentinel value
m. statement
n. string variable
o. syntax
p. TAB function
q. variable

BASIC Commands

r. CLS
s. KEY OFF
t. KEY ON
u. LIST
v. LLIST
w. LOAD
x. NEW
y. RUN
z. SAVE

BASIC Statements

aa. DATA
bb. END
cc. FOR . . . NEXT
dd. GOTO
ee. IF . . . THEN
ff. INPUT
gg. LET
hh. LPRINT
ii. PRINT
jj. READ
kk. REM

Mix and Match

Match the following definitions to the Terms to Remember.

1. ____ statement that displays values of indicated variables on the screen.
2. ____ command that turns on the function key line at bottom of screen.
3. ____ statements used to perform actions based on the value of a given condition.
4. ____ an instruction, with a line number, that is executed only when the program is run.
5. ____ displaying on screen what has been input by the user.
6. ____ clears the screen display without affecting the program in memory.
7. ____ statement that allows user to enter data from a keyboard that is identified by given variable names.
8. ____ symbol indicating which logical operation is to be used in a BASIC IF . . . THEN statement.
9. ____ command that turns off the function key line at bottom of screen.
10. ____ variable that identifies character data.
11. ____ statement that transfers control of the computer to another program statement.
12. ____ instruction immediately executed by the computer after it is entered.
13. ____ command that clears the computer's memory.
14. ____ statement that stops execution; it is usually the last program statement.
15. ____ a number with no decimal places or decimal point.
16. ____ statement that performs arithmetic operations.
17. ____ a division of the screen or paper into 14-column sections used with BASIC output.
18. ____ command that outputs statements on the screen.
19. ____ the end-of-file mark tested for in an IF . . . THEN statement.
20. ____ command that instructs computer to execute program instructions currently in memory.
21. ____ listing of program bugs or mistakes in running an application package.

22. ____ a name that represents a changeable data value under control of a computer program.
23. ____ statement that assigns values in a DATA statement to corresponding variable names.
24. ____ action represented by BASIC command or statement.
25. ____ command that outputs statements on a printer.
26. ____ statement that displays output on a printer.
27. ____ all symbols and numbers to the right of the equal sign in a LET statement.
28. ____ statement containing data for READ statement.
29. ____ the grammar or rules of a programming language.
30. ____ nonexecutable statement that contains programmer's notes; helpful for internal documentation of programs.
31. ____ program instruction that is ignored by the computer.
32. ____ command that copies program in memory onto disk.
33. ____ a number with a decimal point and decimal places.
34. ____ used in PRINT and LPRINT statements. It forces the cursor or print head to start at the specified column.
35. ____ a series of instructions within a computer program that are repeated continuously without exit.
36. ____ statements that surround a block of statements to be repeated a set number of times.
37. ____ command to copy a program from disk into memory.

Review Questions

1. What procedure do you use to load the BASIC translator into the computer's memory?
2. How are BASIC statements different from BASIC commands?
3. What are the flowcharting symbols for start, input, processing, decision, output, and end?
4. How do you correct an error before and after a program instruction is entered into memory?
5. Why are the line numbers in a BASIC program usually incremented by 10?
6. Where must a space be inserted in a BASIC statement?
7. What does the computer display on the screen when it is waiting for the user to input data?
8. What are the rules for naming a BASIC program?

9. Identify which characters are acceptable for numeric constants and which characters are not acceptable.
10. How long can a variable name be?
11. How are parentheses used in a BASIC expression?
12. What is the hierarchy of arithmetic operations in BASIC?
13. How can a user get out of an infinite loop?
14. What are the default print zones in BASIC?
15. How is the output different when semicolons are used instead of commas to separate items in a BASIC PRINT statement?
16. How are headings created as output from a BASIC program?
17. What criterion is used to select a sentinel (trailer) value?
18. What are the six logical operators used in BASIC IF . . . THEN statements?
19. Explain how totals are accumulated and at what point in the program execution they are usually printed.
20. What distinguishes a string variable name from a numeric variable name?
21. Why do programmers use graph paper or a print chart to design a report before writing the program?
22. How long (number of characters) can a BASIC statement be?
23. What happens when a semicolon is placed at the end of a PRINT statement?
24. What distinguishes a string value from a numeric value?
25. How do you separate multiple INPUT values entered on the same line?
26. What are nested FOR . . . NEXT loops?
27. How can a programmer place more than one BASIC statement on the same line?
28. Why would a programmer want to place each statement on its own line and include REM statements?

Applying What You've Learned

The first three exercises use string input/output to produce a report. Your report, in each case, should include appropriate title and carefully centered headings, PRINT USING output of all numeric values, totals for all columns where they are appropriate, and full documentation in the form of REMark statements.

1. Code a BASIC program to produce a listing of the birthdays of your friends. Input consists of name and date.

2. You have been needing a new car and you have been collecting information. You have listed the make, model, year, and price for each car. You also have collected data on the down payment and the number and amount of the monthly payments. Code a BASIC program to display this information, as well as the difference between the price of the car and the sum of the monthly payments plus the down payment.
3. Code a BASIC program that will input information about the courses a student takes. This would vary from one to seven or eight, depending on your school. Input data would include course title, number of credit hours, day(s) it meets, time of the class meeting, building designation, and room number. Your output report should include student name and social security number, all of the other input listed above, and the total number of course hours taken.

The next set of exercises uses FOR . . . NEXT statements.

4. You have a part-time job with hours varying from a low of 10 hours per week to a high of 25 hours per week. Code a BASIC program that will INPUT your rate of pay per hour, and produce a table showing your gross income for the number of hours worked, from 10 to 25 in quarter-hour intervals.
5. Code a BASIC program, using nested FOR . . . NEXT loops that will produce a calendar for the current month. Then modify your program so that it can handle *any* month for which the number of days in the month, and the day on which the first of the month falls, are INPUT.
6. Code a BASIC program that will produce a temperature-conversion table, for all temperatures between freezing and boiling, in both the Fahrenheit and Celsius scales. Your program should ask the user if an F-to-C conversion table, or a C-to-F conversion table, is desired. Use PRINT USING statements, rounding to a tenth of a degree.
7. Code a BASIC program for a kilometers-to-miles or a miles-to-kilometers table, depending upon the wishes of the user. Your table should run from 1 to 100 kilometers or miles and include appropriate headings. Output should be printed with the PRINT USING statement, rounded to tenths.

Answers to Mix and Match

1. ii 2. t 3. ee 4. m 5. b 6. r 7. ff 8. i 9. s 10. n
11. dd 12. a 13. x 14. bb 15. g 16. gg 17. k 18. u
19. l 20. y 21. c 22. q 23. jj 24. h 25. v 26. hh
27. d 28. aa 29. o 30. kk 31. j 32. z 33. e 34. p
35. f 36. cc 37. w

E

Buying a Personal Computer System

- From the User's Point of View
- Needs Analysis
  - Budgets and used computers
  - Application packages
  - User interface
- Hardware Requirements
  - Input
  - Output
  - Storage
  - Expansion slots
  - Configuration
- Complete System Requirements

FROM THE USER'S POINT OF VIEW

Buying a personal computer is like ordering from a large menu. There is a lot from which to choose. Some of the items you don't want; other items you can't afford. Despite the myriad of options for both hardware and software components, the driving force behind choosing a personal computer system is your present and anticipated computing needs. This is the first priority, tempered by an eye on your budget.

You are about to discover that purchasing a computer system is not different than making any other major purchase. Appendix E is designed to help you organize your thoughts, structure your decisions, and ultimately define the computer system that will best satisfy your needs and budget.

NEEDS ANALYSIS

As discussed in Chapter 13, defining system requirements and evaluating alternatives are the first steps in acquiring a new computer system. Deciding on how you want to use a computer sets in motion a search for suitable application packages. Once selected, related software requirements determine minimum hardware specifications. To start, ask yourself some simple questions:

- Do I work primarily with words, numbers, sound, and/or images?
- Will the computer be used at home? school? work?
- Will others be using this system besides myself?
- Who will be using the output from this computer system?
- What things will a computer system let me do that I cannot do now?
- How much can I reasonably afford to pay for a personal computer system?

Budgets and Used Computers

Your budget plays a critical role in this process. Keep in mind that the system includes software, cables, new diskettes, and other items in addition to the hardware. To be realistic, the process of purchasing a personal computer changes drastically if your budget for a basic system is under $1,000. In this situation, consider purchasing a used computer system. Local newspapers and bulletin boards often advertise used personal computer systems.

Advantages to purchasing a used computer:

- best possible price
- software usually is included in the purchase
- you can thoroughly test the system and try the software before purchasing

Disadvantages to purchasing a used computer:

- older technology may not support new application packages
- older technology may not support new peripheral hardware
- increased chance of system failure because of previous usage
- no warranty
- not all of your needs may be met with the system

Much of the decision making discussed in this appendix is reduced when buying a used system. Software and peripheral hardware usually come bundled with it, so you are purchasing a complete package. Computer stores often bundle application packages and system software with a new computer system for the same reason. It makes purchasing a new computer system less intimidating because many of the decisions are already made.

However, personal computer systems can be easily customized to your personal needs with just a little time and effort. What you need to know is covered in this book. Take your time, have fun exploring alternatives, and take comfort in the fact that a computer will help you become more productive.

What follows is a close examination of how to purchase a new computer system when software is not automatically bundled with the hardware. When establishing your budget, you should set aside as much money for software and initial supplies as you do for hardware.

Application Packages

Along the side of Figure E.1 are some of the most common reasons people purchase a personal computer system. The list at the top of the figure contains the types of software packages that may best fit the job. We have rated these packages based on the computing resources each application requires. This rating system is explained in more detail later.

After deciding how you would use a new computer system, you can take a closer look at the computer programs that handle these tasks. To keep things manageable, select the three most important applications and focus on evaluating software that supports these

APPLICATIONS	SOFTWARE							
	Word Processing*	Desktop Publishing	Writing Analyzer	Grammar Checker	Electronic Spreadsheet	Database Management	Presentation Software	Free-drawing Graphics
Writing								
letters and journals	A		A	A				
books and articles	A	C	A	A				
reports and research papers	A	C	A	A		B		
music								
Editing home videos								
Creating brochures newsletters, ads, etc.	A	C	A	A				C
Presentations and speeches	A		A	A	A		B	C
Personal planning address book, calendar, etc.						A		
Personal Finances checkbook balancing, retirement planning, etc.					A			
Personal recordkeeping hobbies, home inventories, etc.	A				A	B		
Social organization or club recordkeeping	A				B	B		
Small business accounting	A		A		B	B		
Small business inventory and order entry					B	B		
Mailing lists	A					B		

*Includes spell checker and thesaurus

A—minimum system B—standard system C—power system

FIGURE E.1
This chart is designed to help you identify personal computer applications and related software packages that will help make you more productive.

APPLICATIONS	SOFTWARE Word Processing*	Desktop Publishing	Writing Analyzer	Grammar Checker	Electronic Spreadsheet	Database Management	Presentation Software	Free-drawing Graphics
Data analysis math, science, business homework					B			
Entertainment								C
Education training, self-improvement, etc.	A	B	A	A		B	B	
Research and information retrieval						B	B	
Interactive shopping								
Graphic arts posters, maps, etc.	A					B	C	C
Graphic design house plans, landscaping, etc.						B	C	
E-mail	A			A				
Fax	A			A				
Programming	A							C
Genealogy	A	B				B		
Computer systems management								

*Includes spell checker and thesaurus

A—minimum system B—standard system C—power system

APPLICATIONS	SOFTWARE Computer-aided Design	Sound Editor	Video Editor	Desktop TSR	Project Management	Statistical Package	Games	Data Communication	Disk Optimization	Data Compression
Writing										
letters and journals										
books and articles										
reports and research papers					B	B				
music		B								
Editing home videos		B	C							
Creating brochures newsletters, ads, etc.					B					
Presentations and speeches		B	C							
Personal planning address book, calendar, etc.				A	B					
Personal Finances checkbook balancing, retirement planning, etc.				A						
Personal recordkeeping hobbies, home inventories, etc.				A						
Social organization or club recordkeeping										
Small business accounting					B					
Small business inventory and order entry					B			A		
Mailing lists								A		

A—minimum system B—standard system C—power system

APPLICATIONS	SOFTWARE: Computer-aided Design	Sound Editor	Video Editor	Desktop TSR	Project Management	Statistical Package	Games	Data Communication	Disk Optimization	Data Compression
Data analysis math, science, business homework						B		A		
Entertainment							A	A		
Education training, self-improvement, etc.		C	C	A	B			A		
Research and information retrieval								A		
Interactive shopping								A		
Graphic arts posters, maps, etc.		C	C		C			A		
Graphic design house plans, landscaping, etc.	C				C	B		A		
E-mail								A		A
Fax								A		A
Programming				A	B					
Genealogy				A				A		
Computer systems management									A	A

A—minimum system B—standard system C—power system

applications. As mentioned in Chapter 3, the best way to get started is by asking friends about how they use their computer systems and by reading software reviews in magazines. Compatibility with software used at school or work is another issue to consider. Finally, try different programs at stores, in a class, or using a friend's PC. Personal experience is the best way to decide on which software packages you like.

In turn, these applications packages work with a specific operating system and hardware. Once you select a personal mix of application packages, the search becomes a little easier because you can now identify a specific operating system and the hardware manufacturers among which to compare prices. This appendix will focus the discussion on the two most popular types of personal computer systems, IBM/compatible and Apple Macintosh.

CONVENTIONAL WISDOM
(When Purchasing a Personal Computer System)

1. Never underbuy. It is usually more expensive and always more aggravating to upgrade your computer system.
2. Graphical user interfaces like Windows and Mac-OS are easier to learn than command-driven interfaces like MS-DOS and PC-DOS.
3. Memory and hard disk requirements never go down. Always buy more than is strictly necessary.
4. Buy the best machine/human interfaces you can afford. This includes the highest-quality color monitor and most comfortable keyboard and pointing device. These peripherals make the system easier and more comfortable to use. The easier it is to use, the more you will use it.
5. Slow disk access makes you wait as often as a slow processor.
6. Buy reputable brands from a reputable source. A one-year on-site warranty does you no good if the company is out of business.
7. Buy the best you can afford and don't look back. Sooner or later (probably sooner) your system will be sold for less than you paid for it.
8. Don't wait until the prices are the lowest they will ever be. You will never buy a computer!

FIGURE E.2
No matter what hardware and software people use, most personal computer users would agree with these basic assumptions.

User Interface

Conventional wisdom (see Figure E.2) supports the premise that new computer users are best served by a graphical user interface (GUI). As a result, your selection of application packages will have you working with one of two operating environments: either a Macintosh using Mac-OS or IBM/compatible running Microsoft's Windows/DOS.

HARDWARE REQUIREMENTS

Many hardware options are available when using either operating environment. The resource ratings in Figure E.1 will help you quantify three hardware variables: processor, memory, and hard disk capacity. Memory and minimum hard disk requirements are determined by the software package. A resource rating of A requires a minimum hardware configuration. A rating of B requires additional resources in the form of a faster processor, more memory, and larger hard disk capacity. A software package rating of C requires state-of-the-art capacities in all three areas.

The table in Figure E.3 will help you decide on the processor, memory, and hard disk that would fit your requirements. The system requirements are as follows:

	Processor (megahertz MHz)	Memory (megabytes MB)	Hard Disk Space (megabytes MB)
* Minimum system:			
IBM/compatible	80486SX @ 25+ MHz	4+ MB	120+ MB
Macintosh	68030 @ 16+ MHz	4+ MB	80+ MB
* Standard system:			
IBM/compatible	80486DX @ 33+ MHz	8+ MB	240+ MB
Macintosh	68030 @ 33+ MHz	8+ MB	160+ MB
* Power system:			
IBM/compatible	80586 @ 66+ MHz (Pentium)	16+ MB	600+ MB
Macintosh	68040 @ 33+ MHz	16+ MB	600+ MB

Use these as general guidelines only. Microprocessor specifications, for instance, are constantly changing. Your future software needs, using multitasking requiring several packages, and having the ability to connect to a network may change processing and storage requirements. A more detailed description of processors and memory is in Chapter 8. Hard disks are discussed in Chapter 10.

FIGURE E.3
The number of application packages a person uses, along with the demand these packages make on system resources, helps users determine the type of microprocessor, memory, and hard disk capacity of their new personal computer system.

Input

For many applications a keyboard, monitor, and printer will suffice as the input/output hardware. Figure E.4 lists additional hardware to consider based upon the applications you want. Notice that in some cases you have a choice. For example, choosing a mouse versus

System Requirements for Processor, Memory, and Hard Disk

Resource Ratings From Figure E.1	Fewer than 6 Applications	6 to 12 Applications	More than 12 Applications
no C ratings	minimum	standard	standard
1 to 3 ratings of B and C	standard	standard	power
more than 3 ratings of B and C	power	power	power

APPLICATIONS	Keyboard	Mouse or Trackball	Scanner	PERIPHERALS Tablet or Digitizer	Joystick	Pen	Color Monitor	Monochrome Monitor
Writing								
letters and journals	X	X				X		X
books and articles	X	X						X
reports and research papers	X	X	X					X
music	X	X						X
Editing home videos	X	X			X		X	
Creating brochures newsletters, ads, etc.	X	X	X				X	
Presentations and speeches	X	X	X		X		X	
Personal planning address book, calendar, etc.	X	X						X
Personal Finances checkbook balancing, retirement planning, etc.	X	X				X		X
Personal recordkeeping hobbies, home inventories, etc.	X	X						X
Social organization or club recordkeeping	X	X						X
Small business accounting	X	X						X
Small business inventory and order entry	X		X			X		X
Mailing lists	X							X

FIGURE E.4
A keyboard, printer, and monitor are basic requirements for any personal computer system. This chart will help you identify other peripherals to consider adding to a shopping list based on your personal mix of application packages.

APPLICATIONS	PERIPHERALS Keyboard	Mouse or Trackball	Scanner	Tablet or Digitizer	Joystick	Pen	Color Monitor	Monochrome Monitor
Data analysis math, science, business homework	X	X				X		X
Entertainment	X	X			X	X	X	
Education training, self-improvement, etc.	X	X	X			X	X	
Research and information retrieval	X	X	X			X	X	
Interactive shopping	X	X				X	X	
Graphic arts posters, maps, etc.	X	X	X	X		X	X	
Graphic design house plans, landscaping, etc.	X	X	X	X			X	
E-mail	X					X		X
Fax	X		X					X
Programming	X	X					X	
Genealogy	X	X	X			X		X
Computer systems management	X	X					X	

APPLICATIONS	PERIPHERALS Printer	Plotter	Sound Card	Microphone	Video Recorder	Speakers	Modem	Fax	CD-ROM	Tape
Writing										
letters and journals	X									
books and articles	X							X		
reports and research papers	X						X	X	X	
music	X		X	X		X				
Editing home videos			X	X	X	X			X	
Creating brochures newsletters, ads, etc.	X							X		
Presentations and speeches	X		X	X	X	X			X	
Personal planning address book, calendar, etc.	X							X		
Personal Finances checkbook balancing, retirement planning, etc.	X						X	X		
Personal recordkeeping hobbies, home inventories, etc.	X									
Social organization or club recordkeeping	X						X	X		
Small business accounting	X						X	X		
Small business inventory and order entry	X						X	X		
Mailing lists	X									

APPLICATIONS	PERIPHERALS Printer	Plotter	Sound Card	Microphone	Video Recorder	Speakers	Modem	Fax	CD-ROM	Tape
Data analysis math, science, business homework	X	X					X			
Entertainment			X			X			X	
Education training, self-improvement, etc.	X		X	X	X	X	X		X	
Research and information retrieval	X						X		X	
Interactive shopping	X		X			X	X			
Graphic arts posters, maps, etc.	X	X							X	
Graphic design house plans, landscaping, etc.	X	X			X		X	X	X	
E-mail	X						X			
Fax	X						X	X		
Programming	X									
Genealogy	X						X	X		
Computer systems management										X

a trackball for doing graphic art work is a matter of personal preference. Some keyboards are designed to "click" as each key is pressed. Others are designed to be as quiet as possible.

Output

Picking a printer depends upon several factors. In Figure E.5, suggestions as to printer type are based on cost, printing speed, and quality of print. Color printers are also available at a premium price.

When choosing a monitor, the first decision is whether to buy one with a monochrome or color display. Figure E.4 has a checkbox that identifies those applications requiring color monitors and those where a monochrome monitor is sufficient. Conventional wisdom says buy the highest-quality color monitor you can afford because color screens are easier on the eyes, and most applications are designed to be used with color monitors. Many computer users think monochrome monitors should be seriously considered an option only when purchasing a portable computer.

While most personal computers have built-in speakers and limited sound capabilities, these speakers are often inadequate for music or multimedia applications. If high fidelity sound is important to you, then seriously considered adding a sound card to the system specifications.

Printer Comparisons

	Dot-matrix	Ink-jet	Laser
Cost – inexpensive	X		
– moderate		X	
– most expensive			X
Speed – slower than 3 pages/minute	X	X	
– 3 pages or more/minute			X
Print Quality – draft quality	X		
– letter quality		X	X

FIGURE E.5
Print quality, speed, and cost are all factored into purchasing a new printer. The fastest printers with the highest-quality output cost the most. Slower printers with draft-quality output are the least expensive.

Storage

Other important decisions relate to the size, storage capacity, access speed, and number of disk drives your system will have. For all practical purposes, the current generation of application software requires access to a hard disk. At least one diskette (floppy disk) drive is also needed to transfer data and programs to the hard disk and for backup. Access time is important when comparing disk drives of similar size and capacity. As you might expect, faster is better and usually more expensive.

Most software packages for IBM/compatible systems have diskettes available in both 5.25″ and 3.5″ sizes. However, the smaller diskette is emerging as a standard. Macintosh computers already routinely use 3.5″ diskettes. Unless you use other computers with disks of varying sizes, most users need only one diskette drive. If you will be transferring data to other IBM/compatible computer systems with different disk drive sizes, consider one drive of each size (see Figure E.6). Review Chapter 10 if you have questions about diskettes and floppy disk drives.

Tape drives provide a fast and an inexpensive way to backup data and program files stored on a hard disk. This type of storage hardware easily fits under the disk drives of most desktop systems. External tape drives are available when needed. The same is true with CD-ROM drives. As multimedia applications become more prevalent, users should seriously consider adding CD-ROM capabilities to their system. Currently, multimedia PC specifications include a CD-ROM drive.

FIGURE E.6
Every personal computer system needs at least one diskette (floppy disk) drive for transferring data and programs between systems. Users look at compatibility and storage issues to decide on the number of drives, along with the disk size and storage capacity.

Diskette Storage Capacity and Size

Single density	(no longer used)
Double density, 3.5"	720 KB
Double density, 5.25"	360 KB
High density, 3.5"	1.44 MB
High density, 5.25"	1.2 MB

Diskette Size

3.5"	Available for all new software packages. Standard on all Macintosh computers.
5.25"	Still available for most software packages. Was standard for IBM/compatibles a few years ago.

Number of Diskette Drives

one	Sufficient for most users if system has enough hard disk space and compatibility is not an issue.
two drives	One of each size. Many people with different needs will be using system.
two drives	Both of same size. Multiple copies of diskettes need to be made from other diskettes.

Expansion Slots

Conventional wisdom says never underbuy because it is more expensive and aggravating to upgrade later (see Figure E.2). Make sure you have enough expansion slots to add that sound card, modem, or CD-ROM drive when you need it. Your best bet is to have several open expansion slots still available when you purchase your new system. In other words, after you have accounted for all your current and foreseeable needs, you should still have room to add a few more expansion boards.

Configuration

The configuration, or arrangement, of the computer system depends on your need for portability and available work space. The flowchart in Figure E.7 can help you determine which size and arrangement of the processing hardware will work best for you. Remember, portable computers are more expensive, easier to steal, and rely on batteries that need recharging after a few hours of operation. They also have smaller keyboards and screens. While these keyboard and screen limitations are acceptable when traveling, long-term usage can place a physical strain on the user. Consider purchasing a full-size keyboard and monitor for use when the portable computer is not "on the road." You will need to make sure the portable computer has additional ports to handle an extra keyboard and monitor.

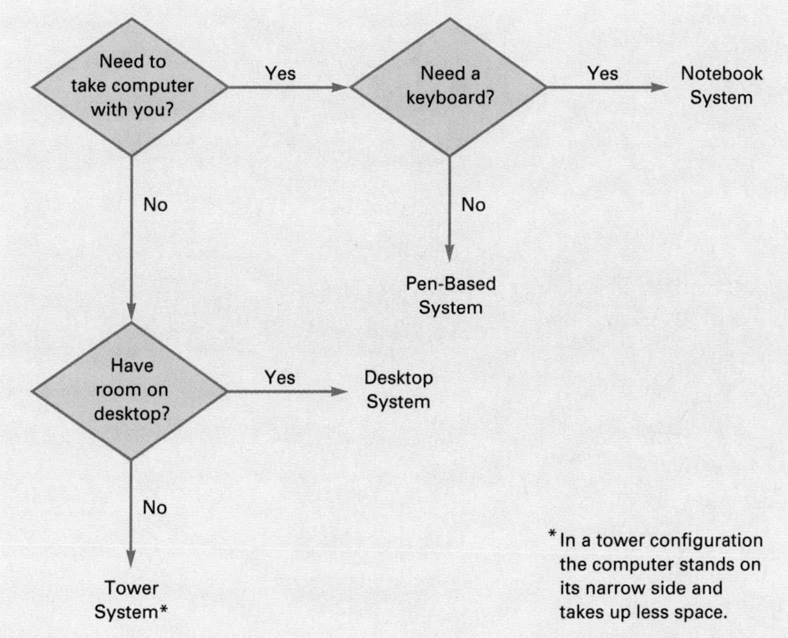

FIGURE E.7
Computers are set up in three basic configurations: those you take with you, those you place on the top of your desk, and those you fit under the desk.

COMPLETE SYSTEM REQUIREMENTS

Regardless of the type of system you are purchasing, some additional decisions must be made at the time of purchase. As mentioned in Chapter 2, training and service provided by full-service computer stores must be weighed against the lower costs offered by discount stores and mail-order houses. Compare computer warranties. How long is the warranty and does it include on-site repair? If on-site repair is not available, where is the closest service center?

Other items should be considered for safe and efficient computing. The miscellaneous shopping list, as seen in Figure E.8, can help you complete your purchases.

To help you organize your hardware and software priorities, Figure E.9 acts as a final worksheet. Use this summary when comparing systems at your local computer store or as you investigate mail-order prices.

Computer System Shopping List–Miscellaneous

- Diskettes, get sufficient number for backup
- Box or holder to store diskettes
- Surge protector
- Paper for printer
- Extra ribbon or ink cartridge for printer
- Necessary cables and extensions
  - monitor
  - keyboard
  - printer
- Covers for keyboard and computer
- Ergonomic desk and chair
- Document stand
- Swivel arm to support monitor
- Screen glare protector
- Anti-static pad
- Lock for portable computer
- On-site service warranty

FIGURE E.8
This list is designed to remind you of the odds and ends you should acquire when purchasing your first computer system.

Personal Computer System Needs Analysis

Software Required for Desired Applications

____________________ ____________________

____________________ ____________________

____________________ ____________________

____________________ ____________________

Software Used Most Often

Software Type	**Computer Required**	**Memory Required**	**Disk Storage Required**
1. ________	________	________	________
2. ________	________	________	________
3. ________	________	________	________

Minimum Memory ________

Minimum Storage ________ (*add* together all software requirements)

Computer Type and Operating System (circle one)	IBM/Compatible with Windows/DOS		APPLE MACINTOSH with Mac-OS	
System Level Required (circle one)	Minimum	Standard	Power	
Processor Required ________	Running at ____ MHz			
Printer Type (circle one)	Dot-matrix	Ink-jet	Laser	
Do you need a color printer? (circle one)	Yes	No		
Monitor Type (circle one)	Monochrome	Color (VGA, SVGA, XGA)		
Configuration (circle one)	Notebook	Pen-based	Desktop	Tower
Diskette Drives	Number ____	Diskette Size ____		
Do you need a sound card?	Yes	No		
Do you need tape backup?	Yes	No		
Do you need a CD-ROM Drive?	Yes	No		
Do you need a modem?	Yes	No		

Peripherals Required

____________________ ____________________

____________________ ____________________

____________________ ____________________

I/O ports needed? Serial ________ Parallel ________

Expansion slots for additional hardware ________

Warranty (circle one) ____ Months On-site? Yes No

Miscellaneous Items to Purchase

____________________ ____________________

____________________ ____________________

____________________ ____________________

FIGURE E.9
When you get serious about purchasing a new computer system, fill out this worksheet and have it handy when evaluating different systems.

Chapter Facts

- Potential microcomputer owners should identify personal needs and applications for a computer before buying one.
- Friends, family, magazines, and computer classes help people learn about and use different application packages.
- Used computers offer affordable prices, but lack a warranty and may not handle newer software specifications.
- Half of the budget for a new personal computer system should be for software and accessories like paper, disks, comfortable chair, etc. The other half is for the computer and peripherals.
- A user's personal mix of application packages determines the operating system, user interface, and basic hardware specifications.
- Microprocessor speeds, memory, and hard disk capacity are determined by the number of applications and related resource requirements.
- Every system should have a keyboard, monitor, printer, hard disk, and at least one diskette drive.
- Potential buyers should not scrimp on machine/human interfaces. Comfortable keyboards and pointing devices, along with high-resolution color monitors, make computers easier to use.
- Printers are evaluated by their speed, print quality, and cost.
- Access speeds are a means of comparing disk drives of similar size and storage capacity.
- Disk drives using 3.5-inch diskettes are becoming a personal computer standard. Include two diskette drives with a new system if you use 3.5- and 5.25-inch disks or if you often make duplicate diskette copies.
- Personal needs and interests may dictate that you include a sound card, modem, CD-ROM drive, or tape drive in your hardware specifications.
- A new computer should have open expansion slots on the motherboard after the minimum hardware specifications have been met.
- When considering portable versus desktop or tower computer configurations, the additional expense and vulnerability of a

portable must be weighed against the convenience of always having access to your computer.

- Training and service provided by full-service computer stores must be weighed against lower costs offered by discount and mail-order stores.
- Compare warranty length and arrangements for repairing problems before buying a new computer system.

Review Questions

1. How would you use a personal computer? (*Hint:* See Figure E.1.)
2. What three software packages do you think you would use most often?
3. Would you purchase an IBM/compatible, Apple Macintosh, or another make of personal computer? How did you make this decision? (*Hint:* See Applying What You've Learned #2.)
4. Would you purchase a used computer system instead of a new one? Explain your rationale.
5. Would you rate your system requirements as minimum, standard, or power, based on Figure E.3?
6. How much memory and what hard disk capacity would you include in a new personal computer system?
7. What are your requirements for a printer? What type of printer would you get?
8. What applications require you to use a color monitor? (*Hint:* See Figure E.4.)
9. How many diskette drives would you need and at what storage capacity?
10. What peripherals do you need beyond a keyboard, monitor, printer, hard disk drive, and diskette drive?
11. What type of configuration (portable, desktop, or tower) best serves your needs?
12. What items besides hardware and software would you need to purchase to make a new computer system operational? (*Hint:* See Figure E.8.)
13. Where would you go to purchase a new computer?

Applying What You've Learned

1. Talk to three friends who have personal computers. Ask them how they use their systems. What software packages do they use the most? What features do they like the best? Would they recommend any specific application packages? What would they do differently if they were purchasing their computers again?
2. For each of your three software priorities, evaluate at least two competing packages. For each package, list the computer it requires (IBM/compatible or Macintosh), its minimum memory requirements, and how much hard disk storage is needed.
3. Compare two of these three types of pointing devices: mouse, trackball, or pen with tablet. Use a free-drawing package or similar graphics software when working with each device. Which input device do you prefer? What are the characteristics that make this device most desirable for your circumstances?
4. Use three different printers. Print the same document, using each printer's highest-quality print mode. Rank the hard-copy output from best to worst. How many pages per minute does each printer output? How much does each cost? Which one, if any, would you purchase? Explain your reasoning.
5. Examine 14-, 15-, and 17-inch color monitors of similar video quality. How much do they weigh? What is the difference in the costs? Which monitor meets your needs most closely? Why?
6. Research the cost of hard disks. Compare equipment produced by three hard disk drive manufacturers as to access speeds and cost per megabyte of storage capacity.
7. Compare the prices and capabilities of two competitive peripherals of your choice. Modems, sound boards, CD-ROM drives, or other peripherals that attach to a personal computer are acceptable. Identify the alternatives and explain why you would purchase one over the other.

GLOSSARY

4GL *see* **fourth generation language.**

absolute cell reference reference to a specific cell address that does not change when it is moved or copied to another worksheet location.

access retrieve data from a storage medium like tape or disk.

access time the time it takes the read/write head to find requested data on a storage medium.

ACM *see* **Association for Computing Machinery.**

acoustic coupler modem a modem that attaches to a telephone handset.

active cell highlighted worksheet cell that receives input data or formula.

active directory directory or subdirectory DOS uses as a default when accessing programs or data files from disk.

activity log a summary of online activities kept for security purposes.

Ada (named after Ada Lovelace) high-level programming language used in scientific applications, especially by the Department of Defense. It is self-structuring but complex, thus difficult to learn.

address unique number assigned to each memory location within a computer's processing hardware.

AI *see* **artificial intelligence.**

algorithm statement of the steps to be followed in solving a problem or performing a process.

alphanumeric data another name for textual data.

American National Standards Institute (ANSI) group that develops programming language standards for use by industry and computer manufacturers.

American Standard Code for Information Interchange (ASCII) code for storing data that uses seven bits to a byte and is commonly used in microcomputers; an extended version of ASCII uses eight bits per byte.

analog signals signals representing data as patterns of frequencies, like sounds.

animation visual images of motions produced by rapid presentation of drawn or computer-generated graphics.

ANSI *see* **American National Standards Institute.**

antivirus software (also known as **vaccine**) computer program that identifies disk files that have been infected with a virus, worm, or other destructive programs. In some cases, the antivirus software can delete unwanted programs and repair damaged files.

Append (Data Management) allows input of data into fields described by the Create operation.

apple icon (Macintosh) displays Finder and other system utility options.

application (Macintosh) application program.

application development team a group of people, including systems analysts and users, responsible for defining specifications, performing feasibility studies, and doing further work on a systems development project.

application generator computer program that works with a data management system to let users design data entry screens, user prompts, and printed reports.

application package software, designed for user-oriented problems, that is packaged with a user's manual and legal contract.

application software class of programs that solve specific user-oriented processing problems.

area graph line graph with the area below the line shaded.

arithmetic operation ability of a computer to do mathematical functions, like addition and subtraction, with numerical data.

artificial intelligence (AI) software application that simulates human thought and judgment by the use of heuristic problem-solving techniques.

ASCII *see* **American Standard Code for Information Interchange.**

Ashton, Alan creator, with Bruce Bastian, of WordPerfect word processing software in the early 1980s.

ASM *see* **Association for System Management.**

assembler language-translating program for converting assembly language into machine language.

assembly language second-generation programming language that uses abbreviations for machine language instructions.

Association for Computing Machinery (ACM) professional organization whose members consist of computer scientists and others involved in computer architecture.

Association for System Management (ASM) professional organization whose members consist of systems personnel, especially systems analysts.

asynchronous transmission communication protocol by which data is sent a single character at a time.

audio-visual data data that people can hear or see—like voice, music, drawings, photographs, and video sequences.

authoring system software package that helps computer professionals create a customized user interface and associated data management system.

automated office *see* **office automation.**

Babbage, Charles (1791–1871) designed the analytical engine in the 1820s. It contained a store for data and punched card programs on a mill. These ideas were later used in designing computers.

backup extra copy of data or programs on a disk or tape that is kept for use in case the original is destroyed.

backup procedures making a copy of important files and programs on another tape or disk.

backward chaining goal-driven problem-solving approach used by expert systems; a problem (goal) is given, and the expert system works backward to identify possible causes.

banner program software allowing users to create and print a variety of banners and awards that may be personalized.

bar code machine-readable collection of bars with varying widths used to identify items.

bar graph graphic showing data as different lengths of bars. A bottom scale indicates what each bar means, while a side scale shows the measurement of the bars. Different shading distinguishes the bars.

Bardeen, John (b. 1908) coinventor, with William Schockley and Walter Brattain, of the transistor and cowinner of the 1956 Nobel Prize in Physics.

BASIC (Beginner's All-purpose Symbolic Instruction Code) high-level programming language used in education and on personal computers. It is easy to learn and is widely used.

BASIC command *see* **command.**

BASIC statement *see* **statement.**

Bastian, Bruce creator, with Alan Ashton, of WordPerfect word processing software in the early 1980s.

batch processing data is collected into groups (batches) and processed at the same time.

baud rate rate at which data is transmitted though a modem or other communication hardware. It is measured as the speed at which a signal changes over a period of time and is often incorrectly equated to bits per second.

BBS *see* **electronic bulletin board system.**

Bednorz, J. George (b. 1950) cowinner, with Karl Müller, of the 1987 Nobel Prize in Physics for work done on superconductivity.

benchmark test compares software and hardware performance against a minimum standard agreed upon by management and the application development team.

Bernoulli disk drive drive using Bernoulli's law relating the actions of air or liquid over a surface. These cartridge disk drives safeguard against head crashes.

beta test prerelease testing of commercial software by potential outside users.

binary code pattern of on/off bits used to represent data or computer operations.

binary digit (also known as **bit**) the on or off state of a single computer circuit, represented as one and zero, respectively.

biometric security device hardware that uses a biological characteristic, like fingerprints or retina patterns, to determine security clearance.

bit (also known as **binary digit**) the on or off state of a single computer circuit, represented as one and zero, respectively.

bit mapping (also known as **pixel graphics**) pattern of pixels making up a graphic image.

bits per second (bps) a measurement of data transmission speed by which the number of zero and one digits per second is counted.

block (Hardware) group of records on tape or disk that are organized together for more efficient input and output.

block (Software) selected text within a document that can be independently moved, copied, or deleted.

boilerplate partially completed document with spaces or codes for specific fields that are added later.

Boole, George (1815–1864) developed two-state (true or false) logic theory for mathematical expressions during the nineteenth century. His theories later became the basis for binary code.

boot to start up a computer system, automatically copying system software into memory.

border worksheet row or column that is printed on every page of printer output.

bps *see* **bits per second.**

Brattain, Walter (1902–1987) coinventor, with John Bardeen and William Shockley, of the transistor and cowinner of the 1956 Nobel Prize in Physics.

Bricklin, Daniel (b. 1951) creator, with Robert Frankston, of Visicalc, the first spreadsheet program.

buffer internal memory set aside for temporary data storage.

bug an error within a computer program.

bulletin board *see* **electronic bulletin board system.**

bus circuitry path that connects the CPU with internal and external hardware.

bus topology network where all nodes are interconnected to each other through a single communications channel.

button labeled icon which initializes or cancels some program option.

Byron, Augusta Ada (Countess of Lovelace) (1815–1852) annotated and published Babbage's work in the 1840s. Her detailed instructions for operation are considered a precursor to modern programming.

byte a group of bits representing a single character or digit of data.

C high-level programming language used in system programming and graphics. It is portable and easy to structure but is a complex language to learn.

cache memory a type of random access memory that holds data for access by the processor. It is faster than disk access.

CAD *see* **computer-aided design.**

CAD/CAM *see* **computer-aided design/computer-aided machining.**

CAM *see* **computer-aided machining.**

camera-ready copy printed document ready to be photographed for a traditional printing plate. Its current meaning is a document ready to be copied.

card data associated with a hypermedia screen display, similar to a data record.

card punch machine that punches holes, representing data, into punched cards.

card reader device that reads and translates the holes on a punched card for use as processing data.

career path series of related jobs.

CASE *see* **computer-aided software engineering tools.**

cashless society a society wherein all financial transactions are done electronically, based upon an individual's universal account number. No cash would be exchanged or needed.

cathode ray tube (CRT) (also known as monitor) an output peripheral by which a visual display is shown on a screen.

CCP *see* **Certificate in Computer Programming.**

Cd (Chdir) internal DOS command to change active directory.

CD *see* **compact disk.**

CD-ROM (compact disk with Read-Only Memory; also known as **CD** or **compact disk)** removable disk that permanently stores data and cannot be changed.

CDP *see* **Certificate in Data Processing.**

cell intersection of a worksheet column and row, which stores a label, value, or formula.

cell address the column letter and row number of a specific worksheet cell.

central processing unit (CPU) the processing hardware of a computer, containing a processor and memory.

Certificate in Computer Programming (CCP) awarded by the Institute for Certification of Computer Professionals to people who pass specialized tests covering business, scientific, and systems programming.

Certificate in Data Processing (CDP) awarded by the Institute for Certification of Computer Professionals to people who pass specialized tests covering data processing hardware; computer programming and software; principles of management; quantitative methods and accounting; and systems analysis and design.

CGA *see* **color graphics adapter.**

channel division of audio data, representing a single voice or instrument.

character smallest unit of data as a single digit, letter, or symbol.

chip a small silicon wafer on which reside integrated circuits and other processing circuitry.

CIM *see* **computer-integrated manufacturing.**

CIS *see* **computer information systems.**

click pressing a mouse button once to select a menu option or icon.

client/server network design in which the client, any end-user's computer, takes on processing tasks traditionally handled by a network server.

clip art graphics and images on paper or disk that are purchased for use by designers.

close box (Macintosh) icon found in the top left corner of a window. Clicking on the close box deactivates the associated window, which usually returns the window back into its original icon.

CLS (BASIC) clears the screen display without affecting the program in memory.

coaxial cable communication channel commonly used for cable television that can handle 80 simultaneous data transmissions at speeds up to 2 million bps.

COBOL (COmmon Business Oriented Language) high-level programming language used for business applications. It is self-documenting, easy to structure, and enjoys widespread use.

Codd, Edgar F. his 12 rules on relational database design, written in the 1970s, are still influencing the field today.

code written program instruction.

coding writing a computer program.

cold site backup facilities, ready for use but not containing hardware, available if an organization's original computer center cannot be used because of an emergency.

collision simultaneous data transmissions from two different computers on the same communication channel.

Color/Contrast Control (Multimedia) editing feature allowing the user to change the colors or brightness of a visual image.

color graphics adapter (CGA) color monitor standard that displays 640 by 200 pixels in 16 colors.

color separation feature of a desktop publishing system to produce a master in each of the colors needed for four-color printing of an image.

COM *see* **computer output microfilm.**

command (BASIC) instruction executed by the computer immediately after it is entered.

command (DOS) instruction that can be executed at any time.

command-driven interface use of keywords and special syntax to initiate program options.

command menu list of operations performed by an electronic spreadsheet.

communication channel the medium by which data communication takes place. Common communication channels include twisted pair wires, coaxial cable, microwave signals, and optical fibers.

communication software system software that transfers data from one computer system to another. These programs usually provide users with data security and error checking capabilities.

compact disk (CD) (also known as **CD-ROM**) removable disk that permanently stores data and cannot be changed.

compact disk with Read-Only Memory (CD-ROM) high-capacity optical disk that is manufactured to permanently store data.

compatibility the ability of software or peripherals to work on a variety of systems.

compiler high-level language translator that checks an entire program for errors while it is translating the code into machine language. If there are syntax errors, a list of errors is output by this program.

computer machine that allows input of facts and figures, processes them, and outputs useful information.

computer-aided design (CAD) application for information technology wherein people use computers to create two- or three-dimensional drawings.

computer-aided design/computer-aided machining (CAD/CAM) communication between CAD and CAM programs that connects design and manufacturing equipment.

computer-aided machining (CAM) use of programmable machines to control manufacturing of products.

computer-aided software engineering (CASE) tools software that helps computer professionals manage systems development projects by integrating through a data dictionary various diagramming and charting tools.

computer application any use for a computer.

computer architect person who specializes in developing processing equipment and associated systems software.

computer architecture an academic program combining computer engineering and computer science.

computer center centralized location for computer hardware and related professionals.

computer center controls equipment is restricted to authorized personnel; activity logs and other usage records are kept; schedules and procedures are stable; emergency recovery procedures exist; and personnel are divided into operations and development groups.

computer engineering computer field specializing in the development, manufacturing, and assembly of hardware.

computer imaging using data, graphics, and mathematics to display complex images.

computer information systems (CIS) an area of specialization concerning the creation of systems in business, science, education, and manufacturing.

computer-integrated manufacturing (CIM) manufacturing system that utilizes the features of CAD/CAM, robotics, and numerical control, linked together by a communications standard.

Computer Matching and Privacy Act of 1988 controls federal use of data banks to cross-reference citizens' information.

computer operator ensures computer hardware is functioning properly and runs different computer programs based on a preset schedule.

computer output microfilm (COM) output onto microfilm or microfiche of computer-generated data.

computer professionals people who work directly with the development and operation of computer technology.

computer program the set of instructions a computer follows in sequence to control the input, processing, output, and storage of data.

computer salesperson sells computer hardware and software.

computer scientist person who specializes in developing techniques for designing system software and their applications in managing data and programs.

computer system collection of components (people, procedures, data, software, and hardware) that work together to solve specific problems.

concurrent update situation that occurs in updating data wherein different users make changes to the same records at the same time. The result is incorrect data in the updated records.

conference a professional meeting covering a broad subject area. It includes concurrent presentations and product displays.

contention two computers trying to use a common communication channel at the same time.

context-sensitive help information displayed when a help screen is activated; relates to the program operation currently being used.

continuing education participation in on-the-job training, workshops, conferences, or other activities associated with the improvement of job skills.

contract programmer computer programmer temporarily employed by an organization to work on a systems development project.

control box (Windows) icon found in the top left corner of the title bar. Clicking on the control box opens the control box menu, which offers options to close, open, or move the associated window. Double-clicking on the control box closes the associated window.

control character special instructions (carriage return, cursor movement, etc.) available from the keyboard.

control clerk schedules when operators load and run computer programs in a computer center and delivers the information to the appropriate users.

control total security procedure in which errors are detected by comparing an independently computed total with the computer-generated equivalent.

conversion (also known as **installation**) changing from an old system to a new system.

Copy (DOS) internal command that creates a duplicate of the designated program or data file.

Copy (Spreadsheet) duplicates contents of selected cells into other worksheet columns or rows.

Copy (Word Processing) operation that duplicates a block of text somewhere else within the same document (internal copy) or to another file (external copy).

copy protection a way of storing software on disk that prevents illegal copying by system utilities.

correspondence-quality character (also called **double-strike**) dot-matrix character that is printed twice, in two slightly different positions, to produce a higher-quality print on a dot-matrix printer.

cost/benefit analysis a report presenting both tangible and intangible costs and benefits of a systems project.

CPU *see* **central processing unit.**

crash computer failure.

Create (Data Management) used to set up the file or database structure by forming new files and describing fields in records.

critical path combination of events within a project PERT chart that requires the most time to complete.

CRT *see* **cathode ray tube.**

cursor blinking line or box that highlights where the computer is going to display the next keyboard entry.

cursor control use of keys on keyboard to move the cursor up, down, left, or right through a document.

Cut and Paste (also known as **Move**) change location of data or formula within a document.

cylinder collection of tracks on a disk pack that can be read at one position of the access mechanism.

data facts, figures, and images.

DATA (BASIC) statement containing data for READ statement.

data administrator individual within an organization who is responsible for establishing files and databases, setting up user rights and restrictions for accessing data, training users in backup procedures, and evaluating the performance of a data management system.

data communication sending data electronically from one location to another.

data compression to reduce data storage space by replacing data redundancies with special notations that take up less space.

data definition language user interface that identifies fields and field characteristics (type and size) for records within a file.

data dictionary a resident index used by CASE software that contains information about the IPOS cycle and other features of a new system.

data drive disk drive storing application programs and data.

data encryption scrambling characters on a disk or transmissions across communication lines to prevent illegal copying of data and programs.

data entry entering numbers and text into a computer for processing.

data entry line area of a worksheet where data and formulas are input and edited before placement in the active cell.

data entry operator inputs data into a computer, usually using a keyboard.

data entry procedures preparation and input of data into a computer system.

data flow diagram visual representation using symbols and arrows to show how data and people interact.

data integrity attribute of a data file where every data field is accurate and properly identified as well as having consistency between duplicate data fields when they exist.

data librarian catalogs and stores tapes and disks in fireproof tape/disk library.

data management program (also known as database management software, data management system, and database program) computer program that creates, stores, and accesses data from data files through the uses of indexes and other techniques.

data management system *see* **data management program.**

data manipulation language user interface that controls the access, updating, and manipulation of data within a file or database.

data model plan computer system uses for storing and accessing data items.

data processing using a computer to convert facts, figures, and images into useful information.

Data Processing Management Association (DPMA) organization whose members consist of computer information systems professionals.

data storage and retrieval capability of computers to store vast amounts of data and later search the data for related information.

database organized collections of data that can be retrieved and cross-referenced by a computer.

database management software (DBMS; also known as **data management program, data management system,** and **database program**) computer program that creates, stores, and accesses data from data files through the uses of indexes and other techniques.

database program *see* **data management program.**

DBMS (database management software) *see* **data management program.**

debugging the process of finding and correcting program errors.

decision support system (DSS) a real-time computer system that aids managers in solving problems through data retrieval and modeling.

default standard assumptions, like hardware connections and formats, that a computer system uses unless otherwise instructed.

default disk drive drive DOS uses when no disk drive is included in an instruction.

Del (DOS) internal command to erase a filename from the designated disk directory.

Delete (Spreadsheet) removes row or column along with associated data and formulas.

Delete (Word Processing) removes text from document. The delete key or other combination of keys is used to remove the indicated text.

density measure of storage media capacity. Computer-based storage media measure density by the number of bytes stored per inch of storage space (bpi).

desktop screen layout associated with graphical user interface, which parallels an actual desktop by using icons that represent documents, file folders, calculators, and other office tools.

desktop publishing software package that integrates text, graphics, and images created by other software packages. It allows users precise control over page layout as well as a wide selection of different fonts and design elements.

detailed report a report showing one output line for each item in a file or database.

device driver file used by operating system to identify operating characteristics of peripherals like a mouse, printer, or scanner.

diagnostic software detects problems in hardware.

dialog box window that prompts the user to enter text, select options from a list, or click on an icon to initiate or cancel some program option.

digital computer computer that accepts programs and data converted to binary digits.

digital signals signals representing bit patterns as on or off electrical voltages.

digitize conversion of a point on a drawing into mathematical coordinates. This is done by using a scanner or stylus on a tablet.

Dir (DOS) internal command to display contents of disk directory on screen.

direct access (also known as random access) the computer system uses an index or other techniques to identify a record's location within a file and can access an individual record without processing other records.

direct-connect modem modem that links a computer to a telephone wall jack.

direct cutover conversion method wherein the old system is removed and the new system is immediately installed.

disaster recovery plan procedures to be followed if an organization's computer center is disabled or destroyed.

discretionary replace as each designated word is found, the user decides whether to replace it or not.

disk a circular platter with concentric tracks that is used as a machine-readable storage medium.

disk address location of data on disk.

disk cartridge hard disk designed to be inserted and removed from the disk drive.

disk directory storage area on a disk that contains the filename, size, date, and time of each data file or program saved on the disk.

disk drive storage hardware that writes data on disk and reads it back into computer's memory upon command.

disk icon (Macintosh) represents a disk that is available for input and storage.

disk operating system (DOS) collection of system software designed to control a computer system using disks for storage.

disk pack collection of hard disks stacked on top of each other to allow access and storage of large amounts of data.

disk track one of the concentric circles on a disk surface where data is stored.

diskette (also known as floppy disk) removable flexible disk, used to store computer-readable data.

diskless workstation personal computer system without a disk drive. A diskless workstation, also known as an intelligent terminal, is always connected to another computer that handles data and program storage.

distributed processing several computers linked together into a communications network to share data processed by end-users.

document (Macintosh) data file.

documentation written instructions, design diagrams, and support materials for a computer program.

domain a specific area of influence or expertise.

DOS *see* **disk operating system.**

DOS prompt screen display of the letter associated with default disk drive and greater than sign, for example, A> or C>. This display indicates the disk operating system is ready to receive instructions. The DOS prompt display is customized by using the Prompt command.

dot-matrix character a type of character made up of dots patterned within a matrix.

dot-matrix printer a printer that forms characters made up of small dots.

double-click pressing a mouse button twice in quick succession to run a program or activate a program operation.

double-strike (also called **correspondence-quality character**) dot-matrix character that is printed twice, in two slightly different positions, to produce a higher-quality print than dot-matrix.

download receiving data or programs directly from another computer.

DPMA *see* **Data Processing Management Association.**

draft-quality printer an impact printer capable of producing dot-matrix characters.

drag move an object on the screen by pointing at it and holding down a mouse button while you move it to a new screen location.

drop-down menu (also known as **pull-down menu**) menu options that stay hidden in a menu bar at the top of the screen until the user selects it. When the menu is selected, the menu opens to list program options. Once an option is selected, the menu rolls back up into the menu bar.

DSS *see* **decision support system.**

E-mail *see* **electronic mail.**

EBCDIC *see* **Extended Binary Coded Decimal Interchange Code.**

Eckert, J. Presper (b. 1919) built the electronic computer ENIAC with John Mauchly in 1946.

EDI *see* **electronic data interchange.**

echo-printing displaying on the screen what has been input by the user.

editing revising text in a document.

EDP *see* **electronic data processing.**

EDP controls security procedures for all computer system components.

Education Privacy Act of 1974 students can examine and correct errors to their academic records. This Act also limits access to this information by others.

EFT *see* **electronic funds transfer.**

EGA *see* **extended graphics adapter.**

electronic bulletin board system (BBS) public access message system that allows users to leave or read messages.

Electronic Communications Privacy Act of 1986 makes interception of electronic mail and other data communications a federal crime.

electronic data interchange (EDI) organizations exchanging orders, bills, and banking information using data communication technology.

electronic data processing (EDP) an old term for data processing.

electronic filing storing documents on disk instead of in a filing cabinet.

electronic funds transfer (EFT) a computer network that allows financial transactions between buyers, sellers, and banks without the actual exchange of money or checks.

electronic mail (E-mail) sending and receiving memos, reports, and personal messages through a computer network.

electronic mailbox personal disk file storing the correspondence for an electronic mail system.

electronic publishing printing technology that runs high-speed printing presses and controls page composition, typography, and file integration.

electronic spreadsheet organizes numbers and associated text into rows and columns for processing and analysis. Financial data, such as budgets and income statements, are often organized in this way.

electronic whiteboard groupware feature that posts drawings, ideas or questions on users' computer screens and allows answers or ideas from others to be physically displayed next to related information.

electrostatic printer printer that uses electrical impulses to put characters on electrostatic paper.

ellipsis series of three periods. When found behind a menu option, an ellipsis indicates that additional user input is necessary.

embedded computer computer built inside a tool or appliance.

emergency procedures actions people take to recover important data after a computer crash.

emulation utility program that mimics the operation of different computer equipment.

END (BASIC) statement that stops execution; it is usually the last program statement.

end-of-file mark (also known as **trailer label**) a record that marks the end of a file on tape or disk.

end-user person who can use computer technology to organize data, stimulate new ideas, solve problems, and communicate the results to others.

end-user computing end-user is responsible for data entry, computer operations, and application of the resulting output.

Enter key key on keyboard that transmits a carriage return.

Erase (DOS) internal command to delete a filename from the designated disk directory.

Erase (Spreadsheet) removing a designated worksheet from disk.

Eraser (Graphics) option whereby, as the eraser icon is moved around the screen, the area beneath it is cleared, like a chalkboard eraser.

ergonomics the study of how tools, furniture, and equipment can be designed to fit the human body.

error correction computer program that checks for data entry errors.

error messages listing of program errors or errors in running an application package. Suggested corrections may be given.

error recovery procedures actions people take to find and eliminate processing mistakes made by people or equipment failures.

ethical standard set of rules a person or organization uses when considering the rights, privileges, and anticipated responses of all persons and groups likely to be affected by a particular action.

exception report a report that lists only those records fulfilling predefined specifications.

execute (also known as **run** or **launch**) having the computer follow the instructions in a program.

execution phase part of processing cycle in which the arithmetic or logic operation is performed by the processor or results are sent from the processor to memory.

executive another name for people at the top management level.

executive information system type of decision support system that is designed to aid in the strategic decisions made by top-level management.

Exit (also known as **Quit**) returns software control to the operating system.

expansion card circuit board designed to fit into an expansion slot of a microcomputer's motherboard to add memory or connect external hardware.

expansion slot places where expansion cards can be plugged into the motherboard, expanding a microcomputer's processing power.

expert system a user interface, inference engine, and knowledge base that contain decision-making rules and probabilities for expected outcomes, based on information available from experts.

exploded pie chart a pie chart wherein one slice is emphasized by separating it from the rest.

export saving data in a file format that enables other software packages to use it.

expression (BASIC) all symbols and numbers to the right of the equal sign in a LET statement.

Extended Binary Coded Decimal Interchange Code (EBCDIC) binary code for storing data that includes eight bits in a byte and is used in minicomputers and mainframes.

extended graphics adapter (EGA) color monitor standard that displays 720 by 350 pixels in 16 colors.

extended graphics array (XGA) color monitor standard that displays 1024 by 768 pixels in 65,536 colors.

external copy copying a block of text from a document to an outside file.

external disk drive disk drive outside of the computer case that is connected to the computer though a parallel port.

external modem standalone modem that directly connects a computer to a communication channel.

facsimile (fax) machine machine that scans, digitizes, and transmits/receives text, images, and other hard-copy formats over communication lines.

Fair Credit Reporting Act of 1970 citizens can examine information held in their credit files and challenge the data if necessary.

FAT *see* **file allocation table.**

Fatbits (Graphics) an area of a graphic image enlarged to show individual bits (pixels). Each pixel can be turned on or off to change the image.

fault-tolerant computer a computer with duplicate processing components designed to switch to one set of components when the other set has problems.

fax *see* **facsimile machine.**

fax board facsimile technology on an expansion board. Installing a fax board lets a computer user work directly with faxed documents.

fax-modem communication hardware with both data communication (modem) and image handling (fax) capabilities.

feasibility study a study done to determine how realistic a systems development project is in terms of time, costs, and resources.

fetch phase part of processing cycle where a processor receives an instruction from memory.

field related group of letters, numbers, and symbols. For example, a name or address.

fifth-generation computer computer system containing natural language interfaces and expert systems software, along with using parallel processors, fiber optics, or superconductors.

file group of related records about people, places, things, ideas, or events.

file allocation table (FAT) index that identifies by sector number where a file is found on a disk. The file allocation table is stored along with the disk directory on a designated disk track.

file folder (also known as **folder**) icon representing a group of related programs and data files. File folder icons represent a specific disk subdirectory.

file management software (also known as **file management system**) computer program that maximizes access to one file at a time.

file management system *see* **file management software.**

file merging feature of a word processing program that merges a letter with a file of names and addresses, resulting in personalized correspondence.

filename unique set of letters, numbers, and symbols that identifies a data file or program.

filename extension a combination of three letters that are added to the end of a filename, preceded by a period, to identify the file format.

Fill Bucket (Graphics) the user chooses a pattern or color, which goes into the Fill Bucket icon. The Fill Bucket is moved to the shape to be filled, and a button is pressed on the mouse. The shape is filled with the chosen pattern or color.

financial data facts and figures about resources that relate to money, such as profit and loss, assets and liabilities, and cash flow.

Find (Spreadsheet) locate a designated label, value, or cell reference.

Find (Word Processing) locates first occurrence of an indicated symbol or phrase in a document.

firmware permanent software programmed onto a memory chip when it is manufactured.

first-generation computer computer manufactured in the late 1940s and early 1950s containing vacuum tubes, having no memory, and using magnetic drums as storage devices.

fixed disk disk permanently installed within the disk drive.

fixed disk drive a drive on which the disk is permanent and protected from destructive environmental elements.

fixed expense regular, known expenses such as rent, mortgages, and consumer loans.

fixed-point constant a number with a decimal point and possibly decimal places.

flash memory uses programmable read-only memory chips to store data. Flash memory is used with portable computers and in other situations where power consumption must be kept to a minimum.

flat file independent data file used by file management software. Flat files are not designed to integrate with other data files.

floppy disk (also known as **diskette**) removable, flexible disk, used to store computer readable data.

flowchart a method of representing program logic by using different symbols and arrows.

folder (also known as **file folder**) icon representing a group of related programs and data files. File folder icons represent a specific disk subdirectory.

font style, weight and size of a printed character.

footer line that appears at the bottom of each document page.

FOR . . . NEXT (BASIC) statements that surround a block of code to be repeated a set number of times.

form feed button on the printer that moves paper to the top of the next page.

Format (DOS) utility program that initializes a disk by creating tracks, sectors, and a root directory.

Format (Spreadsheet) change column widths, fonts and other worksheet display features.

formatting (Word Processing) controlling the final appearance of a document.

formatting (also known as **initialization**) setting identification marks for each track and sector on a disk. A disk directory and file allocation table are also formed.

forward chaining data-driven problem-solving approach used by expert system, which starts with all the known situations or symptoms of a problem and works forward by identifying common parameters that are characteristics of a specific problem.

FORTRAN (FORmula TRANslator) high-level programming language used for scientific and mathematical applications. It handles calculations easily but is difficult to structure.

Fourth Amendment of the U.S. Constitution general rights to privacy including freedom from unreasonable searches of person, house, papers, and effects.

fourth-generation computer computer with processing hardware characterized by very large-scale integrated circuits such as a microprocessor.

fourth-generation language nonprocedural programming language where users indicate IPOS specifications with simple commands.

frame division of visual data like film or video. Each frame can be edited independently. Rapid run through of the frames creates animated movement.

Frame Selection (Multimedia) the ability to find selected frames by using commands or button icons similar to a tape player.

Frankston, Robert creator, with Daniel Bricklin, of Visicalc, one of the first spreadsheet programs.

free-drawing graphics using the computer to create drawings on a screen much as an artist uses a canvas.

Freedom of Information Act of 1970 government-held data is available upon a citizen's request unless it infringes upon someone else's privacy or threatens national security.

front-line management people who make operational decisions about daily activities in an organization.

full character solid-print characters similar to those of a typewriter, producing a high-quality print.

full-duplex transmission communication protocol that allows two-way simultaneous data transmissions between two computers.

full justification both right and left margins of a document are aligned.

full-page monitor screen display that shows an entire page of a word processing or desktop publishing document.

function predefined formula that performs common mathematical, financial, and logical operations.

function keys keys that activate special software features.

Gantt chart a chart showing starting dates and durations for different activities in the systems development process.

Gates, William (Bill) (b. 1955) wrote BASIC interpreter for Altair microcomputer; founded Microsoft Corporation, originators of MS-DOS.

gateway hardware and communication software that acts as an interface to connect different network topologies.

GDSS *see* **group decision support system.**

gigabyte one billion bytes of memory.

GIGO (garbage in, garbage out) errors in data produce useless information.

global replace automatic replacement of all occurrences of a word or phrase in a document without user involvement.

GOTO (BASIC) statement that transfers control of the computer to another program statement.

graphical user interface (GUI) interface that relies on mouse or keyboard input to select menus or icons, which initiate program options.

graphics package generates pictures, drawings, charts, and diagrams on a screen or paper. Some graphics software uses spreadsheet data while others use input from users to create drawings or animated images.

group decision support system (GDSS) groupware application whereby people connected to the same network define problems, discuss solutions, and delegate responsibilities.

group icon organizes related programs and data files available to the system. Double-clicking on a group icon opens a window, but does not execute any software.

groupware software package that supports personal computer users connected through a network with integrated software and compatible data. Groupware applications include common calendars, electronic mail, interactive conference calls, document sharing, and editing sessions with several users.

GUI *see* **graphical user interface.**

hacker self-taught computer expert who tends to try to find ways to access unauthorized computer systems.

half-duplex transmission communication protocol that allows two-way data transmissions between two computers, but in only one direction at a time.

halftone arrangement of different sizes of black dots on white paper to simulate the gray tones of black-and-white photographs.

hard card expansion card with a built-in fixed disk.

hard copy a paper copy of output.

hard-copy terminal a terminal without a screen, producing only paper output.

hard disk nonremovable disk built into disk drive.

hard disk drive hardware used to read and write information on a hard disk. The drive accesses hard disks through access arms containing read/write heads.

hard return a carriage return entered into the text when the user presses the Return or Enter key.

hardware computer and other associated equipment.

hardwired physically connected by wire or cable.

head crash hard disk drive's read/write head touches disk surface, resulting in damage to disk and disk drive.

header line that appears at the top of each document page.

header label record that marks the beginning of a file on disk or tape.

help desk group of computer professionals that answers questions related to personal computer operations, software applications, and hardware problems.

help screen description of software features and explanation of error messages displayed upon demand so the user does not have to refer to a manual.

heuristic the system of applying general rules and experiential information to solve problems by artificial intelligence software.

hidden file file whose name is not displayed as part of the disk directory.

hierarchical model data items and their references are organized in a top-down fashion. Access to data is made only from the top down.

hierarchy chart a graphic representation of the relationship among the modules or objects in a structured program; also called structure chart.

high-level language programming language that resembles human language. Programs written in high-level languages, like BASIC and Pascal, must be translated into the computer's machine language before being used.

highlight changing the intensity of certain characters on a screen for emphasis.

Hoff, Marcian (b. 1937) one of the first inventors of the microprocessor in the 1960s.

Hollerith, Herman (1860–1929) inventor of the punched card and associated hardware in the 1880s.

host the central computer in a star network.

hot site backup facilities, containing ready-to-use hardware, available if an organization's original computer center cannot be used because of an emergency.

Hyatt, George (Gilbert) one of the first inventors of the microprocessor in the 1960s.

hybrid topology a network that incorporates two or more network topologies.

hypermedia multimedia application for data management software wherein users work with a graphical user interface to display information from different cards. Users also have the ability to access cards from different stacks of cards.

hyphenation help word processing software consults a dictionary to inform user of possible places in a word for correct hyphenation.

IC *see* **integrated circuit.**

icon picture of item, action, or computer operation.

icon bar series of icons that represent different software operations as options.

IEEE *see* **Institute of Electrical and Electronic Engineers.**

IF . . . THEN (BASIC) statements used to perform actions based on the value of a given condition.

import adding graphics, images, or text created by other software to a document.

index separate file based on a key field, which identifies the location of a record within a data file.

Index (Data Management) allows user to directly access records in a different key field order while maintaining the file's original record sequencing.

indexed file supports direct access to records through the use of indexes that identify each record's location on disk.

inference engine software within an expert system that retrieves data and makes decisions, based on a set of rules, using data and probabilities from an integrated knowledge base.

infinite loop a series of instructions within a computer program that are repeated continuously without exit.

information knowledge derived by processing data, usually in the form of a printed report or screen display.

information society an area containing a large group of people whose work generates or depends upon information.

information systems manager responsible for the effective and efficient use of an organization's computer resources by ensuring computer professionals complete scheduled jobs on time and within budget.

information utility a commercial service wherein users pay for access to a centralized computer system and its resources, which include E-mail, specialized databases, games, catalogs, and airline schedules.

informed user person who understands how the components of a computer system work together to perform a task, knows its limits, and uses it for personal benefit and for the benefit of others.

initial review a study done by a systems analyst to identify a problem and see if it has a computer-based solution.

initialization (also known as **formatting**) setting identification marks for each track and sector on a disk. A disk directory and file allocation table is also formed.

ink-jet printer printer that sprays drops of ink on paper in patterns to form characters.

INPUT (BASIC) statement that allows a user to enter data from a keyboard that is identified by given variable names.

input, processing, output controls procedures for accepting data and keeping control totals make up the input controls; processing controls depend on good documentation and procedures for processing that are strictly followed, like activity logs and lists of errors; output controls include checking for complete, accurate output and that it is delivered only to authorized personnel.

Insert (Spreadsheet) add new rows or columns.

Insert (Word Processing) adding text to a document. The cursor is put at the place where text must be inserted. Insert key is then pressed and new text is typed in between the existing text.

installation (also known as **conversion**) changing from an old system to a new system.

Institute of Electrical and Electronic Engineers (IEEE) professional association whose members consist of computer and electrical engineers who design and build computer equipment.

integer constant a number with no decimal places or decimal point.

integrated circuit (IC) a small, solid-state circuit placed with other electronic components on a silicon wafer.

integrated software software package that provides user interfaces for several applications and a common data format for sharing data between those applications

intelligent terminal a terminal, often a microcomputer, that has built-in processing and memory capabilities, but no secondary storage capacity.

interactive direct communication with a computer wherein every request is immediately acted upon.

interactive television a television containing a cable control box that lets users communicate through the control box to the television station.

interblock gap area on a magnetic tape that separates blocks of records, similar in use to an interrecord gap.

internal diskette drive disk drive built inside computer housing.

internal modem modem on an expansion card that directly connects computer to communication line.

interpreter program that translates and executes one high-level language instruction at a time until the program logic is completed or an error has been found. Interpreters do not save the translation.

interrecord gap area on magnetic tape that separates records to make room for the read/write head to stop and start between readings.

I/O input and output.

I/O port a plug or connector on a computer where input or output devices are attached.

IPOS (input, processing, output, storage) cycle a four-step computer-related process consisting of the input of data, processing of the data by the computer, output of information in some usable form, and storage of the results for later use.

iteration basic structure of a computer program wherein a sequence of instructions is repeated until some processing condition is changed.

Jacquard, Joseph Marie (1752–1834) developer in 1801 of mechanized looms using punched cards for patterns.

Jobs, Steve (b. 1955) built the Apple I microcomputer in 1976 with Steve Wozniak and later formed Apple Computer Corporation.

Join (Data Management) allows users to merge portions of different database tables together into a new table.

joystick a lever moved around like an automobile stick shift, its action moving a cursor or object on the screen.

justification the alignment of text along the margins.

just-in-time inventory inventory control method that schedules the shipment of parts and raw materials just before they are needed, in order to minimize storage costs and reduce spoilage of time-dependent products.

K *see* **kilobyte.**

Kemeny, John G. (b. 1926) co-creator, with Thomas Kurtz, of BASIC in 1964.

kerning adjusting the spacing between printed characters, based on the shape of the characters.

key field used to identify record in a file.

KEY OFF (BASIC) command that turns off the function key line at bottom of screen.

KEY ON (BASIC) command that turns on the function key line at bottom of screen.

keyboard input hardware, similar to a typewriter, where each keystroke represents a character.

keyboard overlay paper or plastic sheet cut to fit around a keyboard, containing a brief description of keyboard commands.

keypunch machine, operated through a keyboard, that puts patterned holes representing data on punched cards.

keyword action represented by BASIC command or statement.

Kilby, Jack (b. 1923) coinventor of the first working integrated circuit in 1959. Given joint credit with Robert Noyce.

kilobyte (K) approximately one thousand bytes of memory.

knowledge base contains the facts, data relationships, and probabilities of occurrences for activities within a specific domain, for example, medical diagnosis.

knowledge engineer computer professional who designs and tests an expert system.

Kurtz, Thomas E. (b. 1928) co-creator, with John Kemeny, of BASIC in 1964.

label text that is used to describe worksheet or worksheet data. Labels cannot be used in spreadsheet calculations.

label prefix special symbol (',",^, or \) that determines label's placement within a cell and identifies numbers that should be treated as text by an electronic spreadsheet. A single quote left justifies the label, a double quote (") right justifies the label, a caret (^) centers the label, and a backslash (\) repeats the label to fill the cell.

LAN *see* **local area network.**

landscape horizontal layout of a document page.

language translator system program that converts program instructions written in a high-level language into the computer's machine language.

laptop small, portable microcomputer about the size of a notebook with a self-contained power source.

laser printer printer that forms characters on a drum with lasers. The rotating drum uses toner fluid to pick up ink, as in a copy machine, and the characters are printed on paper.

Lasso (Graphics) an area of a graphic image is encircled or lassoed. It can then be moved, copied, or rotated.

launch (also known as **execute** or run) having the computer follow the instructions in a program.

LCD *see* **liquid crystal display.**

left justification alignment of text in a document along only the left edge.

LET (BASIC) statement that performs arithmetic operations.

letter-quality printer a printer using full characters to produce a professional-looking document.

life cycle problem-solving approach to systems design that divides a large job into a series of smaller steps.

light pen a pen that is moved or touches the screen at certain points to select from a menu or make drawings.

line feed button on the printer that moves paper one line at a time through the printer when it is activated.

line graph presentation graphic showing trends in data with a continuous line. The graph has two scales: the bottom one usually shows the passage of time, while the side often measures money or quantity. Different trends are shown as separate lines containing unique symbols.

line number (BASIC) a number before each statement in a program identifying the order in which the statements will be carried out.

line printer impact printer producing one line at a time with speeds of up to 2,000 lines per minute.

linear programming type of modeling wherein an optimum solution for a problem is found for a given set of requirements and constraints.

linker system software that embeds utility programs within a translated version of a high-level-language program.

liquid crystal display (LCD) monitor in which an electric field causes configurations of molecules to align and light up, producing characters.

LIST (BASIC) command that outputs program statements on the screen.

list box displays a list of names or options. When the list is too long to fit in the box, scroll arrows move the list up and down to display different items within the list box.

LLIST (BASIC) command that outputs program statements on a printer.

LOAD (BASIC) command that copies a program from disk into memory.

local area network (LAN) privately owned collection of interconnected computers within a confined service area.

logic error program error that is translatable but does not produce correct results.

logical operation ability of a computer to compare two values to see which is larger or if they are equal.

logical operator symbol (<, >, =) indicating which logical operation is to be used in a BASIC IF . . . THEN statement.

LOGO (from Greek *logos*) high-level programming language used in education. It is easy to learn and allows simple graphing, but has few applications outside education.

LPRINT (BASIC) statement that displays output on a printer.

machine code (also known as machine language) operating language unique to each computer that is made up of bits (0 or 1) representing electronic switches (off or on).

machine language *see* **machine code.**

macro a stored series of spreadsheet operations a user can activate by using a menu or by pressing a few keys.

magnetic ink character recognition (MICR) machine-readable input that uses a scanner to read special magnetized characters at the bottom of checks.

mainframe computer that houses several processors and large amounts of memory and is capable of servicing many users performing different tasks at the same time.

maintenance keeping one or more of a computer system's components up-to-date.

maintenance programmer a person who modifies programs already in use in order to reflect a change in law or company policy.

management controls security procedures by which managers take control of data processing by setting the computer center's direction, not through direct participation in processing activities.

management information system (MIS) collection of systems, both computerized and manual, that provides information to an organization's decision makers.

mass storage storage arrangement in which a strip of magnetic tape is stored in a cell. Hundreds of these cells are arranged in a honeycomb pattern, and a retrieval arm moves from cell to cell, getting the tape and loading it onto a tape drive.

materials requirement planning (MRP) existing inventory and production schedules become data for software that schedules ordering and shipments of raw materials.

math coprocessor microprocessor used by the CPU to speed up mathematical processing.

Mauchly, John (1907–1980) built the electronic computer ENIAC with J. Presper Eckert in 1946.

maximize button (Windows) icon with an up arrow found in the top right corner of the title bar next to the minimize button. Clicking on the maximize button expands the related window to fill the screen.

MB *see* **megabyte.**

McLuhan, Marshall (1911–1980) author of books relating technology to society. His ideas have influenced present-day data communications and multimedia.

Md (Mkdir) internal DOS command to add subdirectory to a designated disk directory.

Measure Selection (Multimedia) the feature allowing a user to find a particular measure of audio data.

megabyte (MB) one million bytes of memory.

megahertz (MHz) one million clock cycles per second; a measurement of processing hardware speed.

memory computer circuitry that temporarily stores data and programs. Usually grouped by storage capacity of thousands (K) or millions (M) of characters; for example, a computer with 8M of memory can store up to 8 million letters, numbers, or symbols.

menu list of program options that allows a user to activate an option by highlighting it or by entering a single letter or number.

menu bar horizontal area that runs across the top of a window and displays menu titles.

message filtering E-mail feature that lets user sort incoming mail into selected mailboxes based on keywords.

MHz *see* **megahertz.**

MICR *see* **magnetic ink character recognition.**

microcomputer small computer with a single processor for use by one person at a time.

microfiche 4- by 6-inch pages of film each holding information equivalent to a 200-page report.

microfilm pages of data stored on a reel of film.

microprocessor a single chip containing input/output control, processing, and some memory circuitry.

microsecond one millionth of a second; used to measure the speed of a computer's processing.

microwave wireless communication channel that handles over 670 simultaneous data transmissions at speeds up to 50 million bps.

middle management people who make tactical decisions about short-term problems.

MIDI *see* **musical instrument digital interface.**

millisecond one thousandth of a second; used to measure the access time of a computer's disk drive.

minicomputer processing hardware that handles a limited number of users and programs at the same time using a single processor.

minimize button (Windows) icon with a down arrow found in the top right corner of the title bar next to the maximize/restore button. Clicking on the minimize button converts window back into an icon.

MIPS million instructions per second; a measurement of a computer's processing speed.

MIS *see* **management information system.**

model mathematical representation of a problem or organizational situation.

modem a device that converts data between analog and digital signals.

Modula-2 high-level programming language similar to Pascal, used for systems programming.

module a subset of a computer program containing code that performs only a single operation.

monitor an output peripheral by which a visual display is shown on a screen.

monochrome a single color, referring to a monitor with one color on a background.

motherboard the primary circuit board in a microcomputer, containing the RAM and ROM chips, microprocessor, and other supporting circuitry.

mouse input device user rolls on a flat surface to control a pointer on screen. User initiates input by positioning pointer over desired screen icon or menu option and pressing a button on the mouse.

Move (Spreadsheet; also known as **Cut and Paste**) change location of data or formula within worksheet.

Move (Word Processing) user blocks off text, which can then be relocated elsewhere in the document.

MRP *see* **materials requirement planning.**

MS-DOS disk operating system developed by the Microsoft Corporation for personal computer systems.

Müller, Karl (b. 1927) co-winner, with J. Georg Bednorz, of the 1987 Nobel Prize in Physics for work done on superconductivity.

multimedia the combination of textual, audio, and visual data under software control for importing, editing, and exporting.

multiplexer a device that combines signals from several incoming transmissions to be sent to the same computer. It can also separate signals from the computer to be sent to several terminals or workstations.

multiprocessing linking several computers together to work on a common problem.

multitasking one computer running two or more independent programs concurrently.

musical instrument digital interface (MIDI) interface that allows musicians to connect instruments and computers for sound synthesizing.

nanomachine extremely small machine.

nanosecond one billionth of a second; used to measure the speed of a computer's processor.

natural language programming language used for decision support and expert systems. Commands closely reflect human languages.

natural language interface relies on spoken words or typed instruction in the user's native tongue to initiate program options.

NC *see* **numerical control.**

nested symbols or statements within each other, like sets of parentheses or FOR...NEXT statements. The innermost set is completed first.

network a system of computers and hardware sharing data and software over communication channels.

network card expansion card that fits into a personal computer's motherboard to connect the computer to the communication channel used by a network.

network model multiple access paths to related data allowing data items to be accessed from different starting points.

network topology design strategy that describes how computers are interconnected within a network.

neural network array of processors integrated into a communication network that mimics neurological connections in the human brain.

NEW (BASIC) command that clears the program from the computer's memory.

node one computer system within a network.

nonexecutable statement program code that is ignored by the computer.

nonprocedural language high-level language where required tasks are defined in terms of operational parameters rather than listing sequential logical steps.

nonvolatile memory type of computer memory that retains its contents when power is turned off.

notepad computer very small portable computer with pen input capable of processing handwritten data.

Noyce, Robert (1927–1990) coinventor of the first working integrated circuit in 1959. Given joint credit with Jack Kilby.

numeric data data containing only numbers (0–9), decimal point, positive (+) and negative (−) signs.

numerical control (NC) ability of machines to use programs representing numeric specifications to produce precise machine parts.

object data item that has meaning by itself. For example, an object may be a photograph or video sequence in a computer-usable format.

object (Programming) section of program code in object-oriented programming (OOP) that contains both the processing code and descriptions of related data to perform a single task.

Object Integration (Multimedia) feature allowing insertion of a video, audio, graphic, or still image clip anywhere within an existing multimedia file.

object-oriented programming (OOP) programming methodology whereby a program is organized into objects, each containing both descriptions of the data and processing operations necessary to perform a task.

obsolescence the rate at which equipment and its associated knowledge become outdated.

OCR *see* **optical character recognition.**

office automation (also known as automated office) office where document processing equipment is networked together.

offline state of hardware when it is not communicating with the computer.

OMR *see* **optical mark recognition.**

online direct input and processing of data by a computer.

online thesaurus word processing software feature that will display possible synonyms for an indicated word.

OOP *see* **object-oriented programming.**

open system interconnection (OSI) mode seven-tier communication standard, developed by the International Standards Organization (ISO), which promotes connectivity between hardware produced by different manufacturers.

operating procedures actions people take when using computer hardware and software correctly.

operating system collection of system programs that oversee the execution of application programs, manage files, and control the computer system's resources—monitor, keyboard, disk drives, memory, etc.

operational decision day-to-day decisions made by front-line managers.

operations personnel persons concerned with the daily IPOS cycle. For example, they may be responsible for data entry, computer operations, or computer center equipment.

optical character recognition (OCR) system of machine-readable input that allows entry of printed or typewritten characters directly with a scanner.

optical computer experimental processing hardware using optical switches for processing and optical fibers to transmit data internally for increased speed.

optical disk high-capacity disk that stores data in a binary format as small holes or flat spots on the disk surface. A low-power laser reads the data from the disk.

optical fiber cable high-speed communication channel made from spun glass filaments, which handles over 2000 simultaneous data transmissions at speeds up to one billion bps.

optical mark recognition (OMR) system of machine-readable input that allows scanners to read pencil marks used on standardized tests and surveys.

OSI *see* **open system interconnection.**

output results of computer processing.

Overwrite (Word Processing) adding text to a document by typing over old text.

page section of a running program that is stored on disk when not in use by a computer system with virtual memory.

page definition language coding of graphics, images, and text for use by laser printers.

page printer printer that produces one page of output at a time with speeds of over 300 pages per minute.

pagination word processing feature that includes counting pages and printing page numbers.

Paintbrush (Graphics) the user chooses a size and style of drawing tool. By moving a mouse, the tool on the screen is moved, creating the drawing.

palette displays the color options available in a graphics package.

paperless office automated offices involving networked technology like word processors, E-mail, and electronic filing systems. Only those documents going outside the office are on paper.

parallel operation conversion method whereby both new and old systems are run side-by-side and results are compared. After one or two successful processing cycles, the old system is removed.

parallel port I/O port sending data one byte at a time.

parallel processing simultaneous processing of the same program through the use of several processing units.

parity bit single bit added to the end of each byte, used to check if data has been correctly read or written.

parity checking each character on tape or disk is represented by an eight-bit code and a parity bit. The number of on (1) bits must be odd or even value for odd or even parity, respectively.

Pascal, Blaise (1623–1662) created the first mechanical adding machine, the Pascaline, in the 1640s.

Pascal (named after Blaise Pascal) high-level programming language used in education and for scientific purposes. It is self-structuring.

password special combination of letters, numbers, or symbols, known only to the user, that allows access to protected computer systems and data.

password protect assigning a unique password to a file. The software allows access to the data only after the correct password is entered.

PC *see* **personal computer.**

PC-DOS operating system IBM licenses from the Microsoft Corporation and distributes with its line of personal computers.

pen-based computer personal computer having a pen as the main or only input hardware.

peripheral equipment attached to processing hardware for storing, entering, and outputting data and programs.

personal computer (PC) processing hardware with a single processor that is designed for use by one person at a time.

personal productivity software general-purpose programs that help people with personal applications, including word processing, spreadsheets, databases, and graphics.

personnel data facts and figures about employees and their productivity, including address, social security number, date-of-hire, and more.

PERT *see* **program evaluation and review technique.**

phased transition piecemeal conversion method whereby part of the new system is put into operation throughout the entire organization. Other parts are added in stages.

physical data data from the environment—for example light, humidity, and pressure.

picosecond one trillionth of a second; used to measure processing speed within a computer's processor.

pie chart a circle divided into sections, each representing the proportion one component has when related to the whole. Each section is labeled with the component name and the actual percentage. Percentages for the entire chart total 100.

pilot operation type of installation whereby the entire new system is tried in just a small part of the organization, then later brought into other areas of the organization.

pitch number of characters printed per inch in a document.

pixel picture element, which is one component of an array or matrix of dots that makes up a visual image.

pixel graphics (also known as bit mapping) pattern of pixels making up a graphic image.

Playback Control (Multimedia) allows the user to change the volume and other special effects measure by measure for audio data.

plotter an output device that produces line drawings by moving pen across paper.

point unit of measure for type size. One point equals 1/72 of an inch.

point-of-sale (POS) type of terminal by which sales data is read from price tags by a scanner and entered directly into the computer/cash register.

portable language programming language that can be used without modification on a variety of computer hardware.

portrait vertical layout of a document page.

POS *see* **point-of-sale.**

presentation graphics common graphics, including pie charts, bar graphs, line graphs, area graphs, and symbol charts, used in business and other applications.

preventive maintenance procedures running diagnostic checks and cleaning computer hardware before a crash occurs.

primary storage another name for a computer's internal memory.

PRINT (BASIC) statement that displays values of indicated variables on the screen.

Print (Spreadsheet) output hard copy of worksheet.

print chart a form that shows how output will appear on paper.

PRINT USING (BASIC) statement that outputs information in a format specified after the keyword USING.

print zone a division of the screen or paper into 14-column sections used with BASIC output.

printer output hardware producing printed information on paper.

Privacy Act of 1974 government agencies must state how collected data will be used and gain permission to use it in other situations.

procedure systematic course of action that helps people use software, hardware, and data.

process control situation wherein a computer constantly monitors and adjusts an activity.

processing the action of a computer on data as it performs calculations or comparisons.

processor computer circuitry that performs arithmetic operations and logical operations using programs and data in memory.

production/sales data facts and figures about products made, products sold, or services provided. Organizations that manufacture products would keep inventory levels and sales figures, while service-oriented organizations maintain data about the number of people served and how they were helped.

program the set of instructions a computer follows in sequence to control a specific IPOS cycle.

program evaluation and review technique (PERT) chart that shows order and time requirements for each task in a project as boxes connected by lines.

program revision change made to existing software to improve operations or comply with changes in laws or company policy.

program specifications part of the systems specifications dealing with the design of software.

programmable the ability of computers and some calculators to follow a stored sequence of instruction for processing input.

programmable read-only memory (PROM) special type of nonvolatile memory that allows updating of data stored there.

programmer person who translates program specifications into computer programs and tests new programs for errors.

Project (Data Management) allows users to create an abbreviated version of an existing database table.

project management software a software package that helps people plan, track, and schedule projects through program features that support time management, job scheduling, resource management, and cost estimations.

projection plate hardware, fitting on an overhead projector, to display computer output on a wall screen.

PROM *see* **programmable read-only memory.**

promotional software software that shows the capabilities of an application package, but restricts the amount of data or number of available program options. Software companies provide promotional software so potential users can try out the package before buying it.

Prompt (DOS) internal command that customizes DOS prompt.

proportional spacing space given to each symbol on a line of type depends upon the width of the symbol.

Protect (Spreadsheet) designating a worksheet or selected cells as read-only.

protected file (also known as read-only file) can be used and copied, but the operating system prevents it from being deleted or changed.

protocol predefined set of procedures for establishing, maintaining, and terminating data communications between remote hardware.

prototyping modeling user interfaces, such as screens and reports, by using applications generator or authoring system.

pseudocode a method of representing program logic by using English phrases in an outline form.

public domain software programs that are free to the general public.

puck small handheld device, moved across a board annotated with CAD commands and options. When desired feature is within the crosshairs of the puck, a button is pushed on the puck to indicate input.

pull-down menu (also known as **drop-down menu**) menu options that stay hidden in a menu bar at the top of the screen until the user selects it. When the menu is selected, the menu opens to list program options. Once an option is selected, the menu rolls back up into the menu bar.

punched card a paper card on which data is represented by rows and columns of holes. Each card has 12 rows and 80 columns.

quality control routine checking of a product or process to make sure it meets a predefined standard.

QBE *see* **query by example.**

query user request to a data management system for information.

query by example (QBE) graphical user interface allows user to structure a query by using a mouse to select desired fields and using the keyboard to identify examples.

Quit (also known as **Exit**) returns software control to operating system.

RAM *see* **random access memory.**

random access (also known as **direct access**) the computer system uses an index or other techniques to identify a record's location within a file and can access an individual record without processing other records.

random access memory (RAM) memory unit with temporary storage for data and programs.

random access memory (RAM) drive volatile memory set aside to temporarily substitute for disk storage. RAM drives have faster access speeds than disk drives, but data must be copied to some type of permanent storage medium before the power is turned off.

range group of cells within a worksheet that are defined by the first and last cells in the block.

range name unique label (name) assigned to a block of cells.

Rd (Rmdir) internal DOS command that removes a subdirectory name from a designated disk directory. All program and data files must be deleted from the subdirectory before it can be removed.

READ (BASIC) statement that assigns values in a DATA statement to corresponding variable names.

read-only file (also known as **protected file**) can be used and copied, but the operating system prevents it from being deleted or changed.

read-only memory (ROM) permanent memory, programmed during manufacturing, which holds systems programs and language translators.

read/write head the mechanism in a tape drive or at the end of a disk drive access arm that picks up or records data.

readers log groupware feature that tracks who has accessed shared documents.

real-time processing the computer system processes a user request as soon as it is input.

record group of related fields about a person, place, thing, idea, or event.

record layout form a form that shows how data fields are organized into records in a file or database.

reduced instruction set computing (RISC) processor designed to achieve faster processing speeds by minimizing intermediary processing steps through limiting the number of complex operations.

relational model data is organized into tables and integrated by joining the tables using fields that are common to both tables.

relative cell reference reference to a cell address within a formula that changes when it is moved or copied in order to maintain the cell relationships in the original formula.

REM (BASIC) nonexecutable statement that contains notes by the programmer; very helpful for internal documentation of programs.

removable disk disk that is designed to be taken out of the disk drive when not in use.

Rename (Ren) internal DOS command that changes the spelling of a filename stored on a specific disk.

repetitive strain injuries (RSI) a group of injuries—usually to neck, back, arms, and hands—that result from repeated movement (as in keyboard typing).

report generator user interface that works with a data management system to support user design and modification of printed documents.

request for proposal (RFP) description of system specifications accompanying a request for bids by vendors.

research data facts and figures about past performance and plans for future projects, such as last year's sales figures, grant applications, and new product designs.

resolution a measure of graphic image sharpness in bits (pixels) per inch or bits per line. The higher the resolution, the sharper the graphic image.

response time the time it takes a computer to process and output user input.

restore button (Windows) icon with double arrows found in the top right corner of the title bar next to the minimize button. Clicking on the restore button returns a maximized window back to its original dimensions.

Retrieve (Spreadsheet) copy designated worksheet from disk into computer's memory.

Retrieve (Word Processing) copy a document from disk into memory.

reverse video putting text into the opposite colors expected on a screen; done for emphasis. For example, black characters on a white background for a monochrome screen.

RFP *see* **request for proposal.**

RGB (red, green, blue) monitor monitor using red, green, and blue pixels in combinations to form a variety of colors.

right justification alignment of text in a document along only the right edge.

Right to Financial Privacy Act of 1978 provides strict guidelines for government agencies reviewing bank accounts.

ring topology a network wherein each node is connected to two other nodes, forming a circle.

RISC *see* **reduced instruction set computing.**

robotics a computer-controlled mechanical arm or device that can be programmed to do repetitive and intricate movements.

ROM *see* **read-only memory.**

root directory primary disk directory that is created when the disk is formatted.

RPG (Report Program Generator) high-level programming language used in business report-generating applications.

RSI *see* **repetitive strain injuries.**

run (also known as **execute** or **launch**) having the computer follow the instructions in a program.

RUN (BASIC) command that instructs computer to execute program instructions currently in memory.

sans-serif lacking tails on printed characters. This results in a simple, block style of text.

SAVE (BASIC) command that copies program in memory onto disk, using designated filename.

Save (Spreadsheet) stores worksheet on disk, using designated filename.

Save (Word Processing) copies the document in memory onto a disk, using designated filename.

scanner input hardware used to sense patterns of bars, dots, images, or characters and convert them into binary codes that can be used by a computer.

screen layout form a form that shows how output will appear on a screen.

screen pointer icon, usually an arrow, on a screen that moves when the mouse or some other pointer device is moved. Program options are activated by using a mouse to move the screen pointer over the desired icon and clicking the mouse button.

screen prompt symbols and/or characters that indicate the computer is ready to accept a new command. The default DOS screen prompt displays an upper-case letter and greater than symbol, for example, A> or C>.

scroll the rolling of data up, down, and sideways on a screen for viewing long or wide documents.

scroll arrows arrow found at either end of a scroll bar. Users change the view of a window or list box by clicking on one of the scroll arrows.

scroll bar area that appears on the right or lower edges of a window or list box when only a partial view is available. A scroll bar contains a scroll box and scroll arrows.

scroll box square within a scroll bar that identifies which portion of the window or list box is currently being viewed. Users can change the view by dragging the scroll box within the scroll bar.

Search and Replace (Spreadsheet) locates and changes designated worksheet data or formula.

Search and Replace (Word Processing) user enters a word or phrase to be found in a document. In a global replace, all occurrences of the phrase are found and automatically replaced. In a discretionary replace, replacement of each occurrence of the word is decided by the user.

search path description of how to find a subdirectory or file by identifying a disk drive and the subdirectory's (or file's) location with respect to the disk's root directory.

second-generation computer computer developed in the mid-to-late 1950s that used transistors as part of the processing hardware. It contained core memory, used an operating system, and was programmed in high-level programming languages.

secondary storage another name for disks or tapes.

sector a division of a disk track used to organize data.

security measures designed to protect computers and information resources against unauthorized activities.

Select (Data Management) retrieves only those records and fields fulfilling user-dictated criteria.

selection basic structure of a computer program whereby one of two alternate sequences of instructions is used, based upon a tested condition.

self-directed work team selected group of people from an organization that have been empowered to make management decisions to solve a specific problem.

seminar also known as **workshop;** a professional educational meeting, concentrating on a single topic.

sensor input peripheral that detects physical data such as heat, light, or pressure.

sentinel value (also known as trailer value) the end-of-file mark tested for in an IF...THEN statement.

sequence basic structure of a computer program whereby instructions are executed in the order they appear in the program.

sequential access the computer system finds a record in a file by starting with the first record and processing each consecutive record until the desired record is found.

serial port I/O port sending data one bit at a time.

serial printer printer producing one character at a time, like a typewriter.

serif short line segments added to a type style to help the reader's eye flow across the page.

server node within a network that handles special tasks for network users, like printing, file management, or database management.

service bureau an outside agency hired by an organization to handle its data processing services.

service technician person who performs repairs and preventive maintenance on computer hardware.

Shape (Graphics) copies preset geometric shapes, like a circle or square, into the drawing.

shareware type of public domain software that is shared by users who are asked to pay a nominal fee to the author. For that fee the user will usually obtain a manual and any program revisions.

shell user interface that uses menus to identify program options and operations instead of commands.

Shockley, William (1910–1989) coinventor, with John Bardeen and Walter Brattain, of the transistor and cowinner of the 1956 Nobel Prize in Physics.

simulation a computer-generated environment that mimics a real-life or imaginary situation.

site license legal copyright restrictions accompanying some software that restricts the number of users as well as the location at which the program can be accessed.

size box (Macintosh) icon found in the bottom right corner of a window. Dragging size box to new screen location changes the size and shape of the associated window.

smart card credit card that contains processor and memory chip that stores and updates owner's credit information.

soft copy data displayed on a monitor.

soft return a carriage return entered into the document by the word wrap operation.

soft-sectored diskette floppy disk with one alignment hole. Sectors on this type of disk are set up during formatting.

soft space blank spaces added between words to fully justify text within the left and right margins.

software programs or instructions for the input, processing, output, and storage of data.

Sort (Data Management) duplicates a file and reorganizes records based on a key value designated by the user.

sound synthesizer output peripheral that generates recognizable sounds, such as warnings and music.

source a file's current location.

SPC *see* **statistical process control.**

speech synthesizer output peripheral that generates human-sounding speech.

Speed Control (Multimedia) control of the presentation speed, in frames per second, for film or video.

spelling checker online word processing feature that compares words in a document to a dictionary and flags words not found.

spooler (Simultaneous Peripheral Operation OnLine) utility program that coordinates the transfer of data between the computer and peripheral hardware.

Spraypaint (Graphics) as the cursor is moved around the screen, a spattering of a chosen color or pattern is sprayed. The speed of movement dictates the density of the spray.

SQL *see* **Structured Query Language.**

stack group of related hypermedia cards, similar to a data file.

stacked bar graph a bar graph in which each bar is broken down to show its components.

star topology a network with a central computer, the host, which has all other nodes attached to it. The host coordinates data communication between the other nodes.

statement a BASIC instruction, with a line number, that is executed only when the program is run.

statistical process control (SPC) procedures used to eliminate quality control problems by statistically selecting certain parts or activities for detailed inspection. A statistical analysis is performed on this data to identify current trends. When trends indicate that product quality is declining, changes are made.

status line area of a worksheet that displays which operation is currently being performed by the electronic spreadsheet program.

stereolithography using computer-controlled infrared beams to solidify a chemical mixture into plastic models.

still presentation camera camera that stores images on disks rather than film for direct input into a computer.

storage media materials on which data is recorded. Tapes and disks are popular storage media.

strategic decision long-term decisions made by top management that determine how an organization is going to achieve its goals.

Stretch (Graphics) lets a user manipulate figures drawn with the Shapes option.

string variable variable name within a computer program that identifies textual data.

structure chart (also known as **hierarchy chart**) a graphic representation of modules or objects in a program.

structured program a program organized to contain only three logical structures: sequence, selection, and iteration.

Structured Query Language (SQL) popular command-driven interface that allows users to access data from a database by using designated keywords and variable names.

structured walkthrough a group review of a program design and/or code done by programmers and supervisors.

stub testing testing modules that will make up a computer program by combining them with stubs or incomplete modules.

style sheet document containing the margin settings, tab locations, justification instructions, line spacing, and other formatting specifications a user wants for an application.

subdirectory additional directory, subordinate to the root directory, that is added to a disk by users.

Subtract (Data Management) compares two database tables and creates a new table containing data the other tables do not have in common.

summary report a report that condenses day-to-day operational data into totals and averages.

super VGA color monitor standard that displays 1024 by 768 pixels in 256 colors.

supercomputer powerful, high-speed computer capable of handling enormous amounts of data.

superconductor material that loses all electrical resistance at a set temperature.

supervisor an operating system program that coordinates all processing activities within a computer system.

switch optional parameter designated by using a slash and letter added to the end of a DOS instruction that identifies special activities user wishes to accomplish. For example, /W added to the Dir command indicates the user wants filenames listed across the screen without date, time, and file size.

symbol chart chart using colors and symbols to represent and highlight data in a presentation graphic.

synchronization coordination of the timing for several audio channels.

synchronous transmission communication protocol whereby data is grouped into blocks for transmission.

syntax word order, spacing, abbreviations, and special symbols used by a command-driven interface or programming language.

syntax error command that is not translatable.

sysop *see* **system operator.**

system a group of elements working together to solve a problem.

system drive disk drive that reads DOS during booting.

system operator (sysop) person responsible for the operation, maintenance, and protection of data and programs found on an electronic bulletin board.

system specifications a document covering in great detail requirements and procedures to be incorporated into a new computer system.

system test part of the software development cycle that includes testing of program modules, testing complete programs, and testing the entire system under realistic operating conditions.

systems analyst computer professional who works with users in developing computer systems that satisfy specific needs.

systems development project steps taken to define and create new system solutions to existing problems.

systems software controls internal computer activities. For example, system software controls flow of data in and out of memory as well as the computer's capacity to store, copy, and remove data on disk.

TAB (BASIC) found in PRINT and LPRINT statements. Acts like tabulation on a typewriter. It forces the cursor or print head to start at the specified column.

table independent file within a relational database that consists of a matrix of rows and columns into which data is placed.

tablet sensitized pad on which the position of a special pen is used as data.

tactical decision short-term decision made by middle managers that impacts when, where, and how an organization's resources are used.

tape a machine-readable medium in which data is stored as magnetic patterns on strips of plastic coated with a metal oxide.

tape cartridge tape within hard plastic shell.

tape drive storage hardware that writes data on tape and reads it back into computer's memory upon command.

tape streaming backing up data from disk to tape by continuous high-speed transfer of the data to tape.

tape track channel on a tape for storing a single bit of data. Data from several tracks is combined together to form the binary code for a specific byte of data.

target where a file is being copied.

task any operation performed by a computer system.

telecommunication long distance communications.

telecommuting working at home or other locations, using computer networks for communications.

teleconferencing meeting in which participants are distantly located and communicate through a network.

teleprocessing central computer system that uses data communication technology to exchange data with physically remote input and output components.

template a worksheet with labels and formulas, but no values, that is formatted for a specific application where it is copied and reused.

terabyte one trillion bytes of memory.

terminal a combination of keyboard with monitor or printer providing input and output to a computer system.

terminate stay resident (TSR) program that resides in the computer's memory, but stays inactive, until a special combination of keys is pressed.

test data sets of data used for program testing that represent all extremes and normal conditions the program would experience.

text another name for textual data.

text box accepts keyboard entries from user to identify new filenames or disk locations. Text boxes are often used within a dialog box.

Text Option (Graphics) a user may type text anywhere on a graphic image. Font and type sizes can be varied.

textual data any combination of letters, numbers, or special characters such as #, $, %, @, etc.

thermal printer dot-matrix printer that uses heated wires to brand the character on special paper.

third-generation computer computer developed during the 1960s that uses integrated circuits as the basis of processing. It normally has multitasking and online processing capabilities.

three-dimensional worksheets series of worksheets visually stacked on top of one another. Data and formulas can easily be moved or copied between worksheets.

time bomb time-dependent computer program that invades a computer system to erase program and data files at a designated day and time. This type of troublemaking program is time activated, hides inside another program, and cannot self-replicate.

timed backup automatic saving of a file to disk after a designated amount of time has passed.

timesharing many users equally share the processing power of a single computer by having the operating system alternate executing each program.

title bar horizontal area across the top of a window that displays the window's title. A window can be moved by clicking on the title bar and dragging it to a new screen location.

title locking freezing selected worksheet columns and/or rows on the screen. Data within locked areas cannot be edited.

token passing communication protocol to avoid data collisions on a network by passing an electronic signal (token) from node to node. A network node can transmit data only when it has the token.

toolbox displays drawing tool options, like brush size and shape, available in a graphics package.

top management people who make long-term strategic decisions involving wide-ranging effects.

total quality management organization-wide philosophy that focuses on customer satisfaction through quality control of every service and product.

touch-sensitive screen monitor whose surface, when touched, becomes an input device.

tower computer housing tipped on its narrow side to take up less floor space.

track storage area on a disk or tape where data is recorded as a series of magnetized areas representing bit patterns.

trackball input device with a ball in a housing. When the user moves the ball, a similar motion is reflected by the screen pointer.

trailer label (also known as **end-of-file mark**) a record that marks the end of a file on tape or disk.

trailer value (also known as **sentinel value**) the end-of-file mark tested for in an IF . . . THEN statement.

transaction exchange of value.

transaction cycle the input, processing, output, and storage of a single transaction.

transaction processing system any system that oversees the input, processing, output, and storage of an organization's transaction data.

transfer rate the speed at which data can be input to or output from the computer's memory and storage media.

transistor small electronic component that can alter a signal in a predefined way. It is the basis of the second-generation computer.

trash icon (Macintosh) temporary storage area for deleted files.

trojan computer program that invades a computer system to erase program and data files. This type of troublemaking program is usually introduced by an outside source, hides inside another program, and cannot self-replicate.

troubleshooting procedure actions people take to detect and eliminate computer system problems.

TSR *see* **terminate stay resident.**

Turing, Alan (1912–1954) developed the Turing test for artificial intelligence and provided some basis for computer science theory.

twisted pair wire communication channel that can handle a single transmission at speeds from 300 bps to 14,400 bps.

Undelete (DOS) internal command that adds a previously deleted filename back to the disk directory. Deleted files are identified by replacing the first character in the filename with a ?. When undeleting a file, the user is asked to reenter the filename's first character.

undo the action of a previous operation is reversed.

unstructured program program using many GOTO statements that are not organized according to structured techniques.

update adding, changing, or deleting data in a file or document.

Update (Data Management) allows user to add records, delete records, or change data fields in records.

upload sending data or programs directly to another computer.

user-developers end-users who design and test their own computer applications.

user friendly an attribute of computers meaning "easy to use."

user interface combination of menu options, icons, and commands people use when working with a computer program.

user's manual information about a software package that includes operating instructions, description of program features, explanation of error messages, and company information.

utility program system program that must be located and loaded into memory before associated instruction is executed.

utility software system software that performs special processing tasks not under the direct control of the operating system. Virus scanning, hardware emulation, and disk optimization are examples of operations performed by utility software.

vaccine another name for antivirus software, it looks for viruses as new files are brought into a system.

vacuum tube a glass tube containing circuitry, which was the processing basis for first-generation computers.

value numeric data within a worksheet.

value-added network (VAN) a wide area network with additional services available to users, such as access to databases and electronic mail.

VAN *see* **value-added network.**

vaporware computer programs that have been promised, but do not exist.

variable a name that represents a changeable data value under control of a computer program.

variable expense changeable expenses under consumer control, such as food or entertainment.

variable name generic name given to a field as a means of identifying different fields within a record.

VDT *see* **video display terminal.**

vector graphics form of graphics wherein any two points can be joined by a solid line rather than a line of pixels.

Ver (DOS) internal command that displays the DOS version number currently running in the computer.

verification person entering data checks it for errors after it is entered, but before processing.

version each new edition of software and documentation.

VGA *see* **video graphics array.**

video display terminal (VDT) a screen that provides temporary output of information.

video graphics array (VGA) color monitor standard that displays 720 by 400 pixels in 256 colors.

Video Privacy Protection Act of 1988 prohibits retailers from releasing video-rental data without customer's permission or a court order.

virtual memory using secondary disk storage as an extension of a computer's main memory unit.

virtual reality computer-generated images displayed as three-dimensional output in a set of goggles and controlled by the physical movements of the user.

virus computer program that invades a computer system by attaching itself to other commonly used programs. Once the virus infects a system, it displays unwanted messages, erases data, or promotes activities that damage hardware.

voice mail computer system that answers telephone calls with a prerecorded message and saves callers' message on disk for later playback.

voice recognition device the capability of a machine to accept spoken commands as input.

volatile memory type of computer memory that is cleared out when the power to the memory is shut off.

volume label 11-character label user adds to disk directory.

WAN *see* **wide area network.**

Watson, Thomas John Sr. (1874–1956) president of IBM from 1924 to 1956. Under his leadership, IBM became the leading computer manufacturer in the world.

white area area of a document containing no text, graphics, or images.

wide area network (WAN) public or private network covering a large geographic area.

window subdivides a screen display to allow the user to look at several menus, dialog boxes, or status reports from more than one program.

window (Spreadsheet) subdivision of electronic spreadsheet display. Screens divided into two windows can display nonadjoining worksheet cells.

window frame border around a window.

Windows Graphical user interface developed by the Microsoft Corporation to be used with MS-DOS or PC-DOS. Windows NT uses the same GUI and is a standalone personal computer operating system.

word a collection of bytes or bits representing the maximum number of bits the CPU can process at one time.

word processing program expedites report and letter writing by enabling users to format, insert, move, copy, erase, save, and print text from a document file.

word wrap when a document is entered without carriage returns, the word processor senses the margins and moves words to the next line as needed.

work group computing people using a network and groupware to share ideas and solve problems.

worksheet related data organized into a row/column format.

workshop (also called **seminar**) a professional educational meeting concentrating on a single topic, that lasts several hours to a few days. Participants are involved in lectures and demonstrations.

workstation the name given to a microcomputer attached to a larger computer system.

worm computer program that invades a computer system from an outside source, is self-contained, and self-replicates until it fills every available memory address.

WORM disk *see* **write once read many disk.**

Wozniak, Steve (1950–) built the Apple I microcomputer in 1976 with Steve Jobs and later formed Apple Computer Corporation.

write once read many (WORM) disk optical disk that can accept data for permanent storage. Once the data is recorded on the disk it cannot be erased, but can be read as many times as needed.

write-protect notch section cut out of the side of a 5.25-inch floppy disk. When covered, a disk drive can read data from the disk, but it cannot write data onto the disk.

write-protect window sliding tab on a 3.5-inch diskette. When open, a disk drive can read data from the disk, but cannot write data onto the disk.

writing analyzer software that analyzes writing style, reading level, passive voice, and complex sentences; highlights jargon; and provides other data about the words used in a document.

WYSIWYG the feature of a word processing or desktop publishing package to show on the monitor exactly how a document will look when printed; acronym for What You See Is What You Get.

XGA *see* **extended graphics array.**

zoom box (Macintosh) icon found in the top right corner of a window. Clicking on the zoom box expands or reduces the size of the associated window.

CREDITS

Photos

Figure 1.1 Sun Microsystems; **1.2** *left* Carolina Power & Light Co., *right* AP/Wide World Photos; **1.3** Ameritech; **1.5** IBM Corp.; **1.9** IBM Corp.; **p. 20** Apple Computer, Inc.; **1.10** Mark Joseph/Ameritech; **p. 22** IBM Corp; **p. 23** National Convenience Stores/Larry Payne; **p. 24** *top* L.A. Schwaber-Barzilay, *bottom* Hewlett-Packard.

Figure 2.2 Mark Joseph/Ameritech; **2.3** IBM Corp.; **2.4** IBM Corp.; **2.6** Intel Corp.; **2.7** IBM Corp.; **2.8** Jeff Smith/GTE Corp.; **2.9** Hewlett-Packard; **2.11** Tandy; **2.13** Autodesk; **pp. 49, 51, 52, 53** Stephen Frisch.

Figure 3.1 IBM Corp.; **3.5** Radio Shack/Tandy Corp.; **3.7** Kemper Service Co.; **3.16** IBM Corp.; **p. 79** Microsoft.

Figure 4.1 IBM Corp.; **4.12** Hewlett-Packard; **4.21** IBM Corp.; **p. 129** WordPerfect; **p. 130** *middle* Radius, *bottom* Hewlett-Packard; **p. 131** IBM Corp.

Figure 5.1 National Convenience Stores/Larry Payne; **5.14** IBM Corp.; **5.15** Morrison Knudson Corp.; **p. 163** IBM Corp.

Figure 6.2 IBM Corp.; **6.11** Macromedia; **6.13** Video Fusion; **6.15** Digital Media; **6.16** Pixar, "Luxo, Jr."; **6.18** *left* Cray Research, Inc., *right* Cray Research, Inc.; **6.19** Evans & Sutherland; **6.21** Microsoft; **6.22** Computer Graphics.

Figure 7.1 New York Stock Exchange; **7.20** Matrix Instruments; **7.21** BCE International; **7.22** © Vickers & Beechler/Automatic Data Processing; **7.23** © Gregory Heisler/NYNEX Corp.; **p. 233** © Canadian Airlines International; **p. 235** Sun Microsystems.

Figure 8.1 Sperry Corp.; **8.2** *lower right* Intel Corp.; **8.3** Bryn Smothers, Houston Industries; **8.9** Silicon Graphics; **8.15, 8.16** IBM Corp.; **8.17** Toshiba America Information Systems; **8.18** Dave Martinez/Apple Computer, Inc.; **8.20** General Electric Corp.; **8.21** Cray Computer, Inc.; **8.22** Hewlett-Packard; **p. 251** AT&T; **p. 261** Texas Instruments; **p. 271** *left* Chuck O'Rear, *right* SPX Corp./Robert Neuman; **p. 272** *upper left* Chuck O'Rear; **p. 373** *upper left* Hewlett-Packard, *bottom* Intel Corp.; **p. 274** *top* Intel Corp., *bottom right* John Greenleigh/Apple Computer Corp.

Figure 9.1 IBM Corp.; **9.2** Microsoft; **9.3** Texas Instruments; **9.6** IBM Corp.; **9.8** *left* Logitech, Inc., *right* Hewlett Packard; **9.10** John Lund/Apple Computer, Inc.; **9.11** IBM Corp.; **9.12** © 1991 Matthew Borkoski; **9.13** IBM Corp.; **9.14** AMP Inc.; **9.16, 9.18** IBM Corp.; **9.19** Hewlett-Packard, **9.22, 9.24** IBM Corp.; **9.25** Cincinatti Milicron; **9.26** Chrysler Corp.; **p. 307** *middle* Visions Photo, Inc./Stephen Shames, *bottom* MEDphone Corp.; **p. 308** *top* Wright State University.

Figure 10.1 Apple Computer, Inc.; **10.3** Hewlett-Packard; **p. 319** Apple Computer, Inc.; **10.8** Seagate Technologies; **10.9** Plus Development Corp.; **10.11** IBM Corp.; **10.14** *top* Federal Bureau of Investigation, *bottom* Archive Corp.; **10.16** IBM Corp.

Figure 11.1 IBM Corp.; **11.7** *top left* US Sprint/United Telecom, *bottom left* BSCE Inc., *middle* IBM Corp.; *right* Obak Arslanian/Pacificorp; **11.11** IBM Corp.; **11.13** Multitech Systems; **11.15** © Gregory Heisler/NYNEX Corp.; **11.16** EO, Inc.; **11.20** Sun Microsystems; **11.21** © Mark Joseph, Inc./Ameritech; **11.24** © Steven Meckler/University of Arizona; **p. 371** Hewlett-Packard.

Figure 12.1 Hewlett-Packard; **12.2** Dana Corp.; **12.4** Johnson & Johnson; **12.5** Brush Wellman; **12.10** © 1991 David Lissy; **12.13** © John Blaustein/Bank of America; **12.14** IBM Corp.; **p. 407** *top* IBM Corp.

Figure 13.1 NASA; **13.4** © Tony Stone Worldwide; **13.13** Intersolv, Inc.

Figure 14.3 Hewlett-Packard; **14.9** Sperry Corp.; **14.12** IBM Corp.; **14.27** Northeast Utilities.

Figure 15.1 Four Phase; **15.2** Mark Joseph/Ameritech; **15.4** Commodore Electronics, Ltd.; **15.8** © Henley & Savage/Figge International; **p. 518** Apple Computer, Inc.; **15.13** © TSW, William S. Helsel; **p. 525** Ogden ERC; **p. 527** IBM Corp.; **p. 528** Mark Segal/TSW.

Figure 16.1 New York Stock Exchange; **16.4** AT&T; **16.5** NASA; **16.7** © John Blaustein; **16.8** AT&T; **16.10** Harmon Industries; **16.13** IBM Corp.; **p. 554** IBM Corp.; **p. 559** *left* Intel Corp., *right* © Manfred Kage/Peter Arnold, Inc.; **p. 560** *top* NASA/Ames, *bottom* Richard S. Muler, Berkeley Sensor & Actuator Center; **p. 561** *top* NEC Corp.

"In the News . . ."

Page 12 "Computer Literacy a Must," reprinted with permission of *Datamation*, 5/1/93, © 1993 by Cahners Publishing Company; **p. 18** "Fighting Fear of Change," 3/15/93, © 1993, reprinted with permission from *Computerworld;* **p. 32** "Computer Chips," *IBM 1990 Annual Report;* **p. 75** "Desktop Operating Systems," 2/22/93, © 1993, reprinted with permission from *Computerworld;* **p. 118** "How to Improve Your Computer Communciation," D. Arnold, *Computers and Society: Impact!* (Mitchell/Mcgraw-Hill, 1991); **p. 123** "10 Ways to Make Your Office Environment-Friendly," John Pivovarnick; **p. 143** "Selecting Software," 12/90, © 1990, reprinted with permission from *Success;* **p. 218** "Characteristics of Good Information," D. Stamper and W. Price, *Database Design and Management* (Mitchell/McGraw-Hill, 1990); **p. 253** "Before Calling Technical Support," *The Personal Computing 500*, 10/89; **p. 291** "Backup Tips," *Info World*, 4/19/93; **p. 293** "Optical Storage Disks," *IBM 1990 Annual Report;* **p. 319** "Ergonomics of Input," Inforworld; **p. 325** "Tips for Reducing Computer Vision Syndrome," 2/8/93, © 1993, reprinted with permission from *Computerworld;* **p. 349** "Don't Be Overloaded: Tips for Fighting E-Mail Overload," 5/17/93, © 1993, reprinted with permission from *Computerworld;* **p. 368** "The Ten Deadly Network Sins," *PC World*, 3/91; **p. 390** "The Winds of Change," *QED Information Sciences, Inc.*, 4/1/93; **p. 395** "Expensive Executive Toys or Productivity Tools?," *Dalton Communications*, 1986; **p. 422** "How Secure Is 'IT'?" *NCSC's Orange Book*, 3/1/93; **p. 428** "A Properly Planned Interview Can Be an Analyst's Best Tool," reprinted by permission, *Data Management* (Data Processing Management Association); **p. 471** "Protyping: Advantages Over Traditional Methods," *Data Management*, 3/86; **p. 510** "Taking a Byte Out of Computer Crime," reprinted by permission of *Management Review;* **p. 521** "Hack-attack Response," *Federal Bureau of Investigation*, 1/25/93; **p. 541** "The Rise of the Visual Communicator," reprinted with permission of *Datamation*, 5/15/93, © 1993 by Cahners Publishing Company.

INDEX

Note: Italicized page numbers refer to illustrations.

Absolute cell reference, 151
Access time, 318, *319*
Accountability, management and, 442
ACM. *See* Association for Computing Machinery
Acoustic coupler modem, 355
Active cell, 145
Active directory, 588
Active window, *644*
Activity log, 524
Ada, 358, 479, *479*
  applications, strengths, weaknesses, *484*
Addition symbol, 148
Address, 257, *257*
  disk, 318
Advertising agency, office automation and, 125
Agriculture, data management systems and, 232
AI. *See* Artificial intelligence
Allen, Paul, 256
Alphanumeric data, 14
Altair microcomputer, 79, 468
Alternative solutions, identification, *425*
American Standard Code of Information Interchange (ASCII), 248–249, *249*
Analog signal, 346, *346*
Analytical engine, 426
Animation, 8, 190–191, *191*
Antivirus software, 515
AP. *See* Associated Press
Append operation, data manipulation language, 215, *215*
Apple I, 20
Apple II, 20, 256
Apple Computer Corporation, 20, 256
Apple icon, 631
Apple Macintosh, 87–92, 628–645
  applications, documents, folders, 640–645, *640*
  initializing diskette, 633–634
  shutting down system, 645
  start-up procedures, 629–632
  using mouse, 632–633
  window features, 637–639
Application, 640–645, *640*
Application development team, 420, *420*
Application generator, 217
Application package, buying, needs analysis, 698–703, *699–702*
Application program languages, *68–69*, *484*
Applications software, 46–48
Architecture, computers and, 8
Area graph, 178, *179*
Arithmetic operation, 12, 250–251
  BASIC, 660, *660*
  symbols, 148
Arithmetic operator, BASIC, 659, *659*
Artificial intelligence (AI), 19, 256, 403, 544–546, *556*
ASCII. *See* American Standard Code of Information Interchange
Ashton, Alan, 110
ASM. *See* Association for System Management
Assembler, 470
Assembly language, 470
Associated Press (AP), 126
Association for Computing Machinery (ACM), 42, 558
  Code of Ethics and Professional Conduct, *506*
Association for System Management (ASM), 557
Asterisk (*), 148
Asynchronous transmission, 360, *360*
Athletics
  electronic spreadsheet and, 160
  graphics software and, 195–196, *195*
ATM. *See* Automatic teller machine
"At" mark (@), 149
AT&T, 186
Attribute name, 213–214
Audio channel, 189
Audio data, 189–190, *190*
Audio-visual data, 14, *38*
  storage, 38
Authoring system, 484
Automatic teller machine (ATM), 353, 523
Automation. *See* Office automation
Automobile, embedded microprocessor, 536, *536*
Automotive repair, data management systems, 231–232, *231*

Babbage, Charles, 243, 358, 426
Backup, tips, 291
Backup procedures, 40
Backward chaining, 406
Bakus, John, 256
Banner program, 128
Bar code, 207, 284
Bar-code scanner, 284–286, *285*
Bardeen, John, 244, 251
Bar graph, 156, 176, *176*
  designing, *180*
  stacked, 176, *176*
BASIC, 74, 83, 247–248, 256, 468, 476, *476*, *477*, 489
  applications, strengths, weaknesses, *484*
  arithmetic operators, 659, *659*
  commands, 652–653
  controlling program loops, 668–674
  designing output, 678–679
  numeric constants, 658
  operation hierarchy, 660, *660*
  performing computations, 657–660
  print zones for output, 664–665, *664*
  repeating program instructions, 661–668
  variables, 658–659, *659*
  working with text, 676–679
BASICA, 651
BASIC code, *655*
BASIC interpreter, 79
  loading, 652
BASIC program, *252*
  batch, 662–663, *663*
  column totals, 671–672
  controlling loops, 668–674
  design, 686–688
  documentation, 688–689
  headings, 665–666, *666*
  listing and running, 656, *656*
  output, *686*, *687*
  output formatting, 672–674, *672*, *673*, *674*
  repeating instructions, 661–668
  saving and loading, 656–657
BASIC programming, 650–689
  defining requirements, 685–686
  flowcharting, 654–655, *654*
  loops, 680–685
  program design, 686–688
Bastian, Bruce, 110
Batch processing, 210
Baudot, 347
Baud rate, 346–347
BBS. *See* Bulletin board system
Bednorz, J. Georg, *554*
Beginner's All-Purpose Symbolic Instruction Code. *See* BASIC
Bell Laboratories, 251, 479
Benchmark test, 432
Bernoulli, Daniel, 322
Beta testing, 486
Binary code, 16, 247–249
Binary digit. *See* Bit
Biometric security device, 520, *521*
Bit, 16, 248
  parity, 331, *332*, 361
  start, 360
  stop, 360
Bit mapping, 171, *172*
Bits per second (bps), 346–347
Block, 104, 327
Boilerplate, 112
Bold, 116, 150
Boole, George, 247, 363
Booting, 48, 76, *76*
  microcomputer, 570–573, *573*, 598–602
Border, 154
Bork, Robert, 504
bps. *See* Bits per second
Brattain, Walter, 244, 251
Bricklin, Daniel, 141, 158, 256
Brown, Jerry, 193
Buffer, 329
Bulletin board system (BBS), 362, *362*
Bus, 252, *253*, *263*
Business
  computers and, 8–9
  multimedia and, 192
Bus topology, 343–344, *344*
Button icon, 72
Byron, Augusta Ada, 358
Byte, 248

C, 74, 83, 479–480, *480*
  applications, strengths, weaknesses, *484*
C++, 256
Cache memory, 257–258
CAD. *See* Computer-aided design
CAD/CAM, 302
Caduceus, 404–406
Calculator, electromechanical, 243
CAM. *See* Computer-aided machining
Camera, still, 290
  characteristics, *292*
Camera-ready copy, 114
Card, 227, *228*, *235*
Cardpunch, 290
  characteristics, *292*
Card reader, 290
  characteristics, *292*
Career path, 550–558
Carpal tunnel syndrome, 304
Carrier sense multiple access with collision detection (CSMA/CD), 350
CASE tools, 431–432, *431*, 447
Cashless society, 542–543, *542*
Cathode-ray tube (CRT), 300–301
CCP. *See* Certificate in Computer Programming
CD. *See* Compact disk
CDC. *See* Centers for Disease Control
Cd command, 588–589, *588*
CDP. *See* Certificate in Data Processing
CD-ROM. *See* Compact disk with read-only memory
CD-ROM disk, access time, transfer rate, storage capacity, *319*
Cell, 141
  active, 145
Cell address, 143
Cell reference
  absolute, 151
  relative, 151
Census Bureau, 42, 256, 328
Centers for Disease Control (CDC), 229–230
Central processing unit (CPU), 250–263
  operations, 258
Certificate in Computer Programming (CCP), *555*
Certificate in Data Processing (CDP), 554–555
CGA. *See* Color graphics adapter
Change, keeping up with, *21*
Channel separation, in multimedia, 189
Character, 36
  control, 248
  correspondence-quality, 295
  dot-matrix, 294
  full, 295
Chart. *See also* Flowchart
  Gantt, 436, *436*
  hierarchy, *465*
  PERT, 448
  pie, 156–157, *157*, 175, *175*
  print, 433, *434*
  structure, 465, *465*
  symbol, 178, *179*
Chdir command, 588–589, *588*
Chip, 32, 245
  memory, 334
  RAM, *257*, 334
  ROM, *255*
Chlorofluorocarbons (CFCs), 123
CIM. *See* Computer-integrated manufacturing

CIS. *See* Computer information system
CL9 Company, 20
Classroom, electronic, 126–128, *128*
Clean room, 273
Clicking, 603, *604*, 632–633, *633*, *636*
Client-server, 353
Client/server network, 353–354, *353*
Clip art, 120, *120*
Clock, 250
Clock speed, 250, 258, 334
Close box, 639
CLS command, 653
Coaxial cable, 347
 communication channels, *348*
COBOL, 74, 83, 256, 468, 474, *475*, 489
 applications, strengths, weaknesses, *484*
 compiler, 471
Codd, Edgar F., 209, 223
Code of Ethics and Professional Conduct, *506*
Cold site, 522
Collision, 349
Collision detection, 349–350
Color, computer graphics, 174
Color and contrast control option, multimedia, 188, *188*
Color graphics adapter (CGA), 301
Color monitor, 300–301
 standards, *300*
Color separation, 121, *121*
Colossus, 42, 243
COM. *See* Computer output microfilm
Command, 577, 652
 BASIC, 652–653
COMMAND.COM, 569, 582, 589, 597, 614–615
 copying, *582*
Command-driven interface, 61–64
Command menu, *144*, 145
COmmon and Business Oriented Language. *See* COBOL
Communication. *See* Data communication
Communication channel, 346, 347–349, *348*
 wireless, 347–348
Communication protocol, 349
Communication software, 48, 81, 359–361
Communications satellite, 348
Compact disk (CD), 45, *45*, 293, 323
Compact disk with read-only memory (CD-ROM), *45*, 323–324, 537, 710, 711
Compatibility, *51*, 131
Competitiveness, computers promoting, 8–9
Compiler, 470–471, *470*
 COBOL, 471
CompuServe, 363
Computed-aided design (CAD), 541
Computed-aided software engineering (CASE), 431–432, *431*
Computer, 6. *See also* Personal computer
 competitiveness and, 8–9
 critical thinking and, 6–7
 digital, 248
 embedded, 14, 43, 268, *536*
 environmental control and, *17*
 fault-tolerant, 270, *270*
 fear of, 20–21
 functions, 17–18
 hearing-impaired and, *19*
 interpersonal relationships and, 19
 laptop, 266–267, *267*, 358
 mainframe, 43, 264–264, *264*
  features compared, *268*
 notepad, 267, *267*, 358, *359*
 optical, 543–544, *544*
 pen-based, 288, *289*
 portable, 561
 processing speed, 16–17
 wearable, 561
Computer-aided design (CAD), 6, 192–194, *194*, 302
Computer-aided machining (CAM), 302, 541
Computer application, 10–11
Computer architect, *557*
Computer architecture, 557
Computer career, 550–558
Computer center, 34–35
Computer center controls, 520–522
 summary, *522*
Computer chip, 32, 245
Computer crime, 508–516
 against computers, 514–516
 examples, 508–512
 signs of potential, 513
 types, 512–513
Computer engineering, 556–557, *557*
Computer graphics. *See also* Graphics
 trends, 174
Computer imaging, 174, 194–195, *194*
Computer information system (CIS), 552–555
 career goals and interests related, *552*
 career specialties, *553*
Computer-integrated manufacturing (CIM), 541
Computer-integrated workplace, 539–541
Computer literacy, 12, *547*
Computer manufacturer, where to find software, 83
Computer Matching and Privacy Act (1988), 504
Computer operator, 35
Computer output microfilm (COM), 299, *299*
Computer professional, 33
 opportunities, *456*
Computer program. *See* Program
Computer retail store, where to find software, 83
Computer salepeople, 33
Computer science, *555*
Computer scientist, *555*
Computer skills, updating, 547–550
Computer software. *See* Software
Computer system, 31. *See also* Personal computer system
 components, 31, *32*, *45*
 requirements, 712, *712*
 secure, *516*
 security
  computer center controls, *520–522*, *522*
  data security controls, 519
  input, processing, and output controls, 522–524, *524*
  management controls, 520, *520*
  physical controls, 517–519, *517*
Computer technology, college curriculum and, *551*
Computer time, theft, 512
Computer trade magazines
 software reviews, *84–85*
 where to find software, 84–85
Computer training, 458
Computer user, 32–33
 informed, *33*
Computer vision syndrome, reducing, 325
Computing
 end-user, 33, *551–552*
 personal, 22–24
 work group, 367–369
Computing Tabulating Recording Company, 396
Concurrent update, 226
Conference, 548–549, *549*
Constant, numeric, 658
Constitution, 503
Consumer electronics, 533–534, *537*
Contention, 349
Contention protocol, 350
Context-sensitive, 74
Context-sensitive help, 605
Continuing education, 549
Contract programmer, 433
Control box, 610
Control character, 248
Control clerk, 35
Control/communication operations, 252–254
Control totals, 523
Conversion, 439, *441*
Coprocessor, math, 254
Copy
 camera-ready, 114
 external, 105
 hard, 283
  screen display, 576
 soft, 283
Copy command, 581–582, *589*
Copy operation
 electronic spreadsheet, 151
 word processing, 105
Correspondence-quality character, 295
Corrigan, Patrick, 368
Corrigan Group, 368
Cost/benefit analysis, 425
Countess of Lovelace, 358, 426
CP/M, 256
CPU. *See* Central processing unit
Crash, 41
Cray-1, 256
Cray Y-MP, 269–270, *269*
Create Directory option, 88
Create operation, data definition language, 213, *213*
Credit card reader, 290
 characteristics, *292*
Crime. *See* Computer crime
Critical thinking, computer and, 6–7
Cross-referencing, 38, 220, 221
CRT. *See* Cathode-ray tube
CSC Index, 18
CSMA/CD. *See* Carrier sense multiple access with collision detection
Cursor, 61–62
 keys controlling, *62*
Cursor control
 electronic spreadsheet, 145
 word processing, 103–104
Cut and paste operation, electronic spreadsheet, 151
Cylinder, 321

Data, 7, 36–39
 alphanumeric, 14
 audio, 189–190, *190*
 audio-visual, 14, *38*
  storage, 38
 demographic, *525*
 financial, 388
 vs. information, 38–39
 integrating, *208*
 management information, 387–389, *388*
 manipulation, 512
 numeric, 14, *678*
 organization, 36–38, *37*
  into reports, 389–392
 personnel, 388
 physical, 14–15
  storage, 38
 presentation graphics, 180
 production/sales, 388–389
 research, 388
 standard codes, 248–249
 string, *678*
 systems design and, 433
 test, 468
 textual, 14
 theft, 512
 types, 14–16
 visual, 186–189, *186*
Data administrator, 212–213
Database, 8
 designs, 221
 hierarchical model, 221–222, *222*
 network model, 222, *222*
 relational, 209
 relational model, 223–225, *223*
Database administrator, 36
Database management, 219–227
Database management software, 212, 219
 user needs, technical support, hardware requirements, *220*
Database management system (DBMS), *219*
 relational, guidelines, 209
Database processing, pros and cons, 226–227, *226*
Database program, 47–48
Database server, 344
Data collision, 349
Data communication, 341–343, *342*, 354–361
 communication channel, 346, 347–349, *348*
 coordinating, 349–350
 hardware, 354–358
 software, 359–361
Data compression, 81, 332
Data definition, file management, 212–214, *213*
Data definition language, 212
 Create operation, 213, *213*
Data dictionary, 431
Data directory, 79
Data drive, 569, 597
Data encryption, 373, 519
Data entry line, 145
Data entry operator, 35, 40
Data entry procedures, 40
Data file, organization into file folder, *614*
Data flow diagram, 420, *421*
Data General, 110
Data integrity, 220
Data librarian, 35
Data management software, applications, 227–232
Data manipulation, file management, 214–216
Data manipulation language, 214–216
Data model, 221
Data processing, 8–9, 207–212, *207*
Data Processing Management Association (DPMA), 558
Data redundancy, 219, 226
Data security, 48
 controls, 519
DATA statement, 662–663, *663*, 665, 669, 688

Data storage media, *319*
Data storage and retrieval, 8
Data transmission
  asynchronous, 360, *360*
  error detection, 361
  full-duplex, 361, *361*
  half-duplex, 360–361, *361*
  modes, 360–361
  rate, 346–347, *347*
  synchronous, 360, *360*
dBASE III PLUS, 489
DBMS. *See* Database management system
Debugging, 473, *473*
Decision making, tools enhancing, 398–406
Decision-support system (DSS), 392–397, *392*
  data analysis using queries, 397, *397*
  group, 400
  modeling, 393–397
Default, 77
Default disk drive, 580
  changing, 580–581, *581*
Defense Department, 269, 474, 479
Delete dialog box, 620–621, *621*
Delete operation
  electronic spreadsheet, 152, *152*
  word processing, 104–105
Delete option, 620
Del instruction, 585
Demodulation, 354–356, *355*
Demographic data, *525*
Density, 319
Desktop, 602, 631
  Macintosh, 631–632, *631*
Desktop operating system, 75
Desktop publishing, 113–122
  file integration, 119–122, *119*
  page composition, 114–117
  software, *113*
  typography, 117–119, *117*
Detailed report, 389, *389*
Device driver file, 77
Diagnostic software, 41
Dialog box, 72–73, *72*, *612*, *635*
  Delete, 620–621, *621*
Difference engine, 426
Digital computer, 248
Digital Research, 256
Digital signal, 346, *346*
Digitized, 172, 289
Direct access, 211–212
Direct cutover, 442
Directory
  active, 588
  data, 79
  disk, 63, 79, 318
    displaying, 583–584, *584*
  displaying, 615–618
  program, 79
  root, 80, 583
Dir instruction, 583
Disaster recovery plan, 522, *523*
Discretionary replace, 106, 153
Disk address, 318
Disk cartridge, 322, *322*
Disk directory, 63, 79, 318
  displaying, 583–584, *584*
Disk drive, 45, 315–318, 335
  default, changing, 580–581, *581*
  external, 322
  read/write head, *316*
Diskette. *See also* Floppy disk
  initializing, 633–634
  soft-sectored, 319
  storage capacity, *710*
  3.5-inch, *315*, 317, 571, 600, *630*, 710
    layout, *572*, *600*
    storage capacity, *320*
Diskette drive
  external, 630
  internal, 630
Disk icon, 631
Diskless workstation, 353–354
Disk operating system (DOS), 48, 87–92
  commands, 577–591
    error correction checklist, *578*
  word processing program and, *102*
Disk pack, 320–321
  access time, transfer rate, storage capacity, *319*
  removable, 321–322, *322*
Disk storage, 318–320
Disk track, 318
Distributed processing, 351–354
Division symbol, 148
Document, 640–645, *640*
  design, general rules, *117*
Documentation, 486–488, *487*
  BASIC, 688–689
Dollar sign ($), 150, 676
Domain, 404
DOS. *See* Disk operating system
DOS prompt, 62, *573*, 602
  customizing, 589
DOS shell, 64
Dot-matrix character, 294
Dot-matrix printer, 50–51, 294–295, *294*, *575*
Double-clicking, 65, 606–607, *607*, 610
Double-strike, 108
Dow Jones News/Retrieval Service, 364
Downloading, 362
DPMA. *See* Data Processing Management Association
Drafting tablet, 289–290
Draft-quality printer, *294*, 295
Dragging, 65, *65*, 604, 616, 632–633, *633*
Drawing tablet, 289–290
Drive icon, clicking, *636*
Drop-down menu, *63*, 72, *73*, 605–606, *605*
Drum plotter, 298
DSS. *See* Decision-support system
Dynatrend, 42

EBCDIC. *See* Extended Binary Coded Decimal Interchange Code
Echo-printing, 663, *664*, 665
Eckert, J. Presper, 42, 243, 256
Economy, global, 542–543
EDI. *See* Electronic data interchange
Editing, 103–107
EDSAC. *See* Electronic Delay Storage Automatic Computer
Education
  computers and, 9
  continuing, 549
  data management systems and, 229
  electronic spreadsheet and, 160
Education Privacy Act (1974), 503
EDVAC. *See* Electronic Discrete Variable Automatic Computer
EFT. *See* Electronic funds transfer
EGA. *See* Extended graphics adapter
Electromechanical calculator, 243
Electronic bulletin board, 362, *362*
  abbreviations and symbols, 118
Electronic classroom, 126–128, *128*
Electronic Communications Privacy Act (1986), 504
Electronic computing, history, 256
Electronic data interchange (EDI), 366–367, *366*, 542
Electronic data processing (EDP) controls, 520
Electronic Delay Storage Automatic Computer (EDSAC), 256
Electronic Discrete Variable Automatic Computer (EDVAC), 256
Electronic filing, 124
Electronic funds transfer (EFT), 365–366, 542
Electronic mail (E-mail), 70, 124, 367–370, 400
  abbreviations and symbols, 118
  security, 373
Electronic mailbox, 124
Electronic Numerical Integrator and Calculator (ENIAC), 42, 243, 256
Electronic office, 122–125
Electronic publishing, 126, *127*
Electronics, consumer, *537*
Electronic spreadsheet, 46, 141–142, *144*
  common operations, 147–155, *147*
  decision support using, *402*
  designing, 162–165
  expanded uses, 156–157
  features and functions, 142–157
  macros, 155
  purchasing, hardware requirements and personal needs, *159*
  uses, 158–161
  worksheet layout, 145–146
Electronic superhighway, 544
Electronic whiteboard, 370
Electrostatic printer, 297
Ellipsis, 72
E-mail. *See* Electronic mail
Embedded computer, 14, 43, 268, *536*
Embedded microprocessor, 268, *269*, 536, *536*
Emergency procedures, 41
Emerging technology, 543–546, *559–561*
Emphasis, desktop publishing, 116–117, *116*
Emulation program, 81
Encryption, 373, 519
End of file (EOF), 492
END statement, 655, 657
End-user, procedures, *39*
End-user computing, 33, 551–552
Engineering, computers and, 8
ENIAC. *See* Electronic Numerical Integrator and Calculator
Environmental control, computers and, *17*
Environmental Defense Fund, 123
EOF. *See* End of file
Equity Funding Corporation, computer crime, 510–511
Erasable optical disk, *325*
Erase instruction, 585
Erase operation, electronic spreadsheet, 155
Eraser option, free-drawing graphics, 184
Ergonomics, 305, 319
Error checking, 48
Error correction, 40
  checklist, *578*
Error detection, data transmission, 361
Error message, 651
Error recovery procedures, 40
Ethernet, 350
Ethical standards, 504
Ethics, 504–508
  guidelines, 505–507, *506*
  issues, 504–505
  responsibilities and opportunities, 507–508
Exception report, 390–391, *391*
Execution phase, 258, *259*
Executive information system, 392
Expansion card, 260
Expansion slot, 260, *263*, 334
  system requirements, 711
Expense
  fixed, 139
  variable, 139
Expert system, 403–408, *405–406*, 545
  developing, 405–406
  interface, *404*
  personal, 545–546, *546*
Expert system shell, 406, 408
Exploded pie chart, 175, *175*
Exported, 156
Expression, 658
Extended Binary Coded Decimal Interchange Code (EBCDIC), 249
Extended graphics adapter (EGA), 301
Extended graphics array (XGA), 301
External copy, 105
External diskette drive, 630
External modem, 356, *356*
Eyegoggles, 538, *539*

Facsimile machine, 357–358, *357*
Fairchild Semiconductor, 256, 261
Fair Credit Reporting Act (1970), 503
FAT. *See* File allocation table
Fatbits option, free-drawing graphics, 184
Fault-tolerant computer, 270, *270*
Fax. *See* Facsimile machine
Fax board, 357
Fax-modem, 358
Feasibility study, 420–422
Fetch phase, 258, *259*
Field, 36–38
  key, 210, 219
File, 36–38
  access
    direct, 211–212
    sequential, 209–210, *210*
  conventions, 68–70
  copying, 614–615
    to file folder, 619–620
    to subdirectory, 589–590, *589*
  creating copy, 581–582, *582*
  cross-referencing, 38
  deleting, 585, *585*, 620–621, *621*
  device driver, 77
  flat, 212
  form letter, *112*
  hidden, 591
  index, 211
  integration, desktop publishing, 119–122, *119*
  merging, 112, *112*
  protected, 79
  readme, 63
  read-only, 79
  renaming, 584, *617*, 618
  undeleting, 585–586
File allocation table (FAT), 318, 583
File folder, 611
  copying file to, 619–620
  creating, 618–619
  icon, *619*
  removing, 621–622
File management, 212–218
  application generator, 217
  data definition, 212–214, *213*

data manipulation, 214–216
operating system, 78–80
queries, 217–218
software, 212
File Manager, 87, 611–622
Filename, 69, 577
changing, *617*, 618
Filename extension, 69, 577
BASIC, *656*
summary, *68–69*
File server, 344
Fill bucket option, free-drawing graphics, 184
Financial data, 388
Financial planning, electronic spreadsheet, 158, *159*
FINDER, 631
Find feature, electronic spreadsheet, 153
Find operation, word processing, 105
Firmware, 255
Fixed disk, access time, transfer rate, storage capacity, *319*
Fixed disk pack, 321–322
Fixed expense, 139
Fixed-point constant, 658
Flash memory, 331
Flat-bed plotter, 298
Flat file, 212
Floppy disk, 45, 315–318. *See also* Diskette
access time, transfer rate, storage capacity, *319*
care, 44
8-inch, 317, *317*
5.25-inch, 317, *317*, 570, 598, 710
layout, *571*, *599*
storage capacity, *320*
formatting, 318, *318*, 577–580, *578*, 612–614
storage capacity, *710*
Flowchart, 466, *466*
program, *669*
Flowcharting, 654–655, *654*
Folder, 640–645, *640*
creating, 640–641
renaming, 641–642
system, *643*
Font, 119
Font futzing, 77
Footer, 108
FOR...NEXT loop, 680–682, *681*, *682*, *683*
nested, 682–685, *683*
FOR...NEXT statement, 680–682
Foreign-language keyboard, *282*
Format feature, electronic spreadsheet, 149–150, *150*
Formatting, 107–109, 318, *318*, 577–580, *578*, 612–614
common operations, *108*
DOS display, *580*
Form feed, 575, *575*
Form letter file, *112*
FORmula TRANSlator. *See* FORTRAN
FORTRAN, 82–83, *82*, 256, 468, 474, *474*
applications, strengths, weaknesses, *484*
Forward chaining, 406
Fourth Amendment, 503
Fourth-generation language (4GL), 482–483, *482*
applications, strengths, weaknesses, *484*
Frame, 186–187
Frame selection option, multimedia, 187
Frankston, Robert, 141, 158, 256
Freedom of Information Act (1970), 503
Free-drawing graphics, 173, 181–185, *183*, *185*
palette, *181*, 182
toolbox, *181*, 182–184
utilities, 184–185
French Revolution, 296
Front-line management, 386
Full character, *295*
Full-duplex transmission, 361, *361*
Full justification, 108
Full-page monitor, 113
Function, 149
Function key, 281–282
Fylstra, Dan, 158

Gantt chart, 436, *436*
Gates, William, 79, 256, 468
Gateway, 345
GDSS. *See* Group decision support system
Gigabyte, 257
GIGO (garbage in, garbage out), 39
Global economy, 542–543
Global format feature, electronic spreadsheet, 150
Global replace, 106, 153
GOTO statement, 661
Graph
area, 178, *179*
bar, 156, 176, *176*
designing, *180*
stacked, 176, *176*
line, 176–178, *177*
x-y, 178
Graphical tools, 171–173
Graphical user interface (GUI), 64–65, 79, 145, 174, 282, 597, 703
Graphics. *See also* Free-drawing graphics; Presentation graphics
applications, 191–197
bit-mapped, *172*
pixel, 171
ready-to-use, 120, *120*
three-dimensional (3D), 543
vector, 172, *173*
Graphics package, 47
Group decision support system (GDSS), 400
Group icon, 603
pointing and clicking, *604*
Groupware, 68–70, *70*, 369, *369*, *370*, 400
applications, 70
GUI. *See* Graphical user interface
GWBASIC, 651

Hacker, 509, *509*
Half-duplex transmission, 360–361, *361*
Halftone, 120–121
Hard card, 321–322, *321*
Hard copy, 283
screen display, *576*
Hard-copy terminal, 283, *283*
characteristics, *292*
Hard disk, 45, 315–318, *316*
system requirements, *704*
Hard return, 104
Hardware, 41–45. *See also* Input hardware; Output hardware; Processing hardware; Storage hardware
communication, 354–358
personal computer, buying, 702–711, *705–708*
systems design and, 432–433
Hardwired, 76
Head crash, 317
Header, 108
Header label, 329
Heading, BASIC, 665–666, *666*
Health care, computers and, 8
Hearing-impaired, computers and, *19*
Heath Group, 512
Help
context-sensitive, 605
hyphenation, 110
Help desk, 34
Help screen, 74, 605
context-sensitive, *74*
Herschel, John, 426
Heuristic, 545
Hidden file, 591
Hierarchical model, 221–222, *222*
Hierarchy chart, *465*
High-level language, 82–83, *82*
Highlighting, 104, *104*
Hoff, Marcian, 245, 261
Hollerith, Herman, 328
Hologram, 561
Homebrew Computer Club, 20
Home entertainment and communications, 537–538
Honeywell Corp., 79
Hopper, Grace, 256
Host, 345
Hot site, 522
House, smart, 534–536, *535*
Human factor, re-engineering and, 18
Human Genome Project, 265
Hyatt, Gilbert, 245, 261
Hybrid topology, 345
Hypermedia, 227, *228*, 233–235
Hyphenation help, 110

IBM. *See* International Business Machines
IBM PC, 110, 256
booting procedures, *573*, *601*
IBM SECC, 396
IC. *See* Integrated circuit
ICCP. *See* Institute for Certification of Computer Professionals
Icon, 10–11, 282
apple, 631
button, 72
disk, 631
double-clicking, 606–607, *607*
dragging, 65, *65*, 604, 616, 632–633, *633*
drive, clicking, *636*
file folder, 611, *619*
group, 603
pointing and clicking, *604*
toolbox, 73, *73*
Icon bar, *144*
IEEE. *See* Institute of Electrical and Electronic Engineers
Image exporting, multimedia, 189
Image processing, 560
Image scanner, 287, *288*
characteristics, *292*
Imaging, 174, 194–195, *194*
Impact printer, 294–295
IN...THEN statement, *669*, 670–671, *670*
Index, 211–212, *211*
Index file, 211
Index operation, data manipulation language, 216
Inference engine, 404
Infinite loop, 661–662, *661*, *662*
Information. *See also* Management information
data vs., 38–39
good, characteristics, 218
Information society, *533–546*, *534*
Information system. *See* Computer information system; Management information system
Information systems manager, 35–36, *35*
Information technology, impact, 16–21
Information utilities, 363–364, 371–373, *537*
service fees, 372–373
Informed user, *33*
Initializing, 633–634
Initial program load (IPL), 76
Initial review, 418–419
Ink-jet printer, 296
Input, 10, 11–12
ergonomics, 319
Input feature, electronic spreadsheet, 147–149
Input hardware, 41, *41*
keyboards, 281–282
pointing devices, 282
scanners, 284–287
system requirements, 704–709, *705–708*
terminals, 283–284
Input/output (I/O), 281
Input peripherals, *292*
Input, processing, output controls, 522–524, *524*
INPUT statement, 655–657, 662, 681, 688
Insert operation
electronic spreadsheet, 152
word processing, 104–105
Installation, 439–442
Institute for Certification of Computer Professionals (ICCP), *554–555*
Institute of Electrical and Electronic Engineers (IEEE), *558*
Integer constant, 658
Integrated circuit (IC), 244–245, *245*, 251, 261, 334
Integrated software, 69–70
Integrated voice/data terminal (IVDT), 395
Integrity. *See* Data integrity
Intel 4004, 246, 256, 261
Intel 8008, 79, 246, 261
Intel 8088, 254
Intel 80386, 254
Intel 80486, 254
Intel Corporation, 256, 261
Intelligent terminal, 284
Intelligent vehicle/highway system (IVHS), *537*
Intel Pentium chip, 256
Interactive, 11
Interactive input device, 290
Interactive television, 538
Interblock gap, 327, *329*
Interface
command-driven, 61–64
expert system, *404*
graphical user, 64–65, 145, 174, 282, 597, 703
natural language, 66
user, 61–66, *62*, *63*, 703
prototype, *430*
Internal diskette drive, 630
Internal modem, 356
International Business Machines (IBM), 32, 82, 254, 256, 328, 396, 554, 569
International Standards Organization (ISO), 350
Interpersonal relationships, computers and, 19
Interpreter, 472, *472*
BASIC, 652
Interrecord gap, 326–327
Interview, personal, 428
Inventory, just-in-time, 399
I/O. *See* Input/output
I/O ports, 262–263, *263*
IPL. *See* Initial program load

IPOS cycle, 10–12, *11*, *33*, 35, 250, 492
ISO. *See* International Standards Organization
Italics, 116, 150
Iteration, 462
Iteration structure, program flowchart, *669*
IVDT. *See* Integrated voice/data terminal
IVHS. *See* Intelligent vehicle/highway system

Jacquard, Joseph Marie, 243, 296
Jobs, Steve, 20, 256
Join operation, relational database, 224, *225*
Journalism, office automation, 125–126
Joystick, 288
  characteristics, *292*
Junction transistor, 251
Junk mail, 123
Justification, 108–109, *109*
  full, 108
  left, 109
  right, 109
Just-in-time inventory, 399

K. *See* Kilobyte
Kapor, Mitch, 256
Kemeny, John G., 256, 468
Kerning, 118
Key, 210
Keyboard, 10, 12, 23, 41, *41*, 62, 281–282
  characteristics, *292*
  foreign-language, *282*
  system requirements, *705–708*
Keyboard overlay, 102
Key field, 210, 219
Keypad, numeric, 282
Keypunch, 290
  characteristics, *292*
Keyword, 654
Kilobyte (K), 257
Kirby, Jack, 256, 261
Knowledge base, 404, 405, 407
Knowledge engineer, 405, 407
Kurtz, Thomas E., 256, 468

Label, 147
  header, 329
  presentation graphics, 180
  tape, 329
  trailer, 329
  volume, 612
Label prefix, 147
LAN. *See* Local area network
Landscape, 114, *115*, 153
Language translator, 74, 82–83, 469–473
La Pascaline, *9*
Laptop computer, 266–267, *267*, 358
Large computer system, security controls, 519–524
Laser printer, 113, 297, *297*
Lasso option, free-drawing graphics, 184
Law enforcement, data management systems, 230–231, *231*
LCD. *See* Liquid crystal display
Left justification, 109
Legend, presentation graphics, 180
Less than (<) symbol, 670–671
LET statement, *655*, *657*, *682*
Letter-quality printer, 295
Libraries, data management systems, 232, *232*
Life cycle, 417
  systems development, *444*
Light pen, 288, *288*, 290
  characteristics, *292*
Linear programming, 393, *394*
Line feed, 574–575, *575*
Line graph, 176–178, *177*
Line printer, 295, *295*
Linker, 472
Liquid crystal display (LCD), 300–301
List box, 72
LIST command, 653, 656, *657*
LLIST command, 653
LOAD command, 657
Local area network (LAN), 351–352, *351*
Lock out, 226
Logical operation, 13, 251–252
  coding, 491
Logical operator, 670
Logic error, 472
LOGO, 83, 477, *478*, 518
  applications, strengths, weaknesses, *484*
Loop
  BASIC programming, 680–685
  FOR...NEXT, 680–682, *681*, *682*, *683*
    nested, 682–685, *683*
Loop structure
  infinite, 661–662, *661*, *662*
  program flowchart, *669*
Lotus 1-2-3, 158, 256, 512
Lotus Development Corporation, 158, 512
LPRINT statement, 661, 665

Machine code, 247–248, *247*
Machine language, 82, 469–470
Macintosh. *See* Apple Macintosh
Macro, 155
Magnetic disk storage, 315–322
Magnetic ink character recognition (MICR), 286, *287*
Magnetic tape, access time, transfer rate, storage capacity, *319*
Magnetic tape cartridge, 326–329
Magnetic tape label, 329
Magnetic tape storage, 326–329, *327*
Mail. *See* Electronic mail; Voice mail
Mainframe, 43, 264, *264*
  features compared, *268*
Maintenance, 443–445
Management
  accountability and, 442
  front-line, 386
  middle, 386, *387*
  top, 386, *387*
Management controls, 520, *520*
Management information
  data, 387–389, *388*
  people using, 384–387, *385*, *386*
Management information system (MIS), 383–392, *384*
  organizing data into reports, 389–392
Manager, ethical issues, *507*
Manual worksheet, 140–141, *140*
Manufacturing, electronic spreadsheet, 161, *161*
Mark I, 243, 396
Mark II, 256
Mass storage, 330, *330*
Materials requirement planning (MRP), 398–399, *399*
Materials resource planning, 541
Math coprocessor, 254
Mauchley, John W., 42, 243, 256
Maximize button, 609
MB. *See* Megabyte
McCarthy, John, 256
McLuhan, Marshall, 193
Measure selection option, multimedia, 189
Medicine
  data management systems, 229–230, *230*
  expert systems, 404–406, *405–406*
Megabyte (MB), 257
Megahertz (MHz), 250
Memory, 43, 254–258
  cache, 257–258
  flash, 331
  operating system and, 77
  programmable read-only, 331
  random access, 255–257
  read-only, 255
  system requirements, *704*
  virtual, 78, *78*
  volatile, 255
Memory chip, 334
Menabrea, Luigi, 358
Menu, 64, 72–73
  drop-down, *63*, 72, *73*, 605–606, *605*
  pull-down, 634–637
Menu bar, 603, 631
Menu option, 64
Merging files, 112, *112*
Message filtering, 369
Meteorology, computers and, *7*
MHz. *See* Megahertz
Michigan State University, computer crime, 508–509
MICR. *See* Magnetic ink character recognition
Microcomputer, 43, *246*, 259–263, 266–267. *See also* Personal computer
  booting, 570–573, *573*, 598–602
  expansion slots and cards, 260
  features compared, *268*
  I/O ports, 262–263, *262*
  shut-down, 591
  start-up procedures, *569–576*
  turning on, 572–573
Microfiche, 299
Microfilm, 299
  computer output, 299, *299*
Microprocessor, 245–246, *245*
  embedded, 268, *269*, 536, *536*
  making, 271–274
  processing speed, 254, *254*
Micropro International, 256
Microsecond, 250
Microsoft Corporation, 79, 186, 256, 597
Microsoft Windows, 75, 79, 87–92, 256, 596–623
  features, 607–610
  File Manager, 611–622
  loading, 602
  Program Manager, 603–607
  system orientation, 597–602
  system shut-down, 622–623, *623*
Microsoft Windows NT, 75, 597
Microwave, 348
  communication channels, *348*
Middle management, 386, *387*
MIDI. *See* Musical Instrumental Digital Interface
Million instructions per second (MIPS), 264
Millisecond, 250
Minicomputer, 43, 265–266, *265*
  features compared, *268*
Minimize button, 610, *610*
Minus sign (-), 148
MIPS. *See* Million instructions per second
MIS. *See* Management information system
Mkdir command, 586
Model, 392
Model 726, 256
Modeling, decision support system, 393–397
Modem, 354–356, 371
  acoustic coupler, 355
  external, 356, *356*
  internal, 356
  modulation/demodulation, *355*
Modula-2, 481, *482*
  applications, strengths, weaknesses, *484*
Modulation, 354–356, *355*
Module, 462–463
Monitor, 43
  color, 300–301
  full-page, 113
  low-frequency emissions, 304–305
  monochrome, 300
  RGB, 300
  system requirements, *705–708*
Monochrome, 300
Moore, Gordon, 256
Motherboard, 259, *260*, 334
Mouse, 41, *41*, *62*, 282, 603–605
  characteristics, *292*
Move operation
  electronic spreadsheet, 151
  word processing, 105
MPC standard, 186
MRP. *See* Materials requirement planning
MS-DOS, 79, 256, 568–591, 597
Muller, Karl, 554
Multimedia, 174, 185–191
  applications, 191–197
  audio data, 189–190, *190*
  data integration, 234
  visual data, 186–189, *186*
Multimedia PC standard, 186
Multiplexer, 356–357, *357*
Multiplication symbol, 148
Multitasking, 71–72, 80–81
Musical Instrumental Digital Interface (MIDI), 196–197, *196*

Nanomachine, 560
Nanosecond, 250
NASA. *See* National Aeronautics and Space Administration
National Aeronautics and Space Administration (NASA), 269
National Cash Register (NCR), 396
National Crime Information Center (NCIC), 230
National Science Foundation, 42
Natural language, 483–484, *483*
  applications, strengths, weaknesses, *484*
Natural language interface, 66
NC. *See* Numerical control
NCIC. *See* National Crime Information Center
NCR. *See* National Cash Register
Nested, 660
Nested FOR...NEXT loop, 682–685, *683*
Network, 17, 343–354
  applications, 361–370
  bus, 343–344, *344*
  client/server, 353–354, *353*
  linking computers, 346–350
  local area, 351–352, *351*
  neural, *559*
  ring, 344–345, *345*
  star, 345, *345*
  token-ring, 350
  value-added, 353
  wide area, 352, *352*
Network administrator, 36

Network card, 352
Network gnash, 77
Networking, mistakes, 368
Network model, 222, *222*
Network topology, 343–345
Neural network, *559*
NEW command, *653*, *657*
New York Stock Exchange, *207*
NeXT Corporation, 20
Node, 343
Nonexecutable statement, 662–663
Nonimpact printer, 296–297
Nonprocedural programming, 481
Notepad computer, 267, *267*, 358, *359*
Noyce, Robert, 256, 261
Numbers, processing, 139–142
Numerical control (NC), 302, *302*, 541
Numeric constant, 658
Numeric data, 14, *678*
Numeric keypad, 282

OA. *See* Office automation
Object, 38, 463
  copying within window, 642–643
  deleting, 642
  moving to different window, 644–645
Object integration feature, multimedia, 189
Object-oriented programming (OOP), 463–465, *464*
Obsolescence, 547–548
OCR. *See* Optical character recognition
Office automation (OA), 122–128
  advertising agency, 125
  journalism, 125–126
Office block, 77
Office environment, user-friendly, 123
Olsten Corp., 12
OMR. *See* Optical mark recognition
Online, 14
Online reference, 109–110
Online thesaurus, 110, *111*, 130
On-the-job training, 547–548
Open Systems Interconnection (OSI) model, 350, *350*
Operating procedures, 40
Operating system, 48, 74, 76–81. *See also* Disk operating system
  booting, 76, *76*
  desktop, *75*
  file management, 78–80
  hardwired, 76
  resource management, 77–78
  task management, 80–81
  user priorities, 66
Operational decision, 387
Optical character recognition (OCR), 286
Optical computer, 543–544, *544*
Optical disk, 323, *323*, *324*
  erasable, 325
Optical disk storage, 293, 323–325
Optical fiber cable, 348–349, *348*
  communication channels, *348*
Optical mark recognition (OMR), 286
Optical storage disk, 293, 323–325
Organizational systems, 264–265
Orlov, Darlene, 505
OS/2, 75
Osborne I, 256
Osborne Computer, 256
Out of DATA message, 668

Output, 10, 11–12
  action, 302–304
  permanent, 293–299
  printed, 43
  sound and speech, 301
  temporary, 299–302
  video display, 300–301
Output formatting, BASIC, 672–674, *672*, *673*, *674*
Output hardware, 43, 293–304
  action output, 302–304
  permanent output, 293–299
  system requirements, 709, *709*
  temporary output, 299–301

Pacific Telephone Company, computer crime, 509
Page, 78
Page composition, 114–117
Page definition language (PDL), 119
Page printer, 295
Page scanner, *288*
Pagination, 108
Paintbrush option, free-drawing graphics, 182
Palette, 73, 200
  free-drawing graphics, *181*, 182
Paperless office, 124–125
Papert, Seymour, 477, 518
Parallel operation, 440–441
Parallel port, 262–263, *262*
Parallel processing, 246
Parentheses, BASIC, 660
Parity bit, 331, *332*, 361
Parity checking, 331–332, 361
Pascal, 74, 83, 256, 478, *478*, 489
  applications, strengths, weaknesses, *484*
Pascal, Blaise, 9, 243, 478
Password, 373, 519
Password-protected, 155, 226
Payroll processing, computer logic, 252
PC. *See* Personal computer
PC-DOS, 568–591, *597*
PDA. *See* Personal digital assistant
PDL. *See* Page definition language
Pen-based computer, 288, *289*
Penn Central Railroad, computer crime, 510
People
  programming and, 455–457
  systems design and, 436
Performing arts, graphics software, 195–196
Peripherals, 45
  design and safety, 304–305
  input, *292*
  special applications, 307–308
Personal applications, electronic spreadsheet, 158–159, *159*
Personal communications devices, 358
Personal computer (PC), 43. *See also* Microcomputer
  automated office, 124
  booting, 570–573, *573*, 598–602
  building, 333–335
  shut-down, 591
  start-up procedures, 569–576
  turning on, 572–573
Personal computer system
  alternatives, 427–429, *427*
  buying, 49–53, 695–713
    conventional wisdom, *703*
    hardware requirements, 703–711
    needs analysis, 697–703, *713*
  design, 437
  requirements, 422–423, *423*
  set-up and maintenance, 445, *445*
  systems specification, *437*
Personal computing, 22–24
Personal digital assistant (PDA), 256, 267, 358
Personal expert system, 545–546, *546*
Personal identification number, 523
Personal interview, 428
Personal privacy. *See* Privacy
Personal productivity software, 46, *47*
  word processing, *102*
Personal Software, 158
Personal systems, 266–267
Personnel data, 388
PERT chart, 448
Phased transition, 441–442
Photoresist, 272
Physical controls, computer security, 517–519, *517*
Physical data, 14–15
  storage, 38
Piaget, Jean, 518
Picosecond, 250
Pie chart, 156–157, *157*, 175, *175*
  exploded, 175
Pilot operation, 442
Pitch, 108, 118
Pixel, 171–172
Pixel graphics, 171
Playback control feature, multimedia, 189
Plotter, 298–299, *298*
  drum, 298
  flat-bed, 298
Plus sign (+), 148
Point, 117
Pointer, handheld, 307
Pointing device, 282
Point-of-sale (POS), 284
Poison Control Center, 230
Port
  parallel, 262–263, *262*
  serial, 262–263, *262*
Portable computer, 561
Portable language, 480
Portrait, 114, *115*, 153
POS. *See* Point-of-sale
PostScript, 119
Presentation graphics, 156–157, *157*, 173–180
  area graphs, 178, *179*
  bar graphs, 176, *176*
  creating, 179–180
  enhancing, 178–179
  line graphs, 176–178, *177*
  pie charts, 175, *175*
  presentation rules of thumb, 177
  software, *175*
  symbol charts, 178, *179*
Presentation perfection, 77
Presentation software, 198–201
Preventive maintenance procedures, 40
Primary storage, 254
Print chart, 433, *434*
Printed output, 43
Printer, 11, 24, 43, 294–297
  comparisons, *709*
  dot-matrix, 50–51, 294–295, *294*, *575*
  draft-quality, *294*, *295*
  electrostatic, 297
  impact, 294–295
  ink-jet, 296
  laser, 113, 297, *297*
  letter-quality, 295
  line, 295, *295*
  malfunctions, *576*
  nonimpact, 296–297
  page, 295
  serial, 295
  setting top of page, 573–575
  system requirements, *705–708*
  thermal, 297
Printer emulation utility, 81
Print operation, electronic spreadsheet, 153–154
Print options, 108–109
Print server, 344
PRINT statement, 655, 657, 665–666, *666*, 668, 671, 673, 678–679, 684, 688
PRINT USING statement, 673, 676, 681, 683–685, 687–688
Print zone, 664–665, *664*
Privacy, 525–527
  invasions, 502–503, *504*
  rights, 503–504, *503*
Privacy Act (1974), 503
Problem definition, program development, 458–459, *459*
Procedures, 39–41
  emergency, 41
  end-user, *39*
  operating, 40
  systems design, 433
Process control, 8
Processing, 10, 11–12
  batch, 210
  data, 8–9, 207–212, *207*
  database, pros and cons, 226–227, *226*
  distributed, 351–354
  image, *560*
  parallel, 246
  payroll, computer logic, 252
  real-time, 212
Processing hardware, 43, *43*, 243–246
  central processing unit, 250–263
  comparison of features, *268*
  first generation, 243–244
  second generation, 244
  third generation, 244–245
  fourth generation, 245–246
  fifth generation, 246
  specialized, 268–270
Processing speed, 16–17
  microprocessor, 254, *254*
  reduced instruction set computing, *255*
Processor, 43, 250–254
  arithmetic operations, 250–251
  control/communication operations, 252–254
  logical operations, 251–252
  reduced instruction set computing, 254
  system requirements, *704*
Prodigy, 363
Production/sales data, 388–389
Productivity, word processing, *102*
Professional organizations, 557–558, *558*
  where to find software, 86
Professional publications, 549–550, *550*
Program, 13–14, *13*. *See also* BASIC program; Software
  banner, 128
  debugging, 473, *473*
  emulation, 81
  flowchart, 466, *466*
  linker, 472
  maintenance, 488
  object-oriented, 463–465, *464*
  organization into file folder, *614*
  structured, 460–463
  supervisor, *75*, *76*
  systems design, 433
  terminate stay resident, 71–72, *71*, 266, 332
  testing, 485
  theft, 512–513
  unstructured, 459–460, *461*

utility, 74, 81, 82, *82*, 577–591
word processing, 46
disk operating system and, *102*
selecting, 129–132
Program code, writing, 469–484
Program design, 458–469
testing, 467–469
tools, 465–467
Program directory, 79
Program Evaluation and Review Technique (PERT), 448
Program flowchart, *669*
Program logic, *671*, *672*
Programmable read-only memory (PROM), 331
Program Manager, 603–607
window, *602*
Programmer, 34, *34*
contract, 433
opportunities, *456*
Programming. *See also* BASIC programming
four-step process, 457, *457*
linear, 393, *394*
misconceptions, 455–457
nonprocedural, 481
object-oriented, 463–465, *464*
people, 455–457
Programming language, 473–484, 489–492
Program revision, 34
Program specifications, 458
Project design structure, 417
Projection plate, 199, 301
Project management software, 446–448, 447
Project operation, relational database, 224
PROM. *See* Programmable read-only memory
Promotional software, 85
Prompt command, 589
Proofreading, 110
symbols, 288
Proportional spacing, 118
Protected file, 79
Protect function, electronic spreadsheet, 154–155
Protocol, 349
Prototype, *430*
Prototyping, 430–431, 471
Pseudocode, 466–467, *467*
Publications, recreational and professional, 549–550, *550*
Public domain software, 86
Public health, data management systems, 229–230, *230*
Publishing. *See also* Desktop publishing
electronic, 126, *127*
Puck, 289, *289*
Pull-down menu, 634–637. *See also* Drop-down menu
Punched card, 256, 290, 328

QBE. *See* Query by Example
Quality control, 401–402
Query, 217–218, *218*
data analysis, 397, *397*
Query by Example (QBE), 218, *218*
QuickBASIC, 476
Quit function, electronic spreadsheet, 155

Radio Broadcast Data System, 537
RAM. *See* Random access memory
RAM chip, *257*, 334
RAM drive, 330
Random access, 211
Random access memory (RAM), 255–257
Range, 149
Range format feature, electronic spreadsheet, 150
Range name, 149
RDBMS. *See* Relational database management system
Rd command, 590–591, *590*
Readers' log, 370
Readme file, 63
Read-only file, 79
Read-only memory (ROM), 255, 334
READ statement, 662–663, *663*
Read/write head, *316*
Reality, virtual, 538–539, *539*
Real-time processing, 212
Record, 36–38
Record layout form, 433, *435*
Recreation, computers and, 8
Recreational publications, 549–550, *550*
Recycling, 123
Reduced instruction set computing (RISC), 254
processing speed, *255*
Redundancy. *See* Data redundancy
Re-engineering, human factor and, 18
Relational database, 209
Relational database management system (RDBMS), guidelines, 209
Relational model, 223–225, *223*
Relative cell reference, 151
Remington Rand, 42
Removable disk pack, 321–322, *322*
access time, transfer rate, storage capacity, *319*
REM statement, 667–668, *668*, 671, 678, 683, 686
Rename command, 584
Rename option, *618*
Repetitive strain injury (RSI), 304
Report
detailed, 389, *389*
exception, 390–391, *391*
summary, 390, *391*
Report generator, 218
Report Program Generator (RPG), 480–481, *481*
applications, strengths, weaknesses, *484*
Request for proposal (RFP), 432–433
Research data, 388
Resource conflict, 447
Resource management, operating system, 77–78
Response time, 212
Restore button, 609
Retrieve feature, electronic spreadsheet, 153
RFP. *See* Request for proposal
RGB monitor, 300
Right to Financial Privacy Act (1978), 504
Right justification, 109
Ring topology, 344–345, *345*
RISC. *See* Reduced instruction set computing
Rmdir command, 590–591, *590*
Robotics, 303, *303*, 541
ROM. *See* Read-only memory
ROM chip, 255, 334, 651
Root directory, 80, 583
Rotated format, 178
RPG. *See* Report Program Generator
RPGII, 480
RPGIII, 480
RPG400, 480
RSI. *See* Repetitive strain injury
Rule of 80–20, 420–421
RUN command, 653, 656
Sans-serif, 119
SAVE command, 657
Save feature, electronic spreadsheet, 153
Save and retrieve operation, word processing, 106–107
SBT, 77
Scanner, 41, 113, 172, 186, 284–287
bar-code, 284–286, *285*
characteristics, *292*
handheld, *285*, *288*
image, 287, *288*
MICR, 286, *287*
OCR, 286
OMR, 286
page, *288*
Schneider, Jerry, 509
Science
computers, 8
electronic spreadsheet, 160–161
multimedia software, 192, *192*
Screen, touch-sensitive, 288–289, *289*, 307
characteristics, *292*
Screen display, hard copy, 576
Screen layout form, 433, *434*
Screen pointer, 63, 64–65, 603, 632
Screen prompt, 61, *63*
Scroll, 72–73
Scroll arrows, 72, 609, 638–639
Scroll bar, 73, 609, 638–639
Scroll box, 73, 609, 639
Scrolling, 146, 638–639
Search path, *587*
Search and replace feature
electronic spreadsheet, 153
word processing, 106, *106*
Secondary storage, *255*
Sector, 318
Security, 422, 516–524
data, 48, *519*
Selection, 461–462
Select operation, data manipulation language, 214–215, *214*
Self-directed work team, 399–400, *400*
Seminar, 548
Sensor, 291, *291*
characteristics, *292*
Sentinel value, 669
Sequence, 460–461
Sequential access, 209–210, *210*
Serial port, 262–263, *262*
Serial printer, 295
Serif, 119
Server, 344
Service bureau, 424
Service technician, 35, 40
Shapes, free-drawing graphics, 182
Shareware, 86
Shell, 64
expert system, 406, 408
Shockley, William, 244, 251
Silicon, 272
Simulation, 8, 193
Site license, 519
Size box, 638
Slash mark (/), 148
Small computer system, security controls, 517–519, *517*
Smart card, 366
Smart house, 534–536, *535*
Smart transportation, 536–537, *536*
Smileys, 118
Soft copy, 283
Soft return, 103
Soft-sectored diskette, 319
Soft space, 108
Software, 13–14, 46–48. *See also* Program
antivirus, *515*
applications, 46–48
communication, 48, 81, 359–361
database management, 212, 219
user needs, technical support, hardware requirements, *220*
data management, applications, 227–232
desktop publishing, *113*
development
program design, 458–469
writing program code, 469–484
diagnostic, 41
evaluating, 66–74
file management, 212
heuristic, *545*
integrated, 69–70
personal productivity, 46, *47*
presentation, 198–201
presentation graphics, *175*
project management, 447
promotional, *85*
public domain, 86
selecting, 143
systems, 48, *48*, 75–83
systems design and, 433
trojan-horse, *515*
protection against, *515*
utility, 74, 81, 82, *82*, 577–591
where to find, 83–86
Software package, *46*
buying, needs analysis, 698–703, *699–702*
user-friendly, *67*
Sort operation, data manipulation language, 216, *216*
Sound output, 301
Sound synthesizer, 301, *301*
Source, *615*
Source, The, 363
Space exploration, graphics applications, 197, *197*
"Spaghetti" code, 460
SPC. *See* Statistical process control
Speech output, 301
Speech synthesizer, 301
Speed control option, multimedia, 187
Spelling checker, 110
SPOOLer utility, 81
Spraypaint option, free-drawing graphics, 182
Spreadsheet. *See* Electronic spreadsheet
Spread web, 77
SQL. *See* Structured Query Language
Stack, 227, *228*, *235*
Stacked bar graph, 176, *176*
Standalone word processor, 101
Stanton, Steven, 18
Start bit, 360
Star topology, 345, *345*
Statement, 654–655
nonexecutable, 662–663
Statistical process control (SPC), 401–402, *401*
Status line, 145
Stereolithography, 540–541, *540*
Still camera, 290
characteristics, *292*
Stop bit, 360
Storage, 10, 11–12
mass, 330, *330*
primary, 254
secondary, 255
Storage hardware, 45, *45*
magnetic disk, 315–3
magnetic tape, 326–
maximizing perform 331–332
optical disk, 323–

specialized, 330–331
system requirements, 710, *710*
Storage media, 315, *315*
Strategic decision, 387
Stretch command, free-drawing graphics, 182
String data, *678*
String variable, 676–677, *677*
Structure chart, 465, *465*
Structured program, 460–463
Structured Query Language (SQL), 217
Structured walkthrough, 467–468, *469*
Stub testing, 485
Style sheet, *107*, 111
Stylus, *282*, 288–289
Subdirectory, 80, *80*, 586
changing from one to another, 588–589, *588*
copying file to, 589–590, *589*
creating, 586–588, *587*
removing from disk, 590–591, *590*
Subtraction symbol, 148
Subtract operation, relational database, 224, *225*
Summary report, 390, *391*
Supercomputer, 269–270, *269*
Superconductivity, *554*
Superconductor, 543, 554
Super VGA, 301
Supervisor, 76
Supervisor program, *75*, *76*
Switch, *579*
Symbol chart, 178, *179*
Synchronization, multimedia, 190
Synchronous transmission, 360, *360*
Syntax, 64, 651
Syntax error, 471
Synthesizer, 196, 301, *301*
Sysop, 362
System 7, 75
System/360, 396
System design, techniques, 430–431
System drive, 569, 597
System folder, *643*
System life cycle, 416–417
System operator, 362
Systems analyst, 33–34, 418–419
Systems development, 33–34
alternative evaluation step, 423–429, *424*, *427*
design step, 429–437, *429*
four-step life cycle, *418*, *444*
implementation step, 438–445, *438*, *443*
life-cycle approach, *416*
requirements step, 418–422, *419*
...s development project, 416
...oftware, 48, *48*, 75–83
...ification, 429
...nputer system, *437*
... 486
...8, 667,

Task management, operating system, 80–81
Technology
computer, college curriculum, *551*
emerging, 543–546, *559–561*
Telecommunication, 341–342
Telecommuting, 364, *364*
Teleconferencing, 364, *365*, 400
Telephone, as interactive input device, 290
characteristics, *292*
Teleprocessing, 342–343
Teletype Corporation, 283
Television, interactive, 538
Template, 160, 200
Terabyte, 257
Terminal, 283–284, *283*
hard-copy, 283, *283*
characteristics, *292*
integrated voice/data, 395
intelligent, 284
video display, 300, *300*
Terminate stay resident (TSR), 71
Terminate stay resident (TSR) program, 71–72, *71*, 266, 332
Test data, 468
Texas Instruments, 256, 261
Text, 14
Text box, 72
Text options, free-drawing graphics, 184
Textual data, 14
Thermal printer, 297
Thesaurus, online, 110, *111*, 130
Three-dimensional (3D) format, 178–179
Three-dimensional worksheet, 146, *148*
Time bomb, 515
Timed backup, 153
Timesharing, 80–81, *81*
Time slice, 356
Title, presentation graphics, 180
Title bar, 607–608, 637–638
Title locking, 146
TMC. *See* Tabulator Machine Company
Token passing, 350
Token-ring network, 350
Toolbox, 73, 200
free-drawing graphics, *181*, 182–184
multimedia, *187*
Top management, 386, *387*
Total quality management, 402–403
Touch-sensitive screen, 288–289, *289*, 307
characteristics, *292*
Track
disk, 318
tape, 326
Trackball, 282, *282*
characteristics, *292*
Trailer label, 329
Training, on-the-job, 547–548
Transaction, 11
Transaction cycle, 387
Transaction processing system, 387
Transfer rate, 318, *319*
Transistor, 244, *245*
junction, 251
Transparent, 48
Transportation, smart, 536–537, *536*
...rojan-horse software, 515
...protection against, *515*
...ubleshooting, *40*
...cedures, 41
...ASIC, 468, 476
..., 79
...R. *See* Terminate stay resident

Turing, Alan, *556*
Turing machine, *556*
Turing Test, *556*
Twisted pair, 347
communication channels, *348*
Two-dimensional (2D) format, 178
Typeface, 119
Typography, 117–119, *117*

Undelete command, *585–586*
Underlining, 108, 116, 150
Undo feature
electronic spreadsheet, 152
word processing, *104*, 105
UNIVAC. *See* Universal Automatic Computer
Universal Automatic Computer (UNIVAC), 43, 243, *244*, 256
Universal Product Code (UPC), 284–286
Unix, 75
Unstructured program, 459–460, *461*
UPC. *See* Universal Product Code
Update, 210
concurrent, 226
Update operation, data manipulation language, 215
Uploading, 362
Uppercase, 116
User-developer, 33
User friendly, 8
User group, where to find software, 86
User interface, 61–66, *62*, *63*, 703
prototype, *430*
User's manual, 73–74
User training, 487–488, *488*
Utility software, 74, 81, 82, *82*, 577–591

Vaccine, 515
Vacuum tube, 243, *245*, 256
Value, 147
Value-added network (VAN), 353
VAN. *See* Value-added network
Vaporware, 83
Variable, 658–659
BASIC, *659*
string, 676–677, *677*
Variable expense, 139
VDT. *See* Video display terminal
Vector graphics, 172, *173*
Venture Development Corp., 395
Ver command, 586
Verification, 40
Version, 488
VGA. *See* Video graphics adapter; Video graphics array
Video display output, 300–301
Video display terminal (VDT), 300, *300*
Video graphics adapter (VGA), 260
Video graphics array (VGA), 301
Video Privacy Protection Act (1988), 504
Virtual memory, 78, *78*
Virtual reality, 538–539, *539*
Virus, 86, 514, *514*
protection against, 515
VisiCalc, 141, 158, 256
Visicorp, 158
Visual BASIC, 476
Visual data, 186–189, *186*
Voice mail, 124, 367–369
Voice-recognition device, 290–291, *290*, 307
characteristics, *292*
Volatile memory, 255
Volume label, 612
Volunteer activities, electronic spreadsheet, 159

von Neumann, John, 256

WAN. *See* Wide area network
Warranty registration, 53
Watson, Thomas, Jr., 396
Watson, Thomas John, Sr., 396
Wearable computer, 561
Weather Bureau, 270
Weather forecasting, computers and, *7*
"What if?" analysis, 142
White space, 114–115
Wide area network (WAN), 352, *352*
Wilkes, Maurice, 256
Window, 71–72. *See also* Microsoft Windows
active, *644*
electronic spreadsheet, 146, *146*
Window frame, 608
Wireless communication channel, 347–348
Wirth, Nicholas, 256, 481
Word, 252
WordPerfect, 110
Word processing, 101–112
editing, 103–107
formatting, 107–109
common operations, *108*
integrated services, 109–112
personal productivity, *102*
software, 46
disk operating system, *102*
selecting, 129–132
Word processor
automated office, 124
standalone, 101
WordStar, 256
Word wrap, 103–104, *103*
Work group computing, 367–369
Work group systems, 265–266
Workplace, computer-integrated, 539–541
Worksheet, 140. *See also* Electronic spreadsheet
budget, *142*
manual, 140–141, *140*
printed, WYSIWYG preview, *154*
three-dimensional, 146, *148*
Worksheet data, expanded uses, 156–157
Workshop, 548–549
Workstation, 264
diskless, 353–354
Work team, self-directed, 399–400, *400*
Worm, 86, 514–515
WORM disk, 324
Wozniak, Steve, 20, 256
Write once read many disk. *See* WORM disk
Write-protect notch, 317, *317*
Write-protect window, 317–318, *317*
Writing analyzer, 111, *111*
WYSIWYG, 113, 130

XGA. *See* Extended graphics array
x-y graph, 178

Zoom box, 639